A CATECHUMEN'S LECTIONARY

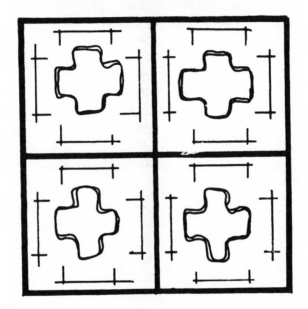

EDITED BY
ROBERT M. HAMMA

Paulist Press ■ New York/Mahwah

D1384736

Interior art by Stella DeVenuta

Copyright © 1988 by

Paulist Press, Inc.

Library of Congress Cataloging-in-Publication Data

A Catechumen's lectionary/edited by Robert M. Hamma.
    p.   cm.
    Text includes the Lectionary for Mass for Sundays and feasts with commentary by various authors.
    ISBN 0-8091-2998-1
    1. Catechumens—Religious life. 2. Lectionaries—Texts.
3. Catholic Church—Liturgy—Texts. 4. Bible—Devotional use.
5. Bible—Liturgical lessons, English. 6. Bible—Commentaries.
I. Hamma, Robert M.   II. Catholic Church. Lectionary for Mass
(U.S.). Sundays and feasts. 1988.
BX1968.C32 1988
264′.029—dc19   88-22498
                                     CIP

Published by Paulist Press, Inc.
997 Macarthur Blvd.
Mahwah, N.J. 07430

www. paulistpress.com

Printed and bound in the United States of America

Contents

Introduction

The Rite of Becoming a Catechumen describes the time of the catechumenate as a journey. As a catechumen, you are invited to walk on the road of faith, following Christ, your loving guide. Having come to know God through the wonder of creation, now the way of the Gospel opens before you. Signed with the cross, you enter the church as the presider says, "We welcome you into the church to share with us at the table of God's word." Then the Gospels are presented to you with these words: "Receive the Gospel, the good news of Jesus Christ, the Son of God." The catechumenate is a journey made with the Scriptures in hand.

Perhaps, at your entrance into the catechumenate, you received this book—the lectionary. The lectionary is the book which contains all the Scriptures to be read at the Eucharist. As the "table of God's word," it offers us a rich banquet from which to be nourished. This edition offers you the Scriptures for all three cycles of the lectionary, along with resources to assist you in praying with the readings. For each Sunday or feast day there is a reflection on the readings, suggestions for prayer, and suggestions for journal keeping.

Each Sunday you will celebrate the liturgy of the word with the entire community. At the conclusion of this first part of the Mass, you will be sent with the other catechumens to reflect on the meaning of the Scriptures you have just heard. This session is a time when you will deepen your understanding of the Scriptures. The Bible is the basis of our faith and you will come to understand the meaning of Catholic faith and tradition through the Scriptures and the liturgy. But most importantly, it is a time when you will hear God calling you personally, inviting you to share more deeply in God's own life and sending you out to share the Gospel with others.

Living the Gospel is not simply a matter of the head. It involves a transformation of the heart, a modeling of oneself after Christ. This conversion happens through prayer. The period of the catechumenate is a time of prayer. For some it may involve learning how to pray. For others it will involve a deepening of a life of prayer already begun. The reflections and suggestions in this book are designed to help you pray, whether you are a beginner or more experienced. Many people find the use of a journal to be a helpful tool. It offers a way of focusing new insights and allows one to see patterns of growth or persistent calls to change. For this reason, suggestions for journal keeping have been included for each

1

week. Prayerful reflection on the Sunday Scriptures, both before and after the catechumenal session, will enrich the time of the session and make you more receptive to God's call.

The contributors to this book are all people of prayer. Out of their experience of praying with the Scriptures, their experience of struggle and growth, they share their faith with you. They are also people committed to the catechumenate. Having worked with catechumens, they share with you what they have found most helpful. Their reflections and suggestions spring from their experience of teaching many others how to pray, of sharing the Catholic tradition of liturgical prayer with other catechumens. Although they are speaking first to catechumens, sponsors, and catechumenal ministers, all Christians will find their suggestions useful.

I would like to express my gratitude to all the contributors. Their enthusiasm and willingness to work under a tight schedule have made it possible to bring out this book. Thanks, too, to Karen Hinman Powell and Joseph P. Sinwell, editors of the three volumes of *Breaking Open the Word of God.* Their helpful suggestions and support enabled me to locate many of the fine contributors to this book. Hopefully it will serve as a resource which enables many to be nourished at the table of God's word.

Robert M. Hamma

Praying with the Lectionary

The lectionary is one of those books we come in contact with most often. For many, its selections from the Old and New Testaments are the only access they have to the Bible. The lectionary, along with the sacramentary with its eucharistic prayers and other special prayers, and the Bible itself, is one of our very special books, one of those shared by Catholics all over the world, and one largely shared by Episcopal and Protestant churches as well. And yet, most Catholics have never had a chance to examine it and become personally familiar with it.

THE LECTIONARY

The lectionary includes all the readings from the Old and New Testaments that we use in the eucharistic liturgy. It has readings for important seasons such as Advent, Christmastime, Lent, and Eastertime, for the Sundays throughout the year, and for solemnities like the feasts of All Saints and the Immaculate Conception, as well as the readings for the daily celebration of the Eucharist.

For Sundays, including some of our greatest feasts, such as Easter and Pentecost, the lectionary includes three great cycles, A, B, and C, each responding to an entire liturgical year, and each drawing its Gospel readings from Matthew, Mark, and Luke, respectively. We read John primarily during Eastertime and during the year of Mark (Cycle B), since Mark is a much shorter Gospel than Matthew and Luke.

For weekdays, the lectionary contains only two readings, but on Sundays and feasts there are three. Usually the first is from the Old Testament and is chosen to prepare us to hear and appreciate the Gospel reading. The second reading is picked independently of the other two. It provides a fairly continuous reading of one of Paul's letters. That way, over the span of three years, we become familiar with much of the Bible or at least with a very good sampling of it.

PRAYING WITH THE LECTIONARY

The liturgical reading of the most important Scripture passages in the eucharistic assembly, especially when accompanied by a good homily, is one of the great formative forces in Christian life. No one assumes, however, that it is enough. Beyond reading and hearing the word of God, and beyond homiletic reflection on it, we need to pray with it, and an excellent way of doing so is to pray with the readings selected for the liturgy that Sunday or that day, as the case may be.

Praying with the lectionary should normally begin with the Gospel reading, since the Gospel text is what governed the choice of the first reading, that from the Old Testament, and the responsorial psalm which moves us beyond stories of faith, prophetic announcements, and wisdom instructions directly into prayer. The same is true of the Alleluia and its verse. After the Gospel, one can then take up the first reading, the psalm and the second reading, in that order. That way we follow the order that governed the formation of the liturgy of the word for each celebration. The second time around, someone may prefer to start with the first reading and follow the order of the liturgy of the word as it is actually celebrated.

In praying with the lectionary for a particular Sunday, it often proves helpful to recall the previous Sunday's readings and even to glance at those for the Sunday that follows. That way the Gospel text will be seen in biblical context as well as in liturgical context. This is especially helpful when the reading is the continuation of a long discourse of Jesus such as we find in the Gospel of John. It is good to recall the concrete setting in which Jesus gave the discourse. Otherwise, the reading appears too abstract, even in the case of something as familiar as the Sermon on the Mount. Sometimes one has to go back several Sundays to find the setting.

In seasons like Advent and Lent, when the Gospel readings for each Sunday are meant to form one continuous Advent Gospel and Lenten Gospel, it is even more helpful to place each Sunday's Gospel reading in the context of the entire season. For example, it is much easier to pray with the Gospel for the First Sunday of Advent which looks to the final return of Christ when we know that it forms the introduction for the Advent Gospel. With it the Church wants us to situate ourselves squarely in our own moment of history. Jesus' life, teaching and miracles, as well as his passion, resurrection and ascension, all are behind us. We are in the era of the Church, looking ahead to the final coming of Christ, his second and definitive advent. Then on the second Sunday, for all three cycles, a Gospel story about John the Baptist and his mission models how we are to prepare the way for Christ's final coming.

PRAYERFUL READING

Prayerful reading is, first of all, a close, attentive reading, open to what the Gospel and the other lessons say to us. This requires that we respect the Gospel's literary form. We do this easiest in the case of actual prayers, like the Lord's Prayer, the Psalms, and the Magnificat, Mary's great song of praise. All of these were meant to be prayed. Even so, a prayer of supplication is not the same as one of repentance or praise, and our prayer must respect the difference. Our attitude should be attuned to the nature of each prayer.

In praying with the little stories told by Jesus, his parables, respecting the literary form includes taking note of the context in which the story was told, to whom Jesus told it, and what occasioned his telling it. The story of the prodigal son, for example, is well understood when we note that it came in response to the complaint of Pharisees and their scribes that Jesus was welcoming tax collectors and others who failed to observe the law and that he was actually eating with them. Only then does it become clear that its principal focus is on the older brother who refused to celebrate the return of his younger brother who had gone astray but had now returned home (Lk 15:1–32). We are never told what the older brother did. Did he persist in resisting his father's pleading? Did he finally overcome his anger and hurt feelings and join in the reconciliation banquet? We do not know. The reading invites us to provide our own feelings and answer those questions on the basis of what we would do. It provides an excellent launching pad for prayer.

Prophetic texts and the letters of Paul speak to us directly in the second person. We need to listen to them, meditate on how they apply to us and ask for the strength to hear their message and live by it. Like some of Jesus' own prophetic statements, which ask that we reform our lives and believe the Gospel, they can be extremely challenging. Even to hear what they ask of us is a difficult and purifying experience.

Then, of course, there are the stories, usually written in the third person. There are stories of Abraham and Sarah, stories of Moses and the exodus, stories of judges, warriors and kings, as well as stories of Jesus, his disciples and the apostolic community. These require special attention.

ENGAGING THE IMAGINATION

In every case, but especially in that of stories, it is most important to engage the imagination. This means we have to resist the temptation to rest satisfied with finding the point of the story. We need to enter the story, that is, think of ourselves among its personages, listening and responding with them to what Jesus and others say. We need to enter eager to join in the dialogue.

There is no engaging the imagination without taking time to picture the place where the event in the story takes place. We need also to pay attention to the time at which it occurs. Being in Jerusalem for Passover is not like being anywhere else at Passover, and eating Passover away from Jerusalem is not the same as eating it in the ancient city of David, Israel's great symbol of freedom, of the Lord's presence, and of every blessed hope.

Only when the imagination is engaged can we follow the contours of the story as participants, attentive to those moments when it invites prayer. The moments of invitation include the sayings and other teachings of Jesus. Sometimes no one in the story responds to them. This silence calls for our response. Other moments consist in questions, such as Jesus' questions to the disciples: "Who do people say that I am? Who do you say that I am?" We know how the disciples and Peter answered. How shall we answer?

The biblical stories are filled with great images: the garden in Eden, the tower of Babel, Mount Sinai, the desert of the exodus, the Jordan crossing, the ascent to Jerusalem, the shores of the Sea of Galilee, Simon's fishing boat, the loaves, the fishes, drinking the cup Jesus drinks—all of these must lodge in our imagination. Then when we leave formal prayer they accompany us throughout the day. What was it like to cross the Sea of Galilee in a little boat when a storm suddenly descended? Does that ever happen to us? Where is the Lord Jesus at those moments? Is he sleeping in the bow of the boat? And what are we to think when Jesus chides his disciples for having so little faith?

The readings in the lectionary ask many questions of us. We too must be able to ask many questions of them. Why does Mark call his Gospel "The beginning of the gospel of Jesus Christ, Son of God"? Was this story of passion and death really a beginning? What does this say to us of moments in our lives which seem to be the end? Might they not, like Mark's Gospel, be new beginnings? Passion and resurrection are over and over again. Ah, yes, Lord! That we may see!

Eugene LaVerdiere, S.S.S.

*Five Steps for Praying
with the Lectionary*

1. Begin with the Gospel, then the first reading, the responsorial psalm and the second reading.
2. Look back and ahead at the Gospels of surrounding weeks to get the concrete setting of this Gospel.
3. Remember the liturgical season (e.g., Advent) and relate this Gospel to the meaning of the season.
4. Look for the literary form that the reading takes. Is it a prayer, a parable, a prophecy, a story? Understanding the kind of reading this is will help you respond appropriately to it.
5. Use your imagination to enter into the scene, to create the characters. Be there in the world of the reading.

Calendar of Celebrations in the Liturgical Year: 2000-2025

Year	Sunday Cycle	1st Sunday of Advent	Ash Wednesday	Easter	Ascension Thursday	Pentecost
2000	B	Nov. 28	Mar. 8	Apr. 23	June 1	June 11
2001	C	Dec. 3	Feb. 28	Apr. 15	May 24	June 3
2002	A	Dec. 2	Feb. 13	Mar. 31	May 9	May 19
2003	B	Dec. 1	Mar. 5	Apr. 20	May 29	June 8
2004	C	Nov. 30	Feb. 25	Apr. 11	May 20	May 30
2005	A	Nov. 28	Feb. 9	Mar. 27	May 5	May 15
2006	B	Nov. 27	Mar. 1	Apr. 16	May 25	June 4
2007	C	Dec. 3	Feb. 21	Apr. 8	May 17	May 27
2008	A	Dec. 2	Feb. 6	Mar. 23	May 1	May 11
2009	B	Nov. 30	Feb. 25	Apr. 12	May 21	May 31
2010	C	Nov. 29	Feb. 17	Apr. 4	May 13	May 23
2011	A	Nov. 28	Mar. 9	Apr. 24	June 2	June 12
2012	B	Nov. 27	Feb. 22	Apr. 8	May 17	May 27
2013	C	Dec. 2	Feb. 13	Mar. 31	May 9	May 19
2014	A	Dec. 1	Mar. 5	Apr. 20	May 29	June 8
2015	B	Nov. 30	Feb. 18	Apr. 5	May 14	May 24
2016	C	Nov. 29	Feb. 10	Mar. 27	May 5	May 15
2017	A	Nov. 27	Mar. 1	Apr. 16	May 25	June 4
2018	B	Dec. 3	Feb. 14	Apr. 1	May 10	May 20
2019	C	Dec. 2	Mar. 6	Apr. 21	May 30	June 9
2020	A	Dec. 1	Feb. 26	Apr. 12	May 21	May 31
2021	B	Nov. 29	Feb. 17	Apr. 4	May 13	May 23
2022	C	Nov. 28	Mar. 2	Apr. 17	May 26	June 5
2023	A	Nov. 27	Feb. 22	Apr. 9	May 18	May 28
2024	B	Dec. 3	Feb. 14	Mar. 31	May 9	May 19
2025	C	Dec. 1	Mar. 5	Apr. 20	May 29	June 8

LET US WALK IN THE LIGHT OF THE LORD

ADVENT

First Sunday of Advent **A**

READING I   Is 2, 1–5

This is what Isaiah, son of Amoz, saw con-
        cerning Judah and Jerusalem.
    In days to come,
The mountain of the Lord's house
        shall be established as the highest moun-
        tain
        and raised above the hills.
All nations shall stream toward it;
        many peoples shall come and say:
"Come, let us climb the Lord's mountain,
        to the house of the God of Jacob,
That he may instruct us in his ways,
        and we may walk in his paths."
For from Zion shall go forth instruction,
        and the word of the Lord from Jerusalem.
He shall judge between the nations,
        and impose terms on many peoples.
They shall beat their swords into plowshares
        and their spears into pruning hooks;
One nation shall not raise the sword against
        another,
        nor shall they train for war again.
O house of Jacob, come,
        let us walk in the light of the Lord!

Responsorial Psalm   Ps 122, 1–2. 3–4. 4–
                                              5. 6–7. 8–9

I rejoiced when I heard them say:
    let us go to the house of the Lord.
I rejoiced because they said to me,
    "We will go up to the house of the Lord."
And now we have set foot
    within your gates, O Jerusalem.
I rejoiced when I heard them say:
    let us go to the house of the Lord.
Jerusalem, built as a city
    with compact unity.
To it the tribes go up,
    the tribes of the Lord.
I rejoiced when I heard them say:
    let us go to the house of the Lord.
According to the decree for Israel,
    to give thanks to the name of the Lord.
In it are set up judgment seats,
    seats for the house of David.
I rejoiced when I heard them say:
    let us go to the house of the Lord.
Pray for the peace of Jerusalem!
    May those who love you prosper!
May peace be within your walls,
    prosperity in your buildings.
I rejoiced when I heard them say:
    let us go to the house of the Lord.

9

Because of my relatives and friends
  I will say, "Peace be within you!"
Because of the house of the Lord, our God,
  I will pray for your good.
I rejoiced when I heard them say:
  let us go to the house of the Lord.

READING II
Rom 13, 11–14

You know the time in which we are living. It is now the hour for you to wake from sleep, for our salvation is closer than when we first accepted the faith. The night is far spent; the day draws near. Let us cast off deeds of darkness and put on the armor of light. Let us live honorably as in daylight; not in carousing and drunkenness, not in sexual excess and lust, not in quarreling and jealousy. Rather, put on the Lord Jesus Christ and make no provision for the desires of the flesh.

GOSPEL
Mt 24, 37–44

Jesus said to his disciples: "The coming of the Son of Man will repeat what happened in Noah's time. In the days before the flood people were eating and drinking, marrying and being married, right up to the day Noah entered the ark. They were totally unconcerned until the flood came and destroyed them. So will it be at the coming of the Son of Man. Two men will be out in the field; one will be taken and one will be left. Two women will be grinding meal; one will be taken and one will be left. Stay awake, therefore! You cannot know the day your Lord is coming.

"Be sure of this: if the owner of the house knew when the thief was coming he would keep a watchful eye and not allow his house to be broken into. You must be prepared in the same way. The Son of Man is coming at the time you least expect."

Reflection on the Readings

Stay awake; be prepared; you cannot know the day your Lord is coming.

Jesus reminds the disciples to be vigilant and to prepare themselves for the Lord's coming. No one knows when the Lord shall come. For Matthew and the early Christian community, the return of the Lord was anticipated daily. For we who live at the dawn of the twenty-first century, is our anticipation as vigilant? How tragic it would be for the Lord's coming to find us unconcerned. Was not that the fate of those of Noah's time, going about their life without regard for tomorrow?

But you who have put on the armor of light are indeed ready. To put on Jesus and to take on the cross speaks of preparation, a making ready of oneself. Those deeds done in darkness are cast aside by the light of Christ.

This preparation that we make daily is done for salvation's sake so that we will be among those called into the reign of God. As Isaiah reminds us, if we turn to the Lord, if we pursue the Lord, if we climb the Lord's mountain, if we listen to the Lord and would be instructed by God's word, if we walk in the path of the Lord, we would receive the promise of fulfillment to dwell in the house of the Lord; a house of peace, a house of joy.

O house of Jacob, come,
Let us walk in the light of the Lord.

Suggestions for Prayer

1. Isaiah 2:3 invites a meditation prayer. In a relaxed position, close your eyes and with your imagination place yourself in the presence of the Lord. Picture yourself receiving instruction from the Lord. What does the Lord wish to teach you to-

day? Allow yourself to hear this instruction repeatedly in your mind.

2. What are the deeds of darkness in your life that must be cast off as you put on the armor of light?

3. Read Psalm 119:33–40 each day this week as a morning and evening reflection.

Suggestion for Journal Keeping

How have you already prepared yourself for the Lord's coming?

What preparation do you now discern is still needed in your life?

John T. Butler

First Sunday of Advent

READING I Is 63, 16–17. 19; 64, 2–7

You, Lord, are our father,
  our redeemer you are named forever.
Why do you let us wander, O Lord, from your ways,
  and harden our hearts so that we fear you not?
Return for the sake of your servants,
  the tribes of your heritage.
Oh, that you would rend the heavens and come down,
  with the mountains quaking before you,
While you wrought awesome deeds we could not hope for,
  such as they had not heard of from of old.
No ear has ever heard, no eye ever seen,
  any God but you
  doing such deeds for those who wait for him.

Would that you might meet us doing right,
  that we were mindful of you in our ways!
Behold, you are angry, and we are sinful;
  all of us have become like unclean men,
  all our good deeds are like polluted rags;
We have all withered like leaves,
  and our guilt carries us away like the wind.
There is none who calls upon your name,
  who rouses himself to cling to you;
For you have hidden your face from us
  and have delivered us up to our guilt.
Yet, O Lord, you are our father;
  we are the clay and you are the potter:
  we are all the work of your hands.

Responsorial Psalm Ps 80, 2–3. 15–16. 18–19

Lord, make us turn to you,
  let us see your face and we shall be saved.
O shepherd of Israel, hearken,
  from your throne upon the cherubim,
    shine forth.
Rouse your power,
  and come to save us.
Lord, make us turn to you,
  let us see your face and we shall be saved.
Once again, O Lord of hosts,
  look down from heaven, and see;
Take care of this vine,
  and protect what your right hand has planted
  [the son of man whom you yourself made strong].
Lord, make us turn to you,
  let us see your face and we shall be saved.
May your help be with the man of your right hand,
  with the son of man whom you yourself made strong.

Then we will no more withdraw from you;
  give us new life, and we will call upon
    your name.
Lord, make us turn to you,
  let us see your face and we shall be saved.

READING II   I Cor 1, 3–9
Grace and peace from God our Father and the Lord Jesus Christ.

I continually thank my God for you because of the favor he has bestowed on you in Christ Jesus, in whom you have been richly endowed with every gift of speech and knowledge. Likewise, the witness I bore to Christ has been so confirmed among you that you lack no spiritual gift as you wait for the revelation of our Lord Jesus [Christ.] He will strengthen you to the end, so that you will be blameless on the day of our Lord Jesus Christ. God is faithful, and it was he who called you to fellowship with his Son, Jesus Christ our Lord.

GOSPEL   Mk 13, 33–37
Jesus said to his disciples: "Be constantly on the watch! Stay awake! You do not know when the appointed time will come. It is like a man traveling abroad. He leaves home and places his servants in charge, each with his own task; and he orders the man at the gate to watch with a sharp eye. Look around you! You do not know when the master of the house is coming, whether at dusk, at midnight, when the cock crows, or at early dawn. Do not let him come suddenly and catch you asleep. What I say to you, I say to all: Be on guard!"

Reflection on the Readings
  As anxious pilgrims we are called to *watch*. "Be constantly on the *watch*! Stay awake!

. . . Be on guard!" (Mark) How are we to understand these words? With *alarm?* (Isaiah: Behold, you are angry and we are sinful.") With *secrecy?* (Isaiah: Would that you might meet us doing right.") With *diligence?* (Isaiah: "Why do you let us wander, O Lord, from your ways?") With *anticipation?* (Isaiah: "No ear has ever heard, no eye ever seen, any God but you doing such deeds for those who wait for him.") With *longing?* (Isaiah: "We are the clay you are the potter; we are all the work of your hands.")

  Most of Chapter 13 of Mark speaks of the second coming and also the destruction of Jerusalem. The tone is certainly ominous. Mark's audience may well have been expecting the "end times," but when the end did not take place, those early listeners had to ask the same questions that we ask today. How shall we *watch?*

  We must be on *watch* day by day as we look for the Lord. If we harbor unrepented sin, certainly the meeting of the Lord is alarming. If we have failed to do the good that we ought, we will be fearful that the Lord will find us out. However, if we have strayed from the path, we will be watching anxiously, with outstretched hand, for the Lord to show us the way. And if we are "ready to go" to follow in his footsteps, we can hardly wait for him to come! And if we know that we love him, and are first loved by him, the *watch* will be much too long as we await the caress of the potter Lord.

  "Be constantly on the watch!"

Suggestions for Prayer

1. Close your eyes. Take a few deep breaths. Place yourself in God's presence. Imagine the caress of the potter

12

Lord. Sit quietly and experience "being loved." Don't worry about words.

2. Pray for unrepentant sinners, especially those who are close to death. Ask the Lord to give them another chance, as he did so often when he walked this earth. Pray for those who are "lost." Ask the Holy Spirit to open their eyes to God's love and goodness. Pray for those who have no one to pray for them.

3. St. Joseph, the foster father of Jesus, is called the Patron of a Happy Death because he had both Jesus and Mary at his side when he died. Ask St. Joseph to pray with you for those who will die today. Pray that their death will be a joyful step into the wondrous life which "no ear has heard, and no eye has seen" (Isaiah). Ask God for the blessing of a happy death for yourself.

Suggestion for Journal Keeping

Describe your own *watch* as a pilgrim. Describe your *watch* as it is *today*. If today you meet the Lord, face to face, are you ready? What is today's message for you?

Joanna Case

First Sunday of Advent C

READING I   Jer 33, 14–16
The days are coming, says the Lord, when I will fulfill the promise I made to the house of Israel and Judah. In those days, in that time, I will raise up for David a just shoot; he shall do what is right and just in the land. In those days Judah shall be safe and Jeru-salem shall dwell secure; this is what they shall call her: "The Lord our justice."

Responsorial Psalm   Ps 25, 4–5. 8–9. 10.
14
To you, O Lord, I lift my soul.
Your ways, O Lord, make known to me;
   teach me your paths,
Guide me in your truth and teach me,
   for you are God my savior,
   and for you I wait all the day.
To you, O Lord, I lift my soul.
Good and upright is the Lord;
   thus he shows sinners the way.
He guides the humble to justice,
   he teaches the humble his way.
To you, O Lord, I lift my soul.
All the paths of the Lord are kindness and
      constancy
      toward those who keep his covenant and
         his decrees.
The friendship of the Lord is with those who
      fear him,
   and his covenant, for their instruction.
To you, O Lord, I lift my soul.

READING II   I Thes 3, 12–4, 2
May the Lord increase you and make you overflow with love for one another and for all, even as our love does for you. May he strengthen your hearts, making them blameless and holy before our God and Father at the coming of our Lord Jesus with all his holy ones.

Now, my brothers, we beg and exhort you in the Lord Jesus that, even as you learned from us how to conduct yourselves in a way pleasing to God—which you are indeed doing—so you must learn to make still

greater progress. You know the instructions we gave you in the Lord Jesus.

GOSPEL   Lk 21, 25–28. 34–36

Jesus said to his disciples: "There will be signs in the sun, the moon and the stars. On the earth, nations will be in anguish, distraught at the roaring of the sea and the waves. Men will die of fright in anticipation of what is coming upon the earth. The powers in the heavens will be shaken. After that, men will see the Son of Man coming on a cloud with great power and glory. When these things begin to happen, stand up straight and raise your heads, for your ransom is near at hand.

"Be on guard lest your spirits become bloated with indulgence and drunkenness and worldly cares. The great day will suddenly close in on you like a trap. The day I speak of will come upon all who dwell on the face of the earth, so be on the watch. Pray constantly for the strength to escape whatever is in prospect, and to stand secure before the Son of Man."

Reflection on the Readings

Advent highlights waiting and expectation. When we wait for a person to come or an event to happen, we prepare. Advent provides a time for each of us to renew the spirit of expecting God. The message of the Gospel says, "Be on guard . . . be on watch." One of the challenges of expectation is to become more conscious of how God comes to us in our everyday life.

God is present in creation in the beauty of the flowers, rivers and mountains and in the changing of the seasons. Our relationships at home, work and play can reveal the presence of God. In the events of our ordinary life, we can discover God. We may need to spend time reflecting and allowing God to become present to us. This waiting will need energy, attention, patience and time. In finding the presence of God, surprises may happen. We may discover the vast richness of God's mercy, the immensity of God's love, and the demands of God's justice. God's presence offers hope.

Each of us is challenged to let God's presence enter our lives and become a living symbol of God's presence to each other. How do we invite God into our lives? How do we prepare for the coming of God?

Suggestions for Prayer

1. Reflect on people, events and things that you could offer to God, and complete the responsorial psalm:
   "To you, O Lord, I lift up _____ ."
2. In the first reading, God is called "the Lord our justice." Reflect on the injustices that exist in your life, community and the world. And ask God to free us. As a response, you could use this form: "From (name injustices), O God, deliver us."
3. Recall people and events today. How was God present in the people and events? Respond to God's presence with your own thoughts or words.

Suggestion for Journal Keeping

God's presence in our lives offers hope. What does hope in God mean for you? How do you offer hope in God to others?

Joseph P. Sinwell

Second Sunday of Advent A

READING I   Is 11, 1–10

On that day
A shoot shall sprout from the stump of Jesse,
  and from his roots a bud shall blossom.
The spirit of the Lord shall rest upon him:
  a spirit of wisdom and of understanding,
A spirit of counsel and of strength,
    a spirit of knowledge and of fear of the
    Lord,
    and his delight shall be the fear of the
    Lord.
Not by appearance shall he judge,
  nor by hearsay shall he decide,
But he shall judge the poor with justice,
  and decide aright for the land's afflicted.
He shall strike the ruthless with the rod of
    his mouth,
    and with the breath of his lips he shall slay
    the wicked.
Justice shall be the band around his waist,
  and faithfulness a belt upon his hips.

Then the wolf shall be a guest of the lamb,
  and the leopard shall lie down with the
  kid;
The calf and the young lion shall browse to-
    gether,
  with a little child to guide them.
The cow and the bear shall be neighbors,
  together their young shall rest;
  the lion shall eat hay like the ox.
The baby shall play by the cobra's den,
  and the child lay his hand on the adder's
  lair.
There shall be no harm or ruin on all my holy
    mountain;
  for the earth shall be filled with knowl-
    edge of the Lord,
  as water covers the sea.

On that day,
The root of Jesse,
  set up as a signal for the nations,
The Gentiles shall seek out,
  for his dwelling shall be glorious.

Responsorial Psalm   Ps 72, 1–2. 7–8. 12–
                                              13. 17

Justice shall flourish in his time,
  and fullness of peace for ever.
O God, with your judgment endow the king,
  and with your justice, the king's son;
He shall govern your people with justice
  and your afflicted ones with judgment.
Justice shall flourish in his time,
  and fullness of peace for ever.
Justice shall flower in his days,
  and profound peace, till the moon be no
  more.
May he rule from sea to sea,
  and from the River to the ends of the
  earth.
Justice shall flourish in his time,
  and fullness of peace for ever.
For he shall rescue the poor man when he
  cries out,
  and the afflicted when he has no one to
  help him.
He shall have pity for the lowly and the
  poor;
  the lives of the poor he shall save.
Justice shall flourish in his time,
  and fullness of peace for ever.
May his name be blessed forever;
  as long as the sun his name shall remain.
In him shall all the tribes of the earth be
  blessed;
  all the nations shall proclaim his happiness.
Justice shall flourish in his time,
  and fullness of peace for ever.

READING II   Rom 15, 4–9

Everything written before our time was written for our instruction, that we might derive hope from the lessons of patience and the words of encouragement in the Scriptures. May God, the source of all patience and encouragement, enable you to live in perfect harmony with one another according to the spirit of Christ Jesus, so that with one heart and voice you may glorify God, the Father of our Lord Jesus Christ.

Accept one another, then, as Christ accepted you, for the glory of God. Yes, I affirm that Christ became the servant of the Jews because of God's faithfulness in fulfilling the promises to the patriarchs whereas the Gentiles glorify God because of his mercy. As Scripture has it, "Therefore I will praise you among the Gentiles and I will sing to your name."

GOSPEL   Mt 3, 1–12

When John the Baptizer made his appearance as a preacher in the desert of Judea, this was his theme: "Reform your lives! The reign of God is at hand." It was of him that the prophet Isaiah had spoken when he said,

> "A herald's voice in the desert:
> 'Prepare the way of the Lord,
> make straight his paths.' "

John was clothed in a garment of camel's hair and wore a leather belt around his waist. Grasshoppers and wild honey were his food. At that time Jerusalem, all Judea, and the whole region around the Jordan were going out to him. They were being baptized by him in the Jordan River as they confessed their sins.

When he saw that many of the Pharisees and Sadducees were stepping forward for this bath, he said to them: "You brood of vipers! Who told you to flee from the wrath to come? Give some evidence that you mean to reform. Do not pride yourselves on the claim, 'Abraham is our father.' I tell you, God can raise up children to Abraham from these very stones. Even now the ax is laid to the root of the tree. Every tree that is not fruitful will be cut down and thrown into the fire. I baptize you in water for the sake of reform, but the one who will follow me is more powerful than I. I am not even fit to carry his sandals. He it is who will baptize you in the Holy Spirit and fire. His winnowing-fan is in his hand. He will clear his threshing floor, and gather his grain into the barn, but the chaff he will burn in unquenchable fire."

Reflection on the Readings

Reform your lives! The reign of God is at hand.

John the Baptist appears to speak a harsh word, calling the Pharisees and Sadducees who were coming forward to be baptized "brood of vipers" and admonishing them to give some proof that they intended to reform their lives. Repentance, change, turning from evil to God is what John preached. It is likely that those whom he addressed felt themselves to be ready. John's challenge invites them to see that something more radical is needed than just the rigid adherence to the law.

How much are we like the Pharisees and Sadducees, assuming that all is well since we follow the law not realizing that more is required of us? Today's Gospel invites us to take seriously our preparation; to take responsibility for the faith we have been given. It invites us to see the deep-rooted change that needs to take place if we are to truly be made ready for the Lord's coming.

Isaiah's vision, in which the wolf shall be a guest of the lamb, is a testimony to the radical nature of the change that is required on our part. The very core of our being must be affected by the peace and love of Christ, if we are to truly reform our lives. Paul's prayer in Romans 15:5–6 affirms this call to perfect peace in Christ.

Suggestions for Prayer

1. If confronted by John the Baptist, what would be the signs of reform evident in your life?
2. The vision of peace that Isaiah reflects on calls for profound change. What prevents you from living in perfect harmony with those around you?
3. Reflect on Psalm 25:4–5 by reciting these verses throughout each day of this week.

Suggestion for Journal Keeping
John the Baptizer warned that every tree that is not fruitful will be cut down and thrown into the fire.

What fruit has been born by you?

John T. Butler

Second Sunday of Advent B

READING I   Is 40, 1–5. 9–11
Comfort, give comfort to my people,
  says your God.
Speak tenderly to Jerusalem, and proclaim to her

that her service is at an end,
  her guilt is expiated;
Indeed, she has received from the hand of the Lord
  double for all her sins.
  A voice cries out:
In the desert prepare the way of the Lord!
  Make straight in the wasteland a highway for our God!
Every valley shall be filled in,
  every mountain and hill shall be made low;
The rugged land shall be made a plain,
  the rough country, a broad valley.
Then the glory of the Lord shall be revealed,
  and all mankind shall see it together;
  for the mouth of the Lord has spoken.

Go up onto a high mountain,
  Zion, herald of glad tidings;
Cry out at the top of your voice,
  Jerusalem, herald of good news!
Fear not to cry out
  and say to the cities of Judah:
  Here is your God!
Here comes with power
  the Lord God,
  who rules by his strong arm;
Here is his reward with him,
  his recompense before him.
Like a shepherd he feeds his flock;
  in his arms he gathers the lambs,
Carrying them in his bosom,
  and leading the ewes with care.

Responsorial Psalm   Ps 85, 9–10. 11–12. 13–14
Lord, let us see your kindness,
  and grant us your salvation.
I will hear what God proclaims;
  the Lord—for he proclaims peace to his people.

17

Near indeed is his salvation to those who
  fear him,
  glory dwelling in our land.
Lord, let us see your kindness,
  and grant us your salvation.
Kindness and truth shall meet;
  justice and peace shall kiss.
Truth shall spring out of the earth,
  and justice shall look down from heaven.
Lord, let us see your kindness,
  and grant us your salvation.
The Lord himself will give his benefits;
  our land shall yield its increase.
Justice shall walk before him,
  and salvation, along the way of his steps.
Lord, let us see your kindness,
  and grant us your salvation.

READING II   2 Pt 3, 8–14
This point must not be overlooked, dear
friends. In the Lord's eyes, one day is as a
thousand years and a thousand years are as
a day. The Lord does not delay in keeping his
promise—though some consider it "delay."
Rather, he shows you generous patience,
since he wants none to perish but all to come
to repentance. The day of the Lord will come
like a thief, and on that day the heavens will
vanish with a roar; the elements will be destroyed by fire, and the earth and all its
deeds will be made manifest.

Since everything is to be destroyed in this
way, what sort of men must you not be! How
holy in your conduct and devotion, looking
for the coming of the day of God and trying
to hasten it! Because of it, the heavens will
be destroyed in flames and the elements will
melt away in a blaze. What we await are
new heavens and a new earth where, according to his promise, the justice of God
will reside. So, beloved, while waiting for

this, make every effort to be found without
stain or defilement, and at peace in his sight.

GOSPEL   Mk 1, 1–8
Here begins the gospel of Jesus Christ, the
Son of God. In Isaiah the prophet, it is written:
    "I send my messenger before you
      to prepare your way:
      a herald's voice in the desert,
        crying,
    Make ready the way of the Lord,
      clear him a straight path.' "
Thus it was that John the Baptizer appeared in the desert proclaiming a baptism
of repentance which led to the forgiveness
of sins. All the Judean countryside and the
people of Jerusalem went out to him in great
numbers. They were being baptized by him
in the Jordan River as they confessed their
sins. John was clothed in camel's hair, and
wore a leather belt around his waist. His
food was grasshoppers and wild honey. The
theme of his preaching was: "One more
powerful than I is to come after me. I am not
fit to stoop and untie his sandal straps. I have
baptized you in water; he will baptize you in
the Holy Spirit."

Reflection on the Readings
  Over and over in Scripture, the term "kingdom of God" or "reign of God" is used. We
learn that it is "at hand," "within us" and in
our "midst." It is a way of "seeing" the world
in God's terms; it is a process of living and
responding to life with goodness and mercy
and justice; it is "now" because the Lord is
in our midst calling us to life as God intends
it; it is "not yet" because God's reign is not
perfect in us; it is a *being* and a *becoming*:

18

"Thy kingdom come, thy will be done on earth as it is in heaven."

Today's readings have a lot of good news about the kingdom! However, if you read *carefully* there is a very insistent theme that is revealed about the kingdom: a change of heart is required. Isaiah says: "Every valley shall be filled in. . . . Then the glory of the Lord shall be revealed." Peter says that the Lord wants "all to come to repentance." Mark says that John the Baptist proclaimed "a baptism of repentance which led to the forgiveness of sins." Repent. Change your heart. Turn around the other way (conversion). All of these words define the Greek term *metanoia*.

As with the chicken and the egg conundrum, repentance occurs when a person is touched by the reign of God, yet God cannot reign in an unrepentant heart. Conversion of life, *metanoia*, goes on and on and on.

Suggestions for Prayer

1. If at all possible, get a record or tape of Handel's *Messiah* and listen to the Isaiah reading set to music. Keep the written words before you as you listen. What words and phrases seem to "jump out" at you? How does it make you feel about God? about yourself? Listen again. Play the tape in your car as you travel the highways (making them straight, of course). Don't forget to praise God for Handel's beautiful music!

2. Read the verses of Psalm 85 that are selected for today's responsorial psalm. Look for the words "justice" and "peace." Remember that Peter spoke of the new heavens and new earth where "the justice of God will reside." Think

about the relationship of justice and the kingdom of God. Ask yourself what you are doing to promote peace and justice? What might you do? "If you want peace, work for justice" (Pope Paul VI).

3. The color of Advent is the color of the sky right before the dawn: blue tinged with a little purple. It is a moment of anticipation as the darkness is expelled. Watch the dawn one morning soon. Then you will know how to feel as the kingdom comes upon us.

Suggestion for Journal Keeping

Chronicle some of the *metanoia* in your own life. How has the Lord called you to change?

Joanna Case

Second Sunday of Advent

READING I   Bar 5, 1–9

Jerusalem, take off your robe of mourning and misery;
> **put on the splendor of glory from God forever:**

Wrapped in the cloak of justice from God, bear on your head the mitre
> **that displays the glory of the eternal name.**

For God will show all the earth your splendor:
> **you will be named by God forever the peace of justice, the glory of God's worship.**

Up, Jerusalem! stand upon the heights;
> **look to the east and see your children**

Gathered from the east and the west
  at the word of the Holy One,
  rejoicing that they are remembered by
  God.
Led away on foot by their enemies they left
  you:
  but God will bring them back to you
  borne aloft in glory as on royal thrones.
For God has commanded
  that every lofty mountain be made low,
And that the age-old depths and gorges
  be filled to level ground,
  that Israel may advance secure in the
  glory of God.
The forests and every fragrant kind of tree
  have overshadowed Israel at God's command;
For God is leading Israel in joy
  by the light of his glory,
  with his mercy and justice for company.

Responsorial Psalm   Ps 126, 1–2. 2–3. 4–
                                              5. 6

The Lord has done great things for us;
  we are filled with joy.
When the Lord brought back the captives of
  Zion,
  we were like men dreaming.
Then our mouth was filled with laughter,
  and our tongue with rejoicing.
The Lord has done great things for us;
  we are filled with joy.
Then they said among the nations,
  "The Lord has done great things for
  them."
The Lord has done great things for us;
  we are glad indeed.
The Lord has done great things for us;
  we are filled with joy.

Restore our fortunes, O Lord,
  like the torrents in the southern desert.
Those that sow in tears
  shall reap rejoicing.
The Lord has done great things for us;
  we are filled with joy.
Although they go forth weeping,
  carrying the seed to be sown,
They shall come back rejoicing,
  carrying their sheaves.
The Lord has done great things for us;
  we are filled with joy.

READING II   Phil 1, 4–6. 8–11
In every prayer I utter, I rejoice as I plead on
your behalf, at the way you have all continually helped promote the gospel from the
very first day.

I am sure of this much: that he who has
begun the good work in you will carry it
through to completion, right up to the day of
Christ Jesus. God himself can testify how
much I long for each of you with the affection of Christ Jesus! My prayer is that your
love may more and more abound, both in
understanding and wealth of experience, so
that with a clear conscience and blameless
conduct you may learn to value the things
that really matter, up to the very day of
Christ. It is my wish that you may be found
rich in the harvest of justice which Jesus
Christ has ripened in you, to the glory and
praise of God.

GOSPEL   Lk 3, 1–6
In the fifteenth year of the rule of Tiberius
Caesar, when Pontius Pilate was procurator
of Judea, Herod tetrarch of Galilee, Philip

his brother tetrarch of the region of Ituraea and Trachonitis, and Lysanias tetrarch of Abilene, during the high-priesthood of Annas and Caiaphas, the word of God was spoken to John son of Zechariah in the desert. He went about the entire region of the Jordan proclaiming a baptism of repentance which led to the forgiveness of sins, as is written in the book of the words of Isaiah the prophet:

"A herald's voice in the desert, crying,
'Make ready the way of the Lord,
    clear him a straight path.
Every valley shall be filled
    and every mountain and hill shall be
    leveled.
The windings shall be made straight
    and the rough ways smooth,
and all mankind shall see the salvation
    of God.' "

Reflection on the Readings

The Gospel centers on announcing the ministry of John the Baptist. John's message is important. He speaks directly to us, saying "Repent." The challenge is to change your life; believing in the risen Christ demands personal conversion. What actions, attitudes and values need your attention?

John the Baptist's message implies that preparing to receive the Lord Jesus makes a difference in one's life. The difference lies in turning to God. Who is the God you look for? The first reading describes a God who is powerfully merciful, just and caring. How does this description compare with your image and experience of God?

John the Baptist proclaimed forgiveness of sins. God forgives us when we fail. Each person must be willing to seek and ask. The forgiveness of God will enable us to be free from the bonds of sin and to grow in love of God and others.

Suggestions for Prayer

1. "The Lord has done great things for us." What are the great things God has done for you? Give thanks to God for each person, event and object.
2. *Reflect on one or more of the following questions:* How do you experience the forgiveness of God? How does my forgiveness of others reflect the forgiveness of God?
3. We need to be open to the call of God in our lives. Pray slowly this prayer of St. Ignatius:

Take, Lord, and receive all my liberty, my memory, my understanding, and my entire will, all that I have and possess.

You have given all to me.

To you, Lord, I return it. All is yours. Dispose of it wholly according to your will. Give me your love and your grace, for this is enough for me.

Suggestion for Journal Keeping

Describe a personal conversion experience. What was God calling you to change? In light of this Sunday's Gospel reading, what is God calling you to change now?

Joseph P. Sinwell

READING I Is 35, 1–6. 10

The desert and the parched land will exult;
   the steppe will rejoice and bloom.
They will bloom with abundant flowers,
   and rejoice with joyful song.
The glory of Lebanon will be given to them,
   the splendor of Carmel and Sharon;
They will see the glory of the Lord,
   the splendor of our God.

Strengthen the hands that are feeble,
   make firm the knees that are weak,
Say to those whose hearts are frightened:
   Be strong, fear not!
Here is your God,
   he comes with vindication;
With divine recompense
   he comes to save you.
Then will the eyes of the blind be opened,
   the ears of the deaf be cleared;
Then will the lame leap like a stag,
   then the tongue of the dumb will sing.
Those whom the Lord has ransomed will return
   and enter Zion singing,
   crowned with everlasting joy;
They will meet with joy and gladness,
   sorrow and mourning will flee.

Responsorial Psalm Ps 146, 6–7. 8–9. 9–
   10

Lord, come and save us.
The Lord God keeps faith forever,
   secures justice for the oppressed,
   gives food to the hungry.
The Lord sets captives free.
Lord, come and save us.

The Lord gives sight to the blind;
   the Lord raises up those that were bowed
   down.
The Lord loves the just;
   the Lord protects strangers.
Lord, come and save us.
The fatherless and the widow he sustains,
   but the way of the wicked he thwarts.
The Lord shall reign forever;
   Your God, O Zion, through all genera-
   tions.
Lord, come and save us.

READING II Jas 5, 7–10

Be patient, my brothers, until the coming of
the Lord. See how the farmer awaits the precious yield of the soil. He looks forward to it
patiently while the soil receives the winter
and the spring rains. You too, must be patient. Steady your hearts, because the coming of the Lord is at hand. Do not grumble
against one another, my brothers, lest you
be condemned. See! The judge stands at the
gate. As your models in suffering hardships
and in patience, brothers, take the prophets
who spoke in the name of the Lord.

GOSPEL Mt 11, 2–11

John in prison heard about the works Christ
performed, and sent a message through his
disciples to ask him, "Are you 'He who is to
come' or do we look for another?" In reply,
Jesus said to them: "Go back and report to
John what you hear and see: the blind recover their sight, cripples walk, lepers are
cured, the deaf hear, dead men are raised to
life, and the poor have the good news
preached to them. Blest is the man who finds
no stumbling block in me."

   As the messengers set off, Jesus began to
speak to the crowds about John: "What did

you go out to the wasteland to see—a reed swaying in the wind? Tell me, what did you go out to see—someone luxuriously dressed? Remember, those who dress luxuriously are to be found in royal palaces. Why then did you go out—to see a prophet? A prophet indeed, and something more! It is about this man that Scripture says,

'I send my messenger ahead of you
to prepare your way before you.'

"I solemnly assure you, history has not known a man born of woman greater than John the Baptizer. Yet the least born into the kingdom of God is greater than he."

Reflection on the Readings

Are you he who is to come or do we look for another?

This question put to Jesus on behalf of John the Baptist offers a point of reflection for us today. Having awaited the Messiah with such anticipation, Jesus does not meet the expectations of those of his day. John the Baptist, who pulls no punches, may have expected Jesus to bring about the destruction of all those who did not remain faithful. Yet, Jesus appears preaching love, healing those who were sick and reconciling sinners.

The question that we might ask is: What kind of Messiah are we looking for? What is it that we expect Jesus to do in our lives and in the world? What kind of Savior do we want? For the Savior who comes gives sight, so that those who fail to see might now see. The Savior who comes empowers and strengthens so that those who are weak are made strong in the ways of the Lord. The Savior who comes brings healing to a world sick with sin. The Savior who comes calls to new life all who are willing to die in faith.

If this is the Savior whom you seek, then steady your heart because the coming of the Lord is at hand.

> Here is your God who comes with vindication,
> with divine recompense, who comes to save you.

Suggestions for Prayer

1. Reflect on the following: What are the signs of Christ's presence in the world today? What are the signs of Jesus' presence in your life?
2. Reflect prayerfully on Psalm 146:6–10 as a morning and evening prayer this week.
3. In a relaxed position, meditate for several minutes on Isaiah 35:4 by personalizing and repeating this verse to yourself:

> Here is my God, who comes to defend and make divine amends for me.
> Here is my God, who comes to save me.

Suggestion for Journal Keeping

Describe an experience of radical change that has already taken place in your life.

John T. Butler

Third Sunday of Advent

READING I   Is 61, 1–2. 10–11

The spirit of the Lord God is upon me,
  because the Lord has anointed me;
He has sent me to bring glad tidings to the lowly,
  to heal the brokenhearted,

To proclaim liberty to the captives
  and release to the prisoners,
To announce a year of favor from the Lord
  and a day of vindication by our God.
I rejoice heartily in the Lord,
  in my God is the joy of my soul;
For he has clothed me with a robe of salvation,
  and wrapped me in a mantle of justice,
Like a bridegroom adorned with a diadem,
  like a bride bedecked with her jewels.
As the earth brings forth its plants,
  and a garden makes its growth spring up,
So will the Lord God make justice and praise
  spring up before all the nations.

Responsorial Psalm   Lk 1, 46–48. 49–50. 53–54

My soul rejoices in my God.
My being proclaims the greatness of the
  Lord,
  my spirit finds joy in God my savior,
For he has looked upon his servant in her
  lowliness;
  all ages to come shall call me blessed.
My soul rejoices in my God.
God who is mighty has done great things for
  me,
  holy is his name;
His mercy is from age to age
  on those who fear him.
My soul rejoices in my God.
The hungry he has given every good thing,
  while the rich he has sent empty away.
He has upheld Israel his servant,
  ever mindful of his mercy.
My soul rejoices in my God.

READING II   I Thes 5, 16–24

Rejoice always, never cease praying, render constant thanks; such is God's will for you in Christ Jesus.

Do not stifle the spirit. Do not despise prophecies. Test everything; retain what is good. Avoid any semblance of evil.

May the God of peace make you perfect in holiness. May you be preserved whole and entire, spirit, soul, and body, irreproachable at the coming of our Lord Jesus Christ. He who calls us is trustworthy, therefore he will do it.

GOSPEL   Jn 1, 6–8. 19–28

There was a man named John sent by God, who came as a witness to testify to the light, so that through him all men might believe— but only to testify to the light, for he himself was not the light.

The testimony John gave when the Jews sent priests and Levites from Jerusalem to ask "Who are you?" was the absolute statement, "I am not the Messiah." They questioned him further, "Who, then? Elijah?" "I am not Elijah," he answered. "Are you the prophet?" "No," he replied.

Finally they said to him: "Tell us who you are, so that we can give some answer to those who sent us. What do you have to say for yourself?" He said, quoting the prophet Isaiah, "I am

  'a voice in the desert, crying out:
  Make straight the way of the Lord!' "

Those whom the Pharisees had sent proceeded to question him further: "If you are not the Messiah, nor Elijah, nor the prophet, why do you baptize?" John answered them: "I baptize with water. There is one among you whom you do not recognize—the one

who is to come after me—the strap of whose sandal I am not worthy to unfasten." This happened in Bethany, across the Jordan, where John was baptizing.

Reflection on the Readings

For the past two Sundays we have traveled with Isaiah and John, Peter and Paul, and today Mary joins us, singing her joyful canticle (Responsorial). Kingdom persons, all of them! Today's readings give an apt description of those who belong to the Kingdom.

How to be a kingdom person:

Isaiah	God calls, "The Spirit of the Lord is upon me."
Isaiah	We respond, "I rejoice heartily in the Lord."
Isaiah	God gives a mission, "He has sent me to bring . . . "
Paul	We respond, "Rejoice always, never cease praying."
Paul	God calls, "Do not stifle the spirit. . . . He who calls us is trustworthy. . . . "
Mary	We respond, "My being proclaims the greatness of the Lord, my spirit finds joy in God my Savior."
John	God gives a mission, "There was a man named John sent by God who came as a witness. . . . "
Mary	We respond, "God who is mighty has done great things for me. Holy is his name."
You	God calls *you,* "The Spirit of the Lord is upon *me.*"
You	*You* respond, "God who is mighty has done great things for *me.*"
You	God gives *you* a mission, "There was *I,* sent by God to _____"
You	*You* respond, "_____ ."

Read all the readings again. Fill in the blanks in your heart.

Suggestions for Prayer

1. Last Sunday Peter spoke of the new heavens and new earth where "the justice of God will reside." Last Sunday we reflected on the kingdom of God. Today Isaiah says: "He has . . . wrapped me in a mantle of justice." Today we reflect on those who respond to the kingdom call. Justice again. Read Isaiah's list again from the point of view of justice. Pray for the brokenhearted, the captives, those who have no glad tidings today.

2. John the Baptist was a prophet, a truth-sayer of God's word. Think about the people in your own experience who have been truth-sayers for you (even the ones you did not want to hear). How did these prophetic voices affect you? Did you change anything in your life? Who are the prophets in the Church? In the world? Has the Lord called you to be a prophet? Pray today for more prophets, more truth-sayers and for more truth-listeners.

3. The Canticle of Mary in today's Responsorial is also known as the Magnificat (from the Latin). This is often set to music as is the Ave Maria (Latin translation of "Hail Mary"). These are often included with Christmas collections of music. Try to find one to listen to this week. (Keep it handy for next week too.)

Suggestion for Journal Keeping

Describe a "kingdom person" that you know (it doesn't have to be one who is already perfect). Is this person also a prophet? Which words from today's Scripture apply to this person?

Joanna Case

Third Sunday of Advent C

READING I   Zep 3, 14–18
Shout for joy, O daughter Zion!
  sing joyfully, O Israel!
Be glad and exult with all your heart,
  O daughter Jerusalem!
The Lord has removed the judgment against you,
  he has turned away your enemies;
The King of Israel, the Lord, is in your midst,
  you have no further misfortune to fear.
On that day, it shall be said to Jeru-
  salem:
  Fear not, O Zion, be not discouraged!
The Lord, your God, is in your midst,
  a mighty savior;
He will rejoice over you with gladness,
  and renew you in his love.
He will sing joyfully because of you,
  as one sings at festivals.

Responsorial Psalm   Is 12, 2–3. 4. 5–6
Cry out with joy and gladness:
  for among you is the great and Holy One
  of Israel.
God indeed is my savior;
  I am confident and unafraid.
My strength and my courage is the Lord,
  and he has been my savior.
With joy you will draw water
  at the fountain of salvation.

Cry out with joy and gladness:
  for among you is the great and Holy One
  of Israel.
Give thanks to the Lord, acclaim his name;
  among the nations make known his deeds,
  proclaim how exalted is his name.
Cry out with joy and gladness:
  for among you is the great and Holy One
  of Israel.
Sing praise to the Lord for his glorious achievement;
  let this be known throughout all the earth.
Shout with exultation, O city of Zion,
  for great in your midst
  is the Holy One of Israel!
Cry out with joy and gladness:
  for among you is the great and Holy One
  of Israel.

READING II   Phil 4, 4–7
Rejoice in the Lord always! I say it again. Rejoice! Everyone should see how unselfish you are. The Lord himself is near. Dismiss all anxiety from your minds. Present your needs to God in every form of prayer and in petitions full of gratitude. Then God's own peace, which is beyond all understanding, will stand guard over your hearts and minds, in Christ Jesus.

GOSPEL   Lk 3, 10–18
The crowds asked John, "What ought we to do?" In reply he said, "Let the man with two coats give to him who has none. The man who has food should do the same."
  Tax collectors also came to be baptized, and they said to him, "Teacher, what are we to do?" He answered them, "Exact nothing over and above your fixed amount."
  Soldiers likewise asked him, "What about

26

us?" He told them, "Do not bully anyone. Denounce no one falsely. Be content with your pay."

The people were full of anticipation, wondering in their hearts whether John might be the Messiah. John answered them all by saying: "I am baptizing you in water, but there is one to come who is mightier than I. I am not fit to loosen his sandal strap. He will baptize you in the Holy Spirit and in fire. His winnowing-fan is in his hand to clear his threshing floor and gather the wheat into his granary, but the chaff he will burn in unquenchable fire." Using exhortations of this sort, he preached the good news to the people.

Reflection on the Readings

The message of the first reading and the Gospel is that God who saves draws close to us. When God is near, how do we react? Do we hesitate because of uncertainty or avoid because of fear? Do we refuse to meet God because of apathy? God comes to us out of love. God comes to us whether we are ready or not. Advent centers on expecting God to come.

Our response to this coming may be joy. We can experience the nearness of God through the actions of others, nature, prayer or reflection. The smile of a friend, the listening of another, the presence of a loved one, the beauty of a sunset or the comfort of silence can reveal God. We may be able to "cry out with joy and gladness."

After this response of joy or gladness, we ask the question of the crowd to John the Baptist: "What ought we to do?" The response in the Gospel to a variety of people, e.g., rich person, tax collector and soldier, is straightforward: be generous and honest, as well as just and fair to others, be conscious of who you are and what are your responsibilities, and perform them with care and unselfishness.

Each of us plays a variety of roles: citizen, worker, professional, laity, clergy, religious, mother, father, sister, etc. We can serve others in these roles. Our challenge is to bring the "good news to the people" and to enable others to share the good news of a God who is near and cares for each person.

Suggestions for Prayer

1. God is present when we experience joy. Remember a time when you were full of joy or happiness.

    What happened? Who was present? Praise God for the events, people and time by repeating slowly these words of the second reading, "Rejoice in the Lord always. Again I say: Rejoice."

2. The Magnificat or Canticle of Mary in the Gospel of Luke announces joy at the nearness and greatness of God. Read Luke 1:46–55 and pray this prayer of the Church.

3. Imagine that God comes to you and speaks. To each phrase below you may respond. God says to you the following:

    I am near to you.
    Dismiss all anxiety.
    Present your needs to me.
    My peace is beyond understanding.

Suggestion for Journal Keeping

Remember a time when you wanted or felt that God was near to you. Describe the experience. How did God come to us. Describe God. What happened after the experience?

How did the experience change you? How does the nearness of God affect you today?

Joseph P. Sinwell

Fourth Sunday of Advent **A**

READING I   Is 7, 10–14
The Lord spoke to Ahaz: Ask for a sign from the Lord, your God; let it be deep as the nether world, or high as the sky! But Ahaz answered, "I will not ask! I will not tempt the Lord!" Then he said: Listen, O house of David! Is it not enough for you to weary men, must you also weary my God? Therefore the Lord himself will give you this sign: the virgin shall be with child, and bear a son, and shall name him Immanuel.

Responsorial Psalm   Ps 24, 1–2. 3–4. 5–6
Let the Lord enter; he is king of glory.
The Lord's are the earth and its fullness;
    the world and those who dwell in it.
For he founded it upon the seas
    and established it upon the rivers.
Let the Lord enter; he is king of glory.
Who can ascend the mountain of the Lord?
    or who may stand in his holy place?
He whose hands are sinless, whose heart is
    clean,
    who desires not what is vain.
Let the Lord enter; he is king of glory.
He shall receive a blessing from the Lord,
    a reward from God his savior.
Such is the race that seeks for him,
    that seeks the face of the God of Jacob.
Let the Lord enter; he is king of glory.

READING II   Rom 1, 1–7
Greetings from Paul, a servant of Christ Jesus, called to be an apostle and set apart to proclaim the gospel of God which he promised long ago through his prophets, as the holy Scriptures record—the gospel concerning his Son, who was descended from David according to the flesh but was made Son of God in power, according to the spirit of holiness, by his resurrection from the dead: Jesus Christ our Lord. Through him we have been favored with apostleship, that we may spread his name and bring to obedient faith all the Gentiles, among whom are you who have been called to belong to Jesus Christ.

To all in Rome, beloved of God and called to holiness, grace and peace from God our Father and the Lord Jesus Christ.

GOSPEL   Mt 1, 18–24
This is how the birth of Jesus Christ came about. When his mother Mary was engaged to Joseph, but before they lived together, she was found with child through the power of the Holy Spirit. Joseph her husband, an upright man unwilling to expose her to the law, decided to divorce her quietly. Such was his intention when suddenly the angel of the Lord appeared in a dream and said to him: "Joseph, son of David, have no fear about taking Mary as your wife. It is by the Holy Spirit that she has conceived this child. She is to have a son and you are to name him Jesus because he will save his people from their sins." All this happened to fulfill what the Lord had said through the prophet:
    "The virgin shall be with child
        and give birth to a son,
        and they shall call him Emmanuel,"
a name which means "God is with us."

When Joseph awoke he did as the angel of the Lord had directed him and received her into his home as his wife.

Reflection on the Readings
Emmanuel, "God is with us."

The promise of God's presence is the promise of salvation. The sign that was sought since before the days of Isaiah is now given to the world through the power of the Holy Spirit and the obedient response of Mary and Joseph.

Our inclination might be to view this story of Jesus' birth from one dimension, to focus exclusively on the virgin birth. Were we to do this, we would miss the perspective that Jewish faith brought to this moment. For the Jewish faith saw the Spirit as the source of God's action in the world. It was the Spirit that taught the prophet what to say and brought God's truth to the people of Israel. It was the Spirit that enabled God's people to recognize the word of God when they heard it and the hand of God when they saw it.

In Jesus, the Holy Spirit was so present as to manifest God to the world. It is Jesus who now brings God's truth to all who open their hearts. This truth, once received, would transform us as it transformed Mary who conceived the child Jesus, and Joseph her faith-filled husband. Thus transformed, Paul reminds us that we are favored with apostleship, so that we might spread his name and bring to obedient faith all who have been called to belong to Jesus Christ.

Suggestions for Prayer

1. The Magnificat, Luke 1:46–55, is a traditional canticle sung at evening prayer. Pray this canticle of Mary each evening of this week.
2. Pray Psalm 111:1–10 daily this week by reading the psalm both quietly and aloud as a morning prayer.
3. Set aside 30–45 minutes to spend in prayerful devotion to the Blessed Virgin Mary reciting the joyful mysteries of the rosary. Ask your sponsor or spiritual guide for help if you do not know how to pray the rosary.

Suggestion for Journal Keeping

Describe an experience when you felt God's presence in a special way in your life.

John T. Butler

Fourth Sunday of Advent

READING I   2 Sm 7, 1–5. 8–11. 16
When King David was settled in his palace, and the Lord had given him rest from his enemies on every side, he said to Nathan the prophet, "Here I am living in a house of cedar, while the ark of God dwells in a tent!" Nathan answered the king, "Go, do whatever you have in mind, for the Lord is with you." But that night the Lord spoke to Nathan and said: "Go, tell my servant David, 'Thus says the Lord: Should you build me a house to dwell in?

" 'It was I who took you from the pasture and from the care of the flock to be commander of my people Israel. I have been with you wherever you went, and I have destroyed all your enemies before you. And I will make you famous like the great ones of

the earth. I will fix a place for my people Israel; I will plant them so that they may dwell in their place without further disturbance. Neither shall the wicked continue to afflict them as they did of old, since the time I first appointed judges over my people Israel. I will give you rest from all your enemies. The Lord also reveals to you that he will establish a house for you. Your house and your kingdom shall endure forever before me; your throne shall stand firm forever.' "

Responsorial Psalm   Ps 89, 2–3. 4–5. 27. 29

For ever I will sing the goodness of the Lord.

The favors of the Lord I will sing forever;
　through all generations my mouth shall proclaim your faithfulness.
For you have said, "My kindness is established forever";
　in heaven you have confirmed your faithfulness.
For ever I will sing the goodness of the Lord.

"I have made a covenant with my chosen one,
　I have sworn to David my servant:
Forever will I confirm your posterity
　and establish your throne for all generations."
For ever I will sing the goodness of the Lord.

"He shall say of me, 'You are my father, my God, the Rock, my savior.'
Forever I will maintain my kindness toward him,
　and my covenant with him stands firm."
For ever I will sing the goodness of the Lord.

READING II   Rom 16, 25–27

To him who is able to strengthen you in the gospel which I proclaim when I preach Jesus Christ, the gospel which reveals the mystery hidden for many ages but now manifested through the writings of the prophets, and, at the command of the eternal God, made known to all the Gentiles that they may believe and obey—to him, the God who alone is wise, may glory be given through Jesus Christ unto endless ages. Amen.

GOSPEL   Lk 1, 26–38

The angel Gabriel was sent from God to a town of Galilee named Nazareth, to a virgin betrothed to a man named Joseph, of the house of David. The virgin's name was Mary. Upon arriving, the angel said to her: "Rejoice, O highly favored daughter! The Lord is with you. Blessed are you among women." She was deeply troubled by his words, and wondered what his greeting meant. The angel went on to say to her: "Do not fear, Mary. You have found favor with God. You shall conceive and bear a son and give him the name Jesus. Great will be his dignity and he will be called Son of the Most High. The Lord God will give him the throne of David his father. He will rule over the house of Jacob forever and his reign will be without end."

Mary said to the angel, "How can this be since I do not know man?" The angel answered her: "The Holy Spirit will come upon you and the power of the Most High will overshadow you; hence, the holy offspring to be born will be called Son of God. Know that Elizabeth your kinswoman has conceived a son in her old age; she who was thought to be sterile is now in her sixth

month, for nothing is impossible with God."

Mary said: "I am the maidservant of the Lord. Let it be done to me as you say." With that the angel left her.

Reflection on the Readings

More good news today! "Nothing is impossible with God!" A young Jewish virgin, by the power of the Holy Spirit, conceives the Son of the Most High God. Nothing is impossible with God. A Jewish woman in her old age also conceives a son. Nothing is impossible with God. God intervenes in history, and nothing will ever be the same. Nothing is impossible with God. The long-awaited one is God-Man. Nothing is impossible with God.

Mary must have been a woman of prayer because she did not seem to be amazed at receiving a message from God. She did seem a bit perplexed about the message itself: "How can this be . . . ?" With a little further explanation, she replied, "Let it be done to me as you say." Mary has become the mother of God. Nothing is impossible with God. Mary is the best example of a kingdom person: God called, she responded, God gave her a special role, she said yes!

When we remain faithful in prayer, listening for God's call in our hearts, watching carefully for opportunities to meet and serve the Lord in each other, then we are eager to say "yes" to God too. Can we really do it? Yes! Nothing is impossible with God.

Suggestions for Prayer

1. Try to imagine the scene described in the Gospel. Try to hear the angel's message and Mary's reply. Then say out loud the last line of Mary's response. Yes! "Let it be done to me as you say." This would be a good way to end all our own prayers too!

2. If you have one, play a recording of an Ave Maria which is the Latin translation of the beautiful prayer of the Church, the Hail Mary. Notice that most of this prayer is directly from Luke's account. Sing or say this prayer slowly today.

> Hail Mary, full of grace, the
> Lord is with thee.
> Blessed art thou among women,
> and blessed is the fruit of
> thy womb, Jesus.
> Holy Mary, mother of God, pray
> for us sinners,
> now and at the hour of our
> death. Amen.

3. Mary was a very young woman, most likely what we would call a teenager. Young people today are really excited when they discover that the most highly-favored person in God's plan was so young. Praise God today for the many wonderful teenagers who respond so lovingly to life on this earth. Pray especially for the ones who need help to turn their lives around.

Suggestion for Journal Keeping

Describe a time when you experienced an "impossible" situation. Did you pray? How did you handle it? Who came to your assistance? Was it really impossible? Is there something in your life now that needs fervent prayer? Nothing is impossible with God.

Joanna Case

Fourth Sunday of Advent

READING I   Mi 5, 1–4

Thus says the Lord:
You, Bethlehem-Ephrathah
  too small to be among the clans of Judah,
From you shall come forth for me
  one who is to be ruler in Israel;
Whose origin is from of old,
  from ancient times.
(Therefore the Lord will give them up, until the time
  when she who is to give birth has borne,
And the rest of his brethren shall return
  to the children of Israel.)
He shall stand firm and shepherd his flock
  by the strength of the Lord,
  in the majestic name of the Lord, his God;
And they shall remain, for now his greatness
  shall reach to the ends of the earth;
  he shall be peace.

Responsorial Psalm   Ps 80, 2–3. 15–16.
                                    18–19

Lord, make us turn to you,
  let us see your face and we shall be saved.
O shepherd of Israel, hearken,
  from your throne upon the cherubim,
  shine forth.
Rouse your power,
  and come to save us.
Lord, make us turn to you,
  let us see your face and we shall be saved.
Once again, O Lord of hosts,
  look down from heaven, and see;
Take care of this vine,
  and protect what your right hand has
    planted
  [the son of man whom you yourself made
    strong].

Lord, make us turn to you,
  let us see your face and we shall be saved.
May your help be with the man of your right
  hand,
  with the son of man whom you yourself
    made strong.
Then we will no more withdraw from you;
  give us new life, and we will call upon
    your name.
Lord, make us turn to you,
  let us see your face and we shall be saved.

READING II   Heb 10, 5–10

On coming into the world Jesus said:
  "Sacrifice and offering you did not desire,
    but a body you have prepared for me;
  Holocausts and sin offerings you took no
    delight in.
  Then I said, 'As is written of me in the
    book,
    I have come to do your will, O God.' "
First he says,
  "Sacrifices and offerings, holocausts and
    sin offerings
  you neither desired nor delighted in."
(These are offered according to the prescriptions of the law.) Then he says,
  "I have come to do your will."
In other words, he takes away the first covenant to establish the second.
  By this "will," we have been sanctified through the offering of the body of Jesus Christ once for all.

GOSPEL   Lk 1, 39–45

Mary set out, proceeding in haste into the hill country to a town of Judah, where she entered Zechariah's house and greeted Elizabeth. When Elizabeth heard Mary's greet-

32

ing, the baby stirred in her womb. Elizabeth was filled with the Holy Spirit, and cried out in a loud voice: "Blessed are you among women and blessed is the fruit of your womb. But who am I that the mother of my Lord should come to me? The moment your greeting sounded in my ears, the baby stirred in my womb for joy. Blessed is she who trusted that the Lord's words to her would be fulfilled."

Reflection on the Readings

God is present to each of us in a variety of ways. The Gospel story points out how Elizabeth is aware of the presence of God in Mary, the mother of Jesus; her response is full of praise, joy and humility. Her response offers the challenge of becoming aware of the presence of God in our own lives.

How do we recognize the presence of God in everyday events? In the hectic pace of modern life, the presence of God can be drowned out by other demands. Several years ago, a popular song stated: "Stop and smell the roses along the way." Recognizing the presence of God in creation, people and events demands that we stop and reflect. God comes to each of us; each of us can find God in our daily lives.

Recognizing God's presence is a first step. Elizabeth welcomes God's presence. She responds. God's presence in our lives demands a personal response. The beauty of nature, experiencing the kindness of a friend or the joy of a child, can reveal the presence of God. Like Elizabeth, we can respond to God. The presence of God can also urge us to deepen our relationship with God and others. Our own actions and words can bear the presence of God to others.

Suggestions for Prayer

1. Say each phrase of the traditional prayer, the Hail Mary. Respond to each phrase with silent reflection or with your words, or pray the joyful mysteries of the rosary.

2. The responsorial psalm expresses a desire for the presence of God: "Lord, make us turn to you; let us see your face and we shall be saved." Another prayer that expresses this desire is:

Day by Day
Thank you, Lord Jesus Christ,
For all the benefits and blessings
   which you have given me,
For all the pains and insults
   which you have borne for me.
Merciful Friend, Brother and Redeemer,
May I know you more clearly,
Love you more dearly,
And follow you more nearly,
Day by day.

St. Richard of Chichester
(twelfth century)

3. Allow yourself to become relaxed. Try to put all thoughts out of your mind. Ask yourself: How is God present to me now? Can you picture or name God's presence? Respond to the presence of God.

Suggestion for Journal Keeping

Review significant events/moments in your life. What was the presence of God to you at that time? How did you respond to the presence of God at those moments?

Joseph P. Sinwell

Christmas

Waiting
for
the first
LIGHT
of Dawn

December 25
Christmas Vigil

READING I   Is 62, 1–5

For Zion's sake I will not be silent,
** for Jerusalem's sake I will not be quiet,**
Until her vindication shines forth like the
**   dawn**
** and her victory like a burning torch.**

Nations shall behold your vindication,
** and all kings your glory;**
You shall be called by a new name
** pronounced by the mouth of the Lord.**
You shall be a glorious crown in the hand of
**   the Lord,**
** a royal diadem held by your God.**
No more shall men call you "Forsaken,"
** or your land "Desolate,"**
But you shall be called "My Delight,"
** and your land "Espoused."**
For the Lord delights in you,
** and makes your land his spouse.**

As a young man marries a virgin,
** your Builder shall marry you;**
And as a bridegroom rejoices in his bride
** so shall your God rejoice in you.**

Responsorial Psalm   Ps 89, 4–5. 16–17.
                                    27. 29

For ever I will sing the goodness of the
      Lord.
I have made a covenant with my chosen one,
** I have sworn to David my servant:**
Forever will I confirm your posterity
** and establish your throne for all genera-**
** tions.**
For ever I will sing the goodness of the
      Lord.
Happy the people who know the joyful
** shout;**
** in the light of your countenance, O Lord,**
** they walk.**
At your name they rejoice all the day,
** and through your justice they are exalted.**
For ever I will sing the goodness of the
      Lord.
He shall say of me, "You are my father,
** my God, the Rock, my savior."**
Forever I will maintain my kindness toward
** him,**
** and my covenant with him stands firm.**
For ever I will sing the goodness of the
      Lord.

37

READING II Acts 13, 16–17. 22–25

[When Paul came to Antioch Pisidia, he entered the synagogue there] and motioning to them for silence, he began: "Fellow Israelites and you others who reverence our God, listen to what I have to say! The God of the people Israel once chose our fathers. He made this people great during their sojourn in the land of Egypt, and 'with an outstretched arm' he led them out of it. God raised up David as their king; on his behalf he testified, 'I have found David son of Jesse to be a man after my own heart who will fulfill my every wish.'

"According to his promise, God has brought forth from this man's descendants Jesus, a savior for Israel. John heralded the coming of Jesus by proclaiming a baptism of repentance to all the people of Israel. As John's career was coming to an end, he would say, 'What you suppose me to be I am not. Rather, look for the one who comes after me. I am not worthy to unfasten the sandals on his feet.' "

GOSPEL Mt 1, 18–25

Now this is how the birth of Jesus Christ came about. When his mother Mary was engaged to Joseph, but before they lived together, she was found with child through the power of the Holy Spirit. Joseph her husband, an upright man unwilling to expose her to the law, decided to divorce her quietly. Such was his intention when suddenly the angel of the Lord appeared in a dream and said to him: "Joseph, son of David, have no fear about taking Mary as your wife. It is by the Holy Spirit that she has conceived this child. She is to have a son and you are to name him Jesus because he will save his people from their sins." All this happened to fulfill what the Lord had said through the prophet:

"The virgin shall be with child
and give birth to a son,
and they shall call him Emmanuel,"

a name which means "God is with us." When Joseph awoke he did as the angel of the Lord had directed him and received her into his home as his wife. He had no relations with her at any time before she bore a son, whom he named Jesus.

Reflection on the Readings

Keeping vigil. A night watch. Awake and waiting. Waiting for the first light of dawn. The Church is keeping vigil during this holy night, waiting, eager to celebrate the light of the world, Jesus the Christ. Again we gather to tell the ancient story "how the birth of Jesus Christ came about." The Church remembers and celebrates.

The virgin shall be with child and give birth to a son, and they shall call him Emmanuel, a name which means "God is with us."

That is the part of the story we need to remember: God is with us! That is the part of the story we gather to celebrate: God is with us! This is the real CHRIST - MASS!

Suggestions for Prayer

1. Make an effort to stay awake through the night and watch for the first light of dawn. Feel the holiness of the night, the silence of the night. Watch the color of the sky change and the light of the daystar come upon you. Anticipation and arrival: God is with us. Jesus. Emmanuel.

38

2. Look again at the list of names in the family record of Jesus in the Gospel account. Now think of the generations and generations in your own family history. Ask all those "saints of old" to gather with you tonight in praising God for Jesus. Ask them to help you to be a light for the world, just as they were in their own lifetimes. Remember them. This is a night for remembering and celebrating.
3. If you have a nativity scene, spend a few minutes gazing. What a wonderfully human story unfolds. How wonderful is the mystery that the Word is made flesh and dwells among us! Holy, holy, holy night!

Suggestion for Journal Keeping
This is a holy night. Describe a moment in your life that was holy, a moment when you experienced God-with-you. Is this a holy moment right now?

Joanna Case

Mass at Midnight

READING I   Is 9, 1–6
The people who walked in darkness
have seen a great light;
Upon those who dwelt in the land of gloom
a light has shone.
You have brought them abundant joy
and great rejoicing,
As they rejoice before you as at the harvest,
as men make merry when dividing spoils.
For the yoke that burdened them,
the pole on their shoulder,

And the rod of their taskmaster
you have smashed, as on the day of Midian.
For every boot that tramped in battle,
every cloak rolled in blood,
will be burned as fuel for flames.
For a child is born to us, a son is given us;
upon his shoulder dominion rests.
They name him Wonder-Counselor, God-Hero,
Father-Forever, Prince of Peace.
His dominion is vast
and forever peaceful,
From David's throne, and over his kingdom,
which he confirms and sustains
By judgment and justice,
both now and forever.
The zeal of the Lord of hosts will do this!

Responsorial Psalm   Ps 96, 1–2. 2–3. 11–12. 13
Today is born our Savior, Christ the Lord.
Sing to the Lord a new song;
sing to the Lord, all you lands.
Sing to the Lord; bless his name.
Today is born our Savior, Christ the Lord.
Announce his salvation, day after day.
Tell his glory among the nations;
Among all peoples, his wondrous deeds.
Today is born our Savior, Christ the Lord.
Let the heavens be glad and the earth rejoice;
let the sea and what fills it resound;
let the plains be joyful and all that is in them!
Then shall all the trees of the forest exult.
Today is born our Savior, Christ the Lord.
They shall exult before the Lord, for he comes;
for he comes to rule the earth.

He shall rule the world with justice
and the peoples with his constancy.
Today is born our Savior, Christ the Lord.

READING II   Ti 2, 11–14
The grace of God has appeared, offering salvation to all men. It trains us to reject godless ways and worldly desires, and live temperately, justly, and devoutly in this age as we await our blessed hope, the appearing of the glory of the great God and of our Savior Christ Jesus. It was he who sacrificed himself for us, to redeem us from all unrighteousness and to cleanse for himself a people of his own, eager to do what is right.

GOSPEL   Lk 2, 1–14
In those days Caesar Augustus published a decree ordering a census of the whole world. This first census took place while Quirinius was governor of Syria. Everyone went to register, each to his own town. And so Joseph went from the town of Nazareth in Galilee to Judea, to David's town of Bethlehem—because he was of the house and lineage of David—to register with Mary, his espoused wife, who was with child.

While they were there the days of her confinement were completed. She gave birth to her first-born son and wrapped him in swaddling clothes and laid him in a manger, because there was no room for them in the place where travelers lodged.

There were shepherds in the locality, living in the fields and keeping night watch by turns over their flock. The angel of the Lord appeared to them, as the glory of the Lord shone around them, and they were very much afraid. The angel said to them: "You have nothing to fear! I come to proclaim good news to you—tidings of great joy to be shared by the whole people. This day in David's city a savior has been born to you, the Messiah and Lord. Let this be a sign to you: in a manger you will find an infant wrapped in swaddling clothes." Suddenly, there was with the angel a multitude of the heavenly host, praising God and saying, "Glory to God in high heaven, peace on earth to those on whom his favor rests."

Reflection on the Readings
"You have nothing to fear! I come to proclaim good news to you—tidings of great joy to be shared by the whole people."

Our joy is that a Savior has been given to us, one who would walk among us, one who would experience what we experience, one who would not receive special favor but would even suffer and die for the sake of all. How fitting it is that Jesus is born in a common courtyard, that he is adorned in simple cloth and laid to rest in a manger. For there was no room in the inn just as there would be no room in the hearts of many who would fail to recognize him as Lord.

How are we to insure that our hearts will always be open to this Savior? How will we guarantee lodging for the one who frees, reconciles and heals us. If we never allow ourselves to be poor, to be empty, if we fill our hearts with earthly desires, if we surround ourselves with distractions and comforts, if we avoid touching the poverty of our hearts and that of the world, then we will fail to see the vacancy into which we would invite this Lord. For it was in poverty that Jesus was born, and it is in the poverty of our hearts that we find space for this Savior to take rest.

The grace of God has appeared offering salvation to all.

Suggestions for Prayer

1. Pray Psalm 96:1–13 as a morning prayer each day of this week.
2. *Reflect on the following:* Isaiah proclaimed, "The people who walked in darkness have seen a great light." In what darkness have you walked? How was the light of the Lord mediated to you?
3. Of what must you empty yourself so that there will be more room for the Lord in your life?

Suggestion for Journal Keeping

How could you be even more open to the Lord than you are now?

John T. Butler

Mass at Dawn

READING I
Is 62, 11–12

See, the Lord proclaims
  to the ends of the earth:
Say to daughter Zion,
  your savior comes!
Here is his reward with him,
  his recompense before him.
They shall be called the holy people,
  the redeemed of the Lord,
and you shall be called "Frequented,"
  a city that is not forsaken.

Responsorial Psalm
Ps 97, 1. 6. 11–12

A light will shine on us this day:
  the Lord is born for us.

The Lord is king; let the earth rejoice;
  let the many isles be glad.
The heavens proclaim his justice,
  and all peoples see his glory.
A light will shine on us this day:
  the Lord is born for us.
Light dawns for the just;
  and gladness, for the upright of heart.
Be glad in the Lord, you just,
  and give thanks to his holy name.
A light will shine on us this day:
  the Lord is born for us.

READING II
Ti 3, 4–7

When the kindness and love of God our Savior appeared, he saved us, not because of any righteous deeds we had done, but because of his mercy. He saved us through the baptism of new birth and renewal by the Holy Spirit. This Spirit he lavished on us through Jesus Christ our Savior, that we might be justified by his grace and become heirs, in hope, of eternal life.

GOSPEL
Lk 2, 15–20

When the angels had returned to heaven, the shepherds said to one another: "Let us go over to Bethlehem and see this event which the Lord has made known to us." They went in haste and found Mary and Joseph, and the baby lying in the manger; once they saw, they understood what had been told them concerning this child. All who heard of it were astonished at the report given them by the shepherds.

Mary treasured all these things and reflected on them in her heart. The shepherds returned, glorifying and praising God for all they had heard and seen, in accord with what had been told them.

Reflection on the Readings

The shepherds returned, glorifying and praising God.

The angels appeared to the shepherds to give the good news of Christ's birth. How fitting it was that the shepherds would be among the first to receive this announcement of God. Shepherds were frequently looked down on by the religious leaders of the day, since they were unable to keep the strict ritual practice of the Jews. Those who lived a simple life, tending the lamb which might be used as a sacrifice to God, were among the first to see Jesus, the lamb of God, who is to be sacrificed for the sins of many.

This encounter with Jesus leaves the shepherds glorifying and praising God and Mary holding these moments in her heart. We, who have come to find Jesus in our lives are filled with joy and as Mary, likewise reflect and treasure these wonders in our hearts. For how profound it is, Paul reminds us, that God our Savior appeared to save us, not because of any righteous deed we have done, but because of God's mercy. This is why our hearts are filled and why we glorify and praise God.

Suggestions for Prayer

1. Pray Psalm 96:1–13 as a morning and evening reflection each day of this week.
2. *Reflect on the following:* What are some of the moments in your faith journey that you treasure? Why are these moments special ones in your life? What do they say about God? What do they say about you?
3. Designate some specific time for meditative prayer this week. After relaxing by reflecting on your breathing for several minutes, allow yourself to feel God's love, kindness and mercy by recalling a special moment you treasure and playing this moment over repeatedly in your mind.

Suggestion for Journal Keeping

Describe one of your most joyful experiences in life.

How was God present in that experience?

John T. Butler

Mass During the Day A B C

READING I Is 52, 7–10

How beautiful upon the mountains
    are the feet of him who brings glad tidings,
Announcing peace, bearing good news,
    announcing salvation, and saying to Zion,
    "Your God is King!"

Hark! Your watchmen raise a cry,
    together they shout for joy,
For they see directly, before their eyes,
    the Lord restoring Zion.
Break out together in song,
    O ruins of Jerusalem!
For the Lord comforts his people,
    he redeems Jerusalem.
The Lord has bared his holy arm
    in the sight of all the nations;
All the ends of the earth will behold
    the salvation of our God.

Responsorial Psalm Ps 98, 1. 2–3. 3–4.
5–6

All the ends of the earth have seen the
    saving power of God.

Sing to the Lord a new song,
  for he has done wondrous deeds;
His right hand has won victory for him,
  his holy arm.
All the ends of the earth have seen the
  saving power of God.
The Lord has made his salvation known:
  in the sight of the nations he has revealed
  his justice.
He has remembered his kindness and his
  faithfulness
  toward the house of Israel.
All the ends of the earth have seen the
  saving power of God.
All the ends of the earth have seen
  the salvation by our God.
Sing joyfully to the Lord, all you lands;
  break into song; sing praise.
All the ends of the earth have seen the
  saving power of God.
Sing praise to the Lord with the harp,
  with the harp and melodious song.
With trumpets and the sound of the horn
  sing joyfully before the King, the Lord.
All the ends of the earth have seen the
  saving power of God.

READING II   Heb 1, 1–6

In times past, God spoke in fragmentary and
varied ways to our fathers through the
prophets; in this, the final age, he has spoken to us through his Son, whom he has
made heir of all things and through whom he
first created the universe. This Son is the reflection of the Father's glory, the exact rep-
resentation of the Father's being, and he
sustains all things by his powerful word.
When the Son had cleansed us from our sins,
he took his seat at the right hand of the Majesty in heaven, as far superior to the angels

as the name he has inherited is superior to
theirs.
  To which of the angels did God ever say,
"You are my son; today I have begotten
you"?
Or again,
"I will be his father, and he shall be my
son"?
And again when he leads his first-born into
the world, he says,
"Let all the angels of God worship him."

GOSPEL   Jn 1, 1–18

  In the beginning was the Word;
  the Word was in God's presence,
  and the Word was God.
  He was present to God in the beginning.
  Through him all things came into being,
  and apart from him nothing came to be.
  Whatever came to be in him, found life,
  life for the light of men.
  The light shines on in darkness,
  a darkness that did not overcome it.
There was a man named John sent by God,
who came as a witness to testify to the light,
so that through him all men might believe—
but only to testify to the light, for he himself
was not the light. The real light which gives
light to every man was coming into the
world.
  He was in the world,
  and through him the world was made,
  yet the world did not know who he was.
  To his own he came,
  yet his own did not accept him.
  Any who did accept him
  he empowered to become children of
  God.
These are they who believe in his name—
who were begotten not by blood, nor by car-

nal desire, nor by man's willing it, but by God.

The Word became flesh
and made his dwelling among us,
and we have seen his glory:
the glory of an only Son coming from
  the Father,
filled with enduring love.
John testified to him by proclaiming, "This is he of whom I said, 'The one who comes after me ranks ahead of me, for he was before me.' "

Of his fullness
we have all had a share—
love following upon love.
For while the law was a gift through Moses, this enduring love came through Jesus Christ. No one has ever seen God. It is God the only Son, ever at the Father's side, who has revealed him.

Reflection on the Readings

In celebrating the event of the birth of Jesus, most people localize the time and place: Bethlehem two thousand years ago. And certainly they celebrate that event in the present in their own cities and homes. But in today's Scripture readings, John and Paul and Isaiah stretch our minds and hearts to consider a great cosmic view, maybe a God's-eye view of salvation. Imagine a camera starting with wide lens, zooming in for a close-up and returning to the larger picture. John starts with the widest possible frame, "In the beginning was the Word; and the Word was in God's presence, and the Word was God." Then God chooses to localize, "The Word became flesh and made his dwelling among us." Isaiah broadens the lens to remind us, "All the ends of the earth will behold the salvation of

our God." And Paul returns us to the opening scene, "When the Son had cleansed us from our sins, he took his seat at the right hand of the Majesty in heaven. . . . "

As much as we like to personalize Christmas, we need to remember that our most loving God intervened in history to call everyone to himself through Jesus. "God so loved the world that he sent his only begotten Son, that whoever believes in him may not die, but may have life eternal" (Jn 3:16).

That is good news for sure! Pass it on!

"How beautiful upon the mountains are the feet of the one who brings glad tidings, announcing peace, bearing good news, announcing salvation, and saying to Zion, ·'Your God is King!' "

Suggestions for Prayer

1. If indeed "all the ends of the earth have seen the salvation of our God," we would not hear of so many global conflicts and wars. Peace on earth requires peacemakers. Pray today for peace. Pray today for peacemakers. Pray that you yourself will "bring glad tidings, announcing peace, bearing good news . . . " in your own little corner of the earth. Make a resolution that you will be a peacemaker.

2. Christmas is a twelve day feast. The custom of gift-giving may vary from culture to culture, but it certainly is an essential of the Christmas celebration. Ask your family and/or friends what *spiritual* gift they would most like to have (e.g., wisdom, humility, courage, faith, prudence, patience, etc.) and tell them you

44

will pray for them, asking God to bestow the requested gift. Pray this way each day of the twelve days (or longer).

3. Christmastime is very difficult for those who are alone. Watch for the lonely and try to share some time with them. Pray for all those who are distressed, or homeless, or lonely.

Suggestion for Journal Keeping

If someone asked you to list the spiritual gifts that you have received from God, what would you say? Write a list in your journal. Don't forget to include a thank-you note.

Joanna Case

Sunday in the Octave of Christmas Holy Family 🅐🅑🅒

READING I   Sir 3, 2–6. 12–14
The Lord sets a father in honor over his children;
    a mother's authority he confirms over her sons.
He who honors his father atones for sins;
    he stores up riches who reveres his mother.
He who honors his father is gladdened by children,
    and when he prays he is heard.
He who reveres his father will live a long life;
    he obeys the Lord who brings comfort to his mother.

My son, take care of your father when he is old;
    grieve him not as long as he lives.
Even if his mind fail, be considerate with him;
    revile him not in the fullness of your strength.
For kindness to a father will not be forgotten,
    it will serve as a sin offering—it will take lasting root.

Responsorial Psalm   Ps 128, 1–2. 3. 4–5
Happy are those who fear the Lord and
    walk in his ways.
Happy are you who fear the Lord,
    who walk in his ways!
For you shall eat the fruit of your handiwork;
    happy shall you be, and favored.
Happy are those who fear the Lord
    and walk in his ways.
Your wife shall be like a fruitful vine
    in the recesses of your home;
Your children like olive plants
    around your table.
Happy are those who fear the Lord and
    walk in his ways.
Behold, thus is the man blessed
    who fears the Lord.
The Lord bless you from Zion:
    may you see the prosperity of Jerusalem
    all the days of your life.
Happy are those who fear the Lord and
    walk in his ways.

READING II   Col 3, 12–21
Because you are God's chosen ones, holy and beloved, clothe yourselves with heartfelt mercy, with kindness, humility, meek-

ness, and patience. Bear with one another; forgive whatever grievances you have against one another. Forgive as the Lord has forgiven you. Over all these virtues put on love, which binds the rest together and makes them perfect. Christ's peace must reign in your hearts, since as members of the one body you have been called to that peace. Dedicate yourselves to thankfulness. Let the word of Christ, rich as it is, dwell in you. In wisdom made perfect, instruct and admonish one another. Sing gratefully to God from your hearts in psalms, hymns, and inspired songs. Whatever you do, whether in speech or in action, do it in the name of the Lord Jesus. Give thanks to God the Father through him.

You who are wives, be submissive to your husbands. This is your duty in the Lord. Husbands, love your wives. Avoid any bitterness toward them. You children, obey your parents in everything as the acceptable way in the Lord. And fathers, do not nag your children lest they lose heart.

GOSPEL **A** Mt 2, 13–15. 19–23
After the astrologers had left, the angel of the Lord suddenly appeared in a dream to Joseph with the command: "Get up, take the child and his mother, and flee to Egypt. Stay there until I tell you otherwise. Herod is searching for the child to destroy him." Joseph got up and took the child and his mother and left that night for Egypt. He stayed there until the death of Herod, to fulfill what the Lord had said through the prophet:

"Out of Egypt I have called my son."
But after Herod's death, the angel of the Lord appeared in a dream to Joseph in Egypt with the command: "Get up, take the child and his mother, and set out for the land of Israel. Those who had designs on the life of the child are dead." He got up, took the child and his mother, and returned to the land of Israel. He heard, however, that Archelaus had succeeded his father Herod as king of Judea, and he was afraid to go back there. Instead, because of a warning received in a dream, Joseph went to the region of Galilee. There he settled in a town called Nazareth. In this way what was said through the prophets was fulfilled: "He shall be called a Nazorean."

GOSPEL **B** Lk 2, 22–40 or 2, 22. 39–40
When the day came to purify them according to the law of Moses, Mary and Joseph brought Jesus up to Jerusalem so that he could be presented to the Lord, for it is written in the law of the Lord, "Every first-born male shall be consecrated to the Lord." They came to offer in sacrifice "a pair of turtledoves or two young pigeons," in accord with the dictate in the law of the Lord.

There lived in Jerusalem at the time a certain man named Simeon. He was just and pious, and awaited the consolation of Israel, and the Holy Spirit was upon him. It was revealed to him by the Holy Spirit that he would not experience death until he had seen the Anointed of the Lord. He came to the temple now, inspired by the Spirit; and when the parents brought in the child Jesus to perform for him the customary ritual of the law, he took him in his arms and blessed God in these words:

"Now, Master, you can dismiss your
    servant in peace;
    you have fulfilled your word.

For my eyes have witnessed your saving
    deed
  displayed for all the peoples to see:
  A revealing light to the Gentiles,
    the glory of your people Israel."
The child's father and mother were marveling at what was being said about him. Simeon blessed them and said to Mary his mother: "This child is destined to be the downfall and the rise of many in Israel, a sign that will be opposed—and you yourself shall be pierced with a sword—so that the thoughts of many hearts may be laid bare."

There was also a certain prophetess, Anna by name, daughter of Phanuel of the tribe of Asher. She had seen many days, having lived seven years with her husband after her marriage and then as a widow until she was eighty-four. She was constantly in the temple, worshiping day and night in fasting and prayer. Coming on the scene at this moment, she gave thanks to God and talked about the child to all who looked forward to the deliverance of Jerusalem.

When the pair had fulfilled all the prescriptions of the law of the Lord, they returned to Galilee and their own town of Nazareth. The child grew in size and strength, filled with wisdom, and the grace of God was upon him.

GOSPEL C   Lk 2, 41–52

The parents of Jesus used to go every year to Jerusalem for the feast of the Passover, and when he was twelve they went up for the celebration as was their custom. As they were returning at the end of the feast, the child Jesus remained behind unknown to his parents. Thinking he was in the party, they continued their journey for a day, looking for him among their relatives and acquaintances.

Not finding him, they returned to Jerusalem in search of him. On the third day they came upon him in the temple sitting in the midst of the teachers, listening to them and asking them questions. All who heard him were amazed at his intelligence and his answers.

When his parents saw him they were astonished, and his mother said to him: "Son, why have you done this to us? You see that your father and I have been searching for you in sorrow." He said to them: "Why did you search for me? Did you not know I had to be in my Father's house?" But they did not grasp what he said to them.

He went down with them then, and came to Nazareth, and was obedient to them. His mother meanwhile kept all these things in memory. Jesus, for his part, progressed steadily in wisdom and age and grace before God and men.

Reflection on the Readings
  You who honor your father atone for sins,
  you who revere your mother store up riches.

On this feast of the Holy Family, the invitation is extended for us to see family as the ground on which the reality of love and virtuous living must be rooted. Sirach recounts some traditional wisdom regarding relations between parents and children, which if taken to heart must challenge us who live in a society which borders on the warehousing of the elderly. Where is the honor for those aging who die quietly and lonely in inner city apartments and suburban homes for the elderly?

Often we resist Paul's exhortation to bear

with one another. Have we not clothed ourselves with heartfelt mercy, with kindness, humility, meekness, and patience? Above all, have we not put on love which binds the rest together and makes perfect our Christ-like response?

Only then can we truly be open to the Lord's guidance as was Joseph (Mt 2:13–15, 19–23) who sought to protect his family from those who would destroy them (Cycle A). Only then can we live in hope as did Simeon and Anna (Lk 2:22–40), standing firm on God's promise to send a Savior (Cycle B). Only then can we in obedient faith grow in knowledge and understanding of what the Lord has in store for us as did Jesus (Lk 2:41–52, Cycle C).

If we would allow the Holy Family to be the model for us in our struggle to be open, faithful and obedient to the Lord, then we might find healing for the fragmented, fractured and disintegrated families in our midst.

Suggestions for Prayer

1. *Reflect on the following:* Which relationships in your family are most comfortable? Why? Which relationships in your family are most difficult? Why?
2. How might you show more fully Christlike love in your family?
3. Pray the prayer of St. Francis as a morning and evening prayer each day this week.

Suggestion for Journal Keeping

After reflecting on the readings and prayer suggestions, what would you want to say to any member of your family?

John T. Butler

January 1—Octave of Christmas Solemnity of Mary, Mother of God Ⓐ Ⓑ Ⓒ

READING I   Nm 6, 22–27

The Lord said to Moses: "Speak to Aaron and his sons and tell them: This is how you shall bless the Israelites. Say to them:
The Lord bless you and keep you!
The Lord let his face shine upon you, and be gracious to you!
The Lord look upon you kindly and give you peace!
So shall they invoke my name upon the Israelites, and I will bless them."

Responsorial Psalm   Ps 67, 2–3. 5. 6. 8
May God bless us in his mercy.
May God have pity on us and bless us;
may he let his face shine upon us.
So may your way be known upon earth;
among all nations, your salvation.
May God bless us in his mercy.
May the nations be glad and exult
because you rule the peoples in equity;
the nations on the earth you guide.
May God bless us in his mercy.
May the peoples praise you, O God;
may all the peoples praise you!
May God bless us,
and may all the ends of the earth fear him!
May God bless us in his mercy.

READING II   Gal 4, 4–7

When the designated time had come, God sent forth his Son born of a woman, born under the law, to deliver from the law those who were subjected to it, so that we might receive our status as adopted sons. The

proof that you are sons is the fact that God has sent forth into our hearts the spirit of his Son which cries out "Abba!" ("Father!"). You are no longer a slave but a son! And the fact that you are a son makes you an heir, by God's design.

GOSPEL   Lk 2, 16–21
The shepherds went in haste to Bethlehem and found Mary and Joseph, and the baby lying in the manger; once they saw, they understood what had been told them concerning this child. All who heard of it were astonished at the report given them by the shepherds.

Mary treasured all these things and reflected on them in her heart. The shepherds returned, glorifying and praising God for all they had heard and seen, in accord with what had been told them.

When the eighth day arrived for his circumcision, the name Jesus was given the child, the name the angel had given him before he was conceived.

Reflection on the Readings
You are no longer slaves, but sons and daughters.

Mary's free acceptance of the responsibility of motherhood resulted in blessings that stretch beyond our imagination. Her yes not only fulfills the Old Testament prophecy but wins for her and for us a privileged place in God's salvific plan. Paul reminds us that we are slaves no more. Because of Christ, we now claim the intimacy that God intended for us, that we would be children of God.

The use of the term "Abba" expresses God as Father, not only to Jesus, but to us who respond to him as openly and willingly as did Mary. Our sonship (daughtership) is rooted in this radical obedience and fidelity to God's will. Therefore, as true sons and daughters of God, we confidently invoke God's name and call forth blessings from the Lord—blessings promised to Moses, Abraham and Sarah, blessings always fulfilled throughout the whole of salvation history.

Suggestions for Prayer

1. *Reflect on the following:* How has the Lord blessed you? How has the Lord kept you?
2. Place yourself in a relaxed position and reflect on the peace that only Christ can give. Spend several minutes each day this week reflecting on this peace.
3. Pray Psalm 67:2–8 as a morning and evening prayer each day this week.

Suggestions for Journal Keeping
Describe what it means for you to be a child of God.

What does God as Father expect from you and/or provide for you?

What does God as Mother expect from you and/or provide for you?

John T. Butler

Epiphany

READING I   Is 60, 1–6
Rise up in splendor, Jerusalem! Your light
    has come,
    the glory of the Lord shines upon you.
See, darkness covers the earth,
    and thick clouds cover the peoples;

But upon you the Lord shines,
  and over you appears his glory.
Nations shall walk by your light,
  and kings by your shining radiance.
Raise your eyes and look about;
  they all gather and come to you:
Your sons come from afar,
  and your daughters in the arms of their
    nurses.
Then you shall be radiant at what you see,
  your heart shall throb and overflow,
For the riches of the sea shall be emptied out
    before you,
  the wealth of nations shall be brought to
    you.
Caravans of camels shall fill you,
  dromedaries from Midian and Ephah;
All from Sheba shall come
  bearing gold and frankincense,
  and proclaiming the praises of the Lord.

Responsorial Psalm   Ps 72, 1–2. 7–8. 10–
                                  11. 12–13
Lord, every nation on earth will adore you.
O God, with your judgment endow the king,
  and with your justice, the king's son;
He shall govern your people with justice
  and your afflicted ones with judgment.
Lord, every nation on earth will adore you.
Justice shall flower in his days,
  and profound peace, till the moon be no
    more.
May he rule from sea to sea,
  and from the River to the ends of the
    earth.
Lord, every nation on earth will adore you.
The kings of Tarshish and the Isles shall offer
    gifts;
  the kings of Arabia and Seba shall bring
    tribute.

All kings shall pay him homage,
  all nations shall serve him.
Lord, every nation on earth will adore you.
For he shall rescue the poor man when he
    cries out,
  and the afflicted when he has no one to
    help him.
He shall have pity for the lowly and the
    poor;
  the lives of the poor he shall save.
Lord, every nation on earth will adore you. .

READING II   Eph 3, 2–3. 5–6
I am sure you have heard of the ministry
which God in his goodness gave me in your
regard. God's secret plan, as I have briefly
described it, was revealed to me, unknown
to men in former ages but now revealed by
the Spirit to the holy apostles and prophets.
It is no less than this: in Christ Jesus the Gen-
tiles are now co-heirs with the Jews, mem-
bers of the same body and sharers of the
promise through the preaching of the gos-
pel.

GOSPEL   Mt 2, 1–12
After Jesus' birth in Bethlehem of Judea dur-
ing the reign of King Herod, astrologers from
the east arrived one day in Jerusalem inquir-
ing, "Where is the newborn king of the
Jews? We observed his star at its rising and
have come to pay him homage." At this
news King Herod became greatly disturbed,
and with him all Jerusalem. Summoning all
of the chief priests and scribes of the people,
he inquired of them where the Messiah was
to be born. "In Bethlehem of Judea," they
informed him. "Here is what the prophet
has written:

'And you, Bethlehem, land of Judah,
are by no means least among the
   princes of Judah,
since from you shall come a ruler
who is to shepherd my people Israel.' "
Herod called the astrologers aside and found
out from them the exact time of the star's appearance. Then he sent them to Bethlehem,
after having instructed them: "Go and get
detailed information about the child. When
you have discovered something, report your
findings to me so that I may go and offer him
homage too."

After their audience with the king, they
set out. The star which they had observed at
its rising went ahead of them until it came to
a standstill over the place where the child
was. They were overjoyed at seeing the star,
and on entering the house, found the child
with Mary his mother. They prostrated
themselves and did him homage. Then they
opened their coffers and presented him with
gifts of gold, frankincense, and myrrh.

They received a message in a dream not to
return to Herod, so they went back to their
own country by another route.

Reflection on the Readings

The Gospel narrates a wonderful story. Astrologers. Star. King. Conflict. Intrigue. Gifts.
Warnings. Return. A great story. But a closer
look might reveal a hidden story. The magi
set out on a spiritual journey, prompted by
the stirrings of their souls through ancient
writings and a wondrous star. They were not
certain of what they would find, but they
were resolute in their intention to pay homage to the newborn king of the Jews. They
found him, and we can imagine that the Isaiah line described them perfectly: "Then you

shall be radiant at what you see, your heart
shall throb and overflow. . . . " One encounter with the Lord and they were never
again the same. They couldn't even go back
the same way; their journey took a different
turn.

We, too, are pilgrims on a journey, seeking
the One who will make our hearts "throb and
overflow." Each time we meet the Lord we
come away changed, our path pointing in a
new direction. Without benefit of star and
messages in dreams, we continue seeking the
Lord in likely and unlikely places. We look
for him in prayer, in good people, in good
deeds, but sometimes he arrives in silence, in
distressing disguises, in emptiness. But we
have set out on our own journey and we must
be resolute. There is no turning back, only
going ahead, and, as Isaiah puts it, "Then
shall you be radiant at what you see, your
heart shall throb and overflow."

Suggestions for Prayer

1. The sun is the daystar for the earth. It
   lights the world. As soon as it is dark, see
   if you can see other stars and the earth's
   moon. The sun, the moon, the stars, the
   galaxy, the universe. Amazing. Overwhelming. Mind-boggling. "We have
   observed his star and have come to pay
   him homage." Praise God.
2. This is "twelfth night." The end of the
   Christmas celebration. Have you noticed that on a spiritual journey, each
   ending only introduces you to another
   beginning? This is going to be a holy
   year for you. Watch for stars that lead
   you to holy places.

The magi brought gold, frankincense, and myrrh. The Little Drummer Boy played his drum. What is your gift? What is your most *precious* gift that you have to give to the Lord?

Joanna Case

Baptism of the Lord A B C

READING I Is 42, 1–4. 6–7

Here is my servant whom I uphold,
my chosen one with whom I am pleased,
Upon whom I have put my spirit;
he shall bring forth justice to the nations,
Not crying out, not shouting,
not making his voice heard in the street.
A bruised reed he shall not break,
and a smoldering wick he shall not quench,
Until he establishes justice on the earth;
the coastlands will wait for his teaching.

I, the Lord, have called you for the victory of justice,
I have grasped you by the hand;
I formed you, and set you
as a covenant of the people,
a light for the nations,
To open the eyes of the blind,
to bring out prisoners from confinement,
and from the dungeon, those who live in darkness.

Responsorial Psalm Ps 29, 1–2. 3–4. 3. 9–10

The Lord will bless his people with peace.
Give to the Lord, you sons of God,
give to the Lord glory and praise,
Give to the Lord the glory due his name;
adore the Lord in holy attire.
The Lord will bless his people with peace.
The voice of the Lord is over the waters,
the Lord, over vast waters.
The voice of the Lord is mighty;
the voice of the Lord is majestic.
The Lord will bless his people with peace.
The God of glory thunders,
and in his temple all say, "Glory!"
The Lord is enthroned above the flood;
the Lord is enthroned as king forever.
The Lord will bless his people with peace.

READING II Acts 10, 34–38

Peter addressed Cornelius and the people assembled at his house in these words: "I begin to see how true it is that God shows no partiality. Rather, the man of any nation who fears God and acts uprightly is acceptable to him. This is the message he has sent to the sons of Israel, 'the good news of peace' proclaimed through Jesus Christ who is Lord of all. I take it you know what has been reported all over Judea about Jesus of Nazareth, beginning in Galilee with the baptism John preached; of the way God anointed him with the Holy Spirit and power. He went about doing good works and healing all who were in the grip of the devil, and God was with him.

GOSPEL A Mt 3, 13–17

Jesus, coming from Galilee, appeared before John at the Jordan to be baptized by him. John tried to refuse him with the protest, "I should be baptized by you, yet you come to me!" Jesus answered, "Give in for now. We must do this if we would fulfill all of God's demands." So John gave in. After Jesus was baptized, he came directly out of

the water. Suddenly the sky opened and he saw the Spirit of God descend like a dove and hover over him. With that, a voice from the heavens said, "This is my beloved Son. My favor rests on him."

GOSPEL B

Mk 1, 7–11

The theme of John's preaching was: "One more powerful than I is to come after me. I am not fit to stoop and untie his sandal straps. I have baptized you in water; he will baptize you in the Holy Spirit."

During that time, Jesus came from Nazareth in Galilee and was baptized in the Jordan by John. Immediately on coming up out of the water he saw the sky rent in two and the Spirit descending on him like a dove. Then a voice came from the heavens: "You are my beloved Son. On you my favor rests."

GOSPEL C

Lk 3, 15–16. 21–22

The people were full of anticipation, wondering in their hearts whether John might be the Messiah. John answered them all by saying: "I am baptizing you in water, but there is one to come who is mightier than I. I am not fit to loosen his sandal strap. He will baptize you in the Holy Spirit and in fire.

When all the people were baptized, and Jesus was at prayer after likewise being baptized, the skies opened and the Holy Spirit descended on him in visible form like a dove. A voice from heaven was heard to say, "You are my beloved Son. On you my favor rests."

Reflection on the Readings

To make a discovery about someone we know or to gain a fresh insight into ourselves is a threshold, a turning point. The deeper our new knowledge, the more we are changed. Once we have passed that threshold, we are never quite the same again.

What is happening in the readings of the recent Sundays and feasts is a progression in the story of the manifestation of Jesus as the Chosen One of God. John the Baptist is the one who has gone before, preparing the way, the hearts of people. John proclaims conversion. Jesus' decision to be baptized indicates his choice—he has passed a threshold, come upon a turning point in his life, as he responds to an inner call. He is making a public statement about his life and his beliefs.

The reading from Isaiah depicting the Servant of God, the Chosen One, is applied by Peter (in the reading from Acts) and by the evangelists to Jesus, identifying him as the beloved servant. The mission of Jesus is that of the servant—to bring forth justice, to be merciful, to heal and to free those in darkness and bondage. Peter's proclamation assures the early Christian community—and us—that Jesus is indeed this servant, the Chosen One of God.

We look first at John, whose whole life of simplicity, preaching and teaching called people to conversion, to a life of holiness and openness to God. We look at Jesus, responding to his call to live as the chosen servant of God. We look then at our own lives, at the call we may be hearing now to follow Jesus. We must respond, as best we can, according to our personal circumstances in life, our gifts. Your response will become visible in your faith life and in your lifestyle.

In our Church community, our individual response to the call to holiness is affirmed and celebrated in many different ways. Your journey as a catechumen will provide opportunities for support, reflection, questioning, affirmation. You will continue to meet and learn from others who have gone before to prepare their own hearts and lives, who have followed their call to holiness.

Suggestions for Prayer

1. Prepare for this prayer time by becoming comfortable, perhaps with pen and paper nearby. You may want some quiet instrumental music in the background. Move away from the distractions of noise, worry and tensions.

   Think of one central, pivotal decision you have made in your life. Name it. Who or what helped prepare you for that decision or brought you to the point of wanting to make a choice? What changes are a result of that decision?
2. Choose and listen to a song which focuses on a theme of conversion, of call and response. Some suggestions may be available from the parish catechumen- ate team or music leaders, many with scriptural themes. As you listen a second time to the song you choose, become aware of a message being given to you— a reassurance of God's love, forgiveness, a renewed call to holiness or prayer, a deeper sense of God's presence in your life.

Suggestion for Journal Keeping

Take time to write a few paragraphs on today's readings and prayer. Ask yourself: What have today's Scripture readings meant to me? What insight has come to me? As you spend time in prayer, write briefly your reflections and thoughts. You may feel comfortable in writing your thoughts as a prayer itself: "Jesus, as I read about your baptism today and thought about your life and my own, I am coming to realize even more that . . ."

Clare M. Colella

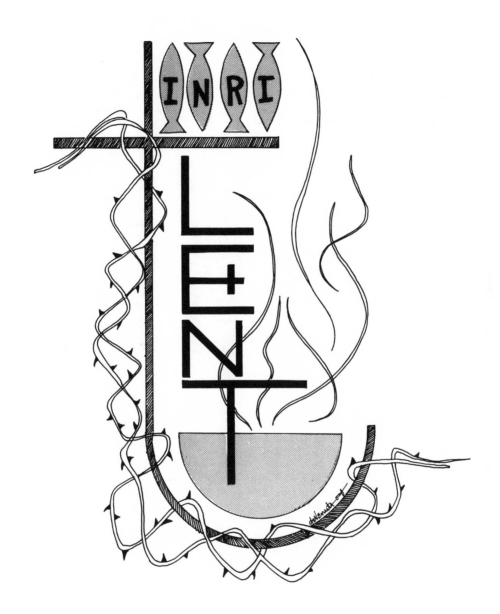

Ash Wednesday

READING I   Jl 2, 12–18

Even now, says the Lord,
  return to me with your whole heart,
  with fasting, and weeping, and mourning;
Rend your hearts, not your garments,
  and return to the Lord, your God.
For gracious and merciful is he,
  slow to anger, rich in kindness,
  and relenting in punishment.
Perhaps he will again relent
  and leave behind him a blessing,
Offerings and libations
  for the Lord, your God.

Blow the trumpet in Zion!
  proclaim a fast,
  call an assembly;
Gather the people,
  notify the congregation;
Assemble the elders,
  gather the children
  and the infants at the breast;
Let the bridegroom quit his room,
  and the bride her chamber.
Between the porch and the altar
  let the priests, the ministers of the Lord,
    weep,
And say, "Spare, O Lord, your people,
  and make not your heritage a reproach,
  with the nations ruling over them!
Why should they say among the peoples,
  'Where is their God?' "
  Then the Lord was stirred to concern for
his land and took pity on his people.

Responsorial Psalm   Ps 51, 3–4. 5–6. 12–
                                    13. 14. 17

Be merciful, O Lord, for we have sinned.
Have mercy on me, O God, in your good-
    ness;
  in the greatness of your compassion wipe
    out my offense.
Thoroughly wash me from my guilt
  and of my sin cleanse me.
Be merciful, O Lord, for we have sinned.
For I acknowledge my offense,
  and my sin is before me always:
"Against you only have I sinned,
  and done what is evil in your sight."
Be merciful, O Lord, for we have sinned.
A clean heart create for me, O God,
  and a steadfast spirit renew within me.
Cast me not out from your presence,
  and your holy spirit take not from me.
Be merciful, O Lord, for we have sinned.
Give me back the joy of your salvation,
  and a willing spirit sustain in me.
O Lord, open my lips,
  and my mouth shall proclaim your praise.
Be merciful, O Lord, for we have sinned.

READING II
2 Cor 5, 20–6, 2

We are ambassadors for Christ, God as it were appealing through us. We implore you, in Christ's name: be reconciled to God! For our sakes God made him who did not know sin to be sin, so that in him we might become the very holiness of God.

As your fellow workers we beg you not to receive the grace of God in vain. For he says, "In an acceptable time I have heard you; on a day of salvation I have helped you." Now is the acceptable time! Now is the day of salvation!

GOSPEL
Mt 6, 1–6. 16–18

Jesus said to his disciples: "Be on guard against performing religious acts for people to see. Otherwise expect no recompense from your heavenly Father. When you give alms, for example, do not blow a horn before you in synagogues and streets like hypocrites looking for applause. You can be sure of this much, they are already repaid. In giving alms you are not to let your left hand know what your right hand is doing. Keep your deeds of mercy secret, and your Father who sees in secret will repay you.

"When you are praying, do not behave like the hypocrites who love to stand and pray in synagogues or on street corners in order to be noticed. I give you my word, they are already repaid. Whenever you pray, go to your room, close your door, and pray to your Father in private. Then your Father, who sees what no man sees, will repay you.

"When you fast, you are not to look glum as the hypocrites do. They change the appearance of their faces so that others may see they are fasting. I assure you, they are already repaid. When you fast, see to it that you groom your hair and wash your face. In that way no one can see you are fasting but your Father who is hidden; and your Father who sees what is hidden will repay you."

Reflection on the Readings

Two themes emerge from the liturgy of today. The more obvious one is the lesson that we are dust, ashes, from which we came and to which we will return. Ashes, blessed as they are, serve to remind us of our humble origins and fragile nature. The sign placed on our foreheads is a sign for our entire selves, our hearts and minds. We are a people set aside, called to become faithful and holy, a redeemed people called to conversion.

Conversion serves as the second theme for today and the setting for the season of Lent. Each of the readings, the same ones proclaimed every year, speak of conversion. Joel, a prophet, calls his people to renew their efforts to live a holy and pleasing life, turning to the Lord as central in their lives. His people, and we, are reminded of the Lord's goodness and mercy; the last line in today's first reading speaks of the ancient covenant: "You will be my people and I will be your God."

Living as the people of God is a process of converting our lives to the Lord. As Paul reminds the Christian community at Corinth: "We are ambassadors for Christ." Therefore our very lives are to be evidence of the grace of God active and fruitful within us. How do we do this? In the Gospel, we hear from Jesus the admonition to give alms, to pray and to fast. What is particularly striking and wonderful about Jesus' message is that we are to do so in simplicity, in our ordinary lives, looking only to God. Three times we hear that it is the Father who sees what is in our hearts.

As we prepare for this day we reflect on our lives, examining our values and lifestyle in comparison with Gospel values. To be signed with ashes, to hear the prayers of the liturgy, is to renew personally our covenant with God. It is to recognize in our own lives the need for continuing conversion, for a deeper understanding of our call to healthy holiness and to strengthen our commitment to live as the redeemed, chosen people of God.

Suggestions for Prayer

1. If at all possible, participate in the liturgy of the Church today. The ashes are made by burning last year's blessed palms. The ashes link us with the death and resurrection of the Lord. If you cannot be in church, but want to reflect on these prayers more thoroughly, a missal or missalette will be of help.

2. The opening prayers of today's liturgy ask for protection in our struggle against evil throughout this season and, in the alternate prayer, for forgiveness and the gift of light. Reflect on your life as it is right now. Recognizing the presence of God in your heart, pray for the light of faith and wisdom to live more faithfully as a follower of Christ.

3. Psalm 51 serves as the responsorial psalm today. Acknowledging our sinfulness, we pray for a clean heart and the joy of salvation. With a spirit of willingness and praise we pray for a sign of our belonging to the Lord. As you pray this psalm, again let your heart and mind become glad and secure in the knowledge that you are forgiven and loved. How, during this Lenten season, will you live out your praise of God?

Suggestion for Journal Keeping

In a quiet setting reflect on those aspects of your life which are central in your faith journey: a spirit of prayer, service to others, simplicity or other qualities. What needs to be changed? What needs to be strengthened? Formulate a personal prayer of resolution—a sort of covenant—to grow in the spirit of Christ.

Clare M. Colella

First Sunday of Lent A

READING I   Gn 2, 7–9; 3, 1–7
The Lord God formed man out of the clay of the ground and blew into his nostrils the breath of life, and so man became a living being.

Then the Lord God planted a garden in Eden, in the east, and he placed there the man whom he had formed. Out of the ground the Lord God made various trees grow that were delightful to look at and good for food, with the tree of life in the middle of the garden and the tree of the knowledge of good and bad.

Now the serpent was the most cunning of all the animals that the Lord God had made. The serpent asked the woman, "Did God really tell you not to eat from any of the trees in the garden?" The woman answered the

serpent: "We may eat of the fruit of the trees in the garden; it is only about the fruit of the tree in the middle of the garden that God said, 'You shall not eat it or even touch it, lest you die.' " But the serpent said to the woman: "You certainly will not die! No, God knows well that the moment you eat of it you will be like gods who know what is good and what is bad." The woman saw that the tree was good for food, pleasing to the eyes, and desirable for gaining wisdom. So she took some of its fruit and ate it; and she also gave some to her husband, who was with her, and he ate it. Then the eyes of both of them were opened, and they realized that they were naked; so they sewed fig leaves together and made loincloths for themselves.

Responsorial Psalm   Ps 51, 3–4. 5–6. 12– 13. 14. 17

Be merciful, O Lord, for we have sinned.

Have mercy on me, O God, in your goodness;
  in the greatness of your compassion wipe out my offense.
Thoroughly wash me from my guilt
  and of my sin cleanse me.
Be merciful, O Lord, for we have sinned.
For I acknowledge my offense,
  and my sin is before me always:
"Against you only have I sinned,
  and done what is evil in your sight."
Be merciful, O Lord, for we have sinned.
A clean heart create for me, O God,
  and a steadfast spirit renew within me.
Cast me not out from your presence,
  and your holy spirit take not from me.
Be merciful, O Lord, for we have sinned.
Give me back the joy of your salvation,
  and a willing spirit sustain in me.

O Lord, open my lips,
  and my mouth shall proclaim your praise.
Be merciful, O Lord, for we have sinned.

READING II   Rom 5, 12–19 or 5, 12. 17–19
Through one man sin entered the world and with sin death, death thus coming to all men inasmuch as all sinned—before the law there was sin in the world, even though sin is not imputed when there is no law—I say, from Adam to Moses death reigned, even over those who had not sinned by breaking a precept as did Adam, that type of the Man to come.

But the gift is not like the offense. For if by the offense of the one man all died, much more did the grace of God and the gracious gift of the one man, Jesus Christ, abound for all. The gift is entirely different from the sin committed by the one man. In the first case, sentence followed upon one offense and brought condemnation, but in the second, the gift came after many offenses and brought acquittal. If death began its reign through one man because of his offense, much more shall those who receive the overflowing grace and gift of justice live and reign through the one man, Jesus Christ. To sum up, then: just as a single offense brought condemnation to all men, a single righteous act brought all men acquittal and life. Just as through one man's disobedience all became sinners, so through one man's obedience all shall become just.

GOSPEL   Mt 4, 1–11
Jesus was led into the desert by the Spirit to be tempted by the devil. He fasted forty days and forty nights, and afterward was hungry. The tempter approached and said to him, "If

you are the Son of God, command these stones to turn into bread." Jesus replied, "Scripture has it:

> 'Not on bread alone is man to live
> but on every utterance that comes from
> the mouth of God.' "

Next the devil took him to the holy city, set him on the parapet of the temple, and said, "If you are the Son of God, throw yourself down. Scripture has it:

> 'He will bid his angels take care of you;
> with their hands they will support you
> that you may never stumble on a
> stone.' "

Jesus answered him, "Scripture also has it:

> 'You shall not put the Lord your God to
> the test.' "

The devil then took him to a lofty mountain peak and displayed before him all the kingdoms of the world in their magnificence, promising, "All these will I bestow on you if you prostrate yourself in homage before me." At this, Jesus said to him, "Away with you, Satan! Scripture says:

> 'You shall do homage to the Lord your
> God;
> him alone shall you adore.' "

At that the devil left him, and angels came and waited on him.

Reflection on the Readings

In today's Gospel, Jesus goes into the desert to be alone: to honestly struggle with all the dimensions of himself. While in the desert, he is confronted with three fundamental temptations: power (turn bread into stones), influence and control (throw himself off the temple), and false glory and idolatry (these kingdoms can be yours). Yet Jesus makes responsible choices. He chooses to live from his inner truth, from his relationship with the Father, rather than allowing the attraction of the temptations to control him.

Jesus' choices are choices we can make. The Genesis text affirms our created goodness: God breathes into Adam's nostril the "breath of life," thus giving Adam life rooted in God. At the center of each of us is this very breath of God which gives life to us. Yet, like Adam and Eve, we can choose to distrust this life of God within us that empowers us for the good and the valuable. When we begin to distrust this breath of God, we begin to make irresponsible and selfish choices (sin), choices that reflect a false center within us, choices similar to those Jesus struggled with in the desert.

But all is not lost. St. Paul reminds us that we are not destined to a life of sin. The obedience of Jesus to his relationship with the Father liberates all of us to share in that new way of life. We can live from our true center: the breath of God within.

Suggestions for Prayer

1. Slowly reread the opening sentence of the Genesis text. Ponder the meaning of the "breath of life" for you and what it means to be a "living being."

2. Find some desert time and space for yourself—time to be alone in silence. Ask God to help you come to an awareness of your own struggles that keep you from living from your true center.

3. Pray Psalm 51 slowly, making explicit for yourself how you have experienced God's mercy (i.e., the abundance of God's love and forgiveness).

Reflect on the last week and the choices you made. List for yourself some of these choices. What do these choices say about your sense of self, sense of relationship with others, sense of God? What do you need from God to help you make more authentic choices?

Thomas H. Morris

First Sunday of Lent B

READING I   Gn 9, 8–15

God said to Noah and to his sons with him: "See, I am now establishing my covenant with you and your descendants after you and with every living creature that was with you: all the birds, and the various tame and wild animals that were with you and came out of the ark. I will establish my covenant with you, that never again shall all bodily creatures be destroyed by the waters of a flood; there shall not be another flood to devastate the earth." God added: "This is the sign that I am giving for all ages to come, of the covenant between me and you and every living creature with you: I set my bow in the clouds to serve as a sign of the covenant between me and the earth. When I bring clouds over the earth, and the bow appears in the clouds, I will recall the covenant I have made between me and you and all living beings, so that the waters shall never again become a flood to destroy all mortal beings."

Responsorial Psalm   Ps 25, 4–5. 6–7. 8–9

Your ways, O Lord, are love and truth,
    to those who keep your covenant.
**Your ways, O Lord, make known to me;
    teach me your paths,**
**Guide me in your truth and teach me.
    for you are God my savior.**
Your ways, O Lord, are love and truth,
    to those who keep your covenant.
**Remember that your compassion, O Lord,
    and your kindness are from of old.**
**In your kindness remember me,
    because of your goodness, O Lord.**
Your ways, O Lord, are love and truth,
    to those who keep your covenant.
**Good and upright is the Lord;
    thus he shows sinners the way.**
**He guides the humble to justice,
    he teaches the humble his way.**
Your ways, O Lord, are love and truth,
    to those who keep your covenant.

READING II   1 Pt 3, 18–22

This is why Christ died for sins once for all, a just man for the sake of the unjust: so that he could lead you to God. He was put to death insofar as fleshly existence goes, but was given life in the realm of the spirit. It was in the spirit also that he went to preach to the spirits in prison. They had disobeyed as long ago as Noah's day, while God patiently waited until the ark was built. At that time, a few persons, eight in all, escaped in the ark through the water. You are now saved by a baptismal bath which corresponds to this exactly. This baptism is no removal of physical stain, but the pledge to God of an irreproachable conscience through the resurrection of Jesus Christ. He went to heaven and is at God's right hand, with angelic rulers and powers subjected to him.

GOSPEL   Mk 1, 12–15
The Spirit sent Jesus out toward the desert. He stayed in the wasteland forty days, put to the test there by Satan. He was with the wild beasts, and angels waited on him.

After John's arrest, Jesus appeared in Galilee proclaiming God's good news: "This is the time of fulfillment. The reign of God is at hand! Reform your lives and believe in the good news!"

Reflection on the Readings

On the day when the Rite of Election takes place, how appropriate that the readings are centered on the symbolism of water and God's establishment of a covenant relationship with us.

In the story of Noah, the flood waters that destroy are the same waters of salvation. They cleanse and purify. God offers salvation to those who live by his law. As this relationship is formed between God and his people, we pray for the grace to keep our part of the covenant. We respond to his endless love.

Today the Rite of Election reminds us of the challenge and meaning of Lent in our lives. For those fully initiated it can be a time of reflection on the past. If it has been a time of self-glorification and falling into temptation, Lent is our time of another conversion. For catechumens journeying toward the font, it is a time of reflecting on the deserts of their life, the hopelessness and lifelessness of the past. Now it is time to listen and respond to the good news. We begin this season of Lent with hope and encouraged in knowing the continued presence of God in our life.

Suggestions for Prayer

1. God has made a covenant with us which is unbreakable. He will always be our God. He always loves us. Reflect on an area of your spiritual life this week that you are not satisfied with. What response will you make to God's love in order to grow in that area?
2. Water can be a symbol of God's power, his gentleness, his cleansing. Take time to refresh yourself by walking near a creek, lake or sea. Reflect on these attributes of God in your own life.
3. Write a letter to God in which you respond to his presence in your life. Prayerfully petition him for continued guidance as you learn his ways.

Suggestion for Journal Keeping

Satan tempted Jesus in order to glorify himself. Instead, Jesus chose to glorify God. Describe a time when you fostered a situation in order to receive self-glorification. What was the outcome? How did you feel about receiving the glory? How could you have acted in a more humble way?

Mary Kay Meier

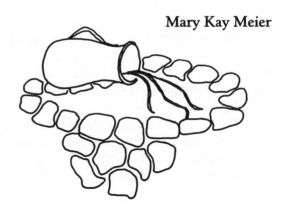

First Sunday of Lent   C

READING I   Dt 26, 4–10

Moses told the people: "The priest shall then receive the basket from you and shall set it in front of the altar of the Lord, your God. Then you shall declare before the Lord, your God, 'My father was a wandering Aramean who went down to Egypt with a small household and lived there as an alien. But there he became a nation great, strong, and numerous. When the Egyptians maltreated and oppressed us, imposing hard labor upon us, we cried to the Lord, the God of our fathers, and he heard our cry and saw our affliction, our toil and our oppression. He brought us out of Egypt with his strong hand and outstretched arm, with terrifying power, with signs and wonders; and bringing us into this country, he gave us this land flowing with milk and honey. Therefore, I have now brought you the first fruits of the products of the soil which you, O Lord, have given me.' And having set them before the Lord, your God, you shall bow down in his presence. Then you and your family, together with the Levite and the aliens who live among you, shall make merry over all these good things which the Lord, your God, has given you.

Responsorial Psalm   Ps 91, 1–2. 10–11.
12–13. 14–15

Be with me, Lord, when I am in trouble.
**You who dwell in the shelter of the Most
    High,**
    who abide in the shadow of the Almighty,
**Say to the Lord, "My refuge and my fortress,
    my God, in whom I trust."**
Be with me, Lord, when I am in trouble.

No evil shall befall you,
    nor shall affliction come near your tent,
For to his angels he has given command
    about you,
    that they guard you in all your ways.
Be with me, Lord, when I am in trouble.
Upon their hands they shall bear you up,
    lest you dash your foot against a stone.
You shall tread upon the asp and the viper;
    you shall trample down the lion and the
    dragon.
Be with me, Lord, when I am in trouble.
Because he clings to me, I will deliver him;
    I will set him on high because he acknowl-
    edges my name.
He shall call upon me, and I will answer him;
    I will be with him in distress;
I will deliver him and glorify him.
Be with me, Lord, when I am in trouble.

READING II   Rom 10, 8–13

What does Scripture say? "The word is near you, on your lips and in your heart (that is, the word of faith which we preach)." For if you confess with your lips that Jesus is Lord, and believe in your heart that God raised him from the dead, you will be saved. Faith in the heart leads to justification, confession on the lips to salvation. Scripture says, "No one who believes in him will be put to shame." Here there is no difference between Jew and Greek; all have the same Lord, rich in mercy toward all who call upon him. "Everyone who calls on the name of the Lord will be saved."

GOSPEL   Lk 4, 1–13

Jesus, full of the Holy Spirit, returned from the Jordan and was led by the Spirit into the desert for forty days, where he was tempted by the devil. During that time he ate nothing, and at the end of it he was hungry. The devil said to him, "If you are the Son of God, command this stone to turn into bread." Jesus answered him, "Scripture has it, 'Not on bread alone shall man live.' "

Then the devil took him up higher and showed him all the kingdoms of the world in a single instant. He said to him, "I will give you all this power and the glory of these kingdoms; the power has been given to me and I give it to whomever I wish. Prostrate yourself in homage before me, and it shall all be yours." In reply, Jesus said to him, "Scripture has it,

'You shall do homage to the Lord your
God; him alone shall you adore.' "

Then the devil led him to Jerusalem, set him on the parapet of the temple, and said to him, "If you are the Son of God, throw yourself down from here, for Scripture has it,

'He will bid his angels watch over you';
and again,

'With their hands they will support you,
that you may never stumble on a
stone.' "

Jesus said to him in reply, "It also says, 'You shall not put the Lord your God to the test.' "

When the devil had finished all this tempting he left him, to await another opportunity.

Reflection on the Readings

With the beginning of the Lenten season, we take time to reflect on what it is we really believe—our faith gives direction and motivation to our Lenten search for holiness.

In the first reading from Deuteronomy, Moses tells his people the story of their origins as the people of God. This story was

retold each year at the Hebrew thanksgiving or harvest festival because it capsulizes God's continuing presence and care for his people, even from the time of Abraham. We connect again with our forebears in faith and strengthen our own spiritual roots.

The responsorial psalm gives voice to our prayer for the protection and support of the Lord and the assurance that we are "delivered" by the Lord because we strive to be faithful. Paul's Letter to the Romans extends to us as well. Our belief in Jesus Christ as the Lord, risen from the dead, leads us to salvation. Our profession of faith affirms our direction toward holiness, a life according to Gospel values.

It is the Gospel that serves as the crowning profession of faith. Each year on this Sunday the Church gives us the story of the temptations of Jesus as he begins his public life. Right after his baptism in the Jordan River, Jesus spent time alone fasting and praying—a soul searching time during which he faced temptations. These are temptations present in our lives as well: to make material comforts foremost in our lives, to seek power and influence for our own use, to be reckless or thoughtless in our self-sufficiency and pride.

Our efforts in the weeks ahead will focus, to some extent, on our purification as individuals and as a community, our efforts to know ourselves better and to be more attentive in our growth toward holiness.

Suggestions for Prayer

1. Use a missal or missalette to read again the opening prayer and other prayers asking for help in our spiritual growth. For us in the catechumenate process, there should be special attentiveness to

our efforts to grow in faith, hope and love. In your own words, formulate a prayer that focuses your Lenten efforts for spiritual growth.

2. In the catechumenate process, some catechumens will be experiencing the Rite of Election at this time. Whether you are participating in the Rite, or are present in support for others in your parish, listen particularly to the prayers of the Rite. They affirm our response to the call to holiness and assure us of the support of the community in our faith journey. Really pray the prayers and reflect on their meaning.

3. The Catholic community professes a summary of our beliefs in a Creed. Familiar to us are two different formulations of our faith: the Apostles' Creed (often prayed in the rosary) and the Nicene Creed, which is proclaimed at Mass. If you do not yet have a copy of the Creed, you may want to ask your sponsor to help you find one. Spend time praying with these statements of belief.

Suggestion for Journal Keeping

Write your own personal creed. Express in it your faith in God, in Jesus, in the Church and in yourself.

Clare M. Colella

Second Sunday of Lent **A**

READING I   Gn 12, 1–4
The Lord said to Abram: "Go forth from the land of your kinsfolk and from your father's house to a land that I will show you.

**"I will make of you a great nation,
    and I will bless you;
I will make your name great,
    so that you will be a blessing.
I will bless those who bless you
    and curse those who curse you.
All the communities of the earth
    shall find blessing in you."
Abram went as the Lord directed him, and Lot went with him. Abram was seventy-five years old when he left Haran.**

Responsorial Psalm   Ps 33, 4–5. 18–19. 20. 22

Lord, let your mercy be on us,
    as we place our trust in you.
**Upright is the word of the Lord,
    and all his works are trustworthy.
He loves justice and right;
    of the kindness of the Lord the earth is full.**
Lord, let your mercy be on us,
    as we place our trust in you.
**See, the eyes of the Lord are upon those who
        fear him,
    upon those who hope for his kindness,
To deliver them from death
    and preserve them in spite of famine.**
Lord, let your mercy be on us,
    as we place our trust in you.
**Our soul waits for the Lord,
    who is our help and our shield.
May your kindness, O Lord, be upon us
    who have put our hope in you.**
Lord, let your mercy be on us,
    as we place our trust in you.

READING II   2 Tm 1, 8–10
Bear your share of the hardship which the gospel entails.

    God has saved us and has called us to a holy life, not because of any merit of ours

66

but according to his own design—the grace held out to us in Christ Jesus before the world began but now made manifest through the appearance of our Savior. He has robbed death of its power and has brought life and immortality into clear light through the gospel.

GOSPEL   Mt 17, 1–9

Jesus took Peter, James, and his brother John and led them up on a high mountain by themselves. He was transfigured before their eyes. His face became as dazzling as the sun, his clothes as radiant as light. Suddenly Moses and Elijah appeared to them conversing with him. Upon this, Peter said to Jesus, "Lord, how good it is for us to be here! With your permission I will erect three booths here, one for you, one for Moses, and one for Elijah." He was still speaking when suddenly a bright cloud overshadowed them. Out of the cloud came a voice which said, "This is my beloved Son on whom my favor rests. Listen to him." When they heard this the disciples fell forward on the ground, overcome with fear. Jesus came toward them and laying his hand on them, said, "Get up! Do not be afraid." When they looked up they did not see anyone but Jesus.

As they were coming down the mountainside Jesus commanded them, "Do not tell anyone of the vision until the Son of Man rises from the dead."

Reflection on the Readings

Our Gospel today relates a rather extraordinary occurrence: the transfiguration of Jesus. This transfiguration is a change in Jesus' appearance that allows the apostles to experience Jesus as he truly was—honest, vulnerable, in his glory. More importantly, however, the apostles experience a particular call from God. The message of the voice from the cloud ends with an active command: Listen to Jesus. The invitation is to trust the way of life of Jesus, to risk following Jesus.

The other readings today continue this message of God's call. In the Genesis reading, we hear God's call to Abraham to leave all his securities—his homeland, his heritage—in order to enter into a deeper relationship with God. In return for his trust, God promises Abraham a blessed future. In the Letter to Timothy, we are reminded again of God's call to lives that are holy. But, like Abraham, we can only respond in trust to this call because of God's presence within us, God's grace.

The transfiguration of Jesus is about our call to a blessed future. When we can trust God's call to follow Jesus, we can let go of all that we hold onto for security (such as prestige, honors, and money) and begin to see the various transfigurations happening all around us whenever women and men embrace honest, vulnerable and authentic lives patterned on the Gospel way of life.

Suggestions for Prayer

1. Reflect on God's call in your life. How is God calling you, and to what is God calling you? Ask God for what you need in order to respond faithfully to God's call in your life.
2. Pray Psalm 33, a psalm of trust. What images and feelings emerge while you pray the psalm?
3. Bring to prayer an experience of your own brokenness that needs to be embraced by the love of God so that it can

be transfigured, so that the true glory of God can shine forth.

Suggestion for Journal Keeping

As we learn to trust, we begin to see more and more transfigurations all around us: people embracing life more fully. Reflect on your own experiences and the experiences of family and friends when life was embraced, such as in the recovery of an alcoholic, or the rebuilding of a life after divorce, or the new life of an infant. How did you meet God in these events?

Thomas H. Morris

Second Sunday of Lent B

READING I   Gn 22, 1–2. 9. 10–13. 15–18
God put Abraham to the test. He called to him, "Abraham!" "Ready!" he replied. Then God said: "Take your son Isaac, your only one, whom you love, and go to the land of Moriah. There you shall offer him up as a holocaust on a height that I will point out to you."

When they came to the place of which God had told him, Abraham built an altar there and arranged the wood on it. Then he reached out and took the knife to slaughter his son. But the Lord's messenger called to him from heaven, "Abraham, Abraham!" "Yes, Lord," he answered. "Do not lay your hand on the boy," said the messenger. "Do not do the least thing to him. I know now how devoted you are to God, since you did not withhold from me your own beloved son." As Abraham looked about, he spied a ram caught by its horns in the thicket. So he went and took the ram and offered it up as a holocaust in place of his son.

Again the Lord's messenger called to Abraham from heaven and said: "I swear by myself, declares the Lord, that because you acted as you did in not withholding from me your beloved son, I will bless you abundantly and make your descendants as countless as the stars of the sky and the sands of the seashore; your descendants shall take possession of the gates of their enemies, and in your descendants all the nations of the earth shall find blessing—all this because you obeyed my command."

Responsorial Psalm   Ps 116, 10. 15. 16–17. 18–19

I will walk in the presence of the Lord,
     in the land of the living.
I believed, even when I said,
     "I am greatly afflicted."
Precious in the eyes of the Lord
     is the death of his faithful ones.
I will walk in the presence of the Lord,
     in the land of the living.
O Lord, I am your servant;
     I am your servant, the son of your handmaid;
     you have loosed my bonds.
To you will I offer sacrifice of thanksgiving,
     and I will call upon the name of the Lord.
I will walk in the presence of the Lord,
     in the land of the living.
My vows to the Lord I will pay
     in the presence of all his people,
In the courts of the house of the Lord,
     in your midst, O Jerusalem.
I will walk in the presence of the Lord,
     in the land of the living.

READING II Rom 8, 31–34

If God is for us, who can be against us? Is it possible that he who did not spare his own Son but handed him over for the sake of us all will not grant us all things besides? Who shall bring a charge against God's chosen ones? God, who justifies? Who shall condemn them? Christ Jesus, who died or rather was raised up, who is at the right hand of God and who intercedes for us?

GOSPEL Mk 9, 2–10

Jesus took Peter, James and John off by themselves with him and led them up a high mountain. He was transfigured before their eyes and his clothes became dazzlingly white—whiter than the work of any bleacher could make them. Elijah appeared to them along with Moses; the two were in conversation with Jesus. Then Peter spoke to Jesus: "Rabbi, how good it is for us to be here. Let us erect three booths on this site, one for you, one for Moses, and one for Elijah." He hardly knew what to say, for they were all overcome with awe. A cloud came, overshadowing them, and out of the cloud a voice: "This is my Son, my beloved. Listen to him." Suddenly looking around they no longer saw anyone with them—only Jesus.

As they were coming down the mountain, he strictly enjoined them not to tell anyone what they had seen before the Son of Man had risen from the dead. They kept this word of his to themselves, though they continued to discuss what "to rise from the dead" meant.

Reflection on the Readings

We are confronted this Sunday with the difficulties as well as the blessings we en-

counter when we answer "yes" to God's call. Abraham says yes and is willing to sacrifice his only son because God has asked it of him. In response to Abraham's obedience God says: "Because you acted as you did, I will bless you abundantly . . . all this because you obeyed my command." Abraham is our example of complete obedience to the will of God. Are we willing to do the same?

The Gospel accounts tell us of Peter, James and John being allowed to share in seeing Christ glorified. However, they are confused by his strict request "not to tell anyone what they had seen, before the Son of Man has risen from the dead." What does "rise from the dead" mean? They fail to comprehend his words. They failed to see that in order to be followers of Christ one must enter into suffering and, perhaps, even death in order to share in his resurrection. For those preparing for initiation as well as for those fully initiated, the good news of today's liturgy reminds us how like Peter, James and John we are. How often do we fail to comprehend Christ's words to us?

Suggestions for Prayer

1. Mark tells us that Christ is glorified before Peter, James and John. From the cloud they hear: "This is my Son. Listen to him." Take time this week and meditate on these words. Clear your mind. Be quiet. Take time to listen.

2. Abraham made a difficult and painful decision. He put his faith in the Lord and the Lord then promised him abundant blessings. Consider a difficult situation in your life right now. How have you handled it so far? Has it gotten less dif-

ficult as a result of your actions? Are you able to follow the example of Abraham and strive to put your faith in God for strength to make the decision?

3. Choose a quiet time and place where you will be undisturbed. Spend a minimum of five minutes in giving thanks and praise to God for blessings received.

Suggestion for Journal Keeping

The faith of Abraham is our example of listening and loving our God above our wants or needs. What still hinders you from doing the same? What are some struggles you have in letting go of controlling the situation? What is preventing you from surrendering to God's will for you?

Mary Kay Meier

Second Sunday of Lent   C

READING I   Gn 15, 5–12. 17–18
God took Abram outside and said: "Look up at the sky and count the stars, if you can. Just so," he added, "shall your descendants be." Abram put his faith in the Lord, who credited it to him as an act of righteousness.

He then said to him, "I am the Lord who brought you from Ur of the Chaldeans to give you this land as a possession." "O Lord God," he asked, "how am I to know that I shall possess it?" He answered him, "Bring me a three-year-old heifer, a three-year-old she-goat, a three-year-old ram, a turtledove, and a young pigeon." He brought him all these, split them in two, and placed each

half opposite the other; but the birds he did not cut up. Birds of prey swooped down on the carcasses, but Abram stayed with them. As the sun was about to set, a trance fell upon Abram, and a deep, terrifying darkness enveloped him.**

When the sun had set and it was dark, there appeared a smoking brazier and a flaming torch, which passed between those pieces. It was on that occasion that the Lord made a covenant with Abram, saying: "To your descendants I give this land from the Wadi of Egypt to the Great River [the Euphrates].

Responsorial Psalm   Ps 27, 1 7–8. 8–9. 13–14

The Lord is my light and my salvation.
**The Lord is my light and my salvation;
    whom should I fear?
The Lord is my life's refuge;
    of whom should I be afraid?**
The Lord is my light and my salvation.
**Hear, O Lord, the sound of my call;
    have pity on me, and answer me.
Of you my heart speaks; you my glance
    seeks.**
The Lord is my light and my salvation.
**Your presence, O Lord, I seek.
    Hide not your face from me;
Do not in anger repel your servant.
    You are my helper: cast me not off.**
The Lord is my light and my salvation.
**I believe that I shall see the bounty of the
    Lord
    in the land of living.
Wait for the Lord with courage;
    be stouthearted, and wait for the Lord.**
The Lord is my light and my salvation.

READING II   Phil 3, 17—4, 1

Be imitators of me, my brothers. Take as your guide those who follow the example that we set. Unfortunately, many go about in a way which shows them to be enemies of the cross of Christ. I have often said this to you before; this time I say it with tears. Such as these will end in disaster! Their god is their belly and their glory is in their shame. I am talking about those who are set upon the things of this world. As you well know, we have our citizenship in heaven; it is from there that we eagerly await the coming of our savior, the Lord Jesus Christ. He will give a new form to this lowly body of ours and remake it according to the pattern of his glorified body, by his power to subject everything to himself.

For these reasons, my brothers, you whom I so love and long for, you who are my joy and my crown, continue, my dear ones, to stand firm in the Lord.

GOSPEL   Lk 9, 28–36

Jesus took Peter, John and James, and went up onto a mountain to pray. While he was praying, his face changed in appearance and his clothes became dazzlingly white. Suddenly two men were talking with him—Moses and Elijah. They appeared in glory and spoke of his passage which he was about to fulfill in Jerusalem. Peter and those with him had fallen into a deep sleep; but awakening, they saw his glory and likewise saw the two men who were standing with him. When these were leaving, Peter said to Jesus, "Master, how good it is for us to be here. Let us set up three booths, one for you, one for Moses, and one for Elijah." (He did not really know what he was saying.) While he was speaking, a cloud came and overshadowed them, and the disciples grew fearful as the others entered it. Then from the cloud came a voice which said, "This is my Son, my Chosen One. Listen to him." When the voice fell silent, Jesus was there alone. The disciples kept quiet, telling nothing of what they had seen at that time to anyone.

Reflection on the Readings

Each year on this Sunday the readings connect the covenant between God and Abram (Abraham) with the transfiguration of Jesus. Having faced our vulnerability with the temptations episode the previous week, we are now assured that we are rooted in the long-standing covenant of God's presence and care. Abraham is our forefather in faith. His relationship with God is a model for us, a deep trust and fidelity that gives us strength. It is the "standing firm in the Lord" of which Paul speaks in the Letter to the Philippians.

When we are strong in the Lord, faithful to our covenant, we experience a continuing conversion. The event of the transfiguration of Jesus is, in a sense, a promise to his followers. Through Jesus we are called to prayer, to a deeper relationship with God and our spiritual forebears. Our reflection on the transfiguration of Jesus is also a call to a process of transformation in our lives. This is a reminder of our continuing Lenten resolve to grow in holiness, to withstand the temptations of pride and selfishness, to become more like Jesus in our lives.

Our lives will become recognizably different—the spiritual energy and growth we experience will make our faith shine. The

71

transfiguration will become real in our lives. The promise from ancient times is renewed through us today.

Suggestions for Prayer

1. Psalm 27 serves as the responsorial psalm, in which we plead for the Lord to be our light and salvation. We pray to recognize the Lord's care and we seek God's encouragement to be strong and persevere in growing in faith. As you pray this psalm slowly, reflect on *your* own conversion to the Lord. What do you ask of Him? Do you truly believe in his presence and care? Create your own personalized prayer springing from the psalm.

2. Transformation of our lives is an outcome of a process of spiritual growth. Take time to envision aspects of your life that are becoming changed as you develop your spiritual life. Pray about your growth, asking the guidance and strength of the Lord. Reflect on ways that care and encouragement come into your life.

3. Just as Jesus spoke with Moses and Elijah, we too have persons in our lives who have given us spiritual roots and spiritual wisdom. Spend time in quiet reflective prayer. Think about those who have helped shape your spiritual life. How are you becoming more transformed to live as a follower of Jesus?

Suggestion for Journal Keeping

As you reflect on the readings and spend time in prayer, track your thoughts in your journal. Reaffirm your resolve to transform your life. We have been calling it your journey of faith, the process of conversion. Your journal is a way for you to make concrete and visible for yourself your on-going spiritual growth.

Clare M. Colella

Third Sunday of Lent A

READING I   Ex 17, 3–7

In their thirst for water, the people grumbled against Moses, saying, "Why did you ever make us leave Egypt? Was it just to have us die here of thirst with our children and our livestock?" So Moses cried out to the Lord, "What shall I do with this people? A little more and they will stone me!" The Lord answered Moses, "Go over there in front of the people, along with some of the elders of Israel, holding in your hand, as you go, the staff with which you struck the river. I will be standing there in front of you on the rock in Horeb. Strike the rock, and the water will flow from it for the people to drink." This Moses did, in the presence of the elders of Israel. The place was called Massah and Meribah, because the Israelites quarreled there and tested the Lord, saying, "Is the Lord in our midst or not?"

Responsorial Psalm   Ps 95, 1–2. 6–7. 8–9
If today you hear his voice,
    harden not your hearts.
**Come, let us sing joyfully to the Lord;
    let us acclaim the Rock of our salvation.
Let us greet him with thanksgiving;
    let us joyfully sing psalms to him.**
If today you hear his voice,
    harden not your hearts.

Come, let us bow down in worship;
let us kneel before the Lord who made us.
For he is our God,
and we are the people he shepherds, the
flock he guides.
If today you hear his voice,
harden not your hearts.
Oh, that today you would hear his voice:
"Harden not your hearts as at Meribah,
as in the day of Massah in the desert,
Where your fathers tempted me;
they tested me though they had seen my
works."
If today you hear his voice,
harden not your hearts.

READING II   Rom 5, 1–2. 5–8

Now that we have been justified by faith, we
are at peace with God through our Lord Jesus Christ. Through him we have gained access by faith to the grace in which we now
stand, and we boast of our hope for the glory
of God. And this hope will not leave us disappointed, because the love of God has been
poured out in our hearts through the Holy
Spirit who has been given to us. At the appointed time, when we were still powerless,
Christ died for us godless men. It is rare that
anyone should lay down his life for a just
man, though it is barely possible that for a
good man someone may have the courage to
die. It is precisely in this that God proves his
love for us: that while we were still sinners,
Christ died for us.

GOSPEL   Jn 4, 5–42

Jesus had to pass through Samaria, and his
journey brought him to a Samaritan town
named Shechem near the plot of land which
Jacob had given to his son Joseph. This was
the site of Jacob's well. Jesus, tired from his
journey, sat down at the well.

The hour was about noon. When a Samaritan woman came to draw water, Jesus
said to her, "Give me a drink." (His disciples
had gone off to the town to buy provisions.)
The Samaritan woman said to him, "You are
a Jew. How can you ask me, a Samaritan and
a woman, for a drink?" (Recall that Jews
have nothing to do with Samaritans.) Jesus
replied:
"If only you recognized God's gift,
and who it is that is asking you for a
drink,
you would have asked him instead,
and he would have given you living
water."
"Sir," she challenged him, "you don't have
a bucket and this well is deep. Where do you
expect to get this flowing water? Surely you
don't pretend to be greater than our ances-
tor Jacob, who gave us this well and drank
from it with his sons and his flocks?" Jesus
replied:
"Everyone who drinks this water
will be thirsty again.
But whoever drinks the water I give him
will never be thirsty;
no, the water I give
shall become a fountain within him,
leaping up to provide eternal life."
The woman said to him, "Give me this water, sir, so that I won't grow thirsty and have
to keep coming here to draw water."

He told her, "Go, call your husband, and
then come back here." "I have no husband," replied the woman. "You are right in
saying you have no husband!" Jesus exclaimed. "The fact is, you have had five, and
the man you are living with now is not your
husband. What you said is true enough."

"Sir," answered the woman, "I can see you are a prophet. Our ancestors worshiped on this mountain, but you people claim that Jerusalem is the place where men ought to worship God." Jesus told her:

"Believe me, woman,
an hour is coming
when you will worship the Father
neither on this mountain
nor in Jerusalem.
You people worship what you do not
    understand,
while we understand what we worship;
after all, salvation is from the Jews.
Yet an hour is coming, and is already
    here,
when authentic worshipers
will worship the Father in Spirit and
    truth.
Indeed, it is just such worshipers
the Father seeks.
God is Spirit,
and those who worship him
must worship in Spirit and truth."

The woman said to him: "I know there is a Messiah coming. (This term means Anointed.) When he comes, he will tell us everything." Jesus replied, "I who speak to you am he."

His disciples, returning at this point, were surprised that Jesus was speaking with a woman. No one put a question, however, such as "What do you want of him?" or "Why are you talking with her?" The woman then left her water jar and went off into the town. She said to the people: "Come and see someone who told me everything I ever did! Could this not be the Messiah?" With that they set out from the town to meet him.

Meanwhile the disciples were urging him, "Rabbi, eat something." But he told them:

"I have food to eat
of which you do not know."

At this the disciples said to one another, "You do not suppose anyone has brought him something to eat?" Jesus explained to them:

"Doing the will of him who sent me
and bringing his work to completion
is my food.
Do you not have a saying:
'Four months more
and it will be harvest!'?
Listen to what I say:
Open your eyes and see!
The fields are shining for harvest!
The reaper already collects his wages
and gathers a yield for eternal life,
that sower and reaper may rejoice to-
    gether.
Here we have the saying verified:
'One man sows; another reaps.'
I sent you to reap
what you had not worked for.
Others have done the labor,
and you have come into their gain."

Many Samaritans from that town believed in him on the strength of the woman's word of testimony: "He told me everything I ever did." The result was that, when these Samaritans came to him, they begged him to stay with them awhile. So he stayed there two days, and through his own spoken word many more came to faith. As they told the woman: "No longer does our faith depend on your story. We have heard for ourselves, and we know that this really is the Savior of the world."

Reflection on the Readings

In today's Gospel, we experience the tenderness and compassion of Jesus as he encounters the Samaritan woman. Jesus helps her come to an awareness of her needs, of her true thirst. We, too, are invited to accept Jesus in order to quench our interior thirst for life, for meaning. It is only in God that we can experience the living waters that can satisfy. This wellspring within us is beautifully described in the text from Romans: the love of God has been poured out into our hearts. The very source of our life, and hence that which can quench our thirst for meaningful life, is God within us.

We see a different response to this thirst in the reading from Exodus. Israel has failed to trust the God who has saved her, the God who has led Israel to freedom. Israel desires to serve herself—and thus threatens violence in order to have her thirst quenched. The Samaritan woman, on the other hand, trusts her experience of Jesus and is freely given living waters. She is then able to witness to God's life within her, thereby bringing others to experience God's gifts of love and life.

Suggestions for Prayer

1. Lead yourself through a guided imagery prayer. Visualize yourself as a well. What is the well made of? What is in the well? What do I need from God to drink more fully from the well of life?
2. Reflect on your thirsts: perhaps thirsts for power, acceptance, relationships, freedom from suffering, etc. Now pray for a deeper awareness of your thirst for God. How is this thirst for God similar to or different than your other thirsts?
3. Slowly and prayerfully chant the responsorial psalm for today, Psalm 95. At the completion of the psalm, allow yourself to sit in the silence to hear the voice of God.

Suggestion for Journal Keeping

The text from Romans proclaims: the love of God has been poured out in our hearts through the Holy Spirit. What does this mean to you? How do you block this gift of love? What does this text from Romans tell you about yourself?

Thomas H. Morris

Third Sunday of Lent B

READING I Ex 20, 1–17

God delivered all these commandments: "I, the Lord, am your God, who brought you out of the land of Egypt, that place of slavery. You shall not have other gods besides me. You shall not carve idols for yourselves in the shape of anything in the sky above or on the earth below or in the waters beneath the earth; you shall not bow down before them or worship them. For I, the Lord, your God, am a jealous God, inflicting punishment for their fathers' wickedness on the children of those who hate me, down to the third and fourth generation; but bestowing mercy down to the thousandth generation, on the children of those who love me and keep my commandments.

"You shall not take the name of the Lord, your God, in vain. For the Lord will not leave unpunished him who takes his name in vain.

"Remember to keep holy the sabbath day. Six days you may labor and do all your work, but the seventh day is the sabbath of the Lord, your God. No work may be done then either by you, or your son or daughter, or your male or female slave, or your beast, or by the alien who lives with you. In six days

the Lord made the heavens and the earth, the sea and all that is in them; but on the seventh day he rested. That is why the Lord has blessed the sabbath day and made it holy.

"Honor your father and your mother, that you may have a long life in the land which the Lord, your God, is giving you.

"You shall not kill.

"You shall not commit adultery.

"You shall not steal.

"You shall not bear false witness against your neighbor.

"You shall not covet your neighbor's house. You shall not covet your neighbor's wife, nor his male or female slave, nor his ox or ass, nor anything else that belongs to him."

Responsorial Psalm   Ps 19, 8. 9. 10. 11
Lord, you have the words of everlasting
    life.
The law of the Lord is perfect,
    refreshing the soul;
The decree of the Lord is trustworthy,
    giving wisdom to the simple.
Lord, you have the words of everlasting
    life.
The precepts of the Lord are right,
    rejoicing the heart;
The command of the Lord is clear,
    enlightening the eye.
Lord, you have the words of everlasting
    life.
The fear of the Lord is pure,
    enduring forever;
The ordinances of the Lord are true,
    all of them just.
Lord, you have the words of everlasting
    life.
They are more precious than gold,
    than a heap of purest gold;

Sweeter also than syrup
    or honey from the comb.
Lord, you have the words of everlasting
    life.

READING II   1 Cor 1, 22–25
Jews demand "signs" and Greeks look for "wisdom," but we preach Christ crucified, a stumbling block to Jews, and an absurdity to Gentiles; but to those who are called, Jews and Greeks alike, Christ is the power of God and the wisdom of God. For God's folly is wiser than men, and his weakness more powerful than men.

GOSPEL   Jn 2, 13–25
As the Jewish Passover was near, Jesus went up to Jerusalem. In the temple precincts he came upon people engaged in selling oxen, sheep and doves, and others seated changing coins. He made a [kind of] whip of cords and drove them all out of the temple area, sheep and oxen alike, and knocked over the moneychangers' tables, spilling their coins. He told those who were selling doves: "Get them out of here! Stop turning my Father's house into a marketplace!" His disciples recalled the words of Scripture: "Zeal for your house consumes me."

At this the Jews responded, "What sign can you show us authorizing you to do these things?" "Destroy this temple," was Jesus' answer, "and in three days I will raise it up." They retorted, "This temple took forty-six years to build, and you are going to 'raise it up in three days'!" Actually he was talking about the temple of his body. Only after Jesus had been raised from the dead did his disciples recall that he had said this, and come to believe the Scripture and the word he had spoken.

While he was in Jerusalem during the Passover festival, many believed in his name, for they could see the signs he was performing. For his part, Jesus would not trust himself to them because he knew them all. He needed no one to give him testimony about human nature. He was well aware of what was in man's heart.

Reflection on the Readings

By the cleansing of the temple Jesus foretells his death followed by the three days before his resurrection. In anger he drives the merchants and money changers from the temple, his Father's house. In doing so he indicates that worship through him, the new temple, will eliminate the need for those elements of sacrifice. The Jewish leaders ask for a sign of his authority. They do not understand his answer to them: "Destroy this temple and in three days I will build it up." How can you tear down something that took forty-six years to build and rebuild it in three days?

Jesus initiates something new. No longer was worship a matter of offering sacrifice in the temple, nor was fidelity simply a matter of obeying the law. As Jesus says to the Samaritan woman, "An hour . . . is already here, when authentic worshipers will worship the Father in Spirit and truth." This message can be as difficult for us as it was for Jesus' hearers. We too want to rely on signs to give us certainty, or worldly wisdom to resolve our questions. Yet the only sign we have is a sign of contradiction, the crucified Jesus. He is the wisdom and power of God on whom we rely.

Suggestions for Prayer

1. In what ways do you base your faith on external signs, obedience to the law, or worldly wisdom? Has there been a time when you discovered that God's folly was wiser than you, or God's weakness stronger than you?
2. Be a sign of Christ's presence in the world today by offering your presence to someone in need. Remember, it is not words or actions, but sometimes our physical presence that is the gift.
3. Take time before retiring to reflect on your day. Have you kept the commandment of Christ this day to love one another? Ask the Lord to continue to show you his way of living and loving.

Suggestion for Journal Keeping

What presently enables you to follow Jesus: the law, his signs, his words? Why? What makes it difficult for you to follow Jesus: the law, his signs, his words? Why?

Mary Kay Meier

Third Sunday of Lent

READING I   Ex 3, 1–8. 13–15

Moses was tending the flock of his father-in-law Jethro, the priest of Midian. Leading the flock across the desert, he came to Horeb, the mountain of God. There an angel of the Lord appeared to him in fire flaming out of a bush. As he looked on, he was surprised to see that the bush, though on fire, was not consumed. So Moses decided, "I must go over to look at this remarkable sight, and see why the bush is not burned."

When the Lord saw him coming over to look at it more closely, God called out to him from the bush, "Moses! Moses!" He an-

swered, "Here I am." God said, "Come no nearer! Remove the sandals from your feet, for the place where you stand is holy ground. I am the God of your father," he continued, "the God of Abraham, the God of Isaac, the God of Jacob." Moses hid his face, for he was afraid to look at God. But the Lord said, "I have witnessed the affliction of my people in Egypt and have heard their cry of complaint against their slave drivers, so I know well what they are suffering. Therefore I have come down to rescue them from the hands of the Egyptians and lead them out of that land into a good and spacious land, a land flowing with milk and honey."

"But," said Moses to God, "when I go to the Israelites and say to them, 'The God of your fathers has sent me to you,' if they ask me, 'What is his name?' what am I to tell them?" God replied, "I am who am." Then he added, "This is what you shall tell the Israelites: I AM sent me to you."

God spoke further to Moses, "Thus shall you say to the Israelites: The Lord, the God of your fathers, the God of Abraham, the God of Isaac, the God of Jacob, has sent me to you.

"This is my name forever;
this is my title for all generations."

Responsorial Psalm   Ps 103. 1–2. 3–4. 6–
7. 8. 11

The Lord is kind and merciful.
**Bless the Lord, O my soul;
and all my being, bless his holy name.
Bless the Lord, O my soul,
and forget not all his benefits.**
The Lord is kind and merciful.
**He pardons all your iniquities,
he heals all your ills.**

He redeems your life from destruction,
he crowns you with kindness and compassion.
The Lord is kind and merciful.
**The Lord secures justice
and the rights of all the oppressed.
He has made known his ways to Moses,
and his deeds to the children of Israel.**
The Lord is kind and merciful.
**Merciful and gracious is the Lord,
slow to anger and abounding in kindness.
For as the heavens are high above the earth,
so surpassing is his kindness toward those
who fear him.**
The Lord is kind and merciful.

READING II   1 Cor 10, 1–6. 10–12
I want you to remember this: our fathers were all under the cloud and all passed through the sea; by the cloud and the sea all of them were baptized into Moses. All ate the same spiritual food. All drank the same spiritual drink (they drank from the spiritual rock that was following them, and the rock was Christ), yet we know that God was not pleased with most of them, for "they were struck down in the desert."

These things happened as an example to keep us from wicked desires such as theirs. Nor are you to grumble as some of them did, to be killed by the destroying angel. The things that happened to them serve as an example. They have been written as a warning to us, upon whom the end of the ages has come. For all these reasons, let anyone who thinks he is standing upright watch out lest he fall!

GOSPEL   Lk 13, 1–9
At that time some were present who told Jesus about the Galileans whose blood Pilate

had mixed with their sacrifices. He said in reply: "Do you think that these Galileans were the greatest sinners in Galilee just because they suffered this? By no means! But I tell you, you will all come to the same end unless you reform. Or take those eighteen who were killed by a falling tower in Siloam. Do you think they were more guilty than anyone else who lived in Jerusalem? Certainly not! But I tell you, you will all come to the same end unless you begin to reform."

Jesus spoke this parable: "A man had a fig tree growing in his vineyard, and he came out looking for fruit on it but did not find any. He said to the vinedresser, 'Look here! For three years now I have come in search of fruit on this fig tree and found none. Cut it down. Why should it clutter up the ground?' In answer, the man said, 'Sir, leave it another year while I hoe around it and manure it; then perhaps it will bear fruit. If not, it shall be cut down.' "

Reflection on the Readings

Throughout the prayers and readings today, we are reminded of the need for ongoing reform in our lives. Persistence and patience are key in a true formation according to the teachings of both Hebrew and Christian Scripture.

In parishes celebrating the rite of Christian Initiation, this is the Sunday of the first scrutiny. That rite serves to focus our reflections today—what are we doing to shape our actions and lives to the Christian values and teachings? As we examine ("scrutinize") our lives, can we affirm areas of growth while we also acknowledge our weaknesses and failures? Where is God in our lives? How central is our relationship with God in the formation of our values?

The first Scripture reading, from the Book of Exodus, has two wonderful insights for those of us consciously endeavoring to grow in faith. First, while shepherding his flock Moses encounters God through a burning bush. It is in the midst of ordinary tasks that we come to recognize the presence and voice of God. Second, God gives himself the name "I am who am." From ancient times on through all generations, God *is*—is present, is close to us, is covenanted with us as our God. He is not distant or unfamiliar. He is compassionate, aware of the suffering of his people. Yet we are often unaware of God. Like the fig tree in the Gospel we can go on year after year without bearing fruit. But eventually there comes a time when the owner of the tree cuts it down if it is fruitless. Lent is for us a time of reckoning. We must look at our lives and ask what fruit we are bearing. Are we responsive to God in our ordinary life, to God who is always with us?

Suggestions for Prayer

1. One task of spiritual growth is to move prayerfully through our ordinary surroundings—to see God in and through our daily lives. Like Moses we are to remove our shoes (habitual ways of seeing and doing) and experience all of life as holy ground. Take time to review the persons and events of the last day or so—pray about them, seeing them as "holy ground." Where do you see God?

2. In the spirit of reforming our lives, we look at, "scrutinize," ourselves, our actions and values. Picture yourself together with Jesus talking about your life. Where are the greatest weaknesses? What needs special care before you

"bear fruit"? Where are your strengths as a follower of Jesus? How regular is your life of prayer, fasting or works of mercy? Because you and Jesus are together, you know you will have strength to be faithful. Let your reflection on your life become a prayer.

3. The catechumenate process is a time of particular attention to our spiritual growth and way of life. Some qualities of holiness are spoken of in today's responsorial psalm—kindness, mercy, compassion, justice, graciousness, forgiveness, being slow to anger. As you pray the psalm again, ponder these qualities.

Suggestion for Journal Keeping

Picture yourself as Moses before the burning bush. Center your attention on your presence with God, however you picture God. God has a message for you. As you hear God's words to you, what is your response? Use your journal to reflect on this time with God.

Clare M. Colella

Fourth Sunday of Lent 🅰

READING I   1 Sm 16, 1. 6–7. 10–13
The Lord said to Samuel: "I am sending you to Jesse of Bethlehem, for I have chosen my king from among his sons.

As Jesse and his sons came to the sacrifice, Samuel looked at Eliab and thought, "Surely the Lord's anointed is here before him." But the Lord said to Samuel: "Do not judge from his appearance or from his lofty stature, be-cause I have rejected him. Not as man sees does God see, because man sees the appearance but the Lord looks into the heart." In the same way Jesse presented seven sons before Samuel, but Samuel said to Jesse, "The Lord has not chosen any one of these." Then Samuel asked Jesse, "Are these all the sons you have?" Jesse replied, "There is still the youngest, who is tending the sheep." Samuel said to Jesse, "Send for him; we will not begin the sacrificial banquet until he arrives here." Jesse sent and had the young man brought to them. He was ruddy, a youth handsome to behold and making a splendid appearance. The Lord said, "There—anoint him, for this is he!" Then Samuel, with the horn of oil in hand, anointed him in the midst of his brothers; and from that day on, the spirit of the Lord rushed upon David.

Responsorial Psalm   Ps 23, 1–3. 3–4. 5. 6
The Lord is my shepherd, there is nothing
          I shall want.
The Lord is my shepherd; I shall not want.
          In verdant pastures he gives me repose;
Beside restful waters he leads me;
          he refreshes my soul.
The Lord is my shepherd, there is nothing
          I shall want.
He guides me in right paths
          for his name's sake.
Even though I walk in the dark valley
          I fear no evil; for you are at my side
With your rod and your staff
          that give me courage.
The Lord is my shepherd, there is nothing
          I shall want.
You spread the table before me
          in the sight of my foes;
You anoint my head with oil;
          my cup overflows.

The Lord is my shepherd, there is nothing
    I shall want.
Only goodness and kindness follow me
    all the days of my life;
And I shall dwell in the house of the Lord
    for years to come.
The Lord is my shepherd, there is nothing
    I shall want.

READING II   Eph 5, 8–14
**There was a time when you were darkness,
but now you are light in the Lord. Well,
then, live as children of light. Light produces
every kind of goodness and justice and truth.
Be correct in your judgment of what pleases
the Lord. Take no part in vain deeds done in
darkness; rather, condemn them. It is
shameful even to mention the things these
people do in secret; but when such deeds are
condemned, they are seen in the light of
day, and all that then appears is light. That
is why we read:**
"Awake, O sleeper,
    arise from the dead,
    and Christ will give you light."

GOSPEL   Jn 9, 1–41
As Jesus walked along, he saw a man who
had been blind from birth. His disciples
asked him, "Rabbi, was it his sin or his parents' that caused him to be born blind?"
"Neither," answered Jesus:
    "It was no sin, either of this man or of
      his parents.
    Rather, it was to let God's works show
      forth in him.
    We must do the deeds of him who sent
      me while it is day.
    The night comes on
    when no one can work.

**While I am in the world
I am the light of the world."**
With that Jesus spat on the ground, made
mud with his saliva, and smeared the man's
eyes with the mud. Then he told him, "Go,
wash in the pool of Siloam." (This name
means "One who has been sent.") So the
man went off and washed, and came back
able to see.

His neighbors and the people who had
been accustomed to see him begging began
to ask, "Isn't this the fellow who used to sit
and beg?" Some were claiming it was he;
others maintained it was not but someone
who looked like him. The man himself said,
"I'm the one, all right." They said to him
then, "How were your eyes opened?" He
answered: "That man they call Jesus made
mud and smeared it on my eyes, telling me
to go to Siloam and wash. When I did go and
wash, I was able to see." "Where is he?"
they asked. He replied, "I have no idea."

Next, they took the man who had been
born blind, to the Pharisees. (Note that it
was on a sabbath that Jesus had made the
mud paste and opened his eyes.) The Pharisees, in turn, began to inquire how he had
recovered his sight. He told them, "He put
mud on my eyes. I washed it off, and now I
can see." This prompted some of the Pharisees to assert, "This man cannot be from
God because he does not keep the sabbath."
Others objected, "If a man is a sinner, how
can he perform signs like these?" They were
sharply divided over him. Then they addressed the blind man again: "Since it was
your eyes he opened, what do you have to
say about him?" "He is a prophet," he replied.

The Jews refused to believe that he had
really been born blind and had begun to see,

until they summoned the parents of this man who now could see. "Is this your son?" they asked, "and if so, do you attest that he was blind at birth? How do you account for the fact that he now can see?" His parents answered, "We know this is our son, and we know he was blind at birth. But how he can see now, or who opened his eyes, we have no idea. Ask him. He is old enough to speak for himself." (His parents answered in this fashion because they were afraid of the Jews, who had already agreed among themselves that anyone who acknowledged Jesus as the Messiah would be put out of the synagogue. That was why his parents said, "He is of age—ask him.")

A second time they summoned the man who had been born blind and said to him, "Give glory to God! First of all, we know this man is a sinner." "I would not know whether he is a sinner or not," he answered. "I know this much: I was blind before; now I can see." They persisted: "Just what did he do to you? How did he open your eyes?" "I have told you once, but you would not listen to me," he answered them. "Why do you want to hear it all over again? Do not tell me you want to become his disciples too?" They retorted scornfully, "You are the one who is that man's disciple. We are disciples of Moses. We know that God spoke to Moses, but we have no idea where this man comes from." He came back at them: "Well, this is news! You do not know where he comes from, yet he opened my eyes. We know that God does not hear sinners, but that if someone is devout and obeys his will he listens to him. It is unheard of that anyone ever gave sight to a person blind from birth. If this man were not from God, he could never have done such a thing." "What!" they exclaimed, "You are steeped in sin from your birth, and you are giving us lectures?" With that they threw him out bodily.

When Jesus heard of his expulsion, he sought him out and asked him, "Do you believe in the Son of Man?" He answered, "Who is he, sir, that I may believe in him?" "You have seen him," Jesus replied. "He is speaking to you now." ["I do believe, Lord," he said, and bowed down to worship him. Then Jesus said:]
"I came into this world to divide it,
to make the sightless see
and the seeing blind."
Some of the Pharisees around him picked this up, saying, "You are not counting us in with the blind, are you?" To which Jesus replied:
"If you were blind
there would be no sin in that.
'But we see,' you say,
and your sin remains.

Reflection on the Readings
Today's readings are filled with images of sight, light, correct vision. Jesus gives glory to God by giving sight to the man born blind. More importantly, Jesus helps the man to gain interior sight—insight—and thus empowers him to accept Jesus and his way of life. Jesus' proclamation—I am the light of the world—helps us realize that we live by an interior guide: the promptings of the heart.

The text from 1 Samuel helps us understand this. God does not see as we see. Our vision is blurred by our prejudices, our own darkness and blindness. Rather, God sees into the heart, the center of our person. Our actions may do one thing, our words may say another, but our heart is living testimony to how we truly live: by the light of God or by our interior darkness. Jesus' invitation today is to be freed from the darkness that keeps us blind, and, as St. Paul tells us, live as children of the light. Living out of our heart, guided by the light of the world, will demand honesty and courage. As the man born blind, we may experience the abuse of those who claim to see, but whose vision has really been blurred by their self-righteousness and sin.

Suggestions for Prayer

1. Return to the Gospel story. Imagine yourself as the person born blind. Hear Jesus ask you: What is your blindness? Respond. Then hear Jesus ask you if you want to recover from this blindness. Respond. Hear Jesus' prayer for you.
2. Pray Psalm 23. Pause between verses and express in your own words what the verse means for you at this moment in your life.
3. In a spirit of repentance, reflect on areas of blindness in your own life. Ask God for what you need to be healed from this blindness.

Suggestion for Journal Keeping

Recall the insight from 1 Samuel: God sees not as we see, but God sees the heart. Write a letter to yourself from God, telling you the quality of your heart, of your authentic center. Describe how you are faithful in your lifestyle to the insights gleaned from the letter.

Thomas H. Morris

Fourth Sunday of Lent B

READING I   2 Chr 36, 14–17. 19–23

All the princes of Judah, the priests and the people added infidelity to infidelity, practicing all the abominations of the nations and polluting the Lord's temple which he had consecrated in Jerusalem.

Early and often did the Lord, the God of their fathers, send his messengers to them, for he had compassion on his people and his dwelling place. But they mocked the messengers of God, despised his warnings, and scoffed at his prophets, until the anger of the Lord against his people was so inflamed that there was no remedy. Then he brought up against them the king of the Chaldeans, who slew their young men in their own sanctuary building, sparing neither young man nor maiden, neither the aged nor the decrepit; he delivered all of them over into his grip. Finally, their enemies burnt the house of God, tore down the walls of Jerusalem, set all its palaces afire, and destroyed all its precious objects. Those who escaped the sword he carried captive to Babylon, where they became his and his sons' servants until the kingdom of the Persians came to power. All this was to fulfill the word of the Lord spoken by Jeremiah: "Until the land has retrieved its lost sabbaths, during all the time it lies waste it shall have rest while seventy years are fulfilled."

In the first year of Cyrus, king of Persia, in order to fulfill the word of the Lord spoken by Jeremiah, the Lord inspired King Cyrus of Persia to issue this proclamation throughout his kingdom, both by word of mouth and in writing: "Thus says Cyrus, king of Persia:

'All the kingdoms of the earth the Lord, the God of heaven, has given to me, and he has also charged me to build him a house in Jerusalem, which is in Judah. Whoever, therefore, among you belongs to any part of his people, let him go up, and may his God be with him!' "

Responsorial Psalm   Ps 137, 1–2. 3. 4–5. 6
Let my tongue be silenced, if I ever forget
    you!

**By the streams of Babylon
    we sat and wept
    when we remembered Zion.
On the aspens of that land
    we hung up our harps.**
Let my tongue be silenced, if I ever forget
    you!

**Though there our captors asked of us
    the lyrics of our songs,
And our despoilers urged us to be joyous:
    "Sing for us the songs of Zion!"**
Let my tongue be silenced, if I ever forget
    you!

**How could we sing a song of the Lord
    in a foreign land?
If I forget you, Jerusalem,
    may my right hand be forgotten!**
Let my tongue be silenced, if I ever forget
    you!

**May my tongue cleave to my palate
    if I remember you not,
If I place not Jerusalem
    ahead of my joy.**
Let my tongue be silenced, if I ever forget
    you!

READING II   Eph 2, 4–10
God is rich in mercy; because of his great love for us he brought us to life with Christ when we were dead in sin. By this favor you were saved. Both with and in Christ Jesus he raised us up and gave us a place in the heavens, that in the ages to come he might display the great wealth of his favor, manifested by his kindness to us in Christ Jesus. I repeat, it is owing to his favor that salvation is yours through faith. This is not your own doing, it is God's gift; neither is it a reward for anything you have accomplished, so let no one pride himself on it. We are truly his handiwork, created in Christ Jesus to lead the life of good deeds which God prepared for us in advance.

GOSPEL   Jn 3, 14–21
Jesus said to Nicodemus:
    **"Just as Moses lifted up the serpent in
        the desert,
    so must the Son of Man be lifted up,
    that all who believe
    may have eternal life in him.
    Yes, God so loved the world
    that he gave his only Son,
    that whoever believes in him may not
        die
    but may have eternal life.
    God did not send the Son into the world
    to condemn the world,
    but that the world might be saved
        through him.
    Whoever believes in him avoids condemnation,
    but whoever does not believe is already
        condemned
    for not believing in the name of God's
        only Son.
    The judgment in question is this:
    the light came into the world,
    but men loved darkness rather than
        light
    because their deeds were wicked.**

> Everyone who practices evil
> hates the light:
> he does not come near it
> for fear his deeds will be exposed.
> But he who acts in truth
> comes into the light,
> to make clear
> that his deeds are done in God."

Reflections on the Readings

> God so loved the world
> that he gave his only Son,
> that whoever believes in him . . .
> may have eternal life.

These words, found in today's Gospel, sum up the heart of the Gospel message. Through the words of the prophets, that same message was given in the Old Testament. Yet at times the word was rejected. We hear, "But they mocked the messengers of God, despised his warnings, scoffed at his prophets." Down through the ages the choice of how we respond to God's love has always been ours.

This gift of God to us, the Christ, raises us up from sin to receive our "place in the heavens." However, we may still choose to live in the darkness—a life of sin, desolation and hopelessness. Or we may accept the light of the life of Christ and live in that light.

We are not unlike the man born blind in the Gospel (Jn 9). Jesus is offering us sight too by inviting us to follow him and to view life with his light. Physical healing is given to the man born blind. Spiritual healing and awakening is offered to us, encouraging us to move from the darkness of sin to the light of Christ.

Suggestions for Prayer

1. Reflect on areas of your life that are still shrouded in darkness. What is left to let go of in order for you to accept the light that Christ offers? This week ask Jesus to continue to sustain you in your quest to grow in faith.

2. As we continue on our Lenten journey we are encouraged to reflect on Christ's death for all people. We are invited to belong to his family. Ask forgiveness for those times we discriminated against members of that family because of race, religion, social status, sex, etc.

3. The themes of forgiveness and reconciliation continue throughout the Lenten season. Is there someone in your life from whom you are alienated? Take steps this week to mend the relationship, to reconcile, to forgive.

Suggestion for Journal Keeping

Read the Gospel of the man born blind (Jn 9). When the blind man is given the gift of sight, he first calls Jesus "a man." Next, he calls him "a prophet." Finally, he professes Jesus as "Lord." Who was Jesus to me when I began my journey as a catechumen? Who is he to me now? What has happened that I have received the gift of sight?

Mary Kay Meier

Fourth Sunday of Lent

READING I   Jos 5, 9. 10–12
The Lord said to Joshua, "Today I have removed the reproach of Egypt from you."

While the Israelites were encamped at Gilgal on the plains of Jericho, they celebrated the Passover on the evening of the fourteenth of the month. On the day after the Passover they ate of the produce of the land in the form of unleavened cakes and parched grain. On that same day after the Passover on which they ate of the produce of the land, the manna ceased. No longer was there manna for the Israelites, who that year ate of the yield of the land of Canaan.

Responsorial Psalm   Ps 34, 2–3. 4–5. 6–7

Taste and see the goodness of the Lord.

I will bless the Lord at all times;
  his praise shall be ever in my mouth.
Let my soul glory in the Lord;
  the lowly will hear me and be glad.

Taste and see the goodness of the Lord.

Glorify the Lord with me,
  let us together extol his name.
I sought the Lord, and he answered me
  and delivered me from all my fears.

Taste and see the goodness of the Lord.

Look to him that you may be radiant with joy,
  and your faces may not blush with shame.
When the afflicted man called out, the Lord heard,
  and from all his distress he saved him.

Taste and see the goodness of the Lord.

READING II   2 Cor 5, 17–21

If anyone is in Christ, he is a new creation. The old order has passed away; now all is new! All this has been done by God, who has reconciled us to himself through Christ and has given us the ministry of reconciliation. I mean that God, in Christ, was reconciling the world to himself, not counting men's transgressions against them, and that he has entrusted the message of reconciliation to us. This makes us ambassadors for Christ, God as it were appealing through us. We implore you, in Christ's name: be reconciled to God! For our sakes God made him who did not know sin to be sin, so that in him we might become the very holiness of God.

GOSPEL   Lk 15, 1–3. 11–32

The tax collectors and the sinners were all gathering around Jesus to hear him, at which the Pharisees and the scribes murmured, "This man welcomes sinners and eats with them." Then he addressed this parable to them: "A man had two sons. The younger of them said to his father, 'Father, give me the share of the estate that is coming to me.' So the father divided up the property. Some days later this younger son collected all his belongings and went off to a distant land, where he squandered his money on dissolute living. After he had spent everything, a great famine broke out in that country and he was in dire need. So he attached himself to one of the propertied class of the place, who sent him to his farm to take care of the pigs. He longed to fill his belly with the husks that were fodder for the pigs, but no one made a move to give him anything. Coming to his senses at last, he said: "How many hired hands at my father's place have more than enough to eat, while here I am starving! I will break away and return to my father, and say to him, "Father, I have sinned against God and against you; I no longer deserve to be called your son. Treat me like one of your hired hands."' With that he set off for his father's house. While he was still a long way off, his father caught sight of him and was deeply moved. He ran out to meet him, threw his arms around his neck, and kissed him. The son said to him, 'Father, I have sinned against God and against you; I no longer deserve to be called your son.' The father said to his servants: 'Quick! bring out the finest robe and put it on him; put a ring on his finger and shoes on his feet. Take the fatted calf and kill it. Let us eat and celebrate because this son of mine was dead and has come back to life. He was lost and is found.' Then the celebration began.

"Meanwhile the elder son was out on the land. As he neared the house on his way home, he heard the sound of music and dancing. He called one of the servants and asked him the reason for the dancing and the music. The servant answered, 'Your brother is home, and your father has killed the fatted calf because he has him back in good health.' The son grew angry at this and would not go in; but his father came out and began to plead with him.

"He said in reply to his father: 'For years now I have slaved for you. I never disobeyed one of your orders, yet you never gave me so much as a kid goat to celebrate with my friends. Then, when this son of yours returns after having gone through your property with loose women, you kill the fatted calf for him.'

" 'My son,' replied the father, 'you are with me always, and everything I have is yours. But we had to celebrate and rejoice! This brother of yours was dead, and has come back to life. He was lost, and is found.' "

Reflection on the Readings

We are at the halfway mark in the Lenten season—a time of renewed energy, a time for recalling God's continuing care. From the first reading we hear of God's providence for his people. While the Hebrews were on the journey, manna was provided for them. On the celebration of this Passover, they ate the food they themselves had grown in their new homeland of Canaan. God had indeed led them into the promised land, and now they are experiencing again God's blessings.

In the reading from Paul's Second Letter to the Corinthians, we are given the image of Jesus Christ as the new Passover who has reconciled us, who gives us the message of forgiveness and redemption.

It is that message of God's continuing care and forgiveness that are highlighted in the memorable and beautiful parable of the Gospel reading. It is the story of a loving and compassionate father, a clear image of God. Each son represents a segment of the people of God. One son is like those who are self-sufficient and proud, but who eventually realize their predicament and return to the father to be forgiven and welcomed. Then there are those of us who stay at home, loyal and perhaps self-righteous. The most wondrous love of this father who has waited for, longed for, the return of his lost son reaches out to his loyal son as well. The elder son was confused and hurt by his father's actions; the father is understanding and compassionate toward him as well.

This is a truly powerful story for meditation. Do we understand the measure of God's deep and constant love for each of us, no matter who we are or what we have done with our lives up to this point? Regardless of our past, whether we are catechumens, candidates, elect or baptized, we all need assurance of God's mercy, love and continued presence with us.

Suggestions for Prayer

1. Reread the Gospel parable and put yourself into the story—perhaps as the runaway son, returning again, or as the loyal stay-at-home elder son, or as an observer. How do you feel about your life? About yourself? About what is going on around you? Spend time with the Father. What does he say to you?

2. In some parishes, the Sunday of the second scrutiny may use the Gospel story of Jesus healing the blind man (Jn 9:1–41). Either Gospel encourages us to look at our lives with the light of faith—to see beyond the immediate situation. We are called to be honest about ourselves. Who is it that heals us, forgives us, welcomes us? How open are we to the action of God in our own lives? Spend some time in quiet reflection, looking at your openness to God's presence and action in your life.

3. Imagine yourself as the son walking the road back home. What thoughts do you have? What do you want to say to your father? Your family? Put these thoughts into a prayer for strength, for mercy and for gladness at being forgiven and welcomed back.

Suggestion for Journal Keeping

Keep your journal ready as you spend time in prayer and reflection. Use it to keep some of the insights and thoughts that come to you. At another time in the week, reread what you wrote. Do new insights come to you? You may want to talk with your sponsor or members of the catechumenate team about your reflections and feelings at this time.

Clare M. Colella

Fifth Sunday of Lent A

READING I   Ez 37, 12–14

Thus says the Lord God: O my people, I will open your graves and have you rise from them, and bring you back to the land of Israel. Then you shall know that I am the Lord, when I open your graves and have you rise from them, O my people! I will put my spirit in you that you may live, and I will settle you upon your land; thus you shall know that I am the Lord. I have promised, and I will do it, says the Lord.

Responsorial Psalm   Ps 130, 1–2. 3–4. 5–6. 7–8

With the Lord there is mercy,
  and fullness of redemption.
Out of the depths I cry to you, O Lord;
  Lord, hear my voice!
Let your ears be attentive
  to my voice in supplication.
With the Lord there is mercy,
  and fullness of redemption.
If you, O Lord, mark iniquities,
  Lord, who can stand?
But with you is forgiveness,
  that you may be revered.
With the Lord there is mercy,
  and fullness of redemption.
I trust in the Lord;
  my soul trusts in his word.
More than sentinels wait for the dawn,
  let Israel wait for the Lord.
With the Lord there is mercy,
  and fullness of redemption.
For with the Lord is kindness
  and with him is plenteous redemption;
And he will redeem Israel
  from all their iniquities.

With the Lord there is mercy,
and fullness of redemption.

READING II   Rom 8, 8–11

Those who are in the flesh cannot please God. But you are not in the flesh; you are in the spirit, since the Spirit of God dwells in you. If anyone does not have the Spirit of Christ, he does not belong to Christ. If Christ is in you, the body is indeed dead because of sin, while the spirit lives because of justice. If the Spirit of him who raised Jesus from the dead dwells in you, then he who raised Christ from the dead will bring your mortal bodies to life also through his Spirit dwelling in you.

GOSPEL   Jn 11, 1–45

There was a certain man named Lazarus who was sick. He was from Bethany, the village of Mary and her sister Martha. (This Mary whose brother Lazarus was sick was the one who anointed the Lord with perfume and dried his feet with her hair.) The sisters sent word to Jesus to inform him, "Lord, the one you love is sick." Upon hearing this, Jesus said:

"This sickness is not to end in death;
rather it is for God's glory,
that through it the Son of God may be
glorified."

Jesus loved Martha and her sister and Lazarus very much. Yet, after hearing that Lazarus was sick, he stayed on where he was for two days more. Finally he said to his disciples, "Let us go back to Judea." "Rabbi," protested the disciples, "with the Jews only recently trying to stone you, you are going back up there again?" Jesus answered:

"Are there not twelve hours of daylight?

If a man goes walking by day he does
not stumble,
because he sees the world bathed in
light.
But if he goes walking at night he will
stumble,
since there is no light in him."

After uttering these words, he added, "Our beloved Lazarus has fallen asleep, but I am going there to wake him." At this the disciples objected, "Lord, if he is asleep his life will be saved." Jesus had been speaking about his death, but they thought he meant sleep in the sense of slumber. Finally Jesus said plainly, "Lazarus is dead. For your sakes I am glad I was not there, that you may come to believe. In any event, let us go to him." Then Thomas (the name means "Twin") said to his fellow disciples, "Let us go along, to die with him."

When Jesus arrived at Bethany, he found that Lazarus had already been in the tomb four days. The village was not far from Jerusalem—just under two miles—and many Jewish people had come out to console Martha and Mary over their brother. When Martha heard that Jesus was coming she went to meet him, while Mary sat at home. Martha said to Jesus, "Lord, if you had been here, my brother would never have died. Even now, I am sure that God will give you whatever you ask of him." "Your brother will rise again," Jesus assured her. "I know he will rise again," Martha replied, "in the resurrection on the last day." Jesus told her:

"I am the resurrection and the life:
whoever believes in me,
though he should die, will come to life;
and whoever is alive and believes in me
will never die.

Do you believe this?" "Yes, Lord," she replied. "I have come to believe that you are the Messiah, the Son of God: he who is to come into the world."

When she had said this she went back and called her sister Mary. "The Teacher is here, asking for you," she whispered. As soon as Mary heard this, she got up and started out in his direction. (Actually Jesus had not yet come into the village but was still at the spot where Martha had met him.) The Jews who were in the house with Mary consoling her saw her get up quickly and go out, so they followed her, thinking she was going to the tomb to weep there. When Mary came to the place where Jesus was, seeing him, she fell at his feet and said to him, "Lord, if you had been here my brother would never have died." When Jesus saw her weeping, and the Jewish folk who had accompanied her also weeping, he was troubled in spirit, moved by the deepest emotions. "Where have you laid him?" he asked. "Lord, come and see," they said. Jesus began to weep, which caused the Jews to remark, "See how much he loved him!" But some said, "He opened the eyes of that blind man. Why could he not have done something to stop this man from dying?" Once again troubled in spirit, Jesus approached the tomb.

It was a cave with a stone laid across it. "Take away the stone," Jesus directed. Martha, the dead man's sister, said to him, "Lord, it has been four days now; surely there will be a stench!" Jesus replied, "Did I not assure you that if you believed you would see the glory of God?" They then took away the stone and Jesus looked upward and said:

"Father, I thank you for having heard me.

I know that you always hear me
but I have said this for the sake of the crowd,
that they may believe that you sent me."

Having said this, he called loudly, "Lazarus, come out!" The dead man came out, bound hand and foot with linen strips, his face wrapped in a cloth. "Untie him," Jesus told them, "and let him go free."

This caused many of the Jews who had come to visit Mary, and had seen what Jesus did, to put their faith in him.

Reflection on the Readings

Jesus is faced with the painful reality of death in today's Gospel. Jesus weeps over the death of his dear friend Lazarus. As a way of pointing out the abundance of God's love, Jesus raises Lazarus back to life. Along with the raising of Lazarus is a central proclamation from Jesus: I am the resurrection and the life. Through the gift of the Spirit, that which was corruptible and broken through death is now made incorruptible and restored to eternal life.

All of the readings today proclaim the God of the living. In the Ezekiel text, we hear God's desire to bring life through the Spirit. In the text from Romans, St. Paul reminds us that because we share in the very Spirit of God, then we will share in fullness of life as experienced in Jesus' resurrection. Lazarus' restoration to life is a witness to the working of God's Spirit. Wherever the Spirit dwells, there life is found in abundance.

Yet these readings also heighten our awareness to that which keeps us from this fullness of life: death, existence without the Spirit, being held bound. The same Spirit that breathes life does so by breaking open the graves that oppress us, by untying the wrappings that keep us enslaved to death.

I am the resurrection and the life—not only for eternal life, but for freedom from sin and oppression in the world now, today. The Spirit is given to restore life where there was apparent death and sin.

Suggestions for Prayer

1. Create and pray a litany celebrating the God of the living. Recite or chant the refrain: "Blessed be the God of the living!" Following the refrain, mention experiences of life from God, such as "For the beauty of creation," "For the gift of my family," etc.
2. Jesus proclaimed: Untie him and let him go free. What are the areas of your life that keep you bound? Pray for what you need to be made free.
3. Return to the Gospel. Prayerfully reflect on the passage when Jesus calls forth Lazarus from the tomb. Hear Jesus call you by your name from your own tomb. Pray for what you need to live a renewed life.

Suggestion for Journal Keeping

Describe areas of your life that have come back to life after being dead. What were the circumstances leading to this renewed life? How were you changed because of this renewed life? Describe your relationship with God because of these experiences.

Thomas H. Morris

READING I   Jer 31, 31–34

The days are coming, says the Lord, when I will make a new covenant with the house of Israel and the house of Judah. It will not be like the covenant I made with their fathers the day I took them by the hand to lead them forth from the land of Egypt; for they broke my covenant, and I had to show myself their master, says the Lord. But this is the covenant which I will make with the house of Israel after those days, says the Lord. I will place my law within them, and write it upon their hearts; I will be their God, and they shall be my people. No longer will they have need to teach their friends and kinsmen how to know the Lord. All, from least to greatest, shall know me, says the Lord, for I will forgive their evildoing and remember their sin no more.

Responsorial Psalm   Ps 51, 3–4. 12–13. 14–15

Create a clean heart in me, O God.
Have mercy on me, O God, in your goodness;
   in the greatness of your compassion wipe out my offense.
Thoroughly wash me from my guilt
   and of my sin cleanse me.
Create a clean heart in me, O God.
A clean heart create for me, O God,
   and a steadfast spirit renew within me.
Cast me not out from your presence,
   and your holy spirit take not from me.
Create a clean heart in me, O God.
Give me back the joy of your salvation,
   and a willing spirit sustain in me.

I will teach transgressors your ways,
  and sinners shall return to you.
Create a clean heart in me, O God.

READING II
Heb 5, 7–9

In the days when Christ was in the flesh, he offered prayers and supplications with loud cries and tears to God, who was able to save him from death, and he was heard because of his reverence. Son though he was, he learned obedience from what he suffered; and when perfected, he became the source of eternal salvation for all who obey him.

GOSPEL
Jn 12, 20–33

Among those who had come up to worship at the feast of Passover were some Greeks. They approached Philip, who was from Bethsaida in Galilee, and put this request to him: "Sir, we should like to see Jesus." Philip went to tell Andrew; Philip and Andrew in turn came to inform Jesus. Jesus answered them:

  "The hour has come
  for the Son of Man to be glorified.
  I solemnly assure you,
  unless the grain of wheat falls to the
    earth and dies,
  it remains just a grain of wheat.
  But if it dies,
  it produces much fruit.
  The man who loves his life
  loses it,
  while the man who hates his life in this
    world
  preserves it to life eternal.
  If anyone would serve me,
  let him follow me;
  where I am,
  there will my servant be.
  Anyone who serves me,

  the Father will honor.
  My soul is troubled now,
  yet what should I say—
  Father, save me from this hour?
  But it was for this that I came to this
    hour.
  Father, glorify your name!"
Then a voice came from the sky:
  "I have glorified it,
  and will glorify it again."
When the crowd of bystanders heard the voice, they said it was thunder. Others maintained, "An angel was speaking to him." Jesus answered, "That voice did not come for my sake, but for yours.

  "Now has judgment come upon this
    world,
  now will this world's prince be driven
    out,
  and I—once I am lifted up from earth—
  will draw all men to myself."
(This statement of his indicated the sort of death he was going to die.)

Reflection on the Readings

New life is the symbol of today's narrative. The Gospel reads, "Unless a grain of wheat falls to the earth and dies, it remains just a grain of wheat. But if it dies, it produces much fruit." Jesus himself follows nature's cycle through his death and burial. New life is resurrected. He had spent his public life telling his followers about the Father's love. Now the hour has almost come. The sign of the love he has shared is about to be given for a final time. John's Gospel reminds us that we are called to follow Christ's example. If we are to share in his glory, we must also die to self.

Jeremiah reminded the people of God's new covenant, "The days are coming . . .

92

when I will make a new covenant with the house of Israel. . . . I will be their God, and they shall be my people." This covenant is extended to us this day as we gather to hear the good news of Christ. It is no longer through observance of the law of the Old Testament, carved in the tablets of stone, that we glorify God. Today we are called to hear the words of Christ and to follow his example. Let us respond to both, and carry them in our hearts.

Suggestions for Prayer

1. As we acknowledge our need for God we also need to acknowledge areas of our life that need to be strengthened. Read and reflect on the responsorial psalm for this week.
2. Take time this week for quiet. Be at peace with your God.

Suggestion for Journal Keeping

Read the Gospel account of the death of Lazarus. Imagine yourself at the tomb. Listen to the words Jesus says: "I am the resurrection and the life: whoever believes in me, though he should die, will come to life; and whoever is alive and believes in me will never die. Do you believe this?" How do you respond?

Mary Kay Meier

Fifth Sunday of Lent   C

READING I   Is 43, 16–21
Thus says the Lord,
  who opens a way in the sea
  and a path in the mighty waters,

Who leads out chariots and horsemen,
  a powerful army,
Till they lie prostrate together, never to rise,
  snuffed out and quenched like a wick.
Remember not the events of the past,
  the things of long ago consider not;
See, I am doing something new!
  Now it springs forth, do you not perceive it?
In the desert I make a way,
  in the wasteland, rivers.
Wild beasts honor me,
  jackals and ostriches,
For I put water in the desert
  and rivers in the wasteland
  for my chosen people to drink,
The people whom I formed for myself,
  that they might announce my praise.

Responsorial Psalm   Ps 126, 1–2. 2–3. 4–5. 6

The Lord has done great things for us;
  we are filled with joy.
When the Lord brought back the captives of Zion,
  we were like men dreaming.
Then our mouth was filled with laughter,
  and our tongue with rejoicing.
The Lord has done great things for us;
  we are filled with joy.
Then they said among the nations,
  "The Lord has done great things for them."
The Lord has done great things for us;
  we are glad indeed.
The Lord has done great things for us;
  we are filled with joy.
Restore our fortunes, O Lord,
  like the torrents in the southern desert.
Those that sow in tears
  shall reap rejoicing.

The Lord has done great things for us;
  we are filled with joy.
**Although they go forth weeping,
  carrying the seed to be sown,
They shall come back rejoicing,
  carrying their sheaves.**
The Lord has done great things for us;
  we are filled with joy.

READING II   Phil 3, 8–14
**I have come to rate all as loss in the light of
the surpassing knowledge of my Lord Jesus
Christ. For his sake I have forfeited everything; I have accounted all else rubbish so
that Christ may be my wealth and I may be
in him, not having any justice of my own
based on observance of the law. The justice
I possess is that which comes through faith
in Christ. It has its origin in God and is based
on faith. I wish to know Christ and the
power flowing from his resurrection; likewise to know how to share in his sufferings
by being formed into the pattern of his
death. Thus do I hope that I may arrive at
resurrection from the dead.**

**It is not that I have reached it yet, or have
already finished my course; but I am racing
to grasp the prize if possible, since I have
been grasped by Christ [Jesus]. Brothers, I
do not think of myself as having reached the
finish line. I give no thought to what lies behind but push on to what is ahead. My entire
attention is on the finish line as I run toward
the prize to which God calls me—life on
high in Christ Jesus.**

GOSPEL   Jn 8, 1–11
**Jesus went out to the Mount of Olives. At
daybreak he reappeared in the temple area;
and when the people started coming to him,
he sat down and began to teach them. The
scribes and the Pharisees led a woman forward who had been caught in adultery. They
made her stand there in front of everyone.
"Teacher," they said to him, "this woman
has been caught in the act of adultery. In the
law, Moses ordered such women to be
stoned. What do you have to say about the
case?" (They were posing this question to
trap him, so that they could have something
to accuse him of.) Jesus simply bent down
and started tracing on the ground with his
finger. When they persisted in their questioning, he straightened up and said to them,
"Let the man among you who has no sin be
the first to cast a stone at her." A second
time he bent down and wrote on the ground.
Then the audience drifted away one by one,
beginning with the elders. This left him
alone with the woman, who continued to
stand there before him. Jesus finally straightened up again and said to her, "Woman,
where did they all disappear to? Has no one
condemned you?" "No one, sir," she answered. Jesus said, "Nor do I condemn you.
You may go. But from now on, avoid this
sin."**

Reflection on the Readings
  One of the joys of reflection on the word of
God in the Scriptures is that we today are
continually learning from words written so
long ago. The words of Scripture are ever
new. This is expressed through Isaiah: "See!
I am doing something new!" Let us take time
to look and see what is new. What is the Lord
doing? We have been on this Lenten journey
for quite a while now—and on our conversion journey for an even longer time. We are
getting to know ourselves better—and getting
to know Jesus as well.
  Today's readings assure us of God's con-

tinued presence and especially his forgiveness. What is made new may well be *us*—we put our past behind us and move on to what is ahead. Though we have done wrong, made mistakes, been weak, we find that God has "remembered not." The first two readings and the responsorial psalm go on to assure us that God has formed us, blessed us, called us to himself. We are forgiven and beloved. Through the Gospel episode, we are enlightened—Jesus speaks not only to the people of his time but to us also. With very few words and a simple action, he teaches us about honesty, forgiveness, conversion, as he challenges the complacent/self-righteous while he accepts and forgives the accused sinner.

This Sunday is the third scrutiny in parishes that are celebrating the catechumenate process. If your parish chooses the Gospel of the raising of Lazarus, read the reflection under Cycle A.

Suggestions for Prayer

1. Reread the Gospel episode of the woman caught in adultery. Picture yourself in this story. Is your life somewhat like the person accused—acknowledging the reality of your life, knowing you are forgiven and that you can begin a new life of discipleship? Or is it more like the accusers who, having found another's weakness, are reluctant to acknowledge their own sinfulness and walk away from the Lord, unconverted? Spend some time in prayer with Jesus as he writes in the sand, then stands up. He knows what is in your heart. What does he say to you? How do you respond?

2. Paul's Letter to the Philippians reveals the deep faith and conviction he has about what is most important in his life. Having found Jesus Christ, nothing else really matters. With the eyes of faith we see things differently—even our sufferings bring us closer to Jesus. Imagine Jesus looking at your life with love and forgiveness. Hear his invitation to you to look at your life through his eyes, with faith and a desire to be a disciple of his.

3. "The Lord has done great things for us; we are filled with joy!" The responsorial psalm proclaims specifically what the other readings and prayers seem only to hint at: that God has done wonderful things in our lives. Picture yourself in a comfortable setting with your friend, the Lord. Take time to get a graphic image of your friend. Feel familiar and comfortable with him. Then let your memory recall some of the good things that have happened in your life.

Suggestion for Journal Keeping

Since your journal is a personal record of your faith journey and your thoughts and prayers along the way, use some quiet time to write about your reflections on the liturgy and readings today. Use your journal to help concretize your prayer—you may want to write your prayer images down and work with them again at a later time.

Clare M. Colella

Passion Sunday
[Palm Sunday]
The Procession with Palms

GOSPEL A   Mt 21, 1–11

As the crowd drew near Jerusalem, entering Bethphage on the Mount of Olives, Jesus sent off two disciples with the instruction: "Go into the village straight ahead of you and you will immediately find an ass tethered and her colt with her. Untie them and lead them back to me. If anyone says a word to you, say, 'The Master needs them.' Then he will let them go at once." This came about to fulfill what was said through the prophet:

> "Tell the daughter of Zion,
> Your king comes to you without display
> astride an ass, astride a colt,
> the foal of a beast of burden."

So the disciples went off and did what Jesus had ordered; they brought the ass and the colt and laid their cloaks on them, and he mounted. The huge crowd spread their cloaks on the road, while some began to cut branches from the trees and laid them along his path. The groups preceding him as well as those following kept crying out:

> "God save the Son of David!
> Blessed be he who comes in the name of the Lord!
> God save him from on high!"

As he entered Jerusalem the whole city was stirred to its depths, demanding, "Who is this?" And the crowd kept answering, "This is the prophet Jesus from Nazareth in Galilee."

GOSPEL B   Mk 11, 1–10

As the crowd drew near Bethphage and Bethany on the Mount of Olives, close to Jerusalem, Jesus sent off two of his disciples with the instruction: "Go to the village straight ahead of you, and as soon as you enter it you will find tethered there a colt on which no one has ridden. Untie it and bring it back. If anyone says to you, 'Why are you doing that?' say, 'The Master needs it but he will send it back here at once.' " So they went off, and finding a colt tethered out on the street near a gate, they untied it. Some of the bystanders said to them, "What do you mean by untying that colt?" They answered as Jesus had told them to, and the men let them take it. They brought the colt to Jesus and threw their cloaks across its back, and he sat on it. Many people spread their cloaks on the road, while others spread reeds which they had cut in the fields. Those preceding him as well as those who followed cried out:

> "Hosannah!
> Blessed be he who comes in the name of the Lord!
> Blessed be the reign of our father David to come!
> God save him from on high!"

OR

96

GOSPEL   Jn 12, 12–16

The great crowd that had come for the feast heard that Jesus was to enter Jerusalem, so they got palm branches and came out to meet him. They kept shouting:

"Hosanna!
Blessed is he who comes in the name of the Lord!
Blessed is the King of Israel!"

Jesus found a donkey and mounted it, in accord with Scripture:

"Fear not, O daughter of Zion!
Your king approaches you
on a donkey's colt."

(At first, the disciples did not understand all this, but after Jesus was glorified they recalled that the people had done to him precisely what had been written about him.)

GOSPEL C   Lk 19, 28–40

Jesus went ahead with his ascent to Jerusalem. As he approached Bethphage and Bethany on the mount called Olivet, he sent two of the disciples with these instructions: "Go into the village straight ahead of you. Upon entering it you will find an ass tied there which no one has yet ridden. Untie it and lead it back. If anyone should ask you, "Why are you untying the beast?' say, 'The Master has need of it.' "

They departed on their errand and found things just as he had said. As they untied the ass, its owners said to them, "Why are you doing that?" They explained that the Master needed it. Then they led the animal to Jesus, and laying their cloaks on it, helped him mount. They spread their cloaks on the roadway as he moved along; and on his approach to the descent from Mount Olivet, the entire crowd of disciples began to rejoice and praise God loudly for the display of power they had seen, saying:

"Blessed be he who comes as king
in the name of the Lord!
Peace in heaven
and glory in the highest!"

Some of the Pharisees in the crowd said to him, "Teacher, rebuke your disciples." He replied, "If they were to keep silence, I tell you the very stones would cry out."

Reflection on the Readings

Hymns of praise resound! Hosanna! Blessed is he who comes in the name of the Lord! Today's proclamation is a reminder of the great excitement and wonder that welcomed Jesus into the city of Jerusalem. Jesus was such a powerful presence to people—in word and action—that the whole city was "stirred to its depths." There were songs of welcome and greetings, great cheers and a great procession.

There was something very simple and sacred about the triumphant entry into Jerusalem. People had been genuinely touched by Jesus. He lived a blessed and holy life that helped them come to know God's gracious love and forgiveness. Because of Jesus, people's lives were changed. And with the same enthusiasm that we would welcome a hero or heroine to our neighborhood, they gather together to greet this special man who comes to them on a borrowed colt, surrounded by his companions.

The initial instinct of the people is to celebrate the gracious presence of God in Jesus. There is gratitude, rejoicing, praise in the air. Soon these same people will turn and run because of their own fear. But for now they welcome the one who has brought the freshness of God into their lives—Jesus.

Suggestions for Prayer

1. Reflect on the text from Matthew. At the end of the text, answer the question posed: Who is this?
2. Lead yourself through a guided imagery of the text from Mark. As you experience Jesus coming into the city, reflect on what you are grateful for that brings you to proclaim: Hosanna!
3. Pray the text from Luke. Recall in your own life the "display of power" from God for which you wish to give praise.

Suggestion for Journal Keeping

The entry into Jerusalem is also an entry into the passion and death of Jesus. Yet Jesus could be obedient because of his profound trust in God. Reflect on your life experience: How have I met God in the very ordinary events of life? For what do I give praise and thanks? How do I describe God's love in my life? Can I trust God? If not, what do I need to trust God? After writing these reflections, recall Jesus' entry into Jerusalem. Continue to journal: Can I go with him? What does this mean for me?

Thomas H. Morris

Passion Sunday
[Palm Sunday] Mass A B C

READING I   Is 50, 4–7

The Lord God has given me
   a well-trained tongue,
That I might know how to speak to the weary
   a word that will rouse them.

Morning after morning
   he opens my ear that I may hear;
And I have not rebelled,
   have not turned back.
I gave my back to those who beat me,
   my cheeks to those who plucked my
   beard;
My face I did not shield
   from buffets and spitting.
The Lord God is my help,
   therefore I am not disgraced;
I have set my face like flint,
   knowing that I shall not be put to shame.

Responsorial Psalm   Ps 22, 8–9. 17–18.
                              19–20. 23–24

My God, my God, why have you abandoned
   me?
All who see me scoff at me;
   they mock me with parted lips, they wag
   their heads:
"He relied on the Lord; let him deliver him,
   let him rescue him, if he loves him."
My God, my God, why have you abandoned
   me?
Indeed, many dogs surround me,
   a pack of evildoers closes in upon me;
They have pierced my hands and my feet;
   I can count all my bones.
My God, my God, why have you abandoned
   me?
They divide my garments among them,
   and for my vesture they cast lots.
But you, O Lord, be not far from me;
   O my help, hasten to aid me.
My God, my God, why have you abandoned
   me?
I will proclaim your name to my brethren;
   in the midst of the assembly I will praise
   you:

"You who fear the Lord, praise him;
   all you descendants of Jacob, give glory to
   him."
My God, my God, why have you abandoned
   me?

READING II   Phil 2, 6–11
Your attitude must be Christ's:
   though he was in the form of God
   he did not deem equality with God
   something to be grasped at.
Rather, he emptied himself
   and took the form of a slave,
   being born in the likeness of men.
He was known to be of human estate,
   and it was thus that he humbled himself,
   obediently accepting even death,
   death on a cross!
Because of this,
   God highly exalted him
   and bestowed on him the name
   above every other name,
So that at Jesus' name
   every knee must bend
   in the heavens, on the earth,
   and under the earth,
   and every tongue proclaim
   to the glory of God the Father:
   JESUS CHRIST IS LORD!

(The Gospels and their related material follow these reflections.)

Reflection on the Readings
   The readings preceeding the Gospel narrative share a common vision: trust in God.
The text from Isaiah, known as the Third Servant Song, speaks of one who has been faithful to proclaiming the message of God
despite persecution and rejection. In Psalm

22, the psalmist moves from a cry of aban-
donment that is a response to the persecution
resulting from trusting in God to the recognition of God's loving presence. And the text
from Philippians recounts Jesus' trust in the
will of the Father, thus being empowered to
empty himself of everything but this loving
relationship. Because of his fidelity to this
truth, Jesus' life is affirmed and confirmed:
God exalts Jesus so we can truly proclaim Jesus as Lord.
   Trust in God—in God's providential love
that will not bring disgrace but help, that will
not leave us abandoned but singing praises,
that will not leave us emptied and dead but
raised up. It is only that kind of trust that can
serve as the backdrop for Jesus' decision to
accept his sentence of death on the cross.

Suggestions for Prayer

1. Reread the text from Isaiah. After sitting
   in silence, offer prayers of petition for
   the men and women in the world who
   stand up for truth and justice, even at the
   cost of their own lives.
2. Recall a painful time in your life when
   you felt abandoned by God. Slowly re-
   tell your experience in your prayer,
   pausing to ask: My God, why have you
   abandoned me? Ask God for the healing
   to be able to see how God was truly
   present with you in this pain.
3. Mantra prayer is a gentle repetition and
   recollection of a short phrase, usually
   accompanied to your breathing. Based
   on the readings and reflection, choose a
   short phrase that reflects your need,
   such as "God, teach me to trust." Slowly
   and prayerfully repeat the phrase in

rhythm to your breathing. Continue to pray the mantra until you feel the need to move either to silence or petition.

Suggestion for Journal Keeping

Recall events in your life (or in the life of family and friends) when you remained firm in your convictions, despite the comments or threats of others. What helped you to remain strong? Looking back on these events, how was God present? How is your experience similar to the experience of trust proclaimed in the readings today?

Thomas H. Morris

GOSPEL **A**   Mt 26, 14–27, 66
The Passion of our Lord Jesus Christ according to Matthew.

One of the Twelve whose name was Judas Iscariot went off to the chief priests and said, "What are you willing to give me if I hand Jesus over to you?" They paid him thirty pieces of silver, and from that time on he kept looking for an opportunity to hand him over.

On the first day of the feast of Unleavened Bread, the disciples came up to Jesus and said, "Where do you wish us to prepare the Passover supper for you?" He said, "Go to this man in the city and tell him, 'The Teacher says, My appointed time draws near. I am to celebrate the Passover with my disciples in your house.' "

The disciples then did as Jesus had ordered, and prepared the Passover supper.

When it grew dark he reclined at table with the Twelve. In the course of the meal he said, "I give you my word, one of you is about to betray me." Distressed at this, they began to say to him one after another, "Surely it is not I, Lord?" He replied: "The man who has dipped his hand into the dish with me is the one who will hand me over. The Son of Man is departing, as Scripture says of him, but woe to that man by whom the Son of Man is betrayed. Better for him if he had never been born."

Then Judas, his betrayer, spoke: "Surely it is not I, Rabbi?" Jesus answered, "It is you who have said it."

During the meal Jesus took bread, blessed it, broke it, and gave it to his disciples. "Take this and eat it," he said, "this is my body." Then he took a cup, gave thanks, and gave it to them. "All of you must drink from it," he said, "for this is my blood, the blood of the covenant, to be poured out in behalf of many for the forgiveness of sins. I tell you, I will not drink this fruit of the vine from now until the day I drink new wine with you in my Father's reign." Then, after singing songs of praise, they walked out to the Mount of Olives.

Jesus then said to them, "Tonight your faith in me will be shaken, for Scripture has it:

'I will strike the shepherd
and the sheep of the flock will be dispersed.'

But after I am raised up, I will go to Galilee ahead of you." Peter responded, "Though all may have their faith in you shaken, mine will never be shaken!" Jesus said to him, "I give you my word before the cock crows tonight you will deny me three times." Peter replied, "Even though I have to die with you, I will never disown you." And all the other disciples said the same.

Then Jesus went with them to a place called Gethsemani. He said to his disciples,

"Stay here while I go over there and pray." He took along Peter and Zebedee's two sons, and began to experience sorrow and distress. Then he said to them, "My heart is nearly broken with sorrow. Remain here and stay awake with me." He advanced a little and fell prostrate in prayer. "My Father, if it is possible, let this cup pass me by. Still, let it be as you would have it, not as I." When he returned to his disciples, he found them asleep. He said to Peter, "So you could not stay awake with me for even an hour? Be on guard, and pray that you may not undergo trial. The spirit is willing but nature is weak." Withdrawing a second time, he began to pray: "My Father, if this cannot pass me by without my drinking it, your will be done!" Once more, on his return, he found them asleep; they could not keep their eyes open. He left them again, withdrew somewhat, and began to pray a third time, saying the same words as before. Finally he returned to his disciples and said to them, "Sleep on now. Enjoy your rest! The hour is on us when the Son of Man is to be handed over to the power of evil men. Get up! Let us be on our way! See, my betrayer is here."

While he was still speaking, Judas, one of the Twelve, arrived accompanied by a great crowd with swords and clubs. They had been sent by the chief priests and elders of the people. His betrayer had arranged to give them a signal, saying, "The man I shall embrace is the one; take hold of him." He immediately went over to Jesus, said to him, "Peace, Rabbi," and embraced him. Jesus answered, "Do what you are here for, friend!" At that moment they stepped forward to lay hands on Jesus, and arrested him. Suddenly one of those who accompanied Jesus put his hand to his sword, drew it, and slashed at the high priest's servant, cutting off his ear. Jesus said to him: "Put back your sword where it belongs. Those who use the sword are sooner or later destroyed by it. Do you not suppose I can call on my Father to provide at a moment's notice more than twelve legions of angels? But then how would the Scriptures be fulfilled which say it must happen this way?"

At that very time Jesus said to the crowd: "Am I a brigand, that you have come armed with swords and clubs to arrest me? From day to day I sat teaching in the temple precincts, yet you never arrested me. Nonetheless, all this has happened in fulfillment of the writings of the prophets." Then all the disciples deserted him and fled.

Those who had apprehended Jesus led him off to Caiaphas the high priest, where the scribes and elders were convened. Peter kept following him at a distance as far as the high priest's residence. Going inside, he sat down with the guards to see the outcome. The chief priests, with the whole Sanhedrin, were busy trying to obtain false testimony against Jesus so that they might put him to death. They discovered none, despite the many false witnesses who took the stand. Finally two came forward who stated: "This man has declared, 'I can destroy God's sanctuary and rebuild it in three days.'" The high priest rose to his feet and addressed him: "Have you no answer to the testimony leveled against you?" But Jesus remained silent. The high priest then said to him: "I order you to tell us under oath before the living God whether you are the Messiah, the Son of God." Jesus answered: "It is you who say it. But I tell you this: Soon you will see the Son of Man seated at the right hand of the Power and coming on the clouds of heaven." At this the high priest tore his robes: "He has blasphemed! What further need have we of witnesses? Remember, you heard the blasphemy. What is your verdict?" They answered, "He deserves death!" Then they began to spit in his face and hit him. Others slapped him, saying: "Play the prophet for us, Messiah! Who struck you?"

Peter was sitting in the courtyard when one of the serving girls came over to him and said, "You too were with Jesus the Galilean." He denied it in front of everyone: "I don't know what you are talking about!" When he went out to the gate another girl saw him and said to those nearby, "This man was with Jesus the Nazorean." Again he denied it with an oath: "I don't know the man!" A little while later some bystanders came over to Peter and said, "You are certainly one of them! Even your accent gives you away!" At that he began cursing and swore, "I don't even know the man!" Just then a rooster began to crow and Peter remembered the prediction Jesus had made: "Before the rooster crows you will three times disown me." He went out and began to weep bitterly.

At daybreak all the chief priests and the elders of the people took formal action against Jesus to put him to death. They bound him and led him away to be handed over to the procurator Pilate.

Then Judas, who had handed him over, seeing that Jesus had been condemned, began to regret his action deeply. He took the thirty pieces of silver back to the chief priests and elders and said, "I did wrong to deliver up an innocent man!" They retorted, "What is that to us? It is your affair!" So Ju-das flung the money into the temple and left. He went off and hanged himself. The chief priests picked up the silver, observing, "It is not right to deposit this in the temple treasury since it is blood money." After consultation, they used it to buy the potter's field as a cemetery for foreigners. That is why that field, even today, is called Blood Field. On that occasion, what was said through Jeremiah the prophet was fulfilled:

"They took the thirty pieces of silver, the value of a man with a price on his head, a price set by the Israelites, and they paid it out for the potter's field just as the Lord had commanded me."

Jesus was arraigned before the procurator, who questioned him: "Are you the king of the Jews?" Jesus responded, "As you say." Yet when he was accused by the chief priests and elders, he had made no reply. Then Pilate said to him, "Surely you hear how many charges they bring against you?" He did not answer him on a single count, much to the procurator's surprise.

Now on the occasion of a festival the procurator was accustomed to release one prisoner, whom the crowd would designate. They had at the time a notorious prisoner named Barabbas. Since they were already assembled, Pilate said to them, "Which one do you wish me to release for you, Barabbas or Jesus the so-called Messiah?" He knew, of course, that it was out of jealousy that they had handed him over.

While he was still presiding on the bench, his wife sent him a message: "Do not interfere in the case of that holy man. I had a dream about him today which has greatly upset me."

Meanwhile, the chief priests and elders

convinced the crowds that they should ask for Barabbas and have Jesus put to death. So when the procurator asked them, "Which one do you wish me to release for you?" they said, "Barabbas." Pilate said to them, "Then what am I to do with Jesus, the so-called Messiah?" "Crucify him!" they all cried. He said, "Why, what crime has he committed?" But they only shouted the louder, "Crucify him!" Pilate finally realized that he was making no impression and that a riot was breaking out instead. He called for water and washed his hands in front of the crowd, declaring as he did so, "I am innocent of the blood of this just man. The responsibility is yours." The whole people said in reply, "Let his blood be on us and on our children." At that, he released Barabbas to them. Jesus, however, he first had scourged; then he handed him over to be crucified.

The procurator's soldiers took Jesus inside the praetorium and collected the whole cohort around him. They stripped off his clothes and wrapped him in a scarlet military cloak. Weaving a crown out of thorns they fixed it on his head, and stuck a reed in his right hand. Then they began to mock him by dropping to their knees before him, saying, "All hail, king of the Jews!" They also spat at him. Afterward they took hold of the reed and kept striking him on the head. Finally, when they had finished making a fool of him, they stripped him of the cloak, dressed him in his own clothes, and led him off to crucifixion.

On their way out they met a Cyrenian named Simon. This man they pressed into service to carry the cross. Upon arriving at a site called Golgotha (a name which means Skull Place), they gave him a drink of wine flavored with gall, which he tasted but refused to drink.

When they had crucified him, they divided his clothes among them by casting lots; then they sat down there and kept watch over him. Above his head they had put the charge against him in writing: "This is Jesus, King of the Jews." Two insurgents were crucified along with him, one at his right and one at his left. People going by kept insulting him, tossing their heads and saying: "So you are the one who was going to destroy the temple and rebuild it in three days! Save yourself, why don't you? Come down off that cross if you are God's Son!" The chief priests, the scribes and the elders also joined in the jeering: "He saved others but he cannot save himself! So he is the king of Israel! Let's see him come down from that cross, then we will believe in him. He relied on God; let God rescue him now if he wants to. After all, he claimed, 'I am God's Son.'" The insurgents who had been crucified with him kept taunting him in the same way.

From noon onward, there was darkness over the whole land until midafternoon. Then toward midafternoon Jesus cried out in a loud tone, "Eli, Eli, lema sabachthani?", that is, "My God, my God, why have you forsaken me?" This made some of the bystanders who heard it remark, "He is invoking Elijah!" Immediately one of them ran off and got a sponge. He soaked it in cheap wine, and sticking it on a reed, tried to make him drink. Meanwhile the rest said, "Leave him alone. Let's see whether Elijah comes to his rescue." Once again Jesus cried out in a loud voice, and then gave up his spirit.

Suddenly the curtain of the sanctuary was torn in two from top to bottom. The earth quaked, boulders split, tombs opened. Many bodies of saints who had fallen asleep were raised. After Jesus' resurrection they came forth from their tombs and entered the holy city and appeared to many. The centurion and his men who were keeping watch over Jesus were terror-stricken at seeing the earthquake and all that was happening, and said, "Clearly this was the Son of God!"

Many women were present looking on from a distance. They had followed Jesus from Galilee to attend to his needs. Among them were Mary Magdalene, and Mary the mother of James and Joseph, and the mother of Zebedee's sons.

When evening fell, a wealthy man from Arimathea arrived, Joseph by name. He was another of Jesus' disciples, and had gone to request the body of Jesus. Thereupon Pilate issued an order for its release. Taking the body, Joseph wrapped it in fresh linen and laid it in his own new tomb which had been hewn from a formation of rock. Then he rolled a huge stone across the entrance of the tomb and went away. But Mary Magdalene and the other Mary remained sitting there, facing the tomb.

The next day, the one following the Day of Preparation, the chief priests and the Pharisees called at Pilate's residence. "Sir," they said, "we have recalled that that impostor while he was still alive made the claim, 'After three days I will rise.' You should issue an order having the tomb kept under surveillance until the third day. Otherwise his disciples may go and steal him and tell the people, 'He has been raised from the dead!' This final imposture would be worse than the first." Pilate told them, "You have a guard. Go and secure the tomb as best you can." So they went and kept it under surveillance of the guard, after fixing a seal to the stone.

Reflection on the Readings

Today's passion narrative from Matthew's Gospel drains us. It is filled with emotions and experience that run very deep—betrayal, love, trust, denial, condemnation, death. For apparently senseless reasons, Jesus is killed. His life was centered on God's love and justice. His ministry helped bring about the liberation and reconciliation of people from all that oppresses and binds. Jesus' words and actions continued to reflect God's abundance, God's graciousness, God's desire to be-on-our-side.

Yet Jesus' obedience to such an authentic life—a life that truly reflected God in the world—not only brought healing and peace, but also stirred up and challenged any way of life that was centered in selfishness and sin. Accepting Jesus' claim that God was truly on-our-side demanded a changed way of life that also reflected this love of God. This made some people uncomfortable, threatening them, unmasking their blindness. Their response was to kill Jesus.

Jesus could have fought back, but then he would have compromised the values he had lived by—the values of the reign of God. Instead, Jesus holds firm to his belief that God's way is truly the way of life, even if it costs death.

The stirrings from the narrative run deep because we hear the same challenge today: Can we live the values of the reign of God, even at the cost of our lives? Is this not what it means to embrace and carry the cross?

Suggestions for Prayer

1. Return to the passion narrative from Matthew. Choose one section that particularly struck you when you heard it proclaimed. Pray that passage slowly. What is God asking of you at this time of your life?
2. Religious art is a special way of entering into prayer. Gaze at either a crucifix or a painting of the crucifixion. What does it mean that Jesus has died for us?
3. Pray the Jesus prayer. Slowly repeat the mantra, "Jesus, Son of the living God, have pity on me, a sinner." Continue to pray the mantra, focusing on Jesus' gift of love for you.

Suggestion for Journal Keeping

"Your will be done." Write about the following: How do I know what God's will is for me? Who can help me understand God's will for me? How do I respond to God's will? What do I need to be able to fully accept God's will?

Thomas H. Morris

GOSPEL B   Mk 14, 1–15, 47
The Passion of our Lord Jesus Christ according to Mark.

The feasts of Passover and Unleavened Bread were to be observed in two days' time, and therefore the chief priests and scribes began to look for a way to arrest Jesus by some trick and kill him. Yet they pointed out, "Not during the festival, or the people may riot."

When Jesus was in Bethany reclining at table in the house of Simon the leper, a woman entered carrying an alabaster jar of perfume made from expensive aromatic nard. Breaking the jar, she began to pour the perfume on his head. Some were saying to themselves indignantly: "What is the point of this extravagant waste of perfume? It could have been sold for over three hundred silver pieces and the money given to the poor." They were infuriated at her. But Jesus said: "Let her alone. Why do you criticize her? She has done me a kindness. The poor you will always have with you and you can be generous to them whenever you wish, but you will not always have me. She has done what she could. By perfuming my body she is anticipating its preparation for burial. I assure you, wherever the good news is proclaimed throughout the world, what she has done will be told in her memory."

Then Judas Iscariot, one of the Twelve, went off to the chief priests to hand Jesus over to them. Hearing what he had to say, they were jubilant and promised to give him money. He for his part kept looking for an opportune way to hand him over.

On the first day of Unleavened Bread, when it was customary to sacrifice the paschal lamb, his disciples said to him, "Where do you wish us to go to prepare the Passover supper for you?" He sent two of his disciples with these instructions: "Go into the city and you will come upon a man carrying a water jar. Follow him. Whatever house he enters, say to the owner, 'The Teacher asks, Where is my guestroom where I may eat the Passover with my disciples?' Then he will show you an upstairs room, spacious, furnished, and all in order. That is the place you are to get ready for us." The disciples went

105

off. When they reached the city they found it just as he had told them, and they prepared the Passover supper.

As it grew dark he arrived with the Twelve. They reclined at table, and in the course of the meal, Jesus said, "I give you my word, one of you is about to betray me, yes, one who is eating with me." They began to say to him sorrowfully, one by one, "Surely not I!" He said, "It is one of the Twelve—a man who dips into the dish with me. The Son of Man is going the way the Scripture tells of him. Still, accursed be that man by whom the Son of Man is betrayed. It were better for him had he never been born."

During the meal he took bread, blessed and broke it, and gave it to them. "Take this," he said, "this is my body." He likewise took a cup, gave thanks and passed it to them, and they all drank from it. He said to them: "This is my blood, the blood of the covenant, to be poured out on behalf of many. I solemnly assure you, I will never again drink of the fruit of the vine until the day when I drink it in the reign of God."

After singing songs of praise, they walked out to the Mount of Olives.

Jesus then said to them: "Your faith in me shall be shaken, for Scripture has it,

'I will strike the shepherd
and the sheep will be dispersed.'

But after I am raised up, I will go to Galilee ahead of you." Peter said to him, "Even though all are shaken in faith, it will not be that way with me." Jesus answered, "I give you my assurance, this very night before the cock crows twice, you will deny me three times." But Peter kept reasserting vehemently, "Even if I have to die with you, I will not disown you." They all said the same.

They went then to a place named Gethsemani. "Sit down here while I pray," he said to his disciples; at the same time he took along with him Peter, James, and John. Then he began to be filled with fear and distress. He said to them, "My heart is filled with sorrow to the point of death. Remain here and stay awake." He advanced a little and fell to the ground, praying that if it were possible this hour might pass him by. He kept saying, "Abba (O Father), you have the power to do all things. Take this cup away from me. But let it be as you would have it, not as I." When he returned he found them asleep. He said to Peter, "Asleep, Simon? You could not stay awake for even an hour? Be on guard and pray that you may not be put to the test. The spirit is willing but nature is weak." Going back again he began to pray in the same words. Once again he found them asleep on his return. They could not keep their eyes open, nor did they know what to say to him. He returned a third time and said to them, "Still sleeping? Still taking your ease? It will have to do. The hour is on us. You will see that the Son of Man is to be handed over into the clutches of evil men. Rouse yourselves and come along. See! My betrayer is near."

Even while he was still speaking, Judas, one of the Twelve, made his appearance accompanied by a crowd with swords and clubs; these people had been sent by the chief priests, the scribes, and the elders. The betrayer had arranged a signal for them, saying, "The man I shall embrace is the one; arrest him and lead him away, taking every precaution." He then went directly over to him and said, "Rabbi!" and embraced him. At this, they laid hands on him and arrested him. One of the bystanders drew his sword and struck the high priest's slave, cutting off his ear. Addressing himself to them, Jesus said, "You have come out to arrest me armed with swords and clubs as if against a brigand. I was within your reach daily, teaching in the temple precincts, yet you never arrested me. But now, so that the Scriptures may be fulfilled. . . ." With that, all deserted him and fled. There was a young man following him who was covered by nothing but a linen cloth. As they seized him he left the cloth behind and ran off naked.

Then they led Jesus off to the high priest, and all the chief priests, the elders and the scribes came together. Peter followed him at a distance right into the high priest's courtyard, where he found a seat with the temple guard and began to warm himself at the fire. The chief priests with the whole Sanhedrin were busy soliciting testimony against Jesus that would lead to his death, but they could not find any. Many spoke against him falsely under oath but their testimony did not agree. Some, for instance, on taking the stand, testified falsely by alleging, "We heard him declare, 'I will destroy this temple made by human hands,' and 'In three days I will construct another not made by human hands.'" Even so, their testimony did not agree.

The high priest rose to his feet before the court and began to interrogate Jesus: "Have you no answer to what these men testify against you?" Jesus remained silent; he made no reply. Once again the high priest interrogated him: "Are you the Messiah, the Son of the Blessed One?" Then Jesus answered: "I am; and you will see the Son of Man seated at the right hand of the Power and coming with the clouds of heaven." At that the high priest tore his robes and said:

"What further need do we have of witnesses? You have heard the blasphemy. What is your verdict?" They all concurred in the verdict "guilty," with its sentence of death. Some of them then began to spit on him. They blindfolded him and hit him, saying, "Play the prophet!" while the officers manhandled him.

While Peter was down in the courtyard, one of the servant girls of the high priest came along. When she noticed Peter warming himself, she looked more closely at him and said, "You too were with Jesus of Nazareth." But he denied it: "I don't know what you are talking about! What are you getting at?" Then he went out into the gateway. At that moment a rooster crowed. The servant girl, keeping an eye on him, started again to tell the bystanders, "This man is one of them." Once again he denied it. A little later the bystanders said to Peter once more, "You are certainly one of them! You're a Galilean, are you not?" He began to curse, and to swear, "I don't even know the man you are talking about!" Just then a second cockcrow was heard and Peter recalled the prediction Jesus had made to him, "Before the cock crows twice you will disown me three times." He broke down and began to cry.

As soon as it was daybreak the chief priests, with the elders and scribes (that is, the whole Sanhedrin), reached a decision. They bound Jesus, led him away, and handed him over to Pilate. Pilate interrogated him: "Are you the king of the Jews?" "You are the one who is saying it," Jesus replied. The chief priests, meanwhile, brought many accusations against him. Pilate interrogated him again: "Surely you have some answer? See how many accusations they are leveling against you." But greatly to Pilate's surprise, Jesus made no further response.

Now on the occasion of a festival he would release for them one prisoner—any man they asked for. There was a prisoner named Barabbas jailed along with the rebels who had committed murder in the uprising. When the crowd came up to press their demand that he honor the custom, Pilate rejoined, "Do you want me to release the king of the Jews for you?" He was aware, of course, that it was out of jealousy that the chief priests had handed him over. Meanwhile, the chief priests incited the crowd to have him release Barabbas instead. Pilate again asked them, "What am I to do with the man you call the king of the Jews?" They shouted back, "Crucify him!" Pilate protested, "Why? What crime has he committed?" They only shouted the louder, "Crucify him!" So Pilate, who wished to satisfy the crowd, released Barabbas to them, and after he had had Jesus scourged, he handed him over to be crucified.

The soldiers now led Jesus away into the hall known as the praetorium; at the same time they assembled the whole cohort. They dressed him in royal purple, then wove a crown of thorns and put it on him, and began to salute him, "All hail! King of the Jews!" Continually striking Jesus on the head with a reed and spitting at him, they genuflected before him and pretended to pay him homage. When they had finished mocking him, they stripped him of the purple, dressed him in his own clothes, and led him out to crucify him.

A man named Simon of Cyrene, the father of Alexander and Rufus, was coming in from the fields and they pressed him into service to carry the cross. When they brought Jesus to the site of Golgotha (which means "Skull Place"), they tried to give him wine drugged with myrrh, but he would not take it. Then they crucified him and divided up his garments by rolling dice for them to see what each should take. It was about nine in the morning when they crucified him. The inscription proclaiming his offense read, "The King of the Jews."

With him they crucified two insurgents, one at his right and one at his left. People going by kept insulting him, tossing their heads and saying, "Ha, ha! So you were going to destroy the temple and rebuild it in three days! Save yourself now by coming down from that cross!" The chief priests and the scribes also joined in and jeered: "He saved others but he cannot save himself! Let the 'Messiah,' the 'king of Israel,' come down from that cross here and now so that we can see it and believe in him!" The men who had been crucified with him likewise kept taunting him.

When noon came, darkness fell on the whole countryside and lasted until midafternoon. At that time Jesus cried in a loud voice, "Eloi, Eloi, lama sabachthani?" which means, "My God, my God, why have you forsaken me?" A few of the bystanders who heard it remarked, "Listen! He is calling on Elijah!" Someone ran off, and soaking a sponge in sour wine, stuck it on a reed to try to make him drink. The man said, "Now let's see whether Elijah comes to take him down."

Then Jesus, uttering a loud cry, breathed his last. At that moment the curtain in the sanctuary was torn in two from top to bottom. The centurion who stood guard over him, on seeing the manner of his death, declared, "Clearly this man was the Son of

God!" There were also women present looking on from a distance. Among them were Mary Magdalene, Mary the mother of James the younger and Joses, and Salome. These women had followed Jesus when he was in Galilee and attended to his needs. There were also many others who had come up with him to Jerusalem.

As it grew dark (it was Preparation Day, that is, the eve of the sabbath), Joseph from Arimathea arrived—a distinguished member of the Sanhedrin. He was another who looked forward to the reign of God. He was bold enough to seek an audience with Pilate, and urgently requested the body of Jesus. Pilate was surprised that Jesus should have died so soon. He summoned the centurion and inquired whether Jesus was already dead. Learning from him that he was dead, Pilate released the corpse to Joseph. Then, having bought a linen shroud, Joseph took him down, wrapped him in the linen, and laid him in a tomb which had been cut out of rock. Finally he rolled a stone across the entrance of the tomb. Meanwhile, Mary Magdalene and Mary the mother of Joses observed where he had been laid.

Reflection on the Readings

The passion narrative from Mark's Gospel is painful: Jesus, who had lived a life of obedience to the will of the Father, is killed because of that very obedience. We are reminded of the various parts of the story that grip us: the sharing of a final meal with his friends, the betrayal from one of his companions, Jesus' own struggle in prayer, the denial of one so close to him, the condemnation to death, the rejection from the crowd that only days earlier welcomed him, the beatings and mockery Jesus endured, and his death on the cross. Painful memories, memories of apparent destruction and violence.

Yet we remember this central story of our faith today precisely because it is in and through the trust Jesus places in the Father that we learn the way of life that brings freedom from all oppression. Jesus died because he was faithful to witnessing to God's love in the world—a love that frees, reconciles, heals, restores order. That witness threatened some, frightened others, and angered enough people to bring Jesus to the cross. Yet Jesus continues to trust that God will be victorious—that the final word will be God's word of justice and love. Even Jesus' followers run in fear, not having developed the level of trust in relationship with the Father.

We are invited to stand at the cross today, to remember the cries of welcome as Jesus enters Jerusalem and the cries of condemnation as he leaves carrying his cross. We come to learn trust with Jesus in the ways of God.

Suggestions for Prayer

1. Prayerfully recall the men and women of our time who have died because of their commitment to the values of justice, mercy, peace and love—in Central and South America, South Africa, Northern Ireland, the Middle East, throughout the world. Pray for the grace to remain strong in your own convictions.

2. Using imaginative prayer, recall the basic story of the passion, walking with Jesus from the gathering to celebrate the passover to his death. As each scene changes, stop and ask God to help you know more deeply the meaning of Jesus' death for the world.

3. The Our Father is the prayer of those

who place their trust in God, the prayer of those who embrace the cross of Jesus. Slowly pray the Our Father, pausing after each line. What does that line mean for you now?

Suggestion for Journal Keeping

What keeps you from trusting God fully? Draw images or list words that capture your feelings as you reflect on your relationship with God, your ability or inability to trust God. What do you need from God to help you trust God more completely?

Thomas H. Morris

GOSPEL **C** Lk 22, 14–23, 56
The Passion of our Lord Jesus Christ according to Luke.

When the hour arrived, Jesus took his place at table, and the apostles with him. He said to them: "I have greatly desired to eat this Passover with you before I suffer. I tell you, I will not eat again until it is fulfilled in the kingdom of God."

Then taking a cup he offered a blessing in thanks and said: "Take this and divide it among you; I tell you, from now on I will not drink of the fruit of the vine until the coming of the reign of God."

Then taking bread and giving thanks, he broke it and gave it to them, saying: "This is my body to be given for you. Do this as a remembrance of me." He did the same with the cup after eating, saying as he did so: "This cup is the new covenant in my blood, which will be shed for you.

"And yet the hand of my betrayer is with me at this table. The Son of Man is following out his appointed course, but woe to that man by whom he is betrayed." Then they began to dispute among themselves as to which of them would do such a deed.

A dispute arose among them about who would be regarded as the greatest. He said: "Earthly kings lord it over their people. Those who exercise authority over them are called their benefactors. Yet it cannot be that way with you. Let the greater among you be as the junior, the leader as the servant. Who, in fact, is the greater—he who reclines at table or he who serves the meal? Is it not the one who reclines at table? Yet I am in your midst as the one who serves you. You are the ones who have stood loyally by me in my temptations. I for my part assign to you the dominion my Father has assigned to me. In my kingdom, you will eat and drink at my table, and you will sit on thrones judging the twelve tribes of Israel.

"Simon, Simon! Remember that Satan has asked for you to sift you all like wheat. But I have prayed for you that your faith may never fail. You in turn must strengthen your brothers." "Lord," he said to him, "at your side I am prepared to face imprisonment and death itself." Jesus replied, "I tell you, Peter, the rooster will not crow today until you have three times denied that you know me."

He asked them, "When I sent you on mission without purse or traveling bag or sandals, were you in need of anything?" "Not a thing," they replied. He said to them: "Now, however, the man who has a purse must carry it; the same with the traveling bag. And the man without a sword must sell his coat and buy one. It is written in Scripture,

'**He was counted among the wicked,'**
and this, I tell you, must come to be fulfilled in me. All that has to do with me approaches

its climax." They said, "Lord, here are two swords!" He answered, "Enough."

Then he went out and made his way, as was his custom, to the Mount of Olives; his disciples accompanied him. On reaching the place he said to them, "Pray that you may not be put to the test." He withdrew from them about a stone's throw, then went down on his knees and prayed in these words: "Father, if it is your will, take this cup from me; yet not my will but yours be done." An angel then appeared to him from heaven to strengthen him. In his anguish he prayed with all the greater intensity, and his sweat became like drops of blood falling to the ground. Then he rose from prayer and came to his disciples, only to find them asleep, exhausted with grief. He said to them, "Why are you sleeping? Wake up, and pray that you may not be subjected to the trial."

While he was still speaking a crowd came, led by the man named Judas, one of the Twelve. He approached Jesus to embrace him. Jesus said to him, "Judas, would you betray the Son of Man with a kiss?" When the companions of Jesus saw what was going to happen, they said, "Lord, shall we use the sword?" One of them went so far as to strike the high priest's servant and cut off his right ear. Jesus said in answer to their question, "Enough!" Then he touched the ear and healed the man. But to those who had come out against him—the chief priests, the chiefs of the temple guard, and the ancients—Jesus said, "Am I a criminal that you come out after me armed with swords and clubs? When I was with you day after day in the temple you never raised a hand against me. But this is your hour—the triumph of darkness!"

They led him away under arrest and brought him to the house of the high priest, while Peter followed at a distance. Later they lighted a fire in the middle of the courtyard and were sitting beside it, and Peter sat among them. A servant girl saw him sitting in the light of the fire. She gazed at him intently, then said, "This man was with him." He denied the fact, saying, "Woman, I do not know him." A little while later someone else saw him and said, "You are one of them too." But Peter said, "No, sir, not I!" About an hour after that another spoke more insistently: "This man was certainly with him, for he is a Galilean." Peter responded, "My friend, I do not know what you are talking about." At the very moment he was saying this, a rooster crowed. The Lord turned around and looked at Peter, and Peter remembered the word that the Lord had spoken to him, "Before the rooster crows today you will deny me three times." He went out and wept bitterly.

Meanwhile the men guarding Jesus amused themselves at his expense. They blindfolded him first, slapped him, and then taunted him: "Play the prophet; which one struck you?" And they directed many other insulting words at him.

At daybreak the council, which was made up of the elders of the people, the chief priests, and the scribes, assembled again. Once they had brought him before their council, they said, "Tell us, are you the Messiah?" He replied, "If I tell you, you will not believe me, and if I question you, you will not answer. This much only will I say: 'From now on, the Son of Man will have his seat at the right hand of the Power of God.'" "So you are the Son of God?" they asked in chorus. He answered, "It is you who say I am." They said, "What need have we of witnesses? We have heard it from his own mouth."

Then the entire assembly rose up and led him before Pilate. They started his prosecution by saying, "We found this man subverting our nation, opposing the payment of taxes to Caesar, and calling himself the Messiah, a king." Pilate asked him, "Are you the king of the Jews?" He answered, "That is your term." Pilate reported to the chief priests and the crowds, "I do not find a case against this man." But they insisted, "He stirs up the people by his teaching throughout the whole of Judea, from Galilee, where he began, to this very place." On hearing this Pilate asked if the man was a Galilean; and when he learned that he was under Herod's jurisdiction, he sent him to Herod, who also happened to be in Jerusalem at the time.

Herod was extremely pleased to see Jesus. From the reports about him he had wanted for a long time to see him, and he was hoping to see him work some miracle. He questioned Jesus at considerable length, but Jesus made no answer. The chief priests and scribes were at hand to accuse him vehemently. Herod and his guards then treated him with contempt and insult, after which they put a magnificent robe on him and sent him back to Pilate. Herod and Pilate, who had previously been set against each other, became friends from that day.

Pilate then called together the chief priests, the ruling class, and the people, and said to them: "You have brought this man before me as one who subverts the people. I have examined him in your presence and have no charge against him arising from your allegations. Neither has Herod, who therefore has sent him back to us; obviously this man has done nothing to deserve death.

Therefore I mean to release him, once I have taught him a lesson." The whole crowd cried out, "Away with this man; release Barabbas for us!" This Barabbas had been thrown in prison for causing an uprising in the city, and for murder. Pilate addressed them again, for he wanted Jesus to be the one he released.

But they shouted back, "Crucify him, crucify him!" He said to them for the third time, "What wrong is this man guilty of? I have not discovered anything about him deserving the death penalty. I will therefore chastise him and release him." But they demanded with loud cries that he be crucified, and their shouts increased in violence. Pilate then decreed that what they demanded should be done. He released the one they asked for, who had been thrown in prison for insurrection and murder, and delivered Jesus up to their wishes.

As they led him away, they laid hold of one Simon the Cyrenean who was coming in from the fields. They put a crossbeam on Simon's shoulder for him to carry along behind Jesus. A great crowd of people followed him, including women who beat their breasts and lamented over him. Jesus turned to them and said: "Daughters of Jerusalem, do not weep for me. Weep for yourselves and for your children. The days are coming when they will say, 'Happy are the sterile, the wombs that never bore and the breasts that never nursed.' Then they will begin saying to the mountains, 'Fall on us,' and to the hills, 'Cover us.' If they do these things in the green wood, what will happen in the dry?"

Two others who were criminals were led along with him to be crucified. When they came to Skull Place, as it was called, they crucified him there and the criminals as well, one on his right and the other on his left. [Jesus said, "Father, forgive them; they do not know what they are doing."] They divided his garments, rolling dice for them.

The people stood there watching, and the leaders kept jeering at him, saying, "He saved others; let him save himself if he is the Messiah of God, the chosen one." The soldiers also made fun of him, coming forward to offer him their sour wine and saying, "If you are the king of the Jews, save yourself." There was an inscription over his head: "THIS IS THE KING OF THE JEWS." One of the criminals hanging in crucifixion blasphemed him, "Aren't you the Messiah? Then save yourself and us." But the other one rebuked him: "Have you no fear of God, seeing you are under the same sentence? We deserve it, after all. We are only paying the price for what we've done, but this man has done nothing wrong." He then said, "Jesus, remember me when you enter upon your reign." And Jesus replied, "I assure you: this day you will be with me in paradise."

It was now around midday, and darkness came over the whole land until midafternoon with an eclipse of the sun. The curtain in the sanctuary was torn in two. Jesus uttered a loud cry and said,

"Father, into your hands I commend my spirit."

After he said this, he expired. The centurion, upon seeing what had happened, gave glory to God by saying, "Surely this was an innocent man." After the crowd assembled for this spectacle witnessed what had happened, they returned beating their breasts. All his friends and the women who had accompanied him from Galilee were standing at a distance watching everything.

There was a man named Joseph, an up-right and holy member of the Sanhedrin, who had not been associated with their plan or their action. He was from Arimathea, a Jewish town, and he looked expectantly for the reign of God. This man approached Pilate with a request for Jesus' body. He took it down, wrapped it in fine linen, and laid it in a tomb hewn out of the rock, in which no one had yet been buried.

That was the day of Preparation, and the sabbath was about to begin. The women who had come with him from Galilee followed along behind. They saw the tomb and how his body was buried. Then they went back home to prepare spices and perfumes. They observed the sabbath as a day of rest, in accordance with the law.

Reflection on the Readings

The passion narrative in Luke's Gospel holds in contrast Jesus' obedience to the will of the Father and the injustice that condemns him to death. Luke is rich in his imagery and stories surrounding the events of these last days of Jesus' life: the sharing of the Passover meal, the dispute over greatness, the agony in the garden and arrest, Jesus' turn to look at Peter after his denial, Jesus' condemnation and crucifixion, the dialogue with the criminals hanging with Jesus, Jesus' death and burial. Over and over again, Jesus is presented with the opportunity to strike back, or to run away. Instead, he remains faithful, refusing to compromise God's values which had directed and empowered him throughout his life and ministry. He remains the innocent victim.

Again and again we see in Luke's account Jesus' choice for self-sacrificing love. Self-sacrificing love means that the values of the reign of God as experienced through Jesus—

113

freedom from oppression, compassion for all, liberation and acceptance, reconciliation and right relationships with God—were more important than Jesus' very own life. When faced with the choice of the reign of God or self-preservation, Jesus chose the reign of God. This does not mean self-annihilation. Rather, it means that Jesus lived from his deepest center—God-within—and responded to all of life in this way, whatever the cost. And now we are invited to lives of self-sacrificing love, of choosing God's values, whatever the cost. We now can choose such love because Jesus—our Liberator and Redeemer—gifts us with the Spirit of God.

Suggestions for Prayer

1. Reflect on incidents of oppression in your neighborhood—racism, sexism, ageism—and pray for the courage to bring God's word of liberation to those situations. Ask God to give you what you need to stand up for the values of the reign of God.

2. Jesus' death frees us from all sin and oppression. Recall areas of your life that are still not free, that are still enslaved. Pray: Come, Lord Jesus, and set me free from . . .

3. Go to your parish church and pray the stations of the cross. Between each station, meditate on the meaning of the station in your life today.

Suggestion for Journal Keeping

The cross is a symbol of Jesus' self-sacrificing love. Recall times in your life when you experienced this self-sacrificing love from another person. Write about: How can I describe this love? How was I changed because of this love? How is God present in this love? What does this love tell me about God's love? What do I need from God to be able to love more freely, to be able to offer self-sacrificing love for others?

Thomas H. Morris

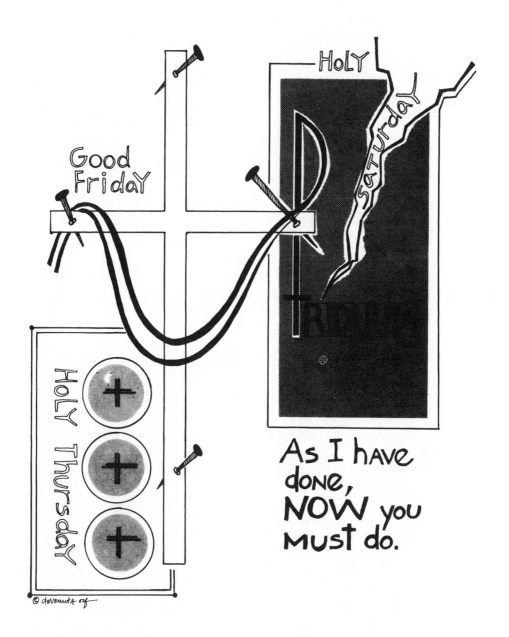

Good Friday

Holy

Saturday

Holy Thursday

As I have done, NOW you must do.

© doremota osf

115

Holy Thursday
Mass of
the Lord's Supper A B C

READING I   Ex 12, 1–8. 11–14

The Lord said to Moses and Aaron in the land of Egypt, "This month shall stand at the head of your calendar; you shall reckon it the first month of the year. Tell the whole community of Israel: On the tenth of this month every one of your families must procure for itself a lamb, one apiece for each household. If a family is too small for a whole lamb, it shall join the nearest household in procuring one and shall share in the lamb in proportion to the number of persons who partake of it. The lamb must be a year-old male and without blemish. You may take it from either the sheep or the goats. You shall keep it until the fourteenth day of this month, and then, with the whole assembly of Israel present, it shall be slaughtered during the evening twilight. They shall take some of its blood and apply it to the two doorposts and the lintel of every house in which they partake of the lamb. That same night they shall eat its roasted flesh with unleavened bread and bitter herbs.

"This is how you are to eat it: with your loins girt, sandals on your feet and your staff in hand, you shall eat like those who are in flight. It is the Passover of the Lord. For on this same night I will go through Egypt, striking down every first-born of the land, both man and beast, and executing judgment on all the gods of Egypt—I, the Lord! But the blood will mark the houses where you are. Seeing the blood, I will pass over you; thus, when I strike the land of Egypt, no destructive blow will come upon you.

"This day shall be a memorial feast for you, which all your generations shall celebrate with pilgrimage to the Lord, as a perpetual institution."

Responsorial Psalm   Ps 116, 12–13. 15–16. 17–18

Our blessing-cup is a communion with the
    blood of Christ.
How shall I make a return to the Lord
    for all the good he has done for me?
The cup of salvation I will take up,
    and I will call upon the name of the Lord.
Our blessing-cup is a communion with the
    blood of Christ.
Precious in the eyes of the Lord
    is the death of his faithful ones.
I am your servant, the son of your hand-
    maid;
    you have loosed my bonds.

Our blessing-cup is a communion with the
blood of Christ.
**To you will I offer sacrifice of thanksgiving,
and I will call upon the name of the Lord.
My vows to the Lord I will pay
in the presence of all his people.**
Our blessing-cup is a communion with the
blood of Christ.

READING II   1 Cor 11, 23–26
**I received from the Lord what I handed on
to you, namely, that the Lord Jesus on the
night in which he was betrayed took bread,
and after he had given thanks, broke it and
said, "This is my body, which is for you. Do
this in remembrance of me." In the same
way, after the supper, he took the cup, saying, "This cup is the new covenant in my
blood. Do this, whenever you drink it, in remembrance of me." Every time, then, you
eat this bread and drink this cup, you proclaim the death of the Lord until he comes!**

GOSPEL   Jn 13, 1–15
**Before the feast of Passover, Jesus realized
that the hour had come for him to pass from
this world to the Father. He had loved his
own in this world, and would show his love
for them to the end. The devil had already
induced Judas, son of Simon Iscariot, to
hand Jesus over; and so, during the supper,
Jesus—fully aware that he had come from
God and was going to God, the Father who
had handed everything over to him—rose
from the meal and took off his cloak. He
picked up a towel and tied it around himself.
Then he poured water into a basin and began
to wash his disciples' feet and dry them with
the towel he had around him. Thus he came
to Simon Peter, who said to him, "Lord, are
you going to wash my feet?" Jesus answered,**

**"You may not realize now what I am doing,
but later you will understand." Peter replied, "You shall never wash my feet!" "If I
do not wash you," Jesus answered, "you will
have no share in my heritage." "Lord," Simon Peter said to him, "then not only my
feet, but my hands and head as well." Jesus
told him, "The man who has bathed has no
need to wash [except for his feet]; he is entirely cleansed, just as you are; though not
all." (The reason he said, "Not all are
washed clean," was that he knew his betrayer.)
After he had washed their feet, he put his
cloak back on and reclined at table once
more. He said to them:
"Do you understand what I just did for
you?
You address me as 'Teacher' and 'Lord,'
and fittingly enough,
for that is what I am.
But if I washed your feet—
I who am Teacher and Lord—
then you must wash each other's feet.
What I just did was to give you an
example:
as I have done, so you must do."**

Reflection on the Readings
Together with the Palm Sunday liturgy, this
Holy Week liturgy continues to offer an
abundance of symbolic celebration, use of
sacramentals, and exposure to the rich ritual
heritage of our Church. Unless you take part
in the liturgy itself, the simple reading of the
prayers and Scripture seem comparatively
barren. It is in the context of the praying community that the liturgy comes to full life.
The evening Mass of the Lord's Supper
connects the first Passover with Jesus' Last
Supper. God's care for his people—through

the exodus event and on through Jesus' washing the feet of his disciples—is part of a covenant. The other part of that covenant is our response to God's presence and care, as shown through our service to others, our prayer, our love and care for others. This liturgy also focuses on the institution of the Eucharist, the Last Supper itself, in which Jesus gives himself through the bread and wine. The Eucharist, celebrated with the community, signifies our oneness with God and one another. If a seder meal is celebrated in your parish, the roots of our sacred meal as a family become more clear. The seder meal recalls the exodus event which becomes the Passover meal of Jewish heritage which is the setting in which Jesus gave us the new Passover—his own self before his passion and death.

The centrality of the holy meal in the life of the community becomes clear when, as catechumens, elect, or baptized members, we regularly gather to worship God and celebrate our life as a community of believers.

Suggestions for Prayer

1. As catechumens, you do not yet celebrate the Eucharist. That fullness of participation comes only after baptism and acceptance into the Church. As you pray with the community, listen to the readings and celebrate to the fullness of your capacity at this time; pray for all those who are members, and particularly those who are preparing for full membership. Let yourself feel a hungering for the Lord in the Eucharist.
2. Washing the feet of members of the community is a sign of the service to others which a leader is called to give.

Modeled after Jesus' actions with his disciples, it is a witness to our care for one another. Spend time praying for God's special blessing on the leaders of your parish.
3. The closing words of the Gospel are Jesus' command to his disciples, "As I have done, now you must do." The example of Jesus is one of service to others. What service, gifts, caring, do you offer to others as a disciple of Jesus? You may want to spend some time thinking and praying about your gifts within the community. How can you be of service to others? You may want to talk with your sponsor or a member of the catechumenate team about your thoughts and questions.

Suggestions for Journal Keeping

The first reading from Exodus describes the Passover meal. These three days are our Passover in Christ, as we journey with him from death to life. Now that Lent has ended, reflect on what you are celebrating. What is your Passover? From what form of death and toward what new life are you moving?

Clare M. Colella

119

Good Friday
The Passion
of the Lord

READING I   Is 52, 13–53, 12

See, my servant shall prosper,
  he shall be raised high and greatly exalted.
Even as many were amazed at him—
  so marred was his look beyond that of
    man,
  and his appearance beyond that of mor-
    tals—
So shall he startle many nations,
  because of him kings shall stand speech-
    less;
For those who have not been told shall see,
  those who have not heard shall ponder it.

Who would believe what we have heard?
  To whom has the arm of the Lord been
    revealed?
He grew up like a sapling before him,
  like a shoot from the parched earth;
There was in him no stately bearing to make
    us look at him,
  nor appearance that would attract us to
    him.
He was spurned and avoided by men,
  a man of suffering, accustomed to infirm-
    ity,
One of those from whom men hide their
    faces,
  spurned, and we held him in no esteem.

Yet it was our infirmities that he bore,
  our sufferings that he endured,
While we thought of him as stricken,
  as one smitten by God and afflicted.
But he was pierced for our offenses,
  crushed for our sins;

Upon him was the chastisement that makes
    us whole,
  by his stripes we were healed.
We had all gone astray like sheep,
  each following his own way;
But the Lord laid upon him
  the guilt of us all.

Though he was harshly treated, he submit-
    ted
  and opened not his mouth;
Like a lamb led to the slaughter
  or a sheep before the shearers,
  he was silent and opened not his mouth.
Oppressed and condemned, he was taken
    away,
  and who would have thought any more of
    his destiny?
When he was cut off from the land of the
    living,
  and smitten for the sin of his people,
A grave was assigned him among the wicked
  and a burial place with evildoers,
Though he had done no wrong
  nor spoken any falsehood.
[But the Lord was pleased
to crush him in infirmity.]

If he gives his life as an offering for sin,
  he shall see his descendants in a long life,
  and the will of the Lord shall be accom-
    plished through him.

Because of his affliction
  he shall see the light in fullness of days;
Through his suffering, my servant shall jus-
    tify many,
  and their guilt he shall bear.
Therefore I will give him his portion among
    the great,
  and he shall divide the spoils with the
    mighty,

120

Because he surrendered himself to death
and was counted among the wicked;
And he shall take away the sins of many,
and win pardon for their offenses.

Responsorial Psalm   Ps 31, 2. 6. 12–13.
                              15–16. 17. 25
Father, I put my life in your hands.
In you, O Lord, I take refuge;
let me never be put to shame.
In your justice rescue me.
Into your hands I commend my spirit;
you will redeem me, O Lord, O faithful
God.
Father, I put my life in your hands.
For all my foes I am an object of reproach,
a laughingstock to my neighbors, and a
dread to my friends;
they who see me abroad flee from me.
I am forgotten like the unremembered dead;
I am like a dish that is broken.
Father, I put my life in your hands.
But my trust is in you, O Lord;
I say, "You are my God."
In your hands is my destiny; rescue me
from the clutches of my enemies and my
persecutors.
Father, I put my life in your hands.
Let your face shine upon your servant;
save me in your kindness.
Take courage and be stouthearted,
all you who hope in the Lord.
Father, I put my life in your hands.

READING II   Heb 4, 14–16; 5, 7–9
**We have a great high priest who has passed
through the heavens, Jesus, the Son of God;
let us hold fast to our profession of faith. For
we do not have a high priest who is unable
to sympathize with our weakness, but one**

who was tempted in every way that we are,
yet never sinned. So let us confidently approach the throne of grace to receive mercy
and favor and to find help in time of need.

**In the days when he was in the flesh,
Christ offered prayers and supplications
with loud cries and tears to God, who was
able to save him from death, and he was
heard because of his reverence. Son though
he was, he learned obedience from what he
suffered; and when perfected, he became
the source of eternal salvation for all who
obey him.**

GOSPEL   Jn 18, 1–19, 42
**The Passion of our Lord Jesus Christ accord-
ing to John.**

**Jesus went out with his disciples across the
Kidron valley. There was a garden there, and
he and his disciples entered it. The place was
familiar to Judas as well (the one who was to
hand him over) because Jesus had often met
there with his disciples. Judas took the cohort as well as police supplied by the chief
priests and the Pharisees, and came there
with lanterns, torches and weapons. Jesus,
aware of all that would happen to him,
stepped forward and said to them, "Who is
it you want?" "Jesus the Nazorean," they replied. "I am he," he answered. (Now Judas,
the one who was to hand him over, was right
there with them.) As Jesus said to them, "I
am he," they retreated slightly and fell to the
ground. Jesus put the question to them
again, "Who is it you want?" "Jesus the Nazorean," they repeated. "I have told you, I
am he," Jesus said. "If I am the one you
want, let these men go." (This was to fulfill
what he had said, "I have not lost one of
those you gave me.")**

Then Simon Peter, who had a sword, drew it and struck the slave of the high priest, severing his right ear. (The slave's name was Malchus.) At that Jesus said to Peter, "Put your sword back in its sheath. Am I not to drink the cup the Father has given me?"

Then the soldiers of the cohort, their tribune, and the Jewish police arrested Jesus and bound him. They led him first to Annas, the father-in-law of Caiaphas who was high priest that year. (It was Caiaphas who had proposed to the Jews the advantage of having one man die for the people.)

Simon Peter, in company with another disciple, kept following Jesus closely. This disciple, who was known to the high priest, stayed with Jesus as far as the high priest's courtyard, while Peter was left standing at the gate. The disciple known to the high priest came out and spoke to the woman at the gate, and then brought Peter in. This servant girl who kept the gate said to Peter, "Aren't you one of this man's followers?" "Not I," he replied.

Now the night was cold, and the servants and the guards who were standing around had made a charcoal fire to warm themselves by. Peter joined them and stood there warming himself.

The high priest questioned Jesus, first about his disciples, then about his teaching. Jesus answered by saying:

> "I have spoken publicly to any who would listen.
> I always taught in a synagogue or in the temple area
> where all the Jews come together.
> There was nothing secret about anything I said.

Why do you question me? Question those who heard me when I spoke. It should be obvious they will know what I said." At this reply, one of the guards who was standing nearby gave Jesus a sharp blow on the face. "Is that any way to answer the high priest?" he said. Jesus replied, "If I said anything wrong produce the evidence, but if I spoke the truth why hit me?" Annas next sent him, bound, to the high priest Caiaphas.

All through this, Simon Peter had been standing there warming himself. They said to him, "Are you not a disciple of his?" He denied: "I am not!" "But did I not see you with him in the garden?" insisted one of the high priest's slaves—as it happened, a relative of the man whose ear Peter had severed. Peter denied it again. At that moment a cock began to crow.

At daybreak they brought Jesus from Caiaphas to the praetorium. They did not enter the praetorium themselves, for they had to avoid ritual impurity if they were to eat the Passover supper. Pilate came out to them. "What accusation do you bring against this man?" he demanded. "If he were not a criminal," they retorted, "we would certainly not have handed him over to you." At this Pilate said, "Why do you not take him and pass judgment on him according to your law?" "We may not put anyone to death," the Jews answered. (This was to fulfill what Jesus had said, indicating the sort of death he would die.)

Pilate went back into the praetorium and summoned Jesus. "Are you the King of the Jews?" he asked him. Jesus answered, "Are you saying this on your own, or have others been telling you about me?" "I am no Jew!" Pilate retorted. "It is your own people and the chief priests who have handed you over to me. What have you done?" Jesus answered:

"My kingdom does not belong to this world.
If my kingdom were of this world,
my subjects would be fighting
to save me from being handed over to the Jews.
As it is, my kingdom is not here."
At this Pilate said to him, "So, then, you are a king?" Jesus replied:
"It is you who say I am a king.
The reason I was born,
the reason why I came into the world,
is to testify to the truth.
Anyone committed to the truth hears my voice."
"Truth!" said Pilate, "What does that mean?"

After this remark, Pilate went out again to the Jews and told them: "Speaking for myself, I find no case against this man. Recall your custom whereby I release to you someone at Passover time. Do you want me to release to you the king of the Jews?" They shouted back, "We want Barabbas, not this one!" (Barabbas was an insurrectionist.)

Pilate's next move was to take Jesus and have him scourged. The soldiers then wove a crown of thorns and fixed it on his head, throwing around his shoulders a cloak of royal purple. Repeatedly they came up to him and said, "All hail, King of the Jews!", slapping his face as they did so.

Pilate went out a second time and said to the crowd: "Observe what I do. I am going to bring him out to you to make you realize that I find no case against him." When Jesus came out wearing the crown of thorns and the purple cloak, Pilate said to them, "Look at the man!" As soon as the chief priests and the temple police saw him they shouted, "Crucify him! Crucify him!" Pilate said,

"Take him and crucify him yourselves; I find no case against him." "We have our law," the Jews responded, "and according to that law he must die because he made himself God's Son." When Pilate heard this kind of talk, he was more afraid than ever.

Going back into the praetorium, he said to Jesus, "Where do you come from?" Jesus would not give him any answer. "Do you refuse to speak to me?" Pilate asked him. "Do you not know that I have the power to release you and the power to crucify you?" Jesus answered:
"You would have no power over me whatever
unless it were given you from above.
That is why he who handed me over to you
is guilty of the greater sin."
After this, Pilate was eager to release him, but the Jews shouted, "If you free this man you are no 'Friend of Caesar.' Anyone who makes himself a king becomes Caesar's rival." Pilate heard what they were saying, then brought Jesus outside and took a seat on a judge's bench at the place called the Stone Pavement—Gabbatha in Hebrew. (It was the Preparation Day for Passover, and the hour was about noon.) He said to the Jews, "Look at your king!" At this they shouted, "Away with him! Away with him! Crucify him!" "What!" Pilate exclaimed. "Shall I crucify your king?" The chief priests replied, "We have no king but Caesar." In the end, Pilate handed Jesus over to be crucified.

Jesus was led away, and carrying the cross by himself, went out to what is called the Place of the Skull (in Hebrew, Golgotha). There they crucified him, and two others with him: one on either side, Jesus in the middle. Pilate had an inscription placed on the cross which read,

JESUS THE NAZOREAN
THE KING OF THE JEWS

This inscription, in Hebrew, Latin and Greek, was read by many of the Jews, since the place where Jesus was crucified was near the city. The chief priests of the Jews tried to tell Pilate, "You should not have written, 'The King of the Jews.' Write instead, 'This man claimed to be king of the Jews.'" Pilate answered, "What I have written, I have written."

After the soldiers had crucified Jesus they took his garments and divided them four ways, one for each soldier. There was also his tunic, but this tunic was woven in one piece from top to bottom and had no seam. They said to each other, "We shouldn't tear it. Let's throw dice to see who gets it." (The purpose of this was to have the Scripture fulfilled:

"They divided my garments among
   them;
for my clothing they cast lots.")
And this was what the soldiers did.

Near the cross of Jesus there stood his mother, his mother's sister, Mary the wife of Clopas, and Mary Magdalene. Seeing his mother there with the disciple whom he loved, Jesus said to his mother, "Woman, there is your son." In turn he said to the disciple, "There is your mother." From that hour onward, the disciple took her into his care.

After that, Jesus, realizing that everything was now finished, to bring the Scripture to fulfillment said, "I am thirsty." There was a jar there, full of common wine. They stuck a sponge soaked in this wine on some hyssop and raised it to his lips. When Jesus took the wine, he said, "Now it is finished." Then he bowed his head, and delivered over his spirit.

Since it was the Preparation Day the Jews did not want to have the bodies left on the cross during the sabbath, for that sabbath was a solemn feast day. They asked Pilate that the legs be broken and the bodies be taken away. Accordingly, the soldiers came and broke the legs of the men crucified with Jesus, first of one, then of the other. When they came to Jesus and saw that he was already dead, they did not break his legs. One of the soldiers ran a lance into his side, and immediately blood and water flowed out. (This testimony has been given by an eyewitness, and his testimony is true. He tells what he knows is true, so that you may believe.) These events took place for the fulfillment of Scripture:

"Break none of his bones."
There is still another Scripture passage which says:

"They shall look on him whom they
   have pierced."

Afterward, Joseph of Arimathea, a disciple of Jesus (although a secret one for fear of the Jews), asked Pilate's permission to remove Jesus' body. Pilate granted it, so they came and took the body away. Nicodemus (the man who had first come to Jesus at night) likewise came, bringing a mixture of myrrh and aloes which weighed about a hundred pounds. They took Jesus' body, and in accordance with Jewish burial custom bound it up in wrappings of cloth with perfumed oils. In the place where he had been crucified there was a garden, and in the garden a new tomb in which no one had ever been laid. Because of the Jewish Preparation

Day they laid Jesus there, for the tomb was close at hand.

Reflection on the Readings

The liturgy of the Church today is unlike that of any other day. It comprises three segments: the liturgy of the word; the veneration of the cross, and a Communion service. The setting and appearance of the church itself is stark and bare today. The quiet, solemn spirit is most appropriate.

A long reading from the prophet Isaiah unfolds a theology of suffering—that pain and suffering are redemptive, through our perseverance and fidelity we grow spiritually. Here we apply the "Suffering Servant" theme to Jesus who, personally innocent, accepted his suffering for all of us. It is he who redeems us through his death and resurrection.

In the passion narrative we hear again, this time from the Gospel according to John, the story of our redemption. This is not an event unconnected with you and me. Jesus is there because of his love for us. The emphasis on suffering should not be understood as an indication that suffering is the only way to grow spiritually. We can grow and gain insight through any occasion or event in our lives. It is fitting, however, at this time, to look at the reality of pain and suffering, and see in it a path to God.

The general intercessions offer both a prayer for many persons within the people of God and a reminder to us of many whom we often neglect to pray for. As a redeemed people of faith, we reaffirm our solidarity with the universal Church and beyond to all those who seek holiness in their respective faith journeys.

The second movement in the service is the veneration of the cross—a time for us to become very aware of the events of Good Friday as we honor the symbol of Jesus' crucifixion and death. Most of the time, the crucifix is an environmental fixture on the wall, a picture, an icon or a hanging. We tend to take it for granted. We are also more conscious of the triumphant resurrection of Jesus; so many times our crucifixes have the image of a resurrected, majestic, triumphant Jesus. But today we focus on the first part of the paschal mystery: Jesus suffered and died on a cross because of his love for us. The prayers and reproaches of this service emphasize God's continuing care for his people throughout time despite their inconsistent fidelity to him.

The final part of this service, for the baptized community, is the Communion service. Even without the usual celebration of Mass, participants desire to receive Jesus into their lives and hearts through the Eucharist. The prayers and reception of Communion serve as a bridge from Holy Thursday to Easter.

Suggestions for Prayer

1. Time to pray is a priority today. In the midst of a hectic pre-Easter schedule of family activities, we especially need an atmosphere of prayer and reflection. If at all possible, join in the parish services. But take personal quiet time to think about the events of the passion and death of Jesus—the great love which moved him to do what he has done for us. Do you really believe you are forgiven, loved, and redeemed by Jesus? What does this mean to you?

2. In a special way, we reflect today on the value of suffering for our purification, spiritual growth, self-knowledge, rela-

tionship with God. All of these are affected by our attitude toward pain and suffering. Take time to think about a time of suffering in your life—physical, emotional, or spiritual. How have you grown through that experience? What are your feelings about suffering in your life? In the lives of loved ones? What are we to learn through suffering in our lives?

3. The reason for Good Friday is the power of love that bursts through death into new life. It is God's overwhelming love for his people, for us, that brought his Son to earth. It is Jesus' love for his Father and for us that brought him to his public life, death and on through to his resurrection. What is the measure of our love in response? To what extent are we willing to suffer because of our love, our discipleship?

Suggestions for Journal Keeping

What has been your experience of death and loss—the loss of a loved one, a painful change in your life, having to let go of someone or something you love? What do you remember about that experience? Have you sensed new growth, new life or wisdom springing from it? Have you learned about yourself? About your relationship with God? Others? God's care for you? As you take time to reflect, use your journal to keep track of your insights and prayer.

Clare M. Colella

READING I   Gn 1, 1–2, 2

In the beginning, when God created the heavens and the earth, the earth was a formless wasteland, and darkness covered the abyss, while a mighty wind swept over the waters.

Then God said, "Let there be light," and there was light. God saw how good the light was. God then separated the light from the darkness. God called the light "day," and the darkness he called "night." Thus evening came, and morning followed—the first day.

Then God said, "Let there be a dome in the middle of the waters, to separate one body of water from the other." And so it happened: God made the dome, and it separated the water above the dome from the water below it. God called the dome "the sky." Evening came, and morning followed—the second day.

Then God said, "Let the water under the sky be gathered into a single basin, so that the dry land may appear." And so it happened: the water under the sky was gathered into its basin, and the dry land appeared. God called the dry land "the earth," and the basin of the water he called "the sea." God saw how good it was. Then God said, "Let the earth bring forth vegetation: every kind of plant that bears seed and every kind of fruit tree on earth that bears fruit with its seed in it." And so it happened: the earth brought forth every kind of plant that bears seed and every kind of fruit tree on earth

that bears fruit with its seed in it. God saw how good it was. Evening came, and morning followed—the third day.

Then God said: "Let there be lights in the dome of the sky, to separate day from night. Let them mark the fixed times, the days and the years, and serve as luminaries in the dome of the sky, to shed light upon the earth." And so it happened: God made the two great lights, the greater one to govern the day, and the lesser one to govern the night; and he made the stars. God set them in the dome of the sky, to shed light upon the earth, to govern the day and the night, and to separate the light from the darkness. God saw how good it was. Evening came, and morning followed—the fourth day.

Then God said, "Let the water teem with an abundance of living creatures, and on the earth let birds fly beneath the dome of the sky." And so it happened: God created the great sea monsters and all kinds of swimming creatures with which the water teems, and all kinds of winged birds. God saw how good it was, and God blessed them, saying, "Be fertile, multiply, and fill the water of the seas; and let the birds multiply on the earth." Evening came, and morning followed—the fifth day.

Then God said, "Let the earth bring forth all kinds of living creatures: cattle, creeping things, and wild animals of all kinds." And so it happened: God made all kinds of wild animals, all kinds of cattle, and all kinds of creeping things of the earth. God saw how good it was. Then God said: "Let us make man in our image, after our likeness. Let them have dominion over the fish of the sea, the birds of the air, and the cattle, and over all the wild animals and all the creatures that crawl on the ground."

God created man in his image;
   in the divine image he created him;
   male and female he created them.
God blessed them, saying: "Be fertile and multiply; fill the earth and subdue it. Have dominion over the fish of the sea, the birds of the air, and all the living things that move on the earth." God also said: "See, I give you every seed-bearing plant all over the earth and every tree that has seed-bearing fruit on it to be your food; and to all the animals of the land, all the birds of the air, and all the living creatures that crawl on the ground, I give all the green plants for food." And so it happened. God looked at everything he had made, and he found it very good. Evening came, and morning followed—the sixth day.

Thus the heavens and the earth and all their array were completed. Since on the seventh day God was finished with the work he had been doing, he rested on the seventh day from all the work he had undertaken.

Responsorial Psalm   Ps 104, 1–2. 5–6. 10.
12. 13–14. 24. 35

Lord, send out your Spirit,
   and renew the face of the earth.
Bless the Lord, O my soul!
   O Lord, my God, you are great indeed!
You are clothed with majesty and glory,
   robed in light as with a cloak.
Lord, send out your Spirit,
   and renew the face of the earth.
You fixed the earth upon its foundation,
   not to be moved forever;
With the ocean, as with a garment, you covered it;
   above the mountains the waters stood.
Lord, send out your Spirit,
   and renew the face of the earth.

You send forth springs into the watercourses
that wind among the mountains.
Beside them the birds of heaven dwell;
from among the branches they send forth
their song.
Lord, send out your Spirit,
and renew the face of the earth.
You water the mountains from your palace;
the earth is replete with the fruit of your
works.
You raise grass for the cattle,
and vegetation for men's use,
Producing bread from the earth.
Lord, send out your Spirit,
and renew the face of the earth.
How manifold are your works, O Lord!
In wisdom you have wrought them all—
the earth is full of your creatures.
Bless the Lord, O my soul! Alleluia.
Lord, send out your Spirit,
and renew the face of the earth.

Reflection on the Reading

In this reading from the Book of Genesis we hear the story of the creation of the world. From darkness came light, from the wasteland came life.

During the season of Lent and continuing into the celebration of Easter, God continues creating through us. There was the darkness of sin and despair; now there is the light of Christ, our hope. There was death and destruction; now there is renewed life through Christ.

In the creation story we hear about the passages of time in which God created new life, the first day, the second day, etc. What is a day in God's time? No doubt it is unlike our perception. But like the creation of life in the world, the creation of our renewed life will take time. And God will see how good it is and be pleased!

Suggestions for Prayer

1. Make a determined effort each day during this Easter season to become more aware of the gifts of creation. Say a prayer of thanksgiving for them.
2. Spend time experiencing new life through relationships, work and recreation.

Mary Kay Meier

READING II   Gn 22, 1–18

God put Abraham to the test. He called to him, "Abraham!" "Ready!" he replied. Then God said: "Take your son, Isaac, your only one, whom you love, and go to the land of Moriah. There you shall offer him up as a holocaust on a height that I will point out to you." Early the next morning Abraham saddled his donkey, took with him his son Isaac, and two of his servants as well, and with the wood that he had cut for the holocaust, set out for the place of which God had told him.

On the third day Abraham got sight of the place from afar. Then he said to his servants: "Both of you stay here with the donkey, while the boy and I go on over yonder. We will worship and then come back to you." Thereupon Abraham took the wood for the holocaust and laid it on his son Isaac's shoulders, while he himself carried the fire and the knife. As the two walked on together, Isaac spoke to his father Abraham. "Father!" he said. "Yes, son," he replied. Isaac continued, "Here are the fire and the wood, but where is the sheep for the holocaust?"

128

"Son," Abraham answered, "God himself will provide the sheep for the holocaust." Then the two continued going forward.

When they came to the place of which God had told him, Abraham built an altar there and arranged the wood on it. Next he tied up his son Isaac, and put him on top of the wood on the altar. Then he reached out and took the knife to slaughter his son. But the Lord's messenger called to him from heaven, "Abraham, Abraham!" "Yes, Lord," he answered. "Do not lay your hand on the boy," said the messenger. "Do not do the least thing to him. I know now how devoted you are to God, since you did not withhold from me your own beloved son." As Abraham looked about, he spied a ram caught by its horns in the thicket. So he went and took the ram and offered it up as a holocaust in place of his son. Abraham named the site Yahweh-yireh; hence people now say, "On the mountain the Lord will see."

Again the Lord's messenger called to Abraham from heaven and said: "I swear by myself, declares the Lord, that because you acted as you did in not withholding from me your beloved son, I will bless you abundantly and make your descendants as countless as the stars of the sky and the sands of the seashore; your descendants shall take possession of the gates of their enemies, and in your descendants all the nations of the earth shall find blessing—all this because you obeyed my command."

Responsorial Psalm Ps 16, 5. 8. 9–10. 11
Keep me safe, O God;
  you are my hope.
**O Lord, my allotted portion and my cup,
  you it is who hold fast my lot.**
I set the Lord ever before me;
  with him at my right hand I shall not be
  disturbed.
Keep me safe, O God;
  you are my hope.
**Therefore my heart is glad and my soul re-
  joices,
  my body, too, abides in confidence;
Because you will not abandon my soul to the
  nether world,
  nor will you suffer your faithful one to undergo corruption.**
Keep me safe, O God;
  you are my hope.
**You will show me the path to life,
  fullness of joys in your presence,
  the delights at your right hand forever.**
Keep me safe, O God;
  you are my hope.

Reflection on the Reading
Abraham and his wife Sarah had been waiting for a child for all of their wedded life. Finally, a miracle happened! Sarah gave birth to a son, even though she was well beyond child-bearing years. Therefore, can you imagine the heartache and pain Abraham must have suffered as he prepared to make a sacrifice of this child? He loved the Lord without question. Without striking bargains or complaining, he accepted the will of God for him. He had passed the test. God's messenger now knew how devoted Abraham was to God. Abraham was blessed abundantly through countless descendants.

We sometimes think that because we love God, life should be easy. How disappointed and angry we can become when we realize daily life can become difficult and messy when we follow Christ. We cannot bargain

129

with Christ, but, like Abraham, we can continue the struggle of putting complete trust in him.

Suggestions for Prayer

1. Reflect on a time when you were going through a difficult time in your life. How did you respond? Did you call upon God at the time? What was the result?
2. Repeat the responsorial psalm (Psalm 16) of the reading daily: "Keep me safe, O God; you are my hope."

Mary Kay Meier

READING III   Ex 14, 15–15, 1

The Lord said to Moses, "Why are you crying out to me? Tell the Israelites to go forward. And you, lift up your staff and, with hand outstretched over the sea, split the sea in two, that the Israelites may pass through it on dry land. But I will make the Egyptians so obstinate that they will go in after them. Then I will receive glory through Pharaoh and all his army, his chariots and charioteers. The Egyptians shall know that I am the Lord, when I receive glory through Pharaoh and his chariots and charioteers."

The angel of God, who had been leading Israel's camp, now moved and went around behind them. The column of cloud also, leaving the front, took up its place behind them, so that it came between the camp of the Egyptians and that of Israel. But the cloud now became dark, and thus the night passed without the rival camps coming any closer together all night long. Then Moses stretched out his hand over the sea, and the Lord swept the sea with a strong east wind throughout the night and so turned it into dry land. When the water was thus divided, the Israelites marched into the midst of the sea on dry land, with the water like a wall to their right and to their left.

The Egyptians followed in pursuit; all Pharaoh's horses and chariots and charioteers went after them right into the midst of the sea. In the night watch just before dawn the Lord cast through the column of the fiery cloud upon the Egyptian force a glance that threw it into a panic; and he so clogged their chariot wheels that they could hardly drive. With that the Egyptians sounded the retreat before Israel, because the Lord was fighting for them against the Egyptians.

Then the Lord told Moses, "Stretch out your hand over the sea, that the water may flow back upon the Egyptians, upon their chariots and their charioteers." So Moses stretched out his hand over the sea, and at dawn the sea flowed back to its normal depth. The Egyptians were fleeing head on toward the sea, when the Lord hurled them into its midst. As the water flowed back, it covered the chariots and the charioteers of Pharaoh's whole army which had followed the Israelites into the sea. Not a single one of them escaped. But the Israelites had marched on dry land through the midst of the sea, with the water like a wall to their right and to their left. Thus the Lord saved Israel on that day from the power of the Egyptians. When Israel saw the Egyptians lying dead on the seashore and beheld the great power that the Lord had shown against the Egyptians, they feared the Lord and believed in him and in his servant Moses.

Then Moses and the Israelites sang this song to the Lord:

I will sing to the Lord, for he is gloriously triumphant;
  horse and chariot he has cast into the sea.

Responsorial Psalm   Ex 15, 1–2. 3–4. 5–6.
                              17–18
Let us sing to the Lord;
  he has covered himself in glory.
I will sing to the Lord, for he is gloriously triumphant;
  horse and chariot he has cast into the sea.
My strength and my courage is the Lord,
  and he has been my savior.
He is my God, I praise him;
  the God of my father, I extol him.
Let us sing to the Lord;
  he has covered himself in glory.
The Lord is a warrior,
  Lord is his name!
Pharaoh's chariots and army he hurled into the sea;
  the elite of his officers were submerged in the Red Sea.
Let us sing to the Lord;
  he has covered himself in glory.
The flood waters covered them,
  they sank into the depths like a stone.
Your right hand, O Lord, magnificent in power,
  your right hand, O Lord, has shattered the enemy.
Let us sing to the Lord;
  he has covered himself in glory.
You brought in the people you redeemed
  and planted them on the mountain of your inheritance.
The place where you made your seat, O Lord,
  the sanctuary, O Lord, which your hands established.
The Lord shall reign forever and ever.

Let us sing to the Lord;
  he has covered himself in glory.

Reflection on the Reading
   In the prayer for the blessing of the baptismal water we hear these words:

> Through the waters of the Red Sea
> you led Israel out of slavery
> to be an image of God's holy people
> set free from sin by baptism.

As we listen to this reading during the Easter vigil we are reminded that the waters of the Red Sea prefigure the water of baptism. As Moses led his people from slavery to freedom through the sea, Jesus leads us from death to life through baptism. Through baptism you will share in Jesus' death and resurrection. You too will go into the water of death and liberation. Like Jesus you will die, leaving sin behind. Like Jesus you will rise, filled with his power and life. Jesus is our Moses, leading us to enter new life in our promised land—the Christian community.

Suggestion for Prayer
   From what slavery do you need to be liberated? What part of you must die if you are to rise with Christ?

                              Robert M. Hamma

READING IV   Is 54, 5–14
He who has become your husband is your Maker;
  his name is the Lord of hosts;
Your redeemer is the Holy One of Israel,
  called God of all the earth.
The Lord calls you back,
  like a wife forsaken and grieved in spirit,

A wife married in youth and then cast off,
 says your God.
For a brief moment I abandoned you,
 but with great tenderness I will take you
 back.
In an outburst of wrath, for a moment
 I hid my face from you;
But with enduring love I take pity on you,
 says the Lord, your redeemer.
This is for me like the days of Noah,
 when I swore that the waters of Noah
 should never again deluge the earth;
So I have sworn not to be angry with you,
 or to rebuke you.
Though the mountains leave their place
 and the hills be shaken,
My love shall never leave you
 nor my covenant of peace be shaken,
 says the Lord, who has mercy on you.
O afflicted one, storm-battered and unconsoled,
 I lay your pavements in carnelians,
 and your foundations in sapphires;
I will make your battlements of rubies,
 your gates of carbuncles,
 and all your walls of precious stones.
All your sons shall be taught by the Lord,
 and great shall be the peace of your children.
In justice shall you be established,
 far from the fear of oppression,
 where destruction cannot come near you.

Responsorial Psalm   Ps 30, 2. 4. 5–6. 11–
                                     12. 13
I will praise you, Lord,
 for you have rescued me.
I will extol you, O Lord, for you drew me
 clear
 and did not let my enemies rejoice over
 me.

O Lord, you brought me up from the nether
 world;
 you preserved me from among those
 going down into the pit.
I will praise you, Lord,
 for you have rescued me.
Sing praise to the Lord, you his faithful ones,
 and give thanks to his holy name.
For his anger lasts but a moment;
 a lifetime, his good will.
At nightfall, weeping enters in,
 but with the dawn, rejoicing.
I will praise you, Lord,
 for you have rescued me.
Hear, O Lord, and have pity on me;
 O Lord, be my helper.
You changed my mourning into dancing;
 O Lord, my God, forever will I give you
 thanks.
I will praise you, Lord,
 for you have rescued me.

Reflection on the Reading
 This reading is filled with very evocative
words. On the one hand there is great sadness—forsaken, abandoned, afflicted, storm-
battered, unconsoled. On the other hand
there is great joy—tenderness, enduring
love, pity. The prophet Isaiah compares our
relationship to the love between a husband
and wife. Our Creator has raised us high and
made us his spouse. Yet we have been unfaithful and so become "a wife forsaken and
grieved in spirit." But now the Lord takes us
back with great tenderness and enduring
love. He promises to be faithful to us even if
we are unfaithful:

 Though the mountains leave their place
  and the hills be shaken,
 My love shall never leave you.

132

God's love is lavished upon us. We are adorned with precious stones.

This is the covenant of fidelity that the Lord makes with you. It is sealed in your baptism.

Suggestion for Prayer

Christian mystics such as John of the Cross have often compared our relationship with the Lord to a marriage. Reflect on God's love for you in this way. Do you find this a helpful image? Why?

Robert M. Hamma

READING V   Is 55, 1–11
Thus says the Lord:
All you who are thirsty,
  come to the water!
You who have no money,
  come, receive grain and eat;
Come, without paying and without cost,
  drink wine and milk!
Why spend your money for what is not bread;
  your wages for what fails to satisfy?
Heed me, and you shall eat well,
  you shall delight in rich fare.
Come to me heedfully,
  listen, that you may have life.
I will renew with you the everlasting covenant,
  the benefits assured to David.
As I made him a witness to the peoples,
  a leader and commander of nations,
So shall you summon a nation you knew not,
  and nations that knew you not shall run to you,
Because of the Lord, your God,
  the Holy One of Israel, who has glorified you.

Seek the Lord while he may be found,
  call him while he is near.
Let the scoundrel forsake his way,
  and the wicked man his thoughts;
Let him turn to the Lord for mercy;
  to our God, who is generous in forgiving.
For my thoughts are not your thoughts,
  nor are your ways my ways, says the Lord.
As high as the heavens are above the earth,
  so high are my ways above your ways
    and my thoughts above your thoughts.
For just as from the heavens
  the rain and snow come down
And do not return there
  till they have watered the earth,
  making it fertile and fruitful,
Giving seed to him who sows
  and bread to him who eats,
So shall my word be
  that goes forth from my mouth;
It shall not return to me void,
  but shall do my will,
  achieving the end for which I sent it.

Responsorial Psalm   Is 12, 2–3. 4. 5–6
You will draw water joyfully from the
    springs of salvation.
God indeed is my savior;
  I am confident and unafraid.
My strength and my courage is the Lord,
  and he has been my savior.
With joy you will draw water
  at the fountain of salvation.
You will draw water joyfully from the
    springs of salvation.
Give thanks to the Lord, acclaim his name;
  among the nations make known his deeds,
  proclaim how exalted is his name.
You will draw water joyfully from the
    springs of salvation.

Sing praise to the Lord for his glorious
  achievement;
  let this be known throughout all the earth.
Shout with exultation, O city of Zion,
  for great in your midst
  is the Holy One of Israel!
You will draw water joyfully from the
  springs of salvation.

Reflection on the Reading

An invitation is given to us. Come to the
water. Come and eat. Come and be re-
freshed. Come and listen. Come and have
new life. Come and renew the covenant with
me.

Conversion is asked of us. Seek the Lord.
Turn to the Lord for mercy. Forsake wicked
ways. Listening to God's word will refresh us.
This was the reason for our creation, to rejoice, celebrate and be made whole through
him.

Suggestion for Prayer

Prayerfully read the responsorial psalm
from Isaiah 12:2–6. Reflect on phrases such
as, "I am confidant and unafraid," "Give
thanks to the Lord," "Sing praise to the Lord
for his glorious achievements" and others
you choose that are meaningful to you.

Mary Kay Meier

READING VI   Bar 3, 9–15. 32–4, 4
Hear, O Israel, the commandments of life:
  listen, and know prudence!
How is it, Israel,
  that you are in the land of your foes,
  grown old in a foreign land,
Defiled with the dead,

accounted with those destined for the
  nether world?
You have forsaken the fountain of wisdom!
  Had you walked in the way of God,
  you would have dwelt in enduring peace.
Learn where prudence is,
  where strength, where understanding;
That you may know also
  where are length of days, and life,
  where light of the eyes, and peace.

Who has found the place of wisdom,
  who has entered into her treasuries?
He who knows all things knows her;
  he has probed her by his knowledge—
He who established the earth for all time,
  and filled it with four-footed beasts;
He who dismisses the light, and it departs,
  calls it, and it obeys him trembling;
Before whom the stars at their posts
  shine and rejoice;
When he calls them, they answer, "Here we
  are!"
  shining with joy for their Maker.
Such is our God;
  no other is to be compared to him:
He has traced out all the way of understanding,
  and has given her to Jacob, his servant,
  to Israel, his beloved son.

Since then she has appeared on earth,
  and moved among men.
She is the book of the precepts of God,
  the law that endures forever;
All who cling to her will live,
  but those will die who forsake her.
Turn, O Jacob, and receive her:
  walk by her light toward splendor.
Give not your glory to another,
  your privileges to an alien race.

Blessed are we, O Israel;
  for what pleases God is known to us!

Responsorial Psalm   Ps 19, 8. 9. 10. 11
Lord, you have the words of everlasting
  life.
The law of the Lord is perfect,
  refreshing the soul;
The decree of the Lord is trustworthy,
  giving wisdom to the simple.
Lord, you have the words of everlasting
  life.
The precepts of the Lord are right,
  rejoicing the heart;
The command of the Lord is clear,
  enlightening the eye.
Lord, you have the words of everlasting
  life.
The fear of the Lord is pure,
  enduring forever;
The ordinances of the Lord are true,
  all of them just.
Lord, you have the words of everlasting
  life.
They are more precious than gold,
  than a heap of purest gold;
Sweeter also than syrup
  or honey from the comb.
Lord, you have the words of everlasting
  life.

Reflection on the Reading
  From the prophet Baruch, we are instructed to walk in the way of God and live
in peace forever. It was when Israel turned
away from God that her enemies destroyed
her.
  God calls us to the light, not the darkness.
He has created all for our joy, not our de-
mise. We are invited into oneness with God,

rather than separation. All ways of giving
glory to God have been revealed to us. It is in
following his ways that we receive enduring
peace. The responsorial psalm of this reading
reminds us, "Lord, you have the words of everlasting life."

Suggestion for Prayer
  In today's culture the advertising world
tells us we can find peace and happiness in
what we eat, drive, wear, or where we live,
etc. This reading tells us we find peace and
happiness in the Lord. Where are you in your
search for peace? What modern day pres-
sures prevent you from responding to God's
invitation to you?

                              Mary Kay Meier

READING VII   Ez 36, 16–28
Thus the word of the Lord came to me: Son
of man, when the house of Israel lived in
their land, they defiled it by their conduct
and deeds. In my sight their conduct was like
the defilement of a menstruous woman.
Therefore I poured out my fury upon them
[because of the blood which they poured out
on the ground, and because they defiled it
with idols]. I scattered them among the na-
tions, dispersing them over foreign lands;
according to their conduct and deeds I
judged them. But when they came among
the nations [wherever they came], they
served to profane my holy name, because it
was said of them: "These are the people of
the Lord, yet they had to leave their land."
So I have relented because of my holy name
which the house of Israel profaned among
the nations where they came. Therefore say
to the house of Israel: Thus says the Lord

God: Not for your sakes do I act, house of Israel, but for the sake of my holy name, which you profaned among the nations to which you came. I will prove the holiness of my great name, profaned among the nations, in whose midst you have profaned it. Thus the nations shall know that I am the Lord, says the Lord God, when in their sight I prove my holiness through you. For I will take you away from among the nations, gather you from all the foreign lands, and bring you back to your own land. I will sprinkle clean water upon you to cleanse you from all your impurities, and from all your idols I will cleanse you. I will give you a new heart and place a new spirit within you, taking from your bodies your stony hearts and giving you natural hearts. I will put my spirit within you and make you live by my statutes, careful to observe my decrees. You shall live in the land I gave your fathers; you shall be my people, and I will be your God.

Responsorial Psalm   Ps 42, 3. 5; 43, 3. 4

Like a deer that longs for running streams,
    my soul longs for you, my God.

**Athirst is my soul for God, the living God.
    When shall I go and behold the face of God?**

Like a deer that longs for running streams,
    my soul longs for you, my God.

**I went with the throng
    and led them in procession to the house of God,
Amid loud cries of joy and thanksgiving,
    with the multitude keeping festival.**

Like a deer that longs for running streams,
    my soul longs for you, my God.

**Send forth your light and your fidelity;
    they shall lead me on**

**And bring me to your holy mountain,
    to your dwelling-place.**

Like a deer that longs for running streams,
    my soul longs for you, my God.

**Then will I go in to the altar of God,
    the God of my gladness and joy;
Then will I give you thanks upon the harp,
    O God, my God!**

Like a deer that longs for running streams,
    my soul longs for you, my God.

Reflection on the Reading

Despite the disobedience and deeds of Israel, God again proclaims his covenant with them, "You shall be my people and I will be your God." At the time Israel turned away from the Lord, they were overcome by enemies and scattered to foreign lands. But now the Lord, once more, welcomes them back to him by washing them clean of their impurities. It is to us he speaks: "I will give you a new heart and place a new spirit within you, taking from your bodies your stony hearts and giving you natural hearts." These words are fulfilled during the baptismal rite of this night's celebration. We are welcomed by the Lord despite our past. We are washed clean in the living waters. We are given new hearts. We are given new spirits.

Suggestions for Prayer

1. In your imagination place yourself at a place of cool water. Imagine yourself touching it, gently. Scooping it into your hands, allow it to run down your face, your arms, your entire self. Reflect on those feelings your imagination has developed.

2. Use Psalm 51, the responsorial psalm of this reading, as your night-time prayer for this week.

Mary Kay Meier

EPISTLE Rom 6, 3–11

Are you not aware that we who were baptized into Christ Jesus were baptized into his death? Through baptism into his death we were buried with him, so that, just as Christ was raised from the dead by the glory of the Father, we too might live a new life. If we have been united with him through likeness to his death, so shall we be through a like resurrection. This we know: our old self was crucified with him so that the sinful body might be destroyed and we might be slaves to sin no longer. A man who is dead has been freed from sin. If we have died with Christ, we believe that we are also to live with him. We know that Christ, once raised from the dead, will never die again; death has no more power over him. His death was death to sin, once for all; his life is life for God. In the same way, you must consider yourselves dead to sin but alive for God in Christ Jesus.

Responsorial Psalm Ps 118, 1–2. 16. 17. 22–23

Alleluia. Alleluia. Alleluia.
Give thanks to the Lord, for he is good,
  for his mercy endures forever.
Let the house of Israel say,
  "His mercy endures forever."
Alleluia. Alleluia. Alleluia.
The right hand of the Lord has struck with power;
  the right hand of the Lord is exalted.
I shall not die, but live,
  and declare the works of the Lord.
Alleluia. Alleluia. Alleluia.
The stone which the builders rejected
  has become the cornerstone.
By the Lord has this been done;
  It is wonderful in our eyes.
Alleluia. Alleluia. Alleluia.

Reflection on the Readings
  Through baptism we die with Christ. Our old self is washed clean. We are no longer slaves to sin but free people living in and with Christ. Christ will never die again. Death has power over him no longer. We are also freed from death, the death we experience from sin. Sin and darkness need control us no longer. Through the death of Christ we are alive in God. It is a time to celebrate! It is a time to praise God's power and might!

Suggestion for Prayer
  As a catechumen still journeying toward the waters of baptism, reflect on this reading often during this week. Converse with God. Share with him your struggles in turning away from darkness to the light, from death of the old self to a new life.

Mary Kay Meier

GOSPEL A Mt 28, 1–10

After the sabbath, as the first day of the week was dawning, Mary Magdalene came with the other Mary to inspect the tomb. Suddenly there was a mighty earthquake, as the angel of the Lord descended from heaven. He came to the stone, rolled it back, and sat on it. In appearance he resembled a flash of lightning while his garments were as

dazzling as snow. The guards grew paralyzed with fear of him and fell down like dead men. Then the angel spoke, addressing the women: "Do not be frightened. I know you are looking for Jesus the crucified, but he is not here. He has been raised, exactly as he promised. Come and see the spot where he was laid. Then go quickly and tell his disciples: 'He has been raised from the dead and now goes ahead of you to Galilee, where you will see him.' That is the message I have for you."

They hurried away from the tomb halfoverjoyed, half-fearful, and ran to carry the good news to his disciples. Suddenly, without warning, Jesus stood before them and said, "Peace!" The women came up and embraced his feet and did him homage. At this Jesus said to them, "Do not be afraid! Go and carry the news to my brothers that they are to go to Galilee, where they will see me."

GOSPEL B
Mk 16, 1–8

When the sabbath was over, Mary Magdalene, Mary the mother of James, and Salome bought perfumed oils with which they intended to go and anoint Jesus. Very early, just after sunrise, on the first day of the week they came to the tomb. They were saying to one another, "Who will roll back the stone for us from the entrance to the tomb?" When they looked, they found that the stone had been rolled back. (It was a huge one.) On entering the tomb they saw a young man sitting at the right, dressed in a white robe. This frightened them thoroughly, but he reassured them: "You need not be amazed! You are looking for Jesus of Nazareth, the one who was crucified. He has been raised up; he is not here. See the place where they

laid him. Go now and tell his disciples and Peter, 'He is going ahead of you to Galilee, where you will see him just as he told you.' " They made their way out and fled from the tomb bewildered and trembling; and because of their great fear, they said nothing to anyone.

GOSPEL C
Lk 24, 1–12

On the first day of the week, at dawn, the women came to the tomb bringing the spices they had prepared. They found the stone rolled back from the tomb; but when they entered the tomb, they did not find the body of the Lord Jesus. While they were still at a loss what to think of this, two men in dazzling garments appeared beside them. Terrified, the women bowed to the ground. The men said to them: "Why do you search for the living One among the dead? He is not here; he has been raised up. Remember what he said to you while he was still in Galilee—that the Son of Man must be delivered into the hands of sinful men, and be crucified, and on the third day rise again." With this reminder, his words came back to them.

On their return from the tomb, they told all these things to the Eleven and the others. The women were Mary of Magdala, Joanna, and Mary the mother of James. The other women with them also told the apostles, but the story seemed like nonsense and they refused to believe them. Peter, however, got up and ran to the tomb. He stooped down but could see nothing but the wrappings. So he went away full of amazement at what had occurred.

Reflection on the Readings

"He is risen." "He is not here." "Go and tell his disciples." These are the words of good news that greet the women when they arrive at the tomb of Jesus. However they probably weren't words of good news when they first heard them! The scene at the tomb was one of mystery, fear, doubt, confusion.

The women were still grieving their loss. They came to the tomb to attend to the ritual of anointing the body as prescribed by the law. Their concerns were getting past the Roman guards stationed at the tomb and rolling the stone away from the tomb. We need only to place ourselves in the scene to begin to imagine their feelings, when, upon their arrival, they are greeted by a man wearing a dazzling white robe telling them their Lord was not there.

Jesus had tried to prepare his followers for the events leading to his death, but even those closest to him did not understand. They tried to protect him in the garden when the soldiers came but, fearing for their own lives, they fled. They were still in hiding on this morning of resurrection. Would you have believed three trembling women when they told you, "He is risen"? The women were the first to receive the news of the resurrection. They were the first to see him in his glory.

They were his first messengers of the good news of his resurrection. Amazed, fearful and confused as they were, they were called to witness what the Lord had accomplished.

Suggestions for Prayer

1. It is the night of nights for Christianity! Celebrate his resurrection with praise and song.
2. Whether you be man or woman, reflect on the happenings of that resurrection morning. Remember a time you doubted Christ's presence or were confused by his words or perhaps frightened by his call. Thank him for "appearing" to you as he did.

Suggestion for Journal Keeping

According to Matthew's account of the resurrection, without warning Jesus stood before the women and said "Peace." Imagine yourself in that scene. How do you respond to him? What do you say? What do you do?

Mary Kay Meier

EASTER

A NEW BIRTH

...A SHARE IN THE RESURRECTION

141

Easter Sunday

READING I Acts 10, 34. 37–43

Peter addressed the people in these words: "I take it you know what has been reported all over Judea about Jesus of Nazareth, beginning in Galilee with the baptism John preached; of the way God anointed him with the Holy Spirit and power. He went about doing good works and healing all who were in the grip of the devil, and God was with him. We are witnesses to all that he did in the land of the Jews and in Jerusalem. They killed him finally, 'hanging him on a tree,' only to have God raise him up on the third day and grant that he be seen, not by all, but only by such witnesses as had been chosen beforehand by God—by us who ate and drank with him after he rose from the dead. He commissioned us to preach to the people and to bear witness that he is the one set apart by God as judge of the living and the dead. To him all the prophets testify, saying that everyone who believes in him has forgiveness of sins through his name."

Responsorial Psalm Ps 118, 1–2. 16–17. 22–23

This is the day the Lord has made;
  let us rejoice and be glad.

Give thanks to the Lord, for he is good,
  for his mercy endures forever.
Let the house of Israel say,
  "His mercy endures forever."
This is the day the Lord has made;
  let us rejoice and be glad.
"The right hand of the Lord has struck with
    power;
  the right hand of the Lord is exalted.
I shall not die, but live,
  and declare the works of the Lord.
This is the day the Lord has made;
  let us rejoice and be glad.
The stone which the builders rejected
  has become the cornerstone.
By the Lord has this been done;
  it is wonderful in our eyes.
This is the day the Lord has made;
  let us rejoice and be glad.

READING II Col 3, 1–4

Since you have been raised up in company with Christ, set your heart on what pertains to higher realms where Christ is seated at God's right hand. Be intent on things above rather than on things of earth. After all, you have died! Your life is hidden now with Christ in God. When Christ our life appears, then you shall appear with him in glory.

OR

READING II   1 Cor 5, 6–8

Do you not know that a little yeast has its effect all through the dough? Get rid of the old yeast to make of yourselves fresh dough, unleavened loaves, as it were; Christ our Passover has been sacrificed. Let us celebrate the feast not with the old yeast, that of corruption and wickedness, but with the unleavened bread of sincerity and truth.

GOSPEL   Jn 20, 1–9

Early in the morning on the first day of the week, while it was still dark, Mary Magdalene came to the tomb. She saw that the stone had been moved away, so she ran off to Simon Peter and the other disciple (the one Jesus loved) and told them, "The Lord has been taken from the tomb! We don't know where they have put him!" At that, Peter and the other disciple started out on their way toward the tomb. They were running side by side, but then the other disciple outran Peter and reached the tomb first. He did not enter but bent down to peer in, and saw the wrappings lying on the ground. Presently, Simon Peter came along behind him and entered the tomb. He observed the wrappings on the ground and saw the piece of cloth which had covered the head not lying with the wrappings, but rolled up in a place by itself. Then the disciple who had arrived first at the tomb went in. He saw and believed. (Remember, as yet they did not understand the Scripture that Jesus had to rise from the dead.)

Reflection on the Readings

In today's first reading Peter proclaims: "God was with Jesus." God worked in and through Jesus. His very name, Jesus, means

"God is our salvation." Thus we might ask ourselves: When we pray or act in the name of Jesus, what are we saying? Are we not saying that we believe in a God who works in us and in the Church too?

Christian prayer is always in the name of Jesus. Praying in the name of Jesus does not necessarily mean that we understand all of what God is doing. Rather, it is an acclamation of faith and trust. It is an act of placing ourselves in God's hands rather than relying on ourselves alone. It is a statement of our intention and desire to enter into fuller union with the will of God.

As individuals, and as a people, we move toward belief. It is always ahead of us. The Gospel makes it clear that the disciples did not understand the consequences of the resurrection of Jesus from the dead, yet they believed. Our task is to ponder the consequences for ourselves, today.

Where are we looking for the Lord? Do we look in the empty tomb, or among the living where healing and reconciliation are happening?

Suggestions for Prayer

1. The word, the name "Jesus" is a prayer. Repeat it often. You can develop your own rhythm. You can add petitions such as "Be with me" or "Give me life."
2. The psalm announces: "This is the day that the Lord has made." Begin your day with these words on your lips. Add your own reasons for giving thanks to God for the day.
3. Pray that God's will shall become more evident. Reflect upon the encounters of your day and ask for God's guidance and wisdom, care and compassion.

Suggestion for Journal Keeping

The Church is sometimes called "the Easter people." Record the names of some of the people who have shared their faith with you, and who have accompanied you in the movement toward belief. How are they like Mary Magdalene, Peter, or the other disciple? How are you a disciple?

Elizabeth S. Lilly

Second Sunday of Easter A

READING I Acts 2, 42–47

The brethren devoted themselves to the apostles' instruction and the communal life, to the breaking of bread and the prayers. A reverent fear overtook them all, for many wonders and signs were performed by the apostles. Those who believed shared all things in common; they would sell their property and goods, dividing everything on the basis of each one's need. They went to the temple area together every day, while in their homes they broke bread. With exultant and sincere hearts they took their meals in common, praising God and winning the approval of all the people. Day by day the Lord added to their number those who were being saved.

Responsorial Psalm Ps 118, 2–4. 13–15. 22–24

Give thanks to the Lord for he is good,
  his love is everlasting.
Let the house of Israel say,
  "His mercy endures forever."
Let the house of Aaron say,
  "His mercy endures forever."
Let those who fear the Lord say,
  "His mercy endures forever."
Give thanks to the Lord for he is good,
  his love is everlasting.
I was hard pressed and was falling,
  but the Lord helped me.
My strength and my courage is the Lord,
  and he has been my savior.
The joyful shout of victory
  in the tents of the just:
Give thanks to the Lord for he is good,
  his love is everlasting.
The stone which the builders rejected
  has become the cornerstone.
By the Lord has this been done;
  it is wonderful in our eyes.
This is the day the Lord has made;
  let us be glad and rejoice in it.
Give thanks to the Lord for he is good,
  his love is everlasting.

READING II 1 Pt 1, 3–9

Praised be the God and Father of our Lord
  Jesus Christ,
he who in his great mercy gave us new birth;
a birth unto hope which draws its life
from the resurrection of Jesus Christ from
  the dead;
a birth to an imperishable inheritance
incapable of fading or defilement,
which is kept in heaven for you
who are guarded with God's power through
  faith;
a birth to a salvation which stands ready
to be revealed in the last days.

  There is cause for rejoicing here. You may
for a time have to suffer the distress of many
trials; but this is so that your faith, which is
more precious than the passing splendor of
fire-tried gold, may by its genuineness lead
to praise, glory, and honor when Jesus Christ

145

appears. Although you have never seen him, you love him, and without seeing you believe in him, and rejoice with inexpressible joy touched with glory because you are achieving faith's goal, your salvation.

GOSPEL   Jn 20, 19–31

On the evening of that first day of the week, even though the disciples had locked the doors of the place where they were for fear of the Jews, Jesus came and stood before them. "Peace be with you," he said. When he had said this, he showed them his hands and his side. At the sight of the Lord the disciples rejoiced. "Peace be with you," he said again.

"As the Father has sent me,
so I send you."
Then he breathed on them and said:
"Receive the Holy Spirit.
If you forgive men's sins,
they are forgiven them;
if you hold them bound,
they are held bound."

It happened that one of the Twelve, Thomas (the name means "Twin"), was absent when Jesus came. The other disciples kept telling him: "We have seen the Lord!" His answer was, "I'll never believe it without probing the nail-prints in his hands, without putting my finger in the nail-marks and my hand into his side."

A week later, the disciples were once more in the room, and this time Thomas was with them. Despite the locked doors, Jesus came and stood before them. "Peace be with you," he said; then, to Thomas: "Take your finger and examine my hands. Put your hand into my side. Do not persist in your unbelief, but believe!" Thomas said in re-

sponse, "My Lord and my God!" Jesus then said to him:

"You became a believer because you saw me.
Blest are they who have not seen and have believed."

Jesus performed many other signs as well—signs not recorded here—in the presence of his disciples. But these have been recorded to help you believe that Jesus is the Messiah, the Son of God, so that through this faith you may have life in his name.

Reflection on the Readings

With Psalm 118, the Church proclaims, "This is the day the Lord has made!" This is the day of Easter, not just twenty-four hours, but the fifty days of Easter, known in the early Church as "the Great Sunday."

On this Second Sunday of Eastertime, as the newly baptized gather with the faithful to celebrate the Eucharist, the Gospel provides a mirror to remind us of the mystery of our assembly. At the disciples' gathering on the first day of the week, the risen Christ appears, breathing the Spirit on them and sending them forth. This is what happens each Sunday. Christ, risen from the dead, is among us and says to us, "Blessed are you who have not seen and have believed."

Although we do not see Jesus as did the apostles, we do see Christ in the ongoing sign of his presence, his body the Church. This community of Christians is called to remain faithful to the teaching of the apostles who are witnesses to the resurrection, to the common life, evidenced by sharing of goods and made possible by the breaking of the bread, and to perseverance in prayer.

Recalling how in Acts the Lord day by day added new members to this community, on the Second Sunday of Easter we rejoice with all the newly baptized whom the Lord has added this year. St. Peter reminds us, however, that baptism is not only initiation into a new community, but a new birth, a share in the resurrection of Jesus Christ. From the womb of the baptismal font come the newborn who already possess an inheritance to be revealed in the last days. Because of this great hope, the baptized see their trials in a new light and look forward to that day anticipated now by the joy and communion of the Great Sunday.

Suggestions for Prayer

1. The members of the early Jerusalem Church shared all their goods in common as a sign of their community life. To what concrete expression of common life do you think the Spirit is guiding you?
2. Peter encourages us to be steadfast during our times of trial. What current situations or experiences in your own life does this bring to mind? What is your response?
3. In your imagination, listen to Jesus speak these words to you. How are you responding? What kind of dialogue ensues?

   Peace be with you.
   As the Father has sent me, so I send you.
   Blest are those that have not seen and have
      believed.

Suggestion for Journal Keeping
   Thomas doubted, yet his doubt led to the strongest affirmation of faith in the New Testament. Do you find yourself ever afraid to doubt in the area of religion? Other areas? Reflect on any experiences you may have had where doubt led to greater faith.

Emily J. Besl

Second Sunday of Easter

READING I   Acts 4, 32–35
The community of believers were of one heart and one mind. None of them ever claimed anything as his own; rather everything was held in common. With power the apostles bore witness to the resurrection of the Lord Jesus, and great respect was paid to them all; nor was there anyone needy among them, for all who owned property or houses sold them and donated the proceeds. They used to lay them at the feet of the apostles to be distributed to everyone according to his need.

Responsorial Psalm   Ps 118, 2–4. 13–15.
                                             22–24
Give thanks to the Lord for he is good,
   his love is everlasting.
**Let the house of Israel say,
   "His mercy endures forever."**
**Let the house of Aaron say,
   "His mercy endures forever."**
**Let those who fear the Lord say,
   "His mercy endures forever."**
Give thanks to the Lord for he is good,
   his love is everlasting.
**I was hard pressed and was falling,
   but the Lord helped me.**
**My strength and my courage is the Lord,
   and he has been my savior.**

The joyful shout of victory
  in the tents of the just:
Give thanks to the Lord for he is good,
  his love is everlasting.
The stone which the builders rejected
  has become the cornerstone.
By the Lord has this been done;
  it is wonderful in our eyes.
This is the day the Lord has made;
  let us be glad and rejoice in it.
Give thanks to the Lord for he is good,
  his love is everlasting.

READING II   1 Jn 5, 1–6
Everyone who believes that Jesus is the
    Christ
  has been begotten by God.
Now, everyone who loves the father
  loves the child he has begotten.
We can be sure that we love God's children
  when we love God
  and do what he has commanded.
The love of God consists in this:
  that we keep his commandments—
  and his commandments are not burden-
    some.
Everyone begotten of God conquers the
    world,
  and the power that has conquered the
    world
  is this faith of ours.
Who, then, is conqueror of the world?
  The one who believes that Jesus is the Son
    of God.
Jesus Christ it is who came through water
    and blood—
  not in water only,
  but in water and in blood.
It is the Spirit who testifies to this,
  and the Spirit is truth.

GOSPEL   Jn 20, 19–31
On the evening of that first day of the week,
even though the disciples had locked the
doors of the place where they were for fear
of the Jews, Jesus came and stood before
them. "Peace be with you," he said. When
he had said this, he showed them his hands
and his side. At the sight of the Lord the disciples rejoiced. "Peace be with you," he said
again.
  "As the Father has sent me,
  so I send you."
Then he breathed on them and said:
  "Receive the Holy Spirit.
  If you forgive men's sins,
  they are forgiven them;
  if you hold them bound,
  they are held bound."
  It happened that one of the Twelve,
Thomas (the name means "Twin"), was absent when Jesus came. The other disciples
kept telling him: "We have seen the Lord!"
His answer was, "I'll never believe it without probing the nail-prints in his hands,
without putting my finger in the nail-marks
and my hand into his side."
  A week later, the disciples were once
more in the room, and this time Thomas was
with them. Despite the locked doors, Jesus
came and stood before them. "Peace be
with you," he said; then, to Thomas: "Take
your finger and examine my hands. Put your
hand into my side. Do not persist in your
unbelief, but believe!" Thomas said in response, "My Lord and my God!" Jesus then
said to him:
  "You became a believer because you
    saw me.
  Blest are they who have not seen and
    have believed."

Jesus performed many other signs as well—signs not recorded here—in the presence of his disciples. But these have been recorded to help you believe that Jesus is the Messiah, the Son of God, so that through this faith you may have life in his name.

Reflection on the Readings

Thomas, like the other disciples, had put all his hope in Jesus of Nazareth. He had dedicated his life to following this great teacher who he believed was the Son of God. When Jesus died, all his hope died too. This was not the way things were supposed to end. In frustration and despair he refused to believe the others when they told him, "We have seen the Lord!" Only when Thomas touched the wounds of Jesus did he finally believe.

When things don't go the way we think they should or when tragedy strikes our life as it did with Thomas in the death of Jesus, we can easily lose faith and fall into despair. Jesus asks us to believe though we do not see. Jesus asks us to have faith even when we do not understand.

It is faith in the risen Lord which transforms a frightened, discouraged group of disciples locked away in a hiding place as described in the Gospel into the strong self-confident community of faith which is described in the reading from Acts. The risen Christ offers them peace and gives them the gift of forgiveness of sins. Christ empowers them and sends them out to preach the good news of the resurrection.

Those who now believe can no longer be defeated. As the First Letter of John proclaims, "Everyone begotten of God conquers the world, and the power that has conquered the world is this faith of ours."

Suggestions for Prayer

1. Reflect on the following questions:
   (a) Was there a time in your life in which you felt alone and afraid like the disciples in the beginning of the Gospel?
   (b) Were you able to find peace? How?
2. Thomas believed because he touched the wounds of Jesus. We can strengthen our faith by touching the wounded in our world. Think of an individual you know personally or a group in our society that is wounded. Ask for God's healing power for them. Ask God how you can help be an instrument of healing.
3. In the Gospel, the disciples proclaim, "We have seen the Lord!" Think of the events and people in your life which help you to say, "I have seen the Lord!"

Suggestion for Journal Keeping

The risen Lord sends us on a mission with the words, "As the Father has sent me, so I send you." Think of these words and ask yourself, "What is God asking of me?" Write in your journal three concrete ways in which you can carry out this mission in your life today.

Kathryn A. Schneider

Second Sunday of Easter

READING I   Acts 5, 12–16
Through the hands of the apostles, many signs and wonders occurred among the people. By mutual agreement they used to meet

in Solomon's Portico. No one else dared to join them, despite the fact that the people held them in great esteem. Nevertheless more and more believers, men and women in great numbers, were continually added to the Lord. The people carried the sick into the streets and laid them on cots and mattresses, so that when Peter passed by at least his shadow might fall on one or another of them. Crowds from the towns around Jerusalem would gather, too, bringing their sick and those who were troubled by unclean spirits, all of whom were cured.

Responsorial Psalm   Ps 118, 2–4. 13–15.
                                22–24
Give thanks to the Lord for he is good,
    his love is everlasting.
Let the house of Israel say,
    "His mercy endures forever."
Let the house of Aaron say,
    "His mercy endures forever."
Let those who fear the Lord say,
    "His mercy endures forever."
Give thanks to the Lord for he is good,
    his love is everlasting.
I was hard pressed and was falling,
    but the Lord helped me.
My strength and my courage is the Lord,
    and he has been my savior.
The joyful shout of victory
    in the tents of the just:
Give thanks to the Lord for he is good,
    his love is everlasting.
The stone which the builders rejected
    has become the cornerstone.
By the Lord has this been done;
    it is wonderful in our eyes.
This is the day the Lord has made;
    let us be glad and rejoice in it.

Give thanks to the Lord for he is good,
    his love is everlasting.

READING II   Rv 1, 9–11. 12–13. 17–19
I, John, your brother, who share with you the distress and the kingly reign and the endurance we have in Jesus, found myself on the island called Patmos because I proclaimed God's word and bore witness to Jesus. On the Lord's day I was caught up in ecstasy, and I heard behind me a piercing voice like the sound of a trumpet, which said, "Write on a scroll what you now see." I turned around to see whose voice it was that spoke to me. When I did so I saw seven lampstands of gold, and among the lampstands One like a Son of Man wearing an ankle-length robe, with a sash of gold about his breast.

When I caught sight of him I fell down at his feet as though dead. He touched me with his right hand and said: "There is nothing to fear. I am the First and the Last and the One who lives. Once I was dead but now I live—forever and ever. I hold the keys of death and the nether world. Write down, therefore, whatever you see in visions—what you see now and will see in time to come."

GOSPEL   Jn 20, 19–31
On the evening of that first day of the week, even though the disciples had locked the doors of the place where they were for fear of the Jews, Jesus came and stood before them. "Peace be with you," he said. When he had said this, he showed them his hands and his side. At the sight of the Lord the disciples rejoiced. "Peace be with you," he said again.

    "As the Father has sent me,
        so I send you."

Then he breathed on them and said:
"Receive the Holy Spirit.
If you forgive men's sins,
they are forgiven them;
if you hold them bound,
they are held bound."

It happened that one of the Twelve, Thomas (the name means "Twin"), was absent when Jesus came. The other disciples kept telling him: "We have seen the Lord!" His answer was, "I'll never believe it without probing the nail-prints in his hands, without putting my finger in the nail-marks and my hand into his side."

A week later, the disciples were once more in the room, and this time Thomas was with them. Despite the locked doors, Jesus came and stood before them. "Peace be with you," he said; then, to Thomas: "Take your finger and examine my hands. Put your hand into my side. Do not persist in your unbelief, but believe!" Thomas said in response, "My Lord and my God!" Jesus then said to him:
"You became a believer because you saw me.
Blest are they who have not seen and have believed."

Jesus performed many other signs as well—signs not recorded here—in the presence of his disciples. But these have been recorded to help you believe that Jesus is the Messiah, the Son of God, so that through this faith you may have life in his name.

Reflection on the Readings

Belief is a gift from God. We do not earn it, but we must choose to receive it. We must be open to faith to discern God's action within us. The Gospel begins with the ac-count of the locked doors. Yet, despite locked doors, God is present.

How often do we place ourselves behind locked doors? We act out of fear and in the search for security. Locked doors are our defenses, barriers between nations and individuals.

The Gospel is about freedom, salvation, and healing. One sign of the attitude of openness to these is the hands that are open and touching. We are called to be open to the peace of God, the gift of God's presence, in an attitude and posture without fear, an attitude that is forgiving.

Suggestions for Prayer

1. Pray for the gift of belief. Like Thomas, we pray that our eyes will be opened to see God. In the name of Jesus, we pray to see God in each other.

2. Pray for a release from fear and for the freedom of the Spirit. You may construct a list or litany of things which bind you and pray with this model: "From (name something such as fear or envy or bitterness) release me, Lord. Fill me with your Spirit of peace."

3. Pray not only with your mind and heart, but with your body also. Find a time and place to rest, a time of quiet, when and where you can sit peacefully. Find a comfortable position. Open your hands and unbind your arms and legs. Feel the presence of God in your midst and sense any tension or tightness. Relax.

Combine this body prayer with the second suggestion. Each time you name that which binds, close your hands into a fist. When you pray for peace, open your hands.

Suggestion for Journal Keeping

Reflect on all of the pressure you feel to preserve your personal security. Reflect on the fears that are raised, such as social rejection or national danger. Note all the instant cures, from beauty aids to massive weapons. Where do you find it easy to move beyond quick answers, and where do you find it difficult to examine more closely your symbol of security? What do you discover about your need for God?

Elizabeth S. Lilly

Third Sunday of Easter A

READING I   Acts 2, 14. 22–28

[On the day of Pentecost] Peter stood up with the Eleven, raised his voice, and addressed them: "You who are Jews, indeed all of you staying in Jerusalem! Listen to what I have to say: Men of Israel, listen to me! Jesus the Nazorean was a man whom God sent to you with miracles, wonders and signs as his credentials. These God worked through him in your midst, as you well know. He was delivered up by the set purpose and plan of God; you even used pagans to crucify and kill him. God freed him from death's bitter pangs, however, and raised him up again, for it was impossible that death should keep its hold on him. David says of him:
'I have set the Lord ever before me,
   with him at my right hand I shall not be
      disturbed.
My heart has been glad and my tongue has
      rejoiced,
   my body will live on in hope,

For you will not abandon my soul to the
      nether world,
   nor will you suffer your faithful one to
      undergo corruption.
You have shown me the paths of life;
   you will fill me with joy in your pres-
      ence.' "

Responsorial Psalm   Ps 16, 1–2. 5. 7–8.
                                          9–10. 11

Lord, you will show us the path of life.
Keep me, O God, for in you I take refuge;
   I say to the Lord, "My Lord are you."
O Lord, my allotted portion and my cup,
   you it is who hold fast my lot.
Lord, you will show us the path of life.
I bless the Lord who counsels me;
   even in the night my heart exhorts me.
I set the Lord ever before me;
   with him at my right hand I shall not be
      disturbed.
Lord, you will show us the path of life.
Therefore my heart is glad and my soul re-
      joices,
   my body, too, abides in confidence;
Because you will not abandon my soul to the
      nether world,
   nor will you suffer your faithful one to
      undergo corruption.
Lord, you will show us the path of life.
You will show me the path to life,
   fullness of joys in your presence,
      the delights at your right hand forever.
Lord, you will show us the path of life.

READING II   1 Pt 1, 17–21

In prayer you call upon a Father who judges each one justly, on the basis of his actions. Since this is so, conduct yourselves reverently during your sojourn in a strange land. Realize that you were delivered from the fu-

152

tile way of life your fathers handed on to you, not by any diminishable sum of silver or gold but by Christ's blood beyond all price: the blood of a spotless, unblemished lamb chosen before the world's foundation and revealed for your sake in these last days. It is through him you are believers in God, the God who raised him from the dead and gave him glory. Your faith and hope, then, are centered in God.

GOSPEL   Lk 24, 13–35

Two disciples of Jesus that same day [the first day of the sabbath] were making their way to a village named Emmaus seven miles distant from Jerusalem, discussing as they went all that had happened. In the course of their lively exchange, Jesus approached and began to walk along with them. However, they were restrained from recognizing him. He said to them, "What are you discussing as you go your way?" They halted in distress, and one of them, Cleopas by name, asked him, "Are you the only resident of Jerusalem who does not know the things that went on there these past few days?" He said to them, "What things?" They said: "All those that had to do with Jesus of Nazareth, a prophet powerful in word and deed in the eyes of God and all the people; how our chief priests and leaders delivered him up to be condemned to death, and crucified him. We were hoping that he was the one who would set Israel free. Besides all this, today, the third day since these things happened, some women of our group have just brought us some astonishing news. They were at the tomb before dawn and failed to find his body, but returned with the tale that they had seen a vision of angels who declared he was alive. Some of our number went to the tomb and found it to be just as the women said; but him they did not see."

Then he said to them, "What little sense you have! How slow you are to believe all that the prophets have announced! Did not the Messiah have to undergo all this so as to enter into his glory?" Beginning, then, with Moses and all the prophets, he interpreted for them every passage of Scripture which referred to him. By now they were near the village to which they were going, and he acted as if he were going farther. But they pressed him: "Stay with us. It is nearly evening—the day is practically over." So he went in to stay with them.

When he had seated himself with them to eat, he took bread, pronounced the blessing, then broke the bread and began to distribute it to them. With that their eyes were opened and they recognized him; whereupon he vanished from their sight. They said to one another, "Were not our hearts burning inside us as he talked to us on the road and explained the Scriptures to us?" They got up immediately and returned to Jerusalem, where they found the Eleven and the rest of the company assembled. They were greeted with, "The Lord has been raised! It is true! He has appeared to Simon." Then they recounted what had happened on the road and how they had come to know him in the breaking of bread.

Reflection on the Readings

To the eucharistic assembly of recently and formerly baptized, as well as catechumens still on the journey, the readings announce in yet another way the mystery of Easter realized anew in the sacraments of initiation.

Today's Gospel recounts how the two disciples on the road to Emmaus had come to know Christ in the breaking of the bread. When he sat down with them to eat, the stranger took bread, blessed it, broke it, and gave it to the disciples. These familiar actions unmistakably brought to mind the Eucharist. Upon recognition Jesus vanished, emphasizing that no longer would he be visible in this glorified body, but in the sacraments. Christ is encountered not only through sacramental symbols, through the meal, but also in the Scriptures. Thus the age-old pattern in Christian worship of word and sacrament is illustrated here as the means by which the risen Christ is made known to us.

God's raising Jesus from the tomb climaxes Peter's summary of the good news in the first reading, foreshadowed in Psalm 16. The redeeming love exemplified in God's rescue of the psalmist is decisively at work in the resurrection of Jesus, and in turn now opens up for us the path of life in baptism.

Eternal life, however, was purchased for us by the ransom of the blood of the Lamb. Here the early Church perceived a reference to the anointing in confirmation. Just as once the blood of the passover lamb anointed the doors of the Israelites, putting the angel of death to flight, so now with the seal of chrism Christ stands guard at our door, shutting out for the initiated the power of death.

Suggestions for Prayer

1. In the responsorial psalm today, we chant the words first applied to Jesus, but now extended to us who are regenerated in the womb of the font. Sing this psalm in prayer this week in thanksgiving for the call to baptism.
2. Christ appears in the Emmaus story as a preacher who explains the Scriptures.

Who have been important preachers in your life? What aspects of their message were significant to you at the time?

3. The image of a path appears in the first reading and the psalm, while the two disciples encounter Jesus on the road. The RCIA is often compared to a journey, with its sequential steps and stages. For what particular moments on the journey do you especially thank God? Which companions on the road have especially been instruments of God for you?

Suggestion for Journal Keeping

At first Jesus is a stranger to the two disciples; they don't recognize him. Their awareness of who he is comes later. In what ways have you grown to gradually recognize the presence of Christ in people or events in your life?

Emily J. Besl

Third Sunday of Easter

READING I Acts 3, 13–15. 17–19

Peter said to the people: "The 'God of Abraham, of Isaac, and of Jacob, the God of our fathers,' has glorified his Servant Jesus, whom you handed over and disowned in Pilate's presence when Pilate was ready to release him. You disowned the Holy and Just One and preferred instead to be granted the release of a murderer. You put to death the Author of life. But God raised him from the dead, and we are his witnesses.

"Yet I know, my brothers, that you acted out of ignorance, just as your leaders did.

God has brought to fulfillment by this means what he announced long ago through all the prophets: that his Messiah would suffer. Therefore, reform your lives! Turn to God, that your sins may be wiped away!"

Responsorial Psalm   Ps 4, 2. 4. 7–8. 9

Lord, let your face shine on us.

When I call, answer me, O my just God,
  you who relieve me when I am in distress;
  Have pity on me, and hear my prayer!
Lord, let your face shine on us.
Know that the Lord does wonders for his faithful one;
  the Lord will hear me when I call upon him.
Lord, let your face shine on us.
O Lord, let the light of your countenance shine upon us!
  You put gladness into my heart.
Lord, let your face shine on us.
As soon as I lie down, I fall peacefully asleep,
  for you alone, O Lord,
  bring security to my dwelling.
Lord, let your face shine on us.

READING II   1 Jn 2, 1–5

My little ones,
  I am writing this to keep you from sin.
But if anyone should sin,
  we have, in the presence of the Father,
Jesus Christ, an intercessor who is just.
  He is an offering for our sins,
  and not for our sins only,
  but for those of the whole world.
The way we can be sure of our knowledge of him
  is to keep his commandments.
The man who claims, "I have known him,"
  without keeping his commandments,

is a liar; in such a one there is no truth.
But whoever keeps his word
  truly has the love of God made perfect in him.

GOSPEL   Lk 24, 35–48

The disciples recounted what had happened on the road to Emmaus and how they had come to know Jesus in the breaking of bread.

While they were still speaking about all this, he himself stood in their midst [and said to them, "Peace to you."] In their panic and fright they thought they were seeing a ghost. He said to them, "Why are you disturbed? Why do such ideas cross your mind? Look at my hands and my feet; it is really I. Touch me, and see that a ghost does not have flesh and bones as I do." [As he said this he showed them his hands and feet.] They were still incredulous for sheer joy and wonder, so he said to them, "Have you anything here to eat?" They gave him a piece of cooked fish, which he took and ate in their presence. Then he said to them, "Recall those words I spoke to you when I was still with you: everything written about me in the law of Moses and the prophets and psalms had to be fulfilled." Then he opened their minds to the understanding of the Scriptures.

He said to them: "Thus it is likewise written that the Messiah must suffer and rise from the dead on the third day. In his name, penance for the remission of sins is to be preached to all the nations, beginning at Jerusalem. You are witnesses of this."

Reflection on the Readings

Because of Jesus' resurrection, there is no unforgivable sin. As Peter reminds the people in this passage from Acts, even though they had handed Christ over to death, God raised him up from the dead. "Therefore, reform your lives! Turn to God that your sins may be wiped away."

Peter spoke from experience. Having encountered the risen Jesus whom he had three times betrayed, he knew of Jesus' forgiveness first-hand. The other disciples also shared this awareness. Jesus' greeting of peace in the Gospel was likewise a word of forgiveness to them who had betrayed him. He communicated that peace through touch, through sharing a meal.

Jesus' forgiveness is offered to all. But in the second reading St. John reminds us that true knowledge of Jesus means putting our sins behind us and living according to his commandments. If we do not do this, our claim to be disciples is a lie. But if we do, God's love is perfected in us.

Suggestions for Prayer

1. *Reflect on one or more of the following questions:*
   - Do you truly believe that there is no unforgivable sin?
   - Is there any sin in your past that blocks you from approaching Jesus?
   - Is there any element of fear in you as you approach him? Why?
2. In your imagination, place yourself in the room with the disciples. Listen to Jesus words:

   Peace to you.
   Look at my hands and feet; it is really I.
   Touch me.

3. Psalm 4, the responsorial psalm, is one of the traditional psalms for night prayer. Read it prayerfully each night before sleep.

Suggestion for Journal Keeping

Describe an experience of betrayal and forgiveness. What were the emotions involved? What light does this shed for you on today's readings?

Robert M. Hamma

Third Sunday of Easter

READING I   Acts 5, 27–32. 40–41

The high priest began the interrogation of the apostles in this way: "We gave you strict orders not to teach about that name, yet you have filled Jerusalem with your teaching and are determined to make us responsible for that man's blood." To this, Peter and the apostles replied: "Better for us to obey God than men! The God of our fathers has raised up Jesus whom you put to death, 'hanging him on a tree.' He whom God has exalted at his right hand as ruler and savior is to bring repentance to Israel and forgiveness of sins. We testify to this. So too does the Holy Spirit, whom God has given to those that obey him." The Sanhedrin ordered the apostles not to speak again about the name of Jesus, and afterward dismissed them. The apostles for their part left the Sanhedrin full of joy that they had been judged worthy of ill-treatment for the sake of the Name.

Responsorial Psalm   Ps 30, 2. 4. 5–6. 11–12. 13

I will praise you, Lord,
   for you have rescued me.
**I will extol you, O Lord, for you drew me clear
   and did not let my enemies rejoice over me.**

O Lord, you brought me up from the nether
world;
  you preserved me from among those
    going down into the pit.
I will praise you, Lord,
  for you have rescued me.
Sing praise to the Lord, you his faithful ones,
  and give thanks to his holy name.
For his anger lasts but a moment;
  a lifetime, his good will.
At nightfall, weeping enters in,
  but with the dawn, rejoicing.
I will praise you, Lord,
  for you have rescued me.
Hear, O Lord, and have pity on me;
  O Lord, be my helper.
You changed my mourning into dancing;
  O Lord, my God, forever will I give you
    thanks.
I will praise you, Lord,
  for you have rescued me.

READING II   Rv 5, 11-14

I, John, had a vision, and I heard the voices
of many angels who surrounded the throne
and the living creatures and the elders. They
were countless in number, thousands and
tens of thousands, and they all cried out:
"Worthy is the Lamb that was slain
  to receive power and riches, wisdom and
    strength,
  honor and glory and praise!"
Then I heard the voices of every creature
in heaven and on earth and under the earth
and in the sea; everything in the universe
cried aloud:
"To the One seated on the throne, and to the
    Lamb,
  be praise and honor, glory and might,
  forever and ever!"
The four living creatures answered,

"Amen," and the elders fell down and worshiped.

GOSPEL   Jn 21, 1-19

At the Sea of Tiberias Jesus showed himself
to the disciples [once again]. This is how the
appearance took place. Assembled were Simon Peter, Thomas ("the Twin"), Nathanael
(from Cana in Galilee), Zebedee's sons, and
two other disciples. Simon Peter said to
them, "I'm going out to fish." "We'll join
you," they replied, and went off to get into
their boat. All through the night they caught
nothing. Just after daybreak Jesus was standing on the shore, though none of the disciples knew it was Jesus. He said to them,
"Children, have you caught anything to
eat?" "Not a thing," they answered. "Cast
your net off to the starboard side," he suggested, "and you will find something." So
they made a cast, and took so many fish they
could not haul the net in. Then the disciple
Jesus loved cried out to Peter, "It is the
Lord!" On hearing it was the Lord, Simon
Peter threw on some clothes—he was
stripped—and jumped into the water.

Meanwhile the other disciples came in the
boat, towing the net full of fish. Actually
they were not far from land—no more than
a hundred yards.

When they landed, they saw a charcoal
fire there with a fish laid on it and some
bread. "Bring some of the fish you just
caught," Jesus told them. Simon Peter went
aboard and hauled ashore the net loaded
with sizable fish—one hundred fifty-three of
them! In spite of the great number, the net
was not torn.

"Come and eat your meal," Jesus told
them. Not one of the disciples presumed to
inquire "Who are you?" for they knew it was

157

the Lord. Jesus came over, took the bread and gave it to them, and did the same with the fish. This marked the third time that Jesus appeared to the disciples after being raised from the dead.

When they had eaten their meal, Jesus said to Simon Peter, "Simon, son of John, do you love me more than these?" "Yes, Lord," Peter said, "you know that I love you." At which Jesus said, "Feed my lambs."

A second time he put his question, "Simon, son of John, do you love me?" "Yes, Lord," Peter said, "you know that I love you." Jesus replied, "Tend my sheep."

A third time Jesus asked him, "Simon, son of John, do you love me?" Peter was hurt because he had asked a third time, "Do you love me?" So he said to him: "Lord, you know everything. You know well that I love you." Jesus told him, "Feed my sheep.

"I tell you solemnly:
as a young man
you fastened your belt
and went about as you pleased;
but when you are older
you will stretch out your hands,
and another will tie you fast
and carry you off against your will."

(What he said indicated the sort of death by which Peter was to glorify God.) When Jesus had finished speaking he said to him, "Follow me."

Reflection on the Readings

Forgiveness is a constant theme in Scripture during this Easter season. We know that Peter had denied Jesus, and Thomas had not believed the accounts of the meetings with the risen Jesus. Yet they are named in particular in today's Gospel. They are in the company of the Lord.

What they come to understand, as we hear in the Acts of the Apostles, is that Jesus' love is a forgiving love. Again and again we, like the apostles, are invited to return to his company even when we have refused or ignored the invitation before.

Not only is each of us forgiven, we are commissioned to share the love of God. To accept forgiveness is to begin to live a forgiving life. The signs of this in today's Gospel are the commands to give nourishment and care to others.

Suggestions for Prayer

1. Meal time is a good time to pause and pray. It is a time to give glory to God and to thank God. It is a good time to ask God's blessing on our lives. The traditional prayer before meals gives us a model.

   Bless us, O Lord, and these your gifts
   which we are about to receive
   from your bounty
   through Christ, our Lord. Amen

2. Place yourself in the presence of God. Remember people who are difficult for you to forgive. Let go of the reasons why forgiveness is difficult. Leave your mind open for the grace of God to be known. Repeat as often as necessary. Spend time with this prayer.

3. Reread the Gospel and hear the words of Jesus spoken personally to you—cast your net, come and eat, tend my lambs, follow me. Imagine you are responding. Which word speaks most urgently to you? Recognize that the Spirit of God is

acting in you in your response. Give thanks for the freedom to respond.

Suggestion for Journal Keeping

Meal time is a time of nourishment, but it is also a time of healing, of reconciling, of building community. Reflect on the meals of your life, past and present. Think of those present, their relationships, the time spent together, the care in the presentation, and any other factors. Do they contribute to community?

Elizabeth S. Lilly

Fourth Sunday of Easter **A**

READING I   Acts 2, 14. 36–41
[On the day of Pentecost] Peter stood up with the Eleven, raised his voice, and addressed them: "Let the whole house of Israel know beyond any doubt that God has made both Lord and Messiah this Jesus whom you crucified."

When they heard this, they were deeply shaken. They asked Peter and the other apostles, "What are we to do, brothers?" Peter answered: "You must reform and be baptized, each one of you, in the name of Jesus Christ, that your sins may be forgiven; then you will receive the gift of the Holy Spirit. It was to you and your children that the promise was made, and to all those still far off whom the Lord our God calls."

In support of his testimony he used many other arguments, and kept urging, "Save yourselves from this generation which has gone astray." Those who accepted his message were baptized; some three thousand were added that day.

Responsorial Psalm   Ps 23, 1–3. 3–4. 5. 6
The Lord is my shepherd;
    there is nothing I shall want.
The Lord is my shepherd; I shall not want.
    In verdant pastures he gives me repose;
Beside restful waters he leads me;
    he refreshes my soul.
The Lord is my shepherd;
    there is nothing I shall want.
He guides me in right paths
    for his name's sake.
Even though I walk in the dark valley
    I fear no evil; for you are at my side
With your rod and your staff
    that give me courage.
The Lord is my shepherd;
    there is nothing I shall want.
You spread the table before me
    in the sight of my foes;
You anoint my head with oil;
    my cup overflows.
The Lord is my shepherd;
    there is nothing I shall want.
Only goodness and kindness follow me
    all the days of my life;
And I shall dwell in the house of the Lord
    for years to come.
The Lord is my shepherd;
    there is nothing I shall want.

READING II   1 Pt 2, 20–25
If you put up with suffering for doing what is right, this is acceptable in God's eyes. It was for this you were called, since Christ suffered for you in just this way and left you an example, to have you follow in his footsteps. He did no wrong; no deceit was found in his mouth. When he was insulted he re-

159

turned no insult. When he was made to suffer, he did not counter with threats. Instead, he delivered himself up to the One who judges justly. In his own body he brought your sins to the cross, so that all of us, dead to sin, could live in accord with God's will. By his wounds you were healed. At one time you were straying like sheep, but now you have returned to the shepherd, the guardian of your souls.

GOSPEL   Jn 10, 1–10
Jesus said:
> "Truly I assure you:
> Whoever does not enter the sheepfold
>   through the gate
> but climbs in some other way
> is a thief and a marauder.
> The one who enters through the gate
> is shepherd of the sheep;
> the keeper opens the gate for him.
> The sheep hear his voice
> as he calls his own by name
> and leads them out.
> When he has brought out [all] those that
>   are his,
> he walks in front of them,
> and the sheep follow him
> because they recognize his voice.
> They will not follow a stranger;
> such a one they will flee,
> because they do not recognize a stranger's voice."

Even though Jesus used this figure with them, they did not grasp what he was trying to tell them. He therefore said [to them again]:
> "My solemn word is this:
> I am the sheepgate.
> All who came before me
> were thieves and marauders
> whom the sheep did not heed.
> "I am the gate.
> Whoever enters through me
> will be safe.
> He will go in and out,
> and find pasture.
> The thief comes
> only to steal and slaughter and destroy.
> I came
> that they might have life
> and have it to the full."

Reflection on the Readings

In the early centuries of Christianity, baptism was imagined as a brand with which Christ marked the sheep belonging to his flock. This ancient tradition is called to mind today by the readings.

Christ is the gate of the sheepfold; it is through him that we have entry into the community of believers, the Church. The life he offers is not mere existence among like-minded friends, but sharing in the fullness of the life of God.

Those whom Christ has marked with the seal of baptism, and who recognize his voice calling each by name, follow their Shepherd as he walks in front of them. The epistle emphasizes a practical aspect of following this Shepherd: the way he walks leads to suffering. But for Christ's flock, accepting suffering is possible because of the promise of resurrection.

Shaken by Peter's preaching, his Pentecost hearers respond to the message about Jesus with conversion and baptism. That journey of initiation is unfolded in the early Church's interpretation of Psalm 23. The green pastures represent catechesis in preparation for baptism where we are nourished on the word of God. Buried with Christ, we pass fearlessly through the dark valley and the shadow of death to the restful waters of baptism. Guided in right paths by the Advocate, the Holy Spirit, our heads are anointed with oil in confirmation, while Jesus spreads the table of the Eucharist before us. The overflowing cup of Christ's saving blood inebriates us with joy as the psalm gives us a foretaste of the peaceful, refreshing garden in which we shall lack nothing good when we at last with our Shepherd are at rest.

Suggestions for Prayer

1. "The sheep hear his voice as he calls his own by name and leads them out." Pray with this passage from the Gospel and allow various images to come to mind. What is it like to hear Jesus call you by name? What name do you hear? Where does he seem to be leading you?
2. In the second reading, Peter urges us to put up with suffering for doing what is right. What experiences does this call to mind? Pray for those who have hurt you and ask for the grace of forgiveness.
3. During the coming week, pray Psalm 23 reflecting on your own journey toward initiation.

Suggestion for Journal Keeping

In the first reading, Peter urges his listeners to reform or repent, while the second reading uses a similar word, "return." These different words are all used to convey the Greek word "metanoia," which literally means a change of heart or change of mind. In what ways has the Good Shepherd prompted you to change

your heart? How have you responded? What obstacles existed? How will this change continue?

Emily J. Besl

Fourth Sunday of Easter

READING I   Acts 4, 8–12
Peter, filled with the Holy Spirit, spoke up: "Leaders of the people! Elders! If we must answer today for a good deed done to a cripple and explain how he was restored to health, then you and all the people of Israel must realize that it was done in the name of Jesus Christ the Nazorean whom you crucified and whom God raised from the dead. In the power of that name this man stands before you perfectly sound. This Jesus is 'the stone rejected by you the builders which has become the cornerstone.' There is no salvation in anyone else, for there is no other name in the whole world given to men by which we are to be saved."

Responsorial Psalm   Ps 118, 1. 8–9. 21–
23. 26. 21. 29
The stone rejected by the builders has
    become the cornerstone.
Give thanks to the Lord, for he is good,
    for his mercy endures forever.
It is better to take refuge in the Lord
    than to trust in man.
It is better to take refuge in the Lord
    than to trust in princes.
The stone rejected by the builders has
    become the cornerstone.

I will give thanks to you, for you have answered me
and have been my savior.
The stone which the builders rejected
has become the cornerstone.
By the Lord has this been done;
it is wonderful in our eyes.
The stone rejected by the builders has
become the cornerstone.
Blessed is he who comes in the name of the Lord;
we bless you from the house of the Lord.
I will give thanks to you, for you have answered me
and have been my savior.
Give thanks to the Lord, for he is good;
for his kindness endures forever.
The stone rejected by the builders has
become the cornerstone.

READING II   1 Jn 3, 1–2

See what love the Father has bestowed on us
in letting us be called children of God!
Yet that is what we are.
The reason the world does not recognize us
is that it never recognized the Son.
Dearly beloved,
we are God's children now;
what we shall later be has not yet come to light.
We know that when it comes to light
we shall be like him,
for we shall see him as he is.

GOSPEL   Jn 10, 11–18

Jesus said:
"I am the good shepherd;
the good shepherd lays down his life for the sheep.
The hired hand, who is no shepherd

nor owner of the sheep,
catches sight of the wolf coming
and runs away, leaving the sheep
to be snatched and scattered by the wolf.
That is because he works for pay;
he has no concern for the sheep.
"I am the good shepherd.
I know my sheep
and my sheep know me
in the same way that the Father knows me
and I know the Father;
for these sheep I will give my life.
I have other sheep
that do not belong to this fold.
I must lead them, too,
and they shall hear my voice.
There shall be one flock then, one shepherd.
The Father loves me for this:
that I lay down my life
to take it up again.
No one takes it from me;
I lay it down freely.
I have power to lay it down,
and I have power to take it up again.
This command I received from my Father."

Reflection on the Readings

The Jewish people at the time of Jesus expected a powerful Messiah. This Savior which had been prophesied for generations was expected to be a great king of Israel who would defeat its enemies and place Israel above all nations. So, when the Messiah came in the form of the humble teacher, Jesus of Nazareth, most were unable to recognize him. He taught, healed, preached and called himself not king, but shepherd.

In the Gospel, Jesus describes himself as the Good Shepherd who lays down his life freely for his sheep. He leads his flock with self-sacrificing love. Those outside his flock do not recognize his voice. But those with faith recognize his voice and follow. This image of the Good Shepherd with its emphasis on gentleness and love is in direct contrast to society's values of power and competition. Those tied to the values of the world fail to recognize Jesus and reject him. Yet those who hear Jesus' voice in faith become children of God.

Children of God run the risk of being rejected as Jesus was. In Acts, Peter and John are arrested for preaching about Jesus' resurrection and for healing a crippled man in Jesus' name. John explains, "The reason the world does not recognize us is that it never recognized the Son." Just as Jesus was the stone rejected by the builders which has become the cornerstone, so too will the followers of Jesus risk being rejected by the world, but find a privileged place in the kingdom of God.

Suggestions for Prayer

1. *Reflect on the following questions:* Are there obstacles in your life which keep you from hearing the voice of Christ, the Good Shepherd? How can you remove those obstacles?
2. We hear the call, the voice of the Good Shepherd, in many ways. Is there a person in your life who helps you to hear the voice of Christ? Bring that person to your mind in your prayer and ask God to help that person to continue to be an instrument of God's call.
3. Prayerfully read Psalm 23.

- Imagine that the waters in the psalm are the waters of baptism.
- Imagine that the table in the psalm is the table of the Eucharist.
- Imagine that the oil in the psalm is the oil of confirmation.
- Now prayerfully reread Psalm 23.

Suggestion for Journal Keeping

In your journal, write down descriptive words which would name the attributes of the Good Shepherd. Do you think these words could also describe values held by our society? How are they the same? How are they different?

Kathryn A. Schneider

Fourth Sunday of Easter

READING I   Acts 13, 14. 43–52
Paul and Barnabas travelled on from Perga and came to Antioch in Pisidia. On the sabbath day they entered the synagogue and sat down. Many Jews and devout Jewish converts became their followers and they spoke to them and urged them to hold fast to the grace of God.

The following sabbath, almost the entire city gathered to hear the word of God. When the Jews saw the crowds, they became very jealous and countered with violent abuse whatever Paul said. Paul and Barnabas spoke out fearlessly, nonetheless: "The word of God has to be declared to you first of all; but since you reject it and thus convict yourselves as unworthy of everlasting life, we now turn to the Gentiles. For thus were we instructed by the Lord: 'I have

made you a light to the nations, a means of salvation to the ends of the earth.' " The Gentiles were delighted when they heard this and responded to the word of the Lord with praise. All who were destined for life everlasting believed in it. Thus the word of the Lord was carried throughout that area.

But some of the Jews stirred up their influential women sympathizers and the leading men of the town, and in that way got a persecution started against Paul and Barnabas. The Jews finally expelled them from their territory. So the two shook the dust from their feet in protest and went on to Iconium. Their disciples knew only how to be filled with joy and the Holy Spirit.

Responsorial Psalm   Ps 100, 1–2. 3. 5
We are his people:
   the sheep of his flock.
Sing joyfully to the Lord, all you lands;
   serve the Lord with gladness;
   come before him with joyful song.
We are his people:
   the sheep of his flock.
Know that the Lord is God;
   he made us, his we are;
   his people, the flock he tends.
We are his people:
   the sheep of his flock.
The Lord is good:
   his kindness endures forever,
   and his faithfulness, to all generations.
We are his people:
   the sheep of his flock.

READING II   Rv 7, 9. 14–17
I, John, saw before me a huge crowd which no one could count from every nation and race, people and tongue. They stood before the throne and the Lamb, dressed in long white robes and holding palm branches in their hands.

Then one of the elders said to me: "These are the ones who have survived the great period of trial; they have washed their robes and made them white in the blood of the Lamb.

"It was this that brought them before God's
   throne:
   day and night they minister to him in his
     temple;
   he who sits on the throne will give them
     shelter.
Never again shall they know hunger or
   thirst,
   nor shall the sun or its heat beat down on
     them,
   for the Lamb on the throne will shepherd
     them.
He will lead them to springs of life-giving
   water,
   and God will wipe every tear from their
     eyes."

GOSPEL   Jn 10, 27–30
Jesus said:
   "My sheep hear my voice.
   I know them,
   and they follow me.
   I give them eternal life,
   and they shall never perish.
   No one shall snatch them out of my
     hand.
   My Father is greater than all, in what he
     has given me,
   and there is no snatching out of his
     hand.
   The Father and I are one."

Reflection on the Readings

"My sheep hear my voice. I give them eternal life. . . . " The word of God is the gift of everlasting life. The word of God is the love that calls forth life, that seeks out life.

The Church is charged with the mission of speaking the word of God in every time and place. Everywhere we turn, we should hear the word of salvation, of love, compassion and life. And we should speak this word; we should echo it in our lives.

What we know of this word of love and life we know because we have first been loved and called to life. Our response to this understanding is to give praise to God. In the Church's constant prayer of praise, we hear the proclamation of love. The more we join the Church in praise, the greater is our experience of God's love and life.

In Christ we already share in the eternal life of God. Our experience of this union and life grows as we experience the love of Jesus and we praise him for his compassion, forgiveness and mercy.

Suggestions for Prayer

1. Prayer is growing in intimacy with God. Identify a place that helps you relax so that intimacy becomes possible. Imagine the lamb held by the shepherd. Then place your needs in the hands of God.
2. Repeat the psalm as a morning prayer. It offers both comfort and an example of prayer. We are the Lord's people and we give thanks and praise.
3. Translate the image of the Good Shepherd with his flock into a contemporary image of compassion, of life giving presence and action. Pray for the grace and courage to bring that life to the relationships and situations that you meet.

Suggestions for Journal Keeping

Select one situation in which you could offer a word or action of comfort. Brainstorm ideas for possible action. Decide to act. Keep a record of your action. Integrate your prayer and your action. Change your course if need be.

Elizabeth S. Lilly

Fifth Sunday of Easter A

READING I   Acts 6, 1–7

In those days, as the number of disciples grew, the ones who spoke Greek complained that their widows were being neglected in the daily distribution of food, as compared with the widows of those who spoke Hebrew. The Twelve assembled the community of the disciples and said, "It is not right for us to neglect the word of God in order to wait on the tables. Look around among your own number, brothers, for seven men acknowledged to be deeply spiritual and prudent, and we shall appoint them to this task. This will permit us to concentrate on prayer and the ministry of the word." The proposal was unanimously accepted by the community. Following this they selected Stephen, a man filled with faith and a Holy Spirit; Philip, Prochorus, Nicanor, Timon, Parmenas and Nicolaus of Antioch, who had been a convert to Judaism. They presented these men to the apostles, who first prayed over them and then imposed hands on them.

The word of God continued to spread, while at the same time the number of the disciples in Jerusalem enormously increased. There were many priests among those who embraced the faith.

Responsorial Psalm   Ps 33, 1–2. 4–5. 18–19

Lord, let your mercy be on us,
  as we place our trust in you.

Exult, you just, in the Lord;
  praise from the upright is fitting.
Give thanks to the Lord on the harp;
  with the ten-stringed lyre chant his praises.
Lord, let your mercy be on us,
  as we place our trust in you.

Upright is the word of the Lord,
  and all his works are trustworthy.
He loves justice and right;
  of the kindness of the Lord the earth is full.
Lord, let your mercy be on us,
  as we place our trust in you.

See, the eyes of the Lord are upon those who fear him,
  upon those who hope for his kindness,
To deliver them from death
  and preserve them in spite of famine.
Lord, let your mercy be on us,
  as we place our trust in you.

READING II   1 Pt 2, 4–9
Come to the Lord, a living stone, rejected by men but approved, nonetheless, and precious in God's eyes. You too are living stones, built as an edifice of spirit, into a holy priesthood, offering spiritual sacrifices acceptable to God through Jesus Christ. For Scripture has it: "See, I am laying a cornerstone in Zion,
  an approved stone, and precious.

He who puts his faith in it shall not be shaken."
  The stone is of value for you who have faith.
For those without faith, it is rather,
"A stone which the builders rejected
  that became a cornerstone."
It is likewise "an obstacle and a stumbling stone." Those who stumble and fall are the disbelievers in God's word; it belongs to their destiny to do so.

You, however, are "a chosen race, a royal priesthood, a consecrated nation, a people he claims for his own to proclaim the glorious works" of the One who called you from darkness into his marvelous light.

GOSPEL   Jn 14, 1–12
Jesus said to his disciples:
  "Do not let your hearts be troubled.
  Have faith in God
  and faith in me.
  In my Father's house there are many dwelling places;
  otherwise, how could I have told you
  that I was going to prepare a place for you?
  I am indeed going to prepare a place for you,
  and then I shall come back to take you with me,
  that where I am you also may be.
  You know the way that leads where I go."
"Lord," said Thomas, "we do not know where you are going. How can we know the way?" Jesus told him:
  "I am the way, and the truth, and the life;
  no one comes to the Father but through me.

**If you really knew me, you would know
my Father also.
From this point on you know him; you
have seen him."**
**"Lord," Philip said to him, "show us the
Father and that will be enough for us."
"Philip," Jesus replied, "after I have been
with you all this time, you still do not know
me?**

**"Whoever has seen me has seen the
Father.
How can you say, 'Show us the Father'?
Do you not believe that I am in the Father
and the Father is in me?
The words I speak are not spoken of
myself;
it is the Father who lives in me accom-
plishing his works.
Believe me that I am in the Father
and the Father is in me,
or else, believe because of the works I
do.
I solemnly assure you,
the man who has faith in me
will do the works I do, and greater far
than these.
Why? Because I go to the Father."**

Reflection on the Readings

As the Easter season continues, the readings carry on their mystagogical task of un-
raveling various facets of Christian initiation
and the Church.

Because of the unity between God and
himself, Jesus stresses that he is the means of
encounter of God; to see Jesus is to see God.
Now, however, his role is carried on by the
Church which also becomes the sacrament of
God in the world and the way, the truth, the
life. The exalted, risen Jesus continues his

words and works in his body, the Church. In
the second reading, Peter urges us to "come
to the Lord," to join ourselves to Christ by
joining fully in the Church. Already the
promise of Jesus in the Gospel to return is fulfilled by his abiding presence in the Church
through the gift of the Spirit.

The "house" of God mentioned in the
Gospel refers not only to heaven, but wherever God is. Thus, the "many dwelling
places" in God's house are the members of
the Church, living stones built into a spiritual
temple on the cornerstone Christ, bonded by
the Spirit. Addressing Christians of different
races and nationalities in the second reading,
Peter boldly emphasizes the unity of baptism
which transcends all such barriers and dis-
tinctions. Living out this unity is not always
easy, however, as is evident in the first reading where the Jerusalem community is threatened by a split between its Greek- and
Hebrew-speaking members.

In assuring that believers will do the works
he does and greater ones, Jesus is not necessarily referring to miracles, but to works of
service and the sacraments. Just as Jesus did
not seek his own glory but God's, so Christians as a "holy priesthood" are dedicated
through baptism to the worship and service of
God. Their very lives are to be an act of worship.

Suggestions for Prayer

1. In the second reading, Peter says that we
   are to offer "spiritual sacrifices" to God
   and to "proclaim the glorious works of
   the One who called you." This is what
   we do in our daily lives, and what is expressed each Sunday in the eucharistic
   prayer. Prayerfully read Eucharistic

Prayer III, reflecting on the works of God which you now proclaim and the sacrifices in your life which you dedicate to God.

2. As demonstrated in the first reading, the Christian community must always organize itself for service of the needy. Who are the needy whom you serve? Do you recognize the face of Christ there?

3. Jesus says, "Whoever sees me has seen the Father." Who in your life is a sign of God for you? What qualities or events come to mind? For whom are you an expression of the love of God?

Suggestion for Journal Keeping

Jesus is the way to God. The path to God lies in patterning our lives after Christ. Describe some instances in which you experienced yourself able to imitate the self-giving love of Christ.

Emily J. Besl

Fifth Sunday of Easter Ⓑ

READING I   Acts 9, 26–31

When Saul arrived back in Jerusalem he tried to join the disciples there; but it turned out that they were all afraid of him. They even refused to believe that he was a disciple. Then Barnabas took him in charge and introduced him to the apostles. He explained to them how on his journey Saul had seen the Lord, who had conversed with him, and how Saul had been speaking out fearlessly in the name of Jesus at Damascus. Saul stayed on with them, moving freely about Jerusalem and expressing himself quite openly in the name of the Lord. He even addressed the Greek-speaking Jews and debated with them. They for their part responded by trying to kill him. When the brothers learned of this, some of them took him down to Caesarea and sent him off to Tarsus.

Meanwhile throughout all Judea, Galilee and Samaria the church was at peace. It was being built up and was making steady progress in the fear of the Lord; at the same time it enjoyed the increased consolation of the Holy Spirit.

Responsorial Psalm   Ps 22, 26–27. 28. 30. 31–32

I will praise you, Lord, in the assembly of
    your people.
**I will fulfill my vows before those who fear
    the Lord.**
The lowly shall eat their fill;
They who seek the Lord shall praise him:
    "May your hearts be ever merry!"
I will praise you, Lord, in the assembly of
    your people.
All the ends of the earth
    shall remember and turn to the Lord;
All the families of the nations
    shall bow down before him.
To him alone shall bow down
    all who sleep in the earth;
Before him shall bend
    all who go down into the dust.
I will praise you, Lord, in the assembly of
    your people.
And to him my soul shall live;
    my descendants shall serve him.
**Let the coming generation be told of the
    Lord**
    **that they may proclaim to a people yet to
    be born**
    the justice he has shown.

I will praise you, Lord, in the assembly of
your people.

READING II   1 Jn 3, 18–24
Little children,
  let us love in deed and in truth
  and not merely talk about it.
This is our way of knowing we are commit-
    ted to the truth
  and are at peace before him
  no matter what our consciences may
    charge us with;
  for God is greater than our hearts
  and all is known to him.

Beloved,
  if our consciences have nothing to charge
    us with,
  we can be sure that God is with us
  and that we will receive at his hands
  whatever we ask.
Why? Because we are keeping his com-
    mandments
  and doing what is pleasing in his sight.
His commandment is this:
  we are to believe in the name of his Son,
    Jesus Christ,
  and are to love one another as he com-
    manded us.
Those who keep his commandments remain
    in him
  and he in them.
and this is how we know that he remains in
    us:
  from the Spirit that he gave us.

GOSPEL   Jn 15, 1–8
Jesus said to his disciples:
  "I am the true vine
  and my Father is the vinegrower.
  He prunes away
every barren branch,
  but the fruitful ones
  he trims clean
  to increase their yield.
You are clean already,
  thanks to the word I have spoken to
    you.
Live on in me, as I do in you.
No more than a branch can bear fruit of
    itself
  apart from the vine,
  can you bear fruit
  apart from me.
I am the vine, you are the branches.
He who lives in me and I in him,
  will produce abundantly,
  for apart from me you can do nothing.
A man who does not live in me
  is like a withered, rejected branch,
  picked up to be thrown in the fire and
    burnt.
If you live in me,
  and my words stay part of you,
  you may ask what you will—
  it will be done for you.
My Father has been glorified
  in your bearing much fruit
  and becoming my disciples."

Reflection on the Readings
  Saul was a great persecutor of the early
Christians until one day, on the road to Damascus, he encountered the risen Lord. Saul,
who would eventually be called Paul, experienced a great conversion. The great persecutor became the great preacher in the name
of Jesus the Lord. His great love for the Lord
drove him to seek entrance into the Christian
community. Many feared him because they
thought he was a spy. Yet Barnabas believed
in Saul, for he saw him risk death to preach

the good news. Saul found new life in Jesus Christ and with the community which proclaimed Jesus as Lord.

In order to have new life, we like Saul must live on in Jesus Christ. Christ is the vine, we are the branches. Cut off from Christ, we wither and die. Yet, if we live on, connected with Christ, we receive the nourishment we need to grow and bear fruit. One way we are able to remain in Christ is through the Church. We receive our nourishment in the form of God's word as proclaimed in Scripture, the celebration of the sacraments and the witness and support of members of the Church community.

As we receive this nourishment, we must bear good fruit. John's letter reminds us that this fruit is love which is expressed in word and deed. Others will know we are committed to the truth not through our words alone. Rather, they will know by how we live our lives and how we love one another.

Suggestions for Prayer

1. Barnabas was Saul's sponsor into the Christian community. Bring your sponsor to mind. Think of how he or she has helped you to feel more welcome in the Christian community. Pray that God may continue to help him or her in witnessing to you.
2. The psalm proclaims, "I will praise you, Lord, in the assembly of your people." Take these words of praise from the eucharistic acclamation in the Mass and meditate on their meaning:

> Christ has died.
> Christ has risen.
> Christ will come again.

3. *Reflect on the following questions:*
   - Have you ever felt cut off from Christ?
   - How did that feel?
   - How is that different from times when you feel connected with Christ?

Suggestion for Journal Keeping

In your journal, list some ways in which you feel you receive nourishment for your life in Jesus Christ. List two or three ways in which you have borne good fruit through your love as expressed in your words and deeds.

Kathryn A. Schneider

Fifth Sunday of Easter

READING I   Acts 14, 21–27

After Paul and Barnabas had proclaimed the good news in Derbe and made numerous disciples, they retraced their steps to Lystra and Iconium first, then to Antioch. They gave their disciples reassurances, and encouraged them to persevere in the faith with this instruction: "We must undergo many trials if we are to enter into the reign of God." In each church they installed elders and, with prayer and fasting, commended them to the Lord in whom they had put their faith.

Then they passed through Pisidia and came to Pamphylia. After preaching the message in Perga, they went down to Attalia. From there they sailed back to Antioch, where they had first been commended to the favor of God for the task they had now completed. On their arrival, they called the congregation together and related all that

God had helped them accomplish, and how he had opened the door of faith to the Gentiles.

Responsorial Psalm   Ps 145, 8–9. 10–11. 12–13

I will praise your name for ever, my king
    and my God.
The Lord is gracious and merciful,
    slow to anger and of great kindness.
The Lord is good to all
    and compassionate toward all his works.
I will praise your name for ever, my king
    and my God.
Let all your works give you thanks, O Lord,
    and let your faithful ones bless you.
Let them discourse of the glory of your
    kingdom
    and speak of your might.
I will praise your name for ever, my king
    and my God.
Let them make known to men your might
    and the glorious splendor of your king-
    dom.
Your kingdom is a kingdom for all ages,
    and your dominion endures through all
    generations.
I will praise your name for ever, my king
    and my God.

READING II   Rv 21, 1–5

I, John, saw new heavens and a new earth. The former heavens and the former earth had passed away, and the sea was no longer. I also saw a new Jerusalem, the holy city, coming down out of heaven from God, beautiful as a bride prepared to meet her husband. I heard a loud voice from the throne cry out: "This is God's dwelling among men. He shall dwell with them and they shall be his people, and he shall be their
God who is always with them. He shall wipe every tear from their eyes, and there shall be no more death or mourning, crying out or pain, for the former world has passed away."**

The One who sat on the throne said to me, "See, I make all things new!"

GOSPEL   Jn 13, 31–33. 34–35

Once Judas had left [the cenacle], Jesus said:
    "Now is the Son of Man glorified
    and God is glorified in him.
    [If God has been glorified in him,]
    God will, in turn, glorify him in himself,
    and will glorify him soon.
    My children, I am not to be with you
    much longer.
    I give you a new commandment:
    Love one another.
    Such as my love has been for you,
    so must your love be for each other.
    This is how all will know you for my dis-
    ciples:
    your love for one another."

Reflection on the Readings

"See, I make all things new!" Change and movement are part of life and they are part of faith. Christians are people coming to faith in God through Jesus the Christ. A life in faith is a life of changing to a new life characterized as a life of moving from sorrow to joy.

"I give you a new commandment: love one another." The model for coming to faith is relationship. Jesus always sees himself in relation to the Father and to others, in a bond of love. Before each of us is the command to love one another. This is not only an individual requirement, but the hallmark of the community of believers.

God opens the door of faith through love.

The Church sustains, encourages, and challenges us to grow in faith. The Church is a community, always in conversion, where encouragement and support come in the form of instruction, worship and discipline.

Suggestions for Prayer

1. Pray for faith. To pray is already an evidence of faith, but we always need to pray for an openness to God's life. The Church gives us a model with the Act of Faith.
2. To become something new means that one must die to something old. In prayer, name the things that are dying, or that need to die in yourself, and ask for the discipline of love to grow in your life. Close your prayer in the name of Jesus.
3. Read the life of someone committed to change in the area of social justice. Reflect upon the place of faith in that person's life and examine the place of faith in your own. In prayer, seek the strength and direction to bring about changes in any unjust situation.

Suggestion for Journal Keeping

Your sponsor is a member of the Church, appointed to walk with you on the journey of conversion. Record any questions you want to discuss and reflect your experience of being with your sponsor. What can you do to make the most of your time together?

Elizabeth S. Lilly

Sixth Sunday of Easter A

READING I   Acts 8, 5–8. 14–17
Philip went down to the town of Samaria and there proclaimed the Messiah. Without exception, the crowds that heard Philip and saw the miracles he performed attended closely to what he had to say. There were many who had unclean spirits, which came out shrieking loudly. Many others were paralytics or cripples, and these were cured. The rejoicing in that town rose to fever pitch.

When the apostles in Jerusalem heard that Samaria had accepted the word of God, they sent Peter and John to them. The two went down to these people and prayed that they might receive the Holy Spirit. It had not as yet come down upon any of them since they had only been baptized in the name of the Lord Jesus. The pair upon arriving imposed hands on them and they received the Holy Spirit.

Responsorial Psalm   Ps 66, 1–3. 4–5. 6–7.
16. 20
Let all the earth cry out to God with joy.
**Shout joyfully to God, all you on earth,
    sing praise to the glory of his name;
    proclaim his glorious praise.**
**Say to God, "How tremendous are your
    deeds!**
Let all the earth cry out to God with joy.

Let all the earth worship and sing praise to
 you,
 sing praise to your name!"
Come and see the works of God,
 his tremendous deeds among men.
Let all the earth cry out to God with joy.
He has changed the sea into dry land;
 through the river they passed on foot;
 therefore let us rejoice in him.
He rules by his might forever.
Let all the earth cry out to God with joy.
Hear now, all you who fear God, while I declare
 what he has done for me.
Blessed be God who refused me not
 my prayer or his kindness!
Let all the earth cry out to God with joy.

READING II   1 Pt 3, 15–18
**Venerate the Lord, that is, Christ, in your
hearts. Should anyone ask you the reason for
this hope of yours be ever ready to reply, but
speak gently and respectfully. Keep your
conscience clear so that, whenever you are
defamed, those who libel your way of life in
Christ may be disappointed. If it should be
God's will that you suffer, it is better to do
so for good deeds than for evil ones.**

**This is why Christ died for sins once for
all, a just man for the sake of the unjust: so
that he could lead you to God. He was put
to death insofar as fleshly existence goes,
but was given life in the realm of the spirit.**

GOSPEL   Jn 14, 15–21
Jesus said to his disciples:
 "If you love me
 and obey the commands I give you,
 I will ask the Father
 **and he will give you another Para-
 clete—**

to be with you always:
 the Spirit of truth,
 whom the world cannot accept,
 since it neither sees him nor recognizes
 him;
 but you can recognize him
 because he remains with you
 and will be within you.
 I will not leave you orphaned;
 I will come back to you.
 A little while now and the world will see
 me no more;
 but you see me
 as one who has life, and you will have
 life.
 On that day you will know
 that I am in my Father,
 and you in me, and I in you.
 He who obeys the commandments he
 has from me
 is the man who loves me;
 and he who loves me will be loved by
 my Father.
 I too will love him
 and reveal myself to him."

Reflection on the Readings
 Anticipating Pentecost, today's readings
focus on the gift of the Spirit, outcome of the
resurrection, bestowed upon the initiated.
 Obedience marks the beginning and end
of today's Gospel. Obeying Christ is proof of
love and condition of receiving the Spirit,
since the words and deeds of the Church reveal the Spirit's presence just as the words
and deeds of Jesus showed he was from God.
A legal term, "paraclete" means an advocate, mediator, or helper. The Spirit is called
"another" mediator because Jesus is the first,
and through the Spirit Jesus will come back
as promised and remain. His departure thus

173

results not in absence, although the world thinks Jesus has disappeared, but rather in continued presence through the Spirit.

Our pledge of triumph, the Spirit among us, gives us basis for hope. Although he was put to death, Christ lives in the Spirit, says the second reading. So we to whom the Spirit gave rebirth in baptism hope to be glorified like Christ. Difficulties and persecution, then, pose no threat since this is the way we share in Christ's victory.

Before his ascension, Jesus announced to the apostles that they would receive the Holy Spirit and be his witnesses to Jerusalem, Judea and Samaria, and even to the ends of the earth—that is, first to the Jews, then to the Gentiles. The first reading presents the spread of the Gospel to Samaria, outcasts of Israel, who joyfully accept the word of God and are baptized. An unusual occurrence, the reception of the Spirit apart from baptism is meant to stress the relationship of the Spirit and the Church. Each new Christian community must be associated with the apostles. It is the Spirit in the Church who brings unity with the apostolic witnesses, with the risen Christ, and through Christ with God.

Suggestions for Prayer

1. Meditate in prayer on these words of Jesus.

I will come back to you.
I am in my Father, and you in me, and I in you.
Another Advocate will be with you always.

2. Peter advises you to be ever ready to reply should anyone ask you the reason for your hope. In what words or images would you express your hope? What would your reply to such a question be?

3. Pray Psalm 66, giving thanks that the Gospel has been preached to "all the earth," and consequently to you. "Listen now while I declare what he has done for me." What thoughts are prompted by this line?

Suggestions for Journal Keeping

"The one who obeys my commandments is the one who loves me." Reflect on an experience in which you obeyed because you loved. What was involved? What light does this shed on your relationship with Christ?

Emily J. Besl

Sixth Sunday of Easter

READING I   Acts 10, 25–26. 34–35. 44–48
Peter entered the house of Cornelius who met him, dropped to his knees before Peter and bowed low. Peter said as he helped him to his feet, "Get up! I am only a man myself."

Peter proceeded to address [the relatives and friends of Cornelius] in these words: "I begin to see how true it is that God shows no partiality. Rather, the man of any nation who fears God and acts uprightly is acceptable to him."

Peter had not finished these words when the Holy Spirit descended upon all who were listening to Peter's message. The circumcised believers who had accompanied Peter were surprised that the gift of the Holy Spirit should have been poured out on the Gentiles

also, whom they could hear speaking in tongues and glorifying God. Peter put the question at that point: "What can stop these people who have received the Holy Spirit, even as we have, from being baptized with water?" So he gave orders that they be baptized in the name of Jesus Christ. After this was done, they asked him to stay with them for a few days.

Responsorial Psalm   Ps 98, 1. 2–3. 3–4
The Lord has revealed to the nations his
   saving power.
Sing to the Lord a new song,
   for he has done wondrous deeds;
His right hand has won victory for him,
   his holy arm.
The Lord has revealed to the nations his
   saving power.
The Lord has made his salvation known:
   in the sight of the nations he has revealed
   his justice.
He has remembered his kindness and his
   faithfulness
   toward the house of Israel.
The Lord has revealed to the nations his
   saving power.
All the ends of the earth have seen
   the salvation by our God.
Sing joyfully to the Lord, all you lands;
   break into song; sing praise.
The Lord has revealed to the nations his
   saving power.

READING II   1 Jn 4, 7–10
Beloved,
   let us love one another
   because love is of God;
   everyone who loves is begotten of God
   and has knowledge of God.

The man without love has known nothing of
   God,
   for God is love.
God's love was revealed in our midst in this
   way:
   he sent his only Son to the world
   that we might have life through him.
Love, then, consists in this:
   not that we have loved God,
   but that he has loved us
   and has sent his Son as an offering for our
   sins.

GOSPEL   Jn 15, 9–17
Jesus said to his disciples:
   "As the Father has loved me,
   so I have loved you.
   Live on in my love.
   You will live in my love
   if you keep my commandments,
   even as I have kept my Father's com-
     mandments,
   and live in his love.
   All this I tell you
   that my joy may be yours
   and your joy may be complete.
   This is my commandment:
   love one another
   as I have loved you.
   There is no greater love than this:
   to lay down one's life for one's friends.
   You are my friends
   if you do what I command you.
   I no longer speak of you as slaves,
   for a slave does not know what his mas-
     ter is about.
   Instead, I call you friends
   since I have made known to you all that
     I heard from my Father.
   It was not you who chose me,

it was I who chose you
to go forth and bear fruit.
Your fruit must endure,
so that all you ask the Father in my
   name
he will give you.
The command I give you is this:
that you love one another."

Reflection on the Readings

God is love. So essential is this love that those who love become children of God and those who do not love know nothing of God. Love becomes the measure. God's love is gracious and open to all. It is hard for us to understand the love of God. As humans, we love some people and do not love others. It is hard to believe that God offers love to all.

Peter came to understand this better when he witnessed the gift of the Holy Spirit given to Cornelius and his friends and relatives. This gift was significant because Cornelius was a Gentile and not a Jew. In the early Church many argued that because Jesus and his first followers were Jews, one must become a Jew before one could be baptized a Christian. Thus, uncircumcised males would have to be circumcised before they could be baptized. Peter came to understand that these were artificial barriers to baptism. Peter realizes that God shows no partiality and that those who respond to God's gracious gift of love with love are worthy to be called children of God. They are worthy to be baptized in the name of Jesus Christ.

In the Gospel of John, Jesus teaches us that God loves us first. Through this love we become friends with God. When we get in touch with this great love in our lives, we respond in love. All Jesus asks of us is this, "Love one another as I have loved you."

Suggestions for Prayer

1. Think of a time when you felt loved by God. What was it like?
2. Is there someone in your life who loves you in a way which reveals God's love to you? Bring that person to your prayer and thank God for him or her.
3. Read today's psalm slowly and prayerfully. Reflect upon how God has revealed himself to all the nations or, in other words, to diverse groups in society.

Suggestion for Journal Keeping

How is God's love different from the way we, as humans, usually love?

How is God calling you to love? Whom is God calling you to love?

Kathryn A. Schneider

Sixth Sunday of Easter

READING I — Acts 15, 1–2. 22–29

Some men came down to Antioch from Judea and began to teach the brothers: "Unless you are circumcised according to Mosaic practice, you cannot be saved." This created dissension and much controversy between them and Paul and Barnabas. Finally it was decided that Paul, Barnabas, and some others should go up to see the apostles and elders in Jerusalem about this question.

It was resolved by the apostles and the elders, in agreement with the whole Jerusalem church, that representatives be chosen from among their number and sent to Antioch along with Paul and Barnabas. Those

chosen were leading men of the community, Judas, known as Barsabbas, and Silas. They were to deliver this letter:

"The apostles and the elders, your brothers, send greetings to the brothers of Gentile origin in Antioch, Syria and Cilicia. We have heard that some of our number without any instructions from us have upset you with their discussions and disturbed your peace of mind. Therefore we have unanimously resolved to choose representatives and send them to you, along with our beloved Barnabas and Paul, who have dedicated themselves to the cause of our Lord Jesus Christ. Those whom we are sending you are Judas and Silas, who will convey this message by word of mouth: 'It is the decision of the Holy Spirit, and ours too, not to lay on you any burden beyond that which is strictly necessary, namely, to abstain from meat sacrificed to idols, from blood, from the meat of strangled animals, and from illicit sexual union. You will be well advised to avoid these things. Farewell.' "

Responsorial Psalm   Ps 67, 2–3. 5. 6. 8
O God, let all the nations praise you!
May God have pity on us and bless us;
   may he let his face shine upon us.
So may your way be known upon earth;
   among all nations, your salvation.
O God, let all the nations praise you!
May the nations be glad and exult
   because you rule the peoples in equity;
   the nations on the earth you guide.
O God, let all the nations praise you!
May the peoples praise you, O God;
   may all the peoples praise you!
May God bless us,
   and may all the ends of the earth fear him!
O God, let all the nations praise you!

READING II   Rv 21, 10–14. 22–23
The angel carried me away in spirit to the top of a very high mountain and showed me the holy city Jerusalem coming down out of heaven from God. It gleamed with the splendor of God. The city had the radiance of a precious jewel that sparkled like a diamond. Its wall, massive and high, had twelve gates at which twelve angels were stationed. Twelve names were written on the gates, the names of the twelve tribes of Israel. There were three gates facing east, three north, three south, and three west. The wall of the city had twelve courses of stones as its foundation, on which were written the names of the twelve apostles of the Lamb.

I saw no temple in the city. The Lord, God the Almighty, is its temple—he and the Lamb. The city had no need of sun or moon, for the glory of God gave it light, and its lamp was the Lamb.

GOSPEL   Jn 14, 23–29
Jesus said to his disciples:
   "Anyone who loves me
   will be true to my word,
   and my Father will love him;
   we will come to him
   and make our dwelling place with him
      always.
   He who does not love me does not keep
      my words.
   Yet the word you hear is not mine;
   it comes from the Father who sent me.
This much have I told you while I was
   still with you;
the Paraclete, the Holy Spirit
whom the Father will send in my name,
will instruct you in everything,
and remind you of all that I told you.
'Peace' is my farewell to you,

my peace is my gift to you;
I do not give it to you as the world gives
    peace.
Do not be distressed or fearful.
You have heard me say,
'I go away for a while, and I come back
    to you.'
If you truly loved me
you would rejoice to have me go to the
    Father,
for the Father is greater than I.
I tell you this now, before it takes place,
so that when it takes place you may
    believe."

Reflection on the Readings

Peace is the gift of God dwelling within us. Peace is the gift of Jesus to the disciples. Peace is our desire, and yet peace seems so often to be absent.

In the first reading we hear that even in some of the early Christian communities, peace was not always evident. We also hear of the model for discerning that peace, that gift of God. The apostles sought to restore peace in the community by uniting their will with the Holy Spirit.

Turning to God, opening ourselves to the work of the Spirit within us, and hearing the word of God in the community of disciples are all important aspects of prayer. Our prayer always follows the model of Jesus. We praise God, and we petition for our needs and the needs of others.

Suggestions for Prayer

1. The sign of the cross is a prayer expressing our faith in the fullness of the gift of God's presence with us. Say this blessing slowly, allowing images, memories, and stories to come to mind with each name—the Father, the Son, and the Holy Spirit. For example, reflect upon God the Creator, the Shepherd, God the Savior, the Anointed One, God who loves us and makes us holy.

2. St. Francis prayed that he would become a channel of God's peace. God's gift to us is not for us alone, but for the good of the world. Pray the Prayer of St. Francis.

3. Acknowledge that you have received the gift of God's peace. Picture the unpeaceful situations of your life as layers that you can peel away. In your imagination, fold back each layer you encounter until you come to rest in God's peace in your heart.

Thank God for peace. Ask for strength to be a peacemaker. Pray in the name of Jesus.

Suggestion for Journal Keeping

Take one couplet from the Prayer of St. Francis, for example, "Where there is hatred, let me sow your love," and reflect on specific situations in your life where you can pray for God's grace of peace.

Elizabeth S. Lilly

Ascension

READING I   Acts 1, 1–11
In my first account, Theophilus, I dealt with all that Jesus did and taught until the day he was taken up to heaven, having first instructed the apostles he had chosen through the Holy Spirit. In the time after his suffering he showed them in many convincing ways

that he was alive, appearing to them over the course of forty days and speaking to them about the reign of God. On one occasion when he met with them, he told them not to leave Jerusalem: "Wait, rather, for the fulfillment of my Father's promise, of which you have heard me speak. John baptized with water, but within a few days you will be baptized with the Holy Spirit."

While they were with him they asked, "Lord, are you going to restore the rule to Israel now?" His answer was: "The exact time it is not yours to know. The Father has reserved that to himself. You will receive power when the Holy Spirit comes down on you; then you are to be my witnesses in Jerusalem, throughout Judea and Samaria, yes, even to the ends of the earth." No sooner had he said this than he was lifted up before their eyes in a cloud which took him from their sight.

They were still gazing up into the heavens when two men dressed in white stood beside them. "Men of Galilee," they said, "why do you stand here looking up at the skies? This Jesus who has been taken from you will return, just as you saw him go up into the heavens."

Responsorial Psalm   Ps 47, 2–3. 6–7. 8–9
God mounts his throne to shouts of joy;
  a blare of trumpets for the Lord.
All you peoples, clap your hands,
  shout to God with cries of gladness,
For the Lord, the Most High, the awesome,
  is the great king over all the earth.
God mounts his throne to shouts of joy;
  a blare of trumpets for the Lord.
God mounts his throne amid shouts of joy;
  the Lord, amid trumpet blasts.

Sing praise to God, sing praise;
  sing praise to our king, sing praise.
God mounts his throne to shouts of joy;
  a blare of trumpets for the Lord.
For king of all the earth is God;
  sing hymns of praise.
God reigns over the nations,
  God sits upon his holy throne.
God mounts his throne to shouts of joy;
  a blare of trumpets for the Lord.

READING II   Eph 1, 17–23
May the God of our Lord Jesus Christ, the Father of glory, grant you a spirit of wisdom and insight to know him clearly. May he enlighten your innermost vision that you may know the great hope to which he has called you, the wealth of his glorious heritage to be distributed among the members of the church, and the immeasurable scope of his power in us who believe. It is like the strength he showed in raising Christ from the dead and seating him at his right hand in heaven, high above every principality, power, virtue and domination, and every name that can be given in this age or the age to come.

He has put all things under Christ's feet and has made him thus exalted, head of the church, which is his body: the fullness of him who fills the universe in all its parts.

GOSPEL   Mt 28, 16–20
The eleven disciples made their way to Galilee, to the mountain to which Jesus had summoned them. At the sight of him, those who had entertained doubts fell down in homage. Jesus came forward and addressed them in these words:

  "Full authority has been given to me
    both in heaven and on earth;

go, therefore, and make disciples of all the nations.

Baptize them in the name
'of the Father,
and of the Son,
and of the Holy Spirit.'

Teach them to carry out everything I have commanded you.

And know that I am with you always, until the end of the world!"

GOSPEL B
Mk 16, 15–20

[Jesus appeared to the Eleven and] said to them: "Go into the whole world and proclaim the good news to all creation. The man who believes in it and accepts baptism will be saved; the man who refuses to believe in it will be condemned. Signs like these will accompany those who have professed their faith: they will use my name to expel demons, they will speak entirely new languages, they will be able to handle serpents, they will be able to drink deadly poison without harm, and the sick upon whom they lay their hands will recover." Then, after speaking to them, the Lord Jesus was taken up into heaven and took his seat at God's right hand. The Eleven went forth and preached everywhere. The Lord continued to work with them throughout and confirm the message through the signs which accompanied them.

GOSPEL C
Lk 24, 46–53

Jesus said to the Eleven: "Thus it is written that the Messiah must suffer and rise from the dead on the third day. In his name, penance for the remission of sins is to be preached to the nations, beginning at Jeru-salem. You are witnesses of all this. See, I send down upon you the promise of my Father. Remain here in the city until you are clothed with power from on high."

He then led them out near Bethany, and with hands upraised, blessed them. As he blessed, he left them, and was taken up to heaven. They fell down to do him reverence, then returned to Jerusalem filled with joy. There they were to be found in the temple constantly, speaking the praises of God.

Reflection on the Readings

Not simply recalling an historical event, the feast of the Ascension celebrates what we are and will be as the Church. Rather than focusing on the departure of Christ, this feast reminds us of his presence manifest in our midst in the Church. As St. Leo preached on this occasion centuries ago, what was previously visible in the Redeemer is now present in the rites. No longer limited by space or time, Christ has gone away only to be available through the Spirit in the sacraments. And because he lives among us, St. Leo says, "Where the Head has gone, the Body hopes to follow." That the ascension of Christ is a promise of what lies ahead for believers is reflected in the prayers of today's liturgy. In the first preface, we remember that Christ left our sight "not to abandon us, but to be our hope," and in the opening prayer we ask, "May we follow him into the new creation, for his ascension is our glory and our hope."

The first two readings are repeated each year. In the first, we have the beginning of Luke's second volume, the Acts of the Apostles, where Jesus' ascension inaugurates the Church's mission of witnessing for Christ, even to the Gentiles. Although the disciples hope for the immediate second coming, Jesus corrects their preoccupation by turning their attention to the Spirit among them: this is the return of Christ for now.

In the second reading, the past event of the ascension is discussed in the context of the present reality of the Church. When St. Paul prays for the Ephesians for knowledge, he does not mean conceptual knowledge, but rather the experience of the power of God among believers. Christ is the sign of such strength, whom God raised and seated at his right hand, making him the head of the Church, his "fullness." Thus the glory of Christ is our hope; we see our inheritance in him.

In Year A, the Gospel is from Matthew. Here Jesus transmits to the apostles the authority he has from God. In sending them out to make disciples by baptizing and teaching, Jesus charges the apostles to continue his ministry. Experiencing Christ's promise fulfilled through the Spirit and the sacraments, the Church witnesses to the resurrection by showing in its life and activity that Jesus lives.

In the Gospel of Mark read in Cycle B, Jesus also commissions the apostles to go forth, preaching the good news leading to baptism. In this way, Christ still continues to work after the ascension—through the disciples. The various signs performed by the believers are indications that the kingdom of God is being established through the work of the Church.

In contrast to his scene in Acts where it marks the beginning of the Church's ministry, Luke's account of the ascension in his Gospel concludes Jesus' ministry on earth on Easter Day. With this farewell scene, Luke describes a definite close to the earthly ministry of Jesus, declaring that no longer can Jesus be known as he was on earth. From now on, Christ will be discovered in the Church.

Suggestions for Prayer

1. The term "apostle" comes from a word meaning to be sent. In prayer this week, consider to whom Christ has sent you. In what ways are you "preaching the good news" or "making disciples" through your daily words or actions?
2. Listen to the Letter to the Ephesians as if it were written to you.
   You may want to dwell especially on these lines.

"the great hope to which he has called you"
"the wealth of his glorious heritage to be distributed among the members of his Church"
"the immeasurable scope of his power in us who believe"

3. In the reading from Acts, the angels ask the apostles, "Why are you standing here looking up at the sky?" What would be your response as you consider the same question?

Suggestion for Journal Keeping

Scripture scholars tell us that the Gospel accounts of the ascension are not literal descriptions of an historical event, but are stories which emphasize the religious truths described above. Reflect this week in your journal on whether or not these conclusions affect your faith, and, if so, in what ways.

Emily J. Besl

181

Seventh Sunday of Easter **A**

READING I
Acts 1, 12–14

[After Jesus was taken up into the heavens,] the apostles returned to Jerusalem from the mount called Olivet near Jerusalem, a mere sabbath's journey away. Entering the city, they went to the upstairs room where they were staying: Peter and John and James and Andrew; Philip and Thomas, Bartholomew and Matthew; James son of Alpheus; Simon, the Zealot party member, and Judas son of James. Together they devoted themselves to constant prayer. There were some women in their company and Mary the mother of Jesus, and his brothers.

Responsorial Psalm
Ps 27, 1. 4. 7–8

I believe that I shall see the good things
 of the Lord in the land of the living.

The Lord is my light and my salvation;
 whom should I fear?
The Lord is my life's refuge;
 of whom should I be afraid?

I believe that I shall see the good things
 of the Lord in the land of the living.

One thing I ask of the Lord;
 this I seek:
To dwell in the house of the Lord
 all the days of my life,
That I may gaze on the loveliness of the Lord
 and contemplate his temple.

I believe that I shall see the good things
 of the Lord in the land of the living.

Hear, O Lord, the sound of my call;
 have pity on me, and answer me.
Of you my heart speaks; you my glance
 seeks.

I believe that I shall see the good things
 of the Lord in the land of the living.

READING II
1 Pt 4, 13–16

Rejoice, insofar as you share Christ's sufferings. When his glory is revealed you will rejoice exultantly. Happy are you when you are insulted for the sake of Christ, for then God's Spirit in its glory has come to rest on you. See to it that none of you suffers for being a murderer, a thief, a malefactor, or a destroyer of another's rights. If anyone suffers for being a Christian, however, he ought not be ashamed. He should rather glorify God in virtue of that name.

GOSPEL
Jn 17, 1–11

Jesus looked up to heaven and said:
 "Father, the hour has come!
 Give glory to your Son
 that your Son may give glory to you,
 inasmuch as you have given him authority over all mankind,
 that he may bestow eternal life on those you gave him.
 (Eternal life is this:
 to know you, the only true God,
 and him whom you have sent, Jesus Christ.)
 I have given you glory on earth
 by finishing the work you gave me to do.
 Do you now, Father, give me glory at your side,
 a glory I had with you before the world began.
 I have made your name known
 to those you gave me out of the world.
 These men you gave me were yours;
 they have kept your word.
 Now they realize
 that all that you gave me comes from you.
 I entrusted to them

the message you entrusted to me,
and they received it.
They have known that in truth I came
    from you,
they have believed it was you who sent
    me.
"For these I pray—
not for the world
but for these you have given me,
for they are really yours.
(Just as all that belongs to me is yours,
so all that belongs to you is mine.)
It is in them that I have been glorified.
I am in the world no more,
but these are in the world
as I come to you."

Reflection on the Readings

Between the feasts of Ascension and Pentecost, we listen to the account which links the two events in the Book of Acts. Listed here are the names of the apostles to whom we are united through the Spirit as suggested by last week's reading. Utterly dependent on God to act, all the community can do is wait and pray. Perhaps we should find here an image of us as the Church persevering in prayer, petitioning God for the gift of the Spirit whose presence we ought never take for granted.

Prayer occurs in the Gospel also, as Jesus prays on behalf of his disciples who must remain in the world. The Spirit will enable them and all Christians to be, as Jesus was, in the world and for the world, yet not of it. In his disciples Jesus has been glorified, through their fidelity as well as their future works of preaching and service. Called to union with one another, the disciples find the model and source of their unity in the communion and mutual love of Father and Son.

The second reading continues from Peter's epistle, repeating the theme of suffering for being a Christian. Baptismal life leads to glory, eternal life, unity, and joy, found paradoxically in the way of suffering. Undergoing persecution for Christ is a cause of joy because the Spirit of God rests on a suffering Church as the pledge of future glory. Nothing, then, can take our joy away because the Holy Spirit is on us.

Suggestions for Prayer

1. Jesus prays for his disciples who must remain in the world but not of the world. Do you ever experience a conflict between Christian values and those of the world? What do you do to resolve this conflict?

2. Reread the epistle from Peter. What experiences come to mind? Have you had to suffer in any way for being a Christian? "Pray for those who persecute you," as Jesus admonishes, and for forgiveness.

3. This week in prayer join those gathered in the upstairs room persevering in prayer and petitioning God for the gift of the Holy Spirit.

Suggestion for Journal Keeping

Empowering the Church, the Spirit prepares each member of the community for ministry. As the season of Easter draws to a close, consider the gifts you have been given and in what way you might use your gifts for the building up of the body of Christ.

Emily J. Besl

Seventh Sunday of Easter B

READING I
Acts 1, 15–17. 20–26

In those days Peter stood up in the midst of the brothers—there must have been a hundred and twenty gathered together. "Brothers," he said, "the saying in Scripture uttered long ago by the Holy Spirit through the mouth of David was destined to be fulfilled in Judas, the one that guided those who arrested Jesus. He was one of our number and he had been given a share in this ministry of ours.

"It is written in the Book of Psalms,
'May another take his office.'

"It is entirely fitting, therefore, that one of those who was of our company while the Lord Jesus moved among us, from the baptism of John until the day he was taken up from us, should be named as witness with us to his resurrection." At that they nominated two, Joseph (called Barsabbas, also known as Justus) and Matthias. Then they prayed: "O Lord, you read the hearts of men. Make known to us which of these two you choose for this apostolic ministry, replacing Judas, who deserted the cause and went the way he was destined to go." They then drew lots between the two men. The choice fell to Matthias, who was added to the eleven apostles.

Responsorial Psalm
Ps 103, 1–2. 11–12. 19–20

The Lord has set his throne in heaven.
Bless the Lord, O my soul;
  and all my being, bless his holy name.
Bless the Lord, O my soul,
  and forget not all his benefits.
The Lord has set his throne in heaven.

For as the heavens are high above the earth,
  so surpassing is his kindness toward those
  who fear him.
As far as the east is from the west,
  so far has he put our transgressions from
  us.
The Lord has set his throne in heaven.
The Lord has established his throne in
  heaven,
  and his kingdom rules over all.
Bless the Lord, all you his angels,
  you mighty in strength, who do his bidding.
The Lord has set his throne in heaven.

READING II
1 Jn 4, 11–16

Beloved,
  if God has loved us so,
  we must have the same love for one another.
No one has ever seen God.
Yet if we love one another
  God dwells in us,
  and his love is brought to perfection in us.
The way we know we remain in him
  and he in us
  is that he has given us of his Spirit.
We have seen for ourselves, and can testify,
  that the Father has sent the Son as savior
  of the world.
When anyone acknowledges that Jesus is the
  Son of God,
  God dwells in him
  and he in God.
We have come to know and to believe
  in the love God has for us.
God is love,
  and he who abides in love
  abides in God,
  and God in him.

GOSPEL   Jn 17, 11–19

Jesus looked up to heaven and prayed:

"**O Father most holy,**
protect them with your name which
you have given me,
[that they may be one, even as we are
one.]
As long as I was with them,
I guarded them with your name which
you gave me.
I kept careful watch,
and not one of them was lost,
none but him who was destined to be
lost—
in fulfillment of Scripture.
Now, however, I come to you;
I say all this while I am still in the world
that they may share my joy completely.
I gave them your word,
and the world has hated them for it;
they do not belong to the world,
[any more than I belong to the world.]
I do not ask you to take them out of the
world,
but to guard them from the evil one.
They are not of the world,
any more than I am of the world.
Consecrate them by means of truth—
'Your word is truth.'
As you have sent me into the world,
so I have sent them into the world;
I consecrate myself for their sakes now,
that they may be consecrated in truth."

Reflection on the Readings

Jesus is the Word of God. When Jesus speaks, God speaks. God's words are truthful and transformative. When we accept God's word as truth and allow this word to touch our lives, our lives are changed. As Jesus states in his prayer, we are no longer of this world. The values of Jesus' kingdom stand in stark contrast to the values of society. Those who allow Jesus' truth to touch them adopt the values of the kingdom and often feel out of step with society. Society can often reject and be cruel to those who do not conform. For this reason, Jesus prays for protection for those who hear God's words and allow their lives to be transformed by them.

The central value of God's kingdom and the message of God's truth is love. God's love is selfless and without limit. It is a love which is showered upon friend and enemy alike. It is a love which stands in stark contrast to society's values of power, self-promotion and materialism. God calls on us to allow ourselves to be touched by this love and to share this love with one another. If we do so, we may risk society's scorn. Yet at the same time, we allow ourselves to share completely in the joy promised by Jesus.

Suggestions for Prayer

1. In the Gospel, Jesus prays to God for his friends. Do you have friends who are in need of your prayers right now? If you do, bring them to your mind in prayer.
2. Psalm 103, the responsorial psalm, is a psalm of praise. Read this psalm prayerfully. At the end, add your own prayer of praise for the good things God has accomplished in your life.
3. Meditate on these words:

   God is love.
   God dwells in me.
   I dwell in God.

185

Write a short prayer based on Jesus' prayer in the Gospel. Include in this prayer how you hope God's word will touch and transform your life.

Kathryn A. Schneider

Seventh Sunday of Easter C

READING I   Acts 7, 55–60

Stephen, filled with the Holy Spirit, looked to the sky above and saw the glory of God, and Jesus standing at God's right hand. "Look!" he exclaimed, "I see an opening in the sky, and the Son of Man standing at God's right hand." The onlookers were shouting aloud, holding their hands over their ears as they did so. Then they rushed at him as one man, dragged him out of the city, and began to stone him. The witnesses meanwhile were piling their cloaks at the feet of a young man named Saul. As Stephen was being stoned he could be heard praying, "Lord Jesus, receive my spirit." He fell to his knees and cried out in a loud voice, "Lord, do not hold this sin against them." And with that he died.

Responsorial Psalm   Ps 97, 1–2. 6–7. 9

The Lord is king, the most high over all the
    earth.
The Lord is king; let the earth rejoice;
    let the many isles be glad.
Justice and judgment are the foundation of
    his throne.
The Lord is king, the most high over all the
    earth.

The heavens proclaim his justice,
    and all peoples see his glory.
All gods are prostrate before him.
The Lord is king, the most high over all the
    earth.
You, O Lord, are the Most High over all the
    earth,
    exalted far above all gods.
The Lord is king, the most high over all the
    earth.

READING II   Rv 22, 12–14. 16–17. 20

I, John, heard a voice saying to me: "Remember, I am coming soon! I bring with me the reward that will be given to each man as his conduct deserves. I am the Alpha and the Omega, the First and the Last, the Beginning and the End! Happy are they who wash their robes so as to have free access to the tree of life and enter the city through its gates!

"It is I, Jesus, who have sent my angel to give you this testimony about the churches. I am the Root and Offspring of David, the Morning Star shining bright."

The Spirit and the Bride say, "Come!" Let him who hears answer, "Come!" Let him who is thirsty come forward; let all who desire it accept the gift of life-giving water.

The One who gives this testimony says, "Yes, I am coming soon!" Amen! Come, Lord Jesus!

GOSPEL   Jn 17, 20–26

Jesus looked up to heaven and said:
    "I do not pray for my disciples alone.
    I pray also for those who will believe in
        me through their word,
    that all may be one
    as you, Father, are in me, and I in you;
    I pray that they may be [one] in us,

186

**that the world may believe that you sent
  me.
I have given them the glory you gave me
that they may be one, as we are one—
I living in them, you living in me—
that their unity may be complete.
So shall the world know that you sent
  me,
and that you loved them as you loved
  me.
Father,
all those you gave me
I would have in my company
where I am,
to see this glory of mine
which is your gift to me,
because of the love you bore me before
  the world began.
Just Father,
the world has not known you,
but I have known you;
and these men have known that you
  sent me.
To them I have revealed your name,
and I will continue to reveal it
so that your love for me may live in
  them,
and I may live in them."**

Reflection on the Readings

Jesus prays for unity, for the oneness of the relationship between the Father and the Son to be the source of union for the believers. The prayer in the Gospel is a petition. It also contains a description and reflection of Jesus' life and a promise of a continuation of the work of unity. The center of the union is the activity of praising God.

Union between loved ones is a normal desire. Family members, friends, lovers, desire to be in each other's company. That union or reunion is life-giving. The desire for union with God is described as thirst. The union with God is described as the very essence of life, as life-giving water.

God's love is inclusive, from beginning to end. God's love is gift. This is not at all simple to grasp in our lives that are surrounded by competition, and by exclusive company and associations. We also experience fragmentation due to the many roles we play or the many hats we wear. Jesus' prayer for unity calls us to wholeness and to an integration of God's will and our lives. The readings express an immediacy about God's love. Union with God is now. And this union includes us.

Suggestions for Prayer

1. Become familiar with a prayer or hymn of praise that is prayed by your community. The Gloria, for example, a prayer of the universal Church, gives praise to God. On a local scale, there are many hymns that are familiar in this country or even a song of your own church. Keep a copy of the words of the prayer and say them daily. Know that when you are doing that you are in union with the Church.

2. Place a basin or bowl of water before you. Touch the water, letting drops splash and circles widen. Pray that this element of creation will become a source of hope and life.

   Recall rivers that divide, and water that has been diverted, polluted, or run dry. Pray that these waters may again flow clear and clean.

   Pray to be fully immersed in God's life-giving water.

Recall the roles you played, the relationships in which you were involved in one day or one week. Where do these converge? How do they bring you to an integrated wholeness?

Elizabeth S. Lilly

Pentecost Sunday A B C

READING I   Acts 2, 1–11

When the day of Pentecost came it found the brethren gathered in one place. Suddenly from up in the sky there came a noise like a strong, driving wind which was heard all through the house where they were seated. Tongues as of fire appeared which parted and came to rest on each of them. All were filled with the Holy Spirit. They began to express themselves in foreign tongues and make bold proclamation as the Spirit prompted them.

Staying in Jerusalem at the time were devout Jews of every nation under heaven. These heard the sound, and assembled in a large crowd. They were much confused because each one heard these men speaking his own language. The whole occurrence astonished them. They asked in utter amazement, "Are not all of these men who are speaking Galileans? How is it that each of us hears them in his native tongue? We are Parthians, Medes, and Elamites. We live in Mesopotamia, Judea and Cappadocia, Pontus, the province of Asia, Phrygia and Pamphylia, Egypt, and the regions of Libya around Cyrene. There are even visitors from Rome—all Jews, or those who have come over to Ju-

daism; Cretans and Arabs too. Yet each of us hears them speaking in his own tongue about the marvels God has accomplished."

Responsorial Psalm   Ps 104, 1. 24. 29–30. 31. 34

Lord, send out your Spirit,
   and renew the face of the earth.
Bless the Lord, O my soul!
   O Lord, my God, you are great indeed!
How manifold are your works, O Lord!
   the earth is full of your creatures.
Lord, send out your Spirit,
   and renew the face of the earth.
If you take away their breath, they perish
   and return to their dust.
When you send forth your spirit, they are
      created,
   and you renew the face of the earth.
Lord, send out your Spirit,
   and renew the face of the earth.
May the glory of the Lord endure forever;
   may the Lord be glad in his works!
Pleasing to him be my theme;
   I will be glad in the Lord.
Lord, send out your Spirit,
   and renew the face of the earth.

READING II   1 Cor 12, 3–7. 12–13

No one can say: "Jesus is Lord," except in the Holy Spirit.

There are different gifts but the same Spirit; there are different ministries but the same Lord; there are different works but the same God who accomplishes all of them in every one. To each person the manifestation of the Spirit is given for the common good.

The body is one and has many members, but all the members, many though they are, are one body; and so it is with Christ. It was in one Spirit that all of us, whether Jew or

Greek, slave or free, were baptized into one body. All of us have been given to drink of the one Spirit.

GOSPEL   Jn 20, 19–23
On the evening of that first day of the week, even though the disciples had locked the doors of the place where they were for fear of the Jews, Jesus came and stood before them. "Peace be with you," he said. When he had said this, he showed them his hands and his side. At the sight of the Lord the disciples rejoiced. "Peace be with you," he said again.

> "As the Father has sent me,
> so I send you."

Then he breathed on them and said:
> "Receive the Holy Spirit.
> If you forgive men's sins,
> they are forgiven them;
> if you hold them bound,
> they are held bound."

Reflection on the Readings
  The psalm proclaims:

> The earth is full of your creatures.
> If you take away their breath,
> they perish and return to dust.
> When you send forth your spirit,
> they are created,
> and you renew the face of the earth.

The Holy Spirit is our breath. God breathes new life into us by sending us the Holy Spirit. We are created anew and together with God we work to renew the face of the earth.

In the Gospel, the disciples are like creatures whose breath had been taken away from them. Jesus, the one in whom all their hope lay, had been taken away and killed. Hidden in a room with doors locked, they are without hope, purpose or identity. It is as if they had perished and returned to dust. Then the risen Lord enters and breathes new life into them. Christ greets them with words of peace and sends them on a mission to continue God's work. Christ gives them the breath of new life by giving them the gift of the Holy Spirit.

This gift manifests itself on the day of Pentecost. In Acts, the Holy Spirit transforms a frightened group of disciples into brave and powerful preachers who make bold proclamations about the marvels God has accomplished.

In his Letter to the Corinthians, Paul reminds us that it is this same Holy Spirit which we receive in baptism. We are made into new creations, united with other Christians in our proclamation, "Jesus is Lord." This same Spirit which unites us provides us with gifts to be used for the common good. Fired with hope, purpose and new identity, the Holy Spirit sends us on our mission to work with God to renew the face of the earth.

Suggestions for Prayer

1. *Reflect on the following questions:* Have you ever felt afraid, without hope or identity? What was that like? How is that different from the times you felt the presence of God in your life?

2. In the reading from Acts, the fact that each spoke a different language proved to be a barrier to hearing the word of God. But then each hears Peter preaching in his or her own tongue. Are there any barriers in your life which keep you from hearing the word of God? Ask God to help you hear and be touched by the word of God.

3. Meditate on this proclamation: *Jesus is Lord!*

Suggestion for Journal Keeping
God asks us to use our gifts to renew the face of the earth. Write in your journal some concrete ways in which you can reach out to others to help renew the face of the earth.

Kathryn A. Schneider

Trinity Sunday A

READING I   Ex 34, 4–6. 8–9
Early in the morning Moses went up Mount Sinai as the Lord had commanded him, taking along the two stone tablets.

Having come down in a cloud, the Lord stood with him there and proclaimed his name, "Lord." Thus the Lord passed before him and cried out, "The Lord, the Lord, a merciful and gracious God, slow to anger and rich in kindness and fidelity." Moses at once bowed down to the ground in worship. Then he said, "If I find favor with you, O Lord, do come along in our company. This is indeed a stiff-necked people; yet pardon our wickedness and sins, and receive us as your own."

Responsorial Psalm   Dn 3, 52. 53. 54. 55. 56

Glory and praise for ever!
Blessed are you, O Lord, the God of our fathers,
praiseworthy and exalted above all forever;
And blessed is your holy and glorious name,
praiseworthy and exalted above all for all ages.
Glory and praise for ever!
Blessed are you in the temple of your holy glory,
praiseworthy and glorious above all forever.
Glory and praise for ever!
Blessed are you on the throne of your kingdom,
praiseworthy and exalted above all forever.
Glory and praise for ever!
Blessed are you who look into the depths from your throne upon the cherubim,
praiseworthy and exalted above all forever.
Glory and praise for ever!
Blessed are you in the firmament of heaven,
praiseworthy and glorious forever.
Glory and praise for ever!

READING II   2 Cor 13, 11–13
Brothers, mend your ways. Encourage one another. Live in harmony and peace, and the God of love and peace will be with you. Greet one another with a holy kiss. All the holy ones send greetings to you. The grace of the Lord Jesus Christ, and the love of God, and the fellowship of the Holy Spirit be with you all!

GOSPEL   Jn 3, 16–18
Jesus said to Nicodemus:
"Yes, God so loved the world
that he gave his only Son,
that whoever believes in him may not die
but may have eternal life.
God did not send the Son into the world
to condemn the world,

190

but that the world might be saved through him.
Whoever believes in him avoids condemnation,
but whoever does not believe is already condemned
for not believing in the name of God's only Son."

Reflection on the Readings

"Blessed be God the Father and his only-begotten Son and the Holy Spirit: for he has shown that he loves us." The entrance antiphon for Trinity Sunday announces what this feast celebrates: God has shown his love for us. Not concerned with pondering abstract metaphysical categories of person and nature, today's readings focus on our *experience* of the triune God as acting *for us* in the work of saving and recreating the world.

Israel's idolatry had provoked Moses to break the tablets of the covenant. But because of Moses' pleas God restored the tablets and turned toward Israel in love and compassion. He is a "merciful and gracious God, slow to anger, rich in kindness and fidelity." Given confidence by this encounter, Moses responds by inviting the Lord to remain and to receive Israel as his own, dwelling among them.

The love which God bestowed on Israel is revealed in Jesus, the decisive sign of God's self-giving, of his commitment not to condemn but to save an alienated world. Allusions to Abraham's willingness to sacrifice his son Isaac are suggested by describing God giving his "only" Son: such is the extent of God's love for us.

The love of God is manifested in Jesus as self-sacrifice, so the disciples of Jesus must express this same kind of love in their lives. Belief in the Trinity, then, requires not mere meditating on an abstraction, but a life lived concretely in harmony and peace expressed in the holy kiss. Often used in the opening rites of Mass, Paul's greeting here sums up Christian faith in the Trinity: Jesus, by ransoming us, has won the grace of our redemption; in Jesus' life and death we encounter the love of God made flesh; this leads us to incorporation in the Church where the Spirit transforms us day by day into the house of God and the image of Christ.

Suggestions for Prayer

1. Meditate on the passage from Exodus describing the mercy and kindness of God. Is your response similar to that of Moses who invited the Lord to "come along"?
2. The responsorial psalm is taken from the well-known Canticle of the Three Young Men in the Book of Daniel, a traditional element of morning prayer. Pray this canticle each morning this week to dedicate your day to God.
3. If we live in harmony and peace, the God of love and peace will be with us, St. Paul says. Consider in prayer how you might be better able to foster harmony in your surroundings.

Suggestion for Journal Keeping

Think of an experience you have had of being loved unconditionally.

Recount the events in light of today's readings, highlighting your response.

Emily J. Besl

READING I   Dt 4, 32–34. 39–40

Moses said to the people: "Ask now of the days of old, before your time, ever since God created man upon the earth; ask from one end of the sky to the other: Did anything so great ever happen before? Was it ever heard of? Did a people ever hear the voice of God speaking from the midst of fire, as you did, and live? Or did any god venture to go and take a nation for himself from the midst of another nation, by testings, by signs and wonders, by war, with his strong hand and outstretched arm, and by great terrors, all of which the Lord, your God, did for you in Egypt before your very eyes? This is why you must now know, and fix in your heart, that the Lord is God in the heavens above and on earth below, and that there is no other. You must keep his statutes and commandments which I enjoin on you today, that you and your children after you may prosper, and that you may have long life on the land which the Lord, your God, is giving you forever."

Responsorial Psalm   Ps 33, 4–5. 6. 9. 18–19. 20. 22

Happy the people the Lord has chosen to be his own.

Upright is the word of the Lord,
   and all his works are trustworthy.
He loves justice and right;
   of the kindness of the Lord the earth is full.
Happy the people the Lord has chosen to be his own.

By the word of the Lord the heavens were made;
by the breath of his mouth all their host.
For he spoke, and it was made;
   he commanded, and it stood forth.
Happy the people the Lord has chosen to be his own.

See, the eyes of the Lord are upon those who fear him,
   upon those who hope for his kindness,
To deliver them from death
   and preserve them in spite of famine.
Happy the people the Lord has chosen to be his own.

Our soul waits for the Lord,
   who is our help and our shield.
May your kindness, O Lord, be upon us
   who have put our hope in you.
Happy the people the Lord has chosen to be his own.

READING II   Rom 8, 14–17

All who are led by the Spirit of God are sons of God. You did not receive a spirit of slavery leading you back into fear, but a spirit of adoption through which we cry out, "Abba!" (that is, "Father"). The Spirit himself gives witness with our spirit that we are children of God. But if we are children, we are heirs as well: heirs of God, heirs with Christ, if only we suffer with him so as to be glorified with him.

GOSPEL   Mt 28, 16–20

The eleven disciples made their way to Galilee, to the mountain to which Jesus had summoned them. At the sight of him, those who had entertained doubts fell down in homage. Jesus came forward and addressed them in these words:

   "Full authority has been given to me
   both in heaven and on earth;

go, therefore, and make disciples of all
the nations.
Baptize them in the name
'of the Father
and of the Son,
and of the Holy Spirit.'
Teach them to carry out everything I
have commanded you.
And know that I am with you always,
until the end of the world!''

Reflection on the Readings

To be a Christian is to live in unity with the Trinity. The words of today's Gospel focus on the mystery into which you will be baptized. The Trinity is a mystery that we can never fully grasp. But the reality of the Trinity reveals to us that God is a community of love. The Father, Son and Holy Spirit exist eternally in a relationship of mutual equality. To be baptized in the name of the Father, the Son and the Holy Spirit is to be immersed into relationship with the Trinity.

In today's second reading Paul points out how our prayer manifests this immersion into the Trinity. In union with our Brother Jesus we cry out, ''Abba!'' This is the name by which Jesus himself called God when he prayed. It is a Hebrew word used by children meaning ''Daddy.'' Both our prayer itself and the very inclination to pray are the works of the Spirit, calling us into relationship with God. Paul says, ''All who are led by the Spirit are sons of God.'' The Holy Spirit unites us with Jesus and we are immersed into his loving union with the Father. We are co-heirs with Christ, sons and daughters of God.

This is the movement of all Christian prayer. In union with Jesus, by the power of the Holy Spirit, we give glory and praise to the Father. This is the mystery into which you will be baptized.

Suggestions for Prayer

1. Sit in a straight-backed chair, feet flat on the floor, hands folded on your lap. Breathe deeply. Each time you exhale pray the word ''Abba!'' Center all your thoughts and energy on this word. Pray this way for about ten minutes.
2. One of the most popular traditional prayers is the Glory Be. In it we praise the triune God:

Glory be to the Father, and to the Son, and to the Holy Spirit. As it was in the beginning, is now, and ever shall be, world without end. Amen.

To grow in your appreciation of this prayer, reflect on Paul's prayer in Ephesians 3:14–21.

Suggestion for Journal Keeping

In today's first reading Moses calls on the Israelites to remember the key events that made them a people. Through God's self-revelation in the burning bush, through signs and wonders worked amidst the Egyptians, and by means of the passage through the Red Sea, God made Israel his own people.

Describe in your journal some key events in your spiritual journey. What is your burning bush? What signs and wonders has God worked for you? What is your Red Sea?

Robert M. Hamma

READING I Prv 8, 22–31

Thus says the Wisdom of God:
"The Lord begot me, the first-born of his ways,
the forerunner of his prodigies of long ago;
From of old I was poured forth,
at the first, before the earth.
When there were no depths I was brought forth,
when there were no fountains or springs of water;
Before the mountains were settled into place,
before the hills, I was brought forth;
While as yet the earth and the fields were not made,
nor the first clods of the world.
"When he established the heavens I was there,
when he marked out the vault over the face of the deep;
When he made firm the skies above,
when he fixed fast the foundations of the earth;
When he set for the sea its limit,
so that the waters should not transgress his command;
Then was I beside him as his craftsman,
and I was his delight day by day,
Playing before him all the while,
playing on the surface of his earth;
and I found delight in the sons of men."

Responsorial Psalm Ps 8, 4–5. 6–7. 8–9
O Lord, our God,
how wonderful your name in all the earth!

When I behold your heavens, the work of your fingers,
the moon and the stars which you set in place—
What is man that you should be mindful of him,
or the son of man that you should care for him?
O Lord, our God,
how wonderful your name in all the earth!
You have made him little less than the angels,
and crowned him with glory and honor.
You have given him rule over the works of your hands,
putting all things under his feet:
O Lord, our God,
how wonderful your name in all the earth!
All sheep and oxen,
yes, and the beasts of the field,
The birds of the air, the fishes of the sea,
and whatever swims the paths of the seas.
O Lord, our God,
how wonderful your name in all the earth!

READING II Rom 5, 1–5

Now that we have been justified by faith, we are at peace with God through our Lord Jesus Christ. Through him we have gained access by faith to the grace in which we now stand, and we boast of our hope for the glory of God. But not only that—we even boast of our afflictions! We know that affliction makes for endurance, and endurance for tested virtue, and tested virtue for hope. And this hope will not leave us disappointed, because the love of God has been poured out in our hearts through the Holy Spirit who has been given to us.

GOSPEL   Jn 16, 12–15

Jesus said to his disciples:

"**I have much more to tell you,**
but you cannot bear it now.
When he comes, however,
being the Spirit of truth
he will guide you to all truth.
He will not speak on his own,
but will speak only what he hears,
and will announce to you the things to
come.
In doing this he will give glory to me,
because he will have received from me
what he will announce to you.
All that the Father has belongs to me.
That is why I said that what he will an-
nounce to you
he will have from me."

Reflection on the Readings

Jesus promises the disciples that the Spirit of truth will come who will guide them to all truth. Our temptation might be to want it all now or to assume that we already have all truth. We live in the promise, opening ourselves to the truth. We will come to truth in God. We do not possess truth, but rather will come to be possessed by truth.

The truth of God is a relational truth. Our experience of God is the loving relationship of the Father, with the Son, in the Spirit. The relationship expressed in the Trinity is one of harmony and peace. This interrelatedness can encompass us.

When we trust in this gift of peace we can begin to live with greater and greater hope. One result of this Spirit-induced hope will be an increase in our awareness and appreciation and participation in the delights of creation.

Suggestions for Prayer

1. Pray for the Spirit of truth, the spirit of wisdom. Reread the first reading and imagine all the places that are described. Imagine yourself, too, created in God's image, an image of delight. After taking some time with these images, thank and praise the creative God.

2. Learn this traditional prayer of praise:

Glory to the Father, and to the Son, and to the Holy Spirit. As it was in the beginning, is now, and ever shall be, world without end. Amen.

Let these traditional words come to your mind in the morning and in the evening. Let them give direction and perspective to your thoughts and your actions.

3. God's hope will not leave us disappointed. Form a statement of faith or belief in God's gift of life and love. Then allow events that might seem hopeless to come to mind. Address each one with your confession of hope, your statement of faith. Ask God to guide you in living in hope. Pray in the name of Jesus.

Suggestion for Journal Keeping

Recollect a relationship that significantly helped you discover who you are. Describe the person and the place and the situation. Was this a single event or did it continue over time? Was your discovery immediate or did you come upon the self-knowledge in reflection?

Elizabeth S. Lilly

Corpus Christi **A**

READING I Dt 8, 2–3. 14–16

Moses said to the people: "Remember how for forty years now the Lord, your God, has directed all your journeying in the desert, so as to test you by affliction and find out whether or not it was your intention to keep his commandments. He therefore let you be afflicted with hunger, and then fed you with manna, a food unknown to you and your fathers, in order to show you that not by bread alone does man live, but by every word that comes forth from the mouth of the Lord.

"Remember, the Lord, your God, who brought you out of the land of Egypt, that place of slavery; who guided you through the vast and terrible desert with its saraph serpents and scorpions, its parched and waterless ground; who brought forth water for you from the flinty rock and fed you in the desert with manna, a food unknown to your fathers."

Responsorial Psalm Ps 147, 12–13. 14–15. 19–20

Praise the Lord, Jerusalem.
Glorify the Lord, O Jerusalem;
praise your God, O Zion.
For he has strengthened the bars of your gates;
he has blessed your children within you.
Praise the Lord, Jerusalem.
He has granted peace in your borders;
with the best of wheat he fills you.
He sends forth his command to the earth;
swiftly runs his word!
Praise the Lord, Jerusalem.

He has proclaimed his word to Jacob,
his statutes and his ordinances to Israel.
He has not done thus for any other nation;
his ordinances he has not made known to them. Alleluia.
Praise the Lord, Jerusalem.

READING II 1 Cor 10, 16–17

Is not the cup of blessing we bless a sharing in the blood of Christ? And is not the bread we break a sharing in the body of Christ? Because the loaf of bread is one, we, many though we are, are one body for we all partake of the one loaf.

GOSPEL Jn 6, 51–58

Jesus said to the crowds of Jews:
"I myself am the living bread
come down from heaven.
If anyone eats this bread
he shall live forever;
the bread I will give
is my flesh, for the life of the world."
At this the Jews quarreled among themselves, saying, "How can he give us his flesh to eat?" Thereupon Jesus said to them:
"Let me solemnly assure you,
if you do not eat the flesh of the Son of Man
and drink his blood,
you have no life in you.
He who feeds on my flesh
and drinks my blood
has life eternal,
and I will raise him up on the last day.
For my flesh is real food
and my blood real drink.
The man who feeds on my flesh
and drinks my blood
remains in me, and I in him.

Just as the Father who has life sent me
and I have life because of the Father,
so the man who feeds on me
will have life because of me.
This is the bread that came down from
heaven.
Unlike your ancestors who ate and died
nonetheless,
the man who feeds on this bread shall
live forever."

Reflection on the Readings

The feast of Corpus Christi, or Body of Christ, celebrates the two dimensions of that mystery: the Eucharist and the Church. The body of Christ that is the Eucharist strengthens and sustains the body of Christ that is the Church.

Prefigured by the manna in the desert, the Eucharist is the food God provides for the journey. Not cultivated or harvested by human efforts, the manna which comes down from heaven is, like the Eucharist, given by God's gracious word, the true source of life. Some early Christian writers saw another reference to the Eucharist in the water from the rock, signifying the blood of Christ as well as the font of baptism: the water and blood flowing from the side of Christ as he hung upon the cross.

A further image of the Eucharist is found in the New Testament in the multiplication of the loaves in which Jesus' discourse in the Gospel occurs. Jesus himself is the living bread from heaven, the "best of wheat" mentioned in Psalm 147. Just as bread exists not for its own sake, but to nourish and give life, so Jesus lives not for self but dies "for the life of the world." We who drink the blessed cup of his blood participate in his sacrificial death, embracing his way of life and trusting in the hope of sharing his resurrection. Communion with Christ now in the Eucharist is a pledge of complete communion with him in the great and promised feast at the end of time.

In contrast to the Corinthians who seem to have had a rather individualistic view of the Lord's supper, Paul stresses that the Eucharist binds us not only to Christ but also to one another. We who eat of the one loaf are really one body. It is through eating the body of Christ that we become the body of Christ, participating in the Eucharist, the sacrament of the Church.

Suggestions for Prayer

1. Spend time in prayer reflecting on the rich image of Christ identified as food. How does it help you to understand or appreciate the mystery of Christ's presence in the Eucharist?
2. Before or after meals, pause for prayer to give thanks to God for sustaining and nourishing you through the gift of food.
3. To share in the eucharistic body of Christ entails patterning one's life after Christ who gave himself for the life of the world. In what ways are you being called to lay down your life for others?

Suggestion for Journal Keeping

Recall an experience of a dinner or other meal in which you felt united with those around the table. What insight does this lend to your experience of the Eucharist?

Emily Besl

Corpus Christi B

READING I   Ex 24, 3–8

When Moses came to the people and related all the words and ordinances of the Lord, they all answered with one voice, "We will do everything that the Lord has told us." Moses then wrote down all the words of the Lord and, rising early the next day, he erected at the foot of the mountain an altar and twelve pillars for the twelve tribes of Israel. Then, having sent certain young men of the Israelites to offer holocausts and sacrifice young bulls as peace offerings to the Lord, Moses took half of the blood and put it in large bowls; the other half he splashed on the altar. Taking the book of the covenant, he read it aloud to the people, who answered, "All that the Lord has said, we will heed and do." Then he took the blood and sprinkled it on the people, saying, "This is the blood of the covenant which the Lord has made with you in accordance with all these words of his."

Responsorial Psalm   Ps 116, 12–13. 15–16. 17–18

I will take the cup of salvation,
  and call on the name of the Lord.
How shall I make a return to the Lord
  for all the good he has done for me?
The cup of salvation I will take up,
  and I will call upon the name of the Lord.
I will take the cup of salvation,
  and call on the name of the Lord.
Precious in the eyes of the Lord
  is the death of his faithful ones.
I am your servant, the son of your handmaid;
  you have loosed my bonds.

I will take the cup of salvation,
  and call on the name of the Lord.
To you will I offer sacrifice of thanksgiving,
  and I will call upon the name of the Lord.
My vows to the Lord I will pay
  in the presence of all his people.
I will take the cup of salvation,
  and call on the name of the Lord.

READING II   Heb 9, 11–15

When Christ came as high priest of the good things which came to be, he entered once for all into the sanctuary, passing through the greater and more perfect tabernacle not made by hands, that is, not belonging to this creation. He entered not with the blood of goats and calves but with his own blood, and achieved eternal redemption. For if the blood of goats and bulls and the sprinkling of a heifer's ashes can sanctify those who are defiled so that their flesh is cleansed, how much more will the blood of Christ, who through the eternal spirit offered himself up unblemished to God, cleanse our consciences from dead works to worship the living God!

This is why he is mediator of a new covenant: since his death has taken place for deliverance from transgressions committed under the first covenant, those who are called may receive the promised eternal inheritance.

GOSPEL   Mk 14, 12–16. 22–26

On the first day of Unleavened Bread, when it was customary to sacrifice the paschal lamb, the disciples said to Jesus, "Where do you wish us to go to prepare the Passover supper for you?" He sent two of his disciples with these instructions: "Go into the city and you will come upon a man carrying a

198

water jar. Follow him. Whatever house he enters, say to the owner, 'The Teacher asks, Where is my guestroom where I may eat the Passover with my disciples?' Then he will show you an upstairs room, spacious, furnished, and all in order. That is the place you are to get ready for us." The disciples went off. When they reached the city they found it just as he had told them, and they prepared the Passover supper.

During the meal he took bread, blessed and broke it, and gave it to them. "Take this," he said, "this is my body." He likewise took a cup, gave thanks and passed it to them, and they all drank from it. He said to them: "This is my blood, the blood of the covenant, to be poured out on behalf of many. I solemnly assure you, I will never again drink of the fruit of the vine until the day when I drink it new in the reign of God."

After singing songs of praise they walked out to the Mount of Olives.

Reflection on the Readings

Most of us are familiar with the slogan of the American Red Cross, "Give the gift of life; give blood." Blood is life, and to give blood is to give life.

In each of today's readings blood plays a central role. In the first reading it is used to seal the bond of unity, the covenant, that God makes with the Israelites. Moses says, "This is the blood of the covenant which the Lord has made with you." And the people respond, "All that the Lord has said, we will heed and do."

In the Gospel, Jesus takes a cup of wine and says, "This is my blood, the blood of the covenant, to be poured out on behalf of many." Jesus recognizes that his obedience to the Father's call will lead to his death, but that this will be "on behalf of many." The gift of his blood forms a new covenant between God and humanity, one which, as Hebrews says, "cleanses our consciences." As the disciples drink of the cup, they say yes to the new covenant.

Today's feast of the Body and Blood of Christ celebrates the life of Christ in us. The Church is his body and he nourishes us through the gift of the Eucharist. Just as the Israelites and Jews responded with obedient fidelity to God, we are called to faithfully give our lives to the Lord. This is true worship of the living God, our ratification of the new covenant.

Suggestions for Prayer

1. Sit quietly. Listen to your heart as it pumps the life blood through your body. Reflect on the importance of your blood for your life. Offer your life again to God.
2. The Eucharist is the spiritual source of our Christian lives. As you prepare for initiation, pray for an increase in your hunger and thirst for the Eucharist.
3. Today's responsorial psalm is read by Christians in light of the Gospel. Join your prayer to that of Jesus as you pray this psalm.

Suggestion for Journal Keeping

Write about what the Eucharist means to you. Discuss this with your sponsor or spiritual guide.

Robert M. Hamma

Corpus Christi C

READING I
Gn 14, 18–20

Melchizedek, king of Salem, brought out bread and wine, and being a priest of God Most High, he blessed Abram with these words:
"Blessed be Abram by God Most High,
   the creator of heaven and earth;
And blessed be God Most High,
   who delivered your foes into your hand."

Responsorial Psalm   Ps 110, 1. 2. 3. 4
You are a priest for ever,
   in the line of Melchizedek.
The Lord said to my Lord: "Sit at my right hand
till I make your enemies your footstool."
You are a priest for ever,
   in the line of Melchizedek.
The scepter of your power the Lord will stretch forth from Zion:
"Rule in the midst of your enemies."
You are a priest for ever,
   in the line of Melchizedek.
"Yours is princely power in the day of your birth, in holy splendor;
   before the daystar, like the dew, I have begotten you."
You are a priest for ever,
   in the line of Melchizedek.
The Lord has sworn, and he will not repent:
   "You are a priest forever, according to the order of Melchizedek."
You are a priest for ever,
   in the line of Melchizedek.

READING II
1 Cor 11, 23–26

I received from the Lord what I handed on to you, namely, that the Lord Jesus on the night in which he was betrayed took bread, and after he had given thanks, broke it and said, "This is my body, which is for you. Do this in remembrance of me." In the same way, after the supper, he took the cup, saying, "This cup is the new covenant in my blood. Do this, whenever you drink it, in remembrance of me." Every time, then, you eat this bread and drink this cup, you proclaim the death of the Lord until he comes!

GOSPEL
Lk 9, 11–17

Jesus spoke to the crowds of the reign of God, and he healed all who were in need of healing.

As sunset approached the Twelve came and said to him, "Dismiss the crowd so that they can go into the villages and farms in the neighborhood and find themselves lodging and food, for this is certainly an out-of-the-way place." He answered them, "Why do you not give them something to eat yourselves?" They replied, "We have nothing but five loaves and two fishes. Or shall we ourselves go and buy food for all these people?" (There were about five thousand men.) Jesus said to his disciples, "Have them sit down in groups of fifty or so." They followed his instructions and got them all seated. Then, taking the five loaves and the two fishes, Jesus raised his eyes to heaven, pronounced a blessing over them, broke them, and gave them to his disciples for distribution to the crowd. They all ate until they had enough. What they had left, over and above, filled twelve baskets.

Reflection on the Readings
One name for the Church is the body of Christ. Today's feast focuses on how the body of Christ is nourished and in turn gives life.

From the Old Testament, from the early Christian community and from the Gospel we hear accounts of blessings associated with the giving of life. The dying and rising of Jesus, the freedom from enemies and the abundance of nourishment give and sustain life.

The Church becomes the body of Christ precisely when it acts in the way of Jesus, e.g., by being present to the hungry and the broken. Sometimes this is on such a grand scale that it becomes news. More often, and perhaps more importantly, are the times when bringing the presence of Jesus into our world is such an ordinary part of the fabric of our lives that we only recognize it when we stop and reflect. For example, sitting with a sick person, feeding a child, preparing a family dinner, and sharing a meal with a stranger are all life-giving acts. These are opportunities to thank God for the gift of life.

Suggestions for Prayer

1. Pray a blessing before each meal. The traditional prayer is given in the suggestions for the Third Sunday of Easter, Cycle C. Vary this with your own prayer, praising God, acknowledging him as the giver of all gifts, and asking for his blessing. Pray in the name of Jesus.
2. We often experience the body of Christ in the dying, the hungry, or the broken. In remembering the saving acts of Jesus' rising, or his feeding the hungry, we enter into communion with God. This remembering is a part of daily Christian life. Pray in remembrance of God's saving action in your life.
3. Pray for wholeness in your body. In the midst of our own sufferings, aches, pains, illness, and brokenness we can turn to God. Pray through these aspects of your life. Pray in hope and trust in the life of God through Jesus.

Suggestion for Journal Keeping

How does the Church remember the life of Jesus in your community today? What are the signs of hope, of life and of healing? Who conveys this message to those searching for meaning, for wholeness? Who brought this good news to you? How are you sharing with others?

Elizabeth S. Lilly

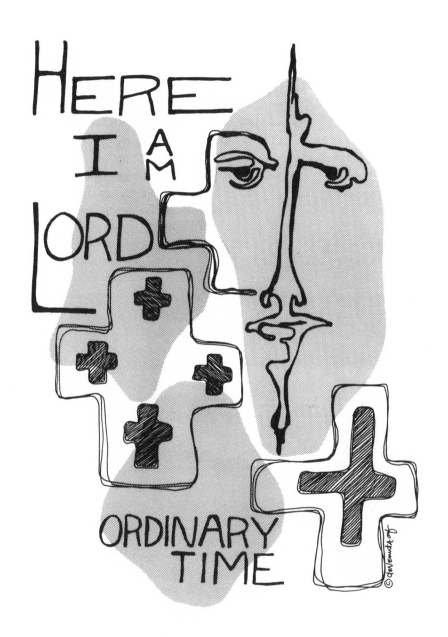

HERE I AM LORD

ORDINARY TIME

Second Sunday of the Year A

READING I   Is 49, 3. 5–6

The Lord said to me: you are my servant,
   Israel, through whom I show my glory.

Now the Lord has spoken
   who formed me as his servant from the
      womb,
That Jacob may be brought back to him
   and Israel gathered to him;
And I am made glorious in the sight of the
      Lord,
   and my God is now my strength!
It is too little, he says, for you to be my ser-
      vant,
   to raise up the tribes of Jacob,
   and restore the survivors of Israel;
I will make you a light to the nations,
   that my salvation may reach to the ends of
      the earth.

Responsorial Psalm   Ps 40, 2. 4. 7–8. 8–9.
                                                   10

Here am I, Lord;
   I come to do your will.
I have waited, waited for the Lord,
   and he stooped toward me and heard my
      cry.
And he put a new song into my mouth,
   a hymn to our God.

Here am I, Lord;
   I come to do your will.
Sacrifice or oblation you wished not,
   but ears open to obedience you gave me.
Holocausts or sin-offerings you sought not;
   then said I, "Behold I come."
Here am I, Lord;
   I come to do your will.
"In the written scroll it is prescribed for me,
   to do your will, O my God, is my delight,
And your law is within my heart!"
Here am I, Lord;
   I come to do your will.
I announced your justice in the vast assem-
      bly;
   I did not restrain my lips, as you, O Lord,
      know.
Here am I, Lord;
   I come to do your will.

READING II   1 Cor 1, 1–3

Paul, called by God's will to be an apostle of
Christ Jesus, and Sosthenes our brother,
send greetings to the church of God which
is in Corinth; to you who have been consecrated in Christ Jesus and called to be a holy
people, as to all those who, wherever they
may be, call on the name of our Lord Jesus
Christ, their Lord and ours. Grace and peace
from God our Father and the Lord Jesus
Christ.

GOSPEL
Jn 1, 29–34

When John caught sight of Jesus coming toward him, he exclaimed:

"Look there! The Lamb of God
who takes away the sin of the world!
It is he of whom I said:
'After me is to come a man
who ranks ahead of me,
because he was before me.'
I confess I did not recognize him, though the very reason I came baptizing with water was that he might be revealed to Israel."

John gave this testimony also:
"I saw the Spirit descend
like a dove from the sky,
and it came to rest on him.
But, as I say, I did not recognize him. The one who sent me to baptize with water told me, 'When you see the Spirit descend and rest on someone, it is he who is to baptize with the Holy Spirit.' Now I have seen for myself and have testified, 'This is God's chosen One.' "

Reflection on the Readings

Today's readings hearken back to last week's feast, the Baptism of the Lord. Jesus' baptism by John was the beginning of his public ministry. Many Scripture scholars believe that it was for Jesus an experience of hearing the Father calling him to his mission. In today's Gospel we hear John the Baptist relate that his baptizing Jesus is a religious experience for him as well. At first, John says, he did not recognize Jesus, even though he was the very reason for John's baptizing. But when he saw the Spirit descend upon him, he recognized Jesus as "God's chosen one." For Jesus, his baptism was a call to ministry; for John, it was a confirmation of his ministry.

As you prepare for your own baptism, to-day's Scriptures can serve as a reminder of the calling you have received. The image of the servant, described by Isaiah in the first reading, can be applied not only to John the Baptist and Jesus, but to you as well. The Lord has also formed you as his servant from the womb. The Lord has given you a mission to be a light for others.

In the second reading, Paul reflects on his call to be an apostle. For Paul, the word apostle does not only apply to the twelve, but to anyone who is sent to preach the good news. All Christians are called to an apostolic life. Furthermore, all the baptized, "who have been consecrated in Christ Jesus," are "called to be a holy people."

Suggestions for Prayer

1. To what kind of mission or service do you sense the Lord is calling you? Reflect on your gifts and the needs you see around you. Respond by praying repeatedly the psalm refrain, "Here am I, Lord; I come to do your will."
2. Reflect on the word "servant." How do the words of John the Baptist in the Gospel express the meaning of being a servant? What kind of a servant was Jesus? What about you?
3. John recognizes Jesus when the Spirit descends upon him and says that Jesus is the one who will baptize with the Holy Spirit. Pray for the gift of the Spirit so that you may fulfill your mission.

Suggestion for Journal Keeping

Reflect on a time—perhaps when you were ill or otherwise needy—when someone was a servant for you. Write down some of the qualities required of a servant. Which of these qualities do you need to grow in? Why?

Robert M. Hamma

Second Sunday of the Year B

READING I   1 Sm 3, 3–10. 19

Samuel was sleeping in the temple of the Lord where the ark of God was. The Lord called to Samuel, who answered, "Here I am." He ran to Eli and said, "Here I am. You called me." "I did not call you," Eli said. "Go back to sleep." So he went back to sleep. Again the Lord called Samuel, who rose and went to Eli. "Here I am," he said. "You called me." But he answered, "I did not call you, my son. Go back to sleep." At that time Samuel was not familiar with the Lord, because the Lord had not revealed anything to him as yet. The Lord called Samuel again, for the third time. Getting up and going to Eli, he said, "Here I am. You called me." Then Eli understood that the Lord was calling the youth. So he said to Samuel, "Go to sleep, and if you are called, reply, 'Speak, Lord, for your servant is listening.' " When Samuel went to sleep in his place, the Lord came and revealed his presence, calling out as before, "Samuel, Samuel!" Samuel answered, "Speak, for your servant is listening."

Samuel grew up, and the Lord was with him, not permitting any word of his to be without effect.

Responsorial Psalm   Ps 40, 2. 4. 7–8. 8–9. 10
Here am I, Lord;
   I come to do your will.

I have waited, waited for the Lord,
   and he stooped toward me and heard my cry.
And he put a new song into my mouth,
   a hymn to our God.
Here am I, Lord;
   I come to do your will.
Sacrifice or oblation you wished not,
   but ears open to obedience you gave me.
Holocausts or sin-offerings you sought not;
   then said I, "Behold I come."
Here am I, Lord;
   I come to do your will.
"In the written scroll it is prescribed for me,
   to do your will, O my God, is my delight,
And your law is within my heart!"
Here am I, Lord;
   I come to do your will.
I announced your justice in the vast assembly;
   I did not restrain my lips, as you, O Lord, know.
Here am I, Lord;
   I come to do your will.

READING II   1 Cor 6, 13–15. 17–20

The body is not for immorality; it is for the Lord, and the Lord is for the body. God, who raised up the Lord, will raise us also by his power.

Do you not see that your bodies are members of Christ? Whoever is joined to the Lord becomes one spirit with him. Shun lewd conduct. Every other sin a man commits is outside his body, but the fornicator sins against his own body. You must know that your body is a temple of the Holy Spirit, who is within—the Spirit you have received from God. You are not your own. You have been purchased, and at what a price! So glorify God in your body.

GOSPEL   Jn 1, 35—42

John was in Bethany across the Jordan with two of his disciples. As he watched Jesus walk by he said, "Look! There is the Lamb of God!" The two disciples heard what he said, and followed Jesus. When Jesus turned around and noticed them following him, he asked them, "What are you looking for?" They said to him, "Rabbi (which means Teacher), where do you stay?" "Come and see," he answered. So they went to see where he was lodged, and stayed with him that day. (It was about four in the afternoon.)

One of the two who had followed him after hearing John was Simon Peter's brother Andrew. The first thing he did was seek out his brother Simon and tell him, "We have found the Messiah!" (which means the Anointed). He brought him to Jesus, who looked at him and said, "You are Simon, son of John; your name shall be Cephas (which is rendered Peter)."

Reflection on the Readings

Responding to a call is only the beginning. A single action or decision affects others as well as ourselves. A choice for God, for Jesus Christ, for an exploration of the faith, or getting to know a community of believers becomes a pivotal time in our lives. Our choices, like our lives, are not in isolation. Once we set a course for ourselves, we continue to make other choices affirming—or changing—that pivotal one.

In the first and third Scripture readings today, we hear stories of "call"—Samuel called by the Lord, the first disciples called by Jesus. Once these persons heard the call, and understood even a little who it was that called them, their response was total: "Here I am!" A second level or implication is indicated in the readings as well: we hear the call through others. There are other people in our lives who advise, guide, lead, listen, and encourage us.

Having heard a message and responded to it, we enter a new community—those who are there to welcome and be with us. During the catechumenate process, we are listening, asking, searching, growing. The important thing is that we continue to be honest with ourselves and others. We do not always know what the end of the journey will be. We don't even have a guarantee of the direction our lives will take on this journey. But we do know that, having said yes, we are learning about ourselves and about others who are also seeking.

In daily life, it is not so simple to hear the call of God or to work out what it means to respond to that call. Sometimes others are most valuable in helping us understand what a call to discipleship means in ordinary terms. As Eli aided Samuel, and Andrew told his brother Simon; there are others who help us. As you are preparing for entrance into the Catholic community, it may be helpful and inspiring to hear other members of the parish who are willing to share their faith and what it means in their lives.

The second reading, from Paul's First Letter to the Corinthians, reminds us of our value as persons, that we are greatly loved by God. The people of Corinth are an example of a community of people who have heard the message and who struggle to remain faithful to it. Being faithful isn't always easy—which is also why getting to know others who are on a faith journey may be helpful at this time.

Suggestions for Prayer

1. Obtain and listen to the song "Here I Am, Lord" (Dan Schutte, S.J., NALR) or "Speak Lord, I'm Listening" (Gary Ault and Damean Music). Listen to the words of the song as if you are praying them as well. Then simply compose your own prayer conversation with the Lord.

2. Recall a time when you were aware of being asked to make a choice that would influence your life. To whom did you turn for help in clarifying the decision and its implications? As you recall the time, keep the persons involved in prayer and thank God for the choice and its aftermath—what you have learned from it.

3. Find a spot where you can see highways, roads or paths. Become aware of these as a way for people to go from one place to another. Watch people—or imagine them—making ordinary choices about directions to go in. Sometimes making decisions about traveling is easier than choices about life directions. Now become aware of Jesus walking with those on the way. Concentrate on Jesus accompanying you, in spirit and through other persons in your life. Talk with Jesus about your choices and decisions right now.

Suggestion for Journal Keeping

What is required of you at this time to respond faithfully, to the best of your abilities, to the call of Jesus: "Come, follow me"? How can you keep a joyous, peace-filled response alive in your life? Reflect, and write down some of the thoughts you have.

Clare M. Colella

Second Sunday of the Year C

READING I Is 62, 1–5

For Zion's sake I will not be silent,
    for Jerusalem's sake I will not be quiet,
Until her vindication shines forth like the dawn
    and her victory like a burning torch.
Nations shall behold your vindication,
    and all kings your glory;
You shall be called by a new name
    pronounced by the mouth of the Lord.
You shall be a glorious crown in the hand of the Lord,
    a royal diadem held by your God.
No more shall men call you "Forsaken,"
    or your land "Desolate,"
But you shall be called "My Delight,"
    and your land "Espoused."
For the Lord delights in you,
    and makes your land his spouse.
As a young man marries a virgin,
    your Builder shall marry you;
And as a bridegroom rejoices in his bride,
    so shall your God rejoice in you.

Responsorial Psalm   Ps 96, 1–2. 2–3. 7–8.
9–10

Proclaim his marvelous deeds to all the
nations.

Sing to the Lord a new song;
sing to the Lord, all you lands.
Sing to the Lord; bless his name.
Proclaim his marvelous deeds to all the
nations.

Announce his salvation, day after day.
Tell his glory among the nations;
Among all peoples, his wondrous deeds.
Proclaim his marvelous deeds to all the
nations.

Give to the Lord, you families of nations,
give to the Lord glory and praise;
give to the Lord the glory due his name!
Proclaim his marvelous deeds to all the
nations.

Worship the Lord in holy attire.
Tremble before him, all the earth;
Say among the nations: The Lord is king.
He governs the peoples with equity.
Proclaim his marvelous deeds to all the
nations.

READING II   1 Cor 12, 4–11
There are different gifts but the same Spirit;
there are different ministries but the same
Lord; there are different works but the same
God who accomplishes all of them in every-
one. To each person the manifestation of the
Spirit is given for the common good. To one
the Spirit gives wisdom in discourse, to an-
other the power to express knowledge.
Through the Spirit one receives faith; by the
same Spirit another is given the gift of heal-
ing, and still another miraculous powers.
Prophecy is given to one; to another power
to distinguish one spirit from another. One
receives the gift of tongues, another that of
interpreting the tongues. But it is one and
the same Spirit who produces all these gifts,
distributing them to each as he wills.

GOSPEL   Jn 2, 1–12
There was a wedding at Cana in Galilee, and
the mother of Jesus was there. Jesus and his
disciples had likewise been invited to the
celebration. At a certain point the wine ran
out, and Jesus' mother told him, "They have
no more wine." Jesus replied, "Woman,
how does this concern of yours involve me?
My hour has not yet come." His mother in-
structed those waiting on table, "Do what-
ever he tells you." As prescribed for Jewish
ceremonial washings, there were at hand six
stone water jars, each one holding fifteen to
twenty-five gallons. "Fill those jars with wa-
ter," Jesus ordered, at which they filled
them to the brim. "Now," he said, "draw
some out and take it to the waiter in
charge." They did as he instructed them.
The waiter in charge tasted the water made
wine, without knowing where it had come
from; only the waiters knew, since they had
drawn the water. Then the waiter in charge
called the groom over and remarked to him:
"People usually serve the choice wine first;
then when the guests have been drinking
awhile, a lesser vintage. What you have
done is keep the choice wine until now." Je-
sus performed this first of his signs at Cana
in Galilee. Thus did he reveal his glory, and
his disciples believed in him.

After this he went down to Capernaum,
along with his mother and brothers [and his
disciples] but they stayed there only a few
days.

Reflection on the Readings

The occasion of a wedding feast becomes the scene for Jesus' first sign of his glory. A miraculous transformation of water into wine opens his disciples into further belief. This transformation is effected quietly. Jesus' mother prompts him with a simple statement, "They have no more wine." And Jesus himself commands, in a simple way, "Now draw some out and take it to the waiter in charge." The way in which this miraculous transformation occurs is not dramatic. But the end result certainly is astounding. Water becomes wine.

In the first reading, Isaiah uses a simple image to convey to the people the effect of God's favor upon Israel. He speaks about a young man marrying his bride. What could be more ordinary? A man and woman stand before their family and friends and proclaim simple words as they vow themselves to one another. The effect, however, is beheld over an entire lifetime of faithfulness. Husband and wife become a "royal diadem" and "glorious crown." God takes to himself a people, Israel, and calls them "espoused" and "my delight."

The culmination of this relationship is to be found in Jesus and his new covenant. The fruit of this covenant is the gift of the Spirit, as St. Paul reminds us in the second reading.

A simple wedding celebration. Jesus' quiet, commanding words effect a powerful transformation. The waters of our lives become the choice, rich wine of his Spirit. Rejoice!

Suggestions for Prayer

1. Spend some quiet time reflecting on one or more of the following: What are the gifts you have been given in your life by Jesus? How does the spirit call you to best use your gifts in service to the needs of others?

2. Imagine Jesus standing before you and commanding, "Now take some and draw it out!" What part of you might he be talking about? Is there an area in your life that needs transforming? Offer that part of yourself to Jesus, and in your prayer use the words of Isaiah, "I shall be called a new name."

Suggestion for Journal Keeping

Describe someone you know who has gone through a personal transformation. What was the cause? What was the cost? In your own estimation, was that transformation positive or negative? Was it the "marvelous deed" proclaimed in the psalm for this Sunday?

Steven M. Lanza

Third Sunday of the Year

READING I   Is 8, 23—9, 3
First he degraded the land of Zebulun and the land of Naphtali; but in the end he has glorified the seaward road, the land west of the Jordan, the District of the Gentiles.
Anguish has taken wing, dispelled is darkness:
   for there is no gloom where but now there was distress.
The people who walked in darkness have seen a great light;
Upon those who dwelt in the land of gloom a light has shone.

You have brought them abundant joy
    and great rejoicing,
As they rejoice before you as at the harvest,
    as men make merry when dividing spoils.
For the yoke that burdened them,
    the pole on their shoulder,
And the rod of their taskmaster
    you have smashed, as on the day of Mi-
    dian.

Responsorial Psalm   Ps 27, 1. 4. 13–14
The Lord is my light and my salvation.
The Lord is my light and my salvation;
    whom should I fear?
The Lord is my life's refuge;
    of whom should I be afraid?
The Lord is my light and my salvation.
One thing I ask of the Lord;
    this I seek:
To dwell in the house of the Lord
    all the days of my life,
That I may gaze on the loveliness of the Lord
    and contemplate his temple.
The Lord is my light and my salvation.
I believe that I shall see the bounty of the
    Lord
    in the land of the living.
Wait for the Lord with courage;
    be stouthearted, and wait for the Lord.
The Lord is my light and my salvation.

READING II   1 Cor 1, 10–13. 17
I beg you; brothers, in the name of our Lord
Jesus Christ, to agree in what you say. Let
there be no factions; rather, be united in
mind and judgment. I have been informed,
my brothers, by certain members of Chloe's
household that you are quarreling among
yourselves. This is what I mean: One of you
will say, "I belong to Paul," another, "I belong to Apollos," still another, "Cephas has
my allegiance," and the fourth, "I belong to
Christ." Has Christ, then, been divided into
parts? Was it Paul who was crucified for
you? Was it in Paul's name that you were
baptized? Christ did not send me to baptize
but to preach the gospel—not with wordy
"wisdom," however, lest the cross of Christ
be rendered void of its meaning!

GOSPEL   Mt 4, 12–23
When Jesus heard that John had been arrested, he withdrew to Galilee. He left Nazareth and went down to live in Capernaum
by the sea near the territory of Zebulun and
Naphtali, to fulfill what had been said
through Isaiah the prophet:
    "Land of Zebulun, land of Naphtali
    along the sea beyond the Jordan,
    heathen Galilee:
    a people living in darkness
    has seen a great light.
    On those who inhabit a land overshad-
        owed by death,
    light has arisen."
From that time on Jesus began to proclaim
this theme: "Reform your lives! The kingdom of heaven is at hand."
    As he was walking along the Sea of Galilee
he watched two brothers, Simon now
known as Peter, and his brother Andrew,
casting a net into the sea. They were fishermen. He said to them, "Come after me and
I will make you fishers of men." They immediately abandoned their nets and became
his followers. He walked along farther and
caught sight of two other brothers, James,
Zebedee's son, and his brother John. They
too were in their boat, getting their nets in

order with their father, Zebedee. He called them, and immediately they abandoned boat and father to follow him.

Jesus toured all of Galilee. He taught in their synagogues, proclaimed the good news of the kingdom, and cured the people of every disease and illness.

Reflection on the Readings

Today's Gospel marks the beginning of Jesus' ministry as recounted by Matthew. Throughout this year the liturgy draws from Matthew. This passage emphasizes two of Matthew's favorite themes: Jesus the fulfillment of the hopes of Israel, and Jesus the teacher.

The first part of the Gospel is a quotation from the prophet Isaiah in today's first reading. Jesus comes from Galilee, a place that was until that time inhabited by Gentiles and held in low regard by the Jews. Matthew sees here a fulfillment of Isaiah's words in which this land, once degraded, is now exalted. Jesus' coming fulfills the hopes expressed by Isaiah and is described with rich imagery.

Jesus begins to teach with the proclamation: "Reform your lives; the kingdom of heaven is at hand." There is much to be said about what the coming of the kingdom means, and Matthew will lead us to understand this in the weeks ahead. Yet already in today's Gospel we see that it calls for a change. This change is dramatically portrayed in the lives of the first disciples who leave their fishing nets to follow Jesus, as well as in the miraculous healing that accompanies Jesus' teaching. So, too, for us, the coming of the kingdom will mean a letting go of something, but also the discovery of something new.

Suggestions for Prayer

1. What do you hope for? How does Jesus fulfill your hopes? Reflect on these questions and conclude by praying the responsorial psalm.
2. What kind of a teacher is Jesus? What do you want to learn from him? What must you let go of in order to learn? Reflect on these questions and pray with Jesus' words to the disciples, "Come after me."
3. One of the changes that the kingdom brings is the end of factions and divisions. Reread the second reading and reflect on how you can be a reconciler.

Suggestion for Journal Keeping

In today's readings from Isaiah, Psalm 27, and Matthew, the theme of light and darkness is emphasized. In your journal make two columns with the headings *Light* and *Darkness*. Under each, list the words that the readings associate with each. In what sense can the words under darkness describe your life? How does Jesus lead you to light? What is required of you for this passage?

Robert M. Hamma

Third Sunday of the Year B

READING I Jon 3, 1–5. 10
The word of the Lord came to Jonah saying: "Set out for the great city of Nineveh, and announce to it the message that I will tell you." So Jonah made ready and went to Nineveh, according to the Lord's bidding. Now

Nineveh was an enormously large city; it took three days to go through it. Jonah began his journey through the city, and had gone but a single day's walk announcing, "Forty days more and Nineveh shall be destroyed," when the people of Nineveh believed God; they proclaimed a fast and all of them, great and small, put on sackcloth.

When God saw by their actions how they turned from their evil way, he repented of the evil that he had threatened to do to them; he did not carry it out.

Responsorial Psalm   Ps 25, 4–5. 6–7. 8–9
Teach me your ways, O Lord.
Your ways, O Lord, make known to me;
  teach me your paths,
Guide me in your truth and teach me,
  for you are God my savior.
Teach me your ways, O Lord.
Remember that your compassion, O Lord,
  and your kindness are from of old.
In your kindness remember me,
  because of your goodness, O Lord.
Teach me your ways, O Lord.
Good and upright is the Lord;
  thus he shows sinners the way.
He guides the humble to justice,
  he teaches the humble his way.
Teach me your ways, O Lord.

READING II   1 Cor 7, 29–31
I tell you, brothers, the time is short. From now on those with wives should live as though they had none; those who weep should live as though they were not weeping, and those who rejoice as though they were not rejoicing; buyers should conduct themselves as though they owned nothing, and those who make use of the world as

though they were not using it, for the world as we know it is passing away.

GOSPEL   Mk 1, 14–20
After John's arrest, Jesus appeared in Galilee proclaiming God's good news: "This is the time of fulfillment. The reign of God is at hand! Reform your lives and believe in the good news!"

As he made his way along the Sea of Galilee, he observed Simon and his brother Andrew casting their nets into the sea; they were fishermen. Jesus said to them, "Come after me; I will make you fishers of men." They immediately abandoned their nets and became his followers. Proceeding a little farther along, he caught sight of James, Zebedee's son, and his brother John. They too were in their boat putting their nets in order. He summoned them on the spot. They abandoned their father Zebedee, who was in the boat with the hired men, and went off in his company.

Reflection on the Readings

Making a decision at one time in our lives doesn't always mean that the case is comfortably closed. Sometimes we have second thoughts about what we are doing. Sometimes we hesitate, waver. Sometimes we need to affirm a choice we have already made.

So it is with the call to holiness. It may be that we are eager for holiness but reluctant to pay the price of discipleship. For others, or at another time in our lives, we may just want to maintain the status quo, being unwilling or unable to invest the energy and time that changes require. We may go through times of wanting to let go of an already made commitment. Our sense of what is important may change. We may simply get tired of trying. There *is* a cost in discipleship.

These ambiguities are part of human nature. Our Scripture readings today deal with this. Jonah, at first reluctant, finally does agree to do what God has asked—to preach conversion to the people of Nineveh. Jonah's efforts are rewarded by the belief and conversion of the people. Jonah was effective. Paul's letter to the people of Corinth is a sort of echo of Jonah—time is short; you are called to lead a holy life. It too is a call for conversion and discipleship.

The Gospel episode opens with Jesus continuing the proclamation of John the Baptist: "Now is the time of fulfillment. Now is the time for conversion." Mark's Gospel recounts this as the time when the disciples responded readily and wholeheartedly to Jesus' invitation to follow, to learn his ways.

The disciples, and we, have made a choice. It is central in our lives; our attitudes, values and priorities may have to change. They may have already changed. We have heard a call to discipleship. Typically, the call from God is indicated in the desires and hopes of our hearts. So we gather, ask, learn, pray, ponder, discern: How do we hear the call? What does it mean to respond to that call? What is being given, promised? What does it mean for me to reform my life and believe the good news? What is being asked of me?

Suggestions for Prayer

1. Reread the Gospel story. Take time to picture graphically in your mind the seashore setting, Jesus walking, seeing Si-

mon and Andrew and calling to them, "Come after me." Picture yourself in that setting. See Jesus approach you, hear his words to the fishermen, watch the others get up to follow him. Does he call to you? What do you feel? What do you do?

2. Think of someone you know who is making a real effort to live a life of goodness, of holiness. Reflect on the qualities and characteristics of one who follows Jesus. Pray the prayer of St. Francis: "Make me a channel of your peace. Where there is hatred, let me sow your love. Where there is injury, pardon; where there is doubt, faith; where there is despair, hope; where there is darkness, light, where there is sadness, joy. O Divine Master, grant that I may seek not so much to be consoled as to console; to be understood as to understand, to be loved as to love. For it is in giving that we receive; it is in pardoning that we are pardoned. It is in dying that we are born to eternal life."

Suggestion for Journal Keeping

Sit in a comfortable position, in a quiet area; let your hands rest, open palms upward, in your lap. Have your journal nearby and ready to write in. With your eyes closed, let your mind picture the important elements in your life right now—your family, loved ones, your home, work. Focus on those you feel are gifts, blessings to you. In the midst of this surrounding, you see Jesus approach you, look at you intently, then ask you to be his follower, his disciple. What do you feel? What is your first response to him? Do you hesitate? Why—or why not? Continue to im-

215

age Jesus and yourself together in the setting of your life. What is changing? Open your eyes and write in your journal.

Clare M. Colella

Third Sunday of the Year C

READING I   Neh 8, 2–4. 5–6. 8–10

Ezra the priest brought the law before the assembly, which consisted of men, women, and those children old enough to understand. Standing at one end of the open place that was before the Water Gate, he read out of the book from daybreak till midday, in the presence of the men, the women, and those children old enough to understand; and all the people listened attentively to the book of the law. Ezra the scribe stood on a wooden platform that had been made for the occasion. Ezra opened the scroll so that all the people might see it (for he was standing higher up than any of the people); and, as he opened it, all the people rose. Ezra blessed the Lord, the great God, and all the people, their hands raised high, answered, "Amen, amen!" Then they bowed down and prostrated themselves before the Lord, their faces to the ground. Ezra read plainly from the book of the law of God, interpreting it so that all could understand what was read. Then [Nehemiah, that is, His Excellency, and] Ezra the priest-scribe [and the Levites who were instructing the people] said to all the people: "Today is holy to the Lord your God. Do not be sad, and do not weep"—for all the people were weeping as they heard the words of the law. He said further: "Go, eat rich foods and drink sweet drinks, and al- lot portions to those who had nothing pre- pared; for today is holy to our Lord. Do not be saddened this day, for rejoicing in the Lord must be your strength!"

Responsorial Psalm   Ps 19, 8. 9. 10. 15
Your words, Lord, are spirit and life.
The law of the Lord is perfect,
   refreshing the soul;
The decree of the Lord is trustworthy,
   giving wisdom to the simple.
Your words, Lord, are spirit and life.
The precepts of the Lord are right,
   rejoicing the heart;
The command of the Lord is clear,
   enlightening the eye.
Your words, Lord, are spirit and life.
The fear of the Lord is pure,
   enduring forever;
The ordinances of the Lord are true,
   all of them just.
Your words, Lord, are spirit and life.
Let the words of my mouth and the thought
   of my heart
   find favor before you,
O Lord, my rock and my redeemer.
Your words, Lord, are spirit and life.

READING II   1 Cor 12, 12–30

The body is one and has many members, but all the members, many though they are, are one body; and so it is with Christ. It was in one Spirit that all of us, whether Jew or Greek, slave or free, were baptized into one body. All of us have been given to drink of the one Spirit. Now the body is not one member, it is many. If the foot should say, "Because I am not a hand I do not belong to the body," would it then no longer belong to the body? If the ear should say, "Because I am not an eye I do not belong to the body," would it then no longer belong to the body? If the body were all eye, what would happen to our hearing? If it were all ear, what would happen to our smelling? As it is, God has set each member of the body in the place he wanted it to be. If all the members were alike, where would the body be? There are, indeed, many different members, but one body. The eye cannot say to the hand, "I do not need you," any more than the head can say to the feet, "I do not need you." Even those members of the body which seem less important are in fact indispensable. We honor the members we consider less honorable by clothing them with greater care, thus bestowing on the less presentable a propriety which the more presentable already have. God has so constructed the body as to give greater honor to the lowly members, that there may be no dissension in the body, but that all the members may be concerned for one another. If one member suffers, all the members suffer with it; if one member is honored, all the members share its joy.

You, then, are the body of Christ. Every one of you is a member of it. Furthermore, God has set up in the church first apostles, second prophets, third teachers, then miracle workers, healers, assistants, administrators, and those who speak in tongues. Are all apostles? Are all prophets? Are all teachers? Do all work miracles or have the gift of healing? Do all speak in tongues, all have the gift of interpretation of tongues?

GOSPEL   Lk 1, 1–4; 4, 14–21
Many have undertaken to compile a narrative of the events which have been fulfilled in our midst, precisely as those events were transmitted to us by the original eye-witnesses and ministers of the word. I too have carefully traced the whole sequence of events from the beginning, and have decided to set it in writing for you, Theophilus, so that Your Excellency may see how reliable the instruction was that you received.

Jesus returned in the power of the Spirit to Galilee, and his reputation spread throughout the region. He was teaching in their synagogues, and all were loud in his praise.

He came to Nazareth where he had been reared, and entering the synagogue on the sabbath as he was in the habit of doing, he stood up to do the reading. When the book of the prophet Isaiah was handed him, he unrolled the scroll and found the passage where it was written:

"The spirit of the Lord is upon me;
    therefore he has anointed me.
He has sent me to bring glad tidings to
    the poor,
    to proclaim liberty to captives,
Recovery of sight to the blind
    and release to prisoners,
To announce a year of favor from the
    Lord."
Rolling up the scroll he gave it back to the assistant and sat down. All in the synagogue had their eyes fixed on him. Then he began by saying to them, "Today this Scripture passage is fulfilled in your hearing."

Reflection on the Readings
Ezra, the priest, reads the words of the law before the people. They react quite strongly: weeping, prostrate on the ground. The ancient scroll from which Ezra reads is the visible, concrete manifestation of God's love to his people; and as the psalm says, the words of the Lord are "spirit and life." The people react as they do because the word of God

217

proclaimed in the law is powerful and life-giving.

And yet, as powerful and life-giving as the words of the old law are, we are gifted with a new law, the ultimate revelation of God's love to us because words written on a scroll are not enough. Just as words between lovers can never quite communicate the depth of their love for one another, God's eternal word to us in the law, or Scripture, is not the whole story. The story is enfleshed in Jesus.

Love must be embodied. It is not enough to say, "I love you." Those words must be acted upon. God has acted upon the words of his law. As Jesus says in the Gospel, "Today this Scripture passage is fulfilled in your hearing." Jesus is the fulfillment of the favor of the Lord God.

Because of that favor, we followers of Jesus are bound together in one body of love. We are many members, united by the living word that Jesus offers us through his real, bodily presence.

Suggestions for Prayer

1. Take some time to reflect on the following:
   - One or two powerful experiences in your life when someone who loved you showed you love-in-action.
   - A time when your family or friends acted together to some good end, where cooperation or unity produced something truly beneficial.
2. Consider when you have been or could have been, in the words of the Gospel:
   "glad tidings to the poor"
   "liberty to captives"
   "sight to the blind"
   "release to prisoners"

3. Think of the times you have attended liturgy with the "one body" of the faithful. Visualize in your prayer those different kinds of people who attend. As you do so, continue to say in your prayer: "Rejoicing in the Lord is our strength!"

Suggestion for Journal Keeping

Jesus stands before you and proclaims, "Today this Scripture passage is fulfilled in your hearing!" How do you feel? How do you react? What glad tidings would that fulfillment entail? What freedom, insight or release?

Steven M. Lanza

Fourth Sunday of the Year A

READING I   Zep 2, 3; 3, 12–13

Seek the Lord, all you humble of the earth,
   who have observed his law;
Seek justice, seek humility;
   perhaps you may be sheltered
   on the day of the Lord's anger.

But I will leave as a remnant in your midst
   a people humble and lowly,
Who shall take refuge in the name of the Lord:
   the remnant of Israel.
They shall do no wrong
   and speak no lies;
Nor shall there be found in their mouths
   a deceitful tongue;
They shall pasture and couch their flocks
   with none to disturb them.

Responsorial Psalm   Ps 146, 6–7. 8–9. 9–10
Happy the poor in spirit;
   the kingdom of heaven is theirs!

The Lord keeps faith forever,
  secures justice for the oppressed,
  gives food to the hungry.
The Lord sets captives free.
Happy the poor in spirit;
  the kingdom of heaven is theirs!
The Lord gives sight to the blind;
  the Lord raises up those that were bowed
  down.
The Lord loves the just;
  the Lord protects strangers.
Happy the poor in spirit;
  the kingdom of heaven is theirs!
The fatherless and the widow the Lord sus-
  tains,
  but the way of the wicked he thwarts.
The Lord shall reign forever;
  your God, O Zion, through all genera-
  tions.
  Alleluia.
Happy the poor in spirit;
  the kingdom of heaven is theirs!

READING II   1 Cor 1, 26–31

**Brothers, you are among those called. Con-
sider your own situation. Not many of you
are wise, as men account wisdom; not many
are influential; and surely not many are well-
born. God chose those whom the world con-
siders absurd to shame the wise, he singled
out the weak of this world to shame the
strong. He chose the world's lowborn and
despised, those who count for nothing, to
reduce to nothing those who were something; so that mankind can do no boasting
before God. God it is who has given you life
in Christ Jesus. He has made him our wisdom and also our justice, our sanctification,
and our redemption. This is just as you find
it written, "Let him who would boast, boast
in the Lord."**

GOSPEL   Mt 5, 1–12

**When Jesus saw the crowds, he went up on
the mountainside. After he had sat down his
disciples gathered around him, and he began
to teach them:**

> **"How blest are the poor in spirit: the
> reign of God is theirs.**
> **Blest too are the sorrowing; they shall
> be consoled.**
> **[Blest are the lowly; they shall inherit
> the land.]**
> **Blest are they who hunger and thirst for
> holiness; they shall have their fill.**
> **Blest are they who show mercy; mercy
> shall be theirs.**
> **Blest are the single-hearted,
> for they shall see God.**
> **Blest too the peacemakers; they shall be
> called sons of God.**
> **Blest are those persecuted for holiness'
> sake; the reign of God is theirs.**
> **Blest are you when they insult you and
> persecute you and utter every kind of
> slander against you because of me.**
> **Be glad and rejoice, for your reward in
> heaven is great."**

Reflection on the Readings

In today's Gospel, Matthew again presents
Jesus as the teacher. Just as Moses ascended
Mount Sinai to receive the law, Jesus, the
new Moses, now goes up on a mountainside
and begins this great sermon. Throughout the
Sermon on the Mount, Jesus proclaims that
the kingdom of God is coming, bringing the
law and the prophets to a new fulfillment and
revising the ways of the world.

The sermon begins with the beatitudes.
These eight sayings announce a new order in
which God's love and justice triumph over
evil. They proclaim where the kingdom of

God is coming and point Jesus' followers in that direction. Understood in this way, we could rephrase the beatitudes as follows: "The reign of God is coming to those who are poor in spirit," or "God is showing mercy to those who are merciful." This perspective allows us to capture Jesus' emphasis on God's action and to go "where the action is." This is the perspective of the responsorial psalm as well. It is the Lord who is securing justice, feeding the hungry, setting captives free.

How? We might follow Paul's lead and go to the "low-born and despised" to find out. There we might discover what the Lord is doing and see what happens to us as well. We might find ourselves beginning to hunger and thirst for the kingdom of God.

Suggestions for Prayer

1. Reflect on the beatitudes in light of your present-day circumstances. Which of the beatitudes is the Spirit calling you to focus on? What must you do to live this beatitude?
2. Do you know anyone whom our society would consider low-born or despised? What can this person teach you? How could you learn from him or her?

Suggestion for Journal Keeping

Following the examples in the reflection, rewrite the beatitudes. Make God the subject of each one. What is God doing in each beatitude, and for whom? Then rewrite the beatitudes again, this time negatively, e.g., "How unhappy are the greedy. The reign of God does not belong to them." What does this exercise teach you?

Robert M. Hamma

Fourth Sunday of the Year B

READING I   Dt 18, 15–20
Moses spoke to the people, saying: "A prophet like me will the Lord, your God, raise up for you from among your own kinsmen; to him you shall listen. This is exactly what you requested of the Lord, your God, at Horeb on the day of the assembly, when you said, 'Let us not again hear the voice of the Lord, our God, nor see this great fire any more, lest we die.' And the Lord said to me, 'This was well said. I will raise up for them a prophet like you from among their kinsmen, and will put my words into his mouth; he shall tell them all that I command him. If any man will not listen to my words which he speaks in my name, I myself will make him answer for it. But if a prophet presumes to speak in my name an oracle that I have not commanded him to speak, or speaks in the name of other gods, he shall die.' "

Responsorial Psalm   Ps 95, 1–2. 6–7. 7–9
If today you hear his voice,
    harden not your hearts.
**Come, let us sing joyfully to the Lord;
    let us acclaim the Rock of our salvation.
Let us greet him with thanksgiving;
    let us joyfully sing psalms to him.**
If today you hear his voice,
    harden not your hearts.
**Come, let us bow down in worship;
    let us kneel before the Lord who made us.
For he is our God,
        and we are the people he shepherds, the
            flock he guides.**
If today you hear his voice,
    harden not your hearts.

Oh, that today you would hear his voice:
"Harden not your hearts as at Meribah,
as in the day of Massah in the desert,
Where your fathers tempted me;
they tested me though they had seen my
works.
If today you hear his voice,
harden not your hearts.

READING II   1 Cor 7, 32–35

I should like you to be free of all worries. The unmarried man is busy with the Lord's affairs, concerned with pleasing the Lord; but the married man is busy with this world's demands and is occupied with pleasing his wife. This means he is divided. The virgin—indeed, any unmarried woman—is concerned with things of the Lord, in pursuit of holiness in body and spirit. The married woman, on the other hand, has the cares of this world to absorb her and is concerned with pleasing her husband. I am going into this with you for your own good. I have no desire to place restrictions on you, but I do want to promote what is good, what will help you to devote yourselves entirely to the Lord.

GOSPEL   Mk 1, 21–28

[In the city of Capernaum,] Jesus entered the synagogue on the sabbath and began to teach. The people were spellbound by his teaching because he taught with authority and not like the scribes.

There appeared in their synagogue a man with an unclean spirit that shrieked: "What do you want of us, Jesus of Nazareth? Have you come to destroy us? I know who you are—the Holy One of God!" Jesus rebuked him sharply: "Be quiet! Come out of the man!" At that the unclean spirit convulsed the man violently and with a loud shriek came out of him. All who looked on were amazed. They began to ask one another: "What does this mean? A completely new teaching in a spirit of authority! He gives orders to unclean spirits and they obey him!" From that point on his reputation spread throughout the surrounding region of Galilee.

Reflection on the Readings

As we grow in love for someone it seems there is always more to get to know about him or her—new insights, new "revelations." Sometimes it is we who change, so we see and understand differently than before. The time we spend reading and reflecting on the Scriptures helps us learn about persons of faith—and hopefully gain insights into ourselves. In particular, reflections on the Gospels give us a deeper knowledge of Jesus Christ, his works and teachings. The readings evoke our personal reflection on our belief in Jesus Christ. We need to be more deeply aware of who it is we have faith in and follow, so that we can be strengthened to live out the Gospel and turn our hearts to God. We may gain insight as well into what barriers we may have to that faith and discipleship.

The readings from Deuteronomy and from Paul's Letter to the Corinthians point to a person who, dedicated to the Lord, serves as a spokesperson for God. Jesus, speaking and acting with authority in the Gospel event, is that person. He teaches and challenges the demons, the barriers which hinder discipleship. The external miracle of casting out demons points to the interior grace of obedience to God and the authority of one who speaks in God's name. It is faith and love that heal—on the part of the penitent (the disciple) as well as on the part of the person assuring forgiveness and healing.

Once we have chosen to begin or renew a life of discipleship we need to look carefully at our lives and into our hearts. What is there that may be a hindrance to our readiness to follow Jesus? What might need to be rooted out, changed radically, so that we might be more faithful to the Gospel teachings?

Brokenness and selfishness are a part of our lives. Part of the process of discipleship is examination of our habits and motivation with a view to changing our lives.

Suggestions for Prayer

1. Write in brief list form several feelings or values you have which may be barriers to discipleship, e.g., materialistic values, holding a grudge against someone, reluctance to help the poor, etc. Choose one to begin with. Meditate on its influence on your life. Concretely imagine how your life will change as that "demon" or problem value is diminished. Pray for strength and perseverance in exorcising that issue from your life. Picture the positive, compassionate values replacing it, influencing your personal spiritual growth. Plan concretely how your life can change.

2. Together with your sponsor or spiritual guide, focus on a value or quality you would like to develop which will help you be a better disciple. Prayerfully reflect on the costs of developing that quality. Picture yourself with Jesus talking over your efforts at growth in holiness. In your own words, pray for

strength and joy as you become a more faithful follower of Jesus.

Suggestion for Journal Keeping

Choose one quality or characteristic you would hope to really develop in your life. Write about it, how you will take concrete, realistic steps to affirm that quality. Create a prayer, in your own words, asking for Jesus' help in your process of growth.

Clare M. Colella

Fourth Sunday of the Year **C**

READING I   Jer 1, 4–5. 17–19

In the days of Josiah the word of the Lord came to me thus:
Before I formed you in the womb I knew you,
  before you were born I dedicated you,
  a prophet to the nations I appointed you.

But do you gird your loins;
  stand up and tell them
  all that I command you.
Be not crushed on their account,
  as though I would leave you crushed before them;
For it is I this day
  who have made you a fortified city,
A pillar of iron, a wall of brass,
  against the whole land:
Against Judah's kings and princes,
  against its priests and people.
They will fight against you, but not prevail over you,
  for I am with you to deliver you, says the Lord.

Responsorial Psalm   Ps 71, 1–2. 3–4. 5–6. 15–17

I will sing of your salvation.

In you, O Lord, I take refuge;
  let me never be put to shame.
In your justice rescue me, and deliver me;
  incline your ear to me, and save me.

I will sing of your salvation.

Be my rock of refuge,
  a stronghold to give me safety,
  for you are my rock and my fortress.
O my God, rescue me from the hand of the
  wicked.

I will sing of your salvation.

For you are my hope, O Lord;
  my trust, O God, from my youth.
On you I depend from birth;
  from my mother's womb you are my
  strength.

I will sing of your salvation.

My mouth shall declare your justice,
  day by day your salvation.
O God, you have taught me from my youth,
  and till the present I proclaim your won-
  drous deeds.

I will sing of your salvation.

READING II   1 Cor 12, 31–13, 13
Set your hearts on the greater gifts.

Now I will show you the way which sur-passes all the others. If I speak with human tongues and angelic as well, but do not have love, I am a noisy gong, a clanging cymbal. If I have the gift of prophecy and, with full knowledge, comprehend all mysteries, if I have faith great enough to move mountains, but have not love, I am nothing. If I give everything I have to feed the poor and hand over my body to be burned, but have not love, I gain nothing.

Love is patient; love is kind. Love is not jealous, it does not put on airs, it is not snob-bish. Love is never rude, it is not self-seek-ing, it is not prone to anger; neither does it brood over injuries. Love does not rejoice in what is wrong but rejoices with the truth. There is no limit to love's forbearance, to its trust, its hope, its power to endure.

Love never fails. Prophecies will cease, tongues will be silent, knowledge will pass away. Our knowledge is imperfect and our prophesying is imperfect. When the perfect comes, the imperfect will pass away. When I was a child I used to talk like a child, think like a child, reason like a child. When I be-came a man I put childish ways aside. Now we see indistinctly, as in a mirror; then we shall see face to face. My knowledge is im-perfect now; then I shall know even as I am known. There are in the end three things that last: faith, hope, and love, and the greatest of these is love.

GOSPEL   Lk 4, 21–30
Jesus began speaking in the synagogue: "To-day this Scripture passage is fulfilled in your hearing." All who were present spoke favor-ably of him; they marveled at the appealing discourse which came from his lips. They also asked, "Is not this Joseph's son?"

He said to them, "You will doubtless quote me the proverb, 'Physician, heal your-self,' and say, 'Do here in your own country the things we have heard you have done in Capernaum.' But in fact," he went on, "no prophet gains acceptance in his native place. Indeed, let me remind you, there were many widows in Israel in the days of Elijah when the heavens remained closed for three and a half years and a great famine spread over the land. It was to none of these that Elijah was sent, but to a widow of Zarephath near Sidon. Recall, too, the many lepers in Israel in the time of Elisha the prophet; yet not one was cured except Naaman the Syrian."

At these words the whole audience in the synagogue was filled with indignation. They rose up and expelled him from the town, leading him to the brow of the hill on which it was built, and intending to hurl him over the edge. But he went straight through their midst and walked away.

Reflection on the Readings

Jeremiah is just like any other human being. He looks and acts pretty much like others around him, except for one major difference. He preaches the word of God. He challenges people to be faithful to God. In the words of the psalm, the prophet "sings of salvation."

But, like Jesus' experience in the Gospel, not everyone wants to hear what the singer sings. Jesus, like Jeremiah, looks like any other human being. He stands up in the synagogue to read from the scrolls of the law and preach on it. His garments look like the garments that all the others are wearing. Those neighbors who listen to him have watched him grow up, like their own sons and daughters. He is one of them. And yet, he is more. The words which Jesus speaks are prophetic, challenging. And he sings of salvation. But because they thought they thoroughly knew him, they were unable to accept his song that day.

As St. Paul reminds us, it is necessary to go beyond the superficial, to become much more mature than we have been. We need to grow up, and to grow into a deeper faithfulness. This means seeing with more than our eyes and going beyond the appearance of things and people to the heart of the matter, to the realities of the kingdom: faith, hope and love.

As Jesus indicates in the Gospel, we must see with our hearts in order to accept his message. We need to be open to his challenge; otherwise, he will walk straight through us, away from our midst, until that time when we are ready.

Suggestions for Prayer

1. Consider the following:
   - What makes the message of Jesus hard for you to hear and accept?
   - Are there times when you have been angry at God? What caused your indignation?
2. Do you have a favorite song about love? If so, play it or recall it and afterward reflect on the following:
   - What makes that song special to you?
   - What feelings does the song create within you? Offer these feelings to God, our loving Redeemer.

Suggestion for Journal Keeping

Jesus has just opened his heart to you, one friend to another. But, for whatever reason, you were not receptive to his message and became upset at what Jesus had revealed to you. Sadly, he walks away. You have second thoughts and run to catch up with him. You tug on his sleeve, turning him around, and you say to him, "I'm sorry. I really do want your friendship. I need you because . . . " Complete the statement.

Steven M. Lanza

Fifth Sunday of the Year A

READING I   Is 58, 7–10

Thus says the Lord:
Share your bread with the hungry,
  shelter the oppressed and the homeless;
Clothe the naked when you see them,
  and do not turn your back on your own.

Then your light shall break forth like the
  dawn,
  and your wound shall quickly be healed;
Your vindication shall go before you,
  and the glory of the Lord shall be your rear
  guard.
Then you shall call, and the Lord will answer,
  you shall cry for help, and he will say:
  Here I am!
If you remove from your midst oppression,
  false accusation and malicious speech;
If you bestow your bread on the hungry
  and satisfy the afflicted;
Then light shall rise for you in the darkness,
  and the gloom shall become for you like
  midday.

Responsorial Psalm   Ps 112, 4–5. 6–7. 8–9
The just man is a light in darkness to the
  upright.
The Lord dawns through the darkness, a light
  for the upright;
  he is gracious and merciful and just.
Well for the man who is gracious and lends,
  who conducts his affairs with justice.
The just man is a light in darkness to the
  upright.
He shall never be moved;
  the just man shall be in everlasting remembrance.

An evil report he shall not fear;
  his heart is firm, trusting in the Lord.
The just man is a light in darkness to the
  upright.
His heart is steadfast; he shall not fear.
  Lavishly he gives to the poor;
His generosity shall endure forever;
  his horn shall be exalted in glory.
The just man is a light in darkness to the
  upright.

READING II   1 Cor 2, 1–5

As for myself, brothers, when I came to you
I did not come proclaiming God's testimony
with any particular eloquence or "wisdom."
No, I determined that while I was with you
I would speak of nothing but Jesus Christ and
him crucified. When I came among you it
was in weakness and fear, and with much
trepidation. My message and my preaching
had none of the persuasive force of "wise"
argumentation, but the convincing power of
the Spirit. As a consequence, your faith rests
not on the wisdom of men but on the power
of God.

GOSPEL   Mt 5, 13–16

Jesus said to his disciples: "You are the salt
of the earth. But what if salt goes flat? How
can you restore its flavor? Then it is good for
nothing but to be thrown out and trampled
underfoot.

   "You are the light of the world. A city set
on a hill cannot be hidden. Men do not light
a lamp and then put it under a bushel basket.
They set it on a stand where it gives light to
all in the house. In the same way, your light
must shine before men so that they may see
goodness in your acts and give praise to your
heavenly Father."

Reflection on the Readings

Most of us would describe our lives as ordinary. There are ups and downs, successes and failures, disappointments and hopes. Sometimes this realization can make us feel unworthy of the Gospel. The Gospel, we think, is a call to heroic love, and we are not often heroic.

Today's readings can help to refute such thinking. The Gospel tells us we are to be salt and light. Of all the seasonings, salt is the most ordinary. Of all life's daily necessities, light is one of the most basic. Jesus affirms the ordinary. He calls us to be salt and light, to be common elements which give flavor to life, which help people find their way.

Writing to the people of Israel in a time of discouragement, Isaiah describes what it means to be a light. Share your bread with the hungry, give shelter to the homeless, remove malicious speech from your midst—then your light will shine. For us to be light, we must actively cast out the darkness both within and around us. Then the light of God will be seen.

The source of our power is the Spirit. As St. Paul says to the Corinthians, their faith does not rest on his wisdom or eloquence, but on the power of God. So for us, our ordinariness, even our weakness, is what the Lord wants to use to make us light and salt for the world.

Suggestions for Prayer

1. Look around you and ask where there is darkness in your world. Who do you know who is suffering, physically, emotionally, spiritually? How can you be a light to this person?

2. What is the "bushel basket" that keeps you from sharing your light? Is it fear, shyness, or perhaps a past hurt? Present your weakness to the Lord and pray for strength. Reflect on the promise of healing in Isaiah to those who share their light.

3. Sit in a quiet and darkened place with a candle lit before you. Focus your attention on it as you pray to Jesus, "You are the light of the world."

Suggestion for Journal Keeping

Today's readings remind us that the best way to get out of our woundedness or discouragement is through love. Is there such an area in your life? If so, reflect on it in your journal. Why do you feel this way? What loving thing can you do to pierce the darkness with the light?

Robert M. Hamma

Fifth Sunday of the Year

READING I   Jb 7, 1–4. 6–7

Job spoke, saying:
Is not man's life on earth a drudgery?
  Are not his days those of a hireling?
He is a slave who longs for the shade,
  a hireling who waits for his wages.
So I have been assigned months of misery,
  and troubled nights have been told off
    for me.

If in bed I say, "When shall I arise?"
  then the night drags on;
  I am filled with restlessness until the
    dawn.

My days are swifter than a weaver's shuttle;
  they come to an end without hope.
Remember that my life is like the wind;
  I shall not see happiness again.

Responsorial Psalm   Ps 147, 1–2. 3–4. 5–6
Praise the Lord who heals the broken-
      hearted.
Praise the Lord, for he is good;
  sing praise to our God, for he is gracious;
  it is fitting to praise him.
The Lord rebuilds Jerusalem;
  the dispersed of Israel he gathers.
Praise the Lord who heals the broken-
      hearted.
He heals the brokenhearted
  and binds up their wounds.
He tells the number of the stars;
  he calls each by name.
Praise the Lord who heals the broken-
      hearted.
Great is our Lord and mighty in power;
  to his wisdom there is no limit.
The Lord sustains the lowly;
  the wicked he casts to the ground.
Praise the Lord who heals the broken-
      hearted.

READING II   1 Cor 9, 16–19. 22–23
Preaching the gospel is not the subject of a boast; I am under compulsion and have no choice. I am ruined if I do not preach it! If I do it willingly, I have my recompense; if unwillingly, I am nonetheless entrusted with a charge. And this recompense of mine? It is simply this, that when preaching I offer the gospel free of charge and do not make full use of the authority the gospel gives me.

Although I am not bound to anyone, I made myself the slave of all so as to win over as many as possible. To the weak I became a weak person with a view to winning the weak. I have made myself all things to all men in order to save at least some of them. In fact, I do all that I do for the sake of the gospel in the hope of having a share in its blessings.

GOSPEL   Mk 1, 29–39
Upon leaving the synagogue, Jesus entered the house of Simon and Andrew with James and John. Simon's mother-in-law lay ill with a fever, and the first thing they did was to tell him about her. He went over to her and grasped her hand and helped her up, and the fever left her. She immediately began to wait on them.

After sunset, as evening drew on, they brought him all who were ill and those possessed by demons. Before long the whole town was gathered outside the door. Those whom he cured, who were variously afflicted, were many, and so were the demons he expelled. But he would not permit the demons to speak, because they knew him. Rising early the next morning, he went off to a lonely place in the desert; there he was absorbed in prayer. Simon and his companions managed to track him down; and when they found him, they told him, "Everybody is looking for you!" He said to them: "Let us move on to the neighboring villages so that I may proclaim the good news there also. That is what I have come to do." So he went into their synagogues preaching the good news and expelling demons throughout the whole of Galilee.

Reflection on the Readings

Today's readings focus on Jesus' great compassion for the poor, the brokenhearted, the sick. In the first reading from the Book of Job we read of one of his poor and downtrodden. Paul affirms that it is in his lowliness and service to others that he carries out the work of the Gospel.

As we seek to know and follow the will of God in our lives, we become more familiar with the varied aspects of Gospel values. Jesus, through his actions as well as by his words, teaches that care for one another, compassion for the needy, and service of others are hallmarks of the Christian disciple.

There is another aspect of today's readings that we may consider: the problem of pain and suffering. By his steadfastness in faith throughout his difficulties, Job exemplifies trust in God, deepened and strengthened through suffering. Through a thoughtful reading of today's Scriptures we are called upon to make a personal response to the suffering of others, according to the example of Jesus. Proclaiming the good news and healing were two aspects of the same event for Jesus. For us and for others, the healing we experience, or nourish in others, may be physical, spiritual, or emotional. While suffering and pain are part of our lives it is also clear that healing the sick and caring for the brokenhearted are integral to the ministry of Jesus and his followers.

Our attitude toward and response to pain and suffering—our own and others'—reflects in some measure our faith and trust in God. Our ready compassion, or lack of it, may well be an indication of how thoroughly we are taking on the mind of Jesus Christ. Do we see the face of God in those who need compassion, mercy, service? Are we aware that our service to others is also a key step in our own growth in faith?

Suggestions for Prayer

1. All around us, daily, are stories and evidence of persons in pain and suffering. Take time to learn just a little more about someone who is in pain. Reflect on a concrete way to make your prayer and faith tangible in the service of others. Then go out to be of service.
2. Recall a time of pain in your own life. Try to understand how you grew through that experience (or are growing as you grapple with it now). In your own words, ask God to help you understand how wisdom and faith can be deepened through such painful experiences. Pray for compassion with others who are suffering.
3. With your sponsor, or on your own, choose and read at least two Gospel stories of Jesus' ministry to the poor, sick, brokenhearted. You may well find a simple pattern of compassion, forgiveness and healing in Jesus' actions. He also asks for conversion, for faith in God, as a response to healing. Take time to read more, to get to know Jesus as a man "who went about doing good."

Suggestion for Journal Keeping

As you take time to work with one of the above prayer suggestions, keep track of your thoughts, questions and efforts in your journal this week. Be honest in your evaluation of your own compassion and sense of service. Affirm that which is good and faith-filled. Specify what you are focusing on in order to grow in a healthy Christian life-style. You may find yourself wanting to talk with your sponsor or spiritual friend. Use opportunities to help others and yourself grow spiritually.

Clare M. Colella

Fifth Sunday of the Year **C**

READING I   Is 6, 1–2. 3–8
In the year King Uzziah died, I saw the Lord seated on a high and lofty throne, with the train of his garment filling the temple. Seraphim were stationed above.

"Holy, holy, holy is the Lord of hosts!" they cried one to the other. "All the earth is filled with his glory!" At the sound of that cry, the frame of the door shook and the house was filled with smoke.

Then I said, "Woe is me, I am doomed! For I am a man of unclean lips, living among a people of unclean lips; yet my eyes have seen the King, the Lord of hosts!" Then one of the seraphim flew to me, holding an ember which he had taken with tongs from the altar.

He touched my mouth with it. "See," he said, "now that this has touched your lips, your wickedness is removed, your sin purged."

Then I heard the voice of the Lord saying, "Whom shall I send? Who will go for us?" "Here I am," I said; "send me!"

Responsorial Psalm   Ps 138, 1–2. 2–3. 4–
                                                    5. 7–8
In the sight of the angels
   I will sing your praises, Lord.
I will give thanks to you, O Lord, with all my
   heart,

[for you have heard the words of my
   mouth;]
in the presence of the angels I will sing
   your praise;
I will worship at your holy temple
   and give thanks to your name.
In the sight of the angels
   I will sing your praises, Lord.
Because of your kindness and your truth;
   for you have made great above all things
   your name and your promise.
When I called, you answered me;
   you built up strength within me.
In the sight of the angels
   I will sing your praises, Lord.
All the kings of the earth shall give thanks to
   you, O Lord,
   when they hear the words of your mouth;
And they shall sing of the ways of the Lord:
   "Great is the glory of the Lord."
In the sight of the angels
   I will sing your praises, Lord.
Your right hand saves me.
   The Lord will complete what he has done
   for me;
Your kindness, O Lord, endures forever;
   forsake not the work of your hands.
In the sight of the angels
   I will sing your praises, Lord.

READING II   1 Cor 15, 1–11
Brothers, I want to remind you of the gospel I preached to you, which you received and in which you stand firm. You are being saved by it at this very moment if you retain it as I preached it to you. Otherwise you have believed in vain. I handed on to you first of all what I myself received, that Christ died for our sins in accord with the Scriptures; that he was buried and, in accord with the Scrip-

tures, rose on the third day; that he was seen by Cephas, then by the Twelve. After that he was seen by five hundred brothers at once, most of whom are still alive, although some have fallen asleep. Next he was seen by James; then by all the apostles. Last of all he was seen by me, as one born out of the normal course. I am the least of the apostles; in fact, because I persecuted the church of God, I do not even deserve the name. But by God's favor I am what I am. This favor of his to me has not proved fruitless. Indeed, I have worked harder than all the others, not on my own but through the favor of God. In any case, whether it be I or they, this is what we preach and this is what you believed.

GOSPEL   Lk 5, 1–11
As the crowd pressed in on Jesus to hear the word of God, he saw two boats moored by the side of the lake; the fishermen had disembarked and were washing their nets. He got into one of the boats, the one belonging to Simon, and asked him to pull out a short distance from the shore; then, remaining seated, he continued to teach the crowds from the boat. When he had finished speaking he said to Simon, "Put out into deep water and lower your nets for a catch." Simon answered, "Master, we have been hard at it all night long and have caught nothing; but if you say so, I will lower the nets." Upon doing this they caught such a great number of fish that their nets were at the breaking point. They signaled to their mates in the other boat to come and help them. These came, and together they filled the two boats until they nearly sank.

At the sight of this, Simon Peter fell at the knees of Jesus saying, "Leave me, Lord. I am a sinful man." For indeed, amazement at the catch they had made seized him and all his shipmates, as well as James and John, Zebedee's sons, who were partners with Simon. Jesus said to Simon, "Do not be afraid. From now on you will be catching men." With that they brought their boats to land, left everything, and became his followers.

Reflection on the Readings
Isaiah is the recipient of a terrifying vision. He sees the Lord God. Yet, he is a sinner, and knows himself to be a sinner. Terror turns to invitation when his sin is removed by the Lord and Isaiah offers to be sent out as God's own prophet.

While Simon Peter is not the recipient of a terrifying vision, he is nonetheless amazed at the miraculous catch of fish and the power of Jesus. Peter probably felt he was a mighty competent fisherman, and yet it is Jesus, the carpenter-preacher, who shows him where all the fish are that day. Amazement turns to realization on the part of Peter and the others. They know themselves to be imperfect. They discover the Master, Jesus, and he in turn invites them to become more than they are, "Do not be afraid. From now on you will be catching men."

St. Paul also encounters the Lord, his Master, and because of that experience becomes more. Indeed, he is transformed from one who persecutes the Church to one who is its biggest promoter among the Gentiles. He knows himself, his previous attitudes and actions, and describes the transformation as being "born out of the normal course."

In all three readings for this Sunday there is self-knowledge, an encounter with divinity and a transformation in Isaiah, Paul and Simon Peter for the greater glory of God's kingdom. The prophet and the disciples experienced what we pray in the psalm: "You built up strength within me."

Suggestions for Prayer

1. After you reread the Gospel passage for this Sunday, set it aside, close your eyes and imagine that scene with Jesus in every detail. Place yourself in Peter's sandals—or in those of one of the other disciples.
   What happens and how do you feel about it?
   When Jesus says, "From now on you will be catching people," how do you react?
2. Transformation or conversion is not usually abrupt, as portrayed in these passages. Conversion to a new way of life usually takes a very long time. Can you reflect on the stages of your own growing and deepening faith in Jesus?

Suggestion for Journal Keeping

In his Letter to the Corinthians, St. Paul says, "I handed on to you first of all what I myself received" (that Christ died, was buried, rose from the dead and was seen by certain witnesses). If you personally were to "hand on" the core of the good news of Jesus, how would you do so? What would you proclaim?

Steven M. Lanza

Sixth Sunday of the Year A

READING I   Sir 15, 15–20
If you choose you can keep the commandments;
  it is loyalty to do his will.
There are set before you fire and water;
  to whichever you choose, stretch forth your hand.
Before man are life and death,
  whichever he chooses shall be given him.
Immense is the wisdom of the Lord;
  he is mighty in power, and all-seeing.
The eyes of God see all he has made;
  he understands man's every deed.
No man does he command to sin,
  to none does he give strength for lies.

Responsorial Psalm   Ps 119, 1–2. 4–5.
                                         17–18. 33–34
Happy are they who follow the law of the Lord!
Happy are they whose way is blameless,
  who walk in the law of the Lord.
Happy are they who observe his decrees,
  who seek him with all their heart.
Happy are they who follow the law of the Lord!
You have commanded that your precepts
  be diligently kept.
Oh, that I might be firm in the ways
  of keeping your statutes!
Happy are they who follow the law of the Lord!
Be good to your servant, that I may live
  and keep your words.
Open my eyes, that I may consider
  the wonders of your law.
Happy are they who follow the law of the Lord!

Instruct me, O Lord, in the way of your
statutes,
that I may exactly observe them.
Give me discernment, that I may observe
your law
and keep it with all my heart.
Happy are they who follow the law of the
Lord!

READING II   1 Cor 2, 6–10
There is, to be sure, a certain wisdom which
we express among the spiritually mature. It
is not a wisdom of this age, however, nor of
the rulers of this age who are men headed
for destruction. No, what we utter is God's
wisdom: a mysterious, a hidden wisdom.
God planned it before all ages for our glory.
None of the rulers of this age knew the mystery; if they had known it, they would never
have crucified the Lord of glory. Of this wisdom it is written:
"Eye has not seen, ear has not heard,
nor has it so much as dawned on man
what God has prepared for those who love
him."
Yet God has revealed this wisdom to us
through the Spirit. The Spirit scrutinizes all
matters, even the deep things of God.

GOSPEL   Mt 5, 17–37
Jesus said to his disciples: "Do not think that
I have come to abolish the law and the
prophets. I have come, not to abolish them,
but to fulfill them. Of this much I assure you:
until heaven and earth pass away, not the
smallest letter of the law, not the smallest
part of a letter, shall be done away with until
it all comes true. That is why whoever
breaks the least significant of these com-

mands and teaches others to do so shall be
called least in the kingdom of God. Whoever
fulfills and teaches these commands shall be
great in the kingdom of God. I tell you, unless your holiness surpasses that of the
scribes and Pharisees you shall not enter the
kingdom of God.
"You have heard the commandment imposed on your forefathers, 'You shall not
commit murder; every murderer will be liable to judgment.' What I say to you is:
everyone who grows angry with his brother
will be liable to judgment; any man who uses
abusive language toward his brother shall be
answerable to the Sanhedrin, and if he holds
him in contempt he risks the fires of Gehenna. If you bring your gift to the altar and
there recall that your brother has anything
against you, leave your gift at the altar, go
first to be reconciled with your brother, and
then come and offer your gift. Lose no time;
settle with your opponent while on your way
to court with him. Otherwise your opponent
may hand you over to the judge, who will
hand you over to the guard, who will throw
you into prison. I warn you, you will not be
released until you have paid the last penny.
"You have heard the commandment, 'You
shall not commit adultery.' What I say to
you is: anyone who looks lustfully at a
woman has already committed adultery
with her in his thoughts. If your right eye is
your trouble, gouge it out and throw it
away! Better to lose part of your body than
to have it all cast into Gehenna. Again, if
your right hand is your trouble, cut it off and
throw it away! Better to lose part of your
body than to have it all cast into Gehenna.
"It was also said, 'Whenever a man divorces his wife, he must give her a decree of

232

divorce.' What I say to you is: everyone who divorces his wife—lewd conduct is a separate case—forces her to commit adultery. The man who marries a divorced woman likewise commits adultery.

"You have heard the commandment imposed on your forefathers, 'Do not take a false oath; rather, make good to the Lord all your pledges.' What I tell you is: do not swear at all. Do not swear by heaven (it is God's throne), nor by the earth (it is his footstool), nor by Jerusalem (it is the city of the great King); do not swear by your head (you cannot make a single hair white or black). Say, 'Yes' when you mean 'Yes' and 'No' when you mean 'No.' Anything beyond that is from the evil one."

Reflection on the Readings

Today's Scriptures again present us with Jesus, our teacher. We have heard his proclamation, "Reform your lives! The kingdom of heaven is at hand." Now we hear him tell us what that means. It is not simply a matter of not murdering or not committing adultery. What Jesus requires is the rooting out of anger and of lust in our lives, actively making peace with those who have harmed us, removing the cause of temptation in our lives.

Jesus calls us to holiness. It is a holiness that must surpass that of the scribes and Pharisees. Our holiness should not focus only on external fulfillment of the law, but must be the result of an internal transformation of our hearts. This holiness is first of all a decision. Your entrance into the catechumenate was your first public commitment to this way of life. At baptism you will finalize your decision to be a disciple, to be holy. Now, as Lent draws near, it is the time to renew your commitment to the process of change and growth.

Holiness is not beyond us. As Sirach says, "If you choose you can keep the commandments." God does not "give strength for lies," but God does give strength for holiness. Nor is the choice a question of something extra. As Sirach tells us, fire and water, life and death are set before us. We receive whatever we choose. But for those who choose life, "no eye has seen what God has prepared for those who love him."

Suggestions for Prayer

1. Is there someone in your life with whom you need to be reconciled? Bring that person before the Lord in your prayer. Ask for the wisdom to understand that person, to see him or her as Jesus does. Pray for the strength to forgive and seek forgiveness.

2. Reflect on the impact that our society has on your approach to sexuality. How have you been influenced by it? To what extent do you see women or men as sex objects? How does that affect your marriage or other relationships?

3. What is Jesus' attitude toward divorce? What is your attitude? Discuss this difficult Scripture passage with your sponsor or another member of the parish catechumenate team.

Suggestion for Journal Keeping

Write out the ten commandments. For each one write what more Jesus calls you to in fulfilling the law.

Robert M. Hamma

Sixth Sunday of the Year B

READING I
Lv 13, 1–2. 44–46

The Lord said to Moses and Aaron, "If someone has on his skin a scab or pustule or blotch which appears to be the sore of leprosy, he shall be brought to Aaron, the priest, or to one of the priests among his descendants. If the man is leprous and unclean, the priest shall declare him unclean by reason of the sore on his head.

"The one who bears the sore of leprosy shall keep his garments rent and his head bare, and shall muffle his beard; he shall cry out, 'Unclean, unclean!' As long as the sore is on him he shall declare himself unclean, since he is in fact unclean. He shall dwell apart, making his abode outside the camp."

Responsorial Psalm   Ps 32, 1–2. 5. 11

I turn to you, Lord, in time of trouble,
   and you fill me with the joy of salvation.
Happy is he whose fault is taken away,
   whose sin is covered.
Happy the man to whom the Lord imputes
   not guilt,
   in whose spirit there is no guile.
I turn to you, Lord, in time of trouble,
   and you fill me with the joy of salvation.
Then I acknowledged my sin to you,
   my guilt I covered not.
I said, "I confess my faults to the Lord,"
   and you took away the guilt of my sin.
I turn to you, Lord, in time of trouble,
   and you fill me with the joy of salvation.
Be glad in the Lord and rejoice, you just;
   exult, all you upright of heart.
I turn to you, Lord, in time of trouble,
   and you fill me with the joy of salvation.

READING II
1 Cor 10, 31–11, 1

Whether you eat or drink—whatever you do—you should do all for the glory of God. Give no offense to Jew or Greek or to the church of God, just as I try to please all in any way I can by seeking not my own advantage, but that of the many that they may be saved. Imitate me as I imitate Christ.

GOSPEL
Mk 1, 40–45

A leper approached Jesus with a request, kneeling down as he addressed him: "If you will to do so, you can cure me." Moved with pity, Jesus stretched out his hand, touched him, and said: "I do will it. Be cured." The leprosy left him then and there, and he was cured. Jesus gave him a stern warning and sent him on his way. "Not a word to anyone, now," he said. "Go off and present yourself to the priest and offer for your cure what Moses prescribed. That should be a proof for them." The man went off and began to proclaim the whole matter freely, making the story public. As a result of this, it was no longer possible for Jesus to enter a town openly. He stayed in desert places; yet people kept coming to him from all sides.

Reflection on the Readings

On the surface two of today's readings deal with physical bodily illness: leprosy and uncleanness. Just below that surface, we are looking at spiritual illness—sin. The balancing of sinfulness and forgiveness gives us hope as we approach the season of Lent. In our search for faith, and through our efforts to know the Catholic community and its beliefs, we both acknowledge our need for help in spiritual growth and affirm the presence of a strong, active faith in the community. For all members of the community, the effort to grow in faith is an on-going experience. We continue to seek to know more about Jesus, to know him better. It is an easy thing to become complacent about our faith, about our relationship with Jesus and our participation in the Church. That is why each year the Church, through its season of Lent, offers us a time of penitence and spiritual re-energizing.

The leper in the Gospel story approached Jesus with the belief that he could be healed. Whether he believed in Jesus' proclamation of the good news or in Jesus' power to forgive, the faith he did have was sufficient. Jesus perceived his desire for healing from leprosy, but he knew on a deeper level the man's need for spiritual strength.

We grow in faith through our experiences, reflection, insight, through being loved and accepted, by being "touched" by the lives of others. When we acknowledge our need for help we can more readily receive the support and care of others; we can grow and learn more fruitfully.

We may even find ourselves, because of that deeper experience, going out to proclaim to others our growing faith. As catechumens we are on the way, engaged in learning, searching. The touch of Jesus may come in a variety of ways, through a variety of persons. But the outreach and compassion are there to the best of the ability of the members of the community. Jesus is present among us.

Suggestions for Prayer

1. As in weeks before, you are encouraged to read more of the Scriptures. Your sponsor may help you this week choose additional stories of Jesus' healing. Par-

ticularly focus on stories which deepen awareness of persons who approached Jesus with faith in his ability to heal. Note how often physical healing is accompanied by forgiveness and a call to conversion. Pray Psalm 32, which is the responsorial psalm in the liturgy today.

2. If you or someone you know has had an experience of healing, physical or spiritual, take time to renew your awareness of that experience. Pray in your own words for a deeper understanding of your relationship with God and the faith that is the outgrowth of that relationship.

3. Often in our society people are made to feel like outcasts when they do not "measure up" to certain arbitrary standards. The mercy and compassionate healing of Jesus were extended to the outcasts in his society. Who are our "outcasts" today? How can you become more aware of them? What can you do to help heal the brokenness in a self-righteous or insensitive society which keeps them outcasts? Take time to look around you, and ask God for wisdom, compassion and energy to somehow help the healing in those situations.

Suggestion for Journal Keeping

In what area of your life have you experienced healing, forgiveness or reconciliation? What wisdom or insight comes to you as a reflection on that experience? Healings may be simple reconciliation between friends who were harsh or angry; they may be as unique as a physical healing. Though we may put other words on the experiences, almost all of us have had a time of healing. As you recall an experience, it may be helpful to write it down, then reflect on what came about because of it. You may also want to talk it over with your sponsor or spiritual guide.

Clare M. Colella

Sixth Sunday of the Year **C**

READING I   Jer 17, 5–8

Thus says the Lord:

Cursed is the man who trusts in human
    beings,
  who seeks his strength in flesh,
  whose heart turns away from the Lord.
He is like a barren bush in the desert
  that enjoys no change of season,
But stands in a lava waste,
  a salt and empty earth.
Blessed is the man who trusts in the Lord,
  whose hope is the Lord.
He is like a tree planted beside the waters
  that stretches out its roots to the stream:
It fears not the heat when it comes,
  its leaves stay green;
In the year of drought it shows no distress,
  but still bears fruit.

Responsorial Psalm   Ps 1, 1–2. 3. 4. 6
Happy are they who hope in the Lord.
**Happy the man who follows not
  the counsel of the wicked
Nor walks in the way of sinners,
  nor sits in the company of the insolent,
But delights in the law of the Lord
  and meditates on his law day and night.**
Happy are they who hope in the Lord.

He is like a tree
  **planted near running water,
That yields its fruit in due season,
  and whose leaves never fade.
  [Whatever he does, prospers.]**
Happy are they who hope in the Lord.
**Not so the wicked, not so;
  they are like chaff which the wind drives
    away.**
For the Lord watches over the way of the
  just,
  but the way of the wicked vanishes.
Happy are they who hope in the Lord.

READING II   1 Cor 15, 12. 16–20
**If Christ is preached as raised from the dead,
how is it that some of you say there is no resurrection of the dead? If the dead are not
raised, then Christ was not raised; and if
Christ was not raised, your faith is worthless. You are still in your sins, and those who
have fallen asleep in Christ are the deadest
of the dead. If our hopes in Christ are limited
to this life only, we are the most pitiable of
men.**

  **But as it is, Christ has been raised from the
dead, the first fruits of those who have fallen
asleep.**

GOSPEL   Lk 6, 17. 20–26
**When Jesus came down the mountain, he
stopped at a level stretch where there were
many of his disciples; a large crowd of people was with them from all Judea and Jerusalem and the coast of Tyre and Sidon. Then,
raising his eyes to his disciples, he said:**

  **"Blest are you poor; the reign of God is
    yours.**

  **Blest are you who hunger; filled you shall
    be.**

Blest are you who are weeping; you shall laugh.

"Blest shall you be when men hate you, when they ostracize you and insult you and proscribe your name as evil because of the Son of Man. On the day they do so, rejoice and exult, for your reward shall be great in heaven. Thus it was that their fathers treated the prophets.

"But woe to you rich, for your consolation is now.

Woe to you who are full; you shall go hungry.

Woe to you who laugh now; you shall weep in your grief.

"Woe to you when all speak well of you. Their fathers treated the false prophets in just this way."

Reflection on the Readings

Jesus is clear and decisive. On one side is offered blessedness. On the other side is offered woefulness. Those who are blessed are poor, hungry, weeping and the followers of Jesus. Those who will be woeful are those who are rich, filled up, well-thought-of, and happy. What is going on here? Choosing Jesus does not necessarily mean comfort and fulfillment here and now. In fact, it may be derision, scorn and hardship.

But St. Paul also knows we are a resurrection people, given a great hope and promise in the new life Jesus holds out to us—even beyond death. In his Letter to the Corinthians, he makes clear that our hope is not limited to this life. To limit the pay-off to this life alone makes our faith worthless. Again, clear and decisive language.

The prophet Jeremiah is just as firm in his message. Trust in God and in God alone. We may be experiencing a "year of drought," our life may be parched, or we may find ourselves in a seemingly hopeless situation, and yet "happy are those who hope in the Lord."

Suggestions for Prayer

1. *Reflect on one of the following:*
   - Are there dry, waterless, parched areas of your life (situations, events, relationships) that you wish to raise up in trust to the Lord?
   - What seemingly hopeless or dead-end situations are reported in today's newspaper or news? Perhaps a particular situation resonates with you. Spend a day abstaining from meat as a form of hopeful prayer regarding this situation.
2. Reread the Gospel passage and then close your eyes, placing yourself in the large crowd of disciples.
   - Are you rich or poor?
   - How do you feel about the words of Jesus?
   - How are the others reacting around you?
   - What will you do about your feelings?

Suggestion for Journal Keeping

Make a list of the affluent aspects of your lifestyle that you would be able to give up in order to embrace Jesus. Make a corresponding list of those aspects you would be unable to give up. Do the words of Jesus in the Gospel hold any challenge to the items placed on either list?

Steven M. Lanza

Seventh Sunday
of the Year 🅐

READING I   Lv 19, 1–2. 17–18

The Lord said to Moses, "Speak to the whole Israelite community and tell them: Be holy, for I, the Lord, your God, am holy.

"You shall not bear hatred for your brother in your heart. Though you may have to reprove your fellow man, do not incur sin because of him. Take no revenge and cherish no grudge against your fellow countrymen. You shall love your neighbor as yourself. I am the Lord."

Responsorial Psalm   Ps 103, 1–2. 3–4. 8.
                                          10. 12–13

The Lord is kind and merciful.
Bless the Lord, O my soul;
    and all my being, bless his holy name.
Bless the Lord, O my soul,
    and forget not all his benefits.
The Lord is kind and merciful.
He pardons all your iniquities,
    he heals all your ills.
He redeems your life from destruction,
    he crowns you with kindness and compassion.
The Lord is kind and merciful.
Merciful and gracious is the Lord,
    slow to anger and abounding in kindness.
Not according to our sins does he deal with us,
    nor does he requite us according to our crimes.
The Lord is kind and merciful.
As far as the east is from the west,
    so far has he put our transgressions from us.

As a father has compassion on his children,
    so the Lord has compassion on those who fear him.
The Lord is kind and merciful.

READING II   1 Cor 3, 16–23

Are you not aware that you are the temple of God, and that the Spirit of God dwells in you? If anyone destroys God's temple, God will destroy him. For the temple of God is holy, and you are that temple.

Let no one delude himself. If any one of you thinks he is wise in a worldly way, he had better become a fool. In that way he will really be wise, for the wisdom of this world is absurdity with God. Scripture says, "He catches the wise in their craftiness"; and again, "The Lord knows how empty are the thoughts of the wise." Let there be no boasting about men. All things are yours, whether it be Paul, or Apollos, or Cephas, or the world, or life, or death, or the present, or the future: all these are yours, and you are Christ's and Christ is God's.

GOSPEL   Mt 5, 38–48

Jesus said to his disciples: "You have heard the commandment, 'An eye for an eye, a tooth for a tooth.' But what I say to you is: offer no resistance to injury. When a person strikes you on the right cheek, turn and offer him the other. If anyone wants to go to law over your shirt, hand him your coat as well. Should anyone press you into service for one mile, go with him two miles. Give to the man who begs from you. Do not turn your back on the borrower.

"You have heard the commandment, 'You shall love your countryman but hate your enemy.' My command to you is: love your

enemies, pray for your persecutors. This will prove that you are sons of your heavenly Father, for his sun rises on the bad and the good, he rains on the just and the unjust. If you love those who love you, what merit is there in that? Do not tax collectors do as much? And if you greet your brothers only, what is so praiseworthy about that? Do not pagans do as much? In a word, you must be perfected as your heavenly Father is perfect."

Reflection on the Readings

The first sentence of the reading from Leviticus and the last sentence from the Gospel offer a striking parallel: Be holy as God is holy; be perfect as your Father is perfect. This is the context in which we should hear Jesus' words in the Gospel. By human standards, what he asks is indeed foolish. But his call is to abandon our human perspective and to take on the perspective of God. We are called to love as God loves—"for his sun rises on the bad and the good."

Not only may this call seem foolish to us, but it may also seem impossible. Who can love like this? We might remember Jesus' words to his disciples when they were shocked by another one of his teachings: "Nothing is impossible with God." We are called not only to love as God loves, but to love *with* God's love. Paul reminds us that we are holy because the Spirit of God already dwells within us. It is the Spirit, the love of God dwelling within us, that enables us to follow the call of Jesus. And when Paul says, "The Spirit of God dwells within you," the *you* is plural. It is in the community of the Church that we find our strength. No one can live Christianity all alone. Nor is it an "all at

once" power. It is a gradual process through which the Spirit of God "perfects" us, as God is perfect.

Suggestions for Prayer

1. Reflect on the following questions:
   Is there anyone for whom you bear hatred in your heart?
   In what ways do you live by the rule "An eye for an eye"?
   How do you respond when people place demands on you?
2. Who is your persecutor? Pray for that person, as well as for those who are considered the enemies of our nation.
3. Spend some time in silence reflecting on the presence of the Holy Spirit dwelling in you. Pray for the love and strength of the Spirit to flow through you. You may find the words of this traditional song helpful:

Spirit of the living God, fall afresh on me.
Melt me, mold me, fill me, use me.

Suggestion for Journal Keeping

Jesus' words in this Gospel are often cited as the foundation for a Christian stance of non-violence. Reflect on this in your journal. How can we as Christians be non-violent in a violent world?

Robert M. Hamma

Seventh Sunday of the Year   B

READING I　　Is 43, 18–19. 21–22. 24–25
Thus says the Lord:
Remember not the events of the past,
　the things of long ago consider not;
See, I am doing something new!
　Now it springs forth, do you not perceive
　　it?
In the desert I make a way,
　in the wasteland, rivers.
The people whom I formed for myself,
　that they might announce my praise.
Yet you did not call upon me, O Jacob,
　for you grew weary of me, O Israel.
You burdened me with your sins,
　and wearied me with your crimes.
It is I, I, who wipe out,
　for my own sake, your offenses;
　your sins I remember no more.

Responsorial Psalm　　Ps 41, 2–3. 4–5. 13–14
Lord, heal my soul,
　for I have sinned against you.
**Happy is he who has regard for the lowly
　　and the poor;
　in the day of misfortune the Lord will de-
　　liver him.**

**The Lord will keep and preserve him;
　he will make him happy on the earth,
　and not give him over to the will of his
　　enemies.**
Lord, heal my soul,
　for I have sinned against you.
**The Lord will help him on his sickbed,
　he will take away all his ailment when he
　　is ill.**
Once I said, "O Lord, have pity on me;
　heal me, though I have sinned against
　　you."
Lord, heal my soul,
　for I have sinned against you.
**But because of my integrity you sustain me
　and let me stand before you forever.
Blessed be the Lord, the God of Israel,
　from all eternity and forever. Amen.
　　Amen.**
Lord, heal my soul,
　for I have sinned against you.

READING II　　2 Cor 1, 18–22
As God keeps his word, I declare that my word to you is not "yes" one minute and "no" the next. Jesus Christ, whom Silvanus, Timothy, and I preached to you as Son of God, was not alternately "yes" and "no"; he was never anything but "yes." Whatever promises God has made have been fulfilled in him; therefore it is through him that we address our Amen to God when we worship together. God is the one who firmly establishes us along with you in Christ; it is he who anointed us and has sealed us, thereby depositing the first payment, the Spirit in our hearts.

GOSPEL　　Mk 2, 1–12
After a lapse of several days Jesus came back to Capernaum and word got around that he

was at home. At that they began to gather in great numbers. There was no longer any room for them, even around the door. While he was delivering God's word to them, some people arrived bringing a paralyzed man to him. The four who carried him were unable to bring him to Jesus because of the crowd, so they began to open up the roof over the spot where Jesus was. When they had made a hole, they let down the mat on which the paralytic was lying. When Jesus saw their faith, he said to the paralyzed man, "My son, your sins are forgiven." Now some of the scribes were sitting there asking themselves: "Why does the man talk in that way? He commits blasphemy! Who can forgive sins except God alone?" Jesus was immediately aware of their reasoning, though they kept it to themselves, and he said to them: "Why do you harbor these thoughts? Which is easier, to say to the paralytic, 'Your sins are forgiven,' or to say, 'Stand up, pick up your mat, and walk again'? That you may know that the Son of Man has authority on earth to forgive sins" (he said to the paralyzed man), "I command you: Stand up! Pick up your mat and go home." The man stood and picked up his mat and went outside in the sight of everyone. They were awestruck; all gave praise to God, saying, "We have never seen anything like this!"

Reflection on the Readings

This week's readings focus on repentance, forgiveness, healing and conversion. The reading from the Book of Isaiah and the responsorial psalm assure us that our sin and the past are forgiven. When we turn our hearts and lives to Jesus, we can leave the past behind us. It is the Lord who "wipes out" our offenses, who, because of his love and forgiveness, remembers our sins no more. We are healed of our sinfulness when we choose to be faithful to the Lord.

The Gospel episode uses a physical healing to point to the power of interior spiritual healing—"Your sins are forgiven." The question of one of the scribes may be somewhat like our hesitancy. We ask, "Am I really forgiven? Does God really forgive me?" Perhaps we do not forgive ourselves, we do not fully seek reconciliation. Perhaps we doubt our own goodness and our ability, with the help of God and the support of others, to become more faithful to the Lord. God has promised his mercy. Paul's Letter to the people of Corinth reminds them of God's fidelity, his presence through the Spirit. The companions of the paralytic, in today's Gospel, must have had some good measure of faith to bring him to Jesus. The miracle of healing is a faith event—an occasion for people to believe in Jesus, his teaching and power. A miracle of this sort is a clearly visible sign of the deeper reality, the inner spiritual healing and forgiveness. It shows God's power active through Jesus' ministry.

Through our reflections on today's Scriptures, we find ourselves challenged as well as comforted. Do we truly believe in God's forgiveness, in his healing power in our lives? What barriers or burdens might we have that we have not yet let go of? What keeps us from spiritual wholistic growth? How strong is our faith, our desire for faith?

Suggestions for Prayer

1. Take a few moments to reflect on your sense of faith in God's forgiving power as it applies to you. Then read the Gospel story inserting yourself into it: Are

you a bystander in the crowd, a skeptical scribe, one of the companions on the rooftop, the paralytic? Think about your presence and your response to Jesus' words and actions. How do you feel? And what insight might you gain as a participant in the imaginative story? Picture yourself alone with Jesus after the event. Talk with him about your feelings and your faith.

2. Are there persons or circumstances in your life that need forgiveness, reconciliation? Are you spontaneous and generous with forgiveness of others? Is there something within you that needs forgiveness? Is that easy or difficult? Picture yourself in a comfortable quiet place with Jesus, a trusted friend. You may want to reread the section from Isaiah, the responsorial psalm, or the Gospel. Talk things over with Jesus. Let your thoughts and prayer come spontaneously. You may want to talk with your sponsor or spiritual companion about forgiveness and reconciliation in your life.

3. Position yourself comfortably, with open hands, palms upward in your lap. In quiet surroundings, let your mind and heart choose an aspect of your life that needs reconciliation and healing. Place that aspect, as if it were a cool dark stone, in thought, in your open palms. With closed eyes, meditate on your stone, letting go of pain, painful memories, self-doubt or fear connected with it. Put behind you the pain of the past. Begin to sense the warming light of love and forgiveness changing the stone— yourself. The love of Jesus, present within you and given vitality through the love of others, can change that stone into a warm, light-filled ball. Image yourself as that warm light source of love. Know that you are loved. Know that you are called to love others. Let your thoughts formulate a prayer.

Suggestion for Journal Keeping

Write your reflections from the prayer experience. Let your thoughts and prayer continue the healing process in your life.

Clare M. Colella

Seventh Sunday of the Year [C]

READING I 1 Sm 26, 2. 7–9. 12–13. 22–23
Saul went off down to the desert of Ziph with three thousand picked men of Israel, to search for David in the desert of Ziph. So David and Abishai went among Saul's soldiers by night and found Saul lying asleep within the barricade, with his spear thrust into the ground at his head and Abner and his men sleeping around him.

Abishai whispered to David: "God has delivered your enemy into your grasp this day. Let me nail him to the ground with one thrust of the spear; I will not need a second thrust!" But David said to Abishai, "Do not harm him, for who can lay hands on the Lord's anointed and remain unpunished? So David took the spear and the water jug from their place at Saul's head, and they got away without anyone's seeing or knowing or awakening. All remained asleep, because the Lord had put them into a deep slumber.

Going across to an opposite slope, David

stood on a remote hilltop at a great distance from Abner, son of Ner, and the troops. He said: "Here is the king's spear. Let an attendant come over to get it. The Lord will reward each man for his justice and faithfulness. Today, though the Lord delivered you into my grasp, I would not harm the Lord's anointed."

Responsorial Psalm   Ps 103, 1–2. 3–4. 8. 10. 12–13

The Lord is kind and merciful.

Bless the Lord, O my soul;
   and all my being, bless his holy name.
Bless the Lord, O my soul,
   and forget not all his benefits.
The Lord is kind and merciful.

He pardons all your iniquities,
   he heals all your ills.
He redeems your life from destruction,
   he crowns you with kindness and compassion.
The Lord is kind and merciful.

Merciful and gracious is the Lord,
   slow to anger and abounding in kindness.
Not according to our sins does he deal with us,
   nor does he requite us according to our crimes.
The Lord is kind and merciful.

As far as the east is from the west,
   so far has he put our transgressions from us.
As a father has compassion on his children,
   so the Lord has compassion on those who fear him.
The Lord is kind and merciful.

READING II   1 Cor 15, 45–49
Scripture has it that Adam, the first man, became a living soul; the last Adam has become a life-giving spirit. Notice the spiritual was not first; first came the natural and after that the spiritual. The first man was of earth, formed from dust, the second is from heaven. Earthly men are like the man of earth, heavenly men are like the man of heaven. Just as we resemble the man from earth, so shall we bear the likeness of the man from heaven.

GOSPEL   Lk 6, 27–38
Jesus said to his disciples: "To you who hear me, I say: Love your enemies, do good to those who hate you; bless those who curse you and pray for those who maltreat you. When someone slaps you on one cheek, turn and give him the other; when someone takes your coat, let him have your shirt as well. Give to all who beg from you. When a man takes what is yours, do not demand it back. Do to others what you would have them do to you. If you love those who love you, what credit is that to you? Even sinners love those who love them. If you do good to those who do good to you, how can you claim any credit? Sinners do as much. If you lend to those from whom you expect repayment, what merit is there in it for you? Even sinners lend to sinners, expecting to be repaid in full.

"Love your enemy and do good; lend without expecting repayment. Then will your recompense be great. You will rightly be called sons of the Most High, since he himself is good to the ungrateful and the wicked.

"Be compassionate, as your Father is compassionate. Do not judge, and you will not be judged. Do not condemn, and you will not be condemned. Pardon, and you shall be pardoned. Give, and it shall be given to you. **Good measure pressed down, shaken together, running over, will they pour into the fold of your garment. For the measure you measure with will be measured back to you."**

Reflection on the Readings

As kingdom people, God requires from us a radical mercy. Our efforts to cooperate with the goodness of God's kingdom focus on others rather than on ourselves—even those who hate and mistreat us. Jesus tells us in the Gospel that the measure of our judgment will be the measure by which we have shown a radical mercy toward others.

This radical mercy is not a new reality. Its roots go back to Old Testament times. The prophet Samuel draws a vivid picture for us of the young David who had within his power Saul's life—a life which he spares out of love of the Lord God.

St. Paul writes of the natural person and the spiritual person. These are not opposing realities. The spiritual builds upon the natural. God's graces build upon what is natural to us. For us to reach for a God-centered radical mercy is not a violation of ourselves, but a progressive movement for those who would be as the Lord is. We will bear the heavenly likeness. As the psalm says, "the Lord is kind and merciful."

Suggestions for Prayer

1. *Examine yourself on one of the following:* David was merciful to Saul. Where have you recently modeled this behavior? Where have you had power over another and yet used that power to show "mercy"? The spiritual builds on the natural. Imagine yourself, what you look like. Imagine your spiritual self. *Now* what do you look like?

2. In the Gospel, Jesus says to be compassionate as our heavenly Father is compassionate. Where have you felt the compassion of God in your life?

Suggestion for Journal Keeping

Reread the Gospel. Set it aside and consider it in silence for a few moments. Imagine yourself as the Pope, speaking before the United Nations. You, the Pope, will use this Gospel as a starting point for your address. What will you say to the representatives of the nations?

Steven M. Lanza

Eighth Sunday of the Year A

READING I Is 49, 14–15

Zion said, "The Lord has forsaken me;
  my Lord has forgotten me."
Can a mother forget her infant,
  be without tenderness for the child of her womb?
Even should she forget,
  I will never forget you.

Responsorial Psalm Ps 62, 2–3. 6–7. 8–9
Rest in God alone, my soul.
Only in God is my soul at rest;
  from him comes my salvation.
He only is my rock and my salvation,
  my stronghold; I shall not be disturbed at all.
Rest in God alone, my soul.

Only in God be at rest, my soul,
    for from him comes my hope.
He only is my rock and my salvation,
    my stronghold; I shall not be disturbed.
Rest in God alone, my soul.
With God is my safety and my glory,
    he is the rock of my strength; my refuge is
    in God.
Trust in him at all times, O my people!
    Pour out your hearts before him.
Rest in God alone, my soul.

READING II   1 Cor 4, 1–5
Men should regard us as servants of Christ
and administrators of the mysteries of God.
The first requirement of an administrator is
that he prove trustworthy. It matters little to
me whether you or any human court pass
judgment on me. I do not even pass judgment on myself. Mind you, I have nothing on
my conscience. But that does not mean that
I am declaring myself innocent. The Lord is
the one to judge me, so stop passing judgment before the time of his return. He will
bring to light what is hidden in darkness and
manifest the intentions of hearts. At that
time, everyone will receive his praise from
God.

GOSPEL   Mt 6, 24–34
Jesus said to his disciples: "No man can
serve two masters. He will either hate one
and love the other or be attentive to one and
despise the other. You cannot give yourself
to God and money. I warn you, then: do not
worry about your livelihood, what you are
to eat or drink or use for clothing. Is not life
more than food? Is not the body more valuable than clothes?

"Look at the birds in the sky. They do not
sow or reap, they gather nothing into barns;
yet your heavenly Father feeds them. Are
not you more important than they? Which of
you by worrying can add a moment to his
lifespan? As for clothes, why be concerned?
Learn a lesson from the way the wild flowers
grow. They do not work; they do not spin.
Yet I assure you, not even Solomon in all his
splendor was arrayed like one of these. If
God can clothe in such splendor the grass of
the field, which blooms today and is thrown
on the fire tomorrow, will he not provide
much more for you, O weak in faith! Stop
worrying, then, over questions like, 'What
are we to eat, or what are we to drink, or
what are we to wear?' The unbelievers are
always running after these things. Your
heavenly Father knows all that you need.
Seek first his kingship over you, his way of
holiness, and all these things will be given
you besides. Enough, then, of worrying
about tomorrow. Let tomorrow take care of
itself. Today has troubles enough of its
own."

Reflection on the Readings
    "Stress management" is an "in" phrase
these days. Chances are you could find a
course on it at your local college. This is not
surprising, given the complexity and fast-
paced nature of our society. There is always
more to do than there are hours in the day.
Often we wish we could just get away from
it all. But except for an occasional vacation,
or day away, that's not a viable solution.
    Today's Gospel provides us with Jesus' ap-
proach to stress management: stop worrying
about what you are to eat, or wear, or any of
the countless concerns that plague you. Instead seek first the kingdom of God. In other
words, trust that God who knows what you
really need will provide that for you. How

245

often are we so preoccupied that we forget to look at the birds in the sky or the flowers in the field? How often are we so busy acquiring things that we forget to give thanks to the one who provides?

The choice Jesus offers between serving God or money is really a choice between the true God and a false god. Money cannot buy what is most precious, or restore it if it is lost. Jesus offers us freedom from slavery to money and the worry that accompanies it. He offers us freedom to love, to be grateful, to build up the values which are truly lasting—those of his kingdom.

Suggestions for Prayer

1. Look around your home and reflect on the plants or pets which you keep there. In what ways can they teach you about trust and reliance on God?
2. How can the complementary images of God as Mother (Isaiah) and Father (Matthew) deepen your own appreciation of God's love for you?
3. Paul calls himself an "administrator" and says that the first quality of an administrator must be trustworthiness. How do you balance your responsibilities with Jesus' call to rely on God?

Suggestion for Journal Keeping

Reflect in your journal on what it means to you to "seek first the kingdom of God and his way of holiness" in your personal life, family life, social life.

Robert M. Hamma

Eighth Sunday of the Year B

READING I   Hos 2, 16.17. 21–22
Thus says the Lord:
I will lead her into the desert
and speak to her heart.
She shall respond there as in the days of her youth,
when she came up from the land of Egypt.
I will espouse you to me forever:
I will espouse you in right and in justice,
in love and in mercy;
I will espouse you in fidelity,
and you shall know the Lord.

Responsorial Psalm   Ps 103, 1–2. 3–4. 8. 10. 12–13

The Lord is kind and merciful.
Bless the Lord, O my soul;
and all my being, bless his holy name.
Bless the Lord, O my soul,
and forget not all his benefits.
The Lord is kind and merciful.
He pardons all your iniquities,
he heals all your ills.
He redeems your life from destruction,
he crowns you with kindness and compassion.
The Lord is kind and merciful.
Merciful and gracious is the Lord,
slow to anger and abounding in kindness.
Not according to our sins does he deal with us,
nor does he requite us according to our crimes.
The Lord is kind and merciful.
As far as the east is from the west,

so far has he put our transgressions from us.

As a father has compassion on his children, so the Lord has compassion on those who fear him.

The Lord is kind and merciful.

READING II   2 Cor 3, 1–6

Do I need letters of recommendation to you or from you as others might? You are my letter, known and read by all men, written on your hearts. Clearly you are a letter of Christ which I have delivered, a letter written not with ink but by the Spirit of the living God, not on tablets of stone but on tablets of flesh in the heart.

This great confidence in God is ours, through Christ. It is not that we are entitled of ourselves to take credit for anything. Our sole credit is from God, who has made us qualified ministers of a new covenant, a covenant not of a written law but of spirit. The written law kills, but the Spirit gives life.

GOSPEL   Mk 2, 18–22

John's disciples and the Pharisees were accustomed to fast. People came to Jesus with the objection, "Why do John's disciples and those of the Pharisees fast while yours do not?" Jesus replied: "How can the guests at a wedding fast as long as the groom is still among them? So long as the groom stays with them, they cannot fast. The day will come, however, when the groom will be taken away from them; on that day they will fast. No one sews a patch of unshrunken cloth on an old cloak. If he should do so, the very thing he has used to cover the hole would pull away—the new from the old—and the tear would get worse. Similarly, no man pours new wine into old wineskins. If he does so, the wine will burst the skins and both wine and skins will be lost. No, new wine is poured into new skins."

Reflection on the Readings

A covenant of love—that's what today's readings focus on. But the term "covenant" may be unfamiliar. How is the covenant described? A love relationship? A relationship of fidelity? Compassionate care between persons? Hosea speaks of God's willingness to take back his unfaithful people, an image particularly powerful because of Hosea's own readiness to accept back his unfaithful wife.

The theme of overwhelming love, forgiveness, acceptance is carried through into Paul's imagery of the covenant being written in our hearts, for it is our faith, our spirit that binds us to God as ministers of that new life-giving covenant. The responsorial psalm phrases it as being kind and merciful. The Gospel uses the covenant imagery of marriage but goes on to use the image of wisdom, matching the new with the new, a relationship of appropriateness. If we are the new people of God, we live in the new covenant of love as taught and modeled by Jesus.

When Jesus (the bridegroom) is present among us, it is most appropriate to celebrate. Do we stand ready to affirm our covenant of love? Are we faithful to him? Has our journey of faith challenged us to make a choice for Jesus, for the Gospel teaching, in our lives? As we grow in faith and love, we may well find the thought of a covenant reassuring and strengthening—a reminder that God is faithful to his promises and to his people. These are the months when, as catechumens and faith community, we take time to read and reflect on the Scriptures, becoming familiar with the themes and teachings of the Word. We look more thoughtfully at the lives and actions of other Catholics, to learn better what it means to live out our faith. We reflect more deeply on our own lives, working out the will of God for us, establishing and deepening our relationship with God. These are the times of forming our covenant with God—uniquely personal yet lived out in the fellowship of other believers.

Suggestions for Prayer

1. The Hebrew people kept alive the stories of covenants between God and their ancestors—from Adam, Noah, Abraham, Jacob, Joseph and Moses on through their prophetic leaders and kings. The sense of being cared for and protected by God was very much a part of their religious heritage. We often do not keep active memories of those times when we sense God's care for us. In deepening your sense of covenant, take time to recall times in your life and the lives of others you know when God's presence, care, love have been evident. Let your thoughts formulate themselves as prayer to God who loves you and cares for you very much.

2. We are called, we are chosen. . . . " The song "Anthem" by Tom Conry (N.A.L.R.) is one of a variety of songs which focus on the caring relationship between God and each one of his people. Find and listen to the words of a song reflecting on God's care for you. Let the song become a prayer for you.

3. The new way of living—the covenant of

love—calls for compassion, forgiveness, concern, acceptance, fidelity, service. Look at your practice of those qualities in your life. They are Gospel values. How will you take steps to grow in these qualities?

Suggestion for Journal Keeping

Write a brief story of at least one event in your life in which you felt especially protected or cared for by God. After some quiet reflection, formulate a prayer expressing your thoughts.

Clare M. Colella

Eighth Sunday of the Year

READING I   Sir 27, 4–7

When a sieve is shaken, the husks appear;
  so do a man's faults when he speaks.
As the test of what the potter molds is in the furnace,
  so in his conversation is the test of a man.
The fruit of a tree shows the care it has had;
  so too does a man's speech disclose the bent of his mind.
Praise no man before he speaks,
  for it is then that men are tested.

Responsorial Psalm   Ps 92, 2–3. 13–14.
                          15–16

Lord, it is good to give thanks to you.
It is good to give thanks to the Lord,
  to sing praise to your name, Most High,
To proclaim your kindness at dawn
  and your faithfulness throughout the night.

Lord, it is good to give thanks to you.
The just man shall flourish like the palm tree,
like a cedar of Lebanon shall he grow.
They that are planted in the house of the
Lord
shall flourish in the courts of our God.
Lord, it is good to give thanks to you.
They shall bear fruit even in old age;
vigorous and sturdy shall they be,
Declaring how just is the Lord,
my Rock, in whom there is no wrong.
Lord, it is good to give thanks to you. ·

READING II   1 Cor 15, 54–58
When the corruptible frame takes on incor-
ruptibility and the mortal immortality, then
will the saying of Scripture be fulfilled:
"Death is swallowed up in victory." "O
death, where is your victory? O death,
where is your sting?" The sting of death is
sin, and sin gets its power from the law. But
thanks be to God who has given us the vic-
tory through our Lord Jesus Christ. Be stead-
fast and persevering, my beloved brothers,
fully engaged in the work of the Lord. You
know that your toil is not in vain when it is
done in the Lord.

GOSPEL   Lk 6, 39–45
Jesus used images in speaking to the disci-
ples: "Can a blind man act as guide to a blind
man? Will they not both fall into a ditch? A
student is not above his teacher; but every
student when he has finished his studies will
be on a par with his teacher.
"Why look at the speck in your brother's
eye when you miss the plank in your own?
How can you say to your brother, 'Brother,
let me remove the speck from your eye,' yet
fail yourself to see the plank lodged in your

own? **Hypocrite, remove the plank from**
your own eye first; then you will see clearly
enough to remove the speck from your
brother's eye.
"A good tree does not produce decayed
fruit any more than a decayed tree produces
good fruit. Each tree is known by its yield.
Figs are not taken from thornbushes, nor
grapes picked from brambles. A good man
produces goodness from the good in his
heart; an evil man produces evil out of his
store of evil. Each man speaks from his
heart's abundance."

Reflection on the Readings
Both the first reading, from the Book of Sirach, and the Gospel, from Luke, center on
speech. In Sirach, the prophet warns not to
judge another until he or she has spoken.
Speech for the prophet is revelatory. It opens
up a horizon toward the other's inner self.
Luke shares with us some powerful images
used by Jesus in speaking to his disciples: a
blind guide, a plank in the eye of one who
wishes to remove another's speck, a good
tree producing decayed fruit. These are powerful images because they are contradictory.
Jesus himself is a powerful Word "spoken"
by his heavenly Father. He is described in the
beginning of the Gospel of John as the eternal
Word with and from God. By his words and
deeds Jesus reveals to us the love of God—a
love so great that God shares our human di-
lemma, our death.
Does this seem contradictory: an all-pow-
erful God who shares with us our powerlessness, a God who dies? But from death springs
life, a life that never ends. Defeat becomes
victory. A more powerful statement could not
be made. The Word who is Jesus is the Word
of life.

Suggestions for Prayer

1. Take the time to speak these phrases aloud. Reflect quietly on each of them.

One's speech reflects one's mind.
Your toil is not in vain when done in the Lord.
O death, where is your sting?

2. The psalm says, "it is good to give thanks to you, Lord." Imagine a Thanksgiving table, loaded down not with food but with everything for which you are thankful to the Lord. What's on the table? What's most important to you on (or around) that table?

Suggestion for Journal Keeping

Jesus uses many powerful images in his speech besides those he uses in this Gospel. Record a handful of these powerful images/words/phrases which Jesus uses—from memory. Why are these words so powerful to you that you recall them?

Steven M. Lanza

Ninth Sunday of the Year　A

READING I　　　　　Dt 11, 18. 26–28
Moses told the people, "Take these words of mine into your heart and soul. Bind them at your wrist as a sign, and let them be a pendant on your forehead.

"I set before you here, this day, a blessing and a curse: a blessing for obeying the commandments of the Lord, your God, which I enjoin on you today; a curse if you do not obey the commandments of the Lord, your God, but turn aside from the way I ordain for you today, to follow other gods, whom you have not known."

Responsorial Psalm　　Ps 31, 2–3. 3–4. 17. 25
Lord, be my rock of safety.
In you, O Lord, I take refuge;
let me never be put to shame.
In your justice rescue me,
incline your ear to me,
make haste to deliver me!
Lord, be my rock of safety.
Be my rock of refuge,
a stronghold to give me safety.
You are my rock and my fortress;
for your name's sake you will lead and
guide me.
Lord, be my rock of safety.
Let your face shine upon your servant;
save me in your kindness.
Take courage and be stouthearted,
all you who hope in the Lord.
Lord, be my rock of safety.

READING II　　　　　Rom 3, 21–25. 28
Now the justice of God has been manifested apart from the law, even though both law and prophets bear witness to it—that justice of God which works through faith in Jesus Christ for all who believe. All men have sinned and hence are deprived of the glory of God. All men are now undeservedly justified by the gift of God, through the redemption wrought in Christ Jesus. Through his blood, God made him the means of expiation for all who believe.

For we hold that a man is justified by faith apart from observance of the law.

GOSPEL   Mt 7, 21–27

Jesus said to his disciples: "None of those who cry out, 'Lord, Lord,' will enter the kingdom of God but only the one who does the will of my Father in heaven. When that day comes, many will plead with me, 'Lord, Lord, have we not prophesied in your name? Have we not exorcised demons by its power? Did we not do many miracles in your name as well?' Then I will declare to them solemnly, 'I never knew you. Out of my sight, you evildoers!'

"Anyone who hears my words and puts them into practice is like the wise man who built his house on rock. When the rainy season set in, the torrents came and the winds blew and buffeted his house. It did not collapse; it had been solidly set on rock. Anyone who hears my words but does not put them into practice is like the foolish man who built his house on sandy ground. The rains fell, the torrents came, the winds blew and lashed against his house. It collapsed under all this and was completely ruined."

Reflection on the Readings

With today's Gospel we come to the conclusion of the Sermon on the Mount. Jesus sums up his preaching with two parallel sayings about words and actions. It is not enough to say, "Lord, Lord." No matter what one's religious credentials are, it is putting Jesus' words into practice that really counts. We must hear his words and do what he says. To do this is to build one's house on rock rather than sand. In both sayings Jesus has as the ultimate horizon the final judgment, pictured as a storm. Here, as we will see in Matthew 25, those who have put his teaching into action are welcomed into his kingdom, while the others are sent out of his sight.

Just as Moses presented the Israelites with two ways, a blessing or a curse, so Jesus, the new Moses, offers us the same choice: a blessing for obeying his commands, a curse if we choose idolatry. As any parent knows, obedience involves listening and doing. Idolatry, on the other hand, is not listening. Idolaters listen only to themselves, making their desires into gods and worshiping them. Idolaters bring the curse upon themselves.

Jesus offers us life. Following his commands strengthens us when the storms of life befall us.

Suggestions for Prayer

1. Moses' words at the beginning of the first reading led to the Jewish custom of wearing a reminder of the covenant on the wrist and around the neck. Christians sometimes wear medals or crosses. Do you consider this helpful to you?
2. Pray with today's responsorial psalm. Do you find the image of God as a rock helpful? Why?
3. Reflect on some of the storms you have experienced in your life. How would your awareness of God today have helped you then? Recall one of these storms in detail, picturing Jesus with you during that time. What does he say or do?

Suggestion for Journal Keeping

The catechumenate is a time of growth in prayer and action. How have you been growing in prayer? How are you putting Jesus' teaching into action?

Robert M. Hamma

Ninth Sunday of the Year **B**

READING I Dt 5, 12–15

"Take care to keep holy the sabbath day as the Lord, your God, commanded you. Six days you may labor and do all your work; but the seventh day is the sabbath of the Lord, your God. No work may be done then, whether by you, or your son or daughter, or your male or female slave, or your ox or ass or any of your beasts, or the alien who lives with you. Your male and female slave should rest as you do. For remember that you too were once slaves in Egypt, and the Lord, your God, brought you from there with his strong hand and outstretched arm. That is why the Lord, your God, has commanded you to observe the sabbath day."

Responsorial Psalm Ps 81, 3–4. 5–6. 6–8. 10–11

Sing with joy to God our help.
Take up a melody, and sound the timbrel,
    the pleasant harp and the lyre.
Blow the trumpet at the new moon,
    at the full moon, on our solemn feast.
Sing with joy to God our help.
For it is a statute in Israel,
    an ordinance of the God of Jacob,
Who made it a decree for Joseph
    when he came forth from the land of
    Egypt.
Sing with joy to God our help.
An unfamiliar speech I hear:
    "I relieved his shoulder of the burden;
    his hands were freed from the basket.
In distress you called, and I rescued you."

Sing with joy to God our help.
"There shall be no strange god among you
    nor shall you worship any alien god.
I, the Lord, am your God
    who led you forth from the land of Egypt."
Sing with joy to God our help.

READING II 2 Cor 4, 6–11

God, who said, "Let light shine out of darkness," has shone in our hearts, that we in turn might make known the glory of God shining on the face of Christ. This treasure we possess in earthen vessels to make it clear that its surpassing power comes from God and not from us. We are afflicted in every way possible, but we are not crushed; full of doubts, we never despair. We are persecuted but never abandoned; we are struck down but never destroyed. Continually we carry about in our bodies the dying of Jesus so that in our bodies the life of Jesus may also be revealed. While we live we are constantly being delivered to death for Jesus' sake, so that the life of Jesus may be revealed in our mortal flesh.

GOSPEL Mk 2, 23–3, 6

It happened that Jesus was walking through standing grain on the sabbath, and his disciples began to pull off heads of grain as they went along. At this the Pharisees protested: "Look! Why do they do a thing not permitted on the sabbath?" He said to them: "Have you never read what David did when he was in need and he and his men were hungry? How he entered God's house in the days of Abiathar the high priest and ate the holy bread which only the priests were permitted to eat? He even gave it to his men." Then he said to them: "The sabbath was made for man, not man for the sabbath. That is why the Son of Man is lord even of the sabbath."

He returned to the synagogue where there was a man whose hand was shriveled up. They kept an eye on Jesus to see whether he would heal him on the sabbath, hoping to be able to bring an accusation against him. He addressed the man with the shriveled hand: "Stand up here in front!" Then he said to them: "Is it permitted to do a good deed on the sabbath—or an evil one? To preserve life—or to destroy it?" At this they remained silent. He looked around at them angrily, for he was deeply grieved that they had closed their minds against him. Then he said to the man, "Stretch out your hand." The man did so and his hand was perfectly restored. When the Pharisees went outside, they immediately began to plot with the Herodians on how they might destroy him.

Reflection on the Readings

The clear theme of today's readings is the keeping of the sabbath, the importance of taking time for rest and worship. What a wonderful message to us who so often get caught up in a hectic daily pace! Keeping the sabbath is for the Hebrew people and for us a time free from routine work in order to remember and renew our relationship with God. Whether on Saturday—for Jews and some other religious groups—or on Sunday, the Christian practice, we are called to make holy our time and actions. We celebrate Sunday as the day of the resurrection. The responsorial psalm today depicts a joyful celebration—our worship.

The myriad of detailed rules about what could or could not be done on the sabbath and the overwhelming legalism of the Jewish leaders in the time of Jesus led him to rebuke the Pharisees: "The sabbath was made for man, not man for the sabbath." It is to be a time of re-creation and renewal. Therefore we are encouraged to take personal and family time on this one day, to pray, to celebrate in worship, to read Scripture, to enjoy fellowship with our parish community, to attend to the spirit.

We need rhythms and changes to keep our sense of balance, perspective and growth. The weekly rhythm of a special day of prayer serves as a reminder and an energizer. It helps us to realize that we are a community of faith. Our busy schedules seldom allow us to take quiet time; we forget to set aside time for the Lord. On Sunday the catechumenate community gathers together to break the word of Scripture. You are spending extra time together on Sunday and perhaps also during the week. This is holy time. How do you feel about this time you share with the parish community? Do you also find a few extra moments to pause, in solitude, to pray, to listen to the Lord in your own life?

Most often we have to plan ahead—we have to *make* time and arrange our activities so that regular quiet time is possible. Even our time driving a car can be made into quiet time by turning off the radio and by putting ourselves in the presence of God.

Suggestions for Prayer

1. In the Book of Exodus 31:12–17 we read of the Lord giving to Moses the rule of keeping the sabbath holy, "a token be-

tween you and me throughout the generations to show that it is I, the Lord, who make you holy." Set aside some quiet time in church to simply be in the presence of the Lord, remembering that it is he who made you, gave you life, gifts, all that you have. Enjoy his presence and listen for the inspiration within you on keeping your relationship with him alive.

2. Really listen to the words of the Mass as the celebrant prays in behalf of the whole community. Notice how the prayers of the community are a balance to our personal prayers—conscious of the whole Church, of our communal worship, of needs and persons we individually do not keep in mind. Use a missal or missalette to reread the prayers of the Mass, taking time to reflect on them.

3. Set aside quiet time on at least three days during the week to create a "sabbath-atmosphere": let go of other tasks, tensions, worries. Hand them to the Lord for a few minutes while you take time to reflect and pray. Be faithful to the prayer time you choose each week, each day.

Suggestion for Journal Keeping

If you are accustomed to making Sunday a special, different kind of day, what will you do to strengthen the spiritual element? If keeping Sunday as a day of prayer and community building is not familiar to you, reflect on how you might begin to develop the sabbath sense. You may want to talk with your family, sponsor and catechumenate team about the changes that may be ahead of you.

Clare M. Colella

Ninth Sunday of the Year C

READING II   1 Kgs 8, 41–43
Solomon prayed in the temple, saying, "To the foreigner, likewise, who is not of your people Israel, but comes from a distant land to honor you (since men will learn of your great name and your mighty hand and your outstretched arm), when he comes and prays toward this temple, listen from your heavenly dwelling. Do all that the foreigner asks of you, that all the peoples of the earth may know your name, may fear you as do your people Israel, and may acknowledge that this temple which I have built is dedicated to your honor.

Responsorial Psalm   Ps 117, 1. 2
Go out to all the world,
    and tell the Good News.
**Praise the Lord, all you nations;
    glorify him, all you peoples!
For steadfast is his kindness toward us,
    and the fidelity of the Lord endures forever.**
Go out to all the world,
    and tell the Good News.

READING II   Gal 1, 1–2. 6–10
Paul, an apostle sent not by men or by any man, but by Jesus Christ and God his Father who raised him from the dead—I and my brothers who are with me, send greetings to the churches in Galatia.

I am amazed that you are so soon deserting him who called you in accord with his

gracious design in Christ, and are going over to another gospel. But there is no other. Some who wish to alter the gospel of Christ must have confused you. For if even we or an angel from heaven should preach to you a gospel not in accord with the one we delivered to you, let a curse be upon him! I repeat what I have just said: if anyone preaches a gospel to you other than the one you received, let a curse be upon him!

Whom would you say I am trying to please at this point—men or God? Is this how I seek to ingratiate myself with men? If I were trying to win man's approval, I would surely not be serving Christ!

GOSPEL — Lk 7, 1–10

When Jesus had finished his discourse in the hearing of the people, he entered Capernaum. A centurion had a servant he held in high regard, who was at that moment sick to the point of death. When he heard about Jesus he sent some Jewish elders to him, asking him to come and save the life of his servant. Upon approaching Jesus they petitioned him earnestly. "He deserves this favor from you," they said, "because he loves our people, and even built our synagogue for us." Jesus set out with them. When he was only a short distance from the house, the centurion sent friends to tell him: "Sir, do not trouble yourself, for I am not worthy to have you enter my house. That is why I did not presume to come to you myself. Just give the order and my servant will be cured. I too am a man who knows the meaning of an order, having soldiers under my command. I say to one, 'On your way,' and off he goes; to another, 'Come here,' and he comes; to my slave, 'Do this,' and he does it." Jesus showed amazement on hearing this, and turned to the crowd which was following him to say, "I tell you, I have never found so much faith among the Israelites." When the deputation returned to the house, they found the servant in perfect health.

Reflection on the Readings

A centurion approaches Jesus through Jewish elders and asks the Lord to heal a valued servant of his. This soldier is a symbol of the occupation force dominating Israel at the time. He is perceived as an enemy. This particular centurion, however, is sensitive to the people. He has built a synagogue for them, and he does not ask Jesus to visit his house. To actually visit would make Jesus ritually impure since this is the home of a non-believer.

Is this centurion truly a non-believer? Not in the eyes of Jesus. The Gospel reports that he is "amazed." This is usually the word given by the evangelists to describe the crowd's reaction to Jesus' teaching (Mt 7:28; Mk 7:37). Instead, Jesus is moved to heal the centurion's servant because of the soldier's great faith in him. This is not the only time in the Gospel story that a centurion exhibits great faith in the Lord. At Jesus' death, in each of the Synoptic Gospels (Mt 27:54, Mk 15:39, Lk 23:47), a centurion reacts with a certain amount of faith.

A seeming non-believer comes to belief in Jesus. Solomon predicts this universal faith in the Most High. Perhaps the temple to which he refers in the first reading can be interpreted, from our point of view, as Jesus himself.

Fidelity to the person of Christ is the message of Paul in the second reading. We must forge intimate bonds of union with the Lord Jesus and in the words of the psalm "go out to all the world and tell the good news." Having met the Lord, perceiving his power and favor, how can we do anything less than tell his wonders?

Suggestions for Prayer

1. What does it mean in your life to go out and spread the good news of Jesus (at home, at work, with family and friends)? How would you do this?
2. In the first reading, Solomon speaks of the "fear" of the Lord by believers. What do you think he means by the word "fear"? Do you fear God?
3. Prayerfully consider the Gospel. Who are you and what do you feel?
   The centurion who wants Jesus' healing for a valued servant/friend?
   The elders who petition for him?
   The people who witness this petition and Jesus' amazement?
   The servant in need of healing?

Suggestion for Journal Keeping

We are commanded by Jesus to spread his good news, to help bring all to belief in the Lord. Spend some time in reflection on the wonderful, transforming and amazing good news of Jesus. Imagine yourself as one of the Gospel evangelists. Spend some time in your journal completing the following:
   "I have good news. Jesus has the power to heal and this is what I have experienced . . ."

Steven M. Lanza

Tenth Sunday of the Year

READING I   Hos 6, 3–6

"Let us know, let us strive to know the Lord;
    as certain as the dawn is his coming,
    and his judgment shines forth like the light of day!
He will come to us like the rain,
    like spring rain that waters the earth."

What can I do with you, Ephraim?
What can I do with you, Judah?
Your piety is like a morning cloud,
    like the dew that early passes away.
For this reason I smote them through the prophets,
    I slew them by the words of my mouth;
For it is love that I desire, not sacrifice,
    and knowledge of God rather than holocausts.

Responsorial Psalm   Ps 50, 1. 8. 12–13. 14–15

To the upright I will show the saving
    power of God.
God the Lord has spoken and summoned the earth,
    from the rising of the sun to its setting.
"Not for your sacrifices do I rebuke you,
    for your holocausts are before me always."
To the upright I will show the saving
    power of God.
"If I were hungry, I should not tell you,
    for mine are the world and its fullness.
Do I eat the flesh of strong bulls,
    or is the blood of goats my drink?"
To the upright I will show the saving
    power of God.

"Offer to God praise as your sacrifice
and fulfill your vows to the Most High;
Then call upon me in time of distress;
I will rescue you, and you shall glorify
me."
To the upright I will show the saving
power of God.

READING II   Rom 4, 18–25

Abraham believed hoping against hope, and so became the father of many nations, just as it was once told him, "Numerous as this shall your descendants be." Without growing weak in faith he thought of his own body, which was as good as dead (for he was nearly a hundred years old), and of the dead womb of Sarah. Yet he never questioned or doubted God's promise; rather, he was strengthened in faith and gave glory to God, fully persuaded that God could do whatever he had promised. Thus his faith was credited to him as justice.

The words, "It was credited to him," were not written with him alone in view; they were intended for us too. For our faith will be credited to us also if we believe in him who raised Jesus our Lord from the dead, the Jesus who was handed over to death for our sins and raised up for our justification.

GOSPEL   Mt 9, 9–13

As Jesus moved about, he saw a man named Matthew at his post where taxes were collected. He said to him, "Follow me." Matthew got up and followed him. Now it happened that, while Jesus was at table in Matthew's home, many tax collectors and those known as sinners came to join Jesus and his disciples at dinner. The Pharisees saw this and complained to his disciples, "What reason can the Teacher have for eating with tax collectors and those who disregard the law?" Overhearing the remark, he said: "People who are in good health do not need a doctor; sick people do. Go and learn the meaning of the words, 'It is mercy I desire and not sacrifice.' I have come to call not the self-righteous, but sinners."

Reflection on the Readings

In the time of Jesus, the tax collectors were among the most despised people in all of Israel. They were seen as traitors, for though they were Jews themselves, they collected taxes for the Roman oppressors. They often overcharged people in order to make a better living for themselves. To befriend and eat with a tax collector was considered to be not only socially unpopular, but also religiously impure. The fact that Jesus befriended and ate with tax collectors and sinners scandalized the religious leaders. Jesus rebuked them for their rigidness. They had become experts at following the letter of the law and at offering sacrifices at the temple. Yet, they had lost the understanding of the spirit of the law, and their sacrifices had become empty and meaningless. Jesus challenges them to reach out to others with love and mercy. He teaches that the meaning of the law is love and that this love is meant for all, especially those who are lost, especially the sinners.

Just as it was easier for the Pharisees in the time of Jesus to offer sacrifice in the temple rather than reach out in mercy to sinners, so too was it easier for the Israelites in the time of Hosea to offer sacrifice rather than form a faith relationship with God. The Israelites to whom Hosea preached had adopted a practice of offering sacrifices to God whenever they were in need, but turned away from God whenever things were going well. Hosea teaches that it is love and knowledge of God that God seeks, not empty sacrifices. It is not through bargaining with God, but through forming a real faith relationship with him that we will, as the psalmist prays, see the saving power of God.

Suggestions for Prayer

1. Reflect with your sponsor on the following questions:
   Do I bargain with God?
   Do I get angry with God when things don't go my way? Why?
2. Who is the "tax collector," "sinner," "social outcast" in your life? Bring that person to your prayer and ask God to help you reach out to that person.
3. Jesus says to Matthew, "Follow me." Repeat these words to yourself prayerfully and silently, and meditate on how Jesus is asking you to follow him.

Suggestion for Journal Keeping
   Write three things that you can do to help build your faith relationship with God.

Kathryn A. Schneider

Tenth Sunday of the Year B

READING I   Gn 3, 9–15
[After Adam had eaten of the tree] the Lord God called him and asked him, "Where are you?" He answered, "I heard you in the garden; but I was afraid, because I was naked, so I hid myself." Then he asked, "Who told you that you were naked? You have eaten, then, from the tree of which I had forbidden you to eat!" The man replied, "The woman whom you put here with me—she gave me fruit from the tree, and so I ate it." The Lord God then asked the woman, "Why did you do such a thing?" The woman answered, "The serpent tricked me into it, so I ate it."
   Then the Lord God said to the serpent:
"Because you have done this, you shall be banned
   from all the animals
   and from all the wild creatures;
On your belly shall you crawl,
   and dirt shall you eat
   all the days of your life.
I will put enmity between you and the woman,
   and between your offspring and hers;
He will strike at your head,
   while you strike at his heel."

Responsorial Psalm   Ps 130, 1–2. 3–4. 5–6. 7–8

With the Lord there is mercy,
   and fullness of redemption.
Out of the depths I cry to you, O Lord;
   Lord, hear my voice!
Let your ears be attentive
   to my voice in supplication.
With the Lord there is mercy,
   and fullness of redemption.
If you, O Lord, mark iniquities,
   Lord, who can stand?
But with you is forgiveness,
   that you may be revered.
With the Lord there is mercy,
   and fullness of redemption.
I trust in the Lord;
   my soul trusts in his word.

258

More than sentinels wait for the dawn,
let Israel wait for the Lord.
With the Lord there is mercy,
and fullness of redemption.
**For with the Lord is kindness
and with him is plenteous redemption;
And he will redeem Israel
from all their iniquities.**
With the Lord there is mercy,
and fullness of redemption.

READING II   2 Cor 4, 13—5, 1
We have that spirit of faith of which the Scripture says, "Because I believed, I spoke out." We believe and so we speak, knowing that he who raised up the Lord Jesus will raise us up along with Jesus and place both us and you in his presence. Indeed, everything is ordered to your benefit, so that the grace bestowed in abundance may bring greater glory to God because they who give thanks are many.

We do not lose heart because our inner being is renewed each day, even though our body is being destroyed at the same time. The present burden of our trial is light enough and earns for us an eternal weight of glory beyond all comparison. We do not fix our gaze on what is seen but on what is unseen. What is seen is transitory; what is not seen lasts forever.

Indeed, we know that when the earthly tent in which we dwell is destroyed we have a dwelling provided for us by God, a dwelling in the heavens, not made by hands, but to last forever.

GOSPEL   Mk 3, 20—35
Jesus came to the house with his disciples and again the crowd assembled, making it impossible for them to get any food what-

ever. When his family heard of this they came to take charge of him, saying, "He is out of his mind"; while the scribes who arrived from Jerusalem asserted, "He is possessed by Beelzebul," and "He expels demons with the help of the prince of demons." Summoning them, he then began to speak to them by way of examples: "How can Satan expel Satan? If a kingdom is torn by civil strife, that kingdom cannot last. If a household is divided according to loyalties, that household will not survive. Similarly, if Satan has suffered mutiny in his ranks and is torn by dissension, he cannot endure; he is finished. No one can enter a strong man's house and despoil his property unless he has first put him under restraint. Only then can he plunder his house.

"I give you my word, every sin will be forgiven mankind and all the blasphemies men utter, but whoever blasphemes against the Holy Spirit will never be forgiven. He carries the guilt of his sin without end." He spoke thus because they had said, "He is possessed by an unclean spirit."

His mother and his brothers arrived, and as they stood outside they sent word to him to come out. The crowd seated around him told him, "Your mother and your brothers and sisters are outside asking for you." He said in reply, "Who are my mother and my brothers?" And gazing around him at those seated in the circle he continued, "These are my mother and my brothers. Whoever does the will of God is brother and sister and mother to me."

Reflection on the Readings

The seasons of our lives are times that let us know all is not perfect or complete. We are on a journey in life—a journey of faith and self-knowledge. With today's readings we recognize the polarizations within ourselves as the same ambiguities all persons share to some extent: weakness and hope, human sinfulness and redemption. Some ambiguities and confusion we learn to live with. Others are more radical and cause us to make a choice: the basic choice of doing good or not—choosing God or choosing evil. The two are not compatible in our lives. As long as we are alive, we continue to make choices. A fundamental choice to seek God as the center of our lives does not clear away all other burdens or difficulties ahead of us. Redemption has been promised, and we can be strong because, as Paul writes, we do not lose heart; we are renewed each day in Jesus through abundant grace.

In the midst of our season of "ordinary time," we see again how our lives are ordinary: common elements of search, question, weakness, failure, blessing, growth are shared by everyone. Yet how individual our life is, how unique in the way we work out our relationship with Jesus! What binds us together as a community of believers (or a community of searchers) is the effort to seek out and do the will of God. That is the assurance Jesus gives us today, that because we seek to follow God's way we are his people. Not because we are perfect; we aren't. But we are called to grow in love: recognizing, acknowledging and overcoming those very human barriers we have to giving and accepting love.

Suggestions for Prayer

1. Reflect on the words of today's opening prayer at Mass: "God of wisdom and love, source of all good, send your Spirit to teach us your truth and guide our actions in your way of peace." What is the truth we seek to learn? How can our actions more and more show the truths we live by?

2. Think of a time in your life when your words or actions have hurt another, and how that hurt you as well. Have you grown beyond that weakness? Are there any "loose ends" that may need to be dealt with or healed? Talk it over with the Lord; listen to his inspiration for your life.

3. As you continue your exploration of the faith and life of the Catholic community, you are becoming yourself a member of this "family of God." As a family we are growing together. Take the time to reflect on your family of faith. How do you feel? What do you think about this family and our faith? Let your thoughts be phrased as prayer. You may choose to talk to your sponsor or the catechumenate team about what you feel and think.

Suggestion for Journal Keeping

What have been the areas of greatest growth for you in recent months—spiritual insights, a specific facet of conversion, relationship to God, to others? Who or what has motivated that growth? Take some time to reflect on these questions. Use your journal to help "track" your growth and developing faith, even your questions and doubts. They are the opening edge of new growth.

Clare M. Colella

READING I
1 Kgs 17, 17–24

The son of the mistress of the house fell sick, and his sickness grew more severe until he stopped breathing. So she said to Elijah, "Why have you done this to me, O man of God? Have you come to me to call attention to my guilt and to kill my son?" "Give me your son," Elijah said to her. Taking him from her lap, he carried him to the upper room where he was staying, and laid him on his own bed. He called out to the Lord: "O Lord, my God, will you afflict even the widow with whom I am staying by killing her son?" Then he stretched himself out upon the child three times and called out to the Lord: "O Lord, my God, let the life breath return to the body of this child." The Lord heard the prayer of Elijah; the life breath returned to the child's body and he revived. Taking the child, Elijah brought him down into the house from the upper room and gave him to his mother. "See!" Elijah said to her, "your son is alive." "Now indeed I know that you are a man of God," the woman replied to Elijah. "The word of the Lord comes truly from your mouth."

Responsorial Psalm   Ps 30, 2. 4. 5–6. 11. 12. 13

I will praise you, Lord,
  for you have rescued me.

I will extol you, O Lord, for you drew me clear
  and did not let my enemies rejoice over me.

O Lord, you brought me up from the nether world;
  you preserved me from among those going
  down into the pit.
I will praise you, Lord,
  for you have rescued me.

Sing praise to the Lord, you his faithful ones,
  and give thanks to his holy name.
For his anger lasts but a moment;
  a lifetime, his good will.
At nightfall, weeping enters in,
  but with the dawn, rejoicing.
I will praise you, Lord,
  for you have rescued me.

Hear, O Lord, and have pity on me;
  O Lord, be my helper.
You changed my mourning into dancing;
  O Lord, my God, forever will I give you thanks.
I will praise you, Lord,
  for you have rescued me.

READING II
Gal 1, 11–19

I assure you, brothers, the gospel I proclaimed to you is no mere human invention. I did not receive it from any man, nor was I schooled in it. It came by revelation from Jesus Christ. You have heard, I know, the story of my former way of life in Judaism. You know that I went to extremes in persecuting the Church of God and tried to destroy it; I made progress in Jewish observances far beyond most of my contemporaries, in my excess of zeal to live out all the traditions of my ancestors.

But the time came when he who had set me apart before I was born and called me by his favor chose to reveal his Son through me, that I might spread among the Gentiles the good tidings concerning him. Immediately, without seeking human advisers or even going to Jerusalem to see those who were apostles before me, I went off to Arabia; later I returned to Damascus. Three years after that I went up to Jerusalem to get to know Cephas, with whom I stayed fifteen days. I did not meet any other apostles except James, the brother of the Lord.

GOSPEL   Lk 7, 11–17

Jesus went to a town called Naim, and his disciples and a large crowd accompanied him. As he approached the gate of the town a dead man was being carried out, the only son of a widowed mother. A considerable crowd of townsfolk were with her. The Lord was moved with pity upon seeing her and said to her, "Do not cry." Then he stepped forward and touched the litter; at this, the bearers halted. He said, "Young man, I bid you get up." The dead man sat up and began to speak. Then Jesus gave him back to his mother. Fear seized them all and they began to praise God. "A great prophet has risen among us," they said; and, "God has visited his people." This was the report that spread about him throughout Judea and the surrounding country.

Reflection on the Readings

In church, when we gather for the liturgy of the word, we hear after each of the readings, "This is the word of the Lord!" All respond, "Thanks be to God."

Thanks be to God, indeed. The word of the Lord is active. It is not just a collection of syllables—subject, verb, object. To those who truly listen, it goes beyond spoken language and effects a change in those who hear the proclamation.

In the first reading for this Sunday, the woman responds to the prophet Elijah and the miracle he works by saying, "The word of the Lord comes truly from your mouth." This word is powerful and is able to restore the breath of life to her son. The word, as given by the prophet through his action, is a word of life.

The only son of the widow of Naim also experienced this powerful word of the Lord and its life-giving potency. Is it any wonder that when the young man is given back his life by the word of God, he too "sat up and began to speak"? The word engenders further words.

St. Paul, in the second reading, conveys this word of life and graphically applies it to his own background. He tells of his own persecution of the Church and how, after the Gospel was revealed to him by Jesus, his whole life was turned around.

The word of God converts us all from darkness to light, from our former ways to those of the Lord. In the words of the Gospel passage, "God visits his people." And those whom he visits are made new.

Suggestions for Prayer

1. The Gospel reading and the first reading are about Elijah and Jesus giving back life to those who are dead. The second reading is about St. Paul who has been given new life by the revelation of Jesus.
   - What areas inside of yourself need the healing presence of the word of the Lord? What keeps you from giving yourself totally to his message?
   - Is there anything you see in the Church itself that keeps you from giv-

ing yourself to the message of Jesus? What might this be?

2. React to the following phrases from the readings:
   - "Have you come to call attention to my guilt?" (First Reading)
   - "I was born and called to his favor." (Second Reading)
   - "The Lord said, 'Do not cry.'" (Gospel Reading)

Suggestion for Journal Keeping

Reread the Gospel passage. Imagine all the sights and sounds. Imagine further that you are the widow of Naim and it has been some months after the miraculous raising of your son by Jesus. At first, you were speechless. Now you are able to say something. Having been given back your son from the dead, write a letter expressing what you feel to Jesus. In what way does this miracle make you a new person?

Steven M. Lanza

Eleventh Sunday of the Year A

READING I   Ex 19, 2–6
The Israelites came to the desert of Sinai [and] pitched camp.

While Israel was encamped here in front of the mountain, Moses went up the mountain to God. Then the Lord called to him and said, "Thus shall you say to the house of Jacob; tell the Israelites: You have seen for yourselves how I treated the Egyptians and how I bore you up on eagle wings, and brought you here to myself. Therefore, if you hearken to my voice and keep my covenant, you shall be my special possession, dearer to me than all other people, though all the earth is mine. You shall be to me a kingdom of priests, a holy nation."

Responsorial Psalm   Ps 100, 1–2. 3. 5
We are his people:
   the sheep of his flock.
**Sing joyfully to the Lord, all you lands;
   serve the Lord with gladness;
   come before him with joyful song.**
We are his people:
   the sheep of his flock.
**Know that the Lord is God;
   he made us, his we are;
   his people, the flock he tends.**
We are his people:
   the sheep of his flock.
**The Lord is good:
   his kindness endures forever,
   and his faithfulness, to all generations.**
We are his people:
   the sheep of his flock.

READING II   Rom 5, 6–11
At the appointed time, when we were still powerless, Christ died for us godless men. It is rare that anyone should lay down his life for a just man, though it is barely possible that for a good man someone may have the courage to die. It is precisely in this that God proves his love for us: that while we were still sinners, Christ died for us. Now that we have been justified by his blood, it is all the more certain that we shall be saved by him from God's wrath. For if, when we were God's enemies, we were reconciled to him by the death of his Son, it is all the more certain that we who have been reconciled will be saved by his life. Not only that; we go so

far as to make God our boast through our Lord Jesus Christ, through whom we have now received reconciliation.

GOSPEL   Mt 9, 36–10, 8

At the sight of the crowds, the heart of Jesus was moved with pity. They were lying prostrate from exhaustion, like sheep without a shepherd. He said to his disciples: "The harvest is good but laborers are scarce. Beg the harvest master to send out laborers to gather his harvest."

Then he summoned his twelve disciples and gave them authority to expel unclean spirits and cure sickness and disease of every kind.

The names of the twelve apostles are these: first Simon, now known as Peter, and his brother Andrew; James, Zebedee's son, and his brother John; Philip and Bartholomew, Thomas and Matthew the tax collector; James, son of Alphaeus, and Thaddaeus; Simon the Zealot party member, and Judas Iscariot, who betrayed him. Jesus sent these men on mission as the Twelve, after giving them the following instructions:

"Do not visit pagan territory and do not enter a Samaritan town. Go instead after the lost sheep of the house of Israel. As you go, make this announcement: 'The reign of God is at hand!' Cure the sick, raise the dead, heal the leprous, expel demons. The gift you have received, give as a gift."

Reflection on the Readings

"I will be your God and you will be my people." This is the essence of the covenant God made with Abraham. God chose the Israelites to be a sign of God's care for and presence in the world. They were to be a nation set apart by virtue of their relationship with and their worship of the one true God. To this covenant God remained ever faithful, though the people of Israel time after time turned away from God. God demonstrated faithfulness when he freed the Israelites from slavery, when he sent Jesus to teach us to love one another, and when he raised Jesus from the dead.

As Christians we are the spiritual heirs to this covenant. To remain faithful, God calls us to follow Jesus Christ and to continue his mission on earth. Jesus came to announce the kingdom of God. He wanted all to know that the kingdom of God was not a kingdom on earth with a powerful leader and a strong defense. Rather, the kingdom of God is the reign of God. The kingdom exists wherever God's will is fulfilled. We glimpse the kingdom every time we see a person reach out to another in genuine love. It is to this harvest that Jesus calls the apostles and each one of us. Just as Jesus called the twelve apostles to announce the reign of God by curing the sick, raising the dead, healing the leprous and expelling demons, so too must we announce the reign of God. Perhaps we think we do not have the powers that were given to the apostles. Yet, we can announce God's reign, God's presence, by the way we love. We can care for those who are sick, mourn with those who have lost a loved one, accept and love those with unpopular diseases and expel the fears of the frightened. Every time we reach out to another in love, we announce through our action that the reign of God is at hand.

Suggestions for Prayer

1. The mission of the apostles and our mission to announce the kingdom of God is

264

the mission of the Church. Speak with your sponsor and ask him/her how the Church attempts to fulfill its mission. In other words, how does the universal Church as well as your local parish work at announcing the kingdom of God?

2. Meditate on these words of the Psalmist:

The Lord is good:
his kindness endures forever;
and his faithfulness to all generations.

Remember these words especially if and when you ever feel unworthy of God's love.

3. The Gospel ends: "The gift you have received, give as a gift." What gift have you received from God that you can share with others?

Suggestion for Journal Keeping
Write one way you can announce the reign of God through your words or actions.

Kathryn A. Schneider

Eleventh Sunday of the Year [B]

READING I   Ez 17, 22–24
Thus says the Lord God:
I, too, will take from the crest of the cedar,
    from its topmost branches tear off a
    tender shoot,
And plant it on a high and lofty mountain;
    on the mountain heights of Israel I will
    plant it.
It shall put forth branches and bear fruit,
    and become a majestic cedar.

Birds of every kind shall dwell beneath it,
    every winged thing in the shade of its
    boughs.
And all the trees of the field shall know
    that I, the Lord,
Bring low the high tree,
    lift high the lowly tree,
Wither up the green tree,
    and make the withered tree bloom.
As I, the Lord, have spoken, so will I do.

Responsorial Psalm   Ps 92, 2–3. 13–14.
                                                    15–16
Lord, it is good to give thanks to you.
It is good to give thanks to the Lord,
    to sing praise to your name, Most High,
To proclaim your kindness at dawn
    and your faithfulness throughout the
    night.
Lord, it is good to give thanks to you.
The just man shall flourish like the palm tree,
    like a cedar of Lebanon shall he grow.
They that are planted in the house of the
    Lord
    shall flourish in the courts of our God.
Lord, it is good to give thanks to you.
They shall bear fruit even in old age;
    vigorous and sturdy shall they be,
Declaring how just is the Lord,
    my Rock, in whom there is no wrong.
Lord, it is good to give thanks to you.

READING II   2 Cor 5, 6–10
We continue to be confident. We know that while we dwell in the body we are away from the Lord. We walk by faith, not by sight. I repeat, we are full of confidence, and would much rather be away from the body and at home with the Lord. This being so, we make it our aim to please him whether we are with him or away from him.

265

The lives of all of us are to be revealed before the tribunal of Christ so that each one may receive his recompense, good or bad, according to his life in the body.

GOSPEL   Mk 4, 26–34

Jesus said to the crowd: "This is how it is with the reign of God. A man scatters seed on the ground. He goes to bed and gets up day after day. Through it all the seed sprouts and grows without his knowing how it happens. The soil produces of itself first the blade, then the ear, finally the ripe wheat in the ear. When the crop is ready he 'wields the sickle, for the time is ripe for harvest.' "

He went on to say: "What comparison shall we use for the reign of God? What image will help to present it? It is like mustard seed which, when planted in the soil, is the smallest of all the earth's seeds, yet once it is sown, springs up to become the largest of shrubs, with branches big enough for the birds of the sky to build nests in its shade." By means of many such parables he taught them the message in a way they could understand. To them he spoke only by way of parable, while he kept explaining things privately to his disciples.

Reflection on the Readings

Hope emerges as a theme from the readings today. But our hope is about lasting things. As Christians, it is about the coming of the reign of God. That is our ultimate hope. The images used are those of planting and harvesting. The hope we have is perhaps like that of a planter of seeds who does his best to assure the fruitful harvest. The mystery of growth, the mystery or gift of faith, is the link between seed and harvest.

The first reading from the prophet Ezekiel

uses the image of God as the planter and care-taker—a wonderful parallel to the Gospel parables. Paul's Letter to the Corinthians here reminds us of God's care: we have every reason to be confident in our hope. We are one with the Lord, his kingdom is within us, we are a part of that kingdom.

Are our lives lived as though we are confident in the Lord's care of us? As catechumens and faith community our faith is always developing, growing, unfolding, as a seed/plant does. Around us there is much that challenges our growth in faith. Forces in society and sometimes even elements within us challenge our hope. As followers of Christ, we have heard the word—the mustard seed of faith. We have our assurance that throughout the growing season and its difficulties, we are cared for by God, the planter, the gardener. We are not left on our own. The good that has been begun in us God will continue to nurture. He will not abandon us. The tension between being planted in faith and not yet fully ready as a harvest is the tension of being "on the way." We have a deep inner-rooted hope, yet we are aware of our fragility. Prayers and readings such as we have today give us the encouragement, the inspiration, to continue in our growth.

Suggestions for Prayer

1. The experience of planting a seed, or transplanting a seedling, is a co-creative experience. We work in partnership to nurture a plant through to its fullness. Take heart—plant some seeds, care for them, watch them grow. Let yourself feel the wonder of the first shoots and leaves as they emerge. Let your care be a reminder of God's care.

2. Reread the Scriptures and the prayers of today's liturgy. Imagine yourself as a disciple of Jesus, in the outdoor setting, hearing the parables of the Gospel. Looking around you see the plants growing—the images Jesus chose are natural to your life. Formulate your own prayer for nourishment in your faith journey.
3. Several traditional prayers of the Catholic Church speak of hope. One of them is called an "Act of Hope." With your sponsor find a copy of that prayer. Reflect on it, coming to understand its meaning. You may want to write your own "Act of Hope."

Suggestion for Journal Keeping

What is your basic outlook on life? Is it an attitude of hope, confidence? Is it harmonious with belief in a loving, nurturing God? Spend some time reflecting on this; then write about it. You may want to talk it over with your sponsor as well.

Clare M. Colella

Eleventh Sunday of the Year C

READING I 2 Sm 12, 7–10. 13

Nathan said to David: "Thus says the Lord God of Israel: 'I anointed you king of Israel. I rescued you from the hand of Saul. I gave you your lord's house and your lord's wives for your own. I gave you the house of Israel and of Judah. And if this were not enough, I could count up for you still more. Why have you spurned the Lord and done evil in his sight? You have cut down Uriah the Hittite with the sword; you took his wife as your own, and him you killed with the sword of the Ammonites. Now, therefore, the sword shall never depart from your house, because you have despised me and have taken the wife of Uriah to be your wife.' " Then David said to Nathan, "I have sinned against the Lord." Nathan answered David: "The Lord on his part has forgiven your sin: you shall not die."

Responsorial Psalm Ps 32, 1–2. 5. 7. 11

Lord, forgive the wrong I have done.
Happy is he whose fault is taken away, whose sin is covered.
Happy the man to whom the Lord imputes not guilt, in whose spirit there is no guile.
Lord, forgive the wrong I have done.
I acknowledged my sin to you, my guilt I covered not.
I said, "I confess my faults to the Lord," and you took away the guilt of my sin.
Lord, forgive the wrong I have done.
You are my shelter; from distress you will preserve me; with glad cries of freedom you will ring me round.
Lord, forgive the wrong I have done.
Be glad in the Lord and rejoice, you just; exult, all you upright of heart.
Lord, forgive the wrong I have done.

READING II Gal 2, 16. 19–21

Knowing that a man is not justified by legal observance but by faith in Jesus Christ, we too have believed in him in order to be justified by faith in Christ, not by observance of the law; for by works of the law no one will be justified. It was through the law that I died to the law, to live for God. I have been crucified with Christ, and the life I live now is not my own; Christ is living in me. I still live my human life, but it is a life of faith in the Son of God, who loved me and gave himself for me. I will not treat God's gracious gift as pointless. If justice is available through the law, then Christ died to no purpose!

GOSPEL   Lk 7, 36—8, 3
There was a certain Pharisee who invited Jesus to dine with him. Jesus went to the Pharisee's home and reclined to eat. A woman known in the town to be a sinner learned that he was dining in the Pharisee's home. She brought in a vase of perfumed oil and stood behind him at his feet, weeping so that her tears fell upon his feet. Then she wiped them with her hair, kissing them and perfuming them with the oil. When his host, the Pharisee, saw this, he said to himself, "If this man were a prophet, he would know who and what sort of woman this is that touches him—that she is a sinner." In answer to his thoughts, Jesus said to him, "Simon, I have something to propose to you." "Teacher," he said, "speak."

"Two men owed money to a certain money-lender; one owed a total of five hundred coins, the other fifty. Since neither was able to repay, he wrote off both debts. Which of them was more grateful to him?" Simon answered, "He, I presume, to whom he remitted the larger sum." Jesus said to him, "You are right."

Turning then to the woman, he said to Simon: "You see this woman? I came to your home and you provided me with no water for my feet. She has washed my feet with her tears and wiped them with her hair. You gave me no kiss, but she has not ceased kissing my feet since I entered. You did not anoint my head with oil, but she has anointed my feet with perfume. I tell you, that is why her many sins are forgiven—because of her great love. Little is forgiven the one whose love is small."

He said to her then, "Your sins are forgiven," at which his fellow guests began to ask among themselves, "Who is this that he even forgives sins?" Meanwhile he said to the woman, "Your faith has been your salvation. Go now in peace."

After this he journeyed through towns and villages preaching and proclaiming the good news of the kingdom of God. The Twelve accompanied him, and also some women who had been cured of evil spirits and maladies: Mary called the Magdalene, from whom seven devils had gone out, Joanna, the wife of Herod's steward Chuza, Susanna, and many others who were assisting them out of their means.

Reflection on the Readings
One of the primary tasks of us Christians is to forgive. When they ask him how they should pray, Jesus himself bids his disciples to petition heaven to "forgive us our sins, as we ourselves forgive everyone who is indebted to us" (Lk 11:4). This does not mean that we do not acknowledge sin or that we cannot challenge one another to holiness as we strive to turn away from sinning. It does mean, however, that while acknowledging sin and challenging one another to holiness, we exercise mercy and forgiveness.

The Lord God certainly treats David in this fashion. In the first reading, God, through the prophet Nathan, accuses David, his anointed king, confronting him with his sins. But even though David has sinned, God does not abandon him or cast him aside. David is the leader of God's people and God does not go back on his covenant, his holy word. That covenanted relationship stands forever, and it is a relationship built on love, a love which funds forgiveness.

Jesus himself is the fulfillment of that Old Testament covenant, offering all men and women a new ultimate covenant based upon his own sacrifice. What greater sign could we be given of God's tremendous love for us? The woman who washes the feet of Jesus with her tears recognizes this great sign of love in Jesus. She does not deny her sins. In coming to Jesus, she acknowledges who she is and what she has done—just as did David before the prophet.

St. Paul tells us that "Christ lives in us." Because of his Spirit, we acknowledge who and what we are, confident that mercy and forgiveness will be given us. In turn, he invites us to act the same way to all those we meet.

Suggestions for Prayer

1. *Spend some time reflecting on one of the following:* Do you believe that Jesus died that our sins might be forgiven? What is the deepest part of yourself that needs Jesus' healing forgiveness? Can you offer that to him in prayer?

2. Spend some quiet time putting yourself into the Gospel scene. Imagine the supper. Imagine the host, Simon, and the honored guest, Jesus. Imagine the others present and the woman who enters. Who are you? Simon? One of the other guests? The woman? What are you feeling? Why?

3. If the prophet Nathan confronted you with a list of transgressions, what would he say? How would you react?

Suggestion for Journal Keeping

Would you assess yourself as a merciful and forgiving person? Why or why not? Is there any relationship(s) of yours at present that needs healing forgiveness? How might this be achieved?

Steven M. Lanza

Twelfth Sunday of the Year A

READING I   Jer 20, 10–13

Jeremiah said:

"Yes, I hear the whisperings of many:
    'Terror on every side!
    Denounce! let us denounce him!'
All those who were my friends
    are on the watch for any misstep of mine.
'Perhaps he will be trapped; then we can prevail,
    and take our vengeance on him.'
But the Lord is with me, like a mighty champion:
    my persecutors will stumble, they will not triumph.
In their failure they will be put to utter shame,
    to lasting, unforgettable confusion.
O Lord of hosts, you who test the just,
    who probe mind and heart,
Let me witness the vengeance you take on them,
    for to you I have entrusted my cause.
Sing to the Lord,
    praise the Lord,

For he has rescued the life of the poor
from the power of the wicked!"

Responsorial Psalm   Ps 69, 8–10. 14. 17.
33–35

Lord, in your great love, answer me.
For your sake I bear insult,
and shame covers my face.
I have become an outcast to my brothers,
a stranger to my mother's sons,
Because zeal for your house consumes me,
and the insults of those who blaspheme
you fall upon me.
Lord, in your great love, answer me.
I pray to you, O Lord,
for the time of your favor, O God!
In your great kindness answer me
with your constant help.
Answer me, O Lord, for bounteous is your
kindness;
in your great mercy turn toward me.
Lord, in your great love, answer me.
"See, you lowly ones, and be glad;
you who seek God, may your hearts be
merry!
For the Lord hears the poor,
and his own who are in bonds he spurns
not.
Let the heavens and the earth praise him,
the seas and whatever moves in them!"
Lord, in your great love, answer me.

READING II   Rom 5, 12–15
**Just as through one man sin entered the
world and with sin death, death thus coming
to all men inasmuch as all sinned—before
the law there was sin in the world, even
though sin is not imputed when there is no
law—I say, from Adam to Moses death
reigned, even over those who had not sinned**
by breaking a precept as did Adam, that type
of the man to come.

**But the gift is not like the offense. For if by
the offense of the one man all died, much
more did the grace of God and the gracious
gift of the one man, Jesus Christ, abound for
all.**

GOSPEL   Mt 10, 26–33
**Jesus said to his apostles: "Do not let men
intimidate you. Nothing is concealed that
will not be revealed, and nothing hidden
that will not become known. What I tell you
in darkness, speak in the light. What you
hear in private, proclaim from the house-
tops.**

**"Do not fear those who deprive the body
of life but cannot destroy the soul. Rather,
fear him who can destroy both body and
soul in Gehenna. Are not two sparrows sold
for next to nothing? Yet not a single sparrow
falls to the ground without your Father's
consent. As for you, every hair of your head
has been counted; so do not be afraid of anything. You are worth more than an entire
flock of sparrows. Whoever acknowledges
me before men I will acknowledge before
my Father in heaven. Whoever disowns me
before men I will disown before my Father
in heaven."**

Reflection on the Readings
Jesus knew that the life of his disciples
would not be easy. After all, in order to
preach his message, they would have to tell
people to love their enemies, to offer the
other cheek to those who strike them, and to
give their riches to those who have nothing.
These were not popular notions, then or
now. For this reason, Jesus tries to reassure
his followers by teaching them that God is

watching over them. He tells them not to fear those who can kill the body, for it is the soul which gains eternal life. He promises that those who follow him and acknowledge him before others, he will acknowledge before God in heaven.

Just as the life of the disciples was not easy, neither was the life of the prophet Jeremiah. People denounced him, and his friends abandoned him. Yet he persevered in his work to call the Israelites back to true faith in God.

Like the prophets, the disciples, and the psalmist who bears insult and becomes an outcast for serving the Lord, we may at times feel alone and abandoned by God. Yet we must remember that God is ever faithful. As Jeremiah proclaims, "The Lord is with me, like a mighty champion." True discipleship carries risk. In living by and witnessing to the message of Jesus Christ, we risk ridicule, rejection and isolation by those who cannot accept Jesus' message of love. Yet, by risking these things, by remaining faithful, we win what is truly important: a privileged place in God's kingdom.

Suggestions for Prayer

1. In the Gospel Jesus tells the disciples not to be afraid. Repeat these words silently and prayerfully and allow God to dispel your fears:

   Do not be afraid.
   I am with you.
   I love you.
2. Many people throughout history have risked much to serve the Lord. Some are famous; most are not. Bring to mind a person who has risked much to remain faithful to God. Perhaps this person is a saint like St. Paul, or a person from recent times like Mother Teresa or Dorothy Day, or perhaps this person is your sponsor or someone in your community. Thank God for this person and ask God to help you nurture one quality of this person in yourself.

Suggestion for Journal Keeping

Are there things that frighten you about being a disciple? List them. Discuss this list with your sponsor or with a close friend.

Kathryn A. Schneider

Twelfth Sunday of the Year B

READING I   Jb 38, 1. 8–11
The Lord addressed Job out of the storm and said:
Who shut within doors the sea,
  when it burst forth from the womb;
When I made the clouds its garment
  and thick darkness its swaddling bands?
When I set limits for it
  and fastened the bar of its door,
And said: Thus far shall you come but no farther,
  and here shall your proud waves be stilled!

Responsorial Psalm   Ps 107, 23–24. 25–26. 28–29. 30–31

Give thanks to the Lord,
  his love is everlasting.
They who sailed the sea in ships,
  trading on the deep waters,

These saw the works of the Lord
  and his wonders in the abyss.
Give thanks to the Lord,
  his love is everlasting.
His command raised up a storm wind
  which tossed its waves on high.
They mounted up to heaven; they sank to the
    depths;
  their hearts melted away in their plight.
Give thanks to the Lord,
  his love is everlasting.
They cried to the Lord in their distress;
  from their straits he rescued them,
He hushed the storm to a gentle breeze,
  and the billows of the sea were stilled.
Give thanks to the Lord,
  his love is everlasting.
They rejoiced that they were calmed,
  and he brought them to their desired
    haven.
Let them give thanks to the Lord for his
    kindness
  and his wondrous deeds to the children of
    men.
Give thanks to the Lord,
  his love is everlasting.

READING II   2 Cor 5, 14–17

The love of Christ impels us who have
reached the conviction that since one died
for all, all died. He died for all so that those
who live might live no longer for themselves,
but for him who for their sakes died and was
raised up.

Because of this we no longer look on anyone in terms of mere human judgment. If at
one time we so regarded Christ, we no
longer know him by this standard. This
means that if anyone is in Christ, he is a new
creation. The old order has passed away;
now all is new!

GOSPEL   Mk 4, 35–41

One day as evening drew on Jesus said to his
disciples, "Let us cross over to the farther
shore." Leaving the crowd, they took him
away in the boat in which he was sitting,
while the other boats accompanied him. It
happened that a bad squall blew up. The
waves were breaking over the boat and it began to ship water badly. Jesus was in the
stern through it all, sound asleep on a cush-
ion. They finally woke him and said to him,
"Teacher, doesn't it matter to you that we
are going to drown?" He awoke and rebuked
the wind and said to the sea: "Quiet! Be
still!" The wind fell off and everything grew
calm. Then he said to them, "Why are you
so terrified? Why are you lacking in faith?"
A great awe overcame them at this. They
kept saying to one another, "Who can this
be that the wind and the sea obey him?"

Reflection on the Readings

This week's readings have a different sense
of hope—there is an urgency, an impact,
quite different from the seed/plant image of
last week. Today we are in the midst of
storms. We hope for safety and rescue.

The parallel in today's readings from Job
and from Mark are linked by the responsorial
psalm: in the midst of the storm, we cry out
in fear, in faith, in hope. The psalm verse is
remarkable in its imagery of storm: Give
thanks to the Lord, his love is everlasting. It is
as if we are to remember, in the midst of our
own life's storms, that the Lord is very present
and very much our protector, if we but turn
to him.

Our lives, individually and as a community, come upon some difficult times. Our
faith may be challenged by some almost un-
answerable questions. Relationships and har-

mony may be devastated by anger, pain, guilt, unforgiveness, selfishness. We all deal with storms. One of the most amazing experiences about storms in nature is that they come to an end. Much fear is engendered; real damage can be done. But storms do come to an end. There is strength that comes from having survived a storm, a sort of natural wisdom. But we do not survive only on our own strength. Prayer in the midst of our storm gives us strength because it helps us remember who we are, beloved people of God, and where our strength truly is, with God. The voice of God addressing Job and the voice of Jesus calming the storm both assure us of God's presence and power in our lives.

Suggestions for Prayer

1. Remember a time of difficulty in your life, a storm on your journey. How did the storm arise? How did you come through it? What have you learned? Write your own prayer from the experience of that storm.
2. Think about what you have been learning in your faith growth. You are stronger than you were before, but you still have a way to go yet. With that in mind, formulate a prayer beginning, "Lord, I know that I can survive a storm in my life when . . . " and continue in your own words. ·
3. Part of the real value in Christian fellowship is that we are not alone—others are there to be our strength and support, inspiration and guide. Who might be the persons in your community who are *there* for you when you need someone? Think of them, and ask God to give them

the strength and grace they need in their lives. You may want to let them know you are praying for them too.

Suggestion for Journal Keeping

Write a letter to God, talking over a storm that is recent in your life. Let God know, in your own words, your fears, doubts, hopes about that storm. Then spend quiet time, open for inspiration and wisdom. Write down your thoughts.

Clare M. Colella

Twelfth Sunday of the Year   C

READING I   Zec 12, 10–11

I will pour out on the house of David and on the inhabitants of Jerusalem a spirit of grace and petition; and they shall look on him whom they have thrust through, and they shall mourn for him as one mourns for an only son, and they shall grieve over him as one grieves over a first-born.

On that day the mourning in Jerusalem shall be as great as the mourning of Hadadrimmon in the plain of Megiddo.

Responsorial Psalm   Ps 63, 2. 3–4. 5–6.
8–9

My soul is thirsting for you, O Lord my God.

O God, you are my God whom I seek; for you my flesh pines and my soul thirsts like the earth, parched, lifeless and without water.

My soul is thirsting for you, O Lord my God.

Thus have I gazed toward you in the
  sanctuary
  to see your power and your glory,
For your kindness is a greater good than life;
  my lips shall glorify you.
My soul is thirsting for you, O Lord my
  God.
Thus will I bless you while I live;
  lifting up my hands, I will call upon your
  name.
As with the riches of a banquet shall my soul
  be satisfied.
  and with exultant lips my mouth shall
  praise you.
My soul is thirsting for you, O Lord my
  God.
You are my help,
  and in the shadow of your wings I shout
  for joy.
My soul clings fast to you;
  your right hand upholds me.
My soul is thirsting for you, O Lord my
  God.

READING II   Gal 3, 26–29
**Each one of you is a son of God because of
your faith in Christ Jesus. All of you who
have been baptized into Christ have clothed
yourselves with him. There does not exist
among you Jew or Greek, slave or freeman,
male or female. All are one in Christ Jesus.
Furthermore, if you belong to Christ you are
the descendants of Abraham, which means
you inherit all that was promised.**

GOSPEL   Lk 9, 18–24
**One day when Jesus was praying in seclusion
and his disciples were with him, he put the
question to them, "Who do the crowds say
that I am?" "John the Baptizer," they re-**
plied, **"and some say Elijah, while others
claim that one of the prophets of old has returned from the dead." "But you—who do
you say that I am?" he asked them. Peter
said in reply, "The Messiah of God." He
strictly forbade them to tell this to anyone.
"The Son of Man," he said, "must first endure many sufferings, be rejected by the elders, the high priests and the scribes, and be
put to death, and then be raised up on the
third day."**

**Jesus said to all: "Whoever wishes to be
my follower must deny his very self, take up
his cross each day, and follow in my steps.
Whoever would save his life will lose it, and
whoever loses his life for my sake will save
it."**

Reflection on the Readings
  St. Paul says that we are all made sons and
daughters of God by our faith in Jesus Christ.
At your baptism you will put on a white robe,
symbolizing that you have put on the Lord by
faith. Because we belong to the Lord, we inherit all that is promised. And what is promised?

  In the first reading, the Lord God promises
to pour out upon the inhabitants of Jerusalem
"a spirit of grace and petition." This spirit is
promised to us. We are inhabitants of the
new Jerusalem through baptism. But it is
clear from the remainder of the reading that
this spirit does not necessarily mean that
everything in our life will go easy or be wonderful. The grace of God can be a difficult
thing. Remember, Jacob wrestled with an angel (Gen 32:24). We, at times, must also
wrestle with the demands of God's grace.

  Like Peter, because we believe, we recognize and proclaim Jesus as the Messiah,

274

the Anointed One of God. We share in this anointing at baptism. But the Anointed One must suffer and die. And we must follow. To live the life of Jesus, we are invited to deny ourselves and take up his cross daily. Living for others, rather than solely for ourselves, is surely a denial of self and perhaps a cross.

John Paul II has said that the Gospel and we Christians are a "sign of contradiction." To live for others, rather than ourselves, to embrace the difficult grace of God, the cross, is a sign of contradiction to an increasingly self-absorbed and egotistical world. Like the psalmist, though, our desires go beyond self-fulfillment. Our soul thirsts for God and what he alone can offer.

Suggestions for Prayer

1. Spend some time in front of a cross or crucifix meditating on Christ's sacrifice.
   • What was that death like?
   • Are you able, as a follower of Jesus, to accept some measure of that same denial of self, to die to self and live for others?
2. At the beginning of Mass, we sign ourselves with the sign of the cross. During the Rite of Becoming a Catechumen your senses were signed with the sign of the cross.
   • What does it mean to you personally when you make this mark upon your own body?
   • Is this gesture so automatic that its significance is lost?
3. In what ways have you suffered and how has this suffering helped others or yourself? Do you offer your suffering to the Lord?

Suggestion for Journal Keeping

In your journal, react to the following statement taken from the Eucharistic Prayer for Reconciliation II.

God our Father, we had wandered far from you,
but through your Son you have brought us back.
You gave him up to death
so that we might turn again to you
and find our way to one another.

Steven M. Lanza

Thirteenth Sunday of the Year A

READING I 2 Kgs 4, 8–11. 14–16

One day Elisha came to Shunem, where there was a woman of influence, who urged him to dine with her. Afterward, whenever he passed by, he used to stop there to dine. So she said to her husband, "I know that he is a holy man of God. Since he visits us often, let us arrange a little room on the roof and furnish it for him with a bed, table, chair, and lamp, so that when he comes to us he can stay there." Sometime later Elisha arrived and stayed in the room overnight.

Later Elisha asked, "Can something be done for her?" "Yes!" Gehazi answered. "She has no son, and her husband is getting on in years." "Call her," said Elisha. When she had been called, and stood at the door, Elisha promised, "This time next year you will be fondling a baby son."

Responsorial Psalm   Ps 89, 2–3. 16–17.
                                    18–19

For ever I will sing the goodness of the
    Lord.
The favors of the Lord I will sing forever;
    through all generations my mouth shall
    proclaim your faithfulness.
For you have said, "My kindness is
    established forever";
    in heaven you have confirmed your
    faithfulness.
For ever I will sing the goodness of the
    Lord.
Happy the people who know the joyful
    shout;
    in the light of your countenance, O Lord,
    they walk.
At your name they rejoice all the day,
    and through your justice they are exalted.
For ever I will sing the goodness of the
    Lord.
For you are the splendor of their strength,
    and by your favor our horn is exalted.
For to the Lord belongs our shield,
    and to the Holy One of Israel, our king.
For ever I will sing the goodness of the
    Lord.

READING II   Rom 6, 3–4. 8–11
Are you not aware that we who were bap-
tized into Christ Jesus were baptized into his
death? Through baptism into his death we
were buried with him, so that, just as Christ
was raised from the dead by the glory of the
Father, we too might live a new life. If we
have died with Christ, we believe that we
are also to live with him. We know that
Christ, once raised from the dead, will never
die again; death has no more power over
him. His death was death to sin, once for all;
his life is life for God. In the same way, you
must consider yourselves dead to sin but
alive for God in Christ Jesus.

GOSPEL   Mt 10, 37–42
Jesus said to his apostles: "Whoever loves fa-
ther or mother, son or daughter, more than
me is not worthy of me. He who will not take
up his cross and come after me is not worthy
of me. He who seeks only himself brings
himself to ruin, whereas he who brings him-
self to nought for me discovers who he is.
    "He who welcomes you welcomes me,
and he who welcomes me welcomes him
who sent me. He who welcomes a prophet
because he bears the name of prophet re-
ceives a prophet's reward; he who wel-
comes a holy man because he is known as
holy receives a holy man's reward. And I
promise you that whoever gives a cup of
cold water to one of these lowly ones be-
cause he is a disciple will not want for his re-
ward."

Reflection on the Readings
    Welcoming a stranger is difficult. Some-
times even welcoming friends is a challenge.
The woman in today's first reading went beyond mere hospitality. She added a room to
her house for the prophet Elisha!
    In the Gospel, Jesus tells us that we will be
rewarded for the welcome we offer to prophets, holy men, and disciples. Jesus knew
about hospitality and he knew about being
sent away unwelcome. He ate in many
homes, and he was driven away from more
than one place.
    We are reminded in today's readings to
make room for Jesus and for holy people. We
have a choice: to welcome or to drive away,
to open our hearts or to close them. Welcoming strangers is difficult. Jesus reminds us that

"whoever welcomes you welcomes me," and that if we open our hearts we "will not want for our reward."

Suggestions for Prayer

1. What is the cross in your life? Are you willing to pick it up and follow Jesus?
2. Have you ever felt welcomed into someone's home? What was it like? What happened? Have you ever felt that way when praying?
3. Spend some time making yourself ready to welcome the Lord. Find a quiet place and ask the Lord to come and visit you. Sit quietly and wait; make time for the Lord!

Suggestion for Journal Keeping

Read over the second reading. Ask yourself what it means to be baptized into Christ's death. What does baptism mean to you at this time?

Michael P. Enright

Thirteenth Sunday of the Year   B

READING I   Wis 1, 13–15; 2, 23–24
God did not make death,
   nor does he rejoice in the destruction of the living.
For he fashioned all things that they might have being;
   and the creatures of the world are wholesome,

And there is not a destructive drug among them
   nor any domain of the nether world on earth,
For justice is undying.
For God formed man to be imperishable;
   the image of his own nature he made him.
But by the envy of the devil, death entered the world,
   and they who are in his possession experience it.

Responsorial Psalm   Ps 30, 2. 4. 5–6. 11. 12. 13
I will praise you, Lord,
   for you have rescued me.
I will extol you, O Lord, for you drew me clear
   and did not let my enemies rejoice over me.
O Lord, you brought me up from the nether world;
   you preserved me from among those going down into the pit.
I will praise you, Lord,
   for you have rescued me.
Sing praise to the Lord, you his faithful ones,
   and give thanks to his holy name.
For his anger lasts but a moment;
   a lifetime, his good will.
At nightfall, weeping enters in,
   but with the dawn, rejoicing.
I will praise you, Lord,
   for you have rescued me.
Hear, O Lord, and have pity on me;
   O Lord, be my helper.
You changed my mourning into dancing;
   O Lord, my God, forever will I give you thanks.
I will praise you, Lord,
   for you have rescued me.

READING II
2 Cor 8, 7. 9. 13–15

Just as you are rich in every respect, in faith and discourse, in knowledge, in total concern, and in our love for you, you may also abound in your work of charity.

You are well acquainted with the favor shown you by our Lord Jesus Christ: how for your sake he made himself poor though he was rich, so that you might become rich by his poverty. The relief of others ought not to impoverish you; there should be a certain equality. Your plenty at the present time should supply their need so that their surplus may in turn one day supply your need, with equality as the result. It is written, "He who gathered much had no excess and he who gathered little had no lack."

GOSPEL
Mk 5, 21–43

When Jesus had crossed back to the other side of the Sea of Galilee in the boat, a large crowd gathered around him and he stayed close to the lake. One of the officials of the synagogue, a man named Jairus, came near. Seeing Jesus, he fell at his feet and made this earnest appeal: "My little daughter is critically ill. Please come and lay your hands on her so that she may get well and live." The two went off together and a large crowd followed, pushing against Jesus.

There was a woman in the area who had been afflicted with a hemorrhage for a dozen years. She had received treatment at the hands of doctors of every sort and exhausted her savings in the process, yet she got no relief; on the contrary, she only grew worse. She had heard about Jesus and came up behind him in the crowd and put her hand to his cloak. "If I just touch his cloth-ing," she thought, "I shall get well." Immediately her flow of blood dried up and the feeling that she was cured of her affliction ran through her whole body. Jesus was immediately conscious that healing power had gone out from him. Wheeling about in the crowd, he began to ask, "Who touched my clothing?" His disciples said to him, "You can see how this crowd hems you in, yet you ask, 'Who touched me?' Despite this, he kept looking around to see the woman who had done it. Fearful and beginning to tremble now as she realized what had happened, the woman came and fell in front of him and told him the whole truth. He said to her, "Daughter, it is your faith that has cured you. Go in peace and be free of this illness."

He had not finished speaking when people from the official's house arrived saying, "Your daughter is dead. Why bother the Teacher further?" Jesus disregarded the report that had been brought and said to the official: "Fear is useless. What is needed is trust." He would not permit anyone to follow him except Peter, James, and James's brother John. As they approached the house of the synagogue leader, Jesus was struck by the noise of people wailing and crying loudly on all sides. He entered and said to them: "Why do you make this din with your wailing? The child is not dead. She is asleep." At this they began to ridicule him. Then he put them all out.

Jesus took the child's father and mother and his own companions and entered the room where the child lay. Taking her hand he said to her, "Talitha, koum," which means, "Little girl, get up." The girl, a child of twelve, stood up immediately and began to walk around. At this the family's astonishment was complete. He enjoined them

strictly not to let anyone know about it, and told them to give her something to eat.

Reflection on the Readings

Touching is one of our basic human senses. We touch others and others touch us in many different ways. We touch others physically by putting our arms around their shoulders, hugging them or kissing them. Others touch us by the look in their eyes, by the words that they speak, by the acts of charity that they do for us. Touching is a beautiful means of communication. By our touch we can communicate comfort and support. We can communicate love and affection. We can communicate a sense of unity. Unfortunately, through touch, we can also communicate sinful desires such as lust or violence.

In the Gospel today, the word "touch" or its equivalent is used at least six times. Jairus says, "My little daughter is desperately sick. Do come and lay your hands on her." The woman suffering from a hemorrhage for twelve years believed that by touching Jesus' cloak, she would be made well again. When the woman touched Jesus' cloak, she was healed, but Jesus experienced power going out of him. It was through touch that the life of Jesus was communicated to the woman and healed her. Jesus also took the dead child by the hand, that is, he touched her, and she was restored to life.

Today God continues to communicate himself to us through the humanity of Jesus. When Jesus touches us and we touch Jesus, we are healed of our sin and ailments and are made one with the Father through him. This happens especially in the sacraments of reconciliation, anointing of the sick, and the Eucharist, and, during the catechumenate, through the laying on of hands and anointing.

Suggestions for Prayer

1. Reflect on one or more of the following questions:
   - Do you believe that Jesus communicates his life, love, and healing through human touch?
   - Can you forgive the times you may have been touched unwholesomely?
   - Do you believe in the healing power of the sacrament of anointing of the sick? Why?
2. In your imagination, you are lying on your sickbed. Jesus is standing beside you, holding your hand. He says: *"Do not be afraid; only have faith." "Go in peace and be free from your complaint."*
3. Pray the responsorial psalm as your evening prayer this week.

Suggestion for Journal Keeping

Describe an experience of a life-giving touch which strengthened you and gave you a sense of unity and belonging. What emotions were involved?

Michael J. Koch

Thirteenth Sunday of the Year C

READING I 1 Kgs 19, 16. 19–21

The Lord said to Elijah: "You shall anoint Elisha, son of Shaphat of Abel-meholah, as prophet to succeed you."

Elijah set out, and came upon Elisha, son of Shaphat, as he was plowing with twelve yoke of oxen; he was following the twelfth. Elijah went over to him and threw his cloak

over him. Elisha left the oxen, ran after Elijah, and said, "Please, let me kiss my father and mother goodbye, and I will follow you." "Go back!" Elijah answered. "Have I done anything to you?" Elisha left him and, taking the yoke of oxen, slaughtered them; he used the plowing equipment for fuel to boil their flesh, and gave it to his people to eat. Then he left and followed Elijah as his attendant.

Responsorial Psalm   Ps 16, 1–2. 5. 7–8.
                          9–10. 11
You are my inheritance, O Lord.
Keep me, O God, for in you I take refuge;
  I say to the Lord, "My Lord are you.
O Lord, my allotted portion and my cup,
  you it is who hold fast my lot.
You are my inheritance, O Lord.
I bless the Lord who counsels me;
  even in the night my heart exhorts me.
I set the Lord ever before me;
  with him at my right hand I shall not be
  disturbed.
You are my inheritance, O Lord.
Therefore my heart is glad and my soul
  rejoices,
  my body, too, abides in confidence;
Because you will not abandon my soul to the
  nether world,
  nor will you suffer your faithful one to
  undergo corruption.
You are my inheritance, O Lord.
You will show me the path to life,
  fullness of joys in your presence,
  the delights at your right hand forever.
You are my inheritance, O Lord.

READING II   Gal 5, 1. 13–18
It was for liberty that Christ freed us. So stand firm, and do not take on yourselves the yoke of slavery a second time!

My brothers, remember that you have been called to live in freedom—but not a freedom that gives free rein to the flesh. Out of love, place yourselves at one another's service. The whole law has found its fulfillment in this one saying: "You shall love your neighbor as yourself." If you go on biting and tearing one another to pieces, take care! You will end up in mutual destruction!

My point is that you should live in accord with the spirit and you will not yield to the cravings of the flesh. The flesh lusts against the spirit and the spirit against the flesh; the two are directly opposed. This is why you do not do what your will intends. If you are guided by the spirit, you are not under the law.

GOSPEL   Lk 9, 51–62
As the time approached when Jesus was to be taken from this world, he firmly resolved to proceed toward Jerusalem, and sent messengers on ahead of him. These entered a Samaritan town to prepare for his passing through, but the Samaritans would not welcome him because he was on his way to Jerusalem. When his disciples James and John saw this, they said, "Lord, would you not have us call down fire from heaven to destroy them?" He turned toward them only to reprimand them. Then they set off for another town.

As they were making their way along, someone said to him, "I will be your follower wherever you go." Jesus said to him, "The foxes have lairs, the birds of the sky have nests, but the Son of Man has nowhere to lay his head." To another he said, "Come after me." The man replied, "Let me bury my father first." Jesus said to him, "Let the dead bury their dead; come away and proclaim the kingdom of God." Yet another said to him, "I will be your follower, Lord, but first let me take leave of my people at home." Jesus answered him, "Whoever puts his hand to the plow but keeps looking back is unfit for the reign of God."

Reflection on the Readings

Anyone who owned twelve oxen in ancient Israel was most likely a very wealthy man. To sacrifice those oxen and burn one's tools for cultivating the soil, one's life work and survival, would have been a radical act. This is precisely what we are told Elisha did in the first reading, as he responded to the call of the Lord given through Elijah, a prophet of God. His response emphasized his understanding of the radical commitment required of one who desires to follow the Lord. For Elisha to follow the Lord meant a total renunciation of all his possessions. He then leaves his land and follows Elijah, becoming a prophet of the Lord.

Jesus' journey to Jerusalem became a witness of his radical commitment to the kingdom of God, and nothing could deter him from being faithful to this commitment. If anyone desired to be Jesus' disciple, that same radical commitment was required from them. But what does that actually mean for the disciple of Jesus? Responding to three potential disciples, Jesus makes it clear that to follow him will require a new single-mindedness that will challenge their current life. No longer will they enjoy a roof over their heads, for they will need to be detached from all things that give security and protection. What they previously understood as their responsibilities under the law or enjoyed as familial relationships will no longer have the same priority as following Jesus.

But perhaps the most important element of being Jesus' disciple is to know that one must also walk the road with Jesus to Jerusalem, the place where all security, all former responsibilities and relationships were surrendered. Jerusalem is the place of the total renunciation and radical sacrifice for all times in the passion and death of Jesus Christ.

Suggestions for Prayer

1. Reflecting on your life in your family, workplace, parish, or neighborhood how do you hear yourself called by God to live a more commited Christian life? What keeps you from living it? After reflecting on this invite God to enter into your life, asking for what you need to help you in your commitment as a Christian.

2. As you reflect on your life today, what is one area or one problem that you would like to become detached from or that you would like to be free from? In silence turn this area of your life over to God.

3. In silent prayer image Jesus standing before you, inviting you to share with him your feelings, fears, concerns, etc. about being his disciple. Listen to Jesus respond to you.

Suggestion for Journal Keeping

In your journal write a dialogue with Jesus about your feelings, fears, concerns, desires, etc., about being his disciple, allowing Jesus to respond to you through your writing. How does Jesus affirm or challenge you? How does he invite you into a greater relationship with him? How does he speak of his love for you?

Kathleen Brown

Fourteenth Sunday of the Year **A**

READING I   Zec 9, 9–10

Rejoice heartily, O daughter Zion,
  shout for joy, O daughter Jerusalem!
See, your king shall come to you;
  a just savior is he,
Meek, and riding on an ass,
  on a colt, the foal of an ass.
He shall banish the chariot from Ephraim,
  and the horse from Jerusalem;
The warrior's bow shall be banished,
  and he shall proclaim peace to the
    nations.
His dominion shall be from sea to sea,
  and from the River to the ends of the
    earth.

Responsorial Psalm   Ps 145, 1–2. 8–9.
                              10–11. 13–14

I will praise your name for ever,
  my king and my God.

I will extol you, O my God and King,
  and I will bless your name forever and
    ever.
Every day will I bless you,
  and I will praise your name forever and
    ever.
I will praise your name for ever,
  my king and my God.

The Lord is gracious and merciful,
  slow to anger and of great kindness.
The Lord is good to all
  and compassionate toward all his works.
I will praise your name for ever,
  my king and my God.

Let all your works give you thanks, O Lord,
  and let your faithful ones bless you.

Let them discourse of the glory of your
    kingdom
  and speak of your might.
I will praise your name for ever.
  my king and my God.

The Lord is faithful in all his words
  and holy in all his works.
The Lord lifts up all who are falling
  and raises up all who are bowed down.
I will praise your name for ever,
  my king and my God.

READING II   Rom 8, 9. 11–13

You are not in the flesh; you are in the spirit,
since the Spirit of God dwells in you. If anyone does not have the Spirit of Christ, he
does not belong to Christ. If the Spirit of him
who raised Jesus from the dead dwells in
you, then he who raised Christ from the
dead will bring your mortal bodies to life
also through his Spirit dwelling in you.

We are debtors, then, my brothers—but
not to the flesh, so that we should live according to the flesh. If you live according to
the flesh, you will die; but if by the spirit you
put to death the evil deeds of the body, you
will live.

GOSPEL   Mt 11, 25–30

On one occasion Jesus spoke thus: "Father,
Lord of heaven and earth, to you I offer
praise; for what you have hidden from the
learned and the clever you have revealed to
the merest children. Father, it is true. You
have graciously willed it so. Everything has
been given over to me by my Father. No one
knows the Son but the Father, and no one
knows the Father but the Son—and anyone
to whom the Son wishes to reveal him.

"Come to me, all you who are weary and
find life burdensome, and I will refresh you.

Take my yoke upon your shoulders and learn from me, for I am gentle and humble of heart. Your souls will find rest, for my yoke is easy and my burden light."

Reflection on the Readings

Jesus liked children, and they seem to have liked him. The disciples tried to send them away, but Jesus rebuked them. In today's Gospel, Jesus lets us in on a secret. He says that the children understand what the "learned and clever" can't quite grasp.

"Come to me, all you who are weary and find life burdensome, and I will refresh you." A simple message, one that a child would believe. Our Savior will come "riding on an ass," and he will proclaim "peace to the nations." Only a child, or a Christian, would believe that.

Adult solutions to problems are much more complex. Adults go to health spas, they work out, they take stress management classes, they spend years in therapy, they get ulcers and high blood pressure. Children take naps, they play; when something hurts them they cry. Children have an easier time than adults do admitting that some things are out of their control, and that Jesus can refresh and renew them.

To recognize our Savior, to rejoice and shout for joy, we must be like children. We must give our cares and concerns to the Lord, take up his yoke and shout for joy!

Suggestions for Prayer

1. Where do you find refreshment? How do you relax in the middle of life's tensions? Do you have a sense of humor about yourself?

2. Imagine Jesus sitting on a rock and talking to a group of children. Where are the children sitting? What are they wearing? What are they saying to each other?

3. Watch some children playing, or watch Sesame Street or Mr. Roger's Neighborhood. What is a child's world like? Make a prayer to God, imagining that you are six years old.

Suggestion for Journal Keeping

Write down a good experience you had as a child that was important to you. Did you feel loved? Did this experience change you or affect your life? How does this experience affect your idea of God?

Michael P. Enright

Fourteenth Sunday of the Year B

READING I   Ez 2, 2–5

Spirit entered into me and set me on my feet, and I heard the one who was speaking say to me: Son of man, I am sending you to the Israelites, rebels who have rebelled against me; they and their fathers have revolted against me to this very day. Hard of face and obstinate of heart are they to whom I am sending you. But you shall say to them: Thus says the Lord God! And whether they heed or resist—for they are a rebellious house—they shall know that a prophet has been among them.

Responsorial Psalm   Ps 123, 1–2. 2. 3–4
Our eyes are fixed on the Lord,
     pleading for his mercy.

To you I lift up my eyes
  who are enthroned in heaven—
As the eyes of servants
  are on the hands of their masters.
Our eyes are fixed on the Lord,
  pleading for his mercy.
As the eyes of a maid
  are on the hands of her mistress,
So are our eyes on the Lord, our God,
  till he have pity on us.
Our eyes are fixed on the Lord,
  pleading for his mercy.
Have pity on us, O Lord, have pity on us,
  for we are more than sated with
    contempt;
Our souls are more than sated
  with the mockery of the arrogant,
  with the contempt of the proud.
Our eyes are fixed on the Lord,
  pleading for his mercy.

READING II   2 Cor 12, 7–10
**As to the extraordinary revelations, in order
that I might not become conceited I was
given a thorn in the flesh, an angel of Satan
to beat me and keep me from getting proud.
Three times I begged the Lord that this might
leave me. He said to me, "My grace is
enough for you, for in weakness power
reaches perfection." And so I willingly boast
of my weaknesses instead, that the power of
Christ may rest upon me.**

**Therefore I am content with weakness,
with mistreatment, with distress, with persecutions and difficulties for the sake of
Christ; for when I am powerless, it is then
that I am strong.**

GOSPEL   Mk 6, 1–6
**Jesus went to his own part of the country fol-
lowed by his disciples. When the sabbath**
came he began to teach in the synagogue in
a way that kept his large audience amazed.
They said: "Where did he get all this? What
kind of wisdom is he endowed with? How is
it such miraculous deeds are accomplished
by his hands? Isn't this the carpenter, the son
of Mary, a brother of James and Joses and Judas and Simon? Aren't his sisters our neighbors here?" They found him too much for
them. Jesus' response to all this was: "No
prophet is without honor except in his native
place, among his own kindred, and in his
own house." He could work no miracle
there, apart from curing a few who were
sick by laying hands on them, so much did
their lack of faith distress him. He made the
rounds of the neighboring villages instead,
and spent his time teaching.**

Reflection on the Readings
One of the most painful experiences we
can have is rejection. Others reject us or we
reject them for a variety of reasons. Rejection
can flow from jealousy or envy. Rejection
can result when someone feels his security is
threatened. Rejection can happen when
someone acts contrary to our expectations.
Often those who challenge us to live more
virtuous lives are rejected. Sometimes people
who are extraordinarily good or unusually
bad are rejected.

The Gospel story today is a story of rejection. When Jesus began his public ministry,
he worked many miracles and gave many
profound teachings. When Jesus cured the
man with the withered hand on the sabbath,
the Pharisees and the scribes rejected him.
When Jesus gave a profound teaching in the
synagogue in Nazareth, his relatives and
townspeople rejected him because they believed he was only a carpenter. Some even

said Jesus was out of his mind. Their minds were so closed that it prompted Jesus to say, "A prophet is only despised in his own country, among his own relatives, and in his own house." Because of their closed minds and their rejection of Jesus, they never did find out who he really was, the living Son of God. They rejected the best that God gave them.

There are many people today who, like the people in the days of the historical Jesus, continue to reject Jesus. Rejection is caused by sin and fear, ignorance and insecurity. People with closed minds are easily prone to reject Jesus when he comes to them in new ways.

Suggestions for Prayer

1. Reflect on one or more of the following questions:
   - Have you experienced rejection because of misunderstanding?
   - How do you feel when you have taken a strong faith stance on something you truly believe in and you are rejected and looked down upon?
   - Can you forgive the people who reject you?
2. In your imagination, you are at a meeting. You have just made a motion in favor of some noble cause. The majority vote you down. Jesus is standing beside you. He says, "A prophet is only despised in his own country, among his own relations, and in his own house."
3. Pray the responsorial psalm as your evening prayer this week.

Suggestion for Journal Keeping

Write in your journal an experience in your life where you went out of your way to be gracious to someone for a long time. Then one day this person rejected you. How do you now feel toward this person? How do you feel toward Jesus?

Michael J. Koch

Fourteenth Sunday of the Year

READING I   Is 66, 10–14

Rejoice with Jerusalem and be glad because of her,
  all you who love her;
Exult, exult with her,
  all you who were mourning over her!
Oh, that you may suck fully
  of the milk of her comfort,
That you may nurse with delight
  at her abundant breasts!
For thus says the Lord:
Lo, I will spread prosperity over her like a river,
  and the wealth of the nations like an overflowing torrent.
As nurslings, you shall be carried in her arms,
  and fondled in her lap;
As a mother comforts her son,
  so will I comfort you;
  in Jerusalem you shall find your comfort.
When you see this, your heart shall rejoice,
  and your bodies flourish like the grass;
The Lord's power shall be known to his servants.

Responsorial Psalm   Ps 66, 1–3. 4–5. 6–7. 16. 20

Let all the earth cry out to God with joy.
Shout joyfully to God, all you on earth,
  sing praise to the glory of his name;
  proclaim his glorious praise.

Say to God, "How tremendous are your deeds!"
Let all the earth cry out to God with joy.
"Let all on earth worship and sing praise to you,
sing praise to your name!"
Come and see the works of God,
his tremendous deeds among men.
Let all the earth cry out to God with joy.
He has changed the sea into dry land;
through the river they passed on foot;
therefore let us rejoice in him.
He rules by his might forever.
Let all the earth cry out to God with joy.
Hear now, all you who fear God, while I declare
what he has done for me.
Blessed be God who refused me not
my prayer or his kindness!
Let all the earth cry out to God with joy.

READING II   Gal 6, 14–18
May I never boast of anything but the cross of our Lord Jesus Christ! Through it, the world has been crucified to me and I to the world. It means nothing whether one is circumcised or not. All that matters is that one is created anew. Peace and mercy on all who follow this rule of life, and on the Israel of God.

Henceforth, let no man trouble me, for I bear the brand marks of Jesus in my body.

Brothers, may the favor of our Lord Jesus Christ be with your spirit. Amen.

GOSPEL   Lk 10, 1–12. 17–20
The Lord appointed a further seventy-two and sent them in pairs before him to every town and place he intended to visit. He said to them: "The harvest is rich but the workers are few; therefore ask the harvest-master to send workers to his harvest. Be on your way, and remember: I am sending you as lambs in the midst of wolves. Do not carry a walking staff or traveling bag; wear no sandals and greet no one along the way. On entering any house, first say, 'Peace to this house.' If there is a peaceable man there, your peace will rest on him; if not, it will come back to you. Stay in the one house eating and drinking what they have, for the laborer is worth his wage. Do not move from house to house.

"Into whatever city you go, after they welcome you, eat what they set before you, and cure the sick there. Say to them, 'The reign of God is at hand.' If the people of any town you enter do not welcome you, go into its streets and say, 'We shake the dust of this town from our feet as testimony against you. But know that the reign of God is near.' I assure you, on that day the fate of Sodom will be less severe than that of such a town."

The seventy-two returned in jubilation saying, "Master, even the demons are subject to us in your name." He said in reply: "I watched Satan fall from the sky like lightning. See what I have done; I have given you power to tread on snakes and scorpions and all the forces of the enemy, and nothing shall ever injure you. Nevertheless, do not rejoice so much in the fact that the devils are subject to you as that your names are inscribed in heaven."

Reflection on the Readings
In a poetic and exultant way the prophet Isaiah calls upon the people of Israel to rejoice and be glad, for they will come to know the joy and the fulfillment of the promises of God. Prosperity, peace and comfort are the promises they shall see and come to know. They can hope in the power of God to trans-

form their mourning into joy, for God is the source of new life. In hope they await the reign of God.

In Jesus the reign of God was brought nearer to the people. Through his ministry of teaching, healing and exorcism Jesus revealed God's power breaking into their world. Jesus also called others to the same ministry, enabling them to be heralds of the coming of the reign of God. Calling first the twelve disciples, Jesus then called seventy-two more to be his disciples. They too went forth, preparing the way for Jesus, like lambs among wolves, announcing the reign of God by their lives, through performing miracles, expelling demons and healing the people in Jesus' name.

Upon return the disciples reported that in the name of Jesus evil has no power in this world. Through Jesus' empowerment the disciples experienced first-hand the breaking into their world of God's reign.

Through Paul's example of his life, he reminds the Galatians that what is really important is understanding the relevance of the cross of Jesus Christ for one's life. All else in the world becomes less important in light of the cross.

Suggestions for Prayer

1. As with the disciples mentioned in the Gospel, we too are called and empowered to be disciples of Jesus. In your life how do you hear yourself called and empowered to be a disciple of Jesus? In what area of your life in particular do you see yourself especially sent as a disciple of Jesus?
2. Reflect on your life, family, workplace, city, world. As you do list all the places and events where you have experienced personally or have seen the power of God active. Throughout the week become more aware of those places in your life and in the world where God's power is active.
3. The invitation to become a new creation is always given to us through God. Where in yourself do you see the need for new life? Envision what the new life would look like for you. In your imagination come before Jesus and hear him inviting you to this new life.

Suggestion for Journal Keeping

After quieting your mind and relaxing your body, journal your responses to one of the above questions. As you write, enter into dialogue with Jesus about your need for his power of healing, hope and love to come into your life.

Kathleen Brown

Fifteenth Sunday of the Year Ⓐ

READING I   Is 55, 10–11
Just as from the heavens
  the rain and snow come down
And do not return there
  till they have watered the earth,
  making it fertile and fruitful,
Giving seed to him who sows
  and bread to him who eats,
So shall my word be
  that goes forth from my mouth;
It shall not return to me void,
  but shall do my will,
  achieving the end for which I sent it.

Responsorial Psalm   Ps 65, 10. 11. 12–13. 14

The seed that falls on good ground
  will yield a fruitful harvest.

You have visited the land and watered it;
  greatly have you enriched it.
God's watercourses are filled;
  you have prepared the grain.

The seed that falls on good ground
  will yield a fruitful harvest.

Thus have you prepared the land: drench-
  ing its furrows,
  breaking up its clods,
Softening it with showers,
  blessing its yield.

The seed that falls on good ground
  will yield a fruitful harvest.

You have crowned the year with your
  bounty,
  and your paths overflow with a rich
  harvest;
The untilled meadows overflow with it,
  and rejoicing clothes the hills.

The seed that falls on good ground
  will yield a fruitful harvest.

The fields are garmented with flocks
  and the valleys blanketed with grain.
  They shout and sing for joy.

The seed that falls on good ground
  will yield a fruitful harvest.

READING II   Rom 8, 18–23

I consider the sufferings of the present to be
as nothing compared with the glory to be revealed in us. Indeed, the whole created
world eagerly awaits the revelation of the
sons of God. Creation was made subject to
futility, not of its own accord but by him
who once subjected it; yet not without hope,
because the world itself will be freed from
its slavery to corruption and share in the glorious freedom of the children of God. Yes,
we know that all creation groans and is in agony even until now. Not only that, but we
ourselves, although we have the Spirit as
first fruits, groan inwardly while we await
the redemption of our bodies.

GOSPEL   Mt 13, 1–23

Jesus, on leaving the house on a certain day,
sat down by the lakeshore. Such great
crowds gathered around him that he went
and took his seat in a boat while the crowd
stood along the shore. He addressed them at
length in parables, speaking in this fashion:

"One day a farmer went out sowing. Part
of what he sowed landed on a footpath,
where birds came and ate it up. Part of it fell
on rocky ground, where it had little soil. It
sprouted at once since the soil had no depth,
but when the sun rose and scorched it, it began to wither for lack of roots. Again, part
of the seed fell among thorns, which grew
up and choked it. Part of it, finally, landed
on good soil and yielded grain at a hundred-
or sixty- or thirty-fold. Let everyone heed
what he hears!"

When the disciples got near him, they
asked him, "Why do you speak to them in
parables?" He answered: "To you has been
given a knowledge of the mysteries of the
reign of God, but it has not been given to the
others. To the man who has, more will be
given until he grows rich; the man who has
not, will lose what little he has.

"I use parables when I speak to them because they look but do not see, they listen
but do not hear or understand. Isaiah's
prophecy is fulfilled in them which says:
  'Listen as you will, you shall not under-
    stand,
  look intently as you will, you shall not
    see.

288

Sluggish indeed is this people's heart.
They have scarcely heard with their
ears,
they have firmly closed their eyes;
otherwise they might see with their
eyes,
and hear with their ears,
and understand with their hearts,
and turn back to me,
and I should heal them.'

"But blest are your eyes because they see
and blest are your ears because they hear. I
assure you, many a prophet and many a saint
longed to see what you see but did not see
it, to hear what you hear but did not hear it.

"Mark well, then, the parable of the
sower. The seed along the path is the man
who hears the message about God's reign
without understanding it. The evil one approaches him to steal away what was sown
in his mind. The seed that fell on patches of
rock is the man who hears the message and
at first receives it with joy. But he has no
roots, so he lasts only for a time. When some
setback or persecution involving the message occurs, he soon falters. What was sown
among briers is the man who hears the message, but then worldly anxiety and the lure
of money choke it off. Such a one produces
no yield. But what was sown on good soil is
the man who hears the message and takes it
in. He it is who bears a yield of a hundred-
or sixty- or thirty-fold."

Reflection on the Readings

Seeds. Plants. Growing things. Jesus was
familiar with these things. Many of the images he used to talk about God and the kingdom were taken from the world of plants. He
spoke of the grain of wheat dying and becoming more than just a grain of wheat. He spoke
of mustard seeds growing to become the largest bushes. He spoke of the vine and the
branches, and today he speaks of the sower.

In Jesus' day, farmers weren't as neat as
they are today. They spread seed far and
wide to ensure a good harvest. They spread
extra seed. They even wasted some! Jesus'
image of the sower is like Isaiah's image of
rain. God's word falls like rain—everywhere.
It will bear fruit in many different ways. It is
plentiful. There is even extra rain!

The harvest from God's word will be plentiful. We are showered with love, and this
love is powerful. We will become like the
valleys and hills. We will rejoice and shout
for joy. We will bear fruit one hundred- and
sixty- and thirty-fold. All we need do is hear
the message of Jesus and take it in.

Suggestion for Prayer

1. Read a newspaper or a magazine, or
   watch the TV news until you find something about hungry people. Pray for
   them and for the farmers who feed them.
   Ask the Lord to send them a rich harvest.
   Ask yourself this question: What do I do
   for the hungry?

2. Look at a plant. Contemplate it. Look at
   its leaves. Study its structure. Marvel
   over its complexity. Wonder how it
   grows. Spend some time (20 minutes)
   doing this, then look at your hand. Move
   your fingers. Thank God for his marvelous craftsmanship.

3. Reread the Gospel. Ask yourself what
   kind of "soil" you are. What is it in you
   that limits God's word bearing fruit in
   your life? Ask God to give you a hand in
   dealing with this.

Suggestion for Journal Keeping

Remember an experience in your life when you loved someone a lot and your love was not accepted. What happened? How did you feel? How does God feel when we turn away from his love?

Michael P. Enright

Fifteenth Sunday of the Year B

READING I Am 7, 12–15

Amaziah (priest of Bethel) said to Amos, "Off with you, visionary, flee to the land of Judah! There earn your bread by prophesying, but never again prophesy in Bethel; for it is the king's sanctuary and a royal temple." Amos answered Amaziah, "I was no prophet, nor have I belonged to a company of prophets; I was a shepherd and a dresser of sycamores. The Lord took me from following the flock, and said to me, Go, prophesy to my people Israel."

Responsorial Psalm Ps 85, 9–10. 11–12. 13–14

Lord, let us see your kindness,
and grant us your salvation.
I will hear what God proclaims;
the Lord—for he proclaims peace to his
people.
Near indeed is his salvation to those who
fear him,
glory dwelling in our land.
Lord, let us see your kindness,
and grant us your salvation.
Kindness and truth shall meet;
justice and peace shall kiss.

Truth shall spring out of the earth,
and justice shall look down from heaven.
Lord, let us see your kindness,
and grant us your salvation.
The Lord himself will give his benefits;
our land shall yield its increase.
Justice shall walk before him,
and salvation, along the way of his steps.
Lord, let us see your kindness,
and grant us your salvation.

READING II Eph 1, 3–14

Praised be the God and Father of our Lord Jesus Christ, who has bestowed on us in Christ every spiritual blessing in the heavens! God chose us in him before the world began, to be holy and blameless in his sight, to be full of love; he likewise predestined us through Christ Jesus to be his adopted sons—such was his will and pleasure—that all might praise the divine favor he has bestowed on us in his beloved.

It is in Christ and through his blood that we have been redeemed and our sins forgiven, so immeasurably generous is God's favor to us. God has given us the wisdom to understand fully the mystery, the plan he was pleased to decree in Christ, to be carried out in the fullness of time: namely, to bring all things in the heavens and on earth into one under Christ's headship.

In him we were chosen; for in the decree of God, who administers everything according to his will and counsel, we were predestined to praise his glory by being the first to hope in Christ. In him you too were chosen; when you heard the glad tidings of salvation, the word of truth, and believed in it, you were sealed with the Holy Spirit who had been promised. He is the pledge of our inheritance, the first payment against the full

redemption of a people God has made his own to praise his glory.

GOSPEL
Mk 6, 7-13

Jesus summoned the Twelve and began to send them out two by two, giving them authority over unclean spirits. He instructed them to take nothing on the journey but a walking stick—no food, no traveling bag, not a coin in the purses in their belts. They were, however, to wear sandals. "Do not bring a second tunic," he said, and added: "Whatever house you find yourself in, stay there until you leave the locality. If any place will not receive you or hear you, shake its dust from your feet in testimony against them as you leave." With that they went off, preaching the need of repentance. They expelled many demons, anointed the sick with oil, and worked many cures.

Reflection on the Readings

Most of us have been sent on an errand. A mother sends her son to the store to buy some groceries. A teacher sends a child home with a message. A page in the government delivers a document for an official. Persons doing errands are sent by someone; they do not go in their own name. The one sent carries a message or does a definite thing. It is not the message of the carrier, but the message of the sender that must be delivered. The carrier need not know the details of the message or its consequences. The carrier must have the commitment necessary to get the message delivered, even if it costs.

In the Gospel today, Jesus sends out his twelve on mission. They are to bring the good news of Jesus to others. Jesus instructs them what to say and do, and he gives them the necessary authority to speak in his name. He instructs them to travel light. All they need is the message. Their creaturely needs will be cared for by the hospitality of those who receive the message. He sends them in pairs for mutual support and to "sacramentalize" the love which they are preaching. They are not to waste their time on those with closed minds and hearts.

Today, Christians by their baptism are mandated to be messengers of the good news. The same criteria apply. We are authorized by Jesus; we are to travel in pairs; we are to travel light. We can expect hospitality from those who accept Christ's message. This is the mission to which you are called and for which you are preparing.

Suggestions for Prayer

1. Reflect on one or more of the following questions?
   - Why did Jesus send out the twelve in pairs?
   - Why is it necessary for the messenger to deliver the message even if he or she doesn't know the content or consequences of the message?
   - Why is it necessary for the apostle or messenger to travel light?
2. In your imagination, Jesus is sending you out to be one of his apostles. With which apostle are you paired? To whom do you go? What is the response to Jesus' message that you bring? What does Jesus say to you when you return?
3. Pray the responsorial psalm as your evening prayer this week.

Suggestion for Journal Keeping

Describe in your journal an event in your life where you were sent on an errand. Did you encounter any opposition? Were you faithful to your commitment even in the face of suffering? How do you feel toward the apostles and Jesus who sent you?

Michael J. Koch

Fifteenth Sunday of the Year C

READING I   Dt 30, 10–14

Moses said to the people: "If only you heed the voice of the Lord, your God, and keep his commandments and statutes that are written in this book of the law, when you return to the Lord, your God, with all your heart and all your soul.

"For this command which I enjoin on you today is not too mysterious and remote for you. It is not up in the sky, that you should say, 'Who will go up in the sky to get it for us and tell us of it, that we may carry it out?' Nor is it across the sea, that you should say, 'Who will cross the sea to get it for us and tell us of it, that we may carry it out?' No, it is something very near to you, already in your mouths and in your hearts; you have only to carry it out."

Responsorial Psalm   Ps 69, 14. 17. 30–31.
33–34. 36. 37

Turn to the Lord in your need, and you will live.
I pray to you, O Lord,
    for the time of your favor, O God!
In your great kindness answer me
    with your constant help.
Answer me, O Lord, for bounteous is your kindness:
    in your great mercy turn toward me.

Turn to the Lord in your need, and you will live.
I am afflicted and in pain;
    let your saving help, O God, protect me.
I will praise the name of God in song,
    and I will glorify him with thanksgiving.
Turn to the Lord in your need, and you will live.
"See, you lowly ones, and be glad;
    you who seek God, may your hearts be merry!
For the Lord hears the poor,
    and his own who are in bonds he spurns not."
Turn to the Lord in your need, and you will live.
For God will save Zion
    and rebuild the cities of Judah.
The descendants of his servants shall inherit it,
    and those who love his name shall inhabit it.
Turn to the Lord in your need, and you will live.

READING II   Col 1, 15–20

Christ Jesus is the image of the invisible God, the first-born of all creatures. In him everything in heaven and on earth was created, things visible and invisible, whether thrones or dominations, principalities or powers; all were created through him, and for him. He is before all else that is. In him everything continues in being. It is he who is head of the body, the church; he who is the beginning, the first-born of the dead, so that primacy may be his in everything. It pleased God to make absolute fullness reside in him and, by means of him, to reconcile everything in his person, everything, I say, both on earth and in the heavens, making peace through the blood of his cross.

GOSPEL   Lk 10, 25–37

On one occasion a lawyer stood up to pose this problem to Jesus: "Teacher, what must I do to inherit everlasting life?" Jesus answered him: "What is written in the law? How do you read it?" He replied:

"You shall love the Lord your God
with all your heart,
with all your soul,
with all your strength,
and with all your mind;
and your neighbor as yourself."

Jesus said, "You have answered correctly. Do this and you shall live." But because he wished to justify himself he said to Jesus, "And who is my neighbor?" Jesus replied: "There was a man going down from Jerusalem to Jericho who fell in with robbers. They stripped him, beat him, and then went off leaving him half-dead. A priest happened to be going down the same road; he saw him but continued on. Likewise there was a Levite who came the same way; he saw him and went on. But a Samaritan who was journeying along came on him and was moved to pity at the sight. He approached him and dressed his wounds, pouring in oil and wine as a means to heal. He then hoisted him on his own beast and brought him to an inn, where he cared for him. The next day he took out two silver pieces and gave them to the innkeeper with the request: 'Look after him, and if there is any further expense I will repay you on my way back.'

"Which of these three, in your opinion, was neighbor to the man who fell in with the robbers?" The answer came, "The one who treated him with compassion." Jesus said to him, "Then go and do the same."

Reflection on the Readings

The lawyer addressing Jesus knew with certainty the letter of the law, but did he understand the spirit of the law? The spirit of the law calls for a person's total engagement, heart, soul, strength and mind, in responding to the commandment to love God, neighbor and self. To illustrate this and to answer the lawyer's inquiry as to who was his neighbor, Jesus told the parable of the good Samaritan. It was a Samaritan, one looked down upon by Jews as unclean, who chose to help the beaten man. Without a doubt the Samaritan showed the greatest awareness of what it means to live the commandment of love. At the end of the parable Jesus charged the lawyer to go and do the same.

The knowledge and ability to live out God's command to love was not foreign to the Israelites. As reflected in the first reading, Moses called on the Israelites to adhere to the commandments with all their heart and soul. This knowledge of God's command is already in our mouths and hearts, and all we need to do is to live it out in our lives.

As expressed in Paul's Letter to the Colossians, the perfection of this love is realized in and through Jesus Christ. It is in Christ Jesus that the fullness of what it means to live a selfless love is best exemplified. Through this selfless love, God reconciled everything on earth and in the heavens bringing peace to all.

Suggestions for Prayer

1. Reflect on one or all of the following questions: Where do you see the

"beaten ones" in your neighborhood, city or world? Who are the Samaritans that are enabling these defenseless ones to live a fuller life?

2. Whom do you identify with in the story: the beaten one, the Levite, the priest, the Samaritan or the lawyer? How do you hear the Lord speaking to you through this reading?

3. Let those people come to your mind who have enabled you or helped you to live your life more fully. Remembering them, thank God for what they have done for you in your life.

Suggestion for Journal Keeping

Recall someone who loves you very much and write that person a letter in your journal, speaking of the meaning and significance of that love for your life, how it enabled you in your journey, how it helped you to get back on the road of life, how it renewed your life, etc. After the letter is written, address Jesus through your writing, giving thanks for this person who has loved you.

Kathleen Brown

Sixteenth Sunday of the Year   Ⓐ

READING I   Wis 12, 13. 16–19

There is no god besides you who have the care of all,
that you need show you have not unjustly condemned.
For your might is the source of justice;

your mastery over all things makes you lenient to all.
For you show your might when the perfection of your power is disbelieved;
and in those who know you, you rebuke temerity.
But though you are master of might, you judge with clemency,
and with much lenience you govern us;
for power, whenever you will, attends you.
And you taught your people, by these deeds, that those who are just must be kind;
And you gave your sons good ground for hope
that you would permit repentance for their sins.

Responsorial Psalm   Ps 86, 5–6. 9–10. 15–16

Lord, you are good and forgiving.
You, O Lord, are good and forgiving,
abounding in kindness to all who call upon you.
Hearken, O Lord, to my prayer
and attend to the sound of my pleading.
Lord, you are good and forgiving.
All the nations you have made shall come and worship you, O Lord,
and glorify your name.
For you are great, and you do wondrous deeds;
you alone are God.
Lord, you are good and forgiving.
You, O Lord, are a God merciful and gracious,
slow to anger, abounding in kindness and fidelity.
Turn toward me, and have pity on me;
give your strength to your servant.
Lord, you are good and forgiving.

READING II   Rom 8, 26–27

The Spirit too helps us in our weakness, for we do not know how to pray as we ought; but the Spirit himself makes intercession for us with groanings which cannot be expressed in speech. He who searches hearts knows what the Spirit means, for the Spirit intercedes for the saints as God himself wills.

GOSPEL   Mt 13, 24–43

Jesus proposed to the crowd another parable: "The reign of God may be likened to a man who sowed good seed in his field. While everyone was asleep, his enemy came and sowed weeds through his wheat, and then made off. When the crop began to mature and yield grain, the weeds made their appearance as well. The owner's slaves came to him and said, 'Sir, did you not sow good seed in your field? Where are the weeds coming from?' He answered, 'I see an enemy's hand in this.' His slaves said to him, 'Do you want us to go out and pull them up?' 'No,' he replied, 'pull up the weeds and you might take the wheat along with them. Let them grow together until harvest; then at harvest time I will order the harvesters. First collect the weeds and bundle them up to burn, then gather the wheat into my barn.' "

He proposed still another parable: "The reign of God is like a mustard seed which someone took and sowed in his field. It is the smallest seed of all, yet when full-grown it is the largest of plants. It becomes so big a shrub that the birds of the sky come and build their nests in its branches."

He offered them still another image: "The reign of God is like yeast which a woman took and kneaded into three measures of flour. Eventually the whole mass of dough began to rise." All these lessons Jesus taught the crowds in the form of parables. He spoke to them in parables only, to fulfill what had been said through the prophet:

"I will open my mouth in parables,
I will announce what has lain hidden since the creation of the world."

Then, dismissing the crowds, he went home. His disciples came to him with the request, "Explain to us the parable of the weeds in the field." He said in answer: "The farmer sowing good seed is the Son of Man; the field is the world, the good seed the citizens of the kingdom. The weeds are the followers of the evil one and the enemy who sowed them is the devil. The harvest is the end of the world, while the harvesters are the angels. Just as weeds are collected and burned, so it will be at the end of the world. The Son of Man will dispatch his angels to collect from his kingdom all who draw others to apostasy, and all evildoers. The angels will hurl them into the fiery furnace where they will wail and grind their teeth. Then the saints will shine like the sun in their Father's kingdom. Let everyone heed what he hears!"

Reflection on the Readings

The kingdom of God is coming. The kingdom of God is here already. These two statements seem to contradict one another, yet both are true. We know that sometime in the future God's reign will reach its fulfillment, but what about right now? How can it be that we are in the kingdom? We read the papers and see the news on TV and experience in our own lives the effects of evil. Where is the kingdom? If it is already here, why do bad things happen?

In the first parable of today's Gospel, Jesus

tells us about the presence of evil. He says that we must be patient and not scandalized about what we see. The weeds, he assures us, will eventually be separated from the wheat.

The second and third parables in today's Gospel reflect another reality of the kingdom. It starts out very small! Mustard seeds and yeast are almost invisible. They grow like mad and make a big difference in their environment. They change things! The kingdom is happening now! The first reading reminds us not to worry. God is "lenient to all," and God, who is just, must be kind.

Even though we know all this, sometimes we are still at a loss for words in prayer. We want to ask God why things happen the way they do. We become angry with our own sinfulness and weakness and with what happens around us. At the same time, we want to show our love for God and let God love us back. We come to prayer distracted, or tired, or joyful or empty. We want to enter into communion with God, but can't.

St. Paul knew about this. In writing to the Romans, he tells them to pray as best they can and let the Spirit speak for them. There are times when the best you can do is sit still and let your heart do the talking. That's O.K., St. Paul tells us, because in our weakness God can speak directly to our hearts.

Suggestions for Prayer

1. Have you ever been angry with God for something that happened? What was it? Have you ever "told God off"? Did you feel that this was acceptable or not?
2. Imagine/remember the worst thing that has ever happened to you. Was God present in the situation? How?

3. Pray with your heart. Become still and try to let God touch you on the inside. Don't talk to God, just listen!

Suggestion for Journal Keeping
Write about your prayer life. How do you pray? When? Where? Does your prayer make a difference to you? To God?

Michael P. Enright

Sixteenth Sunday of the Year B

READING I   Jer 23, 1–6
Woe to the shepherds who mislead and scatter the flock of my pasture, says the Lord. Therefore, thus says the Lord, the God of Israel, against the shepherds who shepherd my people: You have scattered my sheep and driven them away. You have not cared for them, but I will take care to punish your evil deeds. I myself will gather the remnant of my flock from all the lands to which I have driven them and bring them back to their meadow; there they shall increase and multiply. I will appoint shepherds for them who will shepherd them so that they need no longer fear and tremble; and none shall be missing, says the Lord.
Behold, the days are coming, says the Lord,
when I will raise up a righteous shoot to David;
As king he shall reign and govern wisely,
he shall do what is just and right in the land.
In his days Judah shall be saved,
Israel shall dwell in security.

This is the name they give him:
"The Lord our justice."

Responsorial Psalm   Ps 23, 1–3. 3–4. 5. 6
The Lord is my shepherd;
   there is nothing I shall want.
The Lord is my shepherd; I shall not want.
   In verdant pastures he gives me repose;
Beside restful waters he leads me;
   he refreshes my soul.
The Lord is my shepherd;
   there is nothing I shall want.
He guides me in right paths
   for his name's sake.
Even though I walk in the dark valley
   I fear no evil; for you are at my side
With your rod and your staff
   that give me courage.
The Lord is my shepherd;
   there is nothing I shall want.
You spread the table before me
   in the sight of my foes;
You anoint my head with oil;
   my cup overflows.
The Lord is my shepherd;
   there is nothing I shall want.
Only goodness and kindness follow me
   all the days of my life;
And I shall dwell in the house of the Lord
   for years to come.
The Lord is my shepherd;
   there is nothing I shall want.

READING II   Eph 2, 13–18
In Christ Jesus you who once were far off
have been brought near through the blood of
Christ. It is he who is our peace, and who
made the two of us one by breaking down
the barrier of hostility that kept us apart. In
his own flesh he abolished the law with its
commands and precepts, to create in him-
self one new man from us who had been
two, and to make peace, reconciling both of
us to God in one body through his cross
which put that enmity to death. He came
and "announced the good news of peace to
you who were far off, and to those who were
near"; through him we both have access in
one Spirit to the Father.

GOSPEL   Mk 6, 30–34
The apostles returned to Jesus and reported
to him all that they had done and what they
had taught. He said to them, "Come by
yourselves to an out-of-the-way place and
rest a little." People were coming and going
in great numbers, making it impossible for
them to so much as eat. So Jesus and the
apostles went off in the boat by themselves
to a deserted place. People saw them leav-
ing, and many got to know about it. People
from all the towns hastened on foot to the
place, arriving ahead of them.

   Upon disembarking Jesus saw a vast
crowd. He pitied them, for they were like
sheep without a shepherd; and he began to
teach them at great length.

Reflection on the Readings
   You have had a very long and gruelling
day. You are very tired. Nothing appeals to
you more than sitting in an easy chair with
your feet up and listening to a piece of relaxing music. The telephone rings. You answer.
Your neighbor wants you to come over and
help move a scaffold behind his house. What
are you going to say? What are you going to
do?
   In the Gospel today, Jesus and the apostles
find themselves in a similar situation. The
apostles had been out preaching the good
news. Their services were in such great de-

297

mand that they didn't even have time to eat. They returned to Jesus dead-tired. Jesus invited them to come with him to a lonely place so that they could rest a while. They took a boat to a secret place. But the people, like sheep without a shepherd, reached the secret place before Jesus and the apostles. When Jesus stepped ashore, he saw a large crowd waiting for him. Jesus, filled with compassion, took pity on them. In his tiredness, he surrendered his own comfort and set about teaching them at length.

Through baptism, Christians today are engaged in the same ministry as the apostles. Being a witness for Jesus and Gospel values can be very exhausting. The Gospel minister needs time to rest. But even while we rest, someone needs help. How will we respond?

Suggestions for Prayer

1. Reflect on one or more of the following questions:
   - What concern does Jesus show toward the apostles after they have worked hard?
   - What is the place of prayer for the apostles when they are on mission?
   - How does Jesus deal with his own need for rest and the needs of the people who were like sheep without a shepherd?
2. In your imagination, you are sitting in your back yard relaxing after a long day's work. Jesus is standing beside you. He says, "You must come away to some lonely place all by yourselves and rest for a while."
3. Pray the responsorial psalm as your evening prayer this week.

Suggestion for Journal Keeping

Record in your journal an experience in your life where you had worked hard and you needed rest badly. You found yourself in a position of rest. The telephone rang. You answered. A friend was in need. What did you do? How would Jesus have handled this situation?

Michael J. Koch

Sixteenth Sunday of the Year C

READING I Gn 18, 1–10

The Lord appeared to Abraham by the terebinth of Mamre, as he sat in the entrance of his tent, while the day was growing hot. Looking up, he saw three men standing nearby. When he saw them, he ran from the entrance of the tent to greet them; and bowing to the ground, he said: "Sir, if I may ask you this favor, please do not go on past your servant. Let some water be brought, that you may bathe your feet, and then rest yourselves under the tree. Now that you have come this close to your servant, let me bring you a little food, that you may refresh yourselves; and afterward you may go on your way." "Very well," they replied, "do as you have said."

Abraham hastened into the tent and told Sarah, "Quick, three seahs of fine flour! Knead it and make rolls." He ran to the herd, picked out a tender, choice steer, and gave it to a servant, who quickly prepared it. Then he got some curds and milk, as well as the steer that had been prepared, and set

these before them; and he waited on them under the tree while they ate.

"Where is your wife Sarah?" they asked him. "There in the tent," he replied. One of them said, "I will surely return to you about this time next year, and Sarah will then have a son."

Responsorial Psalm   Ps 15, 2–3. 3–4. 5
He who does justice will live in the presence
   of the Lord.
He who walks blamelessly and does justice;
   who thinks the truth in his heart
   and slanders not with his tongue.
He who does justice will live in the presence
   of the Lord.
Who harms not his fellow man,
   nor takes up a reproach against his neigh
   bor;
By whom the reprobate is despised,
   while he honors those who fear the Lord.
He who does justice will live in the presence
   of the Lord.
Who lends not his money at usury
   and accepts no bribe against the innocent.
He who does these things
   shall never be disturbed.
He who does justice will live in the presence
   of the Lord.

READING II   Col 1, 24–28
Even now I find my joy in the suffering I endure for you. In my own flesh I fill up what is lacking in the sufferings of Christ for the sake of his body, the church. I became a minister of this church through the commission God gave me to preach among you his word in its fullness, that mystery hidden from ages and generations past but now revealed to his holy ones. God has willed to
make known to them the glory beyond price which this mystery brings to the Gentiles—the mystery of Christ in you, your hope of glory. This is the Christ we proclaim while we admonish all men and teach them in the full measure of wisdom, hoping to make every man complete in Christ.

GOSPEL   Lk 10, 38–42
Jesus entered a village where a woman named Martha welcomed him to her home. She had a sister named Mary, who seated herself at the Lord's feet and listened to his words. Martha, who was busy with all the details of hospitality, came to him and said, "Lord, are you not concerned that my sister has left me all alone to do the household tasks? Tell her to help me."

The Lord in reply said to her: "Martha, Martha, you are anxious and upset about many things; one thing only is required. Mary has chosen the better portion and she shall not be deprived of it."

Reflection on the Readings
   To extend hospitality to friends is a pleasurable task. Extending hospitality to people whom we do not know, because they are strangers, can be awkward, especially if they arrive unannounced as in the first reading. How many of us would go to as much trouble as Abraham and Sarah to welcome mere strangers? In the Gospel, Martha is concerned about hospitality as well, but not without complaining about Mary's lack of assistance. Both the first reading and the Gospel emphasize the importance of hospitality, but both point to a more important issue.

   At the closing of the first reading, the strangers, speaking to Sarah, predict the birth of a child (Isaac) within a year, fulfilling the promise of God to Abraham that he will have a descendant. Through the strangers God was present to Abraham and Sarah, bringing good news of the fulfillment of the promise. Their openness and presence to the strangers revealed God's presence in their lives.

In the Gospel, Martha, complaining about Mary's not helping with the hospitality, asks Jesus to do something about it. Jesus does not address what Martha believes to be the problem but instead goes to the heart of the issue. While Martha was anxious and worried, Jesus points out to Martha that Mary has chosen the better way. To welcome, to be present, to keep one's life focused on the Lord, is to come to know the presence of God in all of life. For those who remain in the presence of the Lord there is the promise of new life, as with Abraham and Sarah.

Suggestions for Prayer

1. Reflect and respond to the following questions: How do you understand Christian hospitality? How do you extend hospitality in your life to friends and to strangers? Recall a time in your life when hospitality was extended to you as a stranger. How do you hear yourself called to be more hospitable to friends, family and strangers?
2. Have you ever experienced God's presence to you through another person such as a friend, a family member, a stranger, someone at work? Reflect on this experience, the meaning of it for your life, and how it affirmed or challenged your understanding of God's presence in self and others.
3. The Gospel says that Mary had chosen

the better way, to be present and to listen to the Lord. Through your imagination, invite Jesus into your home and your daily life. Speak with him about your concerns, hopes, anxieties, worries, joys, etc.; then listen in silence to his response to you.

Suggestion for Journal Keeping

As you listen to the readings, be aware of what touches you, awakens concerns or desires within you about hospitality or about being more present to the Lord in your life. Journal your responses in a dialogue with Jesus, being sure to allow Jesus to respond to you.

Kathleen Brown

Seventeenth Sunday of the Year A

READING I   1 Kgs 3, 5. 7–12

The Lord appeared to Solomon in a dream at night. God said, "Ask something of me and I will give it to you." Solomon answered: "O Lord, my God, you have made me, your servant, king to succeed my father David; but I am a mere youth, not knowing at all how to act. I serve you in the midst of the people whom you have chosen, a people so vast that it cannot be numbered or counted. Give your servant, therefore, an understanding heart to judge your people and to distinguish right from wrong. For who is able to govern this vast people of yours?"

The Lord was pleased that Solomon made this request. So God said to him: "Because you have asked for this—not for a long life

for yourself, nor for riches, nor for the life of your enemies, but for understanding so that you may know what is right—I do as you requested. I give you a heart so wise and understanding that there has never been anyone like you up to now, and after you there will come no one to equal you."

Responsorial Psalm   Ps 119, 57. 72. 76– 77. 127–128. 129–130
Lord, I love your commands.
I have said, O Lord, that my part
  is to keep your words.
The law of your mouth is to me more precious
    cious
  than thousands of gold and silver pieces.
Lord, I love your commands.
Let your kindness comfort me
  according to your promise to your servants.
    vants.
Let your compassion come to me that I may live,
  live,
  for your law is my delight.
Lord, I love your commands.
For I love your command
  more than gold, however fine.
For in all your precepts I go forward;
  every false way I hate.
Lord, I love your commands.
Wonderful are your decrees;
  therefore I observe them.
The revelation of your words sheds light,
  giving understanding to the simple.
Lord, I love your commands.

READING II   Rom 8, 28–30
We know that God makes all things work together for the good of those who love him, who have been called according to his decree. Those whom he foreknew he predestined to share the image of his Son, that the Son might be the first-born of many brothers. Those he predestined he likewise called; those he called he also justified; and those he justified he in turn glorified.

GOSPEL   Mt 13, 44–52
Jesus said to the crowd: "The reign of God is like a buried treasure which a man found in a field. He hid it again, and rejoicing at his find went and sold all he had and bought that field. Or again, the kingdom of heaven is like a merchant's search for fine pearls. When he found one really valuable pearl, he went back and put up for sale all that he had and bought it.

"The reign of God is also like a dragnet thrown into the lake, which collected all sorts of things. When it was full they hauled it ashore and sat down to put what was worthwhile into containers. What was useless they threw away. That is how it will be at the end of the world. Angels will go out and separate the wicked from the just and hurl the wicked into the fiery furnace, where they will wail and grind their teeth.

"Have you understood all this?" "Yes," they answered; to which he replied, "Every scribe who is learned in the reign of God is like the head of a household who can bring from his store both the new and the old."

This is the gospel of the Lord.

Reflection on the Readings
  How do you find something you're not looking for? You don't. The man in today's Gospel found the treasure because he was looking for it. The merchant found the fine pearl because he was looking for it. Both men found something they were looking for and did what they had to to buy it.
  Today we might think of an antiques buff

who knows Victorian furniture. She looks for original pieces every time she stops at an antique store. One day she sees a table that she recognizes as an original. She asks the price, then races home to get the money she needs. She hurries back, exalted, and snatches up the deal before anyone else can.

Like the men in the Gospel, she sees a valuable thing, recognizes it, and does whatever is necessary to buy the table. The same thing is true for the reign of God. In order to find it, we must be looking for it. We must know what it looks like. We must learn to recognize it. We must, like Solomon, ask the Lord to give us discerning hearts.

Then, when we find evidence of the kingdom, we must do whatever we have to to make it our own. We may have to change some of our usual ways of doing things. We may have to give up old prejudices. We may have to let go of patterns in our lives that blind us to God's love and chain us to our pasts. Once we begin looking for the reign of God, we find it, and once we find it, it demands that we change. Our first step on the journey is the same as Solomon's—asking God to give us wisdom.

Suggestions for Prayer

1. Read today's second reading again. Concentrate on the first sentence. Do you think that God makes all things work together? Turn the first sentence over in your mind. Has God pulled things together in your life?
2. Ask God for wisdom. Think of the problems you have. Tell the Lord about them. Ask for some insight into what you should do.
3. Go for a walk around your neighborhood. Look for signs of the reign of God. See if you can spot the hand of God in what you see. If you find something, pause and give thanks to God.

Suggestion for Journal Keeping

Read over your old journal entries. See if you can spot any patterns. What are they? Can you see yourself moving somewhere?

Michael P. Enright

Seventeenth Sunday of the Year   **B**

READING I   2 Kgs 4, 42–44

A man came from Baal-shalishah bringing to Elisha, the man of God, twenty barley loaves made from the firstfruits, and fresh grain in the ear. "Give it to the people to eat," Elisha said. But his servant objected, "How can I set this before a hundred men?" "Give it to the people to eat," Elisha insisted. "For thus says the Lord, 'They shall eat and there shall be some left over.' " And when they had eaten, there was some left over, as the Lord had said.

Responsorial Psalm   Ps 145, 10–11. 15–16. 17–18

The hand of the Lord feeds us;
  he answers all our needs.
**Let all your works give you thanks, O Lord,
  and let your faithful ones bless you.**
**Let them discourse of the glory of your kingdom
  and speak of your might.**
The hand of the Lord feeds us;
  he answers all our needs.

The eyes of all look hopefully to you,
 and you give them their food in due season;
You open your hand
 and satisfy the desire of every living thing.
The hand of the Lord feeds us;
 he answers all our needs.
**The Lord is just in all his ways
 and holy in all his works.
The Lord is near to all who call upon him,
 to all who call upon him in truth.**
The hand of the Lord feeds us;
 he answers all our needs.

READING II   Eph 4, 1–6

I plead with you as a prisoner for the Lord, to live a life worthy of the calling you have received, with perfect humility, meekness, and patience, bearing with one another lovingly. Make every effort to preserve the unity which has the Spirit as its origin and peace as its binding force. There is but one body and one Spirit, just as there is but one hope given all of you by your call. There is one Lord, one faith, one baptism; one God and Father of all, who is over all, and works through all, and is in all.

GOSPEL   Jn 6, 1–15

Jesus crossed the Sea of Galilee [to the shore] of Tiberias; a vast crowd kept following him because they saw the signs he was performing for the sick. Jesus then went up the mountain and sat down there with his disciples. The Jewish feast of Passover was near; when Jesus looked up and caught sight of a vast crowd coming toward him, he said to Philip, "Where shall we buy bread for these people to eat?" (He knew well what he intended to do but he asked this to test Phil-

ip's response.) Philip replied, "Not even with two hundred days' wages could we buy loaves enough to give each of them a mouthful!"

One of Jesus' disciples, Andrew, Simon Peter's brother, remarked to him, "There is a lad here who has five barley loaves and a couple of dried fish, but what good is that for so many?" Jesus said, "Get the people to recline." Even though the men numbered about five thousand, there was plenty of grass for them to find a place on the ground. Jesus then took the loaves of bread, gave thanks, and passed them around to those reclining there; he did the same with the dried fish, as much as they wanted. When they had had enough, he told his disciples, "Gather up the crusts that are left over so that nothing will go to waste." At this, they gathered twelve baskets full of pieces left over by those who had been fed with the five barley loaves.

When the people saw the sign he had performed they began to say, "This is undoubtedly the Prophet who is to come into the world." At that, Jesus realized that they would come and carry him off to make him king, so he fled back to the mountain alone.

Reflection on the Readings

Were you ever in a situation where there was not enough food to go around? It may have been a family situation, a social function, a disaster, or a third world country. In the group there probably were pessimists who complained of the shortage. On the other hand, there may have been optimists present who used their ingenuity to generate alternative ideas. Were there people who tried to hoard?

In the Gospel today, Jesus finds himself,

the apostles, and a large crowd of people, numbering some five thousand, in a situation of shortage. The only food they had among them was five barley loaves and two fish. But Jesus was an optimist. He asked the troubled people to sit down. Then he took the loaves, gave thanks, and had them distributed. He did the same with the fish. The hunger of all was satisfied, and there were twelve baskets of scraps left over.

St. John tells this story in a way that reflects the Eucharist. Jesus takes bread, gives thanks, and shares it with the multitude. There is a similarity here to the action of the Last Supper in which Jesus takes bread, blesses it, and shares it with his disciples. The abundance of bread which nourishes the five thousand is both a sign of the abundance of life in the Eucharist, and a call to us, as a eucharistic people, to feed the hungry.

Suggestions for Prayer

1. Reflect on one or more of the following questions:
   • Have you ever found yourself in a situation of shortage?
   • What was the attitude of Philip? What was the attitude of Andrew?
   • How did Jesus deal with the situation of shortage of food?
2. In your imagination, place yourself in the large crowd of hungry people. Jesus is saying to you, "Where can we buy some bread for these people to eat?" What answer are you going to give to Jesus?
3. Pray the responsorial psalm as your morning prayer this week. Bear in mind the graciousness of God.

Suggestion for Journal Keeping

In your journal, write about an incident of scarcity in your life. Did you contemplate hoarding? What did you finally do in that situation? Did the example of Jesus' attitude help you in your decision?

Michael J. Koch

Seventeenth Sunday of the Year

READING I Gn 18, 20–32

The Lord said: "The outcry against Sodom and Gomorrah is so great, and their sin so grave, that I must go down and see whether or not their actions fully correspond to the cry against them that comes to me. I mean to find out."

While the two men walked on farther toward Sodom, the Lord remained standing before Abraham. Then Abraham drew nearer to him and said: "Will you sweep away the innocent with the guilty? Suppose there were fifty innocent people in the city; would you wipe out the place, rather than spare it for the sake of the fifty innocent people within it? Far be it from you to do such a thing, to make the innocent die with the guilty, so that the innocent and the guilty would be treated alike! Should not the judge of all the world act with justice?" The Lord replied, "If I find fifty innocent people in the city of Sodom, I will spare the whole place for their sake." Abraham spoke up again: "See how I am presuming to speak to my Lord, though I am but dust and ashes! What

if there are five less than fifty innocent people? Will you destroy the whole city because of those five?" "I will not destroy it," he answered, "if I find forty-five there." But Abraham persisted, saying, "What if only forty are found there?" He replied, "I will forbear doing it for the sake of the forty." Then he said, "Let not my Lord grow impatient if I go on. What if only thirty are found there?" He replied, "I will forbear doing it if I can find but thirty there." Still he went on, "Since I have thus dared to speak to my Lord, what if there are no more than twenty?" "I will not destroy it," he answered, "for the sake of the twenty." But he still persisted: "Please, let not my Lord grow angry if I speak up this last time. What if there are at least ten there?" "For the sake of those ten," he replied, "I will not destroy it."

Responsorial Psalm   Ps 138, 1–2. 2–3. 6–
                                                    7. 7–8
Lord, on the day I called for help, you
    answered me.
I will give thanks to you, O Lord, with all my
    heart,
    [for you have heard the words of my
    mouth;]
    in the presence of the angels I will sing
    your praise;
I will worship at your holy temple
    and give thanks to your name.
Lord, on the day I called for help, you
    answered me.
Because of your kindness and your truth;
    for you have made great above all things
    your name and your promise.
When I called you answered me;
    you built up strength within me.

Lord, on the day I called for help, you
    answered me.
The Lord is exalted, yet the lowly he sees,
    and the proud he knows from afar.
Though I walk amid distress, you preserve
    me;
    against the anger of my enemies you raise
    your hand.
Lord, on the day I called for help, you
    answered me.
Your right hand saves me.
    The Lord will complete what he has done
    for me;
Your kindness, O Lord, endures forever;
    forsake not the work of your hands.
Lord, on the day I called for help, you
    answered me.

READING II   Col 2, 12–14
In baptism you were not only buried with him but also raised to life with him because you believed in the power of God who raised him from the dead. Even when you were dead in sin and your flesh was uncircumcised, God gave you new life in company with Christ. He pardoned all our sins. He canceled the bond that stood against us with all its claims, snatching it up and nailing it to the cross.

GOSPEL   Lk 11, 1–13
One day Jesus was praying in a certain place. When he had finished, one of his disciples asked him, "Lord, teach us to pray as John taught his disciples." He said to them, "When you pray, say:
    "Father,
    hallowed be your name,
    your kingdom come.
    Give us each day our daily bread.

Forgive us our sins
for we too forgive all who do us wrong;
and subject us not to the trial."

Jesus said to them: "If one of you knows someone who comes to him in the middle of the night and says to him, 'Friend, lend me three loaves, for a friend of mine has come in from a journey and I have nothing to offer him'; and he from inside should reply, 'Leave me alone. The door is shut now and my children and I are in bed. I can't get up to look after your needs'—I tell you, even though he does not get up and take care of the man because of friendship, he will find himself doing so because of his persistence and give him as much as he needs.

"So I say to you, 'Ask and you shall receive; seek and you shall find, knock and it shall be opened to you.'

"For whoever asks, receives; whoever seeks, finds; whoever knocks, is admitted. What father among you will give his son a snake if he asks for a fish, or hand him a scorpion if he asks for an egg? If you, with all your sins, know how to give your children good things, how much more will the heavenly Father give the Holy Spirit to those who ask him."

Reflection on the Readings

Prayer is sometimes nothing more than a conversation with God where we express our hopes, concerns, joys. In the first reading, Abraham is engaged in a conversation with God regarding divine justice for Sodom and Gomorrah. Persistent in his pursuit of justice for the people, Abraham draws God into a dialogue in an attempt to preserve the infamous city from being destroyed. But perhaps the most important aspect of this dialogue has to do with what it reveals about God. Ulti-mately, this dialogue reveals a God who is just, who says that even ten innocent people are worth saving the rest of the city and who does not destroy or punish at divine whim. Thus, God's great love for the people is revealed through this prayer dialogue with Abraham.

Although all prayer is essentially a conversation with God, some prayer is not as spontaneous as Abraham's with God. Thus we have received the Lord's Prayer that Jesus gave to his disciples. But all prayer reveals something of the faith of a people and their understanding of who is their God. When the disciples asked Jesus to teach them to pray, he gave them a very simple prayer but one which expressed their nascent faith. To believe in and to call for the coming of God's kingdom, to daily come to God with their basic needs as individuals and community, and to pray both to be forgiven and to forgive as they know themselves to be forgiven by God and to not be asked to endure suffering beyond their capacity—this is how the followers of Jesus were to live their lives. Through parables Jesus continued to speak about the disciples' life of prayer. However, the parables pointed more to the relationship between the disciples and God. On the disciples part, they were to persevere in presenting their needs to God and in their relationship with God. Perseverance in their prayer to God will bear fruit because of who God is.

Suggestions for Prayer

1. Each morning, before beginning the day's activities, slowly and reflectively recite the Lord's Prayer. After each phrase, stop and reflect on the meaning

of it for you, your life in your family, work or neighborhood.

2. Review the growth of your prayer life since your childhood. What was your prayer life like as a child? What is it like now? How do you hear yourself called to pray in your life now? Do you have a daily prayer time and do you persevere in it?

3. Reflectively and slowly read the responsorial psalm every day this week.

Suggestion for Journal Keeping

At the end of the day, record the activities of the day, remembering to forgive those who hurt or offended you and to ask forgiveness from those you may have hurt or offended. In your journal writing include prayer to God expressing your needs and the needs of others.

Kathleen Brown

Eighteenth Sunday of the Year **A**

READING I   Is 55, 1–3
All you who are thirsty,
   come to the water!
You who have no money,
   come, receive grain and eat;
Come, without paying and without cost,
   drink wine and milk!
Why spend your money for what is not bread;
   your wages for what fails to satisfy?
Heed me, and you shall eat well,
   you shall delight in rich fare.

Come to me heedfully,
   listen, that you may have life.
I will renew with you the everlasting covenant,
   the benefits assured to David.

Responsorial Psalm   Ps 145, 8–9. 15–16.
                                                      17–18
The hand of the Lord feeds us;
   he answers all our needs.
The Lord is gracious and merciful,
   slow to anger and of great kindness.
The Lord is good to all
   and compassionate toward all his works.
The hand of the Lord feeds us;
   he answers all our needs.
The eyes of all look hopefully to you,
   and you give them their food in due season;
You open your hand
   and satisfy the desire of every living thing.
The hand of the Lord feeds us;
   he answers all our needs.
The Lord is just in all his ways
   and holy in all his works.
The Lord is near to all who call upon him,
   to all who call upon him in truth.
The hand of the Lord feeds us;
   he answers all our needs.

READING II   Rom 8, 35. 37–39
Who will separate us from the love of Christ? Trial, or distress, or persecution, or hunger, or nakedness, or danger, or the sword? Yet in all this we are more than conquerors because of him who has loved us. For I am certain that neither death nor life, neither angels nor principalities, neither the present nor the future, nor powers, neither height nor depth nor any other creature, will

be able to separate us from the love of God that comes to us in Christ Jesus, our Lord.

GOSPEL   Mt 14, 13–21

When Jesus heard [of the death of John the Baptizer], he withdrew by boat to a deserted place by himself. The crowds heard of it and followed him on foot from the towns. When he disembarked and saw the vast throng, his heart was moved with pity, and he cured their sick. As evening drew on, his disciples came to him with the suggestion: "This is a deserted place and it is already late. Dismiss the crowds so that they may go to the villages and buy some food for themselves." Jesus said to them: "There is no need for them to disperse. Give them something to eat yourselves." "We have nothing here," they replied, "but five loaves and a couple of fish." "Bring them here," he said. Then he ordered the crowds to sit down on the grass. He took the five loaves and two fish, looked up to heaven, blessed and broke them and gave the loaves to the disciples, who in turn gave them to the people. All those present ate their fill. The fragments which remained, when gathered up, filled twelve baskets. Those who ate were about five thousand, not counting women and children.

Reflection on the Readings

Being really hungry is a terrible thing! When you're really hungry, little else matters. All you can think of is the growing emptiness in your stomach. You begin to notice the smell of food, to remember eating, to long for something that will take the hunger away. The need we have to eat transforms itself into a consuming desire that absorbs our thoughts and feelings. When we finally eat, we rejoice in the meal we've been waiting for. Sometimes we even eat too much, so strong is our desire to be filled.

In the Gospel today, Jesus feeds the crowd. His action is a response to his being moved with pity. He sees them like sheep without a shepherd and begins to feed them. What he offers them fills them with hope and joy. He meets their need for healing. He touches their emptiness. They stay around until evening, far away from any food. What they've been feeling is stronger than the gnawing in their stomachs.

The disciples come to Jesus and tell him to send them away, since obviously the crowd has to eat. Jesus again makes his love for them concrete. He has already fed their hearts and now he feeds their bodies. The abundant feast mirrors the feast of Isaiah in the first reading. Free food and drink, and lots of it, come from our covenant with God. Life, life in abundance, springs from Yahweh's love. Jesus fulfills that love and brings life to God's people. We only need to listen and the Lord will fill us with the same life.

Suggestions for Prayer

1. Read the second readings from the 15th to the 18th Sunday of the year (or read Romans 8:18–39). Imagine that what you are reading is a letter written to you. Ask yourself these questions:
   - Is there anything that can separate me from the Love of God?
   - Is there something that worries you and distracts you from remembering that God loves you? What is it?
2. Imagine Jesus talking to you. Remember your own hurts and need for healing.

What could Jesus say to you to heal your deepest wounds? Imagine him saying it to you.

3. Think about your favorite meal of all time. What was your best dining experience? Reread the first reading. Reflect on the promise given. How can you listen to the Lord more carefully?

Suggestion for Journal Keeping

Write down the things that are keeping you from recognizing the love of God in your own life. Can the Lord heal these?

Michael P. Enright

Eighteenth Sunday of the Year B

READING I   Ex 16, 2–4. 12–15

The whole Israelite community grumbled against Moses and Aaron. The Israelites said to them, "Would that we had died at the Lord's hand in the land of Egypt, as we sat by our fleshpots and ate our fill of bread! But you had to lead us into this desert to make the whole community die of famine!"

Then the Lord said to Moses, "I will now rain down bread from heaven for you. Each day the people are to go out and gather their daily portion; thus will I test them, to see whether they follow my instructions or not.

"I have heard the grumbling of the Israelites. Tell them: In the evening twilight you shall eat flesh, and in the morning you shall have your fill of bread, so that you may know that I, the Lord, am your God."

In the evening quail came up and covered the camp. In the morning a dew lay all about the camp, and when the dew evaporated, there on the surface of the desert were fine flakes like hoarfrost on the ground. On seeing it, the Israelites asked one another, "What is this?" for they did not know what it was. But Moses told them, "This is the bread which the Lord has given you to eat."

Responsorial Psalm   Ps 78, 3–4. 23–24. 25. 54

The Lord gave them bread from heaven.
What we have heard and know,
    and what our fathers have declared to us,
We will declare to the generation to come
    the glorious deeds of the Lord and his strength
    and the wonders that he wrought.
The Lord gave them bread from heaven.
He commanded the skies above
    and the doors of heaven he opened;
He rained manna upon them for food
    and gave them heavenly bread.
The Lord gave them bread from heaven.
The bread of the mighty was eaten by men;
    even a surfeit of provisions he sent them.
And he brought them to his holy land,
    to the mountains his right hand had won.
The Lord gave them bread from heaven.

READING II   Eph 4, 17. 20–24

I declare and solemnly attest in the Lord that you must no longer live as the pagans do— their minds empty. That is not what you learned when you learned Christ! I am supposing, of course, that he has been preached and taught to you in accord with the truth that is in Jesus: namely, that you must lay aside your former way of life and the old self

309

which deteriorates through illusion and desire, and acquire a fresh, spiritual way of thinking. You must put on that new man created in God's image, whose justice and holiness are born of truth.

GOSPEL   Jn 6, 24–35
When the crowd saw that neither Jesus nor his disciples were at the place where Jesus had eaten the bread, they too embarked in the boats and went to Capernaum looking for Jesus.

When they found him on the other side of the lake, they said to him, "Rabbi, when did you come here?" Jesus answered them:

"I assure you,
   you are not looking for me because you
      have seen signs
   but because you have eaten your fill of
      the loaves.
   You should not be working for perish-
      able food
   but for food that remains unto life eter-
      nal,
   food which the Son of Man will give
      you;
   it is on him that God the Father has set
      his seal."

At this they said to him, "What must we do to perform the works of God?" Jesus replied:

"This is the work of God:
   have faith in the One he sent."

"So that we can put faith in you," they asked him, "what sign are you going to perform for us to see? What is the 'work' you do? Our ancestors had manna to eat in the desert; according to Scripture, 'He gave them bread from the heavens to eat.' " Jesus said to them:

"I solemnly assure you,
   it was not Moses who gave you bread
      from the heavens;
   it is my Father who gives you the real
      heavenly bread.
God's bread comes down from heaven
   and gives life to the world."

"Sir, give us this bread always," they besought him.

Jesus explained to them:
   "I myself am the bread of life.
   No one who comes to me shall ever be
      hungry,
   no one who believes in me shall thirst
      again."

Reflection on the Readings
   As we go through life, most of us spend a lot of time, money, energy, and other resources on temporal and passing things. At some point in our life, we may place great value on money, a career, education, a house, becoming a sports champion, or physical pleasure. As we go on in life, these values usually wear out or become meaningless. We outgrow them and replace them with more meaningful ones.

   In the Gospel today, Jesus challenges his followers to deeper conversion. Jesus has just finished performing the miracle of the loaves and fish. The crowd follows him wherever he goes. They follow him, not because they wish to grow in faith and spirituality, but because they see Jesus as a source of physical bread. Jesus challenges them, "Do not work for food that cannot last, but work for food that endures to eternal life." A debate ensues. "What does God expect of us?" they ask. Jesus says, "This is working for God: you must believe in the one he has sent." Show us a sign, they say; work a miracle. Jesus then says it was not Moses who gave the manna, but his Father in heaven. The bread of God is that which gives life to the world. "Give us this bread," they say. Jesus answers, "I am the bread of life."

This struggle of conversion is still going on today. Each one of us is called to conversion and faith. We must give "Jesus, the bread of life," priority over mere physical bread.

Suggestions for Prayer

1. Reflect on one or more of the following questions:
   • What are some of the passing "gods" you have served in your life?
   • Have you outgrown any of these "gods"?
   • Do you believe Jesus is the incarnation of the living God?
2. In your imagination, see yourself in a process of conversion. Much of your life and energy is devoted to a "god" whom you hang onto in the hope of finding a meaningful life. Jesus comes and touches you. He says, "I am the bread of life."
3. Pray the responsorial psalm as your morning prayer this week. It will help in your conversion process.

Suggestion for Journal Keeping

Describe a "god" in your life whom you worked for and loved. Describe your parting and good-bye to this "god" when you finally outgrew it. You then embrace Jesus, the bread of life.

Michael J. Koch

Eighteenth Sunday of the Year   **C**

READING I   Eccl 1, 2; 2, 21–23
Vanity of vanities, says Qoheleth, vanity of vanities! All things are vanity! Here is a man who has labored with wisdom and knowledge and skill, and to another, who has not labored over it, he must leave his property. This also is vanity and a great misfortune. For what profit comes to a man from all the toil and anxiety of heart with which he has labored under the sun? All his days sorrow and grief are his occupation; even at night his mind is not at rest. This also is vanity.

Responsorial Psalm   Ps 95, 1–2. 6–7. 8–9
If today you hear his voice,
    harden not your hearts.
Come, let us sing joyfully to the Lord; let us acclaim the Rock of our salvation. Let us greet him with thanksgiving; let us joyfully sing psalms to him.
If today you hear his voice,
    harden not your hearts.
Come, let us bow down in worship; let us kneel before the Lord who made us. For he is our God, and we are the people he shepherds, the flock he guides.
If today you hear his voice,
    harden not your hearts.
Oh, that today you would hear his voice: "Harden not your hearts as at Meribah, as in the day of Massah in the desert, Where your fathers tempted me; they tested me though they had seen my works."

If today you hear his voice,
harden not your hearts.

READING II   Col 3, 1–5. 9–11

Since you have been raised up in company with Christ, set your heart on what pertains to higher realms where Christ is seated at God's right hand. Be intent on things above rather than on things of earth. After all, you have died! Your life is hidden now with Christ in God. When Christ our life appears, then you shall appear with him in glory.

Put to death whatever in your nature is rooted in earth: fornication, uncleanness, passion, evil desires, and that lust which is idolatry. Stop lying to one another. What you have done is put aside your old self with its past deeds and put on a new man, one who grows in knowledge as he is formed anew in the image of his Creator. There is no Greek or Jew here, circumcised or uncircumcised, foreigner, Scythian, slave, or freeman. Rather, Christ is everything in all of you.

GOSPEL   Lk 12, 13–21

Someone in the crowd said to Jesus, "Teacher, tell my brother to give me my share of our inheritance." He replied, "Friend, who has set me up as your judge or arbiter?" Then he said to the crowd, "Avoid greed in all its forms. A man may be wealthy, but his possessions do not guarantee him life."

He told them a parable in these words: "There was a rich man who had a good harvest. 'What shall I do?' he asked himself. 'I have no place to store my harvest. I know!' he said. 'I will pull down my grain bins and build larger ones. All my grain and my goods will go there. Then I will say to myself: You

have blessings in reserve for years to come. Relax! Eat heartily, drink well. Enjoy yourself.' But God said to him, 'You fool! This very night your life shall be required of you. To whom will all this piled-up wealth of yours go?' That is the way it works with the man who grows rich for himself instead of growing rich in the sight of God."

Reflection on the Readings

"Vanity of vanities" is an often quoted line. But what does it mean? Qoheleth, the speaker in the first reading, looks about him and, upon seeing the reality of life and death, wisely concludes that to amass wealth is futile, since we cannot take our material fortunes with us after death.

Jesus, addressed by someone in the crowd who wants him to tell his brother to give him his share of the inheritance, instead tells him the parable of the rich man. This rich man had a good harvest and he wanted to store it and save it. He was a fool for amassing such wealth, for upon his death he could not take it with him. Through the parable Jesus teaches that possessions and wealth are not bad. Rather, it is one's attitude toward possessions that matters. The danger is that one becomes possessed by possessions, keeping focused on things and wealth, rather than having God as the center of one's life. In other words, the danger is greed. Perhaps it would be better to keep a perspective toward possessions similar to Qoheleth.

Paul in addressing the Colossians invites them as well to refocus their attention. It is through the raising of Christ from the dead for us that we are called to rise above those things of the world which keep us from being Christ-like. Setting our hearts and focus on Christ we will grow rich in God.

Suggestions for Prayer

1. Sit in silence, relaxing your whole body. Closing your eyes, envision your favorite place. See yourself in your favorite place, relaxing. Invite Jesus to come and be with you, sitting quietly. Allow his presence to fill you with peace.
2. Reflect on one or all of the following questions: What is your attitude toward things, possessions, money? Do things, possessions or money ever cause you worry or anxiety? How do the readings affirm or challenge your attitudes toward things, possessions or money?
3. Reflect on what it means for you to grow rich in the sight of God. What do you need for this growth to take place? After reflecting on this, come to the Lord presenting your desires and your hopes.

Suggestion for Journal Keeping

Write a letter to God telling about all the blessings you have in your life and giving thanks for everything in your life at this time. Next write in your letter what you really need in your life, presenting these to God as well.

Kathleen Brown

Nineteenth Sunday of the Year   **A**

READING I   1 Kgs 19, 9. 11–13
Elijah came to a cave [from the mountain of God, Horeb], where he took shelter. Then the Lord said, "Go outside and stand on the mountain before the Lord; the Lord will be passing by." A strong and heavy wind was rending the mountains and crushing rocks before the Lord—but the Lord was not in the wind. After the wind there was an earthquake—but the Lord was not in the earthquake. After the earthquake there was fire—but the Lord was not in the fire. After the fire there was a tiny whispering sound. When he heard this, Elijah hid his face in his cloak and went and stood at the entrance of the cave.

Responsorial Psalm   Ps 85, 9. 10. 11–12.
13–14

Lord, let us see your kindness,
    and grant us your salvation.
I will hear what God proclaims;
    the Lord—for he proclaims peace.
Near indeed is his salvation to those who
    fear him,
    glory dwelling in our land.
Lord, let us see your kindness,
    and grant us your salvation.
Kindness and truth shall meet;
    justice and peace shall kiss.
Truth shall spring out of the earth,
    and justice shall look down from heaven.
Lord, let us see your kindness,
    and grant us your salvation.
The Lord himself will give his benefits;
    our land shall yield its increase.
Justice shall walk before him,
    and salvation, along the way of his steps.
Lord, let us see your kindness,
    and grant us your salvation.

READING II   Rom 9, 1–5
I speak the truth in Christ: I do not lie. My conscience bears me witness in the Holy Spirit that there is great grief and constant pain in my heart. Indeed, I could even wish to be separated from Christ for the sake of my brothers, my kinsmen the Israelites.

up and said, "Lord, if it is really you, tell me to come to you across the water." "Come!" he said. So Peter got out of the boat and began to walk on the water, moving toward Jesus. But when he perceived how strong the wind was, becoming frightened he began to sink, and cried out, "Lord, save me!" Jesus at once stretched out his hand and caught him. "How little faith you have!" he exclaimed. "Why did you falter?" Once they had climbed into the boat, the wind died down. Those who were in the boat showed him reverence, declaring, "Beyond doubt you are the Son of God!"

Theirs were the adoption, the glory, the covenants, the lawgiving, the worship, and the promises; theirs were the patriarchs, and from them came the Messiah (I speak of his human origins). Blessed forever be God who is over all! Amen.

GOSPEL   Mt 14, 22–33
[After the crowds had their fill] Jesus insisted that his disciples get into the boat and precede him to the other side. When he had sent them away, he went up on the mountain by himself to pray, remaining there alone as evening drew on. Meanwhile the boat, already several hundred yards out from shore, was being tossed about in the waves raised by strong head winds. At about three in the morning, he came walking toward them on the lake. When the disciples saw him walking on the water, they were terrified. "It is a ghost!" they said, and in their fear they began to cry out. Jesus hastened to reassure them: "Get hold of yourselves! It is I. Do not be afraid!" Peter spoke

Reflection on the Readings

Every once in a while, something happens that we can't quite explain. For some reason, the rules that govern ordinary everyday reality are suspended for a moment and we catch a glimpse of a deeper reality. You've had this experience! It might have been a sunset, or a baby's eyes, or the face of your spouse or son or daughter. It might have been a severe storm, or the first snow, or something a stranger did. Sometime, somehow, you've had an experience that lets you see a different reality. What ordinarily you wouldn't notice, suddenly you see. You can tell this has happened because you remember the experience. You remember that sunset, or that glimpse into someone's eyes. Your heart was touched.

In today's first reading we read of Elijah's experience of God. The Lord God was not present in the earth-shaking "theatrical" ways we might expect. Yahweh was present in a whisper. The special effects were not clues of God's presence. The simplicity of a whisper caused Elijah to hide his face.

The disciples in the boat nearly jumped out

of their skins seeing Jesus approach. Peter put this apparition to the test and was himself tested: Why did you falter? Why did you not believe? Peter's faith was strong enough for him to begin the walk, but he was frightened. We too begin the walk toward the Lord but falter. It's then that Jesus reaches down and picks us up.

The presence of the Lord breaks through the mundane and invites us to a deeper way of seeing. Surprised, we find ourselves appreciating the beauty of our world and knowing God's love for us. We respond to the invitation and begin to move closer to the Lord, only to find our knees weakened. Jesus then reaches out and strengthens us for our journey toward the light.

Suggestions for Prayer

1. Watch a sunset. Give thanks to God for the beauty you see there. Listen hard for a "whisper" that will tell you God is present.
2. Imagine that you're Peter. It's dark and you're on a small boat in a storm. You see Jesus and he calls you toward him. Do you go? What happens?
3. Reread the second reading. Why is Paul grieving? Have you ever been saddened watching someone reject love? What happened?

Suggestion for Journal Keeping

Write down the earliest experience you can remember of seeing something beautiful. How old were you? Why do you think you remember this experience? Did it change you?

Michael P. Enright

Nineteenth Sunday of the Year

READING I   1 Kgs 19, 4–8

Elijah went a day's journey into the desert, until he came to a broom tree and sat beneath it. He prayed for death: "This is enough, O Lord! Take my life, for I am no better than my fathers." He lay down and fell asleep under the broom tree, but then an angel touched him and ordered him to get up and eat. He looked and there at his head was a hearth cake and a jug of water. After he ate and drank, he lay down again, but the angel of the Lord came back a second time, touched him, and ordered, "Get up and eat, else the journey will be too long for you!" He got up, ate and drank; then strengthened by that food, he walked forty days and forty nights to the mountain of God, Horeb.

Responsorial Psalm   Ps 34, 2–3. 4–5. 6–7. 8–9

Taste and see the goodness of the Lord.
I will bless the Lord at all times;
  his praise shall be ever in my mouth.
Let my soul glory in the Lord;
  the lowly will hear me and be glad.
Taste and see the goodness of the Lord.
Glorify the Lord with me,
  let us together extol his name.
I sought the Lord, and he answered me
  and delivered me from all my fears.
Taste and see the goodness of the Lord.
Look to him that you may be radiant with joy,
  and your faces may not blush with shame.
When the afflicted man called out, the Lord heard,
  and from all his distress he saved him.

Taste and see the goodness of the Lord.
The angel of the Lord encamps
   around those who fear him, and delivers
      them.
Taste and see how good the Lord is;
   happy the man who takes refuge in him.
Taste and see the goodness of the Lord.

READING II   Eph 4, 30–5, 2
Do nothing to sadden the Holy Spirit with whom you were sealed against the day of redemption. Get rid of all bitterness, all passion and anger, harsh words, slander, and malice of every kind. In place of these, be kind to one another, compassionate, and mutually forgiving, just as God has forgiven you in Christ.

Be imitators of God as his dear children. Follow the way of love, even as Christ loved you. He gave himself for us as an offering to God, a gift of pleasing fragrance.

GOSPEL   Jn 6, 41–51
The Jews started to murmur in protest because Jesus claimed, "I am the bread that came down from heaven." They kept saying: "Is this not Jesus, the son of Joseph? Do we not know his father and mother? How can he claim to have come down from heaven?" "Stop your murmuring," Jesus told them.
   "No one can come to me
   unless the Father who sent me draws him;
   I will raise him up on the last day.
   It is written in the prophets:
   'They shall all be taught by God.'
   Everyone who has heard the Father
   and learned from him
   comes to me.
   Not that anyone has seen the Father—
   only the one who is from God
   has seen the Father.

Let me firmly assure you,
he who believes has eternal life.
I am the bread of life.
Your ancestors ate manna in the desert,
   but they died.
This is the bread that comes down from
   heaven,
for a man to eat and never die.
I myself am the living bread
come down from heaven.
If anyone eats this bread
he shall live forever;
the bread I will give
is my flesh, for the life of the world."

Reflection on the Readings

Often at a science fair, there is a section on optical illusions. We are entertained by seeing one thing, but the reality is something else. For example, straight lines appear curved. Often we judge others from mere externals. Internally, people are often not what they appear to be externally. We must remain open to new evidence.

In the Gospel today, some Jews are in a state of illusion. They judge Jesus from mere externals. Jesus says, "I am the bread that came down from heaven." But they say, "You are a mere man, the son of Joseph. We know your family and where you grew up." They see only the externals. Because of their negative feelings toward Jesus, they have closed minds. They have already decided who Jesus is, a mere man. They will not accept Jesus' true identity. Jesus says, "I am the living bread which has come down from heaven. Anyone who eats this bread will live forever; and the bread that I shall give is my flesh for the life of the world." To accept Jesus beyond externals requires faith. Faith sees beyond externals.

Throughout the centuries and today, Catholics and other Christians have believed that Jesus is really present in the Eucharist. In a sense, the bread we eat, the wine we drink, is an illusion. Our human eyes see only bread and wine, only externals. Through faith, we go beyond externals and recognize the presence of Jesus in the Eucharist.

Suggestions for Prayer

1. Reflect on one or more of the following questions:
   - Have you ever judged a person from mere externals and later discovered you were not even near to knowing the real person?
   - Why did the Jews in St. John's Gospel have such a hard time with Jesus' true identity?
   - Do you really believe Jesus when he says, "I am the living bread which has come down from heaven. Anyone who eats this bread will live forever"?
2. In your imagination, place yourself at a Sunday eucharistic liturgy after your baptism (or reception into the Church). When the priest holds up the host at the elevation, you acknowledge the presence of Christ in the Eucharist by saying, "My Lord and my God."
3. Pray the responsorial psalm as your evening prayer this week. Delight in the Lord.

Suggestion for Journal Keeping

Record in your journal an experience in your life where you judged a person quite harshly, only to discover later that you saw only externals and that the person was not at all like that. What did you learn from this experience? Does this experience help you to believe in the Real Presence?

Michael J. Koch

Nineteenth Sunday of the Year   C

READING I   Wis 18, 6–9

That night was known beforehand to our fathers,
that, with sure knowledge of the oaths in which they put their faith, they might have courage.
Your people awaited
the salvation of the just and the destruction of their foes.
For when you punished our adversaries,
in this you glorified us whom you had summoned.
For in secret the holy children of the good were offering sacrifice
and putting into effect with one accord the divine institution.

Responsorial Psalm   Ps 33, 1. 12. 18–19. 20–22

Happy the people the Lord has chosen to be his own.

Exult, you just, in the Lord;
praise from the upright is fitting.
Happy the nation whose God is the Lord,
the people he has chosen for his own inheritance.

Happy the people the Lord has chosen to be his own.

See, the eyes of the Lord are upon those who fear him,
upon those who hope for his kindness,

317

To deliver them from death
  and preserve them in spite of famine.
Happy the people the Lord has chosen to be
  his own.
Our soul waits for the Lord,
  who is our help and our shield.
May your kindness, O Lord, be upon us
  who have put our hope in you.
Happy the people the Lord has chosen to be
  his own.

READING II   Heb 11, 1–2. 8–19
Faith is confident assurance concerning
what we hope for, and conviction about
things we do not see. Because of faith the
men of old were approved by God. By faith
Abraham obeyed when he was called, and
went forth to the place he was to receive as
a heritage; he went forth, moreover, not
knowing where he was going. By faith he so-
journed in the promised land as in a foreign
country, dwelling in tents with Isaac and Jacob, heirs of the same promise; for he was
looking forward to the city with foundations, whose designer and maker is God. By
faith Sarah received power to conceive
though she was past the age, for she thought
that the One who had made the promise was
worthy of trust. As a result of this faith, there
came forth from one man, who was himself
as good as dead, descendants as numerous
as the stars in the sky and the sands of the
seashore.

All of these died in faith. They did not
obtain what had been promised but saw
and saluted it from afar. By acknowledging
themselves to be strangers and foreigners on
the earth, they showed that they were seeking a homeland. If they had been thinking
back to the place from which they had
come, they would have had the opportunity

of returning there. But they were searching
for a better, a heavenly home. Wherefore
God is not ashamed to be called their God,
for he has prepared a city for them. By faith
Abraham, when put to the test, offered up
Isaac; he who had received the promises was
ready to sacrifice his only son, of whom it
was said, "Through Isaac shall your descendants be called." He reasoned that God
was able to raise from the dead, and so he
received Isaac back as a symbol.

GOSPEL   Lk 12, 32–48
Jesus said to his disciples: "Do not live in
fear, little flock. It has pleased your Father
to give you the kingdom. Sell what you have
and give alms. Get purses for yourselves that
do not wear out, a never-failing treasure
with the Lord which no thief comes near nor
any moth destroys. Wherever your treasure
lies, there your heart will be.

"Let your belts be fastened around your
waists and your lamps be burning ready. Be
like men awaiting their master's return from
a wedding, so that when he arrives and
knocks, you will open for him without delay.
It will go well with those servants whom the
master finds wide-awake on his return. I tell
you, he will put on an apron, seat them at
table, and proceed to wait on them. Should
he happen to come at midnight or before
sunrise and find them prepared, it will go
well with them. You know as well as I that if
the head of the house knew when the thief
was coming he would not let him break into
his house. Be on guard, therefore. The Son
of Man will come when you least expect
him."

Peter said, "Do you intend this parable for
us, Lord, or do you mean it for the whole
world?" The Lord said, "Who in your opin-

ion is that faithful, farsighted steward whom the master will set over his servants to dispense their ration of grain in season? That servant is fortunate whom his master finds busy when he returns. Assuredly, his master will put him in charge of all his property. But if the servant says to himself, 'My master is taking his time about coming,' and begins to abuse the housemen and servant girls, to eat and drink and get drunk, that servant's master will come back on a day when he does not expect him, at a time he does not know. He will punish him severely and rank him among those undeserving of trust. The slave who knew his master's wishes but did not prepare to fulfill them will get a severe beating, whereas the one who did not know them and who nonetheless deserved to be flogged will get off with fewer stripes. When much has been given a man, much will be required of him. More will be asked of a man to whom more has been entrusted.

Reflection on the Readings

By means of their faith the Hebrew people knew that God would be faithful to them. They waited for the day when the just would be saved and the enemy destroyed. When, through Moses, the Lord called them out of Egypt, they were ready to go. Their faith and courage in the Lord led the way.

Jesus tells the disciples that they are not to fear. Like the Hebrews, they can put their faith in God. And like the Hebrews, they too are called to be prepared for the Lord's coming at any time. Called to be faith-filled, they are to live a life that speaks of their readiness for the coming of the Son of Man. It is a life of constant faithfulness to God in every activity. Because much has been given to them, much will be asked of the disciples of Jesus.

In the Letter to the Hebrews, faith is defined as having confident assurance concerning what we hope for. To be able to recognize the coming of Christ in our life, we need to be as faithful as our Jewish ancestors. Sometimes that faith will require belief in God's faithful promises to us, even when we do not see them fulfilled as we would intend. Abraham and Sarah were promised that their names would be famous, that they would have a land of their own and many descendants. They did not see the fullness of these promises, but future generations would come to know that God was faithful. However, throughout their life, Abraham and Sarah remained faithful to God. As followers of Jesus, we are invited to this same faithfulness even in the midst of suffering.

Suggestions for Prayer

1. Reflect on the following questions: In your own life what has it meant for you to be faithful to friends, to family, to yourself, to God? How have you come to believe in God's faithfulness to you? Where in your life do you desire to be more faith-filled?

2. Reflect on the line from the Gospel, "Do not live in fear, little flock. It has pleased your Father to give you the kingdom." What are your fears, your hopes, your expectations, your needs? In silence, present these to God.

3. Read Genesis 12:1–4, then reread the Letter to the Hebrews. As you read, invite the Lord to speak to you through the readings. Listen to the words or phrases that touch you in your life today. What do the readings have to say to you about your own faith?

Write the story of the Lord's coming into your life, beginning with your childhood and moving into the present. Conclude by writing a letter to God, expressing your thankfulness, your hopes and your desires for the future.

Kathleen Brown

Twentieth Sunday of the Year A

READING I   Is 56, 1. 6–7

Thus says the Lord:
Observe what is right, do what is just;
  for my salvation is about to come,
  my justice, about to be revealed.
The foreigners who join themselves to the
      Lord,
  ministering to him,
Loving the name of the Lord,
  and becoming his servants—
All who keep the sabbath free from profana-
      tion
  and hold to my covenant,
Them I will bring to my holy mountain
  and make joyful in my house of prayer;
Their holocausts and sacrifices
  will be acceptable on my altar,
For my house shall be called
  a house of prayer for all peoples.

Responsorial Psalm   Ps 67, 2–3. 5. 6. 8
O God, let all the nations praise you!
May God have pity on us and bless us;
  may he let his face shine upon us.
So may your way be known upon earth;
  among all nations, your salvation.
O God, let all the nations praise you!

May the nations be glad and exult
  because you rule the peoples in equity;
  the nations on the earth you guide.
O God, let all the nations praise you!
May the peoples praise you, O God;
  may all the peoples praise you!
May God bless us,
  and may all the ends of the earth fear him!
O God, let all the nations praise you!

READING II   Rom 11, 13–15. 29–32

I say this now to you Gentiles: Inasmuch as I am the apostle of the Gentiles, I glory in my ministry, trying to rouse my fellow Jews to envy and save some of them. For if their rejection has meant reconciliation for the world, what will their acceptance mean? Nothing less than life from the dead!

God's gifts and his call are irrevocable. Just as you were once disobedient to God and now have received mercy through their disobedience, so they have become disobedient—since God wished to show you mercy—that they too may receive mercy. God has imprisoned all in disobedience that he might have mercy on all.

GOSPEL   Mt 15, 21–28

Jesus withdrew to the district of Tyre and Sidon. It happened that a Canaanite woman living in that locality presented herself, crying out to him, "Lord, Son of David, have pity on me! My daughter is terribly troubled by a demon." He gave her no word of response. His disciples came up and began to entreat him, "Get rid of her. She keeps shouting after us." "My mission is only to the lost sheep of the house of Israel," Jesus replied. She came forward then and did him homage with the plea, "Help me, Lord!" But he answered, "It is not right to take the food

320

of sons and daughters and throw it to the dogs." "Please, Lord," she insisted, "even the dogs eat the leavings that fall from their masters' tables." Jesus then said in reply, "Woman, you have great faith! Your wish will come to pass." That very moment her daughter got better.

Reflection on the Readings

Whoever you are, rich or poor, there are some places you are not welcome. Whatever your skin color, or age, or sex, there are places where you are not allowed. All of us are victims of discrimination in one way or another. We have all been pre-judged at some time in our lives. We have all been turned away because of our clothes, or our neighborhood, or our family, or our physical characteristics. We know what the Canaanite woman felt.

There is one place, though, where everyone is welcome. There is one place where age, or sex, or sickness, or clothes, or color doesn't make a bit of difference. What does make a difference is our faith. We are all welcome into the house of the Lord. As the first reading tells us, the house of the Lord is a "house of prayer for all peoples." Although it is difficult to live this out in individual parishes, it is true. No one is to be turned away just because we don't like that person. All faithful people are welcome.

This is good news! There is no other place like that on the earth. Even in countries like ours where we are all supposed to be equal, some people are not welcome. At its best, the place where you worship accommodates the whole spectrum of people. It is a sign of the kingdom. The community you want to join opens its arms to you, and to people around the whole earth. You are welcome with all of your strengths and talents and gifts, and with your weaknesses and limits and sinfulness. The only requirement is that your faith is strong.

Suggestions for Prayer

1. Reread the Gospel and imagine the scene. Put yourself into one of the roles: the disciples, the women, or Jesus. How do you feel? What part did you pick? Why?
2. Remember an experience when you felt prejudice. What happened? How did it affect you? What did you learn from it? Imagine Jesus sitting next to you. Tell him about the experience.

Suggestion for Journal Keeping

Write down the prejudices you have. Think of the kind of people you most dislike. Be honest. Write down why you feel the way you do. Read the list over; then write a prayer for these people and yourself.

Michael P. Enright

Twentieth Sunday of the Year

READING I Prv 9, 1–6

Wisdom has built her house,
  she has set up her seven columns;
She has dressed her meat, mixed her wine,
  yes, she has spread her table.
She has sent out her maidens; she calls
  from the heights out over the city:
"Let whoever is simple turn in here;

to him who lacks understanding, I say,
Come, eat of my food,
and drink of the wine I have mixed!
Forsake foolishness that you may live;
advance in the way of understanding.

Responsorial Psalm   Ps 34, 2–3. 10–11.
12–13. 14–15
Taste and see the goodness of the Lord.
I will bless the Lord at all times;
his praise shall be ever in my mouth.
Let my soul glory in the Lord;
the lowly will hear me and be glad.
Taste and see the goodness of the Lord.
Fear the Lord, you his holy ones,
for nought is lacking to those who fear
him.
The great grow poor and hungry;
but those who seek the Lord want for no
good thing.
Taste and see the goodness of the Lord.
Come, children, hear me;
I will teach you the fear of the Lord.
Which of you desires life,
and takes delight in prosperous days?
Taste and see the goodness of the Lord.
Keep your tongue from evil
and your lips from speaking guile;
Turn from evil, and do good;
seek peace, and follow after it.
Taste and see the goodness of the Lord.

READING II   Eph 5, 15–20
Keep careful watch over your conduct. Do
not act like fools, but like thoughtful men.
Make the most of the present opportunity,
for these are evil days. Do not continue in
ignorance, but try to discern the will of the
Lord. Avoid getting drunk on wine that leads
to debauchery. Be filled with the Spirit, addressing one another in psalms and hymns
and inspired songs. Sing praise to the Lord
with all your hearts. Give thanks to God the
Father always and for everything in the
name of our Lord Jesus Christ.

GOSPEL   Jn 6, 51–58
Jesus said to the crowds:
"I myself am the living bread
come down from heaven.
If anyone eats this bread
he shall live forever;
the bread I will give
is my flesh, for the life of the world."
At this the Jews quarreled among themselves, saying, "How can he give us his flesh
to eat?" Thereupon Jesus said to them:
"Let me solemnly assure you,
if you do not eat the flesh of the Son
of Man
and drink his blood,
you have no life in you.
He who feeds on my flesh
and drinks my blood
has life eternal,
and I will raise him up on the last day.
For my flesh is real food
and my blood real drink.
The man who feeds on my flesh
and drinks my blood
remains in me, and I in him.
Just as the Father who has life sent me
and I have life because of the Father,
so the man who feeds on me
will have life because of me.
This is the bread that came down from
heaven.
Unlike your ancestors who ate and died
nonetheless,
the man who feeds on this bread shall
live forever."

Reflection on the Readings

No one is an island. It is part of our nature to be in union, in communion with another. Originally, we were part of our parents. As we became individuated, we felt alone, unbonded. There is a desire in each one of us to be one with another. This hunger can only partially be filled by human intimacy. Ultimately, rest and peace come only when we enjoy union, communion, with God. When we enjoy this communion, we experience ourselves as really real, fully alive.

God our Father has always known this. Jesus is our most profound link with God. When we are in communion with Jesus, we are in union with God. Jesus replies to the unbelievers, "If you do not eat the flesh of the Son of Man and drink his blood, you will not have life in you. Anyone who does eat my flesh and drink my blood has eternal life." Jesus adds, "As I, who am sent by the living Father, myself draw life from the Father, so whoever eats me will draw life from me."

Jesus, at the Last Supper, instituted the Eucharist. Throughout Christian history, Jesus has given himself to us in the Eucharist. Through baptism, we become members of the Church, the body of Christ. Through the Eucharist, we are nourished and kept alive in faith. Every time we partake of the Eucharist, we are reminded whose body we are.

Suggestions for Prayer

1. Reflect on one or more of the following questions:
   - Do you believe that Holy Communion is necessary if you wish to grow in your relationship with Jesus?
   - Do you really believe that when you are in communion with Jesus, you are in union with God?
   - Do you believe that anyone who is an island is already in hell?
2. In your imagination, place yourself in a Catholic church during the rite of Communion. As each person returns to the pew, you recognize Jesus within them. Jesus says to you, "He (she) who eats my flesh and drinks my blood lives in me and I in him (her)."
3. Pray the responsorial psalm as your evening prayer this week. Continue to delight in the Lord.

Suggestion for Journal Keeping

Report in your journal an experience in which you felt very alone. In your goodness you were grossly misunderstood. Identify with Jesus who gave himself totally and yet was rejected.

Michael J. Koch

Twentieth Sunday of the Year

READING I   Jer 38, 4–6. 8–10

The princes said to the king: "Jeremiah ought to be put to death; he demoralizes the soldiers who are left in this city, and all the people, by speaking such things to them; he is not interested in the welfare of our people, but in their ruin." King Zedekiah answered: "He is in your power"; for the king could do nothing with them. And so they took Jeremiah and threw him into the cistern of Prince Malchiah, which was in the quarters of the guard, letting him down with

ropes. There was no water in the cistern, only mud, and Jeremiah sank into the mud.

Ebed-melech went to the Gate of Benjamin from the palace and said to the king: "My lord king, these men have been at fault in all they have done to the prophet Jeremiah, casting him into the cistern. He will die of famine on the spot, for there is no more food in the city." Then the king ordered Ebed-melech the Cushite to take three men along with him, and draw the prophet Jeremiah out of the cistern before he should die.

Responsorial Psalm   Ps 40, 2. 3. 4. 18
Lord, come to my aid!
I have waited, waited for the Lord,
   and he stooped toward me.
Lord, come to my aid!
   The Lord heard my cry.
He drew me out of the pit of destruction,
   out of the mud of the swamp;
He set my feet upon a crag;
   he made firm my steps.
Lord, come to my aid!
And he put a new song into my mouth,
   a hymn to our God.
Many shall look on in awe
   and trust in the Lord.
Lord, come to my aid!
Though I am afflicted and poor,
   yet the Lord thinks of me.
You are my help and my deliverer;
   O my God, hold not back!
Lord, come to my aid!

READING II   Heb 12, 1–4
Since we for our part are surrounded by a cloud of witnesses; let us lay aside every encumbrance of sin which clings to us and persevere in running the race which lies ahead;
let us keep our eyes fixed on Jesus, who inspires and perfects our faith. For the sake of the joy which lay before him he endured the cross, heedless of its shame. He has taken his seat at the right of the throne of God. Remember how he endured the opposition of sinners; hence do not grow despondent or abandon the struggle.

GOSPEL   Lk 12, 49–53
Jesus said to his disciples: "I have come to light a fire on the earth. How I wish the blaze were ignited! I have a baptism to receive. What anguish I feel till it is over! Do you think I have come to establish peace on the earth? I assure you, the contrary is true; I have come for division. From now on, a household of five will be divided three against two and two against three; father will be split against son and son against father, mother against daughter and daughter against mother, mother-in-law against daughter-in-law, daughter-in-law against mother-in-law."

Reflection on the Readings
Jeremiah strongly resisted the call to be a prophet to the king of Israel. He knew that to proclaim the truth and to call Israel to faithfulness would cost him his life. He was not a popular man because he challenged the values and the morals of his day, upsetting important people in high places. But for Jeremiah to be faithful to God was a priority above all else, even above life itself.

In the early Church many thought being a Christian would mean a life of peace and contentment, a life without pain or struggle. Faithfulness and fidelity to Jesus Christ and the proclamation of the values and morals of God's kingdom revealed that to be a disciple of Christ could bring about division among friends and family. The Gospel of Jesus called for a radical way of life that often stood in contradiction to the popular beliefs of the people. And for those who remained radically faithful to the Gospel, it could mean suffering and death.

Complacency is deadly to the fulfillment of the Gospel. In the Letter to the Hebrews, the reader is challenged to persevere and to keep one's eyes focused on Jesus. To be a follower of Jesus, faithful to the Gospel, causes one's life to be challenged to its core. The values and morals of each generation will inevitably come into conflict with the Gospel of Jesus Christ.

Suggestions for Prayer

1. As you watch television, what values and morals do you hear being proclaimed? How are these morals and values in agreement or conflict with your own personal morals and values and those of the Gospel? Where do you hear God affirming or challenging you in your own morals and values?
2. Read the psalm slowly, reflecting on its message for you in your life.
3. Reflect silently on what it means for you to be faithful to the Gospel and to be a prophet of God. Where in your life do you experience the call to be prophetic with your family, friends, workplace, neighborhood? In silence present any fears or concerns that arise to God, asking for strength and courage.

Suggestion for Journal Keeping

Bring to mind someone you consider a modern day prophet. (examples might be Mahatma Gandhi, Dorothy Day, Martin Luther King, Anwar Sadat, etc.). Write a letter to the person, expressing your feelings about him or her, and your own questions and concerns about being a prophet. Through your writing have the person respond to you. At the end of the dialogue, write a prayer that reflects your feelings, your hopes and your concerns about what it means to be a prophet.

Kathleen Brown

Twenty-First Sunday of the Year A

READING I   Is 22, 15. 19–23
Thus says the Lord, the God of hosts:
 Up, go to that official,
 Shebna, master of the palace:
"I will thrust you from your office
 and pull you down from your station.

On that day I will summon my servant
 Eliakim, son of Hilkiah;
I will clothe him with your robe,
 and gird him with your sash,
 and give over to him your authority.
He shall be a father to the inhabitants of
  Jerusalem,
 and to the house of Judah.
I will place the key of the House of David
 on his shoulder;
 when he opens, no one shall shut,
 when he shuts, no one shall open.
I will fix him like a peg in a sure spot,
 to be a place of honor for his family."

Responsorial Psalm   Ps 138, 1–2. 2–3. 6. 8
Lord, your love is eternal;
 do not forsake the work of your hands.

I will give thanks to you, O Lord, with all
   my heart,
   [for you have heard the words of my
      mouth;]
   in the presence of the angels I will sing
      your praise;
I will worship at your holy temple.
Lord, your love is eternal;
   do not forsake the work of your hands.
I will give thanks to your name,
   because of your kindness and your truth:
When I called, you answered me;
   you built up strength within me.
Lord, your love is eternal;
   do not forsake the work of your hands.
The Lord is exalted, yet the lowly he sees,
   and the proud he knows from afar.
Your kindness, O Lord, endures forever;
   forsake not the work of your hands.
Lord, your love is eternal;
   do not forsake the work of your hands.

READING II Rom 11, 33–36

**How deep are the riches and the wisdom
and the knowledge of God! How inscrutable
his judgments, how unsearchable his ways!
For "who has known the mind of the Lord?
Or who has been his counselor? Who has
given him anything so as to deserve return?"
For from him and through him and for him
all things are. To him be glory forever.
Amen.**

GOSPEL Mt 16, 13–20

**When Jesus came to the neighborhood of
Caesarea Philippi, he asked his disciples this
question: "Who do people say that the Son
of Man is?" They replied, "Some say John
the Baptizer, others Elijah, still others Jeremiah or one of the prophets." "And you,"
he said to them, "who do you say that I am?"**

**"You are the Messiah," Simon Peter an-
swered, "the Son of the living God!" Jesus
replied, "Blest are you, Simon son of John!
No mere man has revealed this to you, but
my heavenly Father. I for my part declare to
you, you are 'Rock,' and on this rock I will
build my church, and the jaws of death shall
not prevail against it. I will entrust to you the
keys of the kingdom of heaven. Whatever
you declare bound on earth shall be bound
in heaven; whatever you declare loosed on
earth shall be loosed in heaven." Then he
strictly ordered his disciples not to tell anyone that he was the Messiah.**

Reflection on the Readings

Where does authority come from? To understand today's reading we must first ask
that question. Living in a democracy, our answer naturally is "from the people." The biblical answer is different, and can be hard for
us to accept.

In today's second reading Paul talks about
the wisdom and knowledge of God. God is
the Creator. God needs no counselor. Everything comes from God—everything, including authority.

In the first reading Isaiah prophesies that
Shebna will be pulled down from his position
and Eliakim will take his place. Who makes
the change? Who will fix Eliakim like a peg
in a sure spot? None other than God, who
created the world in the first place!

In the Gospel, Jesus asks the disciples a key
question, "Who am I?" Simon Peter answers,
"The Messiah, the Son of the living God."
With what authority does Jesus speak then?
He then tells Peter that he will be the "rock
of the Church" and gives him authority to
bind and loose sins. Peter's authority comes
from God. The Church's authority comes

from God as well. What gives the whole thing a different slant is Jesus' preaching on authority. Authority is for service. Those in power are not to make their importance felt; rather, they are to be the servants of the people. To be a Christian means to be a servant in God's kingdom.

Suggestions for Prayer

1. Think about the people who have power in your life. Reflect on the way they use their power. Pray for them, that they be reflections of God's authority.
2. Imagine yourself as one of the disciples. Imagine Jesus asking you the question: Who do you say that I am? Think of different answers to the question.
3. Baptized people have the right to participate in the sacrament of reconciliation. What sins would you tell the priest in that sacrament? How would you feel, knowing that these could be forgiven? Ask the Lord to help you get ready for that sacrament.

Suggestion for Journal Keeping

Write down a bad experience you've had with authority. What made it bad? Have you ever used your authority badly?

Michael P. Enright

Twenty-First Sunday of the Year B

READING I   Jos 24, 1–2. 15–17. 18
Joshua gathered together all the tribes of Israel at Shechem, summoning their elders, their leaders, their judges and their officers. When they stood in ranks before God, Joshua addressed all the people: "If it does not please you to serve the Lord, decide today whom you will serve, the gods your fathers served beyond the River or the gods of the Amorites in whose country you are dwelling. As for me and my household, we will serve the Lord."

But the people answered, "Far be it from us to forsake the Lord for the service of other gods. For it was the Lord, our God, who brought us and our fathers up out of the land of Egypt, out of a state of slavery. He performed those great miracles before our very eyes and protected us along our entire journey and among all the peoples through whom we passed. Therefore we also will serve the Lord, for he is our God."

Responsorial Psalm   Ps 34, 2–3. 16–17. 18–19. 20–21. 22–23
Taste and see the goodness of the Lord.
I will bless the Lord at all times;
his praise shall be ever in my mouth.
Let my soul glory in the Lord;
the lowly will hear me and be glad.
Taste and see the goodness of the Lord.
The Lord has eyes for the just,
and ears for their cry.
The Lord confronts the evildoers,
to destroy remembrance of them from the earth.
Taste and see the goodness of the Lord.
When the just cry out, the Lord hears them,
and from all their distress he rescues them.
The Lord is close to the brokenhearted;
and those who are crushed in spirit he saves.
Taste and see the goodness of the Lord.

Many are the troubles of the just man,
  but out of them all the Lord delivers him;
He watches over all his bones;
  not one of them shall be broken.
Taste and see the goodness of the Lord.
Vice slays the wicked,
  and the enemies of the just pay for their
    guilt.
But the Lord redeems the lives of his servants;
  no one incurs guilt who takes refuge in
    him.
Taste and see the goodness of the Lord.

READING II   Eph 5, 21–32
Defer to one another out of reverence for Christ.

Wives should be submissive to their husbands as if to the Lord because the husband is head of his wife just as Christ is head of his body, the church, as well as its savior. As the church submits to Christ, so wives should submit to their husbands in everything.

Husbands, love your wives, as Christ loved the church. He gave himself up for her to make her holy, purifying her in the bath of water by the power of the word, to present to himself a glorious church, holy and immaculate, without stain or wrinkle or anything of that sort. Husbands should love their wives as they do their own bodies. He who loves his wife loves himself. Observe that no one ever hates his own flesh; no, he nourishes it and takes care of it as Christ cares for the church—for we are members of his body.

"For this reason a man shall leave his fa-
    ther and mother,
  and shall cling to his wife,
  and the two shall be made into one."

This is a great foreshadowing; I mean that it refers to Christ and the church.

GOSPEL   Jn 6, 60–69
Many of the disciples of Jesus remarked, "This sort of talk is hard to endure! How can anyone take it seriously?" Jesus was fully aware that his disciples were murmuring in protest at what he had said. "Does it shake your faith?" he asked them.

  "What, then, if you were to see the Son
    of Man
  ascend to where he was before . . . ?
  It is the spirit that gives life;
  the flesh is useless.
  The words I spoke to you
  are spirit and life.
  Yet among you there are some who do
    not believe."

(Jesus knew from the start, of course, the ones who refused to believe, and the one who would hand him over.) He went on to say:

  "This is why I have told you
  that no one can come to me
  unless it is granted him by the Father."

From this time on, many of his disciples broke away and would not remain in his company any longer. Jesus then said to the Twelve, "Do you want to leave me too?" Simon Peter answered him, "Lord, to whom shall we go? You have the words of eternal life. We have come to believe; we are convinced that you are God's holy one."

Reflection on the Readings

The media seem to be eternally puzzled by the teaching of the Catholic Church. Whenever the Church is in the news, one inevitably hears the media litany that the Church is against this or for that. The media, looking at these issues from a mere secular point of view, from a non-faith point of view, could not possibly understand. "This is intolerable teaching. How could anyone accept it."

In the Gospel readings for the last few Sundays, Jesus has been saying, "I am the bread of life; if you eat my flesh and drink my blood, you will have eternal life." Many of the followers of Jesus deserted him. "This is intolerable language. How could anyone accept it." They wanted intellectual answers, answers they could understand. Their faith was too shallow. They did not trust Jesus. Jesus addressed the Twelve: "What about you? Do you want to go away too?" The apostles were just as puzzled; they did not understand either. But because they loved Jesus, they believed, they accepted him without understanding. Peter says, "Lord, to whom shall we go? You have the message of eternal life, and we believe; we know that you are the Holy One of God."

We cannot really understand how Jesus is present in the Eucharist, how bread and wine can become the body and blood of Jesus. However, when we make our act of faith, we are bonded to the Lord in a loving, life-giving way.

Suggestions for Prayer

1. Reflect on one or more of the following questions?
   - How did you respond when you found yourself in a situation where you couldn't understand something? Did loving or not loving the speaker make any difference?
   - Why did Simon Peter answer: Lord, to whom shall we go? You have the message of eternal life and we believe"?

2. In your imagination, pla.... the company of Jesus. teaching. You hear some lowers say, "This is into guage. How could anyone .... Jesus walks up to you and says, "What about you? Do you want to go away too?" How do you respond?

3. Pray the responsorial psalm as your evening prayer this week. Note that the verses are different from the previous two weeks.

Suggestion for Journal Keeping

Recall an experience where you did not understand what was going on. You had some insight, but much more evaded you. How much did you accept or reject? How much did your relationship to the speaker affect your decision? Did Peter's response help you?

Michael J. Koch

Twenty-First Sunday of the Year

READING I   Is 66, 18–21
I come to gather nations of every language; they shall come and see my glory. I will set a sign among them; from them I will send fugitives to the nations: to Tarshish, Put and Lud, Mosoch, Tubal and Javan, to the distant coastlands that have never heard of my fame, or seen my glory; and they shall proclaim my glory among the nations. They shall bring all your brethren from all the nations as an offering to the Lord, on horses

in chariots, in carts, upon mules and romedaries, to Jerusalem, my holy mountain, says the Lord, just as the Israelites bring their offering to the house of the Lord in clean vessels. Some of these I will take as priests and Levites, says the Lord.

Responsorial Psalm Ps 117, 1. 2
Go out to all the world
  and tell the Good News.
Praise the Lord, all you nations;
  glorify him, all you peoples!
Go out to all the world
  and tell the Good News.
For steadfast is his kindness toward us,
  and the fidelity of the Lord endures forever.
Go out to all the world
  and tell the Good News.

READING II Heb 12, 5–7. 11–13
You have forgotten the encouraging words addressed to you as sons:
"My sons, do not disdain the discipline of
    the Lord
  nor lose heart when he reproves you;
For, whom the Lord loves, he disciplines;
  he scourges every son he receives."
Endure your trials as the discipline of God, who deals with you as sons. For what son is there whom his father does not discipline? At the time it is administered, all discipline seems a cause for grief and not for joy, but later it brings forth the fruit of peace and justice to those who are trained in its school. So strengthen your drooping hands and your weak knees. Make straight the paths you walk on, that your halting limbs may not be dislocated but healed.

GOSPEL Lk 13, 22–30
Jesus went through cities and towns teaching—all the while making his way toward Jerusalem. Someone asked him, "Lord, are they few in number who are to be saved?" He replied: "Try to come in through the narrow door. Many, I tell you, will try to enter and be unable. When once the master of the house has risen to lock the door and you stand outside knocking and saying, 'Sir, open for us,' he will say in reply, 'I do not know where you come from.' Then you will begin to say, 'We ate and drank in your company. You taught in our streets.' But he will answer, 'I tell you, I do not know where you come from. Away from me, you evildoers!'

"There will be wailing and grinding of teeth when you see Abraham, Isaac, Jacob, and all the prophets safe in the kingdom of God, and you yourselves rejected. People will come from the east and the west, from the north and the south, and will take their place at the feast in the kingdom of God. Some who are last will be first and some who are first will be last."

Reflection on the Readings
   The good news, as proclaimed by the prophet Isaiah, is that God intends to gather together all the people of the earth. Just as God has saved the Israelites, God will now be the God of all nations. All the peoples of the earth will come to know and see the glory of God.

   Even though the promise of salvation was offered to all, there were some who rejected it and who in consequence are rejected from the feast of the kingdom of God. In response to a question of whether there would be a lot of people saved, Jesus tells the story of the person who desired to get into the master's house, claiming to know the master, to have even eaten with him and to have heard him teach in the streets. The master of the house would not let him in, denying that he ever knew him. Jesus then raised a caution to those who were gathered. No one receives the kingdom because of ancestry. Rather, one must hear the word of God and live it in one's life in order to gain access to the feast of the kingdom. To do this is to come in through the narrow door. Those who fail to hear the word of the Lord and to respond to it will be turned away from the feast.

The Letter to the Hebrews speaks of a narrow door as well, but in terms of discipline. Discipline brings forth the fruit of peace and justice in one's life and in the world. The Gospel asks of us to be strong, to continue to make straight our lives and to endure our trials. Through our lives lived as disciples of Christ, we will come to know and see the glory of God.

Suggestions for Prayer

1. Reflect on the following questions: How do you hear the word of God addressing you in your own life? In what ways do you hear God offering you salvation?
2. As you reread the second reading reflect on what it means to be called to bear the fruit of peace and justice in your personal life, in your neighborhood, in your city, in the country.
3. Reflect on the meaning of God gathering nations of every language. What does this mean for world peace, for unity, for future generations? Compose a prayer that expresses your desires and hopes for the future of all God's people.

Suggestion for Journal Keeping

In your journal write what "to be saved" means for you. Describe an event in your life when you have experienced being rescued, protected or saved. In light of this experience, journal what it means for you to be saved by God. Finish by writing a prayer that expresses your needs, your hopes, your thankfulness.

Kathleen Brown

Twenty-Second Sunday of the Year A

READING I   Jer 20, 7–9
You duped me, O Lord, and I let myself be duped;
  you were too strong for me, and you triumphed.
All the day I am an object of laughter; everyone mocks me.
Whenever I speak, I must cry out, violence and outrage is my message;
The word of the Lord has brought me derision and reproach all the day.
I say to myself, I will not mention him, I will speak in his name no more.
But then it becomes like fire burning in my heart,
  imprisoned in my bones;
I grow weary holding it in, I cannot endure it.

Responsorial Psalm   Ps 63, 2. 3–4. 5–6. 8–9

My soul is thirsting for you, O Lord my God.

O God, you are my God whom I seek;
for you my flesh pines and my soul thirsts
like the earth, parched, lifeless and without water.
My soul is thirsting for you, O Lord my God.
Thus have I gazed toward you in the sanctuary
to see your power and your glory,
For your kindness is a greater good than life;
my lips shall glorify you.
My soul is thirsting for you, O Lord my God.
Thus will I bless you while I live;
lifting up my hands, I will call upon your name.
As with the riches of a banquet shall my soul be satisfied,
and with exultant lips my mouth shall praise you.
My soul is thirsting for you, O Lord my God.
You are my help,
and in the shadow of your wings I shout for joy.
My soul clings fast to you;
your right hand upholds me.
My soul is thirsting for you, O Lord my God.

READING II   Rom 12, 1–2

Brothers, I beg you through the mercy of God to offer your bodies as a living sacrifice holy and acceptable to God, your spiritual worship. Do not conform yourselves to this age, but be transformed by the renewal of your mind, so that you may judge what is God's will, what is good, pleasing and perfect.

GOSPEL   Mt 16, 21–27

From then on Jesus [the Messiah] started to indicate to his disciples that he must go to Jerusalem to suffer greatly there at the hands of the elders, the chief priests, and the scribes, and to be put to death, and raised up on the third day. At this, Peter took him aside and began to remonstrate with him. "May you be spared, Master! God forbid that any such thing ever happen to you!" Jesus turned on Peter and said, "Get out of my sight, you satan! You are trying to make me trip and fall. You are not judging by God's standards but by man's."

Jesus then said to his disciples: "If a man wishes to come after me, he must deny his very self, take up his cross, and begin to follow in my footsteps. Whoever would save his life will lose it, but whoever loses his life for my sake will find it. What profit would a man show if he were to gain the whole world and ruin himself in the process? What can a man offer in exchange for his very self? The Son of Man will come with his Father's glory accompanied by his angels. When he does, he will repay each man according to his conduct.

Reflection on the Readings

To be a Christian is difficult. To be a messenger of God means being uncomfortable. It may even mean death. This is Jesus' message to his disciples. Peter didn't like the sound of Jesus' prediction of his own death. Jesus, though, had a radically different set of values and priorities. What seemed foolish to Peter was part of God's plan.

Jeremiah, a messenger from God, could find no comfort. If he spoke the message, he was laughed to scorn. If he tried to hold it in, it became a burning fire in his heart. He agreed to be a prophet and then suffered because of his role.

The Gospel demands that Christians take a stand. It demands that we stand for a different reality. It demands that we not be conformists but that we learn to judge God's will and do it. Does this mean that we all become fanatics? Does this mean that to live your vocation as a Christian you have to stand on street corners and preach against this age? No, it does not.

What it means is that you are obligated to take up your cross. It means that you will be uncomfortable with injustice. It means that you learn to pray and judge by God's standards. It means that you follow Jesus, through death to resurrection!

Suggestions for Prayer

1. Look back over your life, and try to remember a time when you picked up the cross. What was your cross? How did you pick it up? Did you feel Jesus' presence as you did what you did?
2. Pray the responsorial psalm from today. Imagine yourself "parched, lifeless, and without water." Turn the psalm over in your mind and imagine the right hand of God upholding you.
3. Reflect on the life of one of the martyrs. If you do not know about any, look up Acts 6:8–7:60. Where do you think martyrs get their courage?

Suggestion for Journal Keeping

Write down a time in your life when you stood up for justice. What happened? Was it difficult? Did you feel God's presence in this experience?

Michael P. Enright

Twenty-Second Sunday of the Year

READING I   Dt 4, 1–2. 6–8
Moses told the people: "Now, Israel, hear the statutes and decrees which I am teaching you to observe, that you may live, and may enter in and take possession of the land which the Lord, the God of your fathers, is giving you. In your observance of the commandments of the Lord, your God, which I enjoin upon you, you shall not add to what I command you nor subtract from it. Observe them carefully, for thus will you give evidence of your wisdom and intelligence to the nations, who will hear of all these statutes and say, 'This great nation is truly a wise and intelligent people.' For what great nation is there that has gods so close to it as the Lord, our God, is to us whenever we call upon him? Or what great nation has statutes and decrees that are as just as this whole law which I am setting before you today?"

Responsorial Psalm   Ps 15, 2–3. 3–4. 4–5
He who does justice will live in the
     presence of the Lord.
**He who walks blamelessly and does justice;
     who thinks the truth in his heart
     and slanders not with his tongue.**
He who does justice will live in the
     presence of the Lord.
Who harms not his fellow man,

nor takes up a reproach against his neighbor;
By whom the reprobate is despised,
    while he honors those who fear the Lord.
He who does justice will live in the
    presence of the Lord.
Who lends not his money at usury
    and accepts no bribe against the innocent.
He who does these things
    shall never be disturbed.
He who does justice will live in the
    presence of the Lord.

READING II   Jas 1, 17–18. 21–22. 27
Every worthwhile gift, every genuine benefit comes from above, descending from the Father of the heavenly luminaries, who cannot change and who is never shadowed over. He wills to bring us to birth with a word spoken in truth so that we may be a kind of firstfruits of his creatures.

Humbly welcome the word that has taken root in you, with its power to save you. Act on this word. If all you do is listen to it, you are deceiving yourselves.

Looking after orphans and widows in their distress and keeping oneself unspotted by the world make for pure worship without stain before our God and Father.

GOSPEL   Mk 7, 1–8. 14–15. 21–23
The Pharisees and some of the experts in the law who had come from Jerusalem gathered around Jesus. They had observed a few of his disciples eating meals without having purified—that is to say, washed—their hands. The Pharisees, and in fact all Jews, cling to the custom of their ancestors and never eat without scrupulously washing their hands.

Moreover, they never eat anything from the market without first sprinkling it. There are many other traditions they observe—for example, the washing of cups and jugs and kettles. So the Pharisees and the scribes questioned him: "Why do your disciples not follow the tradition of our ancestors, but instead take food without purifying their hands?" He said to them: "How accurately Isaiah prophesied about you hypocrites when he wrote,

'This people pays me lip service
    but their heart is far from me.
Empty is the reverence they do me
    because they teach as dogmas mere
        human precepts.'
You disregard God's commandment and cling to what is human tradition."

He summoned the crowd again and said to them: "Hear me, all of you, and try to understand. Nothing that enters a man from outside can make him impure; that which comes out of him, and only that, constitutes impurity. Let everyone heed what he hears!"

"Wicked designs come from the deep recesses of the heart: acts of fornication, theft, murder, adulterous conduct, greed, maliciousness, deceit, sensuality, envy, blasphemy, arrogance, an obtuse spirit. All these evils come from within and render a man impure."

Reflection on the Readings
    It is interesting to observe people gathered together in a Sunday eucharistic liturgy. Some have been praying all week. They are very close to the Lord. When they participate in the Sunday worship, one can sense integrity in them. Their responses, gestures, and song come from the heart. Others who come

to the liturgy are quite artificial. Their external behavior has no internal root. Only their external selves are present. They come because of habit, tradition, or law. They come late, gawk around, and leave early. Their hearts are somewhere else.

The Gospel today addresses the question of external practices and internal faith. The Pharisees criticize Jesus and his disciples for not following the Jewish ablution rituals. "Why do your disciples not respect the traditions of the elders but eat their food with unclean hands?" they ask Jesus. Jesus fires back at the Pharisees and scribes and calls them hypocrites. Jesus quotes Isaiah, "This people honors me only with lip service, their hearts are far from me." Jesus says furthermore, "You put aside the commandments of God to cling to human traditions. It is not what goes into a man's stomach that makes him unclean, but what comes out of his heart."

Maintaining integrity is a lifelong project. Our external behavior must flow from internal conviction and life if we are to be authentic. Practices that flow only from habit, tradition, or law—that is, external criteria—destroy integrity.

Suggestions for Prayer

1. Reflect on one or more of the following questions:
   - Do you believe that external religious practice without internal conviction is worthless?
   - Why would the Pharisees and scribes want Jesus and his disciples to "respect the tradition of the elders"?
   - What are some of the things which come out of people that makes them unclean?
2. In your imagination, place yourself in a large church. Jesus comes to the pulpit. He says, "You people honor me only with lip-service, while your hearts are far from me. The worship you offer me is worthless, the doctrines you teach are only human regulations." What is the people's reaction? What is your reaction?
3. Pray the responsorial psalm as your evening prayer this week.

Suggestion for Journal Keeping

Record in your journal some incident in your experience where you truly lacked integrity. Your internal self was miles from your external expression. How did you feel during that time? What did your friends say? What impact did you make?

Michael J. Koch

Twenty-Second Sunday of the Year

READING I   Sir 3, 17–18. 20. 28–29
My son, conduct your affairs with humility,
   and you will be loved more than a giver of gifts.
Humble yourself the more, the greater you are,
   and you will find favor with God.
What is too sublime for you, seek not,
   into things beyond your strength search not.

The mind of a sage appreciates proverbs,
   and an attentive ear is the wise man's joy.
Water quenches a flaming fire,
   and alms atone for sins.

Responsorial Psalm   Ps 68, 4–5. 6–7. 10–11
God, in your goodness, you have made a
   home for the poor.
The just rejoice and exult before God;
   they are glad and rejoice.
Sing to God, chant praise to his name;
   whose name is the Lord.
God, in your goodness, you have made a
   home for the poor.
The father of orphans and the defender of
   widows
   is God in his holy dwelling.
God gives a home to the forsaken;
   he leads forth prisoners to prosperity.
God, in your goodness, you have made a
   home for the poor.
A bountiful rain you showered down, O
   God, upon your inheritance;
   you restored the land when it languished;
Your flock settled in it;
   in your goodness, O God, you provided it
   for the needy.
God, in your goodness, you have made a
   home for the poor.

READING II   Heb 12, 18–19. 22–24
You have not drawn near to an untouchable
mountain and a blazing fire, and gloomy
darkness and storm and trumpet blast, and a
voice speaking words such that those who
heard begged that they be not addressed to
them. No, you have drawn near to Mount
Zion and the city of the living God, the heav-
enly Jerusalem, to myriads of angels in festal
gathering, to the assembly of the first-born
enrolled in heaven, to God the judge of all,

to the spirits of just men made perfect, to Jesus, the mediator of a new covenant.

GOSPEL   Lk 14, 1. 7–14
When Jesus came on a sabbath to eat a meal
in the house of one of the leading Pharisees,
they observed him closely.
   He went on to address a parable to the
guests, noticing how they were trying to get
the places of honor at the table: "When you
are invited by someone to a wedding party,
do not sit in the place of honor in case some
greater dignitary has been invited. Then the
host might come and say to you, 'Make room
for this man,' and you would have to proceed shamefacedly to the lowest place.
What you should do when you have been invited is go and sit in the lowest place, so that
when your host approaches you he will say,
'My friend, come up higher.' This will win
you the esteem of your fellow guests. For
everyone who exalts himself shall be humbled and he who humbles himself shall be
exalted."
   He said to the one who had invited him:
"Whenever you give a lunch or dinner, do
not invite your friends or brothers or relatives or wealthy neighbors. They might invite you in return and thus repay you. No,
when you have a reception, invite beggars
and the crippled, the lame and the blind.
You should be pleased that they cannot repay you, for you will be repaid in the resurrection of the just."

Reflection on the Readings
   Humility is often misunderstood. Some
people believe that to be humble is to put
oneself down, to think less of oneself, denying one's giftedness. In the first reading from
Sirach, the father advises the son to conduct

336

his affairs with humility, not thinking of himself as greater or less than others. Rather, the better way is to stand in a balance, acknowledging oneself with honesty and as an equal to others. To do so is to appreciate the gift of life from God.

When attending a sabbath meal and seeing everyone trying to get the seats of honor, Jesus told those who were gathered not to attempt to sit in the place of honor. After all, the host could ask them to move when someone with greater dignity arrives. Then one would, in shame, have to take a lower place at the table. It is better to be exalted by the host than to exalt oneself.

Jesus goes on to admonish his host about his invited guests. It is not enough to invite only one's friends; rather the lame, the blind, the poor, those rejected by the society of Jesus' time, should be invited.

The questions of where one is to sit and who is to attend the meal are about the feast of the kingdom of God. The good news is that those who do not think themselves worthy will be welcomed at the feast and the lowly will be exalted. The beggars, the crippled, the lame, the blind, will all be cared for and enjoy God's salvation. For in God's eyes all are equal.

Suggestions for Prayer

1. As a child what was your understanding of humility? How has that understanding changed for you? Listen again to the words of the first reading, silently reflecting on their meaning for your life.
2. Prayerfully reread the psalm and reflect on its significance in your life.
3. Reflect on your own attitude toward the poor, the homeless, the jobless, the illit-

erate, different races. How does the Gospel enlighten your understanding of God's presence in them? In your imagination, see Jesus come to you and invite you to meet these people. Listen to them speak to you and hear your response.

Suggestion For Journal Keeping

Write in your journal your experiences of being invited to come to know Jesus. Who are the people that have invited you to come to know you are welcomed and loved by God? Write a letter to God expressing your feelings about this journey toward God and about the people who have invited you onto this road, giving thanks for them in your life.

Kathleen Brown

Twenty-Third Sunday of the Year   A

READING I   Ez 33, 7–9
You, son of man, I have appointed watchman for the house of Israel; when you hear me say anything, you shall warn them for me. If I tell the wicked man that he shall surely die, and you do not speak out to dissuade the wicked man from his way, he [the wicked man] shall die for his guilt, but I will hold you responsible for his death. But if you warn the wicked man, trying to turn him from his way, and he refuses to turn from his way, he shall die for his guilt, but you shall save yourself.

Responsorial Psalm   Ps 95, 1–2. 6–7. 8–9
If today you hear his voice,
   harden not your hearts.

Come, let us sing joyfully to the Lord;
　let us acclaim the Rock of our salvation.
Let us greet him with thanksgiving;
　let us joyfully sing psalms to him.
If today you hear his voice,
　harden not your hearts.
Come, let us bow down in worship;
　let us kneel before the Lord who made us.
For he is our God,
　and we are the people he shepherds, the
　　flock he guides.
If today you hear his voice,
　harden not your hearts.
Oh, that today you would hear his voice:
　"Harden not your hearts as at Meribah,
　as in the day of Massah in the desert,
Where your fathers tempted me;
　they tested me though they had seen my
　　works."
If today you hear his voice,
　harden not your hearts.

READING II　　　　　　　　　　Rom 13, 8–10
Owe no debt to anyone except the debt that
binds us to love one another. He who loves
his neighbor has fulfilled the law. The commandments, "You shall not commit adultery; you shall not murder; you shall not
steal; you shall not covet," and any other
commandment there may be are all summed
up in this, "You shall love your neighbor as
yourself." Love never does any wrong to the
neighbor, hence love is the fulfillment of the
law.

GOSPEL　　　　　　　　　　　　Mt 18, 15–20
Jesus said to his disciples: "If your brother
should commit some wrong against you, go
and point out his fault, but keep it between
the two of you. If he listens to you, you have
won your brother over. If he does not listen,

however, summon another, so that every
case may stand on the word of two or three
witnesses. If he ignores them, refer it to the
church. If he ignores even the church, then
treat him as you would a Gentile or a tax collector. I assure you, whatever you declare
bound on earth shall be held bound in
heaven, and whatever you declare loosed on
earth shall be held loosed in heaven.

"Again I tell you, if two of you join your
voices on earth to pray for anything whatever, it shall be granted you by my Father in
heaven. Where two or three are gathered in
my name, there am I in their midst."

Reflection on the Readings
　What do we do when someone wrongs us?
How do we respond? Writing to the Romans,
Paul reminds us that the greatest commandment is to love our neighbors as ourselves.
Our response should come out of love.
　The response outlined in today's Gospel is
different from our usual response. Our response to being wronged is often enough to
complain to someone else about our hurt
feelings (anger, or whatever). The Gospel response calls for a certain amount of courage
and is motivated by love.
　The first reading also touches on the responsibility we have to correct our brothers
and sisters. It is not a responsibility to be
taken lightly. What is at stake is important—
the health of the individual and of the community.
　What if someone does not respond? The
Gospel outlines the steps to take, and the final resort is to treat the person as a Gentile or
tax collector. To the first Christians, coming
from Jewish origins, Gentiles and tax collectors were outcasts. But if we look once again
to Paul's letter, we find that they too should

be treated with love. Love does not mean accepting everything a person does. It does mean accepting the person.

Suggestions for Prayer

1. Remember the last time someone hurt you. What happened? Have you forgiven the person? Pray for him or her.
2. Reread the second reading. Do you love yourself? Do you love your neighbors? Ask God for forgiveness for when you have not.
3. Read the last part of the Gospel. Gather together with one or two other people and pray for what you need. Remember that Christ will be present with you.

Suggestion for Journal Keeping

Write down a time you tried to correct another person. What happened? Were you motivated by love? Did the person respond? How were things between you later?

Michael P. Enright

Twenty-Third Sunday of the Year B

READING I   Is 35, 4–7
Say to those whose hearts are frightened:
  Be strong, fear not!
Here is your God,
  he comes with vindication;
With divine recompense
  he comes to save you.
Then will the eyes of the blind be opened,
  the ears of the deaf be cleared;

Then will the lame leap like a stag,
  then the tongue of the dumb will sing.
Streams will burst forth in the desert,
  and rivers in the steppe.
The burning sands will become pools,
  and the thirsty ground, springs of water.

Responsorial Psalm   Ps 146, 7. 8–9. 9–10
Praise the Lord, my soul!
The God of Jacob keeps faith forever,
  secures justice for the oppressed,
  gives food to the hungry.
The Lord sets captives free.
Praise the Lord, my soul!
The Lord gives sight to the blind;
  the Lord raises up those that were bowed
  down.
The Lord loves the just;
  the Lord protects strangers.
Praise the Lord, my soul!
The fatherless and the widow the Lord sustains,
  but the way of the wicked he thwarts.
The Lord shall reign forever;
  your God, O Zion, through all generations.
  Alleluia.
Praise the Lord, my soul!

READING II   Jas 2, 1–5
My brothers, your faith in our Lord Jesus Christ glorified must not allow of favoritism. Suppose there should come into your assembly a man fashionably dressed, with gold rings on his fingers, and at the same time a poor man dressed in shabby clothes. Suppose further you were to take notice of the well-dressed man and say, "Sit right here, please;" whereas you were to say to the poor man, "You can stand!" or "Sit over

there by my footrest." Have you not in a case like this discriminated in your hearts? Have you not set yourselves up as judges who hand down corrupt decisions?

Listen, dear brothers. Did not God choose those who are poor in the eyes of the world to be rich in faith and heirs of the kingdom he promised to those who love him?

GOSPEL Mk 7, 31–37

Jesus left Tyrian territory and returned by way of Sidon to the Sea of Galilee, into the district of the Ten Cities. Some people brought him a deaf man who had a speech impediment and begged him to lay his hand on him. Jesus took him off by himself away from the crowd. He put his fingers into the man's ears and, spitting, touched his tongue; then he looked up to heaven and emitted a groan. He said to him, "Ephphatha!" (that is, "Be opened!") At once the man's ears were opened; he was freed from the impediment, and began to speak plainly. Then he enjoined them strictly not to tell anyone; but the more he ordered them not to, the more they proclaimed it. Their amazement went beyond all bounds: "He has done everything well! He makes the deaf hear and the mute speak!"

Reflection on the Readings

Deafness is a serious handicap. Sooner or later, each one of us meets up with a deaf person. Communication with such a person is very difficult and limited. To save embarrassment, people often just walk away from the deaf person. Being a deaf person can be very lonely. While deaf people cannot hear what others are saying, they also cannot speak well because when you cannot hear correctly, you cannot speak correctly.

In today's Gospel, the compassionate Jesus is met by a deaf man who has an impediment in his speech. The deaf man's friends ask Jesus to lay his hands on him and cure him. Jesus takes the man aside and in private cures him to save him embarrassment. Jesus has a sacramental style in his healing. He uses words, materials, and actions. He says, "Ephphatha" which means, "Be opened." Ephphatha was retained to emphasize Jesus' mysterious power. He uses spittle. In those days, spittle was believed to have a curative quality. His actions included looking up to heaven and touching the man's ears and tongue. Looking up to heaven implies that the healing comes from God. Once the deaf man could hear clearly, he could also speak clearly.

Working with and caring for handicapped persons can help us to learn understanding, compassion, and patience. As Jesus cured the physically deaf, so he can also cure the spiritually deaf. Only after we hear the Spirit clearly in our lives can we proclaim the good news of Jesus clearly and emphatically.

Suggestions for Prayer

1. Reflect on one or more of the following questions:
   - Why did Jesus use words, materials, and actions to cure the deaf man?
   - Why did Jesus look up to heaven when he prayed for the cure of the deaf man?
   - Why did the deaf man speak clearly after he had been healed from his deafness?
2. In your imagination, see yourself as a deaf person who cannot speak well. Jesus puts his finger in your ears and

340

touches your tongue with spittle. He says, "Be opened." Describe your new freedom.

3. Pray the responsorial psalm as your evening prayer this week.

Suggestion for Journal Keeping

Describe your journey from spiritual deafness to clearly hearing the word of God. What change has this brought into your life? Describe your journey from spiritual dumbness to joyfully proclaiming God's word. Has this healing made you more mission-conscious?

Michael J. Koch

Twenty-Third Sunday of the Year C

READING I   Wis 9, 13–18

For what man knows God's counsel,
  or who can conceive what the Lord intends?
For the deliberations of mortals are timid,
  and unsure are our plans.
For the corruptible body burdens the soul
  and the earthen shelter weighs down the
  mind that has many concerns.
And scarce do we guess the things on earth,
  and what is within our grasp we find with
  difficulty;
  but when things are in heaven, who can
  search them out?
Or who ever knew your counsel, except you
  had given Wisdom
  and sent your holy spirit from on high?
And thus were the paths of those on earth
  made straight.

Responsorial Psalm   Ps 90, 3–4. 5–6. 12–13. 14–17

In every age, O Lord, you have been our refuge.

You turn man back to dust,
  saying, "Return, O children of men."
For a thousand years in your sight
  are as yesterday, now that it is past,
  or as a watch of the night.
In every age, O Lord, you have been our refuge.

You make an end of them in their sleep;
  the next morning they are like the changing grass,
Which at dawn springs up anew,
  but by evening wilts and fades.
In every age, O Lord, you have been our refuge.

Teach us to number our days aright,
  that we may gain wisdom of heart.
Return, O Lord! How long?
  Have pity on your servants!
In every age, O Lord, you have been our refuge.

Fill us at daybreak with your kindness,
  that we may shout for joy and gladness all our days.
And may the gracious care of the Lord our God be ours;
  prosper the work of our hands for us!
  [Prosper the work of our hands!]
In every age, O Lord, you have been our refuge.

READING II   Phlm 9–10. 12–17

I, Paul, ambassador of Christ and now a prisoner for him, appeal to you for my child, whom I have begotten during my imprisonment. It is he I am sending to you—and that means I am sending my heart!

I had wanted to keep him with me, that he

341

might serve me in your place while I am in prison for the gospel; but I did not want to do anything without your consent, that kindness might not be forced on you but freely bestowed. Perhaps he was separated from you for a while for this reason: that you might possess him forever, no longer as a slave but as more than a slave, a beloved brother, especially dear to me; and how much more than a brother to you, since now you will know him both as a man and in the Lord.

If then you regard me as a partner, welcome him as you would me.

GOSPEL   Lk 14, 25–33

On one occasion when a great crowd was with Jesus, he turned to them and said, "If anyone comes to me without turning his back on his father and mother, his wife and his children, his brothers and sisters, indeed his very self, he cannot be my follower. Anyone who does not take up his cross and follow me cannot be my disciple. If one of you decides to build a tower, will he not first sit down and calculate the outlay to see if he has enough money to complete the project? He will do that for fear of laying the foundation and then not being able to complete the work; at which all who saw it would then jeer at him, saying, 'That man began to build what he could not finish.'

"Or if a king is about to march on another king to do battle with him, will he not sit down first and consider whether, with ten thousand men, he can withstand an enemy coming against him with twenty thousand? If he cannot, he will send a delegation while the enemy is still at a distance, asking for terms of peace. In the same way, none of you can be my disciple if he does not renounce all his possessions."

Reflection on the Readings

Although the first reading stresses the importance of wisdom, it also reminds us that ultimately the secrets of life will elude us. For all of our human wisdom, we cannot understand the ways of God. Wisdom alone knows the mind of God.

In the Gospel, Jesus again speaks about what is necessary to be his disciple. His sayings about building a tower or going into battle emphasize the need for wisdom. Before we do anything in life we need to know what may be required of us. This is wisdom. Before we decide to be a disciple of Jesus, we need to know that it will involve the cross.

In the New Testament, Jesus is revealed as the wisdom of God. Though we attempt to figure life out, it will continue to elude us. The path that leads to wisdom for us is the path that follows Jesus. But to follow Jesus we must take up the cross, letting go of ourselves and our desire to possess, receiving life with all its mystery as a gift.

Suggestions for Prayer

1. Popular culture furnishes us with many so-called words of wisdom: "Go for the gusto in life," "I did it my way," etc. What are some words of wisdom you have lived by? How do these sayings relate to the Gospel?
2. Imagine yourself walking down a path with Jesus. Tell him what it means for you in your life to take up your cross and follow him. Listen as Jesus responds to you.

Discipleship calls us to continually refocus our lives and our thoughts on Jesus and the Gospel. Beginning with your childhood, write a letter to Jesus describing what it has meant for you to be his disciple in the various stages of your life. Then reflect upon how you see your life as his disciple today.

Kathleen Brown

Twenty-Fourth Sunday of the Year **A**

READING I   Sir 27, 30—28, 7
Wrath and anger are hateful things,
 yet the sinner hugs them tight.
The vengeful will suffer the Lord's vengeance,
  for he remembers their sins in detail.
Forgive your neighbor's injustice;
  then when you pray, your own sins will be forgiven.
Should a man nourish anger against his fellows
  and expect healing from the Lord?
Should a man refuse mercy to his fellows,
  yet seek pardon for his own sins?
If he who is but flesh cherishes wrath,
  who will forgive his sins?
Remember your last days, set enmity aside;
  remember death and decay, and cease from sin!
Think of the commandments, hate not your neighbor;
  of the Most High's covenant, and overlook faults.

Responsorial Psalm   Ps 103, 1–2. 3–4.
9–10. 11–12
The Lord is kind and merciful;
  slow to anger, and rich in compassion.
Bless the Lord, O my soul;
  and all my being, bless his holy name.
Bless the Lord, O my soul,
  and forget not all his benefits.
The Lord is kind and merciful;
  slow to anger, and rich in compassion.
He pardons all your iniquities,
  he heals all your ills.
He redeems your life from destruction,
  he crowns you with kindness and compassion.
The Lord is kind and merciful;
  slow to anger, and rich in compassion.
He will not always chide,
  nor does he keep his wrath forever.
Not according to our sins does he deal with us,
  nor does he requite us according to our crimes.
The Lord is kind and merciful;
  slow to anger, and rich in compassion.
For as the heavens are high above the earth,
  so surpassing is his kindness toward those who fear him.
As far as the east is from the west,
  so far has he put our transgressions from us.
The Lord is kind and merciful;
  slow to anger, and rich in compassion.

READING II   Rom 14, 7–9
None of us lives as his own master and none of us dies as his own master. While we live we are responsible to the Lord, and when we die we die as his servants. Both in life and in death we are the Lord's. That is why Christ

died and came to life again, that he might be Lord of both the dead and the living.

GOSPEL   Mt 18, 21–35

Peter came up and asked Jesus, "Lord, when my brother wrongs me, how often must I forgive him? Seven times?" "No," Jesus replied, "not seven times; I say, seventy times seven times. That is why the reign of God may be said to be like a king who decided to settle accounts with his officials. When he began his auditing, one was brought in who owed him a huge amount. As he had no way of paying it, his master ordered him to be sold, along with his wife, his children, and all his property, in payment of the debt. At that the official prostrated himself in homage and said, 'My lord, be patient with me and I will pay you back in full.' Moved with pity, the master let the official go and wrote off the debt. But when that same official went out he met a fellow servant who owed him a mere fraction of what he himself owed. He seized him and throttled him. 'Pay back what you owe,' he demanded. His fellow servant dropped to his knees and began to plead with him, 'Just give me time and I will pay you back in full.' But he would hear none of it. Instead, he had him put in jail until he paid back what he owed. When his fellow servants saw what had happened they were badly shaken, and went to their master to report the whole incident. His master sent for him and said, 'You worthless wretch! I canceled your entire debt when you pleaded with me. Should you not have dealt mercifully with your fellow servant, as I dealt with you?' Then in anger the master handed him over to the torturers until he paid back all that he owed. My heavenly Father will treat you in exactly the same way unless each of you forgives his brother from his heart."

Reflection on the Readings

This week's readings demonstrate the undeniable connection between God's life and our life. Sometimes we experience our relationship with God and we experience our relationship with people and we view them as two separate relationships, in two separate compartments. Have you ever had a conversation in which someone says, "What Jesus would have done is . . ." And then someone else chimes in, "Well, Jesus is God. He's not me. I can't do that. I have to live in the real world."

The Scripture readings today tell us that our world and God's world are the same. God the Father throughout history, and ultimately in the person of Jesus, offers us forgiveness. That wonderful, saving reality from "above" only has meaning, only has power, in the ways in which we forgive each other. There is no relationship to God which is lived out apart from our relationship to each other. An abstract love of God, which does not manifest itself in love of neighbor, simply does not exist. An often quoted Peanuts cartoon sums this up when Linus shouts at Lucy, "I love mankind. It's people I can't stand."

The author of the Book of Sirach states the theme of this week's readings bluntly, "Should a man nourish anger against his fellows and expect healing from the Lord?" Jesus is equally clear, "Should you not have dealt mercifully with your fellow servant, as I have dealt with you?" God forgives us that we might live life with the security and generosity which allows us to forgive each other and thereby respond in truth to the gift of

God's love. The cycle is complete. As St. Paul writes, "Both in life and in death we are the Lord's."

Suggestions for Prayer

1. Reflect on one or more of the following questions:
   - Have you ever been forgiven? How did you feel? How did it impact your life?
   - Did you ever forgive another? Could you imagine Jesus doing the same?
   - Have you ever denied forgiveness to another? How did it make you feel? What can you do with those feelings?
2. Is there any past event in your life from which you still feel guilt? If so, imagine yourself in a room with Jesus. Sit quietly for a while with him. Then tell him of the event. In your imagination look into his eyes. What emotion are they expressing? Listen. What does Jesus say to you?
3. Go to a quiet place with a copy of today's Gospel reading from Matthew. Read the story but imagine you are standing next to Peter when Peter asks Jesus his question. Stay with him and imagine you are there as Jesus answers.

Suggestion for Journal Keeping

Describe an event in your life in which you need forgiveness, and an event in which someone needs your forgiveness. At the end write down the refrain of today's psalm: "The Lord is kind and merciful, slow to anger and rich in compassion."

Douglas Fisher

Twenty-Fourth Sunday of the Year

READING I — Is 50, 4–9

The Lord God opens my ear that I may hear
And I have not rebelled,
have not turned back.
I gave my back to those who beat me,
my cheeks to those who plucked my beard;
My face I did not shield
from buffets and spitting.

The Lord God is my help,
therefore I am not disgraced;
I have set my face like flint,
knowing that I shall not be put to shame.
He is near who upholds my right;
if anyone wishes to oppose me,
let us appear together.
Who disputes my right?
Let him confront me.
See, the Lord God is my help;
who will prove me wrong?

Responsorial Psalm — Ps 116, 1–2. 3–4, 5–6. 8–9

I will walk in the presence of the Lord, in the land of the living.
I love the Lord because he has heard my voice in supplication,
Because he has inclined his ear to me the day I called.
I will walk in the presence of the Lord, in the land of the living.
The cords of death encompassed me; the snares of the nether world seized upon me;
I fell into distress and sorrow,

And I called upon the name of the Lord,
"O Lord, save my life!"
I will walk in the presence of the Lord,
in the land of the living.
Gracious is the Lord and just;
yes, our God is merciful.
The Lord keeps the little ones;
I was brought low, and he saved me.
I will walk in the presence of the Lord,
in the land of the living.
For he has freed my soul from death,
my eyes from tears, my feet from stum-
bling.
I shall walk before the Lord
in the lands of the living.
I will walk in the presence of the Lord,
in the land of the living.

READING II
Jas 2, 14–18

My brothers, what good is it to profess faith
without practicing it? Such faith has no
power to save one, has it? If a brother or sister has nothing to wear and no food for the
day, and you say to them, "Good-bye and
good luck! Keep warm and well fed," but do
not meet their bodily needs, what good is
that? So it is with the faith that does nothing
in practice. It is thoroughly lifeless.

To such a person one might say, "You
have faith and I have works—is that it?"
Show me your faith without works, and I
will show you the faith that underlies my
works!

GOSPEL
Mk 8, 27–35

Jesus and his disciples set out for the villages
around Caesarea Philippi. On the way he
asked his disciples this question: "Who do
people say that I am?" They replied, "Some,
John the Baptizer, others, Elijah, still others,
one of the prophets." "And you," he went
on to ask, "who do you say that I am?" Peter
answered him, "You are the Messiah!" Then
he strictly ordered them not to tell anyone
about him.

He then began to teach them that the Son
of Man had to suffer much, be rejected by
the elders, the chief priests, and the scribes,
be put to death, and rise three days later. He
said this quite openly. Peter then took him
aside and began to remonstrate with him. At
this he turned around and, eyeing the disciples, reprimanded Peter in turn: "Get out of
my sight, you satan! You are not judging by
God's standards but by man's!"

He summoned the crowd with his disciples and said to them: "If a man wishes to
come after me, he must deny his very self,
take up his cross, and follow in my steps.
Whoever would save his life will lose it, but
whoever loses his life for my sake and the
gospel's will save it."

Reflection on the Readings

Rejoice! Today Peter, spokesman of the
disciples, recognizes who Jesus is—the Messiah! Immediately Peter and the other disciples are challenged to rethink their definition
of "Messiah." Jesus is not a military or political savior. He is a suffering, dying and rising
Messiah.

What Jesus said was not popular then. Peter tried to get him to tone it down. It has not
become any more popular over time. But it is
the call of discipleship.

Jesus repeats, even more clearly, to the disciples and the crowd: there is a cost in being
a follower. One must be willing to lose oneself and go where Jesus leads—even if that
means changing perceptions and beliefs, or
suffering injustice, or loss of comforts and
complacency.

The prophet Isaiah speaks of the need for open ears, to hear what Jesus is saying and asking. Christians see in Isaiah's words a prediction of what will happen to Jesus. He closes with a prayer that could be said by the suffering Jesus or any persecuted follower of Christ.

James' Letter seems to turn the table and puts us in the place of the fortunate watching the unfortunate pass by. When we are in that position, it is our call to let go of our comforts and reach out to the other.

Suggestions for Prayer

1. Recall a time when you felt persecuted unjustly. What emotions, fears and anxieties were involved? Read Psalm 116 and reflect on the promises of freedom from that memory and those hurts.
2. Reflect on the following questions:
   - Who do you say Jesus is?
   - Who is Jesus telling you he is?
   - Are there any conflicts between your answers to these questions?
   - How can you resolve or reconcile the conflicts?
3. Imagine walking along a trail in the snow-covered woods. Jesus is immediately ahead of you and you are walking in his footsteps in the snow. After a while you and he sit down on a bench and you tell him what it felt like to follow in his steps.

Suggestion for Journal Keeping

What are the ways you could provide clothing, food, warmth, shelter or other basic necessities to someone in need. What are your obstacles to doing such and how can they be overcome?

Kathleen M. Henry

Twenty-Fourth Sunday of the Year C

READING I   Ex 32, 7–11. 13–14

The Lord said to Moses, "Go down at once to your people, whom you brought out of the land of Egypt, for they have become depraved. They have soon turned aside from the way I pointed out to them, making for themselves a molten calf and worshiping it, sacrificing to it and crying out, 'This is your God, O Israel, who brought you out of the land of Egypt!' I see how stiff-necked this people is," continued the Lord to Moses. "Let me alone, then, that my wrath may blaze up against them to consume them. Then I will make of you a great nation."

But Moses implored the Lord, his God, saying, "Why, O Lord, should your wrath blaze up against your own people, whom you brought out of the land of Egypt with such great power and with so strong a hand? Remember your servants Abraham, Isaac and Israel, and how you swore to them by your own self, saying, 'I will make your descendants as numerous as the stars in the sky; and all this land that I promised, I will give your descendants as their perpetual

heritage.' " So the Lord relented in the punishment he had threatened to inflict on his people.

Responsorial Psalm   Ps 51, 3–4. 12–13.
                                  17. 19

I will rise and go to my father.

Have mercy on me, O God, in your goodness;
   in the greatness of your compassion wipe out my offense.
Thoroughly wash me from my guilt
   and of my sin cleanse me.

I will rise and go to my father.

A clean heart create for me, O God,
   and a steadfast spirit renew within me.
Cast me not out from your presence,
   and your holy spirit take not from me.

I will rise and go to my father.

O Lord, open my lips,
   and my mouth shall proclaim your praise.
My sacrifice, O God, is a contrite spirit;
   a heart contrite and humbled, O God, you
      will not spurn.

I will rise and go to my father.

READING II   1 Tm 1, 12–17
I thank Christ Jesus our Lord, who has strengthened me, that he has made me his servant and judged me faithful. I was once a blasphemer, a persecutor, a man filled with arrogance; but because I did not know what I was doing in my unbelief, I have been treated mercifully, and the grace of our Lord has been granted me in overflowing measure, along with the faith and love which are in Christ Jesus. You can depend on this as worthy of full acceptance: that Christ Jesus came into the world to save sinners. Of these I myself am the worst. But on that very

account I was dealt with mercifully, so that in me, as an extreme case, Jesus Christ might display all his patience, and that I might become an example to those who would later have faith in him and gain everlasting life. To the King of ages, the immortal, the invisible, the only God, be honor and glory forever and ever! Amen.

GOSPEL   Lk 15, 1–32
The tax collectors and sinners were all gathering around to hear Jesus, at which the Pharisees and the scribes murmured, "This man welcomes sinners and eats with them." Then he addressed this parable to them: "Who among you, if he has a hundred sheep and loses one of them, does not leave the ninety-nine in the wasteland and follow the lost one until he finds it? And when he finds it, he puts it on his shoulders in jubilation. Once arrived home, he invites friends and neighbors in and says to them, 'Rejoice with me because I have found my lost sheep.' I tell you, there will likewise be more joy in heaven over one repentant sinner than over ninety-nine righteous people who have no need to repent.

"What woman, if she has ten silver pieces and loses one, does not light a lamp and sweep the house in a diligent search until she has retrieved what she lost? And when she finds it, she calls in her friends and neighbors to say, 'Rejoice with me! I have found the silver piece I lost.' I tell you, there will be the same kind of joy before the angels of God over one repentant sinner."

Jesus said to them: "A man had two sons. The younger of them said to his father, 'Father, give me the share of the estate that is coming to me.' So the father divided up the property. Some days later this younger son collected all his belongings and went off to a distant land, where he squandered his money on dissolute living. After he had spent everything, a great famine broke out in that country and he was in dire need. So he attached himself to one of the propertied class of the place, who sent him to his farm to take care of the pigs. He longed to fill his belly with the husks that were fodder for the pigs, but no one made a move to give him anything. Coming to his senses at last, he said: 'How many hired hands at my father's place have more than enough to eat, while here I am starving! I will break away and return to my father, and say to him, "Father, I have sinned against God and against you; I no longer deserve to be called your son. Treat me like one of your hired hands."' With that he set off for his father's house. While he was still a long way off, his father caught sight of him and was deeply moved. He ran out to meet him, threw his arms around his neck, and kissed him. The son said to him, 'Father, I have sinned against God and against you; I no longer deserve to be called your son.' The father said to his servants: 'Quick! bring out the finest robe and put it on him; put a ring on his finger and shoes on his feet. Take the fatted calf and kill it. Let us eat and celebrate because this son of mine was dead and has come back to life. He was lost and is found.' Then the celebration began.

"Meanwhile the elder son was out on the land. As he neared the house on his way home, he heard the sound of music and dancing. He called one of the servants and asked him the reason for the dancing and the music. The servant answered, 'Your brother is home, and your father has killed the fatted calf because he has him back in good health.' The son grew angry at this and would not go in; but his father came out and began to plead with him.

"He said in reply to his father: 'For years now I have slaved for you. I never disobeyed one of your orders, yet you never gave me so much as a kid goat to celebrate with my friends. Then, when this son of yours returns after having gone through your property with loose women, you kill the fatted calf for him.'

" 'My son,' replied the father, 'you are with me always, and everything I have is yours. But we had to celebrate and rejoice! This brother of yours was dead, and has come back to life. He was lost, and is found.' "

Reflection on the Readings

Today's Gospel contains three parables that speak to us of God's love and mercy. Most especially these stories remind us that no matter how far off the chosen path we may stray, God will be waiting and welcoming us. In the Exodus reading the Israelites have built an altar of gold and brought animals to burn as sacrifice. They have turned their backs on the Lord who brought them out of Egypt. Moses pleads on behalf of his people and God relents, keeping his promise to Abraham, Isaac, and Jacob. Once again we are reminded that it is in our sinfulness that God comes to us. Like the son who returned to his loving father, we too can celebrate with the Lord out of our weakness. For we walk our closest walk with him when we acknowledge our helplessness and utter dependence on God, our Father.

The Church offers us its welcoming arms, too, through the sacraments of baptism and reconciliation. Celebrating these sacraments is encountering the loving Father as he welcomes us or calls us back to the family of believers. But, like the son, we must acknowledge our sin, turn away, and return to the Father. How often we fail to do this, telling ourselves, "The sin is too great," or "Next time I'll deal with this." We doubt the unlimited mercy of God, and deny the need to have his help in getting back "on track."

Suggestions for Prayer

1. Remember in prayer those individuals "who are lost." Pray that you may be used as the Lord's instrument in helping to bring them home. Use the responsorial psalm as you pray.
2. Pray that this day you may be especially aware of your utter dependence on the Father. Use 2 Corinthians 3:4–5 as you pray.
3. The Lord rejoices over the sinner who is repentant. Rejoice and give thanks with the Lord, remembering that it is in our sinfulness that we are especially loved. Psalm 103:1–5 might be helpful.

Suggestion for Journal Keeping

All of these parables remind us of our importance to God. He loves us as if we were the only person on earth. Write your feelings in regard to that. How do you respond to this kind of love and mercy?

Khris S. Ford

Twenty-Fifth Sunday of the Year   A

READING I   Is 55, 6–9

Seek the Lord while he may be found,
   call him while he is near.
Let the scoundrel forsake his way,
   and the wicked man his thoughts;
Let him turn to the Lord for mercy;
   to our God, who is generous in forgiving.
For my thoughts are not your thoughts,
   nor are your ways my ways, says the Lord.
As high as the heavens are above the earth,
   so high are my ways above your ways
   and my thoughts above your thoughts.

Responsorial Psalm   Ps 145, 2–3. 8–9.
                                        17–18

The Lord is near to all who call him.
Every day will I bless you,
   and I will praise your name forever and
   ever.
Great is the Lord and highly to be praised;
   his greatness is unsearchable.
The Lord is near to all who call upon him.
The Lord is gracious and merciful,
   slow to anger and of great kindness.
The Lord is good to all
   and compassionate toward all his works.
The Lord is near to all who call upon him.
The Lord is just in all his ways
   and holy in all his works.
The Lord is near to all who call upon him,
   to all who call upon him in truth.
The Lord is near to all who call upon him.

READING II   Phil 1, 20–24. 27
Christ will be exalted through me, whether
I live or die. For, to me, "life" means Christ;

hence dying is so much gain. If, on the other hand, I am to go on living in the flesh, that means productive toil for me—and I do not know which to prefer. I am strongly attracted by both: I long to be freed from this life and to be with Christ, for that is the far better thing; yet it is more urgent that I remain alive for your sakes. Conduct yourselves, then, in a way worthy of the gospel of Christ.

GOSPEL   Mt 20, 1–16

Jesus told his disciples this parable: "The reign of God is like the case of the owner of an estate who went out at dawn to hire workmen for his vineyard. After reaching an agreement with them for the usual daily wage, he sent them out to his vineyard. He came out about midmorning and saw other men standing around the marketplace without work, so he said to them, 'You too go along to my vineyard and I will pay you whatever is fair.' At that they went away. He came out again around noon and midafternoon and did the same. Finally, going out in late afternoon he found still others standing around. To these he said, 'Why have you been standing here idle all day?' 'No one has hired us,' they told him. He said, 'You go to the vineyard too.' When evening came the owner of the vineyard said to his foreman, 'Call the workmen and give them their pay, but begin with the last group and end with the first.' When those hired late in the afternoon came up they received a full day's pay, and when the first group appeared they supposed they would get more; yet they received the same daily wage. Thereupon they complained to the owner, 'This last group did only an hour's work, but you have put

them on the same basis as us who have worked a full day in the scorching heat.' 'My friend,' he said to one in reply, 'I do you no injustice. You agreed on the usual wage, did you not? Take your pay and go home. I intend to give this man who was hired last the same pay as you. I am free to do as I please with my money, am I not? Or are you envious because I am generous?' Thus the last shall be first and the first shall be last."

Reflection on the Readings

Today's Gospel offers us a powerful insight into the logic of God. We hear Jesus tell his disciples a parable in which people come to work at all different hours of the day but all are paid the same in the end. Any business man would say this is not a good way to run a vineyard. A person should be paid according to the hours worked. But God is not constrained by our logic. God cannot be locked into the way we do things. God may choose to be exceedingly generous—at times and in places we may never have predicted.

The reading from Isaiah adds another dimension to this theme. "Seek the Lord while he may be found, call him while he is near," says the prophet. Where may the Lord be found? Perhaps we think of a church, or of quiet mountaintops, or of holy people. But the prophet refuses to let us confine God to the places we expect to find him. God could be anywhere because God's thoughts are not our thoughts and God's ways are not our ways. Seek God where he may be found and that may be in very unlikely places, circumstances and people. What will God be like when we find him? Isaiah tells us: "Our God is generous and forgiving."

351

1. Reflect on one or more of the following questions:
   - Where do you expect to find the presence of God?
   - Have you ever experienced generosity from an unexpected source?
   - What does it mean that God's ways are not our ways? Does that make you feel insecure or hopeful?
2. Imagine yourself there with the disciples when Jesus told this parable. What are your thoughts and feelings? What do you feel when Jesus says, ''Thus the last shall be first and the first shall be last.''
3. Read the responsorial psalm slowly to yourself. Substitute ''me'' for ''all'' so that you are saying, ''The Lord is near to me when I call him.''

Suggestion for Journal Keeping

Describe a time in your life when you were depressed, lonely or afraid. How did you come through that time? Could the Lord have been present in the small events, in the people, and in your own heart as you passed through that time?

Douglas Fisher

Twenty-Fifth Sunday of the Year **B**

READING I   Wis 2, 12. 17–20

[The wicked say:]
Let us beset the just one, because he is obnoxious to us;
  he sets himself against our doings,

Reproaches us for transgressions of the law and charges us with violations of our training.
Let us see whether his words be true;
  let us find out what will happen to him.
For if the just one be the son of God, he will defend him
and deliver him from the hand of his foes.
With revilement and torture let us put him to the test
that we may have proof of his gentleness and try his patience.
Let us condemn him to a shameful death;
  for according to his own words, God will take care of him.

Responsorial Psalm   Ps 54, 3–4. 5. 6–8
The Lord upholds my life.
O God, by your name save me,
  and by your might defend my cause.
O God, hear my prayer;
  hearken to the words of my mouth.
The Lord upholds my life.
For haughty men have risen up against me,
  and fierce men seek my life;
  they set not God before their eyes.
The Lord upholds my life.
Behold, God is my helper;
  the Lord sustains my life.
Freely will I offer you sacrifice;
  I will praise your name, O Lord, for its goodness.
The Lord upholds my life.

READING II   Jas 3, 16–4, 3
Where there are jealousy and strife, there also are inconstancy and all kinds of vile behavior. Wisdom from above, by contrast, is first of all innocent. It is also peaceable, le-

nient, docile, rich in sympathy and the kindly deeds that are its fruit, impartial and sincere. The harvest of justice is sown in peace for those who cultivate peace.

Where do the conflicts and disputes among you originate? Is it not your inner cravings that make war within your members? What you desire you do not obtain, and so you resort to murder. You envy and you cannot acquire, so you quarrel and fight. You do not obtain because you do not ask. You ask and you do not receive because you ask wrongly, with a view to squandering what you receive on your pleasures.

GOSPEL   Mk 9, 30–37
Jesus and his disciples came down the mountain and began to go through Galilee, but he did not want anyone to know about it. He was teaching his disciples in this vein: "The Son of Man is going to be delivered into the hands of men who will put him to death; three days after his death he will rise." Though they failed to understand his words, they were afraid to question him.

They returned to Capernaum and Jesus, once inside the house, began to ask them, "What were you discussing on the way home?" At this they fell silent, for on the way they had been arguing about who was the most important. So he sat down and called the Twelve around him and said, "If anyone wishes to rank first, he must remain the last one of all and the servant of all." Then he took a little child, stood him in their midst, and putting his arms around him, said to them, "Whoever welcomes a child such as this for my sake welcomes me. And whoever welcomes me welcomes, not me, but him who sent me."

Reflection on the Readings
The wisdom necessary to follow Jesus is not the world's. This is a key lesson any disciple must learn. Jesus is not looking for self-important people or those who strive to be on top at the expense of others. To follow Jesus means to be a servant of others. Being a disciple means welcoming and honoring children, the lowly and unprotected. It means changing our priorities, standards and goals from the world's to Jesus'.

James expounds on the fruits of wisdom which come from God. He contrasts these qualities with those which do not characterize a follower of Jesus and warns of the dangers and consequences of such conduct.

The Book of Wisdom, speaking from the wicked's perspective, gives insight into what Jesus and James are saying. The wicked cannot stand the wise. The just one's ways, by being in conflict with the wicked, reproach and charge them. The gentleness and patience of the wise upset the wicked, who choose hostile and ugly ways to retaliate.

Jesus provides us with a wonderful reassurance and promise: when we welcome the lowly, the outcast, the unclean of our society, we welcome Jesus into our life. And, in welcoming Jesus, God, Father, Son and Spirit, comes to dwell in us.

Suggestions for Prayer

1. Read Psalm 54 and ask yourself these questions:
   • Where have I been confronted or upset by injustice today?
   • Where can I see God's help and sustaining power in the situation?
   • How can I thank and praise God in the situation?

2. Imagine yourself among the disciples when Jesus said that the Son of Man is going to die and then rise in three days. What questions are going through your mind? What questions do you overhear the disciples asking among themselves? Which of the questions would you be willing to ask Jesus?
3. You are the little child Jesus put his arms around. Feel Jesus' arms around you. What parts of yourself are you glad Jesus is embracing? What parts of yourself are you having difficulty letting Jesus embrace?

Suggestion for Journal Keeping

Where are origins of conflict and dispute among your family and close friends? What inner cravings do you have that are in conflict with your body, mind, spirit or emotions? What gifts and riches has our nation received and squandered? As a result of reflecting on today's readings, what can you do in any of the situations you have just outlined?

Kathleen M. Henry

Twenty-Fifth Sunday of the Year   C

READING I   Am 8, 4–7

Hear this, you who trample upon the needy
  and destroy the poor of the land!
"When will the new moon be over," you ask,
  "that we may sell our grain,
  and the sabbath, that we may display the wheat?

We will diminish the ephah,
  add to the shekel,
  and fix our scales for cheating!
We will buy the lowly man for silver,
  and the poor man for a pair of sandals;
  even the refuse of the wheat we will sell!"
The Lord has sworn by the pride of Jacob:
  Never will I forget a thing they have done!

Responsorial Psalm   Ps 113, 1–2. 4–6. 7–8

Praise the Lord who lifts up the poor.
Praise, you servants of the Lord,
  praise the name of the Lord.
Blessed be the name of the Lord
  both now and forever.
Praise the Lord who lifts up the poor.
High above all nations is the Lord;
  above the heavens is his glory.
Who is like the Lord, our God, who is enthroned on high
  and looks upon the heavens and the earth below?
Praise the Lord who lifts up the poor.
He raises up the lowly from the dust;
  from the dunghill he lifts up the poor
To seat them with princes,
  with the princes of his own people.
Praise the Lord who lifts up the poor.

READING II   1 Tm 2, 1–8

First of all, I urge that petitions, prayers, intercessions, and thanksgivings be offered for all men, especially for kings and those in authority, that we may be able to lead undisturbed and tranquil lives in perfect piety and dignity. Prayer of this kind is good, and God our savior is pleased with it, for he wants all men to be saved and come to know the truth. And the truth is this:
  "God is one.

One also is the mediator between God and
men,
the man Christ Jesus,
who gave himself as a ransom for all."
This truth was attested at the fitting time. I
have been made its herald and apostle (believe me, I am not lying but speak the truth),
the teacher of the nations in the true faith.

It is my wish, then, that in every place the
men shall offer prayers with blameless hands
held aloft, and be free from anger and dissension.

GOSPEL Lk 16, 1–13
Jesus said to his disciples: "A rich man had a
manager who was reported to him for dis-
sipating his property. He summoned him
and said, 'What is this I hear about you?
Give me an account of your service, for it is
about to come to an end.' The manager
thought to himself, 'What shall I do next?
My employer is sure to dismiss me. I cannot
dig ditches. I am ashamed to go begging. I
have it! Here is a way to make sure that people will take me into their homes when I am
let go.'

"So he called in each of his master's debtors, and said to the first, 'How much do you
owe my master?' The man replied, 'A
hundred jars of oil.' The manager said, 'Take
your invoice, sit down quickly, and make it
fifty.' Then he said to a second, 'How much
do you owe?' The answer came, 'A hundred
measures of wheat,' and the manager said,
'Take your invoice and make it eighty.'

"The owner then gave his devious em-
ployee credit for being enterprising! Why?
Because the worldly take more initiative
than the other-worldly when it comes to
dealing with their own kind.

"What I say to you is this: Make friends for
yourselves through your use of this world's
goods, so that when they fail you, a lasting
reception will be yours. If you can trust a
man in little things, you can also trust him in
greater; while anyone unjust in a slight matter is also unjust in greater. If you cannot be
trusted with elusive wealth, who will trust
you with lasting? And if you have not been
trustworthy with someone else's money,
who will give you what is your own?

"No servant can serve two masters. Either
he will hate the one and love the other or be
attentive to the one and despise the other.
You cannot give yourself to God and
money."

Reflection on the Readings
The "good news" in today's readings may
strike us as confusing. Is Jesus condoning the
shrewd acts of the manager? Is he asking us
to act in this way? The confusion may cause
us to reflect on our material possessions and
our use of them to examine our skills as man-
agers of these gifts. It is in this way that our
puzzlement may indeed become "good
news." Today we are challenged to look at
our management skills, to examine those
people and/or things that we have authority
over. What kind of stewards are we? The
Gospel calls us to use our gifts of intelligence
and perception. It is our privilege and duty to
exercise these gifts by keeping ourselves well
informed in matters of the world and of our
faith. We are promised that we shall be welcomed into an eternal dwelling if we use our
gifts to build friendship and to give life in our
world.

The reading from Amos calls us to continue
to look at our business dealings and all of our

dealings with people. Are we honest in these relationships? Are we using our gifts to call forth the best in each situation? If our answer is a consistent "no" and we continue to worship and prepare for initiation into the midst of this kind of living, we scandalize the sacraments. For baptism, confirmation and the Eucharist call us to be more, to be Christ-like in all our doings. Our worship is not authentic if there is no intent to truly give "worth" to God in our life.

Suggestions for Prayer

1. Identify one area of your life where you are not exercising wise use of your gifts. What must you do to change this? What will this cost you? Pray for the courage and the strength to change.
2. Pray that Christ may truly be master of your life, asking for the grace to be honest with yourself and God. What must you do to make him more fully your master?
3. Name those people who have authority over you in various areas of your life. Pray that these individuals will be graced with true wisdom, be guided by God, and be willing to use their gifts for the betterment of the kingdom.

Suggestion for Journal Keeping

Make a list of your gifts (talents, material blessings, etc.). When you are finished take time to look over your list and become more aware of each one as a gift. Remember that these are gifts from God, unearned, undeserved, yet freely given. Write about your feelings when you reflect on this. Take time to respond by writing a prayer of thanksgiving.

Khris S. Ford

Twenty-Sixth Sunday of the Year A

READING I Ez 18, 25–28

You say, "The Lord's way is not fair!" Hear now, house of Israel: Is it my way that is unfair, or rather, are not your ways unfair? When a virtuous man turns away from virtue to commit iniquity, and dies, it is because of the iniquity he committed that he must die. But if a wicked man, turning from the wickedness he has committed, does what is right and just, he shall preserve his life; since he has turned away from all the sins which he committed, he shall surely live, he shall not die.

Responsorial Psalm Ps 125, 4–5. 6–7. 8–9

Remember your mercies, O Lord.

**Your ways, O Lord, make known to me;
teach me your paths,
Guide me in your truth and teach me,
for you are God my savior.**

Remember your mercies, O Lord.

**Remember that your compassion, O Lord,
and your kindness are from of old.
The sins of my youth and my frailties remember not;
in your kindness remember me,
because of your goodness, O Lord.**

Remember your mercies, O Lord.

Good and upright is the Lord;
   thus he shows sinners the way.
He guides the humble to justice,
   he teaches the humble his way.
Remember your mercies, O Lord.

READING II   Phil 2, 1–11
In the name of the encouragement you owe
me in Christ, in the name of the solace that
love can give, of fellowship in spirit, compassion, and pity, I beg you: make my joy
complete by your unanimity, possessing the
one love, united in spirit and ideals. Never
act out of rivalry or conceit; rather, let all
parties think humbly of others as superior to
themselves, each of you looking to others'
interests rather than his own. Your attitude
must be Christ's:
   Though he was in the form of God,
   he did not deem equality with God
   something to be grasped at.
Rather, he emptied himself
   and took the form of a slave,
   being born in the likeness of men.
He was known to be of human estate
   and it was thus that he humbled himself,
   obediently accepting even death,
   death on a cross!
Because of this,
   God highly exalted him
   and bestowed on him the name
   above every other name,
So that at Jesus' name
   every knee must bend
   in the heavens, on the earth,
   and under the earth,
   and every tongue proclaim
   to the glory of God the Father:
JESUS CHRIST IS LORD!

GOSPEL   Mt 21, 28–32
Jesus said to the chief priests and elders of
the people: "What do you think of this case?
There was a man who had two sons. He approached the elder and said, 'Son, go out
and work in the vineyard today.' The son replied, 'I am on my way, sir'; but he never
went. Then the man came to his second son
and said the same thing. This son said in reply, 'No, I will not'; but afterward he re-
gretted it and went. Which of the two did
what the father wanted?" They said, "The
second." Jesus said to them, "Let me make
it clear that tax collectors and prostitutes are
entering the kingdom of God before you.
When John came preaching a way of holiness, you put no faith in him; but the tax collectors and the prostitutes did believe in
him. Yet even when you saw that, you did
not repent and believe in him."

Reflection on the Readings
   In today's reading from Matthew's Gospel,
we hear Jesus tell us of two sons. The one son
says he will work for his father but does not.
The second son refuses to work but ultimately
does. The responses of the two sons reflect
two different journeys in faith. Some people
experience God's love and say they are going
to share it with others, but they never do.
Other people resist God's love. They say no
to the presence of God in their life. But later
on they do lead loving lives. They overcome
their initial resistance to God's call—and
there lies growth, grace and greatness.
   Jesus goes on to say that the least likely
people, the prostitutes and tax collectors, enter heaven before those who are religious but
do not love. This happens because these people need God's love and they know it. They

want a Savior. They are open to God coming into their lives and changing them. Sometimes people are in love with being in love with God. They like the security of religion. They like the feeling of being certain they look good and neat. Jesus argues vehemently with people who want the "things" of religion—the ritual, the rules, the secure way of life—more than they want God. The sinners know they need God. And our God, who needs to be needed because he created us for no other reason than to love us, escorts them into the kingdom of God.

Suggestions for Prayer

1. Reflect on one or more of the following questions:
   - Did you ever say yes to some good and worthy cause and then did not follow through? How did you feel?
   - Do you know anyone personally or in history who led a sinful life and then did something unselfish and loving?
   - Have you ever said no to God's invitation to love and worship him? What led you to consider saying yes?
2. Contact someone you know who works with the poor. Ask him or her what it is like. Ask him or her if it is easier to look for God there.
3. Take the reading from Paul's Letter to the Philippians and read it out loud to yourself. Read it again. What does it feel like to proclaim: "Jesus Christ is Lord"? What kind of Lord is he?

Suggestion for Journal Keeping

Write down a time when you really needed someone—a time you were poor or depressed or abandoned. Now think of that situation with Jesus present. What happens? Write down your thoughts.

Douglas Fisher

Twenty-Sixth Sunday of the Year B

READING I   Nm 11, 25–29

The Lord came down in the cloud and spoke to Moses. Taking some of the spirit that was on him, he bestowed it on the seventy elders; and as the spirit came to rest on them, they prophesied.

Now two men, one named Eldad and the other Medad, were not in the gathering but had been left in the camp. They too had been on the list, but had not gone out to the tent; yet the spirit came to rest on them also, and they prophesied in the camp. So, when a young man quickly told Moses, "Eldad and Medad are prophesying in the camp," Joshua, son of Nun, who from his youth had been Moses' aide, said, "Moses, my lord, stop them." But Moses answered him, "Are you jealous for my sake? Would that all the people of the Lord were prophets! Would that the Lord might bestow his spirit on them all!"

Responsorial Psalm   Ps 19, 8. 10. 12–13. 14
The precepts of the Lord give joy to the heart.
The law of the Lord is perfect, refreshing the soul;
The decree of the Lord is trustworthy, giving wisdom to the simple.
The precepts of the Lord give joy to the heart.

The fear of the Lord is pure,
  enduring forever;
The ordinances of the Lord are true,
  all of them just.
The precepts of the Lord give joy to the
  heart.
Though your servant is careful of them,
  very diligent in keeping them,
Yet who can detect failings?
  Cleanse me from my unknown faults!
The precepts of the Lord give joy to the
  heart.
From wanton sin especially, restrain your
  servant;
  let it not rule over me.
Then shall I be blameless and innocent
  of serious sin.
The precepts of the Lord give joy to the
  heart.

READING II   Jas 5, 1–6
You rich, weep and wail over your impending miseries. Your wealth has rotted, your fine wardrobe has grown moth-eaten, your gold and silver have corroded, and their corrosion shall be a testimony against you; it will devour your flesh like a fire. See what you have stored up for yourselves against the last days. Here, crying aloud, are the wages you withheld from the farmhands who harvested your fields. The shouts of the harvesters have reached the ears of the Lord of hosts. You lived in wanton luxury on the earth; you fattened yourselves for the day of slaughter. You condemned, even killed, the just man; he does not resist you.

GOSPEL   Mk 9, 38–43. 45. 47–48
John said to Jesus, "Teacher, we saw a man using your name to expel demons and we tried to stop him because he is not of our company." Jesus said in reply: "Do not try to stop him. No man who performs a miracle using my name can at once speak ill of me. Anyone who is not against us is with us. Any man who gives you a drink of water because you belong to Christ will not, I assure you, go without his reward. But it would be better if anyone who leads astray one of these simple believers were to be plunged in the sea with a great millstone fastened around his neck.

"If your hand is your difficulty, cut it off! Better for you to enter life maimed than to keep both hands and enter Gehenna, with its unquenchable fire. If your foot is your undoing, cut it off! Better for you to enter life crippled than to be thrown into Gehenna with both feet. If your eye is your downfall, tear it out! Better for you to enter the kingdom of God with one eye than to be thrown with both eyes into Gehenna, where 'the worm dies not and the fire is never extinguished.' "

Reflection on the Readings

God is not limited by our restrictions or shortsightedness. God moves where he wills, bestowing gifts for the good of all. God chooses whom he wills, with criteria frequently different than ours.

When Moses took some of the gift God gave him and passed it on, the elders who were meant to receive the spirit did so whether present in the tent or left behind in the camp. The power to expel demons in Jesus' name was bestowed on one, not of the disciples, who was using Jesus name. God today has gifts to bestow. We should be vigilant in encouraging such outpourings of God's Spirit.

Jesus provides us with guidelines for measuring the purity of our actions and motivations. No one who acts in Jesus' name can, at the same time, speak against Jesus. If we speak in his name, we can provide wisdom, comfort and healing to those around us.

Jesus warns us against false teachers and personal failings. The consequences of leading others astray from Jesus' way or of wandering off ourselves are severe. James further expounds on the dangers of putting riches and possessions above God's ways and our fellow human beings.

Suggestions for Prayer

1. What talent would you like to develop which could be used to help others? Spend some time each day this week asking God to give you that gift.
2. If you were one of the elders upon whom Moses bestowed some of the spirit God gave him, what would you do with it? How would you want to use the gift for others?
3. Think of some small and ordinary aspect or attribute you have, or a possession you own, or a way you act toward others that moves you or others away from God. How can you remove this from your life? Ask Jesus to help you change.

Suggestion for Journal Keeping

At the end of each day this week, write down some small action you did or you received that represented you giving someone a drink of water because he or she belonged to Christ or where you received a drink of water from someone because you represented Christ to him or her.

Kathleen M. Henry

Twenty-Sixth Sunday of the Year

READING I   Am 6, 1. 4–7
Woe to the complacent in Zion!
Lying upon beds of ivory,
  stretched comfortably on their couches,
They eat lambs taken from the flock,
  and calves from the stall!
Improvising to the music of the harp,
  like David, they devise their own accompaniment.
They drink wine from bowls
  and anoint themselves with the best oils;
  yet they are not made ill by the collapse of Joseph!
Therefore, now they shall be the first to go into exile,
  and their wanton revelry shall be done away with.

Responsorial Psalm   Ps 146, 7. 8–9. 9–10
Praise the Lord, my soul!
Happy he who keeps faith forever,
  secures justice for the oppressed,
  gives food to the hungry.
The Lord sets captives free.
Praise the Lord, my soul!
The Lord gives sight to the blind.
  The Lord raises up those that were bowed down;
The Lord loves the just.
  The Lord protects strangers.
Praise the Lord, my soul!
The fatherless and the widow he sustains,
  but the way of the wicked he thwarts.
The Lord shall reign forever;
  your God, O Sion, through all generations.

Alleluia.
Praise the Lord, my soul!

READING II   1 Tm 6, 11–16

Man of God that you are, seek after integrity, piety, faith, love, steadfastness, and a gentle spirit. Fight the good fight of faith. Take firm hold on the everlasting life to which you were called when, in the presence of many witnesses, you made your noble profession of faith. Before God, who gives life to all, and before Christ Jesus, who in bearing witness made his noble profession before Pontius Pilate, I charge you to keep God's command without blame or reproach until our Lord Jesus Christ shall appear. This appearance God will bring to pass at his chosen time. He is the blessed and only ruler, the King of kings and Lord of lords who alone has immortality and who dwells in inapproachable light, whom no human being has ever seen or can see. To him be honor and everlasting rule! Amen.

GOSPEL   Lk 16, 19–31

Jesus said to the Pharisees: "Once there was a rich man who dressed in purple and linen and feasted splendidly every day. At his gate lay a beggar named Lazarus who was covered with sores. Lazarus longed to eat the scraps that fell from the rich man's table. The dogs even came and licked his sores. Eventually the beggar died. He was carried by angels to the bosom of Abraham. The rich man likewise died and was buried. From the abode of the dead where he was in torment, he raised his eyes and saw Abraham afar off, and Lazarus resting in his bosom.

"He called out, 'Father Abraham, have pity on me. Send Lazarus to dip the tip of his finger in water to refresh my tongue, for I am tortured in these flames.' 'My child,' replied Abraham, 'remember that you were well off in your lifetime, while Lazarus was in misery. Now he has found consolation here, but you have found torment. And that is not all. Between you and us there is fixed a great abyss, so that those who might wish to cross from here to you cannot do so, nor can anyone cross from your side to us.'

" 'Father, I ask you, then,' the rich man said, 'send him to my father's house where I have five brothers. Let him be a warning to them so that they may not end in this place of torment.' Abraham answered, 'They have Moses and the prophets. Let them hear them.' 'No, Father Abraham,' replied the rich man. 'But if someone would only go to them from the dead, then they would repent.' Abraham said to him, 'If they do not listen to Moses and the prophets, they will not be convinced even if one should rise from the dead.' "

Reflection on the Readings

The message in today's readings is pointed and perhaps harsh. Lazarus and the rich man are the models of the "have nots" and the "haves." Could this be a microcosm of what often happens between these two groups in our own society today? Coupled with this story is the reading from Amos which warns us of the attitude which says "we deserve" our blessings.

All we have and are is a gift from God. When we truly understand and believe that, then we can begin to live as one with all men and women. To recognize our complete giftedness is to know that without God we are nothing. In this "nothingness" we can identify with the poor, the sick, the victims of injustice—with all peoples.

As followers of Christ we are called to recognize and live out a sense of "connectedness" with all humans. When we do this we model Christ.

Suggestions for Prayer

1. Pray for those who are victims of injustice in our world. Try to identify groups or individuals within your own community. Pray that you may be an instrument of justice in your activities this day and ask the Lord to guide you to respond to those who are oppressed.
2. Reread the Gospel story. Put yourself in the place of Lazarus as he is carried to the door of the rich man to eat the scraps. Pray that you may be sensitive to such victims of injustice.
3. Remembering that all that we are and have is a gift from God, focus on one or two of your blessings. Place them in your hands, symbolically. Reflect on them. Then offer them to the Lord's use. Let go of your possession of them.

Suggestion for Journal Keeping

What was your initial reaction to this Gospel story?

With whom did you identify? Why? Then write what it would be like to identify with the other character.

Khris S. Ford

Twenty-Seventh Sunday of the Year **A**

READING I　　　　　　　　　　　Is 5, 1–7
Let me now sing of my friend,
 my friend's song concerning his vineyard.

My friend had a vineyard
 on a fertile hillside;
He spaded it, cleared it of stones,
 and planted the choicest vines;
Within it he built a watchtower,
 and hewed out a wine press.
Then he looked for the crop of grapes,
 but what it yielded was wild grapes.
Now, inhabitants of Jerusalem and men of Judah,
 judge between me and my vineyard:
What more was there to do for my vineyard
 that I had not done?
Why, when I looked for the crop of grapes,
 did it bring forth wild grapes?
Now, I will let you know
 what I mean to do to my vineyard:
Take away its hedge, give it to grazing,
 break through its wall, let it be trampled!
Yes, I will make it a ruin:
 it shall not be pruned or hoed,
 but overgrown with thorns and briers;
I will command the clouds
 not to send rain upon it.
The vineyard of the Lord of hosts is the house of Israel,
 and the men of Judah are his cherished plant;
He looked for judgment, but see, bloodshed!
 for justice, but hark, the outcry!

Responsorial Psalm　　　Ps 80, 9. 12. 13–14.
　　　　　　　　　　　　　　　15–16. 19–20
The vineyard of the Lord is the house of Israel.

A vine from Egypt you transplanted;
 you drove away the nations and planted it.
It put forth its foliage to the Sea,
 its shoots as far as the River.

The vineyard of the Lord is the house of
  Israel.
Why have you broken down its walls,
  so that every passer-by plucks its fruit,
The boar from the forest lays it waste,
  and the beasts of the field feed upon it?
The vineyard of the Lord is the house of
  Israel.
Once again, O Lord of hosts,
  look down from heaven, and see;
Take care of this vine,
  and protect what your right hand has
  planted
  [the son of man whom you yourself made
  strong].
The vineyard of the Lord is the house of
  Israel.
Then we will no more withdraw from you;
  give us new life, and we will call upon
  your name.
O Lord of hosts, restore us;
  if your face shine upon us, then we shall
  be safe.
The vineyard of the Lord is the house of
  Israel.

READING II   Phil 4, 6–9

**Dismiss all anxiety from your minds. Present
your needs to God in every form of prayer
and in petitions full of gratitude. Then God's
own peace, which is beyond all understanding, will stand guard over your hearts and
minds, in Christ Jesus.**

**Finally, my brothers, your thoughts
should be wholly directed to all that is true,
all that deserves respect, all that is honest,
pure, admirable, decent, virtuous, or worthy of praise. Live according to what you
have learned and accepted, what you have
heard me say and seen me do. Then will the
God of peace be with you.**

GOSPEL   Mt 21, 33–43

**Jesus said to the chief priests and elders of
the people: "Listen to another parable.
There was a property owner who planted a
vineyard, put a hedge around it, dug out a
vat, and erected a tower. Then he leased it
out to tenant farmers and went on a journey.
When vintage time arrived he dispatched his
slaves to the tenants to obtain his share of
the grapes. The tenants responded by seizing
the slaves. They beat one, killed another,
and stoned a third. A second time he dispatched even more slaves than before, but
they treated them the same way. Finally he
sent his son to them, thinking, 'They will respect my son.' When they saw the son, the
tenants said to one another, 'Here is the one
who will inherit everything. Let us kill him
and then we shall have his inheritance!'
With that they seized him, dragged him outside the vineyard, and killed him. What do
you suppose the owner of the vineyard will
do to those tenants when he comes?" They
replied, "He will bring that wicked crowd to
a bad end and lease his vineyard out to others who will see to it that he has grapes at
vintage time." Jesus said to them, "Did you
never read in the Scriptures,**

  'The stone which the builders rejected
  has become the keystone of the struc-
  ture.
  It was the Lord who did this
  and we find it marvelous to behold'?
**For this reason, I tell you, the kingdom of
God will be taken away from you and given
to a people that will yield a rich harvest."**

Reflection on the Readings

One of the best and most interesting ways
to teach is to tell a story. Jesus of Nazareth
knew this and used his story-telling skills to

challenge us to look at our lives in a new way. Jesus tells a story in today's Gospel which had a specific meaning in his time but still carries a powerful message to us today.

Jesus told the story of the vineyard to explain why he devotes time and energy to the poor and sinners. The chief priests of Judaism, like the tenants in the story, have rejected God's messenger. So Jesus turns to those who will bear fruit, and it is the unlikely sinners who accept the Gospel.

What does this parable have to say to us today? It seems that religious people can be tempted with that same attitude that characterized chief priests and elders: complacency in the underlying belief that we are God's chosen people, that we have the truth, that we have our salvation guaranteed. This complacency shows itself in narrow-mindedness, lack of creativity, lack of passion, and smug self-assurance. The "chosen people" of Jesus' era did not have a monopoly on those qualities. And, as the parable makes clear, if we do not choose to respond, God will find those who will.

Suggestions for Prayer

1. Reflect on one or more of the following questions:
   - Have you ever heard a story, whether from another person, from a book, from a movie, from the news, which really moved you? What was that story?
   - Were you ever involved in religion before and then as a result became smug and complacent? How can that be avoided?
   - Why did Jesus spend so much time reaching out to the poor? What is your attitude to the poor?
2. Imagine that Jesus has just had an argument with a smug, complacent religious person. Now he sees you. What does he say?
3. Try to envision what your life might be like for the next few days. Imagine Jesus with you, present as you meet every person, every situation.

Suggestion for Journal Keeping

Think of a time when you might have been narrow-minded and set in your ways. In writing, describe that time. Describe yourself now.

Douglas Fisher

Twenty-Seventh Sunday of the Year   B

READING I   Gn 2, 18–24

The Lord God said: "It is not good for the man to be alone. I will make a suitable partner for him." So the Lord God formed out of the ground various wild animals and various birds of the air, and he brought them to the man to see what he would call them; whatever the man called each of them would be its name. The man gave names to all the cattle, all the birds of the air, and all wild animals; but none proved to be the suitable partner for the man.

So the Lord God cast a deep sleep on the man, and while he was asleep, he took out one of his ribs and closed up its place with

flesh. The Lord God then built up into a woman the rib that he had taken from the man. When he brought her to the man, the man said:

"This one, at last, is bone of my bones
and flesh of my flesh;
This one shall be called 'woman,'
for out of 'her man' this one has been
taken."

That is why a man leaves his father and mother and clings to his wife, and the two of them become one body.

Responsorial Psalm   Ps 128, 1–2. 3. 4–5. 6

May the Lord bless us
all the days of our lives.

**Happy are you who fear the Lord,
who walk in his ways!
For you shall eat the fruit of your handiwork;
happy shall you be, and favored.**

May the Lord bless us
all the days of our lives.

**Your wife shall be like a fruitful vine
in the recesses of your home;
Your children like olive plants
around your table.**

May the Lord bless us
all the days of our lives.

**Behold, thus is the man blessed
who fears the Lord.
The Lord bless you from Zion:
may you see the prosperity of Jerusalem
all the days of your life.**

May the Lord bless us
all the days of our lives.

**May you see your children's children.
Peace be upon Israel!**

May the Lord bless us
all the days of our lives.

READING II   Heb 2, 9–11

Jesus was made for a little while lower than the angels, that through God's gracious will he might taste death for the sake of all men. Indeed, it was fitting that, when bringing many sons to glory, God, for whom and through whom all things exist, should make their leader in the work of salvation perfect through suffering. He who consecrates and those who are consecrated have one and the same Father. Therefore, he is not ashamed to call them brothers.

GOSPEL   Mk 10, 2–16

Some Pharisees came up and as a test began to ask Jesus whether it was permissible for a husband to divorce his wife. In reply he said, "What command did Moses give you?" They answered, "Moses permitted divorce and the writing of a decree of divorce." But Jesus told them: "He wrote that commandment for you because of your stubbornness. At the beginning of creation God made them male and female; for this reason a man shall leave his father and mother and the two shall become as one. They are no longer two but one flesh. Therefore let no man separate what God has joined." Back in the house again, the disciples began to question him about this. He told them, "Whoever divorces his wife and marries another commits adultery against her; and the woman who divorces her husband and marries another commits adultery."

People were bringing their little children to him to have him touch them, but the disciples were scolding them for this. Jesus became indignant when he noticed it and said to them: "Let the children come to me and do not hinder them. It is to just such as these that the kingdom of God belongs. I assure you that whoever does not accept the kingdom of God like a little child shall not enter into it." Then he embraced them and blessed them, placing his hands on them.

Reflection on the Readings

Our call from God is a lifelong one, toward perfection. In Genesis, God was creating a new and pure world, a world before the fall, a world of harmony and love. Jesus, by his coming, recalls that perfection created by God. He returns again to the indissolubility of marriage and uses children as an example of purity of heart and soul.

Today we still live in an imperfect time. We still have much to learn. But Jesus has come to teach us and set us free, if we are willing. All were welcome around Jesus. Jesus spoke to Pharisees and children alike, he ate with sinners and leaders, he invited rich and poor, men and women to gather around him, he touched the unclean and healed the sick.

Paul speaks further of what Jesus willingly did to begin the reconciliation and return to a time of harmony. Jesus became less than who he was, and by doing so raised us up. Jesus suffered and died for us so that we could live a new life and a new hope.

We must be willing to follow the example of Jesus. People and groups we consider less than ourselves are our equal before God. They are our brothers and sisters. We are called to embrace and bless them as Jesus did.

Suggestions for Prayer

1. We all know people who have been through a divorce. Bring one such person and his or her hurts and worries before Jesus. Tell Jesus your concerns about him or her and ask Jesus to take care of that person. Imagine the person being embraced and blessed by Jesus. Ask Jesus if there is anything he wants you to do for the person.

2. You are the parent who is bringing a child to Jesus. You are scolded by the disciples and you become discouraged. Just then, Jesus invites your child forward and blesses your child. After you return home you notice differences in your child and yourself. What will you tell Jesus the next time you see him?

3. Take a walk in nature (woods, park, beach, lakeside, etc.). Thank God for each act of creation that comes to mind.

Suggestion for Journal Keeping

Take a group of people you have difficulty believing are your equal (for example: homeless, unemployed, women, homosexuals). Write down all the reasons why you think or know Jesus loves them. Reread the second reading from Hebrews and see if you can add any more reasons to your list.

Kathleen M. Henry

Twenty-Seventh Sunday of the Year **C**

READING I   Hb 1, 2–3; 2, 2–4
How long, O Lord? I cry for help
    but you do not listen!
I cry out to you, "Violence!"
    but you do not intervene.

Why do you let me see ruin;
  why must I look at misery?
Destruction and violence are before me;
  there is strife, and clamorous discord.
Then the Lord answered me and said:
  Write down the vision
Clearly upon the tablets,
  so that one can read it readily.
For the vision still has its time,
  presses on to fulfillment, and will not dis-
    appoint;
If it delays, wait for it,
  it will surely come, it will not be late.
The rash man has no integrity;
  but the just man, because of his faith, shall
    live.

Responsorial Psalm   Ps 95, 1–2. 6–7. 8–9
If today you hear his voice,
  harden not your hearts.
Come, let us sing joyfully to the Lord;
  let us acclaim the Rock of our salvation.
Let us greet him with thanksgiving;
  let us joyfully sing psalms to him.
If today you hear his voice,
  harden not your hearts.
Come, let us bow down in worship;
  let us kneel before the Lord who made us.
For he is our God,
  and we are the people he shepherds, the
    flock he guides.
If today you hear his voice,
  harden not your hearts.
Oh, that today you would hear his voice:
  "Harden not your hearts as at Meribah,
  as in the day of Massah in the desert,
Where your fathers tempted me;
  they tested me though they had seen my
    works.
If today you hear his voice,
  harden not your hearts.

READING II   2 Tm 1, 6–8. 13–14
I remind you to stir into flame the gift of God
bestowed when my hands were laid on you.
The Spirit God has given us is no cowardly
spirit, but rather one that makes us strong,
loving and wise. Therefore, never be
ashamed of your testimony to our Lord, nor
of me, a prisoner for his sake; but with the
strength which comes from God bear your
share of the hardship which the gospel entails.

Take as a model of sound teaching what
you have heard me say, in faith and love in
Christ Jesus. Guard the rich deposit of faith
with the help of the Holy Spirit who dwells
within us.

GOSPEL   Lk 17, 5–10
The apostles said to the Lord, "Increase our
faith," and he answered: "If you had faith
the size of a mustard seed, you could say to
this sycamore, 'Be uprooted and transplanted into the sea,' and it would obey you.

"If one of you had a servant plowing or
herding sheep and he came in from the
fields, would you say to him, 'Come and sit
down at table'? Would you not rather say,
'Prepare my supper. Put on your apron and
wait on me while I eat and drink. You can eat
and drink afterward'? Would he be grateful
to the servant who was only carrying out his
orders? It is quite the same with you who
hear me. When you have done all you have
been commanded to do, say, 'We are useless
servants. We have done no more than our
duty.' "

Reflection on the Readings
The key words in today's Gospel might be
"faith" and "duty." At first reading it may
seem that the two have little connection. Je-

sus responds to the apostles' desire for greater faith by telling them two stories. One story illustrates the power of faith and the other tells us to regard our Christian service as duty, never expecting reward or recognition.

One link between these two stories may be found if we ponder the faith-filled life of someone we know who serves God diligently. Faith grows and is nurtured by service to others. In our service we recognize our helplessness and powerlessness. Thus we rely on God much more and our faith in turn is strengthened. Secondly, one who is truly alive in faith desires to serve in response to this great gift. Just as we have been touched by God, we desire others to experience this new life. We expect no reward and realize that it is a privilege to serve God.

This is what Paul calls Timothy to do in the second reading. As we serve the Lord and prepare for the sacraments of initiation, the Spirit is at work in us, making us "strong, loving, and wise."

Suggestions for Prayer

1. Pray for an increase in your faith. Recognize that as you grow in faith, you may be called to further action. Using the refrain to the responsorial psalm, pray that you will say yes to the Lord.
2. Give thanks for the privilege of serving the Lord. Identify one or two times when you may have been blessed in your service to others. Reflect on the second reading in light of this experience.
3. Faith is a gift. Spend a few moments identifying individuals who may have been "instruments" in your faith growth. Pray for these people, offering

thanks for their faith, asking for courage to be used in this manner.

Suggestion for Journal Keeping

The Gospel uses the phrase "useless servants." How do you feel when you hear that phrase? In what way is it true of you? Why is it only a partial description of you?"

Khris S. Ford

Twenty-Eighth Sunday of the Year Ⓐ

READING I   Is 25, 6–10

On this mountain the Lord of hosts
    will provide for all peoples
A feast of rich food and choice wines,
    juicy, rich food and pure, choice wines.
On this mountain he will destroy
    the veil that veils all peoples,
The web that is woven over all nations;
    he will destroy death forever.
The Lord God will wipe away
    the tears from all faces;
The reproach of his people he will remove
    from the whole earth; for the Lord has
    spoken.

On that day it will be said:
"Behold our God, to whom we looked to
    save us!
    This is the Lord for whom we looked;
    let us rejoice and be glad that he has saved
    us!"
For the hand of the Lord will rest on this
    mountain.

Responsorial Psalm   Ps 23, 1–3. 3–4. 5. 6

I shall live in the house of the Lord
  all the days of my life.

The Lord is my shepherd; I shall not want.
  In verdant pastures he gives me repose;
Beside restful waters he leads me;
  he refreshes my soul.

I shall live in the house of the Lord
  all the days of my life.

He guides me in right paths
  for his name's sake.
Even though I walk in the dark valley
  I fear no evil; for you are at my side
With your rod and your staff
  that give me courage.

I shall live in the house of the Lord
  all the days of my life.

You spread the table before me
  in the sight of my foes;
You anoint my head with oil;
  my cup overflows.

I shall live in the house of the Lord
  all the days of my life.

Only goodness and kindness follow me
  all the days of my life;
And I shall dwell in the house of the Lord
  for years to come.

I shall live in the house of the Lord
  all the days of my life.

READING II   Phil 4, 12–14. 19–20
**I am experienced in being brought low, yet
I know what it is to have an abundance. I
have learned how to cope with every circumstance—how to eat well or go hungry,
to be well provided for or do without. In him
who is the source of my strength I have
strength for everything.**

**Nonetheless, it was kind of you to want to
share in my hardships.**

**My God in turn will supply your needs
fully, in a way worthy of his magnificent
riches in Christ Jesus. All glory to our God
and Father for unending ages! Amen.**

GOSPEL   Mt 22, 1–14
**Jesus began to address the chief priests and
elders of the people, once more using parables. "The reign of God may be likened to a
king who gave a wedding banquet for his
son. He dispatched his servants to summon
the invited guests to the wedding, but they
refused to come. A second time he sent
other servants, saying: 'Tell those who were
invited, See, I have my dinner prepared! My
bullocks and corn-fed cattle are killed;
everything is ready. Come to the feast.'
Some ignored the invitation and went their
way, one to his farm, another to his business. The rest laid hold of his servants, insulted them, and killed them. At this the king
grew furious and sent his army to destroy
those murderers and burn their city. Then he
said to his servants: 'The banquet is ready,
but those who were invited were unfit to
come. That is why you must go out into the
byroads and invite to the wedding anyone
you come upon.' The servants then went out
into the byroads and rounded up everyone
they met, bad as well as good. This filled the
wedding hall with banqueters.**

**"When the king came in to meet the
guests, however, he caught sight of a man
not properly dressed for a wedding feast.
'My friend,' he said, 'how is it you came in
here not properly dressed?' The man had
nothing to say. The king then said to the attendants, 'Bind him hand and foot and throw
him out into the night to wail and grind his**

teeth.' The invited are many, the elect are few."

Reflection on the Readings

What is heaven like? The human mind and imagination have long sought the answer to the question. Children often imagine the answer in terms of playing forever without the imposition of school and homework. The elderly may see it as a time to be reunited with loved ones. Artists and saints may think of mystical union with God. The poor and oppressed hope for a better life with justice, free from suffering. Of course, no one knows exactly what heaven will be like, but that has never stopped us from using our own experience to try to imagine it.

The first reading today from the Book of Isaiah envisions a heavenly banquet in which all sin and suffering will be overcome. Jesus uses this image to talk about his favorite topic: the reign of God. The coming of the reign of God was the central message of Jesus. Jesus was not primarily a teacher of ethics but a person of faith with a distinctly religious perspective. His goal was not simply to get people to act differently, but to change their entire view of life and life's meaning. At the heart of Jesus' message of the kingdom of God was his insistence that the kingdom had already begun. A new way of life reflecting that final banquet was possible now if men and women would turn their hearts to God.

The readings today offer us a vision of heaven as a banquet and feast. The Gospel parable shows us the urgency of the vision. Heaven is not wishful thinking. God's reign has broken through now.

In a society where there is a great distinction between the haves and the have-nots, the image of the heavenly banquet might glare at us like an indictment. All are welcome in the kingdom. The kingdom cannot be confined to our own private vision, but is a life in love with God and neighbor.

Suggestions for Prayer

1. Reflect on one or more of the following questions:
   - How do you envision heaven? What will make it heavenly?
   - Jesus envisions the kingdom as a banquet. What are your family meals like? Are they a sign of community and love? How could you make them that way?
   - How do you feel about the idea of the kingdom beginning now? Is that true in your experience, or is the kingdom for you something in the future?
2. Imagine yourself walking along some back road. Suddenly Jesus appears and invites you to a banquet with him. How do you feel? What do you say to him?
3. Stay with that same scene from suggestion #2. As you walk along with Jesus you come across someone you consider a "bad" person. Jesus invites that person as well. What do you feel about this person? What do you feel toward Jesus?

Suggestion for Journal Keeping

Describe a time you were rejected by someone or some organization. Now imagine Jesus inviting you to the kingdom of God. Write down what you feel and what you say to Jesus.

Douglas Fisher

Twenty-Eighth Sunday of the Year   **B**

READING I   Wis 7, 7–11

I prayed, and prudence was given me;
   I pleaded, and the spirit of Wisdom came
      to me.
I preferred her to scepter and throne,
And deemed riches nothing in comparison
      with her,
   nor did I liken any priceless gem to her;
Because all gold, in view of her, is a little
      sand,
   and before her, silver is to be accounted
      mire.
Beyond health and comeliness I loved her,
And I chose to have her rather than the light,
   because the splendor of her never yields
      to sleep.
Yet all good things together came to me in
      her company,
   and countless riches at her hands.

Responsorial Psalm   Ps 90, 12–13. 14–15.
                                                    16–17

Fill us with your love, O Lord,
   and we will sing for joy!
Teach us to number our days aright,
   that we may gain wisdom of heart.
Return, O Lord! How long?
   Have pity on your servants!
Fill us with your love, O Lord,
   and we will sing for joy!
Fill us at daybreak with your kindness,
   that we may shout for joy and gladness all
      our days.
Make us glad, for the days when you af-
      flicted us,
   for the years when we saw evil.

Fill us with your love, O Lord,
   and we will sing for joy!
**Let your work be seen by your servants
   and your glory by their children;
And may the gracious care of the Lord our
      God be ours;
   prosper the work of our hands for us!
   [Prosper the work of our hands!]**
Fill us with your love, O Lord,
   and we will sing for joy!

READING II   Heb 4, 12–13

**God's word is living and effective, sharper
than any two-edged sword. It penetrates and
divides soul and spirit, joints and marrow; it
judges the reflections and thoughts of the
heart. Nothing is concealed from him; all
lies bare and exposed to the eyes of him to
whom we must render an account.**

GOSPEL   Mk 10, 17–30

**As Jesus was setting out on a journey a man
came running up, knelt down before him
and asked, "Good Teacher, what must I do
to share in everlasting life?" Jesus answered,
"Why do you call me good? No one is good
but God alone. You know the commandments:**
      **'You shall not kill;
      You shall not commit adultery;
      You shall not steal;
      You shall not bear false witness;
      You shall not defraud;
      Honor your father and your mother.' "
He replied, "Teacher, I have kept all these
since my childhood." Then Jesus looked at
him with love and told him, "There is one
thing more you must do. Go and sell what
you have and give to the poor; you will then
have treasure in heaven. After that come
and follow me." At these words the man's**

face fell. He went away sad, for he had many possessions. Jesus looked around and said to his disciples, "How hard it is for the rich to enter the kingdom of God!" The disciples could only marvel at his words. So Jesus repeated what he had said: "My sons, how hard it is to enter the kingdom of God! It is easier for a camel to pass through a needle's eye than for a rich man to enter the kingdom of God."

They were completely overwhelmed at this, and exclaimed to one another, "Then who can be saved?" Jesus fixed his gaze on them and said, "For man it is impossible but not for God. With God all things are possible."

Peter was moved to say to him: "We have put aside everything to follow you!" Jesus answered: "I give you my word, there is no one who has given up home, brothers or sisters, mother or father, children or property, for me and for the gospel who will not receive in this present age a hundred times as many homes, brothers and sisters, mothers, children and property—and persecution besides—and in the age to come, everlasting life."

Reflection on the Readings

When Jesus looked at the young man, he spoke only a few words. Those words clearly affected the young man with the power of God's word as described in Hebrews. They penetrated and laid bare the difficulty the man was having with Jesus' call. And the young man went away.

The disciples became very concerned with the apparent impossibility of salvation. Jesus' response was twofold. The invitation is gift, surrounded by love. When Jesus spoke to the young man, Jesus looked at him with love. The call of God's love is strong; once accepted, it becomes so strong that one is willing to give up even family to follow Jesus and the Gospel.

The first reading from Wisdom confirms the pull of God. The author clearly prefers God's wisdom to any earthly possession or physical reality.

But this gift is a two-edged sword. The way of Jesus Christ cuts through the world's ways. And the world objects with violence, ridicule and derision. Jesus, however, promises much good and the greatest gift of all, everlasting life, to those who follow.

Suggestions for Prayer

1. What is the one more thing Jesus is asking of you at this moment in time? Ask for Jesus' help so that it will not become an impossible stumbling block.
2. Pray Psalm 90 daily this week while asking yourself these questions:
   • How have I recognized God's majesty today?
   • How have I felt apart from God today?
   • How have I rejoiced at God's graciousness toward me today?
3. Think of an area in your life where it would help if you had wisdom. Are you willing to pray and plead for the spirit of wisdom? Tell God what the gift would mean to you.

Suggestion for Journal Keeping

Think of a situation where you felt totally overwhelmed and confounded. Write down how it felt. Describe how you felt when the

372

solution was discovered. What assistance does this recalling give you in reflecting on the Gospel?

Kathleen M. Henry

Twenty-Eighth Sunday of the Year   C

READING I   2 Kgs 5, 14–17
Naaman went down and plunged into the Jordan seven times at the word of Elisha, the man of God. His flesh became again like the flesh of a little child, and he was clean [of his leprosy].

He returned with his whole retinue to the man of God. On his arrival he stood before him and said, "Now I know that there is no God in all the earth, except in Israel. Please accept a gift from your servant."

"As the Lord lives whom I serve, I will not take it," Elisha replied; and despite Naaman's urging, he still refused. Naaman said: "If you will not accept, please let me, your servant, have two mule-loads of earth, for I will no longer offer holocaust or sacrifice to any other god except to the Lord."

Responsorial Psalm   Ps 98, 1. 2–3. 3–4
The Lord has revealed to the nations
    his saving power.
Sing to the Lord a new song,
  for he has done wondrous deeds;
His right hand has won victory for him,
  his holy arm.
The Lord has revealed to the nations his
    saving power.

The Lord has made his salvation known:
  in the sight of the nations he has revealed
    his justice.
He has remembered his kindness and his
  faithfulness
  toward the house of Israel.
The Lord has revealed to the nations his
    saving power.
All the ends of the earth have seen
  the salvation by our God.
Sing joyfully to the Lord, all you lands:
  break into song; sing praise.
The Lord has revealed to the nations his
    saving power.

READING II   2 Tm 2, 8–13
Remember that Jesus Christ, a descendant of David, was raised from the dead. This is the gospel I preach; in preaching it I suffer as a criminal, even to the point of being thrown into chains—but there is no chaining the word of God! Therefore I bear with all of this for the sake of those whom God has chosen, in order that they may obtain the salvation to be found in Christ Jesus and with it eternal glory.
  You can depend on this:
If we have died with him
  we shall also live with him;
If we hold out to the end
  we shall also reign with him.
But if we deny him he will deny us. If we are unfaithful he will still remain faithful; for he cannot deny himself.

GOSPEL   Lk 17, 11–19
On his journey to Jerusalem Jesus passed along the borders of Samaria and Galilee. As he was entering a village, ten lepers met

him. **Keeping their distance, they raised their voices and said, "Jesus, Master, have pity on us!" When he saw them, he responded, "Go and show yourselves to the priests." On their way there they were cured. One of them, realizing that he had been cured, came back praising God in a loud voice. He threw himself on his face at the feet of Jesus and spoke his praises. This man was a Samaritan.**

Jesus took the occasion to say, "Were not all ten made whole? Where are the other nine? Was there no one to return and give thanks to God except this foreigner?" He said to the man, "Stand up and go your way; your faith has been your salvation."

Reflection on the Readings

Naaman is healed by faith, and comes to profess his belief in the one, true God. The leper is healed through faith and returns to give thanks and to praise God. Both are healed and both deepen in faith as they proclaim their healing and give praise to the source of healing. Though we probably have not experienced such miraculous physical healing, we have experienced God's healing touch in our lives. If we respond in gratitude and praise, we are doubly blessed. Ten lepers came upon Jesus. All of them had enough faith to ask for healing and to follow Jesus' directions. Upon arrival all ten were cured of their leprosy. Yet only one returned to Jesus to give praise and thanksgiving. Only one recognized the true source of the healing, and was thus more fully healed. One only both was healed and received the gift of salvation.

How often we take for granted the blessings we have been given! It's not so much that we aren't thankful. We just forget to stop

and express our gratitude, to recognize and praise the source of all goodness.

Suggestions for Prayer

1. Pray a special prayer of thanksgiving for the gift of life itself. As you pray, be particularly aware of your heartbeat, a powerful sign of life within us. Take a few moments just to be present to God, the source of that life.
2. As Naaman plunged into the Jordan he was healed. As you prepare for your own baptismal bath, pray that the Lord may help you to discern what healing you should seek.
3. Pray the responsorial psalm. Read it slowly and deliberately, allowing more time for those words and phrases which seem to express your feelings.

Suggestion for Journal Keeping

Recall a time when you were healed from some sickness, broken relationship, or even a weakened trust in God. Describe the situation, the healing, your response, and your relationship to God afterward. How was your faith deepened as you acknowledged your healing?

Khris S. Ford

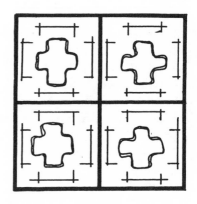

Twenty-Ninth Sunday of the Year   A

READING I   Is 45, 1. 4–6

Thus says the Lord to his anointed, Cyrus,
  whose right hand I grasp,
Subduing nations before him,
  and making kings run in his service,
Opening doors before him
  and leaving the gates unbarred:
For the sake of Jacob, my servant,
  of Israel, my chosen one,

I have called you by your name,
  giving you a title, though you knew me
    not.
I am the Lord and there is no other,
  there is no God besides me.
It is I who arm you, though you know me
    not,
  so that toward the rising and the setting of
    the sun
  men may know that there is none besides
    me.
I am the Lord, there is no other.

Responsorial Psalm   Ps 96, 1. 3. 4–5. 7–8.
                                                         9–10

Give the Lord glory and honor.
Sing to the Lord a new song;
  sing to the Lord, all you lands.
Tell his glory among the nations;
  among all peoples, his wondrous deeds.
Give the Lord glory and honor.
For great is the Lord and highly to be
  praised;
  awesome is he, beyond all gods.
For all the gods of the nations are things of
  nought,
  but the Lord made the heavens.

Give the Lord glory and honor.
Give to the Lord, you families of nations,
  give to the Lord glory and praise;
  give to the Lord the glory due his name!
Bring gifts, and enter his courts.
Give the Lord glory and honor.
Worship the Lord in holy attire;
  tremble before him, all the earth;
Say among the nations: The Lord is king,
  he governs the peoples with equity.
Give the Lord glory and honor.

READING II   1 Thes 1, 1–5

**Paul, Silvanus, and Timothy, to the church
of Thessalonians who belong to God the Father and the Lord Jesus Christ. Grace and
peace be yours.**

  **We keep thanking God for all of you and
we remember you in our prayers, for we
constantly are mindful before our God and
Father of the way you are proving your faith,
and laboring in love, and showing constancy
in hope in our Lord Jesus Christ. We know,
too, brothers beloved of God, how you were
chosen. Our preaching of the gospel proved
not a mere matter of words for you but one
of power; it was carried on in the Holy Spirit
and out of complete conviction.**

GOSPEL   Mt 22, 15–21

**The Pharisees went off and began to plot how
they might trap Jesus in speech. They sent
their disciples to him, accompanied by Herodian sympathizers, who said: "Teacher,
we know you are a truthful man and teach
God's way sincerely. You court no one's favor and do not act out of human respect.
Give us your opinion, then, in this case. Is it
lawful to pay tax to the emperor or not?" Jesus recognized their bad faith and said to**

them, "Why are you trying to trip me up, you hypocrites? Show me the coin used for the tax." When they handed him a small Roman coin he asked them, "Whose head is this, and whose inscription?" "Caesar's," they replied. At that he said to them, "Then give to Caesar what is Caesar's, but give to God what is God's."

Reflection on the Readings

Jesus' statement in this week's Gospel has been quoted out of context numerous times. "Give to Caesar what is Caesar's, but give to God what is God's." Let's look at this quote in the context of the times and then apply it in its truth to our lives.

The Herodian sympathizers supported the puppet ruler of Israel, Herod Antipas. They would have supported the tax because Herod's power was totally dependent on Rome. The Pharisees, however, being the most devout of all Jews, would have opposed the tax and Roman rule, although they would not have gone as far as the Zealots (anti-Roman insurrectionists) who would have refused to pay the tax. If Jesus says payment is licit, he may be portrayed as a Roman sympathizer. If he says that payment to Rome is not to be obeyed, he is then a subversive.

Jesus refuses to be trapped by the question. By answering as he does, he demonstrates the relative value of all commitments in comparison to the commitment to love God. Everything else will find its meaning in relation to that. Jesus is not giving a definitive teaching on taxes or government. He is saying that love of one's country and allegiance to its leaders have a value, but a relative one. The value of nationalism easily becomes a vice when it is understood in the tribal sense of "us" against "them." Unthinking, uncritical patriotism is simply a form of idolatry. Perhaps St. Thomas More captured the meaning of Jesus saying in his own life. A man who deeply loved his country, he was convicted of treason for his refusal to acknowledge the king as the supreme head of the Church in England. His words were: "I am the king's good servant, but God's first."

Suggestions for Prayer

1. Reflect on one or more of the following questions:
   - In what ways is being an American an obstacle to being Christian? How is it an aid?
   - Can you imagine taking a public stance against a government policy because of your faith?
   - In what ways do you think the Church should be involved in the realm of political decision-making?
2. Imagine yourself in the crowd that day when Jesus was confronted by the Pharisees. You hear what he has to say. You go up to him afterward and ask him further questions. What do you ask?
3. Think about an upcoming election. How would a person of faith vote? How will you vote?

Suggestion for Journal Keeping

Describe a time when you were torn as to how to vote. How did you decide? What values were brought into the decision? Are any of these values Christian values?

Douglas Fisher

Twenty-Ninth Sunday of the Year **B**

READING I
Is 53, 10–11

[But the Lord was pleased
  to crush him in infirmity.]
If he gives his life as an offering for sin,
  he shall see his descendants in a long life,
  and the will of the Lord shall be accomplished through him.

Because of his affliction
  he shall see the light in fullness of days;
Through his suffering, my servant shall justify many,
  and their guilt he shall bear.

Responsorial Psalm
Ps 33, 4–5. 18–19. 20. 22

Lord, let your mercy be on us,
  as we place our trust in you.
Upright is the word of the Lord,
  and all his works are trustworthy.
He loves justice and right;
  of the kindness of the Lord the earth is full.
Lord, let your mercy be on us,
  as we place our trust in you.
See, the eyes of the Lord are upon those who
    fear him,
  upon those who hope for his kindness,
To deliver them from death
  and preserve them in spite of famine.
Lord, let your mercy be on us,
  as we place our trust in you.
Our soul waits for the Lord,
  who is our help and our shield.
May your kindness, O Lord, be upon us
  who have put our hope in you.
Lord, let your mercy be on us,
  as we place our trust in you.

READING II
Heb 4, 14–16

We have a great high priest who has passed through the heavens, Jesus, the Son of God; let us hold fast to our profession of faith. For we do not have a high priest who is unable to sympathize with our weakness, but one who was tempted in every way that we are, yet never sinned. So let us confidently approach the throne of grace to receive mercy and favor and to find help in time of need.

GOSPEL
Mk 10, 35–45

Zebedee's sons, James and John, approached Jesus. "Teacher," they said, "we want you to grant our request." "What is it?" he asked. They replied, "See to it that we sit, one at your right and the other at your left, when you come into your glory." Jesus told them, "You do not know what you are asking. Can you drink the cup I shall drink or be baptized in the same bath of pain as I?" "We can," they told him. Jesus said in response, "From the cup I drink of you shall drink; the bath I am immersed in you shall share. But sitting at my right or my left is not mine to give; that is for those for whom it has been reserved." The other ten, on hearing this, became indignant at James and John. Jesus called them together and said to them: "You know how among the Gentiles those who seem to exercise authority lord it over them; their great ones make their importance felt. It cannot be like that with you. Anyone among you who aspires to greatness must serve the rest; whoever wants to rank first among you must serve the needs of all. The Son of Man has not come to be served but to serve—to give his life in ransom for the many."

Reflection on the Readings

Isaiah, the Old Testament prophet, spoke about the Suffering Servant. Isaiah foretold that the Servant would give his life as an offering for our sins. As Christians, we understand that Jesus is the Suffering Servant. The will of God, that we be reconciled to him, is accomplished in Jesus.

Jesus invites us to come and follow him. And, just as James and John did, we shall experience what it means to follow Jesus. We will daily discover opportunities to give our life for others. And we shall feel pain.

Paul offers us hope for such occasions. Jesus sympathizes with our weaknesses. He understands temptation and difficulties. Jesus experienced such things. By living among us Jesus has made God approachable. We can ask for and receive mercy and favor and help in times of need.

But we must not become puffed up and proud because God has chosen us. Rather, we must make it an opportunity to bring others to Jesus. Jesus becomes approachable to others when they see that we are different and do not act in worldly ways. When we practice humility, charity or love, when we serve those in need, when we comfort and stand with the downtrodden, we represent the approachable God who calls all.

Suggestions for Prayer

1. Read Psalm 33 at the end of the day and think of the ways that the psalm has come alive for you throughout the day.
2. Imagine Jesus handing you the cup to drink. What are your reservations about drinking from the cup? Are you willing to ask for Jesus' help in such times of need?
3. Talk with Jesus about the definition of servant. What is your definition? What do you hear Jesus offering as his definition? How do they differ? Are you willing to adopt Jesus' definition where it is different from yours?

Suggestion for Journal Keeping

Recall a time when you chose to be humble rather than exalting yourself or letting others honor you. What was the experience like? List the positive and negative feelings it raised. How would being humble be the same or different for Jesus?

Kathleen M. Henry

Twenty-Ninth Sunday of the Year   C

READING I   Ex 17, 8–13

Amalek came and waged war against Israel. Moses, therefore, said to Joshua, "Pick out certain men, and tomorrow go out and engage Amalek in battle. I will be standing on top of the hill with the staff of God in my hand." So Joshua did as Moses told him: he engaged Amalek in battle after Moses had climbed to the top of the hill with Aaron and Hur. As long as Moses kept his hands raised up, Israel had the better of the fight, but when he let his hands rest, Amalek had the better of the fight. Moses' hands, however, grew tired; so they put a rock in place for him to sit on. Meanwhile Aaron and Hur supported his hands, one on one side and one on the other, so that his hands remained

steady till sunset. And Joshua mowed down Amalek and his people with the edge of the sword.

Responsorial Psalm   Ps 121, 1–2. 3–4. 5–6. 7–8

Our help is from the Lord
  who made heaven and earth.
I lift up my eyes toward the mountains;
  whence shall help come to me?
My help is from the Lord,
  who made heaven and earth.
Our help is from the Lord
  who made heaven and earth.
May he not suffer your foot to slip;
  may he slumber not who guards you:
Indeed he neither slumbers nor sleeps,
  the guardian of Israel.
Our help is from the Lord
  who made heaven and earth.
The Lord is your guardian; the Lord is your
  shade;
  he is beside you at your right hand.
The sun shall not harm you by day,
  nor the moon by night.
Our help is from the Lord
  who made heaven and earth.
The Lord will guard you from all evil;
  he will guard your life.
The Lord will guard your coming and your
  going,
  both now and forever.
Our help is from the Lord
  who made heaven and earth.

READING II   2 Tm 3, 14—4, 2
You must remain faithful to what you have learned and believed, because you know who your teachers were. Likewise, from your infancy you have known the sacred Scriptures, the source of the wisdom which through faith in Jesus Christ leads to salvation. All Scripture is inspired of God and is useful for teaching—for reproof, correction, and training in holiness so that the man of God may be fully competent and equipped for every good work.

In the presence of God and of Christ Jesus, who is coming to judge the living and the dead, and by his appearing and his kingly power, I charge you to preach the word, to stay with this task whether convenient or inconvenient—correcting, reproving, appealing—constantly teaching and never losing patience.

GOSPEL   Lk 18, 1–8
Jesus told his disciples a parable on the necessity of praying always and not losing heart: "Once there was a judge in a certain city who respected neither God nor man. A widow in that city kept coming to him saying, 'Give me my rights against my opponent.' For a time he refused, but finally he thought, 'I care little for God or man, but this widow is wearing me out. I am going to settle in her favor or she will end by doing me violence.'" The Lord said, "Listen to what the corrupt judge has to say. Will not God then do justice to his chosen who call out to him day and night? Will he delay long over them, do you suppose? I tell you, he will give them swift justice. But when the Son of Man comes, will he find any faith on the earth?"

Reflection on the Readings
  Surely if a corrupt judge would give in to the pleas of this persistent widow, our God will hear our persistent cries. Persistence

paid off for the widow, and so will we be rewarded if we persist in our prayers to God. Like the widow, we are asked to stay strong in our faith, even when the going gets difficult. It is easy to persist in the good times, when life is smooth. But, what of our strong faith when we are persecuted or when we just don't feel the presence of God? The Gospel tells us that swift justice is due those who are persistent in calling upon the Lord.

In the second reading Paul reminds Timothy of the sources of his faith—his family, his teachers and, most importantly, the Scriptures. It is this formation that strengthens Timothy for the task at hand, the preaching of the word. During this time of baptismal preparation, the Scriptures are a key source to strengthen our faith so that we may be prepared for the tasks that lie ahead.

Suggestions for Prayer

1. Prayer is the work of the Spirit in us, not our own doing. Pray for the grace to be persistent in prayer, especially during those "desert" times.
2. Is there something or someone that you've given up on? Offer this to God once again. Consciously pray with confidence in the Father.
3. If this is a particularly good time in your life, bask in the goodness and give thanks in prayer. In doing this, your faith is strengthened for a time when things are more difficult.

Suggestion for Journal Keeping
"But, when the Son of Man comes will he find any faith on the earth?" Look about you.

Reflect on your life situation. What are some signs of faith that help to sustain you?

Khris S. Ford

Thirtieth Sunday of the Year A

READING I   Ex 22, 20–26
"You shall not molest or oppress an alien, for you were once aliens yourselves in the land of Egypt. You shall not wrong any widow or orphan. If ever you wrong them and they cry out to me, I will surely hear their cry. My wrath will flare up, and I will kill you with the sword; then your own wives will be widows, and your children orphans.

"If you lend money to one of your poor neighbors among my people, you shall not act like an extortioner toward him by demanding interest from him. If you take your neighbor's cloak as a pledge, you shall return it to him before sunset; for this cloak of his is the only covering he has for his body. What else has he to sleep in? If he cries out to me, I will hear him; for I am compassionate."

Responsorial Psalm   Ps 18, 2–3. 3–4. 47. 51

I love you, Lord, my strength.
I love you, O Lord, my strength,
   O Lord, my rock, my fortress, my deliverer.
I love you, Lord, my strength.
My God, my rock of refuge,
   my shield, the horn of my salvation, my stronghold!

Praised be the Lord, I exclaim,
and I am safe from my enemies.

I love you, Lord, my strength.

**The Lord live! And blessed be my Rock!
Extolled be God my savior.**

**You who gave great victories to your king
and showed kindness to your anointed.**

I love you, Lord, my strength.

READING II   1 Thes 1, 5–10

You know as well as we do what we proved to be like when, while still among you, we acted on your behalf. You, in turn, became imitators of us and of the Lord, receiving the word despite great trials, with the joy that comes from the Holy Spirit. Thus you became a model for all the believers of Macedonia and Achaia. The word of the Lord has echoed forth from you resoundingly. This is true not only in Macedonia and Achaia; throughout every region your faith in God is celebrated, which makes it needless for us to say anything more. The people of those parts are reporting what kind of reception we had from you and how you turned to God from idols, to serve him who is the living and true God and to await from heaven the Son he raised from the dead—Jesus, who delivers us from the wrath to come.

GOSPEL   Mt 22, 34–40

When the Pharisees heard that Jesus had silenced the Sadducees, they assembled in a body; and one of them, a lawyer, in an attempt to trip him up, asked him, "Teacher, which commandment of the law is the greatest?" Jesus said to him:

**" 'You shall love the Lord your God
with your whole heart,
with your whole soul,
and with all your mind.'**

**This is the greatest and first commandment.
The second is like it:**

'You shall love your neighbor as yourself.'

On these two commandments the whole law is based, and the prophets as well."

Reflection on the Readings

The key insight of this week's Gospel is Jesus combination of two commandments as the central meaning of life. This insight, although not unique to Jesus, was one of the abiding principles of his life and teaching: love of God and love of one's neighbor form an inseparable unity. This is evident not only in what Jesus says, but also in how he acts. In Jesus there is total openness and devotion to the Father. His relationship with the Father is the source of his life. Yet that relationship is not simply a private one. It flows out into the compassion and truth of his relationships with people.

In trying to describe the relationship between love of God and love of one's neighbor, spiritual writers sometimes use the phrases "vertical" (relationship with God) and "horizontal" (relationships with others). It seems that the key is to maintain a healthy and positive relationship between the two and to allow each to enrich the other. A one-sided vertical relationship degenerates into illusion and escapism from the real challenges of love. A one-sided horizontal relationship loses sight of the ultimate goal and source of its loving. It collapses under the weight of becoming its own god and has no measure outside itself.

Perhaps there is one more aspect of this commandment that we are ignoring. The law says: Love your neighbor as yourself. It has become commonplace in religious education to say that Jesus is teaching that we must love ourselves as well. In fact, he is simply assuming it as the condition for loving others. Jesus never explicitly talks about self-love. It is more of a modern concept. However, there is no doubt that Jesus was a champion of the healthy and proper love of oneself. For Jesus, this fundamental self-love is very different from many of its contemporary narcissistic manifestations. A person's basic worth is not derived from anything less than God's unconditional love for all of his children and the dignity inherent to that status.

Suggestions for Prayer

1. Reflect on one or more of the following questions:
   - Do you see any aspects of narrow legalism in Christianity?
   - How can you enrich the "vertical" aspect of your spirituality?
   - How do you see the connection between the "vertical" and "horizontal" in your life?
   - How do you understand a healthy love of self?
2. Think of a circumstance in your life where you consistently feel bad about yourself. Imagine Jesus walking into this situation. What happens?
3. Have you ever tried to love someone at a time when you felt bad about yourself? What happened? Reflect on this question and then reread Matthew 22:34–40.

Suggestion for Journal Keeping

Describe a person you know who loves God but does not seem to love people. Describe a person who is generous and unselfish but is not religious. Which person do you identify with? What can you do to integrate the two?

Douglas Fisher

Thirtieth Sunday of the Year B

READING I   Jer 31, 7–9
Thus says the Lord:
Shout with joy for Jacob,
  exult at the head of the nations;
  proclaim your praise and say:
The Lord has delivered his people,
  the remnant of Israel.
Behold, I will bring them back
  from the land of the north;
I will gather them from the ends of the world,
  with the blind and the lame in their midst,
The mothers and those with child;
  they shall return as an immense throng.
They departed in tears,
  but I will console them and guide them;
I will lead them to brooks of water,
  on a level road, so that none shall stumble.
For I am a father to Israel,
  Ephraim is my first-born.

Responsorial Psalm   Ps 126, 1–2. 2–3. 4–
5. 6

The Lord has done great things for us;
  we are filled with joy.
When the Lord brought back the captives of Zion,
  we were like men dreaming.
Then our mouth was filled with laughter,
  and our tongue with rejoicing.

The Lord has done great things for us;
  we are filled with joy.
Then they said among the nations,
  "The Lord has done great things for
them."
The Lord has done great things for us;
  we are glad indeed.
The Lord has done great things for us;
  we are filled with joy.
Restore our fortunes, O Lord,
  like the torrents in the southern desert.
Those that sow in tears
  shall reap rejoicing.
The Lord has done great things for us;
  we are filled with joy.
Although they go forth weeping,
  carrying the seed to be sown,
They shall come back rejoicing,
  carrying their sheaves.
The Lord has done great things for us;
  we are filled with joy.

READING II   Heb 5, 1–6
Every high priest is taken from among men
and made their representative before God,
to offer gifts and sacrifices for sins. He is
able to deal patiently with erring sinners, for
he is himself beset by weakness and so must
make sin offerings for himself as well as for
the people. One does not take this honor on
his own initiative, but only when called by
God as Aaron was. Even Christ did not glo-
rify himself with the office of high priest; he
received it from the One who said to him,
  "You are my son;
    today I have begotten you";
just as he says in another place,
  "You are a priest forever,
    according to the order of Melchize-
    dek."

GOSPEL   Mk 10, 46–52
As Jesus was leaving Jericho with his disci-
ples and a sizable crowd, there was a blind
beggar Bartimaeus ("son of Timaeus") sit-
ting by the roadside. On hearing that it was
Jesus of Nazareth, he began to call out, "Je-
sus, Son of David, have pity on me!" Many
people were scolding him to make him keep
quiet, but he shouted all the louder, "Son of
David, have pity on me!" Then Jesus stopped
and said, "Call him over." So they called the
blind man over, telling him as they did so,
"You have nothing whatever to fear from
him! Get up! He is calling you!" He threw
aside his cloak, jumped up and came to Je-
sus. Jesus asked him, "What do you want me
to do for you?" "Rabboni," the blind man
said, "I want to see." Jesus said in reply, "Be
on your way! Your faith has healed you."
Immediately he received his sight and
started to follow him up the road.

Reflection on the Readings

The blind man is a model for approaching
Jesus in faith. He was an active participant in
his healing. He persisted in his attempts to attract Jesus' attention, even when others tried
to discourage him. He told Jesus what he
wanted; he was clear and specific. And he
believed in Jesus and his power. The blind
man's faith caused his healing.

By the man's willingness to approach Jesus, he revealed his faith in Jesus. That faith
was then strengthened by the encounter with
Jesus. Thereafter, he followed Jesus up the
road.

Jesus met and responded to the man even
though he was blind. He approaches us even
when we are blind. In our encounters with Jesus we are given the opportunity to express
our faith. As a result, our relationship be-

comes stronger and it becomes easier to follow Jesus up the road.

Paul reassures us that we can have faith in Jesus. He is our high priest representative before God. Jesus speaks to God on our behalf from the perspective of one who has stood in our shoes. We have nothing to fear in approaching Jesus.

The prophet Jeremiah had foretold an age when God would deliver and gather his people, consoling and leading them. Jesus' coming has inaugurated that time. In Mark's Gospel we see that the blind and lame, women and children, lowly and sinners are welcomed by Jesus. No one is turned away.

Suggestions for Prayer

1. The reading from Jeremiah is a prophecy of comfort in times of distress, a promise of a better future. Think of an area in your life or relationships where you need to know that things will get better. Slowly read and reflect on the reading, savoring its promises.
2. Imagine Jesus as the high priest presenting you to God the Father and the Holy Spirit. Listen to the positive things Jesus says about you.
3. Recall when you were sitting by the roadside and you first decided to approach Jesus. What is it that attracted you to Jesus? Tell Jesus the things that made you decide to find out more about him and caused you to begin exploring the possibility of following him.

Suggestion for Journal Keeping

Write down an area in your life where you have come to realize that you are blind. Imagine Jesus approaching you and asking:

"What do you want me to do for you?" Write down the stumbling blocks to asking Jesus for sight in that area. Continue with this exercise until, when Jesus approaches and asks the question, you can ask for sight.

Kathleen M. Henry

Thirtieth Sunday of the Year **C**

READING I   Sir 35, 12–14. 16–18
The Lord is a God of justice,
   who knows no favorites.
Though not unduly partial toward the weak,
   yet he hears the cry of the oppressed.
He is not deaf to the wail of the orphan,
   nor to the widow when she pours out her
      complaint.

He who serves God willingly is heard;
   his petition reaches the heavens.
The prayer of the lowly pierces the clouds;
   it does not rest till it reaches its goal,
Nor will it withdraw till the Most High responds,
   judges justly and affirms the right.

Responsorial Psalm   Ps 34, 2–3. 17–18.
                                    19. 23
The Lord hears the cry of the poor.
I will bless the Lord at all times;
   his praise shall be ever in my mouth.
Let my soul glory in the Lord;
   the lowly will hear me and be glad.
The Lord hears the cry of the poor.
The Lord confronts the evildoers,
   to destroy remembrance of them from the
      earth.

When the just cry out, the Lord hears them,
   and from all their distress he rescues
   them.
The Lord hears the cry of the poor.
The Lord is close to the brokenhearted;
   and those who are crushed in spirit he
   saves.
The Lord redeems the lives of his servants;
   no one incurs guilt who takes refuge in
   him.
The Lord hears the cry of the poor.

READING II   2 Tm 4, 6–8. 16–18
**I am already being poured out like a libation.
The time of my dissolution is near. I have
fought the good fight, I have finished the
race, I have kept the faith. From now on a
merited crown awaits me; on that Day the
Lord, just judge that he is, will award it to
me—and not only to me but to all who have
looked for his appearing with eager longing.**

**At the first hearing of my case in court, no
one took my part. In fact, everyone abandoned me. May it not be held against them!
But the Lord stood by my side and gave me
strength, so that through me the preaching
task might be completed and all the nations
might hear the gospel. That is how I was
saved from the lion's jaws. The Lord will
continue to rescue me from all attempts to
do me harm and will bring me safe to his
heavenly kingdom. To him be glory forever
and ever. Amen.**

GOSPEL   Lk 18, 9–14
**Jesus spoke this parable addressed to those
who believed in their own self-righteousness
while holding everyone else in contempt:
"Two men went up to the temple to pray;
one was a Pharisee, the other a tax collector.
The Pharisee with head unbowed prayed in**
**this fashion: 'I give you thanks, O God, that
I am not like the rest of men—grasping,
crooked, adulterous—or even like this tax
collector. I fast twice a week. I pay tithes on
all I possess.' The other man, however, kept
his distance, not even daring to raise his eyes
to heaven. All he did was beat his breast and
say, 'O God, be merciful to me, a sinner.'
Believe me, this man went home from the
temple justified but the other did not. For
everyone who exalts himself shall be humbled while he who humbles himself shall be
exalted.''**

Reflection on the Readings
   Today we are given some guidance in how
we should pray. We are offered this guidance
in the form of a story about two men who
prayed. One prayed with head held high, list-
ing the many sacrifices he had made for the
Lord, and separating himself from the sinners. The other, head and eyes bowed, acknowledged his sinfulness and begged God's
mercy. We are told that the second man shall
be exalted and the first shall be humbled.
Our prayer is to be in humility, raising up
God's name in praise, and recognizing our
complete dependence on him.
   Sirach affirms this in saying that the
"prayer of the lowly pierces the clouds.'' In
our lowliness we are joined with all people.
We dare not stand in judgment of anyone.
Paul too displays this attitude when he forgives those who have betrayed him. He
learned how to depend on the Lord alone.

Suggestions for Prayer

1. Pray for the grace of humility. Look at
   one specific area of your life where you
   most need this grace.

2. Pray the words: "Jesus Christ, Son of God, Savior of the world, have mercy on me, a sinner." Repeat this several times, saying the words slowly. Emphasize a different word each time. Allow the words to soak into your being.
3. Pray that this day you will judge no man or woman, and that you will seek your identity only in Christ. Use Philippians 2:3–9.

Suggestion for Journal Keeping

With which person did you identify in the Gospel story?

Are you the tax collector or the Pharisee? Why?

Khris S. Ford

Thirty-First Sunday of the Year A

READING I   Mal 1, 14–2, 2. 8–10
A great King am I, says the Lord of hosts,
   and my name will be feared among the nations.
If you do not lay it to heart,
   to give glory to my name, says the Lord of hosts,
I will send a curse upon you
   and of your blessing I will make a curse.
Yes, I have already cursed it,
   because you do not lay it to heart.
You have turned aside from the way,
   and have caused many to falter by your instruction;
You have made void the covenant of Levi,
   says the Lord of hosts.

I, therefore, have made you contemptible
   and base before all the people,
Since you do not keep my ways,
   but show partiality in your decisions.
Have we not all the one Father?
   Has not the one God created us?
Why then do we break faith with each other,
   violating the covenant of our fathers?

Responsorial Psalm   Ps 131, 1. 2. 3
In you, Lord, I have found my peace.
O Lord, my heart is not proud,
   nor are my eyes haughty;
I busy not myself with great things,
   nor with things too sublime for me.
In you, Lord, I have found my peace.
Nay rather, I have stilled and quieted
   my soul like a weaned child.
Like a weaned child on its mother's lap,
   [so is my soul within me.]
In you, Lord, I have found my peace.
O Israel, hope in the Lord,
   both now and forever.

READING II   1 Thes 2, 7–9. 13
While we were among you we were as gentle as any nursing mother fondling her little ones. So well disposed were we toward you, in fact, that we wanted to share with you not only God's tidings but our very lives, you had become so dear to us. You must recall, brothers, our efforts and our toil: how we worked day and night all the time we preached God's good tidings to you in order not to impose on you in any way. That is why we thank God constantly that in receiving his message from us you took it, not as the word of men, but as it truly is, the word of God at work within you who believe.

GOSPEL   Mt 23, 1–12

Jesus told the crowds and his disciples: "The scribes and the Pharisees have succeeded Moses as teachers; therefore, do everything and observe everything they tell you. But do not follow their example. Their words are bold but their deeds are few. They bind up heavy loads, hard to carry, to lay on other men's shoulders, while they themselves will not lift a finger to budge them. All their works are performed to be seen. They widen their phylacteries and wear huge tassels. They are fond of places of honor at banquets and the front seats in synagogues, of marks of respect in public and of being called 'Rabbi.' As to you, avoid the title 'Rabbi.' One among you is your teacher, the rest are learners. Do not call anyone on earth your father. Only one is your father, the One in heaven. Avoid being called teachers. Only one is your teacher, the Messiah. The greatest among you will be the one who serves the rest. Whoever exalts himself shall be humbled, but whoever humbles himself shall be exalted."

Reflection on the Readings

"Practice what you preach" is a line all of us have heard many times in many different contexts. In today's Gospel Jesus addresses it to religious people. When we look at all four Gospels, we see that Jesus is continually frustrated and angered by people who put on ornate religious rituals without making the love of God and neighbor part of their everyday living.

Jesus also says that people should not be called "rabbi," "teacher" or "father." The meaning of this passage is very important although the specifics need to be placed in context. The heart of Jesus' message here is that people in leadership positions should not think they are better than everyone else, or that they have the right to demand blind obedience from others. In addition, Jesus does not want people to follow leaders as cult-like figures. We have numerous examples of religious leaders abusing power in our own day. The actual calling of someone "father," "teacher" or "rabbi" is not at the heart of what Jesus is saying and can be interpreted differently in various cultures and historical settings.

We hear many people labeled "great" by our media, but Jesus has a narrow definition of the term. Greatness is determined by service. "The greatest among you will be the one who serves the rest." Service is given by someone who is humble, that is, as we saw in last week's Gospel, someone who loves himself or herself and therefore can love another knowing that he or she has something wonderful to give.

Suggestions for Prayer

1. Reflect on one or more of the following questions:
   - Have you ever gone to a religious ceremony, knowing that the people attending were not living what they were saying? How did that make you feel?
   - Jesus says that you are great when you serve another. Is there a way open to you now where you could serve?
   - What is the true meaning of humble? Could you be a humble person?
2. Take a couple of the prayers from Sunday's liturgy of the word and meditate on them. How could you make them real in your daily living?

387

3. Think of people who serve others. What are their qualities? Do you think they are great?

Suggestion for Journal Keeping

Describe a time in your life when you were humble and then were exalted. How did it make you feel? How can a person live humbly and what do you believe it will result in?

Douglas Fisher

Thirty-First Sunday of the Year B

READING I   Dt 6, 2–6

Moses told the people: Fear the Lord, your God, and keep, throughout the days of your lives, all his statutes and commandments which I enjoin on you, and thus have long life. Hear then, Israel, and be careful to observe them, that you may grow and prosper the more, in keeping with the promise of the Lord, the God of your fathers, to give you a land flowing with milk and honey. "Hear, O Israel! The Lord is our God, the Lord alone! Therefore, you shall love the Lord, your God, with all your heart, and with all your soul, and with all your strength. Take to heart these words which I enjoin on you today."

Responsorial Psalm   Ps 18, 2–3. 3–4. 47. 51

I love you, Lord, my strength.
I love you, O Lord, my strength,
   O Lord, my rock, my fortress, my deliverer.
I love you, Lord, my strength.

My God, my rock of refuge,
   my shield, the horn of my salvation, my stronghold!
Praised be the Lord, I exclaim,
   and I am safe from my enemies.
I love you, Lord, my strength.
The Lord live! And blessed be my Rock!
   Extolled be God my savior.
You who gave great victories to your king
   and showed kindness to your anointed.
I love you, Lord, my strength.

READING II   Heb 7, 23–28

Under the old covenant there were many priests because they were prevented by death from remaining in office; but Jesus, because he remains forever, has a priesthood which does not pass away. Therefore he is always able to save those who approach God through him, since he forever lives to make intercession for them.

It was fitting that we should have such a high priest: holy, innocent, undefiled, separated from sinners, higher than the heavens. Unlike the other high priests, he has no need to offer sacrifice day after day, first for his own sins and then for those of the people; he did that once for all when he offered himself. For the law sets up as high priests men who are weak, but the word of the oath which came after the law appoints as priest the Son, made perfect forever.

GOSPEL   Mk 12, 28–34

One of the scribes came up to Jesus, and asked him, "Which is the first of all the commandments?" Jesus replied: "This is the first:

   'Hear, O Israel! The Lord our God is Lord alone!

388

**Therefore you shall love the Lord your God
with all your heart,
with all your soul,
with all your mind,
and with all your strength.'
This is the second,
'You shall love your neighbor as yourself.'
There is no other commandment greater than these." The scribe said to him: "Excellent, Teacher! You are right in saying, 'He is the One, there is no other than he.' Yes, 'to love him with all our heart, with all our thoughts and with all our strength, and to love our neighbor as ourselves' is worth more than any burnt offering or sacrifice."
Jesus approved the insight of this answer and told him, "You are not far from the reign of God." And no one had the courage to ask him any more questions.**

Reflection on the Readings

Moses instructed the people to fear the Lord and to keep his laws so that they would prosper and receive the bounty of God's promises. They were to follow and love God above all else.

When Jesus was asked about the greatest commandment, he began with Moses' admonishment from Deuteronomy. Jesus then coupled it with a second directive whose basis can be found in Leviticus 19:18. Jesus, by story and example, expanded the definition of neighbor. He expands neighbor to include not just one's family and friends, but also one's enemies, as well as those with whom one disagrees and those we dislike. Jesus also commands us to love ourselves. Jesus loves us and wants us to love ourselves as we love God and neighbor.

Jesus, by refusing to stop with the first commandment and by joining the two directives, is saying that to follow him is not just to be in relationship with God. We need to also love ourselves and others. Salvation is not just between me and God but is lived out in community, with others and with myself.

Paul reminds us that Jesus is available to us. He is forever ready and willing to stand before the Father on our behalf. Paul sets out a great promise that should not be overlooked or underrated: Jesus is always able to save those who approach God through him.

Suggestions for Prayer

1. Psalm 18 is a wealth of drama and promises fulfilled. Read it this week as follows. Day 1: verses 1–7; Day 2: verses 8–20; Day 3: verses 21–31; Day 4: verses 32–39; Day 5: verses 40–46; Day 6: verses 47–51; Day 7: reread and reflect on the portion that meant the most to you.
2. Reflect on the following:
   • How can I love God with my heart and emotions?
   • How can I love God with my soul and essence?
   • How can I love God with my mind and intellect?
   • How can I love God with my strength and body?
3. We can approach God through Jesus. Jesus has taught us how to pray to the Father. Slowly pray the Our Father reflecting on the words you are saying.

Do you believe and mean what you are saying to God the Father?

Suggestion for Journal Keeping

Draw a picture that represents why you are having a difficult time loving a particular person. The picture can be of how you see the person, the emotions you are feeling in relation to him or her, or the circumstances that are creating the difficulty. Show the picture to Jesus and write down all the things Jesus tells you that he loves about you in the situation.

Kathleen M. Henry

Thirty-First Sunday of the Year **C**

READING I   Wis 11, 22—12, 1
Before the Lord the whole universe is as a grain from a balance
  or a drop of morning dew come down upon the earth.
But you have mercy on all, because you can do all things;
  and you overlook the sins of men that they may repent.
For you love all things that are
  and loathe nothing that you have made;
  for what you hated, you would not have fashioned.
And how could a thing remain, unless you willed it;
  or be preserved, had it not been called forth by you?
But you spare all things, because they are yours, O Lord and lover of souls,
  for your imperishable spirit is in all things!

Responsorial Psalm   Ps 145, 1–2. 8–9.
                                  10–11. 13. 14
I will praise your name for ever, my
  king and my God.
I will extol you, O my God and King,
  and I will bless your name forever and ever.
Every day will I bless you,
  and I will praise your name forever and ever.
I will praise your name for ever, my King
  and my God.
The Lord is gracious and merciful,
  slow to anger and of great kindness.
The Lord is good to all
  and compassionate toward all his works.
I will praise your name for ever, my King
  and my God.
Let all your works give you thanks, O Lord,
  and let your faithful ones bless you.
Let them discourse of the glory of your kingdom
  and speak of your might.
I will praise your name for ever, my King
  and my God.
The Lord is faithful in all his words
  and holy in all his works.
The Lord lifts up all who are falling
  and raises up all who are bowed down.
I will praise your name for ever, my King
  and my God.

READING II   2 Thes 1, 11—2, 2
We pray for you always that our God may make you worthy of his call, and fulfill by his power every honest intention and work of faith. In this way the name of our Lord Jesus may be glorified in you and you in him, in accord with the gracious gift of our God and of the Lord Jesus Christ.

On the question of the coming of our Lord Jesus Christ and our being gathered to him, we beg you, brothers, not to be so easily agitated or terrified, whether by an oracular utterance or rumor or a letter alleged to be ours, into believing that the day of the Lord is here.

GOSPEL   Lk 19, 1–10
Jesus, upon entering Jericho, passed through the city. There was a man there named Zacchaeus, the chief tax collector and a wealthy man. He was trying to see what Jesus was like, but being small of stature, was unable to do so because of the crowd. He first ran on in front, then climbed a sycamore tree which was along Jesus' route, in order to see him. When Jesus came to the spot he looked up and said, "Zacchaeus, hurry down. I mean to stay at your house today." He quickly descended, and welcomed him with delight. When this was observed, everyone began to murmur, "He has gone to a sinner's house as a guest." Zacchaeus stood his ground and said to the Lord: "I give half my belongings, Lord, to the poor. If I have defrauded anyone in the least, I pay him back fourfold." Jesus said to him: "Today salvation has come to this house, for this is what it means to be a son of Abraham. The Son of Man has come to search out and save what was lost."

Reflection on the Readings

The story in today's Gospel is familiar to many of us. It is the story of Zacchaeus, the chief tax collector, who climbed up a tree to catch a glimpse of Jesus as he was traveling into Jericho. The importance of his public office and his reputation with the people mattered little as this man scurried up the tree. In his desire to get a good look at Jesus, to see him clearly, he forgot everything. How surprised he must have been when Jesus stopped beneath that tree and called up to him, personally. Not only had he seen Jesus, but more importantly Jesus had seen and spoken to him. How often we are caught off guard when we encounter Christ in the events of our daily life. Sometimes we totally miss his presence.

This familiar story ends as Jesus has visited Zacchaeus' home and eaten with him. Zacchaeus is a changed man as he offers to make reparation for those whom he has cheated. Salvation has come to Zacchaeus' house. He was once unable to see Christ clearly; now his vision is restored. He is a new creation.

Suggestions for Prayer

1. Reread the first reading. Let the Lord address these words to you personally. Then respond to God by praying the responsorial psalm.
2. Review the events of the day. Pray for the grace to recognize Christ as he comes to you in the events and people of the day.
3. "Zacchaeus hurried down and welcomed him with great joy." What words of welcome would you offer Jesus? Welcome him into your heart in prayer.

Suggestion for Journal Keeping

Consider an unexpected home-visit from Jesus. You've met him in the subway, in the grocery store, or along the corridor of your office. He plans to join you for dinner. Write down your thoughts and feelings. Are there some areas of your life that you would want to change immediately? How would you respond to such a visit?

Khris S. Ford

Thirty-Second Sunday of the Year A

READING I Wis 6, 12–16

Resplendent and unfading is Wisdom,
  and she is readily perceived by those who love her,
  and found by those who seek her.
She hastens to make herself known in anticipation of men's desire;
  he who watches for her at dawn shall not be disappointed,
  for he shall find her sitting by his gate.
For taking thought of her is the perfection of prudence,
  and he who for her sake keeps vigil shall quickly be free from care;
Because she makes her own rounds, seeking those worthy of her,
  and graciously appears to them in the ways,
  and meets them with all solicitude.

Responsorial Psalm Ps 63, 2. 3–4. 5–6. 7–8

My soul is thirsting for you, O Lord my God.

O God, you are my God whom I seek;
  for you my flesh pines and my soul thirsts
  like the earth, parched, lifeless and without water.
My soul is thirsting for you, O Lord my God.

Thus have I gazed toward you in the sanctuary
  to see your power and your glory,
For your kindness is a greater good than life;
  my lips shall glorify you.
My soul is thirsting for you, O Lord my God.

Thus will I bless you while I live;
  lifting up my hands, I will call upon your name.
As with the riches of a banquet shall my soul be satisfied,
  and with exultant lips my mouth shall praise you.
My soul is thirsting for you, O Lord my God.

I will remember you upon my couch,
  and through the night-watches I will meditate on you:
You are my help,
  and in the shadow of your wings I shout for joy.
My soul is thirsting for you, O Lord my God.

READING II 1 Thes 4, 13–18

We would have you be clear about those who sleep in death, brothers; otherwise you might yield to grief like those who have no hope. For if we believe that Jesus died and rose, God will bring forth with him from the dead those also who have fallen asleep believing in him. We say to you, as if the Lord himself had said it, that we who live, who survive until his coming, will in no way have an advantage over those who have fallen asleep. No, the Lord himself will come down from heaven at the word of command, at the sound of the archangel's voice and God's trumpet; and those who have died in Christ will rise first. Then we, the living, the survivors, will be caught up with them in the clouds to meet the Lord in the air. Thenceforth we shall be with the Lord unceasingly. Console one another with this message.

GOSPEL   Mt 25, 1–13

Jesus told this parable to his disciples: "The reign of God can be likened to ten bridesmaids who took their torches and went out to welcome the groom. Five of them were foolish, while the other five were sensible. The foolish ones, in taking their torches, brought no oil along, but the sensible ones took flasks of oil as well as their torches. The groom delayed his coming, so they all began to nod, then to fall asleep. At midnight someone shouted, 'The groom is here! Come out and greet him!' At the outcry all the virgins woke up and got their torches ready. The foolish ones said to the sensible, 'Give us some of your oil. Our torches are going out.' But the sensible ones replied, 'No, there may not be enough for you and us. You had better go to the dealers and buy yourselves some.' While they went off to buy it the groom arrived, and the ones who were ready went in to the wedding with him. Then the door was barred. Later the other bridesmaids came back. 'Master, master!' they cried. 'Open the door for us.' But he answered, 'I tell you, I do not know you.' The moral is: keep your eyes open, for you know not the day or the hour."

Reflection on the Readings

Part of the human journey through life is the quest for wisdom. Today's first reading is from an Old Testament work called the Book of Wisdom. Wisdom, in this book, is a personified attribute of God, i.e., it is spoken of as a person. It is closely identified with the Spirit of God. Wisdom is, then, not a quality acquired by study and discipline (as for the pagans) but rather a favor to be asked of God. It is not merely an ideal toward which to strive in human life, but the power enabling one to live a meaningful life.

To lead godly lives in a corrupt and temptation-ridden society one needs help, and help is near at hand. God's Wisdom has a radiance that makes her easy to find. Furthermore, while people search for Wisdom, Wisdom actively goes about seeking those worthy of her. The ungodly who seek their own life, their own wisdom, have abandoned God and are headed for destruction. Those, however, who put their trust in the Lord can be confident that in seeking true Wisdom, they will be found by true Wisdom.

The Gospel reading from Matthew tells us more about wisdom. The wise virgins keep a torch lit waiting for the Lord. They look around their world not just with their own eyes, as do the foolish virgins, but they have help to see in the darkness. For us today, the parable seems to say that believers and unbelievers all peer into the darkness. But the Christian can see more when aided by the light of Christ. Believers and unbelievers experience the same world of joy and suffering, life and death, but the believer sees more in those events. The believers perceive God's presence.

Suggestions for Prayer

1. Reflect on one or more of the following questions:
   • In your life, how have you gone about seeking wisdom?
   • In the parable, with whom do you identify? Do you feel as though you

are peering into the darkness and seeing nothing, or do you look at the world and see meaning, hope and salvation?

- Reflect on the last line of the Gospel. Have you allowed your heart to grow weary of God's absence in a world of violence and evil?

2. Spend some time praying in a room lit only by a candle. Ask yourself: What is the light in my life? What helps me to see the world in a clearer way?

3. Today's responsorial psalm is often used in the Church's morning prayer. Try to pray it a number of times this week as your own morning prayer.

Suggestion for Journal Keeping

Describe an event in your life in which you gained wisdom. What did you learn? How did it change your life?

Douglas Fisher

Thirty-Second Sunday of the Year B

READING I   1 Kgs 17, 10–16

Elijah [the prophet] went to Zarephath. As he arrived at the entrance of the city, a widow was gathering sticks there; he called out to her, "Please bring me a small cupful of water to drink." She left to get it, and he called out after her, "Please bring along a bit of bread." "As the Lord, your God, lives," she answered, "I have nothing baked; there is only a handful of flour in my jar and a little oil in my jug. Just now I was collecting a couple of sticks, to go in and prepare something

for myself and my son; when we have eaten it, we shall die." "Do not be afraid," Elijah said to her. "Go and do as you propose. But first make me a little cake and bring it to me. Then you can prepare something for yourself and your son. For the Lord, the God of Israel, says, 'The jar of flour shall not go empty, nor the jug of oil run dry, until the day when the Lord sends rain upon the earth.' " She left and did as Elijah had said. She was able to eat for a year, and he and her son as well; the jar of flour did not go empty, nor the jug of oil run dry, as the Lord had foretold through Elijah.

Responsorial Psalm   Ps 146, 7. 8–9. 9–10
Praise the Lord, my soul!
The Lord keeps faith forever,
secures justice for the oppressed,
gives food to the hungry.
The Lord sets captives free.
Praise the Lord, my soul!
The Lord gives sight to the blind.
The Lord raises up those that were bowed down;
The Lord loves the just.
The Lord protects strangers.
Praise the Lord, my soul!
The fatherless and the widow he sustains,
but the way of the wicked he thwarts.
The Lord shall reign forever;
your God, O Zion, through all generations. Alleluia.
Praise the Lord, my soul!

READING II   Heb 9, 24–28

Christ did not enter into a sanctuary made by hands, a mere copy of the true one; he entered heaven itself that he might appear before God now on our behalf. Not that he might offer himself there again and again, as

394

the high priest enters year after year into the sanctuary with blood that is not his own; were that so, he would have had to suffer death over and over from the creation of the world. But now he has appeared, at the end of the ages to take away sins once for all by his sacrifice. Just as it is appointed that men die once, and after death be judged, so Christ was offered up once to take away the sins of many; he will appear a second time not to take away sin but to bring salvation to those who eagerly await him.

GOSPEL Mk 12, 38–44

In the course of his teaching Jesus said: "Be on guard against the scribes, who like to parade around in their robes and accept marks of respect in public, front seats in the synagogues, and places of honor at banquets. These men devour the savings of widows and recite long prayers for appearance' sake; it is they who will receive the severest sentence."

Taking a seat opposite the treasury, he observed the crowd putting money into the collection box. Many of the wealthy put in sizable amounts; but one poor widow came and put in two small copper coins worth about a cent. He called his disciples over and told them: "I want you to observe that this poor widow contributed more than all the others who donated to the treasury. They gave from their surplus wealth, but she gave from her want, all that she had to live on."

Reflection on the Readings

Today's Scripture readings present us with two stories of widows with limited resources but generous spirits. In both the central figure is a second class citizen, a poor woman,

alone, with little resources. Yet both women gave freely out of what they had.

Elijah's widow had a spirit of hospitality for the stranger. She gave and received a year's supply of flour and oil for her generosity.

Jesus' widow had a spirit of humility. Though she did not have much, she did not delay contributing from what she had. She recognized the call to give to God and she did not let the possibility that her gift might appear shabby next to the others deter her. For her effort she received Jesus' praise and attention.

The contrast with the rich is striking. They gave sizable amounts, but merely from their excess. It cost them little yet it made them appear great. Jesus dug under the surface, uncovered the injustice which was the source of their funds, and condemned them. God focuses on the purity of the gift, not on its outward appearance.

Paul continues the theme of Jesus as the perfect high priest standing before God on our behalf. Jesus has removed our sins and moved us from the Mosaic law to the new covenant. Paul also promises a time in the future when Jesus will come again.

Suggestions for Prayer

1. Imagine yourself as the widow in the story from Kings. You and your son are so poor and there is so little food left that you expect to die soon. You are approached by a stranger who asks you to share. Tell God what your emotions and conflicts are about giving up what little you have for yourself and your child to this stranger.

2. Like the widow in the story, you invite the stranger to share what you have.

Wonder of wonders, he promises you a year's supply of staples for you and your son. Reflect on the changes in your attitudes and actions because you know you have a year's supply of food.

3. Read Psalm 146. Praise God for his care of you. Renew your trust in God.

Suggestion for Journal Keeping

Imagine yourself as an observer of the events Mark describes. What do you think the widow's life is like? You hear what Jesus says. Write down what you can do for the growing number of elderly and single women with children in your own geographic area who are living on fixed incomes.

Kathleen M. Henry

Thirty-Second Sunday of the Year C

READING I   2 Mc 7, 1–2. 9–14

It happened that seven brothers with their mother were arrested and tortured with whips and scourges by the king, to force them to eat pork in violation of God's law. One of the brothers, speaking for the others, said: "What do you expect to achieve by questioning us? We are ready to die rather than transgress the laws of our ancestors."

At the point of death the second brother said: "You accursed fiend, you are depriving us of this present life, but the King of the world will raise us up to live again forever. It is for his laws that we are dying."

After him the third suffered their cruel sport. He put out his tongue at once when told to do so, and bravely held out his hands, as he spoke these noble words: "It was from Heaven that I received these; for the sake of his laws I disdain them; from him I hope to receive them again." Even the king and his attendants marveled at the young man's courage, because he regarded his sufferings as nothing.

After he had died, they tortured and maltreated the fourth brother in the same way. When he was near death, he said, "It is my choice to die at the hands of men with the God-given hope of being restored to life by him; but for you, there will be no resurrection to life."

Responsorial Psalm   Ps 17, 1. 5–6. 8. 15
Lord, when your glory appears,
    my joy will be full.
Hear, O Lord, a just suit;
    attend to my outcry;
    hearken to my prayer from lips without
        deceit.
Lord, when your glory appears,
    my joy will be full.
My steps have been steadfast in your paths,
    my feet have not faltered.
I call upon you, for you will answer me, O
        God;
    incline your ear to me; hear my word.
Lord, when your glory appears,
    my joy will be full.
Keep me as the apple of your eye,
    hide me in the shadow of your wings.
But I in justice shall behold your face;
    on waking I shall be content in your pres-
        ence.
Lord, when your glory appears,
    my joy will be full.

READING II   2 Thes 2, 16—3, 5

May our Lord Jesus Christ himself, may God our Father who loved us and in his mercy gave us eternal consolation and hope, console your hearts and strengthen them for every good work and word.

For the rest, brothers, pray for us that the word of the Lord may make progress and be hailed by many others, even as it has been by you. Pray that we may be delivered from confused and evil men. For not everyone has faith; the Lord, however, keeps faith; he it is who will strengthen you and guard you against the evil one. In the Lord we are confident that you are doing and will continue to do whatever we enjoin. May the Lord rule your hearts in the love of God and the constancy of Christ.

GOSPEL   Lk 20, 27—38

Some Sadducees came forward (the ones who claim there is no resurrection) to pose this problem to Jesus: "Master, Moses prescribed that if a man's brother dies leaving a wife and no child, the brother should marry the widow and raise posterity to his brother. Now there were seven brothers. The first one married and died childless. Next, the second brother married the widow, then the third, and so on. All seven died without leaving her any children. Finally the widow herself died. At the resurrection, whose wife will she be? Remember, seven married her.

Jesus said to them: "The children of this age marry and are given in marriage, but those judged worthy of a place in the age to come and of resurrection from the dead do not. They become like angels and are no longer liable to death. Sons of the resurrection, they are sons of God. Moses in the pas-

sage about the bush showed that the dead rise again when he called the Lord the God of Abraham, and the God of Isaac, and the God of Jacob. God is not the God of the dead but of the living. All are alive for him."

Reflection on the Readings

The Sadducees in today's Gospel provide us with a model of a people without hope. Their cynical question portrays their unbelief in the resurrection of the dead. Thus they live only for today.

As Christians we may wonder about what life after death will be like. We may try to imagine what heaven will be. Even though our faith does not provide us with a picture of heaven, it fills us with hope for an everlasting life of intimacy with God, the source of all love. As we reflect on death, we are rooted in this hope. It gives us cause to live our lives differently. Our God is a God of the living. We are called to live as witnesses of this life.

We do this as we share daily in the paschal mystery. By recognizing in our life the pattern of Jesus' life, death, and resurrection, we are filled with hope.

Suggestions for Prayer

1. Christians are called to be a sign of hope for the world. Pray for the grace to respond to that call. Recognize how you are already responding and deepening in that commitment.

2. At the beginning of the second reading Paul prays that the Thessalonians will be filled with hope. Pray with his words and make them your own.

3. How have you entered into Christ's death and resurrection these past few

days? Are you experiencing some kind of dying in your life? Is it a physical dying, giving up a destructive habit, or the letting go of someone or something for the sake of another? Pray that you may accept that death and truly know new life as you come through the experience.

Suggestion for Journal Keeping

Describe your thoughts and feelings as you think about your death?

How are these changing as you grow in relationship with the Lord?

Khris S. Ford

Thirty-Third Sunday of the Year A

READING I   Prv 31, 10–13. 19–20. 30–31
When one finds a worthy wife,
   her value is far beyond pearls.
Her husband, entrusting his heart to her,
   has an unfailing prize.
She brings him good, and not evil,
   all the days of her life.
She obtains wool and flax
   and makes cloth with skillful hands.
She puts her hands to the distaff,
   and her fingers ply the spindle.
She reaches out her hands to the poor,
   and extends her arms to the needy.
Charm is deceptive and beauty fleeting;
   the woman who fears the Lord is to be
      praised.
Give her a reward of her labors,
   and let her works praise her at the city
      gates.

Responsorial Psalm   Ps 128, 1–2. 3. 4–5
Happy are those who fear the Lord.
Happy are you who fear the Lord,
   who walk in his ways!
For you shall eat the fruit of your handiwork;
   happy shall you be, and favored.
Happy are those who fear the Lord.
Your wife shall be like a fruitful vine
   in the recesses of your home;
Your children like olive plants
   around your table.
Happy are those who fear the Lord.
Behold, thus is the man blessed
   who fears the Lord.
The Lord bless you from Zion:
   may you see the prosperity of Jerusalem
   all the days of your life.
Happy are those who fear the Lord.

READING II   1 Thes 5, 1–6
As regards specific times and moments, brothers, we do not need to write you; you know very well that the day of the Lord is coming like a thief in the night. Just when people are saying, "Peace and security," ruin will fall on them with the suddenness of pains overtaking a woman in labor, and there will be no escape. You are not in the dark, brothers, that the day might catch you off guard, like a thief. No, all of you are children of light and of the day. We belong neither to darkness nor to night; therefore let us not be asleep like the rest, but awake and sober!

GOSPEL   Mt 25, 14–30
Jesus told this parable to his disciples: "A man was going on a journey. He called in his servants and handed his funds over to them according to each man's abilities. To one he disbursed five thousand silver pieces, to a

second two thousand, and to a third a thousand. Then he went away. Immediately the man who received the five thousand went to invest it and made another five. In the same way, the man who received the two thousand doubled his figure. The man who received the thousand went off instead and dug a hole in the ground, where he buried his master's money. After a long absence, the master of those servants came home and settled accounts with them. The man who had received the five thousand came forward bringing the additional five. 'My lord,' he said, 'you let me have five thousand. See, I have made five thousand more.' His master said to him, 'Well done! You are an industrious and reliable servant. Since you were dependable in a small matter I will put you in charge of larger affairs. Come, share your master's joy!' The man who had received the two thousand then stepped forward. 'My lord,' he said, 'you entrusted me with two thousand and I have made two thousand more.' His master said to him, 'Cleverly done! You too are an industrious and reliable servant. Since you were dependable in a small matter I will put you in charge of larger affairs. Come, share your master's joy!'

"Finally the man who had received the thousand stepped forward. 'My lord,' he said, 'I knew you were a hard man. You reap where you did not sow and gather where you did not scatter, so out of fear I went off and buried your thousand silver pieces in the ground. Here is your money back.' His master exclaimed: 'You worthless, lazy lout! You know I reap where I did not sow and gather where I did not scatter. All the more reason to deposit my money with the bankers, so that on my return I could have had it back with interest. You, there! Take the thousand away from him and give it to the man with the ten thousand. Those who have, will get more until they grow rich, while those who have not, will lose even the little they have. Throw this worthless servant into the darkness outside, where he can wail and grind his teeth.' "

Reflection on the Readings

It wasn't too long ago that Catholics spoke of the urgency of "saving one's soul." It usually meant to stay out of trouble, to defend oneself against the snares of the world, the flesh, and the devil. It was, for many, a largely negative concept meant to keep a person out of sin. Although well-intentioned, it was often sadly self-centered. The focus of life was to save my soul.

How do we think about the meaning of salvation? What relationship do we see between our lives now and the final judgment? To whom does life ultimately belong? The answer in the parable is clear: all that we have is a gift given to us. Life comes from God and ultimately belongs to God. To live solely for oneself is to live an illusion. When we are aware that our lives are part of a bigger reality than ourselves, we can be free to live with a new creativity, seeing our lives as a gift received and a gift given.

Today's Gospel attacks the notion of faith as a security system for heaven. Such a notion is based more on fear than on faith. Like the action of the men in the Gospel who are unafraid to invest their silver pieces, faith for us is a risk, a letting go, a willingness to walk. Salvation is not "saving one's soul," but generously expanding and donating it. It is finding one's life wrapped up in the concerns of God and freed from petty self-preoccupations.

Understanding ourselves as stewards of God's gifts can drastically affect our lives. Our wives, husbands and children are not "ours" at all. They have been entrusted to us. Our neighbors, our parishes, our country, our planet have all been entrusted to us. In the end, we decide how we will care for these gifts or use them. In deciding that, we decide our very selves and our ultimate destiny.

Suggestions for Prayer

1. Reflect on one or more of the following questions:
   - Do you understand faith as something that encourages creativity or conformity? Why?
   - St. Irenaeus once wrote, "The glory of God is man fully alive." Do you associate holiness with human wholeness? How do you think spiritual and personal growth are related to each other?
   - Of the three men mentioned in the parable, with whom do you identify?
2. Write down your abilities and talents. How have you used them? Have you used them for personal gain only or have you enriched the lives of others?
3. Have you ever helped someone at great personal risk? What was the result? Did you come away a richer person?

Suggestion for Journal Keeping

Describe a time in your life when you left a "small world" for a larger one. It might be when you went away to college, or started a family, or began a new job. What were your feelings? What were the risks? If you join the Church, what are the risks? Can you imagine it expanding your world? In what way?

Douglas Fisher

Thirty-Third Sunday of the Year

READING I   Dn 12, 1–3
At that time there shall arise
  Michael, the great prince,
  guardian of your people;
It shall be a time unsurpassed in distress
  since nations began until that time.
At that time your people shall escape,
  everyone who is found written in the book.
Many of those who sleep
  in the dust of the earth shall awake;
Some shall live forever,
  others shall be an everlasting horror and disgrace.
But the wise shall shine brightly
  like the splendor of the firmament,
And those who lead the many to justice
  shall be like the stars forever.

Responsorial Psalm   Ps 16, 5. 8. 9–10. 11
Keep me safe, O God;
  you are my hope.
O Lord, my allotted portion and my cup,
  you it is who hold fast my lot.
I set the Lord ever before me;
  with him at my right hand I shall not be disturbed.
Keep me safe, O God;
  you are my hope.

Therefore my heart is glad and my soul rejoices,
my body, too, abides in confidence;
Because you will not abandon my soul to the nether world,
nor will you suffer your faithful one to undergo corruption.
Keep me safe, O God;
you are my hope.
You will show me the path to life,
fullness of joys in your presence,
the delights at your right hand forever.
Keep me safe, O God;
you are my hope.

READING II   Heb 10, 11–14. 18

Every other priest stands ministering day by day, and offering again and again those same sacrifices which can never take away sins. But Jesus offered one sacrifice for sins and took his seat forever at the right hand of God; now he waits until his enemies are placed beneath his feet. By one offering he has forever perfected those who are being sanctified. Once sins have been forgiven, there is no further offering for sin.

GOSPEL   Mk 13, 24–32

Jesus said to his disciples: "During that period after trials of every sort the sun will be darkened, the moon will not shed its light, stars will fall out of the skies, and the heavenly hosts will be shaken. Then men will see the Son of Man coming in the clouds with great power and glory. He will dispatch his messengers and assemble his chosen from the four winds, from the farthest bounds of earth and sky. Learn a lesson from the fig tree. Once the sap of its branches runs high and it begins to sprout leaves, you know that summer is near. In the same way, when you see these things happening, you will know that he is near, even at the door. I assure you, this generation will not pass away until all these things take place. The heavens and the earth will pass away, but my words will not.

"As to the exact day or hour, no one knows it, neither the angels in heaven nor even the Son, but only the Father."

Reflection on the Readings

Jesus and the prophet Daniel speak of a time when the world, as we know it, will end. The physical order we currently rely on will disappear and we will have to look to God for new directions.

Daniel says it will be a time of great distress. Jesus expounds and says that not only will there be many trials, but our own physical surroundings will fail us. Daniel promises a different kind of light to lead us then. The wise shall shine brightly and those who lead others to justice shall be like bright stars.

The descriptions are scary but we should be aware of the promises within them. Jesus' words will not pass away. In times of such turmoil, we can cling to and rely on God's word and the awareness that Jesus is among us. The second reading continues to remind us that, in times of stress and upheaval, we have a spokesman at the right hand of God who loves us and died for us.

Suggestions for Prayer

1. As you say yes to following Jesus, reflect on those areas in your life where you see that the old way of doing things is no longer working. Ask Jesus for the courage to make the necessary changes.

2. Psalm 16 says:

I set the Lord ever before me;
with him at my right hand I shall not be
    disturbed.

Begin the day by asking the Lord to be at your right hand. Throughout the day take moments to sense God's presence. At the end of the day thank the Lord for being with you throughout the day.

Suggestion for Journal Keeping

From today's readings it is clear that God's ways are not the world's and will survive the end of the world's order. The world we know today can end in many ways—accident, illness, death, or loss of a job, to name just a few. What are the things in your life that would survive such a change? How precious are those things to you now? Do you need to rethink your priorities?

Kathleen M. Henry

Thirty-Third Sunday of the Year   C

READING I   Mal 3, 19–20

Lo, the day is coming, blazing like an oven,
    when all the proud and all evildoers will
        be stubble,
And the day that is coming will set them on
        fire,
    leaving them neither root nor branch,
    says the Lord of hosts.

But for you who fear my name, there will arise
    the sun of justice with its healing rays.

Responsorial Psalm   Ps 98, 5–6. 7–8. 9
The Lord comes to rule the earth with
    justice.
**Sing praise to the Lord with the harp,
    with the harp and melodious song.
With trumpets and the sound of the horn
    sing joyfully before the King, the Lord.**
The Lord comes to rule the earth with
    justice.
**Let the sea and what fills it resound,
    the world and those who dwell in it;
Let the rivers clap their hands,
    the mountains shout with them for joy.**
The Lord comes to rule the earth with
    justice.
**Before the Lord, for he comes,
    for he comes to rule the earth,
He will rule the world with justice
    and the peoples with equity.**
The Lord comes to rule the earth with
    justice.

READING II   2 Thes 3, 7–12
You know how you ought to imitate us. We did not live lives of disorder when we were among you, nor depend on anyone for food. Rather, we worked day and night, laboring to the point of exhaustion so as not to impose on any of you. Not that we had no claim on you, but that we might present ourselves as an example for you to imitate. Indeed, when we were with you we used to lay down the rule that anyone who would not work should not eat.

We hear that some of you are unruly, not keeping busy but acting like busybodies. We

enjoin all such, and we urge them strongly in the Lord Jesus Christ to earn the food they eat by working quietly.

GOSPEL   Lk 21, 5–19

Some were speaking of how the temple was adorned with precious stones and votive offerings. Jesus said, "These things you are contemplating—the day will come when not one stone will be left on another, but it will all be torn down." They asked him, "When will this occur, Teacher? And what will be the sign it is going to happen?" He said, "Take care not to be misled. Many will come in my name, saying, 'I am he' and 'The time is at hand.' Do not follow them. Neither must you be perturbed when you hear of wars and insurrections. These things are bound to happen first, but the end does not follow immediately."

He said to them further: "Nation will rise against nation and kingdom against kingdom. There will be great earthquakes, plagues and famines in various places—and in the sky fearful omens and great signs. But before any of this, they will manhandle and persecute you, summoning you to synagogues and prisons, bringing you to trial before kings and governors, all because of my name. You will be brought to give witness on account of it. I bid you resolve not to worry about your defense beforehand, for I will give you words and a wisdom which none of your adversaries can take exception to or contradict. You will be delivered up even by your parents, brothers, relatives and friends, and some of you will be put to death. All will hate you because of me, yet not a hair of your head will be harmed. By patient endurance you will save your lives."

Reflection on the Readings

"Lo, the day is coming," says the prophet Malachi. Jesus too says, "The day will come . . . Both Jesus and Malachi use the expression to refer to a time of upheaval, a time of judgment, an apocalyptic time. Although "the day" may sometimes refer to the end of the world, in both these readings it refers to the end of a world. It is a time of violent transition, a birth into a new reality.

Malachi describes the twofold effect of "the day." For the proud and the evildoers it will be like a blazing oven which consumes them. But for those who trust in the Lord, it will be a day of justice and healing.

In the Gospel Jesus uses "the day" to refer to the destruction of the temple. This destruction of the temple in 70 A.D. was indeed a time of upheaval and transition for both Christians and Jews. For the Jews it was a crushing defeat at the hand of the Romans and led to a transition of their focus away from the temple as their spiritual center. For Christians, it marked the emergence of Christianity from Judaism and was followed by the persecutions Jesus goes on to describe in this Gospel. Suffering and persecution were indeed the marks of the early Church and led to the deaths of many believers. Yet in the midst of the tumult, Jesus reminds his followers that they are not alone—the Holy Spirit will give them guidance and by patient endurance the Church will survive.

Suggestions for Prayer

1. Reflect on the symbol of fire which the prophet Malachi uses to describe the action of God. How has the Lord's love for you been like a "blazing oven"? How

403

has it been like the "healing rays" of the sun?

2. What are the situations in your life that call for "patient endurance"? Reflect on Jesus' pledge to be with his disciples in times of difficulty and renew your trust in him.

3. Paul called the Thessalonians to imitate him, especially in the way he worked to support himself. Reflect on the work you do. How can you be a better worker?

Suggestion for Journal Keeping

The Gospel depicts the sufferings that the first Christians endured. Has your decision to become a Catholic brought about changes in your life, in your relationships with your parents, brothers, sisters, spouse, relatives or friends? How are you dealing with any friction that may have arisen? Is there anything that you would like to work harder on?

Robert M. Hamma

Christet the King   A

READING I   Ez 34, 11–12. 15–17

Thus says the Lord God: I myself will look after and tend my sheep. As a shepherd tends his flock when he finds himself among his scattered sheep, so will I tend my sheep. I will rescue them from every place where they were scattered when it was cloudy and dark. I myself will pasture my sheep; I myself will give them rest, says the Lord God. The lost I will seek out, the strayed I will bring back, the injured I will bind up, the sick I will heal [but the sleek and the strong I will destroy], shepherding them rightly.

As for you, my sheep, says the Lord God, I will judge between one sheep and another, between rams and goats.

Responsorial Psalm   Ps 23, 1–2. 2–3. 5–6

The Lord is my shepherd;
    there is nothing I shall want.

The Lord is my shepherd; I shall not want.
    In verdant pastures he gives me repose.

The Lord is my shepherd;
    there is nothing I shall want.

Beside restful waters he leads me;
    he refreshes my soul.

He guides me in right paths
    for his name's sake.

The Lord is my shepherd;
    there is nothing I shall want.

You spread the table before me
    in the sight of my foes;

You anoint my head with oil;
    my cup overflows.

Only goodness and kindness follow me
    all the days of my life;

And I shall dwell in the house of the Lord
    for years to come.

The Lord is my shepherd;
    there is nothing I shall want.

READING II   1 Cor 15, 20–26. 28

Christ has been raised from the dead, the first fruits of those who have fallen asleep. Death came through a man; hence the resurrection of the dead comes through a man also. Just as in Adam all die, so in Christ all will come to life again, but each one in proper order: Christ the first-fruits and then, at his coming, all those who belong to him. After that will come the end, when, after having destroyed every sovereignty, authority, and power, he will hand over the kingdom to God the Father. Christ must reign

until God has put all enemies under his feet, and the last enemy to be destroyed is death. When, finally, all has been subjected to the Son, he will then subject himself to the One who made all things subject to him, so that God may be all in all.

GOSPEL   Mt 25, 31–46

Jesus said to his disciples: "When the Son of Man comes in his glory, escorted by all the angels of heaven, he will sit upon his royal throne, and all the nations will be assembled before him. Then he will separate them into two groups, as a shepherd separates sheep from goats. The sheep he will place on his right hand, the goats on his left. The king will say to those on his right: 'Come. You have my Father's blessing! Inherit the kingdom prepared for you from the creation of the world. For I was hungry and you gave me food, I was thirsty and you gave me drink. I was a stranger and you welcomed me, naked and you clothed me. I was ill and you comforted me, in prison and you came to visit me.' Then the just will ask him: 'Lord, when did we see you hungry and feed you or see you thirsty and give you drink? When did we welcome you away from home or clothe you in your nakedness? When did we visit you when you were ill or in prison?' The king will answer them: 'I assure you, as often as you did it for one of my least brothers, you did it for me.'

"Then he will say to those on his left: 'Out of my sight, you condemned, into that everlasting fire prepared for the devil and his angels! I was hungry and you gave me no food, I was thirsty and you gave me no drink. I was away from home and you gave me no welcome, naked and you gave me no clothing. I was ill and in prison and you did not come to comfort me.' Then they in turn will ask: 'Lord, when did we see you hungry or thirsty or away from home or naked or ill or in prison and not attend you in your needs?' He will answer them: 'I assure you, as often as you neglected to do it to one of these least ones, you neglected to do it to me.' These will go off to eternal punishment and the just to eternal life."

Reflection on the Readings

The title of today's feast is somewhat misleading because in order to understand the kingship of Christ we have to forget our preconceptions about kings. The notion of monarchies and kings usually recalls a social and political system repugnant to democratic American sensibilities. The notion of the king often conjures up the image of someone who is set apart from the common people. But the lordship of Jesus does not separate him from us; rather it unites us.

In the second reading, Paul tells us that in the resurrection Jesus has destroyed death which separates and divides and has restored life. This reconciliation has come through Jesus' humanity: "Death came through a man; hence the resurrection of the dead comes through a man also." It is Jesus' complete and total identification with us that brings us life and unity.

The Gospel today makes the point even more strongly. The last few Sundays we have been focusing on the end-time and the final judgment. Today's Gospel leaves no questions about the pre-requisites for entrance into the kingdom: feed the hungry, welcome the stranger, clothe the naked, comfort the sick, visit the imprisoned. To love our neighbor (without boundaries) is to love our king. The king is totally identified with the most humble of his subjects: "As often as you did it for the least of my brothers, you did it for me."

The feast of Christ the King forces us to re-evaluate our notions of power and authority. The king is one whose power lies in his love and service, one who seeks out the lost, brings back the stray, binds up the injured and heals the sick (see today's first reading from Ezekiel). In the Gospels, the kingship of Christ is revealed most deeply on the cross: "Jesus of Nazareth, King of the Jews." In his death, the king has become one of us in the darkest moment of our humanity.

Suggestions for Prayer

1. Reflect on one or more of the following questions:
   • How do you use your power and authority?
   • Do you have a commitment to the poor? How is it lived out?
   • How do you imagine a final judgment?
2. Think of a time in your life when you helped someone who was down and out. How did it make you feel? Imagine the event and imagine Jesus witnessing your actions.
3. The responsorial psalm comes from Psalm 23. Sit in a quiet place and read this psalm slowly and thoughtfully.

Suggestion for Journal Keeping

Make a list of the things you worry about in life, leaving a line blank after each item. When you are finished write on the blank lines: "The Lord is my shepherd; I shall not want." Now slowly and prayerfully read what you have written.

Douglas Fisher

Christt the King

READING I   Dn 7, 13–14
**As the visions during the night continued, I
    saw
One like a son of man coming,
    on the clouds of heaven;
When he reached the Ancient One
    and was presented before him,
He received dominion, glory, and kingship;
    nations and peoples of every language
        serve him.
His dominion is an everlasting dominion
    that shall not be taken away,
    his kingship shall not be destroyed.**

Responsorial Psalm   Ps 93, 1. 1–2. 5
The Lord is king;
    he is robed in majesty.
**The Lord is king, in splendor robed;
    robed is the Lord and girt about with
        strength.**
The Lord is king;
    he is robed in majesty.
**And he has made the world firm,
    not to be moved.
Your throne stands firm from of old;
    from everlasting you are, O Lord.**

The Lord is king;
   he is robed in majesty.
Your decrees are worthy of trust indeed;
   holiness befits your house,
   O Lord, for length of days.
The Lord is king;
   he is robed in majesty.

READING II   Rv 1, 5–8
Jesus Christ is the faithful witness, the first-born from the dead and ruler of the kings of earth. To him who loves us and freed us from our sins by his own blood, who has made us a royal nation of priests in the service of his God and Father—to him be glory and power forever and ever! Amen.
See, he comes amid the clouds!
   Every eye shall see him,
   even of those who pierced him.
All the peoples of the earth
   shall lament him bitterly.
   So it is to be! Amen!
   The Lord God says, "I am the Alpha and the Omega, the One who is and who was and who is to come, the Almighty!"

GOSPEL   Jn 18, 33–37
Pilate said to Jesus: "Are you the king of the Jews?" Jesus answered, "Are you saying this on your own, or have others been telling you about me?" "I am no Jew!" Pilate retorted. "It is your own people and the chief priests who have handed you over to me. What have you done?" Jesus answered:
   "My kingdom does not belong to this world.
   If my kingdom were of this world,
   my subjects would be fighting
   to save me from being handed over to the Jews.

As it is, my kingdom is not here."
At this Pilate said to him, "So, then, you are a king?" Jesus replied:
   "It is you who say I am a king.
   The reason I was born,
   the reason why I came into the world,
   is to testify to the truth.
   Anyone committed to the truth hears my voice."

Reflection on the Readings
   "My kingdom does not belong to this world." Both the first and second readings tell about the broad reaches of God's kingdom.

   Daniel's vision is physically expansive, covering all the earth as well as the heavens. The "Son of Man" receives all dominion and power from God forever. Majesty and power are emphasized.

   In the Book of Revelation, Jesus comes on a cloud and is the Almighty, the beginning and the end. Jesus, the faithful witness, has made us a royal nation of priests who serve. The focus is on service.

   How difficult it was for the people of Jesus' time to see and understand what Jesus was professing and inviting people to join. The idea of a ruler who serves was as foreign then as it is now. Jesus' kingdom still does not belong to this world. Instead we are called to move from worldly ways and values into God's way.

   Because we live in this world as much as Daniel or Pilate or John, we have a limited understanding of what exactly God's reign looks like. However, our entrance is through Jesus. Whoever is committed to knowing the truth hears Jesus and follows his ways of love and service to others.

1. Jesus says that those committed to the truth hear him. Place a difficult situation before Jesus and ask to be shown the way.
2. Christ is our King. Think of those areas of your life where Jesus is Lord. Spend time thanking and praising God for his kingship in those areas.
3. Read Psalm 93 and reflect on a time when God saved you from turmoil and distress that seemed to be overpowering you. Tell God how your trust has increased as a result of that experience.

Suggestions for Journal Keeping

Write about what it means to you to be in Jesus' royal nation of priests. How does it feel to be a priest, a leader? How does it feel to be royalty? As a royal priest of the order of Jesus, how are you fulfilling the call to service?

Kathleen M. Henry

Christ the King C

READING I 2 Sm 5, 1–3

All the tribes of Israel came to David in Hebron and said: "Here we are, your bone and your flesh. In days past, when Saul was our king, it was you who led the Israelites out and brought them back. And the Lord said to you, 'You shall shepherd my people Israel and shall be commander of Israel.' " When all the elders of Israel came to David in Hebron, King David made an agreement with them there before the Lord, and they anointed him king of Israel.

Responsorial Psalm Ps 122, 1–2. 3–4. 4–5

I rejoiced when I heard them say:
  let us go to the house of the Lord.
I rejoiced because they said to me,
  "We will go up to the house of the Lord."
And now we have set foot
  within your gates, O Jerusalem.
I rejoiced when I heard them say:
  let us go to the house of the Lord.
Jerusalem, built as a city
  with compact unity.
To it the tribes go up,
  the tribes of the Lord.
I rejoiced when I heard them say:
  let us go to the house of the Lord.
According to the decree for Israel,
  to give thanks to the name of the Lord.
In it are set up judgment seats,
  seats for the house of David.
I rejoiced when I heard them say:
  let us go to the house of the Lord.

READING II Col 1, 12–20

Give thanks to the Father for having made you worthy to share the lot of the saints in light. He rescued us from the power of darkness and brought us into the kingdom of his beloved Son. Through him we have redemption, the forgiveness of our sins.

He is the image of the invisible God, the firstborn of all creatures. In him everything in heaven and on earth was created, things visible and invisible, whether thrones or dominations, principalities or powers; all were created through him, and for him. He is before all else that is. In him everything continues in being. It is he who is head of the body, the church; he who is the beginning, the first-born of the dead, so that primacy may be his in everything. It pleased God to make absolute fullness reside in him and, by means of him, to reconcile everything in his person, everything, I say, both on earth and in the heavens, making peace through the blood of his cross.

GOSPEL   Lk 23, 35–43

The people stood there watching, and the leaders kept jeering at Jesus, saying, "He saved others; let him save himself if he is the Messiah of God, the chosen one." The soldiers also made fun of him, coming forward to offer him their sour wine and saying, "If you are the king of the Jews, save yourself." There was an inscription over his head:

"THIS IS THE KING OF THE JEWS." One of the criminals hanging in crucifixion blasphemed him, "Aren't you the Messiah? Then save yourself and us." But the other one rebuked him: "Have you no fear of God, seeing you are under the same sentence? We deserve it, after all. We are only paying the price for what we've done, but this man has done nothing wrong." He then said, "Jesus, remember me when you enter upon your reign." And Jesus replied, "I assure you: this day you will be with me in paradise."

Reflection on the Readings

Today we hear the story of the crucifixion of Jesus, how the soldiers threw dice for his clothes, mocked him, and offered him cheap wine. It is in the context of this Gospel reading that we celebrate the solemnity of Christ the King. What a perfect illustration of the paradox that Christ lived!

This is a king like no other we have known, and the contrast is evident as we ponder the scene of his death on the cross. We see his throne to be the cross, no gold-laden vestments, only nakedness before his people, no armored guards on his right and left, only two thieves that share in his painful death. Even more, we see no attitude of revenge or anger. Rather we witness a man who is willing to forgive and offers himself completely for the very men who kill him. He even promises one of the thieves that he will share paradise with him. This is Christ the King whose kingship serves as a model for our living.

Today's Gospel calls us to commit ourselves to be followers of this King and to the building of his kingdom. To do this we must model the King himself.

Suggestions for Prayer

1. Respond to this call to follow Christ the King. Begin your prayer by saying, "Christ, my King . . ."
2. The cross is the banner or emblem of our King. Begin your prayer with a slow signing of yourself with the cross. Spend some time in silence and reflect on the emblem that you have claimed.
3. Pray with the second reading from Colossians. Read through it slowly one time. Then read it again, pausing for prayer after each sentence. Then read it a third time all the way through.

Suggestion for Journal Keeping

In Jesus' last moments on the cross he assured the thief of his place in paradise. Why is that an important part of this story? What does it mean for your personal story?

Khris S. Ford

August 15
The Assumption of the Blessed Virgin Mary

READING I   Rv 11, 19, 12, 1–6. 10

God's temple in heaven opened and in the temple could be seen the ark of his covenant.

A great sign appeared in the sky, a woman clothed with the sun, with the moon under her feet, and on her head a crown of twelve stars. Because she was with child, she wailed aloud in pain as she labored to give birth. Then another sign appeared in the sky: it was a huge dragon, flaming red, with seven heads and ten horns; on his head were seven diadems. His tail swept a third of the stars from the sky and hurled them down to the earth. Then the dragon stood before the woman about to give birth, ready to devour her child when it should be born. She gave birth to a son—a boy who is destined to shepherd all the nations with an iron rod. Her child was snatched up to God and to his throne. The woman herself fled into the desert, where a special place had been prepared for her by God.

Then I heard a loud voice in heaven say:
"Now have salvation and power come,
    the reign of our God and the authority of
        his Anointed One."

Responsorial Psalm   Ps 45, 10. 11. 12. 16

The queen stands at your right hand,
    arrayed in gold.

**The queen takes her place at your right hand
in gold of Ophir.**

The queen stands at your right hand, arrayed in gold.

**Hear, O daughter, and see; turn your ear,
forget your people and your father's
house.**

The queen stands at your right hand, arrayed in gold.

**So shall the king desire your beauty;
for he is your lord.**

The queen stands at your right hand, arrayed in gold.

**They are borne in with gladness and joy;
they enter the palace of the king.**

The queen stands at your right hand, arrayed in gold.

READING II   1 Cor 15, 20–26

Christ has been raised from the dead, the first fruits of those who have fallen asleep. Death came through a man; hence the resurrection of the dead comes through a man also. Just as in Adam all die, so in Christ all will come to life again, but each one in proper order: Christ the first fruits and then, at his coming, all those who belong to him. After that will come the end, when, after having destroyed every sovereignty, authority, and power, he will hand over the kingdom to God the Father. Christ must reign until God has put all enemies under his feet.

GOSPEL   Lk 1, 39–56

Mary set out, proceeding in haste into the hill country to a town of Judah, where she entered Zechariah's house and greeted Elizabeth. When Elizabeth heard Mary's greeting, the baby stirred in her womb. Elizabeth was filled with the Holy Spirit and cried out in a loud voice: "Blessed are you among women and blessed is the fruit of your womb. But who am I that the mother of my

Lord should come to me? The moment your greeting sounded in my ears, the baby stirred in my womb for joy. Blessed is she who trusted that the Lord's words to her would be fulfilled."

Then Mary said:

"My being proclaims the greatness of the Lord,
my spirit finds joy in God my savior,
For he has looked upon his servant in her lowliness;
all ages to come shall call me blessed.
God who is mighty has done great things for me,
holy is his name;
His mercy is from age to age
on those who fear him.
"He has shown might with his arm;
he has confused the proud in their inmost thoughts.
He has deposed the mighty from their thrones
and raised the lowly to high places.
The hungry he has given every good thing,
while the rich he has sent empty away.
He has upheld Israel his servant,
ever mindful of his mercy;
Even as he promised our fathers,
promised Abraham and his descendants forever."

Mary remained with Elizabeth about three months and then returned home.

Reflection on the Readings

The feast of the Assumption is a celebration of Mary's sharing in the fullness of God's love in her death. More importantly, though, the feast points to the promised future for all. Mary reminds us of our own desire for com-

pletion and union with God. She also reminds us that the fulfillment of that desire can only come when we live lives that are faithful to God's values as proclaimed by Jesus. Mary, because of her obedience to God's ways, now lives in the fullness of life with God: what we all will be in Christ.

The Gospel text today highlights these values of God. Mary's canticle of praise is a proclamation of God's unending love and compassion that calls us to justice, reconciliation, love and community. It is a recognition that in Jesus the reign of God has begun. This reign of God will be fully realized when all creation is drawn up into the fullness of God's embrace, thus experiencing reconciliation, transformation and redemption. We, the followers of Jesus, participate in this reign of God by our witness through our lives of justice and compassion.

Jesus has redeemed us fully. Mary shares in the fullness of this redemption because of her active obedience to God's life in her, the demands of the reign of God. Mary becomes a symbol of hope for our future.

Suggestions for Prayer

1. Reflect on the following: What are my hopes for the future? What are the promises of God for me? What do I need to trust God's promises for life and love?
2. Pray the traditional mantra prayer, the rosary, reflecting on the symbol of the assumption of Mary. Pause between each decade, asking God to help you become more aware of your need to hope in God.
3. Return to the Gospel text for today. Slowly pray the canticle of praise, being

aware of the call to lives of justice and mercy contained in the prayer.

Suggestion for Journal Keeping

Recall the opening lines to the canticle of praise in today's Gospel. For what in your life and in our world do you proclaim God's greatness, finding joy in God? How does such an awareness call you to be a person of justice and mercy?

Thomas H. Morris

November 1
All Saints

READING I   Rv 7, 2–4. 9–14

I, John, saw another angel come up from the east holding the seal of the living God. He cried out at the top of his voice to the four angels who were given power to ravage the land and the sea, "Do no harm to the land or the sea or the trees until we imprint this seal on the foreheads of the servants of our God." I heard the number of those who were so marked—one hundred and forty-four thousand from every tribe of Israel.

After this I saw before me a huge crowd which no one could count from every nation, race, people, and tongue. They stood before the throne and the Lamb, dressed in long white robes and holding palm branches in their hands. They cried out in a loud voice, "Salvation is from our God, who is seated on the throne, and from the Lamb!" All the angels who were standing around the throne and the elders and the four living creatures fell down before the throne to worship God. They said: "Amen! Praise and glory, wisdom, thanksgiving, and honor, power and might to our God forever and ever. Amen!"

Then one of the elders asked me, "Who do you think these are, all dressed in white? And where have they come from?" I said to him, "Sir, you should know better than I." He then told me, "These are the ones who have survived the great period of trial; they have washed their robes and made them white in the blood of the Lamb.

Responsorial Psalm   Ps 24, 1–2. 3–4. 5–6

Lord, this is the people that longs to see your face.

The Lord's are the earth and its fullness;
    the world and those who dwell in it.
For he founded it upon the seas
    and established it upon the rivers.

Lord, this is the people that longs to see your face.

Who can ascend the mountain of the Lord?
    or who may stand in his holy place?
He whose hands are sinless, whose heart is clean,
    who desires not what is vain.

Lord, this is the people that longs to see your face.

He shall receive a blessing from the Lord,
    a reward from God his savior.
Such is the race that seeks for him,
    that seeks the face of the God of Jacob.

Lord, this is the people that longs to see your face.

READING II   1 Jn 3, 1–3

See what love the Father has bestowed on us in letting us be called children of God!
Yet that in fact is what we are.
The reason the world does not recognize us
Is that it never recognized the Son.

412

Dearly beloved,
we are God's children now;
what we shall later be has not yet come to
   light.
We know that when it comes to light
we shall be like him,
for we shall see him as he is.
Everyone who has this hope based on him
keeps himself pure, as he is pure.

GOSPEL   Mt 5, 1–12
When Jesus saw the crowds he went up on
the mountainside. After he had sat down his
disciples gathered around him, and he began
to teach them:
   "How blest are the poor in spirit: the
   reign of God is theirs.
   Blest too are the sorrowing; they shall
   be consoled.
   [Blest are the lowly; they shall inherit
   the land.]
   Blest are they who hunger and thirst for
   holiness;
   they shall have their fill.
   Blest are they who show mercy; mercy
   shall be theirs.
   Blest are the single-hearted, for they
   shall see God.
   Blest too the peacemakers; they shall be
   called sons of God.
   Blest are those persecuted for holiness'
   sake; the reign of God is theirs.
   Blest are you when they insult you and
   persecute you and utter every kind of
   slander against you because of me.
   Be glad and rejoice, for your reward in
   heaven is great."

Reflection on the Readings
   The feast of All Saints is a celebration of all
those women and men who lived in fidelity
to the call of the Gospel: those named by our
community as saints and those whose names
we do not know. We set them aside not because they led extraordinary lives, but rather
because in their very ordinary lives they believed that the cross of Jesus Christ made all
the difference. This feast also reminds us that
we are all called to be saints, to be holy.
   Today's Gospel invites us to be disciples of
Jesus. The beatitudes present a new way of
life not centered on personal gain but on self-
sacrificing love, a love that witnesses to the
gracious and compassionate presence of
God that liberates and redeems. Jesus raises
up as the way of the holy—the women and
men of the reign of God—crucial attitudes
toward life and our relationships: being poor,
so we know the only source of power is God;
the solidarity and compassion of the sorrowing; the gentle who do not bring violence; the
true longing for a holy justice; the plentiful-
ness and abundance of mercy; the singleness
of heart that acknowledges the one desire
that informs all our other desires—to know
God; the active stand for restoration, reconciliation and harmony. If we live faithfully
these values, then surely we will disrupt the
status quo, we will bring upon us the wrath
of others, as Jesus did. But we have cause to
rejoice, to be glad, for it is in our fidelity to
these values of the reign of God that we share
in God's very life. Then, as we heard in the
text from the Book of Revelation, we will proclaim salvation from our God as one of the
saints, the holy women and men of God.

Suggestions for Prayer

1. Remember the women and men in our
   Christian community who have died
   and share in the new life of Jesus. Slowly

and prayerfully recite or chant their names, recognizing your solidarity with them: "Holy Mary, Mother of God . . . St. Paul . . . St. Mary Magdalene . . . St. Thomas . . . St. Francis . . . " adding names of family, friends and contemporary saints.

2. Bring the needs of your neighborhood to prayer. Who are the women and men who are leading selfless lives, bringing God's love to others? Ask God for the grace to bring holiness to the life of your family and neighborhood.

3. Pray the Gospel text, the beatitudes. Stop between each beatitude asking God to give you the needed grace to live this value.

Suggestion for Journal Keeping

List for yourself what you consider important and necessary for a happy life. Now reflect on your need for God. What keeps you from recognizing your need for God? How are your "essentials" similar or different from the values of the beatitudes?

Thomas H. Morris

December 8
Immaculate Conception

READING I Gn 3, 9–15, 20

After Adam had eaten of the tree the Lord God called to the man and asked him, "Where are you?" He answered, "I heard you in the garden; but I was afraid, because I was naked, so I hid myself." Then he asked, "Who told you that you were naked? You have eaten, then, from the tree of which I had forbidden you to eat!" The man replied, "The woman whom you put here with me— she gave me fruit from the tree, and so I ate it." The Lord God then asked the woman, "Why did you do such a thing?" The woman answered, "The serpent tricked me into it, so I ate it."

Then the Lord God said to the serpent: "Because you have done this, you shall be banned
from all the animals
and from all the wild creatures;
On your belly shall you crawl,
and dirt shall you eat
all the days of your life.
I will put enmity between you and the woman,
and between your offspring and hers;
He will strike at your head,
while you strike at his heel."
The man called his wife Eve, because she became the mother of all the living.

Responsorial Psalm Ps 98, 1. 2–3. 3–4
Sing to the Lord a new song,
  for he has done marvelous deeds.

Sing to the Lord a new song,
  for he has done wondrous deeds;
His right hand has won victory for him,
  his holy arm.
Sing to the Lord a new song,
  for he has done marvelous deeds.

The Lord has made his salvation known:
  in the sight of the nations he has revealed
  his justice.
He has remembered his kindness and his
  faithfulness
  toward the house of Israel.
Sing to the Lord a new song,
  for he has done marvelous deeds.

All the ends of the earth have seen
   the salvation by our God.
Sing joyfully to the Lord, all you lands;
   break into song; sing praise.
Sing to the Lord a new song,
   for he has done marvelous deeds.

READING II   Eph 1, 3–6. 11–12

Praised be the God and Father of our Lord
Jesus Christ, who has bestowed on us in
Christ every spiritual blessing in the heavens! God chose us in him before the world
began, to be holy and blameless in his sight,
to be full of love; likewise he predestined us
through Christ Jesus to be his adopted
sons—such was his will and pleasure—that
all might praise the divine favor he has bestowed on us in his beloved.

In him we were chosen; for in the decree
of God, who administers everything according to his will and counsel, we were predestined to praise his glory by being the first to
hope in Christ.

GOSPEL   Lk 1, 26–38

The angel Gabriel was sent from God to a
town of Galilee named Nazareth, to a virgin
betrothed to a man named Joseph, of the
house of David. The virgin's name was
Mary. Upon arriving, the angel said to her:
"Rejoice, O highly favored daughter! The
Lord is with you. Blessed are you among
women." She was deeply troubled by his
words, and wondered what his greeting
meant. The angel went on to say to her: "Do
not fear, Mary. You have found favor with
God. You shall conceive and bear a son and
give him the name Jesus. Great will be his
dignity and he will be called Son of the Most
High. The Lord God will give him the throne
of David his father. He will rule over the

house of Jacob forever and his reign will be
without end."

Mary said to the angel, "How can this be
since I do not know man?" The angel answered her: "The Holy Spirit will come upon
you and the power of the Most High will
overshadow you; hence, the holy offspring
to be born will be called Son of God. Know
that Elizabeth your kinswoman has conceived a son in her old age; she who was
thought to be sterile is now in her sixth
month, for nothing is impossible with God."

Mary said: "I am the maidservant of the
Lord. Let it be done to me as you say." With
that the angel left her.

Reflection on the Readings

The feast of the Immaculate Conception is
a celebration of Mary's beginnings, of God's
free choice to surround Mary from the moment of conception with God's love or grace.
Mary reminds us of the possibility of this new
life now available to all of us because of Jesus, the Christ. We use many images to say
this: freedom from sin, life of grace, God's
abiding presence.

Yet the Gospel text points us to the announcement of the conception of Jesus, not
of Mary. Why? Because Mary is able to trust
God's presence within her (what we call
grace), overcoming her own fears and confusions. In the Genesis text, we hear the vivid
story of the human community's choice not
to live faithfully in relationship with God,
thus embracing sin. Mary stands in sharp
contrast to this life of sin because of her trust
in God's love and presence, and therefore
can accept God's invitation to be the mother
of Jesus.

Mary is held before us as a model of Christian living: men and women who can trust

415

God present-with-us, and therefore open to the possibilities of life (grace) and not death (sin).

Suggestions for Prayer

1. Take a few moments, quiet down, and gently recall God who is already present with you. Imagine yourself surrounded with God's love. What does this love look like, feel like? Now imagine that same love penetrating you, completely filling you: What does this love look like, feel like? Sit in the recognition of yourself as loved by God.

2. Imagine yourself with Mary at the angel's visitation. Hear the angel turn to you and ask you a special favor from God. What is that favor? Hear your response. What does your response tell you about your relationship with God?

3. Slowly recite the Hail Mary. Be sensitive to Mary's role as advocate and companion with you on your journey of faith.

Suggestion for Journal Keeping

Recall some of the times when you chose to close in on yourself, to not trust, to be afraid, to not have hope. Write images and words that describe the feelings and capture your sense of fear. Now recall times when you believed in your goodness, used your gifts, took important risks. Write out images and words to express those feelings. Relate this experience to today's feast of trusting in God's loving presence, the gift of grace.

Thomas H. Morris

Contributors

EMILY J. BESL holds an M.A. in Liturgical Studies from the University of Notre Dame. Presently she teaches part-time in the Theology Department at Xavier University in Cincinnati, Ohio, and serves as a consultant to the Archdiocese of Cincinnati Worship Office. A member of the Archdiocesan Worship Commission, she also is a frequent speaker and lecturer.

KATHLEEN BROWN is a pastoral minister in the Diocese of Tucson and was formerly a member of the staff at the North American Forum on the Catechumenate. She received her Master's in Theology from St. Paul University in Ottawa, Canada. Ms. Brown has also served as the Adult Education Coordinator and Catechumenate Director for a parish in Tempe, Arizona.

JOHN T. BUTLER is director of parish services for the Archdiocese of Washington. He is a Team Member for the North American Forum on the Catechumenate as well as Catechumenate Director at St. Augustine Church. He is a contributing author of *Breaking Open the Word of God, Cycles A and B* (Paulist Press). He holds a Master's degree in Education and is currently pursuing a Master's in Theology.

JOANNA CASE has been Director of the Catechumenate at St. Patrick's Cathedral, Charlotte, North Carolina, since 1980. She works as a Team Member at workshops sponsored by the North American Forum on the Catechumenate. She teaches Religious Studies at Charlotte Catholic High School and is currently working on a Master's Degree through Loyola University of New Orleans.

CLARE M. COLELLA is Director of Electronic Communications for the Diocese of San Bernardino. She formerly was Director of the Office of Sacramental Formation there and continues to serve them as resource person, as well as being on her parish catechumenate team. For several years she served on the Board of the North American Forum on the Catechumenate. Mrs. Colella holds a Master's in Religious Education from Seattle University.

REV. MICHAEL P. ENRIGHT is Associate Pastor at Blessed Agnes Parish in Chicago. He serves on the Archdiocesan Catechumenate Board and has written articles for *Liturgy 80, The Chicago Catechumenate* and *Upturn.*

417

DOUGLAS FISHER is a book editor and video director for Paulist Press. His productions include *Becoming an R.C.I.A. Sponsor* and *Becoming an R.C.I.A. Catechist* (Paulist Press). He is also managing editor of the quarterly *Service: Resources for Pastoral Ministry*. He holds an M. Div. degree from Immaculate Conception Seminary, Huntington, NY.

KHRIS S. FORD serves as R.C.I.A. Facilitator for the Diocese of Galveston-Houston. Formerly she served as a Parish Catechumenate Director and was a teacher for many years. A member of the North American Forum on the Catechumenate Institutes Team, she is also a contributor to *Breaking Open the Word of God, Cycles A and C* (Paulist Press). She holds a Master's Degree in Education.

ROBERT M. HAMMA is an editor at Paulist Press with special responsibility for the development of R.C.I.A. materials. He is a contributing author of the religious education series *This Is Our Faith* (Silver Burdett) and is the co-author of the video *Becoming an R.C.I.A. Sponsor* (Paulist Press). He holds an M. Div. degree as well as a Master's in Liturgical Studies from the University of Notre Dame.

KATHLEEN M. HENRY has five years of experience in R.C.I.A. Presently she is a parish RCIA Director and a member of the Oakland Diocese's Christian Initiation Committee. Kathleen is co-founder of Resources for Ministry and Christian Initiation, providing formation and continuing support for parish ministries of initiation. She is a certified spiritual director and has spent eight years in small faith sharing communities. She is a college lecturer and an attorney in private practice.

REV. MICHAEL J. KOCH is pastor of St. Philip Neri Church in Saskatoon, Canada. He received his education at the University of Saskatchewan and St. Joseph Seminary, Edmonton. He also studied at the University of San Francisco and in Jerusalem. Father Koch is a member of the steering committee of the North American Forum on the Catechumenate, and a contributing author to *Breaking Open the Word of God, Cycles A, B, C* (Paulist Press).

REV. STEVEN M. LANZA is Associate Pastor of St. Michael Church in Orland Park, IL. He has been active in pastoral work in parishes for six years and serves as a member of the Chicago Archdiocesan Catechumenate Board.

REV. EUGENE A. LAVERDIERE, SSS is the editor of *Emmanuel* magazine and an associate editor of *The Bible Today*. He holds a doctorate in New Testament and Early Christian Literature from the University of Chicago. Father LaVerdiere is the author of many books as well as audio and video cassettes. His most recent books include *The New Testament in the Life of the Church* and *When We Pray* (both Ave Maria Press). He was also a contributing author to *Breaking Open the Word of God, Cycles A, B, C* (Paulist Press).

ELIZABETH S. LILLY is the Liturgy Coordinator for the five churches of Saint Thomas Aquinas Parish in Palo Alto, California. For seven years she directed the Catechumenate in Saint William Parish, Los Altos, California.

During those years she contributed to the three cycles of *Breaking Open the Word of God* (Paulist Press). She has been a member of the Liturgy Commission of the Diocese of San Jose and continues to serve on the committees on the Catechumenate and Environment and Art. She is a graduate of the University of California with a Master's degree in the History of Art.

MARY KAY MEIER is a member of the Catechumenate Team of St. Irenaeus Parish in Cypress, CA. She also serves as a member of the Steering Committee of the North American Forum on the Catechumenate. Active in spiritual direction and team formation, she holds a B.A. in education from Wisconsin State University.

THOMAS H. MORRIS is a member of the pastoral team at St. Rose of Lima parish, Gaithersburg, MD and former Assistant Director for the Office for Religious Education, Archdiocese of Washington. He is also a Team Member of the North American Forum on the Catechumenate and Instructor in Pastoral Theology at DeSales School of Theology, Washington, DC. He holds graduate degrees in theology and spirituality and is a doctoral candidate in Christian spirituality at The Catholic University of America. His publications include contributions to Paulist Press' *Breaking Open the Word of God* (Cycles A and B) and *The RCIA: Transforming the Church* (Paulist).

KATHRYN A. SCHNEIDER is Director of Religious Education at St. Anthony's Church in Nanuet, NY. She has been involved in the development of the R.C.I.A. and has done pastoral work in Texas, North Dakota, and Brazil. She holds an M. Div. degree from the University of Notre Dame.

JOSEPH P. SINWELL currently serves as Diocesan Director of Religious Education for the Diocese of Providence and as Co-Director of the Rhode Island Catechumenate. He is a founding member of the North American Forum on the Catechumenate. His articles have appeared in *Christian Initiation Resources, Today's Parish, Christian Adulthood* and *Catechist*. He is also the co-editor of *Breaking Open the Word of God*, Cycles A, B, and C (Paulist Press). He holds Master's degrees in Religious Education and Agency Counseling and is a candidate for a Doctor of Ministry degree at St. Mary's University in Baltimore.